INVITATION TO
WORLD RELIGIONS

INVITATION TO
World Religions

FIFTH EDITION

JEFFREY BRODD
California State University, Sacramento

LAYNE LITTLE
University of California, Davis

BRADLEY NYSTROM
California State University, Sacramento

ROBERT PLATZNER
California State University, Sacramento

RICHARD SHEK
California State University, Sacramento

ERIN STILES
University of Nevada, Reno

OXFORD
UNIVERSITY PRESS

OXFORD
UNIVERSITY PRESS

Oxford University Press is a department of the University of Oxford.
It furthers the University's objective of excellence in research, scholarship,
and education by publishing worldwide. Oxford is a registered trade mark
of Oxford University Press in the UK and in certain other countries.

Published in the United States of America by Oxford University Press
198 Madison Avenue, New York, NY 10016, United States of America.

Library of Congress Cataloging-in-Publication Data

Names: Brodd, Jeffrey, author.
Title: Invitation to world religions / Jeffrey Brodd, California State
  University, Sacramento, Layne Little, University of California, Davis,
  Bradley Nystrom, California State University, Sacramento, Robert
  Platzner, California State University, Sacramento, Richard Shek,
  California State University, Sacramento, Erin Stiles, University of
  Nevada, Reno.
Identifiers: LCCN 2024022889 (print) | LCCN 2024022890 (ebook) | ISBN
  9780197771341 (paperback) | ISBN 9780197771358 (ebook)
Subjects: LCSH: Religions.
Classification: LCC BL80.3 .B754 2024 (print) | LCC BL80.3 (ebook) | DDC
  200—dc23/eng/20240628
LC record available at https://lccn.loc.gov/2024022889
LC ebook record available at https://lccn.loc.gov/2024022890

Printed by Sheridan Books, Inc., United States of America

⬤ BRIEF CONTENTS

CONTENTS

3 ● Indigenous Religions of Africa 67

4 ● Hinduism 99

5 ● Buddhism 153

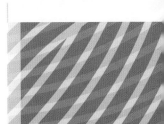

PREFACE

THE WORLD'S RELIGIOUS TRADITIONS have offered answers to the weightiest questions of human existence, contributed to the formation of political and social institutions, inspired masterpieces of art and literature, and provided many of the cultural values and ideals on which entire civilizations have been based. Today, religions continue to play a powerful role in shaping the ways in which people understand themselves, the world they live in, and how they should live.

Invitation to World Religions welcomes students to the study of religion. In these pages, we open the doors and invite the reader to explore with wonder and respect. We describe the essential features of the world's major religions and show how they have responded to basic human needs and to the cultural settings in which they developed. We also compare the answers religions have offered us regarding some of the most essential human questions: Why are wc here? What is the nature of the universe? How should we live? Our aim has been to balance concision and substance in an introductory text that is accessible, as well as challenging.

A team of authors cooperated in writing this book, each one of us bringing a particular scholarly expertise—as well as years of teaching experience—to the respective chapters. We wrote with important learning goals in mind. We want students to gain an objective understanding of the beliefs and practices associated with the world's religions, but we also encourage an empathetic appreciation of what their beliefs and actions actually *mean* to adherents. By emphasizing the connections between religious traditions and their cultural contexts, we seek to heighten awareness of the extent to which religions have influenced, and been influenced by, politics and society, literature, the arts, and philosophy. We also examine the role of religions in our contemporary world as global cultures are transformed by social, political, and technological change and are becoming more reliant on science regarding matters once explained by religions alone. A thoughtful reading of this book will provide a clear understanding of the characteristics that are unique to individual religions and highlight many of their shared qualities and concerns. Finally, we trust that every reader will find here a means of making sense of other ways of believing and living and of finding a solid basis for the tolerance and respect that are so critically important in times like ours.

Religions are multidimensional. Accordingly, all but the first and last chapters examine three primary aspects of each religion: teachings, historical development, and way of life (practices and experiences). These three aspects are presented in the same order in every chapter in which they appear. Although they appear in the same order, we do not devote equal attention to each category. To do so would be to ignore the varying nature of the religious traditions. Judaism, for example, naturally calls for extensive attention to historical development; Jainism, for which an early historical record barely exists, does not. In each case, we shape our coverage in the way that seems most natural given the characteristics of the tradition under discussion.

Teachings

Commonly found in scriptures, myths, creeds, and ethical codes, the basic teachings of a religious tradition convey its answers to fundamental questions, such as: What is the human condition? How can the human condition be improved or transcended? What is the nature of the world? What is ultimate reality, and how is it revealed? Will there eventually be an end of the world, and if so, how and when? The authority on which a religion answers questions such as these is also important. Are its truths revealed? Are they the products of intellectual effort? Are they insights gained in moments of profound psychological experience? Or are they simply traditional ways of looking at reality and our place within it that have been passed down from generation to generation?

Historical Development

Every religious tradition has a history that reveals how and why it developed its distinctive features, including its system of beliefs, leadership and governance structures, social institutions, and forms of artistic expression. Sometimes the forces that generate change arise largely from within a tradition, as in the case of conflict between opposing sects or schools of thought. At other times they operate from the outside, as with the influence exerted by Western powers on foreign colonies and spheres of influence or through the expansion of a tradition into a new cultural milieu. A religion's history also functions to unite the individual with others in a shared memory of the past that helps to explain the present.

Way of Life

By way of life we mean practices—the things people *do* in making practical application of their beliefs, such as engaging in prayer, meditation, communal worship or various other forms of ritual, or working to enhance social justice or to care for the environment. Closely related to practices are modes of experience, the ways in which a religion's adherents actually experience the consequences of applying its teachings. These might include a sense of inner peace, a more acute sense of community with others, a greater awareness of the divine, or a state of profound enlightenment.

ORGANIZATION

Our survey begins in Chapter 1 with an introductory essay on the academic study of religions. After considering what religion *is*, the chapter identifies some of the other important questions scholars ask: What do religions do? What issues of universal concern do they address? What do scholars mean when they speak of mystical experience or of transcendence? What are the constituent parts of religious traditions? How are religions today being affected by the forces of modernization, urbanization, globalization, and science? What is the relationship between religion and such issues as gender identity and roles, environmental causes, and violence? Finally, the chapter explains why a multidisciplinary approach is necessary in any serious attempt to understand the world's religions.

Chapter 1 is followed by two chapters on indigenous traditions. The book concludes with a chapter on new religions. The ten chapters in the middle are organized according to geographical and (roughly) chronological order, as follows: first, the religions of South Asian origin (Hinduism, Buddhism, Jainism, Sikhism); next, those of East Asian origin (Chinese religions, Japanese religions); and, finally, those of West Asian (or Middle Eastern) origin (Zoroastrianism, Judaism, Christianity, Islam). By studying the indigenous traditions first, students will gain an appreciation not only for the many living traditions that continue to thrive but also for certain ways of being religious (such as emphasis on oral transference of myths and other sacred lore) that at one time were predominant in most of today's major world religions. By studying new religions last, students will likewise gain an appreciation for living traditions, along with glimpsing the sorts of innovations that occur within the old traditions, too, as religions respond to the cultural, technological, social, and cultural changes and challenges of the world around them.

NEW TO THE FIFTH EDITION

- **Learning objectives to ensure purposeful reading** Learning objectives clearly stated at the beginning of each section help students to organize their learning experience with an awareness of what matters most.
- **Chapter conclusions on "engaging with the world"** These concluding sections emphasize the relevance of the religious traditions for issues of concern in today's world, such as environmentalism, gender roles, personal identity, inclusion, and other topics relating to social justice.
- **Improved organization of material and a more uniform writing style** We have reorganized material in the interest of enhancing clarity. In the history sections, material on recent events, previously set forth in box features, is now more effectively integrated into the overall presentation. In general, we have continued to streamline the presentation of material and to employ a more

uniform writing style, all the while benefiting from many helpful reviewer suggestions.

Along with the general features described here, chapter-specific revisions of particular note include the following:

- Chapter 1, "An Invitation to the Study of World Religions," features new consideration of the realities of "lived religion" or, to use another phrase popular in contemporary scholarship, "religion on the ground," realities which sometimes stand in contrast to religious ideals.
- Chapter 1 also includes a new section on religious engagement with politics, noting that religion often affects political positions and sometimes is thoroughly manifested in the form of a theocracy (now a bold-faced Glossary term).
- Chapter 2, "Indigenous Religions of North America," sets forth new material on Native North American religions and conflicts over lithium mining.
- Chapter 3, "Indigenous Religions of Africa," features enhanced consideration of the influence of African religions in the Americas.
- Chapter 4, "Hinduism," includes expanded attention to the political influence of the Bharatiya Janata Party (BJP) and Prime Minister Narendra Modi, as the future of Hinduism seems more than ever inextricably tied to politics and the fortunes of the BJP.
- Chapter 5, "Buddhism," features enhanced clarity in both textual and graphic descriptions of Buddhist teachings, particularly those of Mahayana Buddhism.
- Chapter 13, "Islam," contains enriched material on Islam and politics in the modern world, and provides enhanced attention to contemporary social justice issues such as gender identity and environmentalism.
- Chapter 5, "Buddhism," Chapter 7, "Sikhism," Chapter 12, "Christianity," and Chapter 13, "Islam," feature new "Voices" interviews that focus on the meaning and utility of the religion in the interviewee's life.

FEATURES AND PEDAGOGY

Because the concepts and contexts of the world's religions are immeasurably complex, we have worked to present a clear and accessible introductory text. Our tone throughout, while deeply informed by scholarship, is both accessible and appropriate for a wide range of undergraduate students. Consistent chapter structure also helps students to focus on *content* inasmuch as they do not have to navigate each chapter anew. With the exception of Chapters 1 and 14, every chapter in the book includes three core modules: the teachings of the religion, the history of the religion, and the religion as a way of life. This modular and predictable structure is also highly flexible, allowing instructors to easily create a syllabus that best reflects their own scholarly interests, as well as their students' learning needs.

The study of religions can be daunting to newcomers, who must plunge into a sea of unfamiliar words, concepts, and cultures. For this reason, we have provided a variety of ways for students to engage with important ideas, personalities, and visuals:

Voices: In personal, candid interviews, a diverse array of people share the ways they live their religion.

Visual Guide: A key to important religious symbols, provided in an easy-to-read table for quick reference and comparison, is included in each "Way of Life" section.

Maps and Timelines: Each chapter begins with a map to provide geographical context for a religion's development. Key features and places mentioned in the chapter are called out on the map. A timeline at the beginning of each chapter provides social and political context to help students situate each religion and trace its development. Finally, a comprehensive timeline of all the main religions covered in the book appears on the inside front and back covers.

Seeking Answers: After each chapter's Conclusion, we revisit three essential questions that religions strive to answer. This feature helps students to review the chapter's key concepts and informs their ability to *compare* constructively the ways in which different religions address the same fundamental human questions:

> What is ultimate reality?
> How should we live in this world?
> What is our ultimate purpose?

Other elements that facilitate teaching and learning include the following:

Glossary: Important terms are printed in bold type at their first occurrence and are explained in the Glossary that follows each chapter, with pronunciation guides as needed. In addition, a glossary at the back of the book includes all of the key terms from the entire text.

End-of-Chapter Questions: Each chapter concludes with two sets of questions to help students review, retain, and reflect upon chapter content. For Review questions prompt students to recall and rehearse key chapter concepts; For Further Reflection questions require students to think critically about the chapter's nuances and encourage both discussion and personal response by inviting students to engage in a more penetrating analysis of a tradition or taking a comparative approach.

Suggestions for Further Reading: These annotated lists of some of the best and most recent works on each tradition, as well as online resources, encourage students to pursue their exploration of the world's religions.

Rich, Robust, and Relevant Visuals: Finally, we have filled the pages of *Invitation to World Religions* with an abundance of color photographs and illustrations that add visual experience to our verbal descriptions of sacred objects, build-ings, art, and other material aspects of religious life.

SUPPLEMENTS

A rich set of supplemental resources is available to support teaching and learning in this course.

The Oxford University Press **Oxford Learning Link (OLL)** at https://learninglink.oup.com/access/brodd5e houses the following **Instructor's Resources**:

- A LMS Test Bank, including multiple-choice, true/false, and essay questions
- An Instructor's Manual, including
  - A pencil-and-paper version of the LMS Test Bank
  - Chapter Summaries
  - Chapter Learning Objectives
  - Suggested Web Links and other Media Resources
  - Web Links to Sacred Texts, accompanied by brief descriptions of their content
  - Lists of Key Terms and their definitions from the text
- PowerPoint lecture outlines
- PowerPoint art database
- **Oxford Learning Link Direct** cartridges to import Instructor and Student Resources into Canvas, Blackboard, D2L, and Moodle.

The **Student Resources** on the **OLL** contain the following:

- Enhanced eBook, which integrates the text's narrative with a rich assortment of interactive content (video and flashcards) and self-assessment
- Student Quizzes
- Flashcards of Key Terms from the text
- Video clips on significant beliefs, practices, and places related to a variety of traditions covered in *Invitation to World Religions*, accompanied by multiple-choice questions
- Extended "Voices" interviews with adherents of Buddhism, Sikhism, Shinto, Christianity, and Islam
- Interactive timelines of the world religions, including comparisons of Indian, Chinese, and Abrahamic religions, accompanied by multiple-choice questions
- Interactive maps of key locations for the world religions, accompanied by multiple-choice questions

ACKNOWLEDGMENTS

This book has been a long time in the making. Along the way, family members, friends, and colleagues have supported us with love, patience, insights, and suggestions. We also are grateful to the people who kindly granted us interviews. Although there is no way we can adequately thank them here, we can at least acknowledge them: Edward Allen, Dr. Onkar Bindra, Jill Brodd, Jon Brodd, Mary Chapman, Linda Dekker, Tunay Durmaz, Hadi Eltahlawi, Lin Estes, Rev. Dr. Christopher Flesoras, Rustom Ghadiali, Avigayil Halpern, George and Kausalya Hart, Susan Hotchkiss, Kathleen Kelly, Hari Krishnan, Sammy Letoole, Ray and Marilyn Little, Terrie McGraw, Brian Melendez, Watanabe Minoru, Annie Nystrom, Festus Ogunbitan, Susan Orr, Rev. Bob Oshita, Mia Sasaki, Girish Shah, Kitty Shek, Akal-Ustat Singh, Davesh Soneji, Jason Ch'ui-hsiao Tseng, Kaitlyn Ugoretz, Archana Venkatesan, Krishna and Jayashree Venkatesan, Father Art Wehr, S.J., Dr. Xinyu David Zhang, and members of the Sacramento Dharma Center.

We have also benefited immensely from the hard work and good suggestions of colleagues across the country. In particular, we would like to thank:

Vivian Arendall, University of Memphis

Ryan M. Armstrong, Oklahoma State University

Michael Bobo, Norco College

Jeffrey Brackett, Ball State University

Eric Breault, Northern Arizona University

Christopher S Chandler, Indiana University of Pennsylvania

Jeanine Diller, University of Toledo

Sarah R. Egelman, Central New Mexico Community College

Peter Fraser-Morris, James Madison University

Robert Gall, West Liberty University

Blayne Harcey, Arizona State University

Yaroslav Komarovski, University of Nebraska—Lincoln

Court Lewis, Pellissippi State Community College

Mac McGoldrick, Colorado State University

Martha Roberts, Fullerton College

Nancy Rourke, Canisius College

Elijah Siegler, College of Charleston

Jason Sprague, University of Michigan-Dearborn

Jason Staples, North Carolina State University

We extend our special thanks to Yaroslav Komarovski of the University of Nebraska–Lincoln, who so generously provided valuable suggestions, and to Ravi Gupta of Utah State University, who responded so very helpfully to our request for expert advice.

We would also like to acknowledge the suggestions of reviewers for the previous four editions, which continued to inform our work on this fifth edition:

Asad Q. Ahmed, Washington University in St. Louis

Kenneth Atkinson, University of Northern Iowa

Kenneth Bass, Central Texas College

John Baumann, University of Oregon

Todd M. Brenneman, University of Central Florida

Robert E. Brown, James Madison University

David Bush, Shasta College

Dexter E. Callender, Jr., University of Miami

Kenneth Claus, Miami Dade College–Kendall Campus

Sharon Coggan, University of Colorado–Denver

John L. Crow, Florida State University

Philip R. Drey, Kirkwood Community College–Cedar Rapids

James Ford, Rogers State University

Matthew Hallgarth, Tarleton State University

Kathleen Hladky, Florida State University

T. Christopher Hoklotubbe, Cornell College

Barbara Hornum, Drexel University

Mordechai Inbari, University of North Carolina–Pembroke

Jon Inglett, Oklahoma City Community College

Maria Jaoudi, California State University–Sacramento

Jeffrey Kaplan, University of Wisconsin–Oshkosh

Brad Karelius, Saddleback College

Kate S. Kelley, University of Missouri–Columbia

Erik Larson, Florida International University

Finally, we owe a debt of gratitude to the editorial staff at Oxford University Press. Our thanks go to Jeff Marshall, Portfolio Manager for Philosophy and Religion, who has overseen development of the Fifth Edition, with assistance from Sonya Venugopal, Lauren Thompson, Maeve O'Brien, Mia Cirillo, Melissa Emanoilidis, and Julia Hartheimer. We are very grateful for their diligent work. The Fourth Edition was overseen by Andy Blitzer, Acquisitions Editor for Philosophy and Religion. The previous editions were overseen by then Executive Editor Robert Miller, who originally invited us to publish with Oxford and who put us in the excellent care of Content Development Manager Meg Botteon, whose professionalism and skill all along have been an essential guiding force. Our thanks also go to Ashli MacKenzie for managing the final stages of the book's production.

INVITATION TO
WORLD RELIGIONS

An Invitation to the Study of World Religions

1

Chapter Outline

1.1 Explain the study of world religions as an academic inquiry, clarifying how it is distinguishable from theology.

1.2 Identify prominent definitions of religion.

1.3 Summarize what religions do with regard to significant questions they answer.

1.4 Identify significant features of and issues pertaining to religions in the modern world.

1.5 Identify strategies of a sound academic approach to the study of the world's religions.

ON MOST AMERICAN COLLEGE CAMPUSES, signs of the world's religions are readily observable. Bulletin boards display fliers announcing upcoming events pertaining to Buddhist meditation or Hindu sacred art or the Islamic observance of Ramadan. Campus religious groups engage in outreach activities at tables alongside walkways or in student unions. Some students might wear a yarmulke or dress in hijab, while others wear a cross pendant or a tattoo of the yin/yang symbol.

To study the world's religions is to progress from mere observation of outward signs to understanding their meaning and relevance. Anyone who observes the yin-yang symbol can appreciate the beauty of its spiraling symmetry, but studying Chinese religion reveals a much more complex meaning. Mysterious in their origins, yin and yang are complementary primal energies that give rise to all creation. For the human being, to maintain a perfect balance of yin and yang is to live an ideal life. The nearly ubiquitous symbol of the cross similarly takes on new depths of meaning, even for many who identify themselves as Christian,

Candlelight vigils typically draw together people of different
religious perspectives in times of sorrow as well as celebration.

when approached through the study of world religions. To Christians, God, the creator of all things, having taken on human form in the person of Jesus Christ, willingly suffered the painful death of crucifixion on the cross to save humanity from the power of sin. We can expand on our understanding of the meaning and cultural relevance of these two icons through a comparative study. Chinese religion, with its belief in the creative, complementary energies of yin and yang, has no need for a creator such as the Christian God. The Christian concept of sin and the corresponding need for salvation are alien to the Chinese quest for balance of yin and yang. These two icons, in other words, signify profoundly different cultural orientations.

T o study the world's religions is to enhance one's understanding and appreciation of the rich variety of cultures around the globe. This chapter introduces this field of study by exploring the significance, examining the foundational concepts, and describing appropriate strategies for the academic exploration of religion.

1.1 Approaching the Study of World Religions

In order to be an educated person today, one must have an awareness of world religions. To learn about world religions is to increase one's cultural literacy—the objective that lies at the heart of this study. The religious traditions examined in this book are foundational aspects of cultures around the globe. Religion plays a crucial role in shaping, transforming, and transmitting cultures. Interacting with other cultural aspects—politics, economics, aesthetics—religion is a potent force in culture, in ways both constructive and destructive. When people believe they are acting in a manner that is condoned by a transcendent power or is in keeping with timeless tradition, they tend to act more fervently and with greater conviction. In other words, religions are powerful, sometimes even dangerous. Knowing about them is crucial for negotiating our complex world.

"World Religions" has been a course of study in American colleges and universities for nearly a century. Recently, the category has come under scrutiny by some scholars, as has the so-called world religions discourse that often accompanies it.[1] Although such scrutiny sometimes loses sight of the obvious—that "world religions" as an academic category is here to stay and that learning about its subject matter is vitally important—critics are correct to demand sound academic approaches to the study. A primary concern is that the study of world religions, and indeed the entire enterprise of the academic study of religion, arose within a predominantly Christian European intellectual culture that assumed that Christianity was a model of what a religion ought to be and, commonly, that it was the only *true* religion. Until the late decades of the nineteenth century, theorists applied the term *world religion* (in the singular) only to Christianity. Eventually Buddhism, Judaism, and occasionally Islam were grouped with Christianity as "world religions" (or "the world's religions"). By the 1930s, the list had grown to include the ten to twelve religions that still today are normally categorized as world religions.

And so, to the basic need for knowing about the world religions (however they came to be categorized), we can add another vital need: that we study them appropriately through awareness of what we might call the "do's and don'ts" of religious studies, which this chapter explores in some detail. An appropriate study of world religions does not privilege any religion as being somehow exemplary or the model with which others are to be compared. We also need to avoid terms and categories that are rooted in such privileging. For example, "faith" is a natural term to use when studying Christianity, but it is far less applicable to the study of Confucianism or Shinto. Other important issues involve underlying motives or assumptions that can too easily creep in. A common assumption to avoid is that all religions ultimately say the same thing. Although this possibility is intriguing, it is impossible to prove by way of a sound academic approach—that is, well-reasoned theorizing based on careful analysis of the evidence.

The challenge of mastering the "do's" and avoiding the "don'ts" only enriches our study. We begin by considering the rise of the modern academic field of religious studies.

Religion as a Subject of Academic Inquiry

The academic study of religion, commonly known as "religious studies" (or sometimes as "comparative religion" or "history of religions") is a relatively recent development. Prior to the European Enlightenment of the eighteenth century, it rarely occurred to anyone to think of a religion as an entity that could be separated from other aspects of culture, and therefore as something that could be defined as a distinct category and studied as such. Enlightenment thinkers, most influentially the German philosopher Immanuel Kant (1724–1804), conceived of religion as something separate from the various phenomena the human mind is capable of perceiving.[2] This impulse toward categorically separating religion, coupled with European exploration of distant lands and their unfamiliar "religions," launched efforts to understand religion that have continued to the present day. This shift means that we modern observers need to be cautious when appraising the religious aspects of other cultures, lest we make the error of assuming that all peoples have recognized religion as a distinctive category. Most cultures throughout history have had neither the conceptual category nor a term meaning "religion."

The academic study of religion is not an intentionally religious enterprise and is thus generally distinct from

William James defined religion as "the feelings, acts and experiences of individual men in their solitude." This Orthodox Christian priest sits alone in the Amhara region of northwestern Ethiopia.

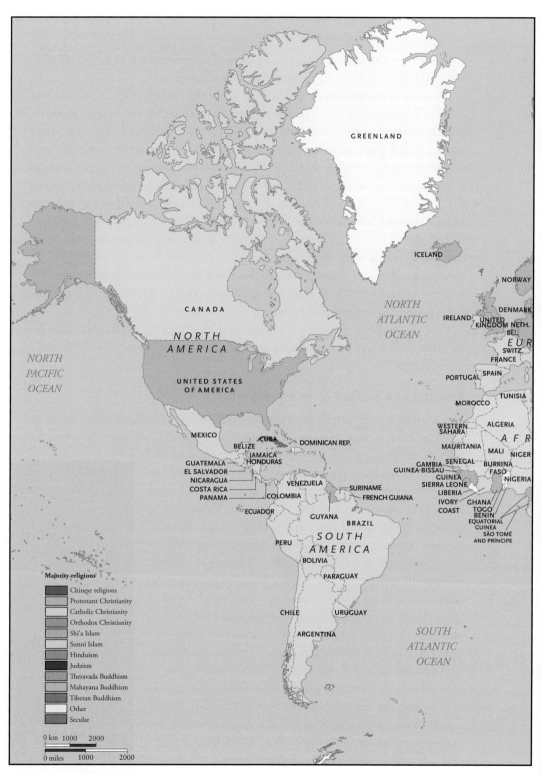

Religious affiliations of majority populations in the world today. Some countries have large populations of minority affiliations. In Germany, for example, there are nearly as many Catholics as Protestants.

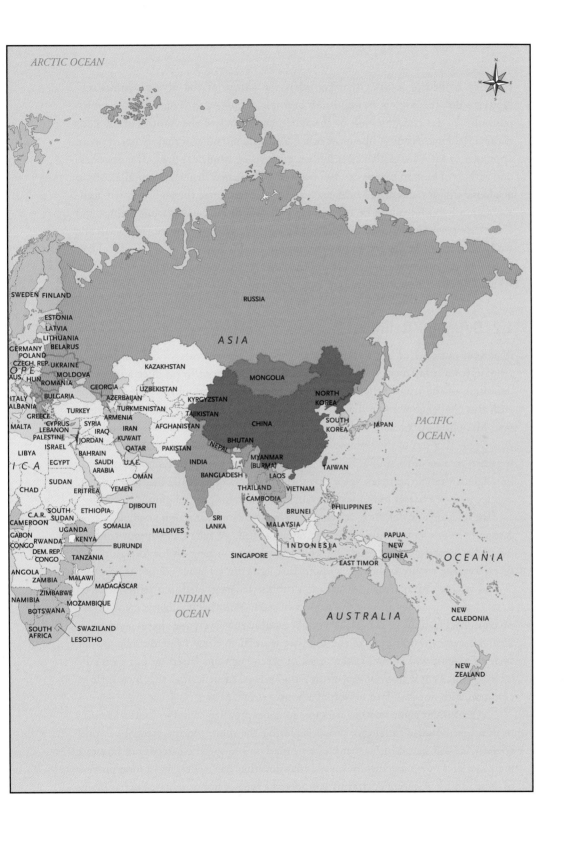

theology, a field of inquiry that considers the nature of the divine. Unlike religious studies, theology is an important example of *doing* and *being* religious, which naturally invites consideration of the supernatural and of the "truth" of religious claims. Religious studies, like most other academic pursuits, is mainly based on an approach to knowledge that depends on analysis of empirical data. The discourse and actions of human beings can be observed and studied through normal means of academic inquiry; empirical evidence can be gathered, and through rational argumentation hypotheses can be formulated and supported. Supernatural beings and events are beyond the reach of empirically based academic inquiry. The academic study of religion, as understood by the authors of this book, is therefore not theology, however much we might admire theologians and enjoy studying their work, which is itself an important human enterprise and a major component of religion.

1.2 Defining "Religion"

A natural outcome of the Enlightenment impulse toward categorically separating religion from other aspects of culture has been the attempt to produce a universal definition of the term. Scholars from various academic disciplines have struggled with this challenge without having produced a single definition that pleases everyone. Many theorists today dismiss the challenge as futile, and some even go so far as to argue that use of the term *religion* in academic study should be abandoned altogether because of its ambiguity and misleading inferences. Most scholars involved in religious studies, however, agree that they are studying basically the same subject, and for lack of a better term most are content with calling it "religion."

The relevance of defining "religion" can be understood through an analogy that compares religions to houses. Embarking on a study of religions without concern over *what*, exactly, we are studying would be akin to setting off for foreign places to explore the nature of houses without first agreeing on what counts as a house. Would we include apartments? Vacation cabins? Palaces? Defining terms helps us draw clear boundaries around the subject of study. Another challenge involves our preconceived notions of things. We might assume that everyone shares a common idea of a typical "house" (like the kind we learned to draw in grade school), but such an assumption is mainly the result of preconceptions based on our own culture's norms. People from other cultures might dwell in structures that have little in common with our standard notion of a house.

Let's consider some notable attempts to conceptualize "religion" while keeping in mind our "house" analogy. When exploring the more specific category "world religion," it will be useful to think of a similarly more specific category of house: a mansion, and more specifically, an old mansion that has undergone a long process of refurbishing. Although certainly considered a type of house, a mansion has many rooms that serve a wide variety of functions and styles. Imagine an old mansion that has kept the same foundation and basic structure over the years, but to which various inhabitants have made changes that have enabled the structure to survive into modern times. Our study of the world's religions is an invitation to explore several extraordinary "old mansions." Our tools of study—beginning with considerations of definition—are designed to help us make the most of our explorations, to take in fully the teachings, the histories, and the practices of the world's religions.

Three Classic Definitions

The history of the attempt to define "religion" is intriguing. In many instances, definitions reveal as much about the historical era and about the intentions of the individual theorist as they do about the nature of religion.

The following well-known definitions of "religion" are from notable theorists in different fields:

> A religion is a unified system of beliefs and practices relative to sacred things, that is to say, things set apart and forbidden—beliefs and practices which unite into one single moral community called a Church, all those who adhere to them.[3]
>
> —*Émile Durkheim*

> [Religion is] . . . the feelings, acts and experiences of individual men in their solitude, so far as they apprehend themselves to stand in relation to whatever they may consider the divine.[4]
>
> —*William James*

> [T]he religious aspect points to that which is ultimate, infinite, unconditional in man's spiritual life. Religion, in the largest and most basic sense of the word, is ultimate concern.[5]
>
> —*Paul Tillich*

French sociologist Émile Durkheim (1858–1917), a founding figure of the sociological study of religion, emphasizes in his definition the *social* nature of religion. He insists on the unification brought about by "beliefs and practices," culminating in a "moral community called a Church." Durkheim surely hits on some central functions of religion, but most scholars contend that he overemphasizes this social orientation. In contrast, American psychologist William James (1842–1910) emphasizes the *individual* nature of religion. Although this aspect is also clearly important, his definition omits any mention of religion's social nature. The definitions put forth by Durkheim and James, therefore, are insufficient.

Protestant theologian Paul Tillich (1886–1965) naturally connects religion to a focus on "man's spiritual life." His notion of religion as "ultimate concern," though influential for several decades, is very broad, and says nothing regarding the specific content of religious traditions. In emphasizing the existential concerns of religion, it neglects social and institutional aspects. People commonly claim to be "spiritual" while also denying that they belong to a religion. A sound definition needs to accommodate this distinction or else avoid this ambiguity altogether.

Two Prominent Definitions

Let us now consider two definitions of "religion" that currently enjoy wide favor and that avoid these sorts of shortcomings. The *HarperCollins Dictionary of Religion*, a popular reference work, states: "One may clarify the term religion by defining it as a system of beliefs and practices that are relative to superhuman beings."[6] This definition encompasses a wide array of cultural phenomena, while at the same time restricting the category, most especially with the concept "superhuman beings."

Bruce Lincoln (b. 1948), a prominent theorist of religion, asserts in his book *Holy Terrors: Thinking about Religion after September 11* that a religion always consists of four "domains"—discourse, practice, community, and institution:

1. A discourse whose concerns transcend the human, temporal, and contingent, and that claims for itself a similarly transcendent status. . . .
2. A set of practices whose purpose is to produce a proper world and/or proper human subjects, as defined by a religious discourse to which these practices are connected. . . .
3. A community whose members construct their identity with reference to a religious discourse and its attendant practices. . . .
4. An institution that regulates religious discourse, practices, and community, reproducing them over time and modifying them as necessary, while asserting their eternal validity and transcendent value.[7]

By basing religion on the notion of the "transcendent" rather than on "supernatural beings" or the like, Lincoln's definition is helpfully inclusive. The religions featured in this textbook conform to Lincoln's definition. Notably, it encompasses Confucianism and forms of Buddhism that do not focus on belief in supernatural beings. This is not to say that Lincoln, or for that matter any other theorist, has determined what religion "truly" is. In the words of sociologist Peter Berger (1929–2017), commenting on the challenge of defining religion, "a definition is not more or less true, only more or less useful."[8] For purposes of our study, Lincoln's definition provides a useful means of categorizing the subject matter. It clarifies why the traditions featured in this book qualify as religions while also, especially with its insistence that a religion involves an "institution," establishing helpful limits. The general category "spirituality," for example, would not necessarily qualify as religion based on Lincoln's definition.

We now shift our focus from what religions *are* to consider what religions *do*. In the next section, we analyze various functions of religion, concentrating especially on the fundamental questions to which religious traditions provide answers.

1.3 What Religions Do

Whatever one thinks a religion *is*, this much remains certain: a religion *does*. This fact is closely related to the challenge of defining religion. Theorists who emphasize this functional side of religion in their explanations risk *explaining away* or *reducing* religion to being an effect or result of other forces. Underlying Durkheim's definition, for example, is a theory that reduces religion to being an effect of societal forces, a mechanism that, having been produced in the first place by societal needs, functions in turn to promote social unity. This demonstrates that sometimes definitions reveal as much about the intentions of the theorist as they do about the nature of religion: Durkheim is a founder of sociology, and so it is not surprising that he emphasizes the social aspects of religion. Consider also this assertion from psychologist Sigmund Freud (1856–1939):

> Religion would thus be the universal obsessional neurosis of humanity; like the obsessional neurosis of children, it arose out of the Oedipus complex, out of the relation to the father.[9]

Freud was an atheist whose psychological theory held religion to be undesirable. Political philosopher Karl Marx (1818–1883), likewise an atheist, offers an even more antagonistic assessment:

> *Man makes religion*, religion does not make man. In other words, religion is the self-consciousness and self-feeling of man who has either not yet found himself or has already lost himself again. But *man* is no abstract being squatting outside the world. Man is the *world of man*, the state, society. . . . Religion is the sigh of the oppressed creature, the heart of a heartless world, just as it is the spirit of a spiritless situation. It is the *opium* of the people.[10]

Marx, affected by what he perceived as the economic disparities of the Industrial Revolution, was a materialist who dismissed all forms of ideology as obstacles to the pursuit of true well-being. Freud similarly regarded religion as an effect of other forces, viewing it as a by-product of psychological influences. According to Freud, religion functions as an unhealthy but soothing buffer against the inner terrors of the psyche. For Marx, religion functions in a similarly unhealthy manner, as an opiate that deters the suffering individual from attending to the true cause of affliction (namely the class struggle).

Contemporary scholars largely regard these functionalist explanations as severely limited. Perhaps religions *do* function in these ways at certain times in certain situations; but surely religions do much more. In fact, neither Freud nor Marx ever actually tried to define religion; rather, they tried to explain it away. This does not diminish, however, the enduring relevance of these theorists for attempting to understand the role religion plays in the lives of individuals and in societies.

At sites like this Confucian temple in Beijing, China, Confucius (Master K'ung) is honored for his enduring contributions to Chinese culture. Sound definitions of "religion" are flexible enough to include Confucianism as a religious tradition.

We can widen our vantage point on the functions of religion and produce a fairer and more accurate depiction by considering the variety of life's challenges that these traditions help people to face and to overcome.

Religious Questions and Challenges

It might seem disrespectful or even blasphemous to ask, Why do religions exist? Yet this is a perfectly legitimate question. As human enterprises, religions naturally respond to human needs and readily acknowledge reasons for their doctrines and rituals. A typical reason has to do with some kind of perceived separation from the sacred or estrangement from a state of perfection or fulfillment. The human condition, as ordinarily experienced, is regarded as being disconnected from the fulfillment that lies at the end of a spiritual path. Of the questions and challenges addressed by religions, we will focus on these three:

1. What is ultimate reality?
2. How should we live in this world?
3. What is our ultimate purpose?

The rest of this book's chapters explore the ways major religions answer these questions. For now, let's consider these questions more broadly.

What Is Ultimate Reality?

It is difficult to imagine a religion that has nothing to say about ultimate reality—even if this involves asserting that "ultimate" reality consists of no more than the natural world and we human beings who inhabit it. Religions typically assert that ultimate reality is somehow divine, and explanation of the nature and role of the divine is fundamental to a religion's belief system. But the "divine" is not necessarily thought of as God or gods. When it is, we refer to that religion as a **theistic** (from Greek *theos*, or god) belief system. When it is not, the religion is said to be **nontheistic**. Some forms of Buddhism, such as Zen, are clearly nontheistic. A helpful middle ground term is **transtheistic**, acknowledging the existence of gods—but of gods that are not vital with regard to the most crucial religious issues, such as the quest for enlightenment or salvation.[11]

Theistic religions can be further categorized. **Polytheism** (from Greek *polys*, or many) is the belief in many gods ("gods" is considered a gender-neutral term and can—and often does—include goddesses). **Monotheism** (from Greek *monos*, or only one) is the belief in only one god (in which case the term is normally capitalized—God—a proper noun referring to a specific being). Here, a kind of middle ground is **henotheism** (from Greek *hen*, the number one), which acknowledges a plurality of gods but elevates one of them to special status. Some forms of Hindu devotion to a particular god such as Vishnu or Shiva are henotheistic.

Pantheism (from Greek *pan*, or all) is the belief that the divine is identical to nature or the material world. Although not one of the world's living religions, the ancient Greek and Roman religious philosophy known as Stoicism is an example. It is important to bear in mind, too, that the world's religions often feature entities (such as angels, demons, and the monsters of myths) that are supernatural and yet are not necessarily gods. The *theos* in the "polytheism" of such non-Western religions therefore often refers to a very different type of being than does the *theos* in "monotheism." Simplistic application of such terms is misleading.

Nontheistic belief systems include those that uphold **atheism**, which in a modern context is a perspective that denies the existence of God or gods (Chapter 14). In ancient times, a person could be labeled an atheist for denying the significance of deities, even while believing that they exist. Among the ancient Greeks and Romans, for example, Epicureans were considered to be atheists. Even according to the modern meaning of atheism, some atheists nevertheless could be regarded as religious—depending on how one defines "religion." The *HarperCollins Dictionary of Religion* definition, with its basis in "supernatural beings," likely would not leave room for atheism, whereas Bruce Lincoln's definition could. Current trends in religiosity among young people suggest that atheism, along with its less insistent relative, agnosticism (which only refuses to assert the existence of God or gods, rather than outright denying it), are becoming more prevalent. A May 2015 Pew Forum study indicates that 22.8 percent of people in the United States identify themselves as atheist, agnostic, or "nothing in particular"—a group that is labeled "Unaffiliated" or religious "nones." This marks a sharp increase. (For more on the Pew Forum study, see the Online Resources list at the end of this chapter.)

Related to the category of nontheism is **monism**, the belief that all reality is ultimately one. An example of monism is the belief of some Hindus in many gods and goddesses while simultaneously holding that Brahman, ultimately indescribable, is the essence of all. Those Hindus therefore embrace monism, which is also described as nondualistic, because there is no distinction between the divine reality, on one hand, and the rest of reality, including human individuals, on the other.

These attempts at categorizing perspectives on ultimate reality involve some complications. Some Hindus are monistic because they understand all reality ultimately to be one thing: Brahman. But some of those same monistic Hindus also pay homage to a variety of supernatural and divine beings, and thus might also be described as polytheists.

Along with asserting the existence of ultimate reality, religions describe how this reality is revealed to human beings. Episodes of **revelation** are frequently recorded in sacred texts, or scriptures. In the case of theistic religions,

This painting, produced in 1810, depicts the Hindu deities Shiva and Parvati with their children, Ganesha and Kartikeya. Hindus believe in many gods and goddesses; these four—especially Shiva—are among the most popular.

Ka'ba, Mecca.

scriptures describe the role of God or the gods in history and also include pronouncements directly attributed to the divine. In the Jewish and Christian Bible, for example, God's will regarding ethical behavior is expressed directly in the Ten Commandments. The giving of the Ten Commandments is described in the narrative about the Exodus of the Israelites from Egypt, in which God is said to have played a central role.

Among nontheistic religions in particular—but also among the mystical traditions that form part of every religious tradition—revelation often combines textual transmission with a direct experience of revelation. Revelation is usually experienced by a founding figure of the religion, whose experiences are later written about; subsequent believers can then experience similar types of revelation, which requires their own participation. Buddhists, for example, have scriptural records that describe the Buddha's experience of nirvana, as well as pronouncements by deities praising the ultimate value of that experience. Followers must then connect to such revelation through practices such as meditation.

Another helpful way of thinking about revelation is offered by historian of religions Mircea Eliade (1907–1986), who describes a phenomenon he calls "hierophany," or "the *act of manifestation* of the sacred," which helps a people to establish its cosmology, or religious understanding, of the order of the world.[12] Eliade emphasizes how this concept applies to indigenous or small-scale traditions. But the phenomenon of the hierophany is readily apparent within the world's major religions, often, but not always, as a theophany, a manifestation of God or of gods. The role of hierophanies in establishing places of special significance can be observed in many of the sites related to the founding figures and events of the major religions: Christianity's Church of the Nativity (and other sacred sites related to the life of Christ); Islam's sacred city of Mecca; Buddhism's Bodh Gaya, site of Gautama's foundational experience of Enlightenment; and so on. Sacred moments establish sacred spatial monuments, thus establishing a sense of centrality and spatial order.

Religions also have much to say about *this* world. Human beings have always asked searching questions about the origin and status of our planet and of the universe, and how the world is ordered. This category of religious understanding is **cosmology** (from *kosmos*, the Greek term for world or universe). Typically, these issues—origin, status, and order—are intertwined. If our world was intentionally fashioned and ordered by a creator god, for instance, then it bears the stamp of divine affirmation. Thus, the early chapters of the book of Genesis in the Hebrew

Bible (the Christian Old Testament) describe the creative activity of God, including the creation of humankind. In contrast, the creation stories of some religious traditions deemphasize the role of the divine will in bringing about the world, sometimes (as in the religion of the ancient Greeks) describing the advent of the principal deities *after* the universe itself has been created. The gods, like humans, come into a world that is already established; gods and humans are depicted as sharing the world, which naturally affects the relationship between human and divine. In other religions, notably Hinduism, Buddhism, and other traditions that embrace liberation as the ultimate religious objective, this world is depicted as a kind of illusion; liberation involves being completely freed from the confines of this world.

In certain respects, modern scientific explanations set forth cosmologies that are intriguingly similar to some religious cosmologies taught by religious personages of the distant past, such as Gautama the Buddha or Epicurus, a Greek philosopher who espoused a theory of atomism, arguing that reality is composed entirely of a very large number of very small particles. (Recall that the Epicureans were labeled "atheists" because they denied the significance of the gods.)

Of course, a particular religion's cosmology strongly influences the degree to which its adherents are involved in caring for the world. On the one hand, religions that are indifferent or hostile toward the natural world are not apt to encourage anything akin to environmentalism. On the other hand, a religion that teaches that the world is inherently sacred naturally encourages a sense of stewardship toward the natural world. Native American traditions, for example, are notably environmentally oriented.

Cosmologies often describe how the world will end. On this issue, most of the religions considered in this text can roughly be divided into two categories. Some, including Judaism and, more stridently, Christianity and Islam, envision a divinely orchestrated end of the world as we know it. This end is a one-time event, often said to be accompanied by judgment and eternal reward for the good and punishment for the evil. Some forms of Western monotheism, such as Adventism and Jehovah's Witnesses (both explored in Chapter 14), have placed special emphasis on predictions of precise dates for this cataclysmic end. Religions belonging to the other category, which includes most forms of Hinduism, Buddhism, Jainism, and Sikhism, understand this world to be a temporary phenomenon that is part of an eternal cycle of creation and eventual destruction, to be followed repeatedly by another round.

How Should We Live in This World?

All religions are human enterprises. Their teachings are communicated in human languages, their rituals are practiced by human participants, and their histories are entwined with the development of human societies and cultures. Religions also explain what it is to be a human being, which includes ethical or moral considerations. Are we by nature good, evil, or somewhere in between? Religions tend to recognize that human beings do not always do the right thing, and they commonly offer teachings and disciplines directed toward moral or ethical improvement. On the one hand, to say that we are by nature good, and at the same time to recognize moral failings, is to infer that some cause external to our nature is causing the shortcoming. If we are by nature evil, on the other hand, or at least naturally prone to doing wrong, then the moral challenge lies within and the means of improvement would need to be directed inwardly.

Religions typically prescribe right behavior and condemn wrong behavior, based on a set of ethical tenets, such as the Jewish and Christian Ten Commandments. In fact, the prospects of improving the human condition and of faring well in an afterlife are often understood to depend upon right ethical behavior. The ethical teachings of many religions are notably similar. The so-called Golden Rule ("Do unto others what you would have them do unto you"[13]) in the Christian New Testament is reflected in the scriptures of virtually all of the world's major traditions.

The religions differ, however, over the source of ethical truth. Some emphasize **revealed ethics**, asserting that God, or some other supernatural force such as Hindu dharma (ethical duty), has established what constitutes right behavior and has revealed this to human beings. Others, such as some forms of Buddhism, emphasize the role of conscience in an individual's moral deliberations. These two emphases are not necessarily mutually exclusive. Some religions, Christianity among them, teach that both revealed ethics and individual conscience work together to distinguish right from wrong.

What Is Our Ultimate Purpose?

The challenge of mortality—the fact that we are destined to die—is sometimes cited as the primary motivating force behind religion. And although it is true that all religions have something to say about death, the diversity of perspectives is striking. For example, whereas Christianity, with its focus on the resurrection of Christ and the hope of eternal life, makes mortality a central concern, Zen Buddhism, drawing inspiration from the classic Daoist texts, simply acknowledges the natural place of death in the order of things.

Both the challenge of mortality and the issue of our moral nature relate to questions regarding the human condition. In many faiths, how we conduct ourselves in this world will determine our fates after we die. Most religions do, of course, acknowledge that human beings are destined to die (although some, such as Daoism, have aspired to discover the means of inducing physical immortality). While some religions have little to say about the prospects of an afterlife, most do provide explanations regarding the fate of the individual after death—although their explanations vary widely.

Hinduism, Buddhism, Jainism, and Sikhism all maintain belief in samsara, the "wheel of life" that implies a series of lives, deaths, and rebirths for every individual. The ultimate aim of each of these religions is liberation from samsara. But most of the adherents of these religions anticipate that death will lead to rebirth into another life form (not necessarily human), one in a long series of rebirths. Furthermore, the reborn are destined for any one of multiple realms, including a variety of hells and heavens.

Other religions, including Christianity and Islam, teach that individuals are destined for some sort of afterlife, usually a version of heaven or of hell. Sometimes the teachings are more complicated. The traditional Catholic doctrine of purgatory, for example, anticipates an intermediary destiny somewhere between the bliss of heaven and the agony of hell, where an individual can gradually be purified from sin, ultimately achieving salvation and entry to heaven.

Sixteenth-century triptych (altar painting) depicting the creation of Eve (center), the eating of the forbidden fruit (left), and the expulsion from the Garden of Eden (right). This story of humankind's first sin sets forth basic biblical perspectives on the human condition.

Given what a religion says about the human condition, what ultimate purpose is the religious life intended to achieve? Is there a state of existence to which the religious person can hope to aspire that perfectly completes or even transcends the human condition, overcoming entirely its cares and shortcomings?

One such state of existence is what Protestant theologian and philosopher of religion Rudolf Otto (1869–1937) in his classic work *The Idea of the Holy* (1923) describes as the **numinous experience**. Otto describes the encounter with "the Holy" as "numinous," a term he developed from the Latin *numen*, meaning spirit or divinity. A genuine numinous experience, Otto asserts, is characterized by two powerful and contending forces: ***mysterium tremendum*** and *__fascinans__*. *Mysterium tremendum* is the feeling of awe that overwhelms a person who experiences the mysterious and majestic presence of the "wholly other." *Fascinans* (Latin, "fascinating") is the contrasting feeling of overwhelming attraction. The encounter with the Holy is thus alluring (*fascinans*) even as it is frightening on account of the awe-inspiring mystery (*mysterium tremendum*). The biblical phenomenon of the "fear of God" fits this description, as the God who is being feared is at the same time recognized as the source of life and the hope for salvation. Otto's analysis of the numinous experience remains an important contribution to religious studies, although it suffers from a significant limitation: based in his Protestant Christian outlook, it may ring true to a Protestant; from a global perspective, however, the analysis is rather narrow. For example, Otto discounts the **mystical experience**, a category that includes such phenomena as Buddhist nirvana, the complete dissolution of an individual's sense of selfhood said by Buddhists to be a state of perfect bliss and ultimate fulfillment.

According to Otto, nirvana involves too much *fascinans* without enough *mysterium tremendum*.

Recall that Bruce Lincoln's definition of "religion" is based on the notion of the transcendent. Both the numinous experience and nirvana are examples of transcendent states of existence. For Otto, the numinous experience depends on the existence of "the Holy," or God. For many Buddhists, the experience of nirvana does not depend whatsoever on belief in God or gods. Most world religions, whether or not they embrace belief in a supernatural being, assert the possibility of such a transcendent state of existence, an ultimate objective of the religious life that brings complete spiritual fulfillment. For a Buddhist who has experienced nirvana, there is, paradoxically, no longer a need for Buddhism. The religious life has been lived to its fullest extent, and the ultimate objective has been reached. Because nirvana involves the complete extinction of individual existence, it is truly transcendent of the human condition. Other religions, in varying ways, also set forth ultimate objectives, whether or not they imply the complete transcendence of the human condition. In some cases, spiritual fulfillment consists of living in harmony with nature. Others acknowledge the supernatural—usually God (or gods)—and the need for human beings to live in perfect relationship with it. Christianity, for example, offers salvation from the effects of sin, which otherwise estrange the individual from God. Sometimes spiritual fulfillment is thought to be achievable in this lifetime; other times it is projected into the distant future, after many lifetimes.

Of course, improving upon the human condition does not have to involve complete transcendence. Every day around the world, religious people improve upon the human condition in all sorts of ways. Belief in a loving God gives hope and fortitude in the face of life's uncertainties. Meditation and prayer bring tranquility. Charitable acts are motivated by religious beliefs. Belonging to a religious group offers social benefits that can be deeply fulfilling. Even for individuals who do not participate directly in a religious tradition, sacred art, architecture, and music can bring joy.

Moses and the Burning Bush (1990), charcoal and pastel on paper by Hans Feibusch. In the drawing, God reveals himself to Moses in a bush that is on fire but not consumed by the flames. The event is described in Exodus, the second book of the Hebrew Bible (Old Testament).

Religious Ideals and the Realities of Lived Religions

The previous section on religious questions and challenges emphasizes what "should" be done according to religious ideals. Naturally, religious teachings set forth ideals regarding what to believe and how to act. But the realities of religions as they are actually lived by individuals and communities—or, to use a term that has recently become popular in scholarship, "religion on the ground"—often do not match with those high ideals.

Surely most of this lived religion is not notably egregious, and often even the highest standards of formal teachings are met. But everyone in today's world recognizes that actions are done in the name of religion that hardly seem compatible with ideals or moral imperatives. News surfaces quite frequently about the moral failings of religious leaders or the usurpation of religious institutions by groups that pervert and exploit their teachings. Even more troubling is the constant barrage of reports regarding acts of terrorism and other forms of violence committed in the name of religion. Could there be something about religion itself that motivates such harmful acts?

Religion and Violence   Religion, as noted at the beginning of this chapter, is a potent force, in ways that are both constructive and destructive. Consider again Bruce Lincoln's four-domain definition of a "religion," and note that it does not portray religion as necessarily being a force for peace in the world. The "discourse" that claims a "transcendent status," and the "practices," "community," and "institution" related to this discourse need not necessarily be based on avoiding violence. As Lincoln argues later in *Holy Terrors: Thinking about Religion after September 11*, religion has the potential to facilitate and even to escalate violence. Lincoln concludes his book with a list of fourteen "Theses on Religion and Violence," the last of which states:

> Just as the use of violence tends to elicit a violent riposte, so the religious valorization of violence prompts its victims to frame their violent responses in religious terms. In doing so, they normally invert the signs through which their adversaries mark one side as sacred and the other profane. When both sides experience their struggle in religious terms, the stage is set for prolonged, ferocious, and enormously destructive combat.[14]

This is a frightening and, we can hope, an unlikely scenario. But as we observe frequently in today's world, even when just one side in a conflict justifies actions by belief in "transcendent" authority, there is a risk of religiously motivated violence, even to the point of taking the lives of others and of losing one's own.

Religion and Politics   Short of inflicting violence in order to exert force on worldly affairs, religious acts and perspectives often have a political edge. The history of religious engagement in politics reaches back to the advent of civilizations and continues to this day, in many cases overtly and with highly significant consequences. Through the centuries, many religious systems have served simultaneously to provide governing systems, situations that typically involve **theocracy**: a governmental system that claims power and guidance based on divine authority.

In less pronounced ways, religion often affects political positions and influences voting decisions and other ways in which populations are involved in governance. This is obvious when we consider, for example, the political influence of evangelical Christianity in the United States, or the recent rise and current dominance of India's BJP (Bharatiya Janata Party) and Prime Minister Narendra Modi. Similar examples could be cited for many countries around the globe.

1.4 Religions in the Modern World

A sound analysis of the world's religions must take account of the rapid changes that characterize the modern world. Historical transformations, accelerated during the past several centuries by colonialism, the scientific revolution, and economic globalization, have reshaped religious traditions. This book takes into account such factors whenever appropriate. Here we introduce four phenomena that will reappear frequently: modernization, urbanization, globalization, and multiculturalism. We give special attention to two features of modernization that are especially noteworthy for our study: the increasingly visible place of women within religious traditions and the encounter of religion and science.

Modernization and Related Phenomena

Modernization is the general process through which societies transform economically, socially, and culturally to keep pace with an increasingly competitive global marketplace. Its net effects include increased literacy, improved education, enhanced technologies, self-sustaining economies, the increased roles of women in various aspects of society, and the greater involvement of the general populace in government (as in democracies). All these effects involve corresponding changes within religious traditions. Higher literacy rates and improved education, for example, facilitate increased access to religious texts that previously were controlled by and confined to the religious elite. Technological advances, strengthened economies, and increased participation in government all nurture greater equality for and empowerment of the common people. Moreover, a general feature of modernity is its tendency to deny the authority of tradition and the past. Traditional patriarchal modes, for example, have tended over time to be diminished. Around the globe, we are witnessing a general erosion of long-standing power structures within religions. Obviously, this is not the case in all circumstances; changes have tended to occur in different societies at different times, and some religious institutions are better equipped to resist change.

Urbanization   **Urbanization**, the shift of population centers from rural, agricultural settings to cities, is a significant demographic effect of modernization. A century ago, only about 10 percent of the global population lived in cities; today, this figure has risen to more than 50 percent. Many religious traditions developed within primarily rural settings, with calendars of holy days and rituals patterned around

agricultural cycles. For most religious people, such patterns have far less relevance today.

Globalization   **Globalization** is the linking and intermixing of cultures. It accelerated quickly during the centuries of exploration and colonization and has been nurtured considerably by the advanced technologies brought about by modernization. The extent of this linking and intermixing is evinced in the very term *World Wide Web*, and the pronounced and rapidly evolving effects of the Internet and other technologies have been extraordinary. The almost instantaneous exchange of information that this technology allows is more or less paralleled by better means of transportation. In sum, we now live in a global community that could hardly have been imagined a few decades ago.

Multiculturalism   The most pronounced religious effects of globalization pertain to the closely related phenomenon of **multiculturalism**, the coexistence of different peoples and their cultural ways in one time and place. Many people today live in religiously pluralistic societies, no longer sheltered from the presence of religions other than their own. This plurality increases the degree of influence exerted by one religion on another, making it difficult for many individuals to regard any one religious tradition as the *only* viable one. This circumstance, in turn, fosters general questioning and critical assessment of religion. To some extent, such questioning and critical assessment erodes the authority traditionally attributed to religion. Globalization, then, like modernization, has nurtured the notably modern process of **secularization**, the general turning away from traditional religious authority and institutions.

Bongeunsa Temple, founded in 794 CE, is surrounded by the ultramodern cityscape of Seoul, South Korea.

Gender Issues in Religions

One of the more pronounced effects of modernization on world religions has involved issues pertaining to gender identity and roles. The most obvious effect has been the increased visibility and prominence of women within many traditions. Other issues include norms regarding sexuality and the status of LGBTQ persons, with regard to both a religion's adherents and those in positions of leadership, such as clergy and rabbis. As the text's chapters will show, the various religions—and divisions within each religion—maintain a diversity of positions on such issues. There is a strong tendency, however, in modern times for religions to be more inclusive with regard to gender issues.

To some extent, the increased visibility of women also has *caused* the furtherance of modernization. As women increasingly feel themselves empowered and are afforded opportunities to effect change, their momentum propels modernizing transformations. Traditional patriarchal modes have tended to give way to more egalitarian ones, and old assumptions have gradually receded. To cite just one example, in the last twenty years the percentage of clergy in Protestant Christian churches who are women has risen quite dramatically. While in 1999 only 5 percent of senior pastors were female, ten years later this figure had doubled to 10 percent.[15] According to a recent study, in 2016 the percentage of women clergy was 20.7 percent.[16]

Corresponding to the increased visibility and prominence of women in many religions has been the dramatic development over the past five decades of feminist theory and its application to the study of religion. Sometimes referred to as women's studies or as gender studies, academic approaches based in feminist theory have revealed the strong historical tendency of religious traditions to subordinate women and to enforce the perpetuation of patriarchal systems. On the one hand, these studies have revealed contributions of women through the ages that have hitherto been largely ignored, while on the other hand they have prompted changes within some religions that have expanded the roles of women and have provided opportunities for their greater prominence. In other words, studies based in feminist theory have to some extent *changed* the religions themselves, along with providing new and potent means of studying them.

A miniature illustration from the "Automata of al-Jazari," a Muslim scholar, inventor, engineer, mathematician, and astronomer who lived from 1136 to 1206.

The Encounter of Religion and Science

Perhaps no single feature of modernization has been more challenging to traditional religious ways—and more nurturing of secularization—than the encounter of religion with science. One need only think of the impact of Charles Darwin's *Origin of Species* (1859) and its theory of evolution to note the potential for conflict between scientific and traditional religious worldviews. The question of whether the biblical account of creation should be taught alongside the theory of evolution in schools is a divisive issue in some predominantly Christian societies today. In the domain of cosmology, too, science has tended to overwhelm traditional perspectives, such as the idea that the Earth is somehow the center of the cosmos, as implied in the Bible and in the creation myths of many traditions.

Many more examples could be drawn from the history of religions and the history of science to illustrate the ongoing potential for conflict between these two domains. Of course, religions are not always hostile to science. In fact, as we have already noted, sometimes modern scientific theories seem almost to converge with ancient religious outlooks. Acquiring a more sophisticated perspective on the encounter of religion and science requires us to consider the underlying reasons for both conflict and convergence.

Fundamental to the scientific method is dependence on empirical data, the observable "facts" of any given situation. To a large extent, religions do not rely only on the observable as a source of determining truth. Religious belief is often characterized precisely by commitment to the *non*observable, such as a supernatural being. This term, "supernatural," indicates another point of contention between religion and science. For whereas science takes it for granted that the universe consistently obeys certain laws of nature, religions commonly embrace belief in beings and events that are not subject to these laws.

And yet these issues of natural laws and of the observable versus the unobservable also lead to points of convergence between science and religion. Certain basic and extremely significant scientific questions remain unanswered. For example, what is the ground of consciousness? What causes gravity? What, if anything, existed prior to the Big Bang, and what caused *its* existence? Science and religion can perhaps generally agree on one point: mystery abounds. Granted, the scientific response to a mystery is "let's solve it," whereas the religious response typically is "this is a mystery and is meant to be." But in the meantime, mystery abides, allowing for a certain kind of convergence. It is probably no accident that the percentage of scientists in the United States who regularly attend religious services is almost the same as the percentage for the general population.[17]

Religion and the Environment   Another topic that involves the relationship of religion and science is perspectives on the environment. As the following chapters will show, for the most part, recently such perspectives are not characterized by conflict in this regard; on the contrary, environmentalists in most of the world's religions readily accept the facts and projections as established by science, and they look to their traditions for ways of understanding and responding to them.

Currently, the fact of climate change caused by greenhouse gas emissions resulting from human activities is on the forefront of many environmental concerns. But the upsurge in concern among religiously minded people has been growing for several decades, from times when other environmental problems loomed large, such as pollution, of land, water, and air, and the threat of nuclear disasters, as experienced all too tangibly at Three Mile Island in 1979 and Chernobyl in 1986. The gas leak disaster at Bhopal in 1984 singlehandedly launched environmentalist movements in India.

Environmental responses to these and other threats have varied depending on specificities of place, time, and cultural predispositions, but for every religious tradition, activists draw upon deeply rooted beliefs regarding the sanctity of the natural world and humanity's appropriate role, oftentimes seen as divinely sanctioned, in caring for it.

1.5 Methods for Studying the World's Religions

Scholars approach the study of religion in a variety of ways. And although there is no *single* correct approach, it is helpful to keep some basic concepts and strategies in mind. We begin with consideration of effective means of categorizing religious phenomena.

Dimensions of Religions

Sound definitions strive to be universal in scope. Along with a sound definition, a means of categorizing the common, though not necessarily universal, components of a subject of study can often prove beneficial. We now explore possibilities for identifying religious phenomena, in part to bring home the important point that there is no "right" or "wrong" way to go about categorizing them. Instead, we seek the most useful means given the task at hand. This will lead naturally to clarifying how this book goes about organizing its presentation of material.

Some scholarly approaches to the world's religions feature specific categories of phenomena as the primary means of organizing information. Religious scholar Ninian Smart's (1927–2001) "dimensional" scheme, for example, divides the various aspects of religious traditions into seven dimensions:

- The mythic (or sacred narrative)
- The doctrinal (or philosophical)
- The ethical (or legal)
- The ritual (or practical)
- The experiential (or emotional)
- The social
- The material[18]

Such an approach to the content of religious traditions is very useful, especially if one focuses on a comparative analysis that emphasizes particular motifs (that is, "dimensions" or aspects thereof).

Three Categories: Teachings, Historical Development, and Way of Life

We will continue to explore Smart's dimensions and their interrelationships as we proceed with an overview of the three main categories employed in this book, the organization scheme for which is based on Smart's dimensional approach. Although each chapter of this book is organized around these three main categories, we do not devote equal attention to each category. To do so would be to ignore the varying nature of the religious traditions and to force an inappropriately rigid structure. Judaism, for example, calls for extensive attention to historical development in order to best understand the context of its teachings and practices; Jainism, for which an early historical record barely exists, does not.

Teachings Obviously, religions tend to involve beliefs. But as long as they remain private to the individual, beliefs are problematic for the student of religion. Once they are given outward expression in the form of a religion's teachings, however, beliefs can be observed and interpreted. Such public beliefs are manifested as doctrines or creeds—sets of concepts that are *believed in*. (The term *creed* derives from the Latin verb *credo*, meaning "I believe.") Among the world's major religions, Christianity most emphasizes doctrines. Most Christians, for example, regularly acknowledge belief in the statements of the Nicene Creed.

Religious teachings include another significant category, often referred to as **myth** (as noted in Smart's "mythic" dimension). In contrast to the modern connotation of myth as a falsehood, myth as understood by the academic field of religious studies is a powerful source of sacred truth. Set forth in narrative form and originally conveyed orally, myths do not depend on empirical verifiability or rational coherence for their power. Believers simply accept them as true accounts, often involving events of primordial time that describe the origin of things.

As we have noted previously, religions typically include ethical instructions, whether doctrinal or mythic, among their teachings. And as Smart readily acknowledges, the various dimensions are closely interrelated; the ethical dimension, for example, extends into the doctrinal and the mythic, and so forth.

Meditating Buddha, sixth century CE (Thai). Sculptures of the Buddha typically depict the serene calm of the enlightened state.

Historical Development The world's major religions—all of which are many centuries old—have long and intricate histories. Thus, the historical development of religious traditions incorporates a vast sweep of social, artistic, and other cultural phenomena.

The wide array of artistic, architectural, and other aspects of material culture generated within religious traditions is obvious to anyone who has studied art history. The ornate Hindu temple sculptures, the majestic statues of Jain tirthankaras, the mathematically ordered architectural features of Islamic arabesque décor—all attest to the role of religion in the nurturing of material culture. Other forms of artistic creation, most prominently music and theater, also are significant features of religions. And, as Smart helpfully clarifies when discussing the material dimension of religion, some traditions designate natural entities (mountains, rivers, wooded groves) as sacred.

Social institutions and phenomena, such as economic activities, politics, social class structures, and hierarchies, interact with the historical development of religious traditions. As we have observed, Marx and Durkheim went as far as to reduce religion to being entirely the effect

Devils Tower, located in northeastern Wyoming, is regarded as a sacred place by many Native Americans.

of economic and societal forces, respectively. Even for theorists who opt not to go nearly as far as they did, the relevance of such phenomena is obvious.

Way of Life   This main category features two types of religious phenomena: practices and modes of experience, both of which are included among Smart's seven dimensions of religion, as the ritual (or practical) and the experiential (or emotional) dimensions. Some such elements are tangible and readily observable and describable, such as a **ritual** like the exchange of marriage vows or the procession of pilgrims to a shrine. Others are highly personal and therefore hidden from the outsider's view. One of the great challenges of studying religions rests precisely in this personal, private quality. Modes of experience such as Buddhist nirvana are by definition beyond the reach of empirical observation and of description. Rudolf Otto, throughout his analysis, emphasizes the impossibility of fully describing the "numinous" experience. Even common practices such as prayer and meditation involve an inner aspect that is inaccessible to anyone who is not sharing the experience. Although the present book can adequately illustrate and explain these experiential phenomena, it cannot be expected to provide a full disclosure at certain points. Such is the nature of religion.

Balance and Empathy

A vital concept for studying world religions is the maintenance of a healthy balance between the perspective of an insider (one who practices a given religion) and the perspective of an outsider (one who studies the religion without practicing it). For, although an insider arguably has the best vantage point on the lived realities of the religion, presumably the insider is primarily concerned with *being* religious and not in explaining the religion in a manner that will be most effective for those who hold other religious (or nonreligious) perspectives. It is quite natural for an insider to be biased in favor of his or her own religion. The outsider, however, has no reason to feel such bias. At the same time, the outsider would not have the benefit of experiencing the religion firsthand. It is analogous to trying to understand a goldfish in a pond. An outsider can describe the fish's color, its movements, and its eating habits, but can say very little about what it is actually like to be a goldfish.[19]

The academic approach to the study of religions attempts to balance the perspectives of insider and outsider, thereby drawing upon the benefits of each. It is not an intentionally religious enterprise. As we have noted previously, unlike theology, it is not *doing* religion or *being* religious. Instead, the academic approach strives to analyze and describe religions in a way that is accurate and fair for all concerned—insiders and outsiders alike. An instructive parallel can be drawn from the discipline of political science. Rather than advocating a particular political point of view, and rather than *being* a politician, a political scientist strives to analyze and describe political viewpoints and phenomena in a fair, neutral manner. A good political scientist could, for instance, belong to the Democratic Party but still produce a fair article about a Republican politician—without ever betraying personal Democratic convictions. A good scholar of religion, of whatever religious (or nonreligious) persuasion, attends to religious matters with a similarly neutral stance.

Another basic concept for the academic approach to religion is **empathy**, the capacity for seeing things from another's perspective. Empathy works in tandem with the usual tools of scholarship—the observation and rational assessment of empirical data—to yield an effective academic approach to the study of religions. The sometimes cold, impersonal procedures of scholarship are enlivened by the personal insights afforded by empathy.

Comparative and Multidisciplinary Approaches

Along with empathy, the study of the world's religions benefits from a comparative approach. Friedrich Max Müller (1823–1900), who is generally regarded as the founder of the modern field of religious studies, asserted that to know just one religion is to know none. That is, to understand the phenomena of any given tradition, it is necessary to observe such phenomena as they occur in other traditions. This requires that the study of world religions be cross-cultural.

This is not to say that comparison should be undertaken haphazardly or only to discover similarities while ignoring differences. Those critics mentioned earlier who deride the "world religions discourse" tend to be suspicious of attempts at comparison, claiming that too often similarities are indeed valued over differences and that the categories used to make comparisons tend to privilege Christianity over other traditions. Sometimes the results of the comparison of religion differentiate religions into groups that are too sweepingly general: for example, "Eastern" and

"Western" religions. Still, the benefits of comparative analysis outweigh the risks, and the potential pitfalls that these critics appropriately warn against can indeed be avoided through a conscientious approach.

Along with being cross-cultural, religious studies is multidisciplinary, or poly-methodic, drawing on the contributions of anthropology, history, sociology, psychology, philosophy, feminist theory, and other disciplines and fields of study.

This chapter has frequently used the term *culture*, the study of which is especially the domain of anthropology. We have noted that religion plays a crucial role in molding, transforming, and transmitting cultures and that it interacts with other cultural aspects. An effective study of the world's religions requires consideration of the interrelationship between religion and culture; in other words, it requires a healthy dose of cultural anthropology.

Contributions from other disciplines are similarly vital. Religions are historical and social phenomena, and so the disciplines of history and sociology play significant roles. Especially when trying to make sense of the modes of religious experience, psychology offers important inroads to understanding. Along with Freud and James, Swiss psychologist Carl Jung (1875–1961) deserves mention for his vital contributions to the study of religious symbolism and of the role of the unconscious mind in the religious life. The philosophy of religion, which in certain respects is the closest to actually *doing* religion (or theology), endeavors to assess critically the truth claims and arguments set forth by religions. Questions involving the existence of God, for example, are among those taken up by philosophers. We have already noted the important contributions of feminist theory. The natural sciences also have contributed substantially, at a pace that is accelerating rapidly. Especially striking innovations have come from cognitive science, which studies both the physical capacity for thinking (i.e., the "brain"—although this category can also include computers and other systems of artificial intelligence) and mental functions (i.e., the "mind"). Cognitive science is itself a multidisciplinary field with contributors including neuroscientists, evolutionary biologists, and computer scientists, along with specialists from the social sciences.

The multidisciplinary nature of religious studies accounts for its very *existence* as an academic discipline. Without the involvement of its many subdisciplines, there could be no academic field of religious studies. In recent years, these various disciplines and subdisciplines have been pushed in new directions, with exciting results. The list of "tags" used by the Society of Biblical Literature for categorizing papers delivered at its meetings provides a glimpse of the range of disciplines and perspectives (see Online Resources at the end of this chapter). Even in this relatively confined field—although the society oversees study of much more than just the Bible—there are forty-four "Interpretive Approaches," which is only one of twelve subcategories listed under the main heading, "Methods" (the other main heading is "Texts"). These diverse Interpretive Approaches include such subdisciplines as African and African American criticism, deconstruction, disability studies, gender and sexuality criticism, Marxist criticism, postcolonial criticism, and theological interpretation. As Ninian Smart was known to say, those who study religion are "polymethod-doodling all da-day long."

Studying Religions and Being Religious

We have noted that the rest of this book's chapters feature a threefold organizational scheme consisting of teachings, historical development, and way of life. Although these chapters, with their focus on the religious traditions themselves, naturally are quite different from this introduction, it is worth noticing that in this chapter, too, we have featured historical development—of both the attempts to explain or define religion and the approaches to studying it—and teachings, most especially the theories of various notable contributors to religious studies. The "way of life" aspect perhaps has been less obvious, but in fact it deserves consideration as we end the chapter. On more than one occasion, we have drawn a distinction between the academic study of religion and *doing* religion or *being* religious. Where, then, does this leave the individual who wants to do (and be) both? Ultimately, this question is left for the individual reader to ponder. But it might prove helpful to know that the degree of *being* religious among scholars of religion spans the spectrum of possibilities, from not religious at all to highly devout. Either way (or someplace in between), one thing is true for all who study the world's religions: we are investigating enduring aspects of human cultures around the globe. Our understanding of things that matter is certain to be enriched.

REVIEW QUESTIONS

For Review

1. Who is Émile Durkheim, and what is notable about his definition of "religion"?
2. Bruce Lincoln, in his definition of a "religion," identifies four "domains." What are they?
3. What is "revelation," and how is it pertinent to the question, What is ultimate reality?
4. Identify and briefly describe Ninian Smart's seven "dimensions" of religion.
5. What is "empathy," and how is it relevant for the academic study of religion?

For Further Reflection

1. Sigmund Freud and Karl Marx, while tending to be dismissive of the enduring importance of religion, asserted explanations that continue to provoke and to enrich academic consideration of the role of religion. Based on their statements included in this chapter, how might their perspectives be provocative and enriching in this respect?
2. This book poses three prominent questions with regard to the challenges addressed by the world's religions: What is ultimate reality? How should we live in this world? What is our ultimate purpose? Drawing on the examples and ideas presented in this chapter, discuss to what extent and in what ways these three questions are interrelated.
3. Explore the interrelationship of these features of religions in the modern world: globalization, secularization, and multiculturalism.

GLOSSARY

atheism Perspective that denies the existence of God or gods.

cosmology Understanding of the nature of the world that typically explains its origin and how it is ordered.

empathy The capacity for seeing things from another's perspective, and an important methodological approach for studying religions.

globalization The linking and intermixing of cultures; any process that moves a society toward an internationalization of religious discourse.

henotheism The belief that acknowledges a plurality of gods but elevates one of them to special status.

modernization The general process through which societies transform economically, socially, and culturally to become more industrial, urban, and secular; any transformation of societies and cultures that leads to the abandonment of traditional religious values.

monism The belief that all reality is ultimately one.

monotheism The belief in only one god.

multiculturalism The coexistence of different peoples and their cultural ways in one time and place.

mysterium tremendum and **fascinans** The contrasting feelings of awe-inspiring mystery and of overwhelming attraction that are said by Rudolf Otto to characterize the numinous experience.

mystical experience A general category of religious experience characterized in various ways, for example, as the union with the divine through inward contemplation or as the dissolution of the sense of individual selfhood.

myth A story or narrative, originally conveyed orally, that sets forth basic truths of a religious tradition and that often involves events of primordial time that describe the origins of things.

nontheistic Term denoting a religion that does not maintain belief in God or gods.

numinous experience Rudolf Otto's term for describing an encounter with "the Holy"; it is characterized by two powerful and contending forces, *mysterium tremendum* and *fascinans.*

pantheism The belief that the divine reality is identical to nature or the material world.

polytheism The belief in many gods.

revealed ethics Truth regarding right behavior believed to be divinely established and intentionally made known to human beings.

revelation The expression of the divine will, commonly recorded in sacred texts.

ritual Formal worship practice.

secularization The general turning away from traditional religious authority and institutions; any tendency in modern society that devalues religious worldviews or seeks to substitute scientific theories for religious beliefs.

theistic Term denoting a religion that maintains belief in God or gods.

theocracy A governmental system that claims power and guidance based on divine authority.

transtheistic Term denoting a theological perspective that acknowledges the existence of gods while denying that the gods are vital with regard to the most crucial religious issues, such as the quest for salvation.

urbanization The shift of population centers from rural, agricultural settings to cities.

SUGGESTIONS FOR FURTHER READING

Eliade, Mircea. *The Sacred and the Profane: The Nature of Religion.* Translated by Willard R. Trask. New York: Harper and Row, 1961. Eliade's most accessible work, offering a rich analysis of sacred space and time.

Hinnels, John, ed. *The Routledge Companion to the Study of Religion.* 2nd ed. Oxford: Routledge, 2010. Coverage of significant issues in religious studies by leading scholars.

Masuzawa, Tomoko. *The Invention of World Religions: Or, How European Universalism Was Preserved in the Language of Pluralism.* Chicago: University of Chicago Press, 2005. Careful historical analysis of the term and category "world religions."

Pals, Daniel. *Nine Theories of Religion*. 3rd ed. New York: Oxford University Press, 2015. The best introduction to the history of religious studies as an academic field, including chapters on Karl Marx, William James, Sigmund Freud, Émile Durkheim, and Mircea Eliade.

Segal, Robert A., and Kocku von Stuckrad, eds. *Vocabulary for the Study of Religion*. Leiden, The Netherlands: Brill, 2015. 3 vols. Also available online, this recent, thorough work provides encyclopedic coverage of all important topics in the field of religious studies.

Smart, Ninian. *Dimensions of the Sacred: An Anatomy of the World's Beliefs*. Berkeley: University of California Press, 1996. An engaging presentation of Smart's "dimensions."

Smith, Jonathan Z. *Imagining Religion: From Babylon to Jonestown*. Chicago Studies in the History of Judaism. Chicago: University of Chicago Press, 1982. One among various collections of essays that exemplify Smith's impressively wide-ranging and astute approach to the study of religion.

Taylor, Mark C., ed. *Critical Terms for Religious Studies*. Chicago: University of Chicago Press, 1998. Articles on various central topics for the study of religions, written by leading scholars in the field.

ONLINE RESOURCES

American Academy of Religion

The largest and most influential North American academic society for the study of religion.

Society of Biblical Literature

A companion organization to the American Academy of Religion, the Society of Biblical Literature is the premier academic organization for scholars in biblical studies and much more. The diversity and innovative nature of the Society is evidenced in its extensive list of "tags" that are used to help categorize papers presented at its various meetings:

Pew Research Religion and Public Life Project

Excellent source of information on issues involving social and political aspects of religion. The Pew Research Center has revealed startling statistics with regard to the rapid decline recently of traditional forms of religion in the United States.

The Pluralism Project at Harvard University

Organization that offers an impressive array of helpful resources, especially with regard to the world's religions in North America.

Indigenous Religions of North America

2

Chapter Outline

2.1 Summarize the key beliefs and practices central to indigenous religions of North America.

2.2 Identify how indigenous religions of North America conceive of humanity's place in nature.

2.3 Discuss the emergence of early religions in North America.

2.4 Describe the impact of conquest and colonization on North American religions.

2.5 Summarize contemporary issues in North American indigenous religions, such as resistance movements and revitalization.

2.6 Describe various modes of indigenous North American religious observance.

2.7 Identify important stages in the life cycle, and how they are marked with ritual in indigenous religions of North America.

2.8 Associate specific traditions and rituals with stages in the life cycle and gender identity.

2.9 Describe the state of indigenous religions of North America in today's world.

THE HOT AFTERNOON SUN beats down on the eighteen men and women who dance in patterned formation in the midst of a circular enclosure. Caleb, a twenty-six-year-old medical technician from Rapid City, South Dakota, is one of the Eagle Dancers. Caleb and the others dance to the rhythmic beating of a large drum, their faces turned upward to the eastern sky. This is the sixth time this day that the group has danced, each time for forty minutes, each time gradually shifting formation in order to face all four directions, honoring the spirit beings of the East, the South, the West, and the North. One more session of dancing, later this afternoon, will bring to an end this year's annual

This photo from 1910 shows several Cheyenne people gathered in preparation for a Sun Dance ceremony.

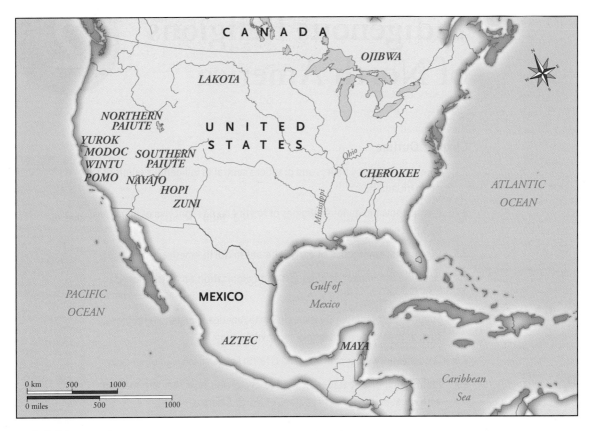

Indigenous peoples of North America that are discussed in this chapter.

Sun Dance. The Sun Dance is a midsummer Native American ritual that spans nearly two weeks, culminating in four days of dancing. This Sun Dance, in the wilderness of the Pacific Northwest, is open to all participants—from all Native American nations and even non-Native Americans.

In the center of the circular enclosure stands a remarkable tree. Perhaps a hundred bundles of colorful cloth hang from its boughs. Its central limbs hold a branch of chokecherry, from which hang effigies of a buffalo and of a man. The cottonwood tree was carefully selected months in advance for this purpose, and then ceremoniously felled the day before the dancing began and carried many miles to be positioned at the enclosure's center.

The tree's significance for all those gathered at the Sun Dance can hardly be overstated. Due to the ritual of the dancing, the circle for these four days is sacred space. The tree stands at the center and marks the most sacred space of all. In fact, it is the tree that *establishes* the circle and defines the sacred space. Added to this is the significance of its verticality. By reaching upward, the tree is thought to be the point of contact with the spirit world that connects the sacred expanse of the sky to the sacred space of the circle and to Caleb and the dancers. In every respect, the cottonwood tree is a kind of **axis mundi** (Latin, "the center of the world"), a symbol that scholars of religious studies and mythology have recognized in cultures and traditions globally. Planted in the Earth, reaching skyward, and establishing the sacred enclosure of the Sun Dance, the tree is perceived by the participants as being the center of the world—and of reality itself.

Caleb is a member of the Lakota Nation, a people of the Northern Plains. Caleb is a special type of dancer known as an Eagle Dancer. He and the two other Eagle Dancers dance attached to ropes that are strung from the tree's trunk and looped around skewers that were pierced through the skin of their chests on the first day of dancing. At the end of the fourth day, they will fall back on their ropes, pulling the skewers free from their flesh. This act is considered a sacrifice to the Great Spirit, or God, a gift of the one thing that is truly one's own to give—one's being. The Eagle Dancers spend almost the entire four days in the midst of the sacred circle, enduring the days' heat and the nights' chill, and taking neither food nor drink. Though he is a young man, Caleb has spent several years preparing for this Sun Dance, the first summer of three in which he will be an Eagle Dancer. Training under the guidance of a Lakota healer, Caleb has practiced the difficult arts of fasting and enduring the heat.

As the temperature hovers near 100 degrees, the dancers gradually complete this round. The challenges of the fast and the hot sun are especially daunting for the three Eagle Dancers. As the youngest and least experienced of the Eagle dancers, Caleb has difficulty enduring the harsh conditions and the rigors of the dance. He nearly faints on several occasions.

The Sun Dance incorporates many ritual features: the sounds of the beating drum, often accompanied by chanting of sacred words; the sights of the tree and the dancers; the smell of cedar smoke used to ritually purify the grounds and participants; and, for the Eagle Dancers, the experiences of fasting and the acts of sacrifice. The cumulative effects of these features are self-evident to Caleb and the others involved. The perception of sacred space, with the tree as the axis mundi, is complemented and enhanced by the perception of sacred *time*.

TIMELINE
Indigenous Religions of North America

1500 BCE–200 BCE	Olmec period in Mesoamerica.
600 BCE–300 CE	Zapotec period in Mesoamerica.
300–900 CE	The Mayan culture flourishes; elements of *Popol Vuh* seen in hieroglyphic script.
300–400 CE	City of Teotihuacan reaches peak population of 200,000 people.
700–1400	Mississippian culture flourishes; the city of Cahokia is inhabited.
900–1519	The Mayan cities decline; major urban centers are deserted.
800s–1100s	The first pueblos are built in the American Southwest. Pueblo cultures thrive.
1100–1519	The Aztec civilization thrives.
1513	The Spanish arrive in Florida.
1519–1521	The Spanish arrive in Mexico; Hernán Cortés. Collapse of Aztec Empire.
1540s	The Spanish arrive in American Southwest.
1607	The English establish Jamestown.
1700s	The *Popol Vuh* written in Quiché Mayan language in Roman script.
1819	The Civilization Fund Act is passed.
1870	The First Ghost Dance.
1889	Wovoka's vision.
1890	The Second Ghost Dance.
December 29, 1890	Tragic battle at Wounded Knee ends the Ghost Dance.
1904	The Sun Dance banned in the United States.
1918	The Native American Church is founded.
1978	The American Indian Religious Freedom Act is passed.
1995	The use of peyote is made legal for religious purposes.
2016–2017	Standing Rock resistance to Dakota Access Pipeline/#NoDAPL resistance.

The usual partitioning of everyday life is superseded by the ritualized stages of the dancing and of the ceremony at large. For Native Americans like Caleb, these effects tend to induce a state of heightened awareness of the spirit world—and of the Great Spirit, or god.

The Sun Dance has been practiced for centuries by many Native American tribes of the Northern Plains. Details have varied, depending on particular tribal traditions. The Sun Dance retains its importance today and is becoming more popular as Native peoples strive to rediscover and to nurture traditions rooted in the past. No one ritual, however important or popular, can exemplify the religious practices of all Native Americans. Still, the Sun Dance features certain elements—such as the axis mundi, the perception of sacred space and sacred time, and the communing with the spirit world—that are quite common to the religions of North America.

In this chapter, we will explore the indigenous religions of North America. The chapter focuses primarily on the practices and beliefs of peoples in what is today the contiguous United States, and also draws examples from indigenous Canadian, Mexican, and Central American traditions. Because these spiritual traditions are so numerous, we will not attempt to discuss them all but rather will select examples from a few. It is important to observe that these religions are not relics of the past. Although they are practiced on a smaller scale, they are not simpler or more basic than large-scale religions like Christianity, Buddhism, or Islam. Therefore, they should not be considered evidence of a "primitive" or less developed religious mentality. Rather, indigenous North American religions are highly complex systems of belief and practice, with sophisticated cosmologies and firm ethical principles. Although followers, like Caleb, certainly inherit ideas and practices from their ancestors, the religions are not simply copies of ancient religions. They have changed—and continue to change—in response to interaction with other belief systems, other cultures, and technological advances.

Although we explore these religions together in a single chapter, it is important to note that there are many indigenous religions in North America. Today, more than 700 tribal nations are recognized in the United States alone. In the past, there were many more. The human landscape of North America changed dramatically with the arrival of Europeans. Prior to European contact, the population of the Americas as a whole was estimated to be as high as 100 million. However, due to disease and conquest, the Native population throughout the Americas was decimated, and it is likely that some religious traditions were lost forever.

There is much diversity in indigenous North American religious traditions, but there are also some common patterns in religious practice, teachings, and historical development. Ritual practices like the Sun Dance are found in many traditions. Also, many religions share the belief that the sacred coexists with and infuses everyday life. Similarly, many share a recognition of the interconnectedness of all things and thus emphasize the importance of reciprocal relationships between humans and other elements of the natural world. Also, although these religions each have individual histories, they have faced similar issues and events in early modern and modern times, particularly with the European conquest of the Americas.

2.1 The Teachings of Indigenous Religions of North America: Core Precepts

We will begin our exploration of Native religions by looking at the belief systems and teachings of some of these religions. Because they are complex and varied, we will focus our attention primarily on elements of belief that are common to many Native religions. We will look particularly closely at beliefs about creation and human origins, the interrelationship of humanity and other elements of the world, and the nature of sacred language.

Most Native religions do not have a specific creed or statement of belief. Rather, essential teachings are revealed in mythic narratives and are shared and enacted through religious practice. As we learned in Chapter 1, all religions have a mythic component. The religions of North America have especially rich and detailed sacred narratives. Myths contain sacred knowledge about the world, humanity, and the meaning of existence. It is through hearing and retelling myths that people commit this knowledge to heart and pass it on to the next generation. In most Native religions, knowledge is highly valued, and those people who hold it are greatly respected. With their intriguing characters and compelling stories, myths are a powerful way for people everywhere to learn about their origins, the supernatural, and ethics and morality. As in other religions, the myths of Native religions also provide guidelines for human behavior, relationships, and ritual practice.

Creation and Origins

Creation stories abound in the myths of Native North America, and there is a remarkable variety in the types of creation narratives. Some myths focus on the creation of the earth and the origins of humans in general, and others simply account for the origins of one particular people. Some myths tell of people coming to the surface of the Earth from deep underground, and others tell of humans being fashioned from corn by creator gods.

The Creators and Sacred Power In Native myths, acts of creation are most often attributed to superhuman beings, often referred to simply as "creators." Because of the vast differences among Native religions, it is difficult to make generalizations about Native conceptions of superhuman beings. Some Native religions, like those of the Great Plains tribes, hold a belief in a supreme being, sometimes known as the Great Spirit. Such religions, like that of the Lakota, may also teach that all elements of creation, both animate and inanimate, contain the spiritual essence of the Great Spirit. Sometimes the supreme being is thought to be somewhat removed from the day-to-day lives of human beings. Spirits or lesser deities, however, may be more active in everyday human affairs.

Many Native religions also share a belief in a supreme force or sacred power. This sacred power may be manifest in different ways. It may be inherent in parts of the natural world, or it may be an important quality of gods or other supernatural beings. The Navajo of the southwestern United States teach of a **Holy Wind**, which is a spiritual force that inhabits every element of creation. The Holy Wind enters living beings through their own breath and directs their actions and thoughts. In this way, the Holy Wind connects all living things.

The Aztecs of central Mexico recognized a sacred power that infused elements of everyday life and supernatural beings. The Aztecs also recognized many different deities who possessed different aspects of sacred power. Some deities were associated with the power of creation and fertility, and others with the sun. The god **Quetzalcoatl**, who is often depicted as a feathered serpent, was thought to possess the sacred power of creation. Many mythic narratives surround Quetzalcoatl. One myth teaches that he assisted with creation by providing food and nourishment for the Aztec people. As a result, he is regarded as an important culture hero in Mexico.[1]

Human Origins and Human Ancestors
The creation narratives of indigenous North American religions differ significantly from each other in their accounts of the origin of humans. Some myths describe how humans were created, and others focus on how they came to live in a particular geographic locale. Despite such differences, Native myths often teach that human beings and human ancestors originated in the Americas. This belief contradicts anthropological theories that the Americas were settled by people from Asia tens of thousands of years ago.

The Mayan people of Mexico and Central America have complex creation narratives. Mayan cultural roots go back thousands of years. Although most myths of the Americas have been transmitted orally, the Maya have an ancient written language and texts that contain their mythic heritage. The Quiché Maya, one of several Mayan ethnic groups, are from the highlands of Guatemala. The Quiché creation epic, known as the ***Popol Vuh***, contains stories about creation, the exploits of the gods, and the first humans. The written text of *Popol Vuh* in the Quiché language dates back several centuries.

The *Popol Vuh* contains a dramatic account of the creation of the first humans. The creator gods attempted to make humans several times but failed in their first three attempts. The first time, the gods succeeded in creating animals, but they could only squawk and chatter—they could not speak. This disappointed the gods, who wanted humans to be able to worship them with spoken language. The second time, the creators made humans out of mud, but the clumsy figures just melted away. The third time, the gods fashioned wooden manikins. The manikins looked human and could talk, but they were cruel and heartless. The *Popol Vuh* tells that these manikins became the first monkeys. Finally, the creators mixed cornmeal with water to fashion human beings. This attempt was successful, and the humans could talk, think, and worship the gods.[2]

Other Native myths do not describe the creation of humans but instead account for their emergence on the surface of the Earth. The Zuni live in the southwestern United States. In Zuni mythology, a god called Awonawilona created the world from his own breath and body. At the time of creation, the ancestors of the Zuni lived underground in dark and unpleasant conditions. Eventually, two warrior gods were created. They led the ancestors out from under the Earth to live on its surface in the sun. Zuni mythology teaches that the Zuni were the first people on the surface of the Earth, but every few years the Earth would open again and another people would emerge. The Zuni regard the other Southwest peoples who followed them, like the Navajo and the Hopi, as their younger siblings.[3]

Navajo creation myths similarly describe the ancestors of humans, sometimes known as **Holy People**, emerging from under the surface of the Earth. The myths tell that ancestors of the Navajo lived a stressful and conflict-ridden life underground. This unpleasantness was due to the inherent chaos of their environment—there was neither order nor purpose to life under the Earth, and people behaved badly toward one another. To escape the turmoil, the ancestors traveled through many subterranean worlds in search of one in which order would prevail. They finally emerged on the surface of the Earth. First Man and First Woman were born, and it was their responsibility to help create this world.

The ancestors prepared the world for humans through specific rituals using special objects. The rituals established order and served as the foundation for Navajo religious practice, even as practiced today. In one ritual, the ancestors created a painting on the ground, in which they depicted all that was going to exist in the world. Then, through prayer and song, the real world came to be from this won-derful painting. In stark contrast to the chaos underground, the world was perfectly balanced and ordered. Eventually, an important figure known as **Changing Woman** was born. She gave birth to heroic twins, who prepared the way for humanity by vanquishing monsters that roamed the Earth. Then, Changing Woman created the first Navajo people from her own body.[4]

In some religions, ancestors are the spiritual representations of what humans can hope to become. The Pueblo peoples are cultures of the Four Corners region of the

This seventh- or eighth-century vase from Guatemala depicts scenes from the *Popol Vuh*.

American Southwest that include the Hopi and the Zuni. Among the Pueblo peoples, ancestral spirits are known as **kachinas**. Kachinas, which may take the form of animals, plants, or humans, represent the spiritually perfect beings that humans become after they die. The Hopi believe that in this life, humans are spiritually imperfect. But in the afterlife, the Hopi leave their human nature behind and become unsullied spirits. Humanity's spiritual imperfection is represented in public dances and ceremonies by clowns. This is because, in Hopi mythology, a clown led human beings as they emerged from the ground. In some of these ceremonies, masked dancers portraying the kachina spirits tell the clowns to mend their imperfect ways and strive to be better human beings. When the dancers don the masks, the kachina spirits inhabit and inspire them.[5]

Life Lessons in Myths

Native mythologies contain teachings about how to live properly in the world. From myths, people learn to live respectfully with others in society, to make a living off of the land, and to understand the meaning of life. In many Native myths, these lessons are taught through the exploits of a character known as a **trickster**. The trickster figure is often an animal who has adventures and engages in all manner of mischief. In many myths, the trickster suffers repercussions because of his failure to follow established rules about social behavior. Therefore, those hearing the myth are warned about the importance of proper behavior. One trickster tale featuring Coyote comes from the Pima of Arizona. In the past, Bluebird was an unattractive color. The bird decided to bathe in a special blue lake every morning for four days. After the fourth dip in the lake, the bird grew beautiful blue feathers. Coyote, who was green at the time, saw the new color and asked Bluebird how he could become beautiful, too. The bird explained his method, and Coyote turned blue. Coyote was very proud, and he looked around arrogantly as he walked to make sure he was being admired. But he did not watch where he was going, and he tripped and fell in the dirt. When he got up, he was the color of dirt, and now all coyotes are dirt-colored.[6] This short tale teaches an important lesson about the dangers of arrogance.

Myths of North America may also account for the origins of subsistence activities, such as hunting and farming. Often, the subsistence practices of a people are said to have been determined by the gods. This divine origin of daily activity casts everyday life and everyday activities, such as planting crops or preparing food, in a sacred dimension.[7]

Consider, for example, the many diverse myths about the origins of corn. Corn, or maize, has been a staple crop of great importance throughout North America. Some myths explain that human beings have a special duty to raise corn. Myths may tell of a particular god who is responsible for providing the crop or for protecting the fertility of the Earth. The Cherokee, historically of the southeastern United

States, tell a myth in which the goddess Corn Woman produced corn through the treachery of her son and his playmate. In the myth, Corn Woman rubbed her body to produce food. One day, the two boys saw her doing this. They thought she was practicing witchcraft and so decided to kill her. After they attacked her, she instructed the boys to drag her injured body over the ground. Wherever her blood fell, corn grew. This myth teaches about the relationship between life and death: the blood that causes death can also produce life.[8]

Many other myths teach about life and death. The following passage from the *Popol Vuh* is a moving speech made by the heroic twin gods to the maiden Blood Moon. At this point in the myth, the lords of the underworld have defeated the twins. The severed head of one of the twins has been placed in a tree, and his skull impregnates the maiden with his spittle when she holds out her hand. Blood Moon will eventually bear the next generation of hero twins who avenge their fathers' deaths and prepare the world for the arrival of humans. In the twins' poignant speech to the maiden, we learn something about the Mayan view of the meaning of life: even after death, we live on in our children.

Mount Shasta, in Northern California, is regarded as sacred by many tribes in the region.

And then the bone spit out its saliva, which landed squarely in the hand of the maiden. . . .

"It's just a sign I have given you, my saliva, my spittle. This, my head, has nothing on it—just bone, nothing of meat. It's just the same with the head of a great lord: It's just the flesh that makes his face look good. And when he dies, people get frightened by his bones. After that, his son is like his saliva, his spittle, in his being whether it be the son of a lord or the son of a craftsman, an orator. The father does not disappear, but goes on being fulfilled. Neither dimmed nor destroyed is the face of a lord, a warrior, a craftsman, orator. Rather, he will leave his daughters and sons. So it is that I have done likewise through you. Now go up there on the face of the earth; you will not die. Keep the word. So be it."[9]

Stories of heroic twins are also common in other indigenous American mythologies. This shows an important degree of continuity among traditions throughout regions of North America. As you recall, Navajo mythology includes a similar tale of heroic twins preparing the world for humanity. The Apache, also of the southwestern United States, share a similar tale.

2.2 The Teachings of Indigenous Religions of North America: Humanity and the Environment

Many indigenous North American religions emphasize the interrelationship of all things. As we saw earlier, the elements of creation, humans included, are often thought to share a common spiritual energy or sacred power. This may be understood as a life force or as the presence of the supreme being.

The Importance of Balance

This interrelationship is beautifully captured by the words of **Black Elk** (1863–1950), a famous Lakota religious leader. In a book titled *Black Elk Speaks* (1932), he tells of his life and of a great vision. He opens by saying: "It is the story of all life that is holy and is good to tell, and of us two-leggeds sharing in it with the four-leggeds and the wings of the air and all green things; for these are the children of one mother and their father is one spirit."[10]

This interconnectedness often extends to humanity's relationship with animals. In some teachings, humanity is created as the companion of other creatures—not as their master. In other traditions, humans are thought to be descended from animal or animal-like ancestors. A myth of the Modoc of Northern California tells of the special relationship between humans and grizzly bears. The Sky God created all creatures and also created Mount Shasta, a 14,000-foot volcanic peak, which served as the home for the Sky God's family. One day, his daughter fell to Earth from the top of the mountain. She was adopted and raised by a family of grizzly bears, who could talk and walk on two feet. Eventually, she married one of the bears, and from this union were born the first people. When the Sky God eventually found his daughter, he was angry that a new race was born that he had not created. He then cursed the grizzly bears to forever go about on all fours.[11]

As a result of this interconnectedness, many Native religions emphasize the importance of maintaining balance among all things. Often, this is viewed as the primary responsibility of humanity. A critical part of religious practice is therefore focused on developing and preserving harmonious relationships between humans and other elements of the world. As we have learned, Navajo myths tell that the ancestors learned to maintain this balance as an example to later generations. The myths of the Yurok of Northern California similarly describe a time when the Immortals inhabited the Earth. The Immortals knew how to maintain balance, but humans did not. Thus, the Immortals taught the Yurok people ceremonies that they could use to restore the balance of the Earth.[12]

Sacred Places and Spaces
The focus on balance extends to the physical landscape. In many Native spiritual traditions, humanity is often thought to live in a reciprocal relationship with the land: each relies on and must care for the other, and all are part of a sacred whole. Certain geographical features, like rivers, mountains,

and rocks, may be permeated with sacred power. Such places often feature prominently in mythology and are infused with power because of what happened there in the mythic past. One such place is Mount Shasta in Northern California. Many tribes of the region regard the mountain as sacred because of its importance in mythology. Myths tell that the creator made the mountain so that he could reach the Earth from the heavens. (As we saw in the Modoc myth, the creator resided in the mountain with his family.) Because of its sacred history, areas of Mount Shasta are powerful places where Native religious experts can make contact with the spirit world. To this day, leaders from several tribes use the area for religious ceremonies.

Among the White Mountain Apache of Arizona, the significance of certain places comes alive in the stories people tell about them. Tales about the local landscape are an important part of Apache cultural and religious knowledge, and they convey important moral teachings. The landscape is thus imbued with life lessons. An Apache woman named Annie Peaches (b. 1900) told the anthropologist Keith Basso (1940–2013) about a place called "Big Cottonwood Trees Stand Here and There." In the tale, the Apaches and the neighboring Pima were fighting near the big cottonwood trees. The fighting awakened a sleeping old woman, but she thought the noise was simply her son-in-law cursing her daughter. She yelled at him and told him to stop picking on the young woman. The Pima heard her, rushed in, and killed her. The tale illustrates the danger of disregarding appropriate behavior: in Apache culture, a woman should not criticize her son-in-law unless her daughter asks her to intervene. The old woman suffered dire consequences from interfering; when Apache people pass the place known as Big Cottonwood Trees Stand Here and There, they are reminded of this social rule.[13]

Myths that cast the land in a sacred light may also teach people how to build their communities. Thus, even architecture has a sacred dimension. Among the Navajo, the guidelines for building the sacred dwelling known as a **hogan** are found in myth. The Holy People taught that a hogan should be built as a representation of Navajo lands and the cosmos. Four posts, which represent four sacred mountains that surround the Navajo homeland, support the hogan. The roof represents Father Sky, and the

The tipi, a typical structure of the peoples of the Great Plains, has a sacred blueprint. Each tipi can be understood as an image of the universe.

Navajo hogans are built to represent the Navajo lands and the cosmos.

floor is Mother Earth. The **tipi**, a typical structure of the tribes of the Great Plains, has a similar sacred blueprint. Each tipi is an image of the universe. The perimeter of the tipi is the edge of the universe, and the lit fire in the center represents the center of all existence. Joseph Epes Brown (1920–2000), a scholar of Native religions, writes that the smoke from the fire, which escapes the tipi through a hole in the ceiling, can carry messages to the spirit world.[14] The tipi is thus another axis mundi, connecting different planes of existence.

Sacred Language and Sacred Time

In many Native cultures, conceptions of time reflect the cycles of nature; thus, time is regarded as circular, not linear. Therefore, events that happened at one point on the circle of time are not simply past; they will be experienced again. Beliefs about death further illustrate this concept. In many Native religions, death is considered to be an important spiritual transition. During old age, death may be welcomed and prepared for, and funeral rituals ease the transition of the deceased into the next stage in the afterlife. In many cultures, the transition of a person from birth to death is thought to be comparable to the cyclical nature of the seasons of the year.[15] Accordingly, just as winter precedes spring, human death is connected to the reemergence of life. Recall the Cherokee myth about the origins of corn, which emphasizes the necessity of death to produce life. As you read the next passage, think about cyclical time and the nature of death. Joseph Epes Brown tells us how Black Elk explained this to him:

> This cyclical reality was beautifully expressed . . . when I noticed how the dignified old Lakota man Black Elk would relate to little children. He would get down on his hands and knees and pretend he was a horse, and the children would squeal with joy. . . . There obviously was no generation gap; he fully connected with children. I once asked him how it was that he could so relate to the children, and he replied "I who am an old man am about to return to the Great Mysterious and a young child is a being who has just come from the Great Mysterious, so it is that we are very close together."[15]

The words of Black Elk illustrate the important relationship between the elderly and the very young. In many Native religions, elders teach youngsters about their religious heritage through myths. Often, the telling of myths is regarded as sacred speech. Because of the cyclical nature of time, the events related in myths are not thought to be a part of a distant and irrecoverable past but rather are representative of another place on the circle of time. Recounting a myth re-creates the events of the myth, transporting listeners into mythic time.[16]

In some Native cultures of California and the southwestern United States, deaths are marked by special **cry ceremonies**, which involve sacred mourning songs and tales, dances, and sharing stories about the deceased, all of which aid the spirit of the deceased in transition to the next world. In the nineteenth century, Native communities in Nevada and California held the cry annually as a collective mourning rite for all the deceased. Eventually, peoples in the region like the Southern Paiute began to hold cries for individuals.[17] For the Southern Paiute today, the cry ceremony helps guide the spirit to the next world, and emotional talk about the deceased is thought to give strength to the spirit on a difficult journey.[18] In this chapter's "Voices" interview with Brian Melendez, attending cry ceremonies with his community was one of the first spiritual practices he recalled as a child.

Earlier in this chapter, we learned how the ancestors of the Navajo sang and painted the world into existence. Thus, words and language were the building blocks of creation. The rituals of the ancestors provide the foundation for Navajo ceremonial practice, which is focused on maintaining order in the world. This is primarily done through practices known as **chantways**. Chantways involve ritualized singing and chants and may take place over several days. Like the cry ceremonies, the songs and chants retell the stories of creation and thus, through language, bring the power of the time of creation into the present. Chantways are used in many contexts, such as marriages, births, and puberty rites, and are thought to have the power to bring great benefit. The chantways are used for healing by aiming to bring afflicted individuals into harmony with their surroundings. Normally, the ceremonies take place in hogans.

VOICES: An Interview with Brian Melendez

Brian Melendez is of Northern Paiute, Southern Paiute, and Western Shoshone descent. He is a member of the Reno-Sparks Indian Colony, in Nevada, and is from the Hungry Valley tribal community.

What is your background?

I am Northern-Southern Paiute and Western Shoshone. I'm from three different Great Basin cultures. As a Great Basin person, I don't just have one isolated tribal identity. Growing up in Hungry Valley [the Reno-Sparks Indian Colony], I was

Brian Melendez.

fortunate that my family fostered a mixture of different belief systems. We lived together in modest tribal housing and often shared space with extended families. Times were very difficult back then. There was never a shortage of dysfunction in my community. We had countless issues and collectively struggled. The Reno-Sparks Indian Colony is made up Paiute, Shoshone, and Washoe people. As a tribe, we maintain three distinct languages and cultural mechanisms, happening all at the same time. Today, most young people, like me, are some combination of all three groups.

In your view, what is the nature of the world? What is humanity's place in it?

Tribal people embrace the art of storytelling and introspection, and much of our cultural identity is based on what is shared with us through stories. Our stories emphasize that we have a purpose to provide a certain balance within nature: I believe that our innate occupation is to protect family, community, and nature. In my opinion, nature is the greatest equalizer, to address imbalances of humanity. I think that there is a justice in nature. Spiritually, when we wanted to know something, to gain power, or to heal, we would go out into the world, and on our own merit we would stand before creation for those answers. Our ancestors were impeccable in their understandings of these actions. Today, we are not as ingenious as they once were, or as resourceful . . . but I like to think we do our best to live as natural as possible. We understood that we would have to travel to where the food and water was—we had to move with nature, otherwise we wouldn't exist. I think that modern people don't look at nature that way. Modern people want nature to be convenient. For us, we feel that we owe something to our environment, as stewards of the land. Moreover, we feel that that there is a need to preserve the integrity of the planet. Protection of the planet may be the most agreed-upon platform among tribal peoples in this country. Our cultural identities, belief systems, and complex languages are derived from our relationship with nature: everything we are as Indigenous people is connected to the environments we've existed in. The justice of nature, and our role in nature, keeps my culture in harmony.

Could you describe your religious practice and your personal spirituality?

My spiritual identity began as a young child. I can recall participating in cry ceremonies associated with death. Putting someone to rest culturally is a substantial ritual. Even though some belief systems conflicted, almost everyone in my community would participate in burials: mourning is a universal part of our collective faith. As Great Basin people, our communal foundations and much of our spirituality are based on the cycles of life and death. Ideally, the respect we have for life should be equal to the respect we have for death.

In 2001, my little brother died tragically. He was preparing to participate in the Sun Dance that summer with our family, and never made it. Reluctantly, I attended in his place. Overpowered by grief, it was during the Sun Dance that I had the proverbial "coming to God" experience. It was at that moment I knew that I could not go back to living the way I had been. I said to myself, "I don't know what this ceremony is, but I know that my brother is here, and whatever I have to do to be with him in this circle, I'll do it." My relatives were able to direct me to areas where I could learn: with an open mind and heart, I found various sweat lodges and Sun

Dances. I went to all types of ceremonies when I began my spiritual path, travel-ing the country for a couple of years figuring myself out. Over the years, I have become a practical-minimalist, I'm a pretty pragmatic guy. I contribute my time and energy for my community to sing, dance, and pray in our mountains, the way our people once did. The fruits of these labors have been beautiful.

What opportunities and challenges do you face as a member of a Native community in the United States today?

The federal government definitely had a plan when they taught our people to be carpenters and housemaids. They weren't giving us hard science and philosophy so that we could be equal to each other. Today, we understand the range of multi-ple educations and how to use them all. In terms of spiritual practices, parents are supposed to teach their children, but when they were separated during the board-ing school era, they weren't able to do this. Thus, our grandparents were forcefully removed from their cultural and tribal roles. This was especially devastating for my parents' generation. For my parents . . . they were in a state of confusion and strug-gling with their own identities. They couldn't teach what they didn't know. It cre-ated direct trauma for them, and indirect trauma for us. My generation is currently working to heal this trauma.

The upside is that, today, tribal people in this country have never been more mobile. We have more access to technology, to academics, to economic capital, to larger communities. Tribes are able to stay up to speed with what other tribes are doing; this is forcing us to evolve. When it comes to spirituality, we are able to observe what neighboring tribes are doing to retain their cultures. Tribes are problem-solving to find something that works, for who they are today. This is helping tribal people adapt and adopt new practices, which assist communities as they self-regulate. We were at a spiritual ground zero—we were struggling to main-tain customs and rituals, some more than others. Not all transitions are easy or even welcomed; sometimes these changes create tension with the older genera-tion. Some people are wishing for a revival of old ways, some people are working towards a revolution of change: there's no one right way or wrong way. This is all happening internally in Indian Country right now.

2.3 The History of Indigenous Religions of North America: Origins

As we have seen thus far in this chapter, the beliefs and teachings of indigenous religions of North America are complex and multifaceted. Just as in other religions, these traditions have developed historically and have both resisted and accommo-dated cultural changes. However, because the region is so diverse, it is difficult to generalize about historical change in this large region. Thus, this section briefly re-views some of the major historical events and empires in North America, and what we know about religion during these periods.

Later in this section, we will look at how Native North American religions have responded to the social and political changes in the modern period. As you read this section, think about how indigenous American religions have adapted and endured despite colonialism, encroaching Christianity, and culture change.

Religion in Early Civilizations and States

Although archaeologists think that the first peoples arrived in North America from Asia between 15,000 and 18,000 years ago, as we have seen, indigenous sacred narratives frequently hold that peoples of the Americas originated in America, not elsewhere. For millennia, it is likely that most Americans were hunter-gatherers living in small mobile communities. Hunter-gatherers leave little material record, and as a result we do not know a great deal about their history or their religious practices and ideas.

However, we know quite a bit about religion in later, larger-scale civilizations. Numerous major civilizations arose in Mesoamerica, such as the Olmec (1500–200 BCE) and later the Zapotec (600 BCE–800 CE). Many ancient Mesoamerican peoples shared religious ideas, practices, and gods. The Mayan civilization thrived for centuries in what is today southern Mexico, Belize, and Guatemala, and Mayan people of the region today are their descendants. The height of Mayan civilization was from about 300 to 900 CE. The ancient Mayans had sophisticated architecture and built large pyramids in many urban centers. They had a complex social organization and written language. Mayan religion recognized a complex pantheon of gods, and a three-layered cosmos, with an underworld, a middle world, and an upper world; we discussed Mayan religious teachings earlier in this chapter. Many ritual practices were part of Mayan religious life and included penitential bloodletting. Evidence of religious ideas abounds in architecture; for example, the origins of a complex ball game are in sacred narratives like the *Popol Vuh*, and ball courts can be found at many Mayan sites. After 900 CE, Mayan civilization began to decline, and Mayan cities were eventually abandoned. Although scholars do not agree on why this happened, many think that overpopulation and a changing climate and accompanying drought were factors. Despite the abandonment of cities, Mayan cultures and religious ideas and practices persist to the present day.

Farther to the west in Mexico, the city of Teotihuacan thrived from 200 BCE to 900 CE. Scholars believe that the city was very important as a religious and ritual center. The huge city is best known today for its two enormous pyramids, known as the Pyramid of the Sun and the Pyramid of the Moon. There are numerous other structures that were likely temples, including one dedicated to the feathered serpent god Quetzalcoatl, who was recognized in many Mesoamerican religions. The orientation of structures to celestial bodies suggests sophisticated astronomical knowledge and the likelihood that religious practices and ideas were calendrical. Archaeological evidence shows that numerous offerings, including sacrifices of animals, were likely made to various gods and goddesses at the site.

Somewhat later, the Aztec civilization thrived in the same region from about 1100 until the early 1500s CE. The Aztec city of Tenochtitlan had as many as 200,000 inhabitants by the 1500s, and it was the largest city in the Americas. Like many other Mesoamerican civilizations, the Aztecs were known for monumental architecture and agricultural sophistication. Scholars know quite a bit about Aztec religion due to surviving manuscripts, archaeological evidence, and written accounts of the Spanish. Aztec religion was complex and recognized many deities, including Quetzalcoatl. Numerous ritual practices, including sacrifices, focused on pleasing and honoring the deities. As a result of internal conflicts in the empire and the eventual Spanish siege of Tenochtitlan, the Aztec Empire collapsed in 1521 CE.

Large-scale civilizations also arose further north, in what is today the United States, although not nearly as many as in Mesoamerica. The Mississippian culture flourished from around 700 to 1400 CE. The Mississippian city of Cahokia, in what is today Illinois, was the largest preconquest city north of Mexico. Cahokia is known for the huge earthen mounds built by its founders. We do not know a great deal about Cahokian religion. However, archaeologists think that some of the mounds were "shrine houses," which likely served a religious or ritual purpose, and that the mound cities like Cahokia drew people for religious reasons.[19]

Around the same time but further west, the first pueblos, a term for communal urban dwellings something like apartments, were built in what is today the American Southwest. One of these sites is Canyon de Chelly, in Arizona, which was first inhabited nearly 5,000 years ago. Much later, around 1000 CE, the ancestors of contemporary Navajo and Pueblo peoples built permanent settlements in the area, including pueblo dwellings and *kiva*s, which are special chambers dug into the ground that were used for ritual and social purposes; kivas are still in use today by Pueblo peoples. Canyon de Chelly was eventually abandoned around 1300 CE, though scholars do not agree on why. Hopi and Zuni people trace their ancestors to the first inhabitants of the pueblos, and the Navajo people arrived centuries later.

Chaco Canyon, in New Mexico, is another ancestral site of the Pueblo peoples. The site flourished from the 800s to 1100s CE, and its residents built impressive architectural structures, such as large multi-story "great houses" and very large underground kivas. As with sites farther south in Mexico, such as Teotihuacan, structures of Chaco Canyon were oriented according to the positions of the sun and moon, showing astronomical expertise and the importance of the solar or lunar calendar in the ritual year. Trade goods from Mesoamerica, such as macaw feathers and cacao, show important connections with peoples to the south, and perhaps shared ritual practices.

2.4 The History of Indigenous Religions of North America: Conquest and Colonization

The expansion of European imperialism from the sixteenth through the early twentieth centuries ravaged and radically influenced indigenous religious traditions in the Americas. Throughout North America, the effects of colonialism on Indigenous peoples were disastrous: indigenous populations were devastated by disease and warfare, forced to move far away from their ancestral homelands, and sometimes enslaved or indentured to work for the colonists.

The Impact of Christianity

Spanish, British, and French colonial powers sent Christian missionaries to their imperial holdings (and beyond) in North and Central America with the aim of "saving" Indigenous peoples from what were viewed as their pagan ways. As a result, many Indigenous peoples converted (forcibly or by choice) to the Christianity of the colonizers. Some colonizers, such as the Spanish, also believed that they could bring about the second coming of Christ by completing the work of taking the gospel to the ends of the Earth.

More recently, in the nineteenth and twentieth centuries, Native American children in the United States and Canada were forcibly removed from their homes and sent to boarding schools, where they were taught that their cultural and religious ways were wrong. In the United States, the 1819 Civilization Fund Act, which aimed to educate Native children in an effort to "civilize" them, led to the development of many of these boarding schools. As another example, in the southwestern United States, Navajo children were adopted by white families and raised in Latter-day Saint (Mormon) or other Christian traditions. In Canada, many of the schools were run by Christian missionaries until the late twentieth century, and Christian education was a key goal.

Indigenous religious traditions were never entirely eradicated, however, even when Native peoples identified as Christians. When the Spanish conquistadors arrived in Mesoamerica, the indigenous religion of the Mayan peoples was banned, written versions of holy texts were burned, and the Maya were often forcibly converted to Roman Catholicism. Although many Mayan people today identify as Catholic, elements of indigenous religion remain. Catholic saints may be equated with Mayan gods, and some Maya have equated Jesus and Mary with the sun and the moon in Mayan cosmology. Today, many Mayan people may draw on elements of both Catholic and Mayan religion in their beliefs and practice.

In the United States today, many Native Americans identify as Catholics, Protestants, or nondenominational Christians. However, as with the Maya, this does not necessarily mean that the beliefs and practices of Native religions are no longer relevant. Furthermore, some Native Christians understand Christianity as an indigenous American religion. Among the White Mountain Apache of Arizona, some religious leaders claim that they "have always had the Bible."[20] As with the Navajo, an important part of Apache girls' initiation is the assumption of the powers of Changing Woman. In Apache mythology, Changing Woman was distressed about the difficulty of life on Earth and prayed to God to change it. God answered her prayers by impregnating her with the rays of the sun, and she gave birth to a heroic son, who made the Earth safe for humans. Some Apache religious leaders interchange the names of Jesus and Mary for Changing Woman and her son. Furthermore, at the girls' puberty ceremony, participants draw parallels between other sacred Apache narratives and the stories of Genesis. It is in such contexts that practitioners argue that Christianity is indeed an indigenous American religion that predated colonization.[21] For other Apache Christians, however, traditional religion is viewed not as a complement to Christianity but as a relic of the past that good Christians should reject.

2.5 The History of Indigenous Religions of North America: The Modern Age

Many Native communities resisted European American expansion in North America. Such movements have often had an overtly religious dimension and many have emphasized social and environmental justice—particularly in the twenty-first century. Indigenous religious leaders have frequently been at the forefront of resistance movements. Many movements have had influence far and wide and might thus be understood as "pan-Indian" religious movements.

Resistance Movements and Social Justice

One influential resistance movement was the **Ghost Dance**. In the late nineteenth century, a religious leader of the Northern Paiute claimed to have had a vision that taught him that the white occupiers would leave if the Native people performed a special dance described by the spirits. This event was called the Ghost Dance because of the belief that it would usher in the destruction and rebirth of the world and that dead ancestors would return. Versions of the Ghost Dance spread rapidly throughout the western United States in 1870 because many Native people embraced the possibility that the dance not only could allow them to communicate with deceased ancestors but also could revive the Native cultures in the face of European domination.

In 1890, another Northern Paiute man of Nevada named **Wovoka** (1856–1932), who had studied Paiute religion and participated in the first Ghost Dance, founded a second Ghost Dance. In 1889, Wovoka experienced a powerful vision in which the Creator told him the ancestors would rise up. If people demonstrated their belief through dances, human misery and death would come to an end. The dances spread quickly across the Great Basin and to the Sioux of the northern Midwest and other Plains peoples.

Regrettably, many white Americans feared the dances, and the US government interpreted the widespread dances as an armed resistance movement. The Ghost Dance came to a tragic end on December 29, 1890, at Wounded Knee,

In Chichicastenango, Guatemala, Mayan men take part in a religious ceremony where saints are taken to the streets by members of religious brotherhoods.

A photograph of Wovoka (seated).

South Dakota. American troops killed hundreds of Lakota people, including women and children, who had gathered for a dance. The Ghost Dance came at a critical time in the history of Native peoples and was seen by many participants as a final attempt to revive the ways of the past. Although the second Ghost Dance ended in catastrophe, the movement brought together people of different Native backgrounds and helped create a shared sense of identity, history, and purpose among peoples of diverse origins.

Although the massacre at Wounded Knee is perhaps the most well-known attempt by the US government to control Native religious practice, government suspicions of indigenous religions continued well into the twentieth century. In 1904, the Sun Dance was officially banned because it was considered chaotic and dangerous. And as we have learned, for much of the nineteenth and twentieth centuries, the US government backed a program in which young Native American children were taken from their homes and relocated to specially built boarding schools, where they were forced to leave behind their religious beliefs, languages, and other cultural practices while adopting the ways of European Americans. In the accompanying "Voices" interview, Brian Melendez describes the devastating impact of the boarding schools on his own family and community in Nevada.

The **Native American Church** can be considered another resistance movement in the United States. In the early twentieth century, followers of **peyote** religion formed this church to protect their religious practice. The hallucinogenic peyote cactus has been used for thousands of years in indigenous religions of northern Mexico. In the late nineteenth and early twentieth centuries, use of the plant spread to Native communities in the United States, particularly in the Plains. Around 1890, a Comanche chief called **Quanah Parker** (1845–1911) spread the call for Native Americans to embrace peyote religion. He had been introduced to peyote use in the 1890s when he was treated with peyote for an injury, and he became an important defender of the use of the plant against detractors. Peyote is not habit-forming and is primarily used for healing purposes and to facilitate encounters with the spirit world. However, Christian missionaries and other activists in the United States preached against peyote use, and federal and state governments eventually outlawed its use. (Centuries earlier, the Spanish colonizers had also prohibited the use of peyote in religious practice as a result of a decree of the Spanish Inquisition.) In 1918, followers of peyote religion incorporated as the Native American Church to request legal protection for practicing religion.

In 1978, the **American Indian Religious Freedom Act** was passed in an effort to give Native peoples the right to express and practice their beliefs according to the

First Amendment of the US Constitution. However, Native peoples have not always been able to protect their rights to religious freedom by referencing the Act. Some practices, like the use of peyote for religious purposes, continued to face challenges from the government for years. Since 1995, however, the use of peyote has been legally permissible.

In 2016, a resistance movement drew the attention of the world to North Dakota and the Standing Rock Sioux reservation. What has become known as the Standing Rock movement is nonviolent resistance to the construction of the Dakota Access Pipeline (DAPL) across the sacred lands and waters of the Lakota Sioux. Although the movement began with members of the Standing Rock Sioux Nation, it attracted thousands of supporters from around the United States and around the world, many of whom remained in camps during the cold winter of 2016–2017. The resistance movement has focused on the US government's violation of treaty rights with the Sioux, and the profound environmental impact of the pipeline, which threatens sacred lands and waters. The Standing Rock Sioux argue that the pipeline construction violates an 1851 treaty between the US government and the Sioux. Furthermore, the pipeline crosses the Missouri River and could contaminate the water the Sioux depend on. Indeed, many members of the camp referred to themselves as "water protectors," and the rallying cry "Water Is Life" (*Mni Wiconi* in Lakota) remains an important symbol of the resistance movement. In an interview with CNN in 2016, Faith Spotted Eagle, who traveled from the Yankton Sioux Reservation in South Dakota to support the movement, described the importance of the water. She observed that water is not simply the sustainer of life, but it purifies, and also hears and has a memory. The water, therefore, will remember what happened at Standing Rock and will tell future generations.

It is important to understand the movement within a framework of Native spirituality and the sacred nature of the land and the water, which we discussed earlier in this chapter. In 2016, the leader of the Standing Rock Sioux, David Archambault Jr., made a statement to the United Nations Human Rights Council describing the pipeline project as the "deliberate destruction" of sacred lands by oil companies. Professor Rosalyn LaPier, a member of the Blackfoot Nation, has argued that Standing Rock has become a place of spiritual practice and pilgrimage for both Native peoples and non-Natives who support them: the movement drew supporters from over 300 North American tribes. Although the

The Oceti Sakowin Camp at Cannon Ball, North Dakota, in January 2017. Campers were protesting the North Dakota Access Pipeline.

resistance was peaceful, the state of North Dakota called in the National Guard and militarized the police force in an attempt to protect the pipeline construction.

In December 2016, the Standing Rock Sioux seemed victorious, as the Army Corps of Engineers announced they would cease work on the pipeline. After Donald Trump was inaugurated, however, he immediately approved construction of the pipeline and it became fully operational on June 1, 2017. Two weeks later, however, a federal court ruled that the DAPL did not go through full vetting for environmental concerns. In July 2020, a US District Judge ordered the DAPL to shut down pending environmental review. However, an appeals court reversed the order and permitted the pipeline to continue running. In 2022, a federal court ordered another environmental impact statement, and this is expected in late 2024.

The proposal for a lithium mine in northern Nevada's Thacker Pass has drawn similar criticism from Native peoples, who fought a legal battle beginning in 2021 to halt progress on the mine. The mine is near the Nevada-Oregon border, and it is situated near the site of the 1865 massacre of Native people by the US Army. The land is considered sacred by many Paiute and Shoshone peoples of the region. In July 2023, a federal appeals court rejected the suit brought by Native and environmental groups to halt the progress of the mine.

Global Interest in Indigenous Religions of North America

The Standing Rock movement, which also became known on social media as the #NoDAPL (No Dakota Access Pipeline) resistance, attracted the attention of the world. It is fair to say that it truly became a global movement. Social media sites like Facebook and Twitter rapidly spread news of Standing Rock around the world, and thousands of people traveled to the Standing Rock reservation in person to show support for the Sioux people protesting the pipeline. Hashtags like #WeStandwithStandingRock and #WaterisLife have circulated worldwide. Many supporters of the Standing Rock movement made connections to the challenges faced by other indigenous communities involving conflicts over land. For example, Palestinians showed support for the movement and argued that their concerns about land and displacement mirrored the Sioux concerns in the United States. In September 2016, the Palestinian Youth Movement even sent a delegation to North Dakota. The organization Jewish Voices for Peace also declared their support for Standing Rock. The Maori, the Indigenous people of New Zealand, showed their support of the #NoDAPL movement by sending videos of hakas, the Maori war dance, through social media like Facebook. One Maori man created a Facebook page called "Haka for Standing Rock" to allow people to share images and videos of their hakas.

Maori man Kereama Te Ua, who traveled from New Zealand to Standing Rock to perform this haka in solidarity with protesters.

Despite the history of antagonism toward Native religions in North America, many non-Natives are interested in learning about Native religious traditions. Today, many non-Native people are attracted to what they view as the nature-centered focus of the indigenous religions of North America. And since the late twentieth century, some have started following the religious practices, rituals, and beliefs of Native religions as an alternative to what they perceive as drawbacks of Western religious traditions like Christianity and Judaism.

Maori women performing a traditional haka at Standing Rock.

In the 1960s, many of those involved in the so-called countercultural movement began to develop an interest in the teachings and practices of Native religions. Some were attracted to teachings about the interconnectedness of all things and found what they thought to be an appealing lack of materialism in Native religions. Others were particularly interested in practices that involved the use of hallucinogenic plants like peyote.

Some Native Americans appreciate the growing interest of non-Natives in indigenous religions. However, Native thinkers have also criticized non-Native interest in indigenous religious practices. These critics argue that selective adoption of certain practices, like peyote use, removes the activity from the cultural and historical context in which it developed. Sometimes conflicts arise over the use of sacred places. For example, non-Native Americans have felt the pull of Mount Shasta, in Northern California. Their interest has not always been welcomed by Native peoples—primarily because of a perception that non-Natives are appropriating Native spirituality without proper understanding or proper training. Among the Native people of the region, the springs and meadows of Mount Shasta are treated with great reverence, and a person should not approach these places without proper guidance from an expert or elder with great religious knowledge. Non-Native spiritual seekers, however, often bathe in sacred springs or play music in sacred groves and meadows without the advice or permission of religious leaders in the area, which offends some Native practitioners. Indigenous views of the sacred nature of the land often conflict with the aims and goals of non-Native Americans, many of whom see the potential for development on the lands that Native people consider sacred.[22] This is evident in the controversies over the Dakota Access Pipeline and the Thacker Pass lithium mine.

2.6 Indigenous Religions of North America as a Way of Life: Observance

Followers of Native American religions do not usually make stark distinctions between what is "religious" and what is "secular." As we have seen, myths instill everyday life with a sacred quality by providing explanations even for seemingly mundane activities such as planting or preparing food. Therefore, many actions have a religious dimension.

Healing

In Native American religions, healing the sick is often part of religious practice. Healers may use religious knowledge to cure physical and mental illnesses. In addition, healers are frequently well-known for their understanding of local plant remedies. Some healers undergo years of training to acquire great depths of religious knowledge. Others are considered specialists not because of particular training but because they have an inherent ability to interact with the spirit world or have been selected by a spirit to become healers. In many Native traditions, healers are also religious leaders.

In addition to the Navajo chantways we learned about earlier in this chapter, Navajo healing ceremonies also use an art form known as **sand painting**. The Holy People gave the paintings to the Navajo people. As the name suggests, sand paintings are created using vivid colors of sand and other dry materials such as pollen. The paintings are created on the floors of hogans and treat illnesses by bringing individuals into alignment with nature. A healer, or singer, selects the subjects of the painting in consultation with the family of the person being treated; these may include animals, plants, and mythic figures.

During the ceremony, the afflicted person is seated in the center of the painting, which tells one of the creation stories. As sand is applied to his body, he identifies with the Holy People depicted in the painting. During the treatment, the painted figures are thought to come to life to aid in the healing of the patient. After the ceremony is complete, the painting is destroyed and the sand is removed. In the past, Navajo people never kept permanent copies of the paintings because it was thought

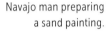

Navajo man preparing a sand painting.

that it would diminish their healing power. Today, small paintings are sometimes produced for sale, but ideally these permanent paintings should not represent or depict the important figures and symbols used in healing practice.

Medicine bundles may also be an important part of healing in Navajo communities. The bundles contain a variety of religiously significant objects, and some items may be very old. Navajo singers usually own their own bundles and use the powers of the items in the bundle in healing. Other Native communities use similar bundles in healing.[23]

Women have often been highly regarded for their expertise in healing. A well-known twentieth-century spiritual healer was **Mabel McKay** (1907–1993), a Pomo woman of Northern California. As a young woman, Mabel was called to be a liaison between her people and the spirit world. Spirit guides told her that she would develop a special gift of healing. Here, Mabel McKay's close friend Greg Sarris describes how a spirit called her to be a healer.

> The spirit talked to her constantly now. . . . Sometimes it felt as if her own tongue were moving, shaping the words she was hearing. This happened when she sang the songs that came loud and clear. "Am I going crazy?" she asked once. . . . "No," the spirit said, "it's me. And what is happening is that you have an extra tongue. Your throat has been fixed for singing and sucking out the diseases I've been teaching you about. It's talking. It's me in you." "Well, how am I to suck?" Mabel asked. "You'll know when you get to that point. You will have a basket to spit out the disease. All your baskets will come from me. Like I told you. Watch how things turn out."[24]

Rites of Renewal and Purification

As we learned earlier in this chapter, many Native American religions focus on humanity's important role in maintaining balance with other elements of creation. This goal forms the foundation of many kinds of ritual practice, specifically those ceremonies known as **rites of renewal**. Like the term suggests, rites of renewal seek to renew the sacred balance of all things. Such rites are often seasonal because they are designed to correspond with the cycle of planting and harvesting or moving herd animals for grazing. They may aim to enhance natural processes such as rainfall or the growth of crops.

As mentioned earlier, the Yurok tell of the knowledge given to human beings by the Immortals, who lived on Earth before humans. The Immortals taught human beings a ritual known as the **Jump Dance**, which restores the balance of the Earth and renews the harmony that was present in the time of the Immortals. Along with a number of other rituals, the Jump Dance is performed during the World Renewal Ceremonial Cycle. This is a cycle of ceremonies that are performed by many Northern California peoples at various times of the year, and the purpose is to maintain the balance of all living things. In the Jump Dance, men march to a special place that

This Hopi kachina doll from the twentieth century might be used to remind children of the qualities of the kachinas.

has been sanctified by a priest, where they dance. By engaging in this religious practice, which imitates and repeats the words and actions that the Immortals taught humans, the mythic time is called into the present, and the Earth is renewed. And because an entire community may participate in rites of renewal, they also enhance group solidarity.[25]

In North American religions from Mexico to Alaska, **sweat lodge** ceremonies are used to ritually purify and cleanse the body. They are rites of purification. In these ceremonies, participants build an enclosed structure that is filled with heated stones. Pouring water over the stones generates steam. The steam has the power to cleanse the body and clear the mind of anything that might distract an individual from focusing on the divine. A sweat bath may be used to prepare for other ritual activities, such as the Sun Dance described in the opening part of this chapter. The ritual use of the sweat lodge encourages a bond between all those who bathe in it. And sometimes the cleansing power extends even beyond the inhabitants of the lodge to other elements of creation.[26] In this way, this rite of purification also serves as a rite of renewal. The ritual use of the sweat bath is such an important part of religious practice that some states have been ordered by federal judges to provide Native prisoners access to sweat lodges.[27]

Among Pueblo peoples such as the Hopi and Zuni, kachina dances are a type of renewal rite. As we discussed earlier in this chapter, when dancers wear the masks of the kachinas, they are thought to become imbued with the spirit of the kachina. Kachinas have the power to bring rain and enhance fertility. Among the Hopi, who recognize over 200 kachina spirits, several dances take place during the part of the year between the winter solstice and the summer solstice. The songs used with the dances often call for fertility of the land, for rainfall, and for the flourishing of crops. Rites of renewal also often have significance beyond these material aims. The Hopi dance for rain calls for nourishment not just of crops but also the cosmos. In the Hopi belief system, the spiritual qualities of rain underlie all of existence. Thus, rain dances rejuvenate the entire cosmos, not just the crops in a particular locale.[28]

The kachina dances also teach young people about ethics and morality. Children are not allowed to see the dancers without their masks. This is so the children will strongly associate the dancers with the kachinas and think of them only as representing the idealized qualities the kachinas possess. However, when they are old enough, children learn that their parents or other relatives are behind the masks. This disillusionment is part of their religious development, as children learn that the world is not always as it seems.[29]

2.7 Indigenous Religions of North America as a Way of Life: Life-Cycle Events

In North America, indigenous traditions have many different ways of marking important developments and transitions in the life cycle, and they are often connected to ideals and values from sacred narratives. In this section, we will explore of a few of these events in different indigenous communities.

Rites of Passage

Like other religions around the world, Native American traditions use rituals to recognize important changes in a person's social status. Such rituals are known as **rites of passage**. Often, rites of passage mark the transition from childhood to adulthood. Many Native cultures have elaborate rites marking this transition for young women and men. In this section, we will examine two rites of passage. First, we will look at the **Kinaalda**, which marks a Navajo girl's transition to adulthood. Then we will examine a spiritual rite of passage known as a **vision quest**.

The *Kinaalda*   The Navajo puberty rite for girls is known as the *Kinaalda*. It takes place soon after a girl begins menstruating. Each girl undergoing *Kinaalda* has a sponsor. This is an older woman who serves as a guide and role model and teaches her about the expectations of her as a Navajo woman. The ceremonial activities last several days and are part of the chantways. Thus, the ritual has its foundation in mythology. Changing Woman experienced the first *Kinaalda*, which is the model ritual for all girls. Indeed, girls are believed to take on the identity and spiritual qualities of Changing Woman during the ritual. Because she takes on the identity of Changing Woman, a girl going through the rites is thought to have special healing powers. People may visit her to request healing for their ailments.

An important *Kinaalda* activity is baking a giant cake of cornmeal. The initiate prepares the cake with the assistance of her family. She grinds the corn and prepares the batter carefully, since it is believed that if a cake turns out well, she will have a full and productive life. A poorly made cake bodes ill for her future.

The Vision Quest   One rite of passage that is common to many North American religions is the vision quest. This is the attempt by an individual to communicate with the spirit world. It is especially well known among peoples of the Great Plains and Great Lakes regions of Canada and the United States, such as the Sioux and the Ojibwa. Men or women may undertake the quest, depending on the culture, and it may occur once or at several points in an individual's life. In some cultures, the vision quest marks the transition from childhood to adulthood.

Usually, the goal of the vision quest is for an individual to make contact with the spirit world. This is frequently accomplished through contact with a spirit guide. Often, the spirit guide takes an animal form, which may be revealed during the quest. Sometimes, individuals report that the spirit guide appeared to them directly. Others learned the identity of the guide by spotting a particular animal during the quest. In other vision quests, the focus is not on a spirit guide but rather on accessing a spiritual power more generally.

In most quests, the initiate will remove himself or herself from normal society by spending several days alone in the wilderness. The vision quest can be both mentally and physically demanding, as it may require long periods of isolation and fasting. A vision quest teaches a person about the importance of seeking and following guidance from the spirit world and has the potential to cultivate a mental and physical hardiness that will serve the individual throughout his or her life.[30] Among the Ojibwa, boys normally undertook the vision quest at puberty. After a period of preparation, a boy was taken deep into the woods where he would remain by himself, fasting, until he received a vision. For many boys, visions were journeys into the spirit world, and spirit guides would help the boy figure out his life's path. Boys who were not able to endure the fast could try again at a later time.[31]

Gender and Identity

Gender roles and conceptions of gender vary across Native American religious traditions. As you have learned, the sacred narratives of Native American religions often include tales of important female spiritual beings, like Changing Woman. Furthermore, women have often had prominent roles in certain aspects of religious practice, such as healing, and many Native religions mark the transition from girlhood to womanhood in a profound manner. For example, as mentioned earlier, young Navajo girls embody Changing Woman during the *Kinaalda*.

Among the Iroquois, balance and reciprocity have long been emphasized in the relations between men and women, and many scholars regard the historical Iroquois as a fine example of a gender-egalitarian society, in which neither men nor women dominated. This emphasis on balance has been reflected in both religious symbols and religious practice. In the Iroquois Longhouse Religion, which is practiced today, the house of worship is divided into male and female spaces, and male and female religious leaders known as "faithkeepers" are of equal importance in spiritual matters.[32] The ceremonial year is very important in regulating ceremonies honoring Creator and spirits, and historically women and men have each been in charge of ceremonies during half of the Iroquois year.

For example, women's songs are sung to accompany the planting of corn to encourage fertility.[33]

Two Spirit   Many Native North American cultures have historically recognized the existence of a third gender—people who are regarded as being neither male nor female. A **Two Spirit** person might be biologically male but adopt the dress, occupations, and behaviors of a woman. Collectively, such individuals are sometimes called "Two Spirit" because they are regarded as having the spirits of both men and women. Historically, Two Spirit persons were treated with respect and were regarded as having special spiritual abilities, and many took on a special religious role in the community. With the arrival and domination of Europeans, however, the role of Two Spirit individuals was suppressed. European binary understandings of gender did not acknowledge third or fourth genders, and those with Two Spirits were often regarded as deviant rather than occupying a special social role. Today, many Native peoples are proudly reclaiming a Two Spirit identity. The Montana Two Spirit Society, for example, is an organization founded by member of the Pikunii Blackfeet Nation that advocates for LGBTQ and Two Spirit issues and histories. For twenty-five years, the society has held regular gatherings for Native Two Spirit people and their families and friends.

VISUAL GUIDE
North American Religions

Among Pueblo peoples such as the Hopi and Zuni, kachina dances are a type of renewal rite. When dancers wear the masks of the kachinas, they are thought to become imbued with the spirit of the kachinas. Kachinas have the power to bring rain and enhance fertility. This is a Hopi kachina doll, representing a kachina, from Arizona. The doll dates to before 1901 and is made of painted wood, feathers, and pine needles.

In North American religions from Mexico to Alaska, sweat lodge ceremonies ritually purify and cleanse the body. In these ceremonies, participants build an enclosed structure that is filled with heated stones.

The tipi, a typical structure of the tribes of the Great Plains, has religious significance. Each tipi is an image of the universe. The perimeter of the tipi is the edge of the universe, and the lit fire in the center represents the center of all existence.

2.8 Indigenous Religions of North America as a Way of Life: Engaging with the World

Native American religions are not relics of the past. Rather, they are living traditions that continue to develop, change, and engage with the broader world in meaningful ways. Today, more than 700 tribal nations are recognized in the United States, and Canada recognizes 650 First Nations. Mexico does not recognize tribal nations in the way the United States and Canada do, but it has a larger indigenous population: nearly 20 percent of the people of Mexico identify as indigenous, as opposed to only

1–2 percent in the United States and about 5 percent in Canada. One of the major challenges Native American religions have faced throughout North America is the spread of Christianity, particularly through European colonialism. However, even in those areas that have seen widespread conversion to other religions, elements of indigenous religions have often been maintained and even incorporated into the practice of the colonizing religions.

In many communities, Native Americans are advocating a resurgence of indigenous religious ways in engaging with contemporary issues and challenges. Pan-Indian or intertribal interest in certain types of religious practice and modes of mobilization has been important thus far in the twenty-first century. Although it is important to understand the diversity of Native American religious traditions, it is also essential to acknowledge that pan-tribal movements and ceremonies can be an important means of fostering a collective Native American identity. An emphasis on resurgence has been particularly important in environmental justice movements such as the Standing Rock resistance to the Dakota Access Pipeline, which we discussed earlier in this chapter, and in discourses concerning mitigation of the effects of climate change, as we will explore in the next section.

Environmental Stewardship

Native communities in North America have historically utilized very sophisticated and complex practices to preserve and maintain the environment. In recent years, the western United States has suffered from increasingly devastating wildfires. This is in large part due to climate change, as temperatures rise and droughts become more common. An additional factor, however, is that over the past century, the United States adopted a policy of suppression—most forest fires were extinguished rather than letting forests burn through a cycle of rejuvenation. Historically, many Native communities have practiced prescribed "cultural burns" to foster this cycle. In California, for example, the Karuk people regarded the land and fire as sacred, and engaged in such burns. However, in the nineteenth century, the state legislature criminalized these cultural burns. Today many Native communities are fighting to preserve sacred lands and forests using indigenous methods. The Karuk Tribe and Western Klamath Restoration Partnership is proposing fire solutions like cultural burns, which focus on indigenous methods and leadership. Bill Tripp, a Karuk member, wrote the following response to the devastating 2020 fires in California:

> Our land was taken from us long ago and our Indigenous stewardship responsibility was taken from us too. The land is still sacred and it will forever be part of us. We hold the knowledge of fire, forests, water, plants and animals that is needed to revitalize our human connection and responsibility to this land. If enabled, we can overcome our current situation and teach others how to get it done across the western United States[34]

SEEKING ANSWERS

What Is Ultimate Reality?

Myths contain sacred knowledge about ultimate reality and the nature of the world. In Native American religions, the world is believed to have been created by creator deities. The entire world and the many elements within it—including human beings—may be believed to be infused by the spiritual essence of a supreme being, or Great Spirit.

How Should We Live in This World?

In most Native American religions, myths provide the foundations for the way people should live their lives. Humans are one part of the general order of existence and live in a reciprocal relationship with the land, plants, and other animals. Myths teach that it is the responsibility of humans to maintain balance, order, and right relationships with other elements of creation.

What Is Our Ultimate Purpose?

Native American religions differ in terms of humanity's ultimate purpose. Some religions focus on humanity's role in maintaining balance with the natural world, and certain religious practices, such as the Jump Dance, aim to do this. Maintaining this balance can improve the human condition, and upsetting the balance can have terrible consequences. Many Native American religions conceive of life and death as cyclical in nature. In Native religions, the transition of a person from birth to death is thought to be comparable to the cyclical nature of the seasons of the year. In some religions, the deceased transitions to the land of the dead, which may resemble this life.

REVIEW QUESTIONS

For Review

1. Why is it difficult to make generalizations about Native American religions?
2. Many Native American religions emphasize the interconnectedness of all things. How does this play out in religious practice?
3. What are some common themes in Native American mythology? What do these themes teach the listeners?
4. What was the significance of the Ghost Dance? Do you see any parallels to more recent resistance movements?

For Further Reflection

1. How do Native American traditions answer some of the great questions that many religions address? What is unique to Native traditions? What do they share with other traditions?
2. How are Native American religions tied to specific places and landscapes? What are some examples of the significance of this connection? Do you see this in other religions described in this book? Why do you think some religions emphasize ties to specific locales?

GLOSSARY

American Indian Religious Freedom Act 1978 US law to guarantee freedom of religious practice for Native Americans.

axis mundi (ak'suhs moon'dee; Latin) An academic term for the center of the world, which connects the Earth with the heavens.

Black Elk Famous Lakota religious leader.

Changing Woman Mythic ancestor of the Navajo people who created the first humans.

chantway The basis of Navajo ceremonial practice; includes chants, prayers, songs, and other ritual practice.

cry ceremony Sacred mourning ceremony involving songs, dances, and stories about the deceased, all of which aid the spirit of the deceased in transition to the next world.

Ghost Dance Religious resistance movements in 1870 and 1890 that originated in Nevada among Paiute peoples.

hogan (hoh'gahn; Pueblo) A sacred structure of Pueblo peoples.

Holy People Ancestors to the Navajo people, described in mythic narratives.

Holy Wind Navajo conception of a spiritual force that inhabits every element of creation.

Jump Dance Renewal dance of Yurok people.

kachinas (kah-chee'nah; Hopi) Pueblo spiritual beings.

Kinaalda (kee-nahl'dah) Rite of passage for young Navajo women.

McKay, Mabel A Pomo woman who was well known as a healer and basket weaver.

Native American Church A church founded in the early twentieth century based on peyote religion.

Parker, Quanah Comanche man who called for the embrace of peyote religion.

peyote (pay-oh'tee) Hallucinogenic cactus used in many Native American religions.

Popol Vuh (poh-pohl voo'; Quiché Mayan, "council book") The Quiché Mayan book of creation.

Quetzalcoatl (ket-zuhl-kuh-wah'tuhl; Aztec) Aztec god and important culture hero in Mexico.

rites of passage Rituals that mark the transition from one social stage to another.

rites of renewal Rituals that seek to enhance natural processes, like rain or fertility, or to enhance the solidarity of a group.

sand painting A painting made with sand used by Navajo healers to treat ailments.

Sun Dance Midsummer ritual common to many Native American religions; details vary across cultures.

sweat lodge A structure built for ritually cleansing and purifying the body.

tipi (also teepee) A typical conical structure of the tribes of the Great Plains which is often constructed with a sacred blueprint.

trickster A common figure in North American mythologies; trickster tales often teach important moral lessons.

Two Spirit An additional gender identity in many Native North American cultures; often thought to have special spiritual powers.

vision quest A ritual attempt by an individual to communicate with the spirit world.

Wovoka A Paiute man whose visions started the Ghost Dance of 1890.

SUGGESTIONS FOR FURTHER READING

Brown, Joseph Epes. *Teaching Spirits: Understanding Native American Religious Tradition.* New York: Oxford University Press, 2001. A comprehensive look at Native American religions, including topics such as geography, creativity, and ritual.

DeLoria, Vine, Jr. *God Is Red: A Native View of Religion.* New York: Dell Publishing Company, 2003. A seminal work on Native American spirituality from a Native perspective.

Gill, Sam. *Native American Religions: An Introduction.* Boston: Thomson Wadsworth, 2005.

Hirschfelder, Arlene, and Paulette Molin. *An Encyclopedia of Native American Religions.* New York: Facts on File, 1992. A useful encyclopedia with detailed entries on many aspects of Native American religious belief and practice.

Kehoe, Alice Beck. *The Ghost Dance: Ethnohistory and Revitalization.* Long Grove, IL: Waveland

Press, 2006. A detailed look at the Ghost Dance in its cultural and historical context.

LaPier, Rosalyn R. *Invisible Realities: Storytellers, Storytakers, and the Supernatural World of the Blackfeet*. Omaha: University of Nebraska Press, 2017.

Neihardt, John G., and Black Elk. *Black Elk Speaks: Being the Life Story of a Holy Man of the Oglala Sioux*. Omaha: University of Nebraska Press, (1932) 1961. An intimate account of the religious visions and worldview of the Lakota religious leader Black Elk.

ONLINE RESOURCES

Montana Two Spirit Society
Informative website of an advocacy organization for Two Spirit and LGBTQ issues.

National Museum of the American Indian
This museum, part of the Smithsonian Institution, has many materials about the research collection online.

National Archives
This portal page at the website of the National Archives leads to the Archives' research materials on federally recognized tribes.

Indigenous Religions of Africa

3

Chapter Outline

3.1 Understand the significance of oral narrative to African religions.

3.2 Summarize the key beliefs and practices about humanity in many indigenous religions of Africa.

3.3 Discuss the emergence of early religions in Africa.

3.4 Describe the impact of the spread of Islam, and then conquest and colonization by European empires, on African religions.

3.5 Describe the impact of the transatlantic slave trade and the spread and transformation of African religions in the Americas.

3.6 Describe resistance movements and revitalization in the modern history of African indigenous religions.

3.7 Describe various modes of observance in African religions.

3.8 Associate specific African traditions and rituals with stages in the life cycle.

3.9 Identify ways in which African religions engage with issues in the contemporary world.

TEPILIT OLE SAITOTI is a Maasai man from Tanzania, a country in East Africa. The Maasai are a cattle-herding people, most of whom live in Kenya and Tanzania. As a promising young student, Tepilit eventually studied in the United States and Europe. In 1988, he published his autobiography, *The Worlds of a Maasai Warrior*. In the book, he describes the initiation ceremony that transformed him from a young boy into a warrior.

When Maasai boys reach adolescence, they are circumcised in a public ritual to mark their transition to the status of warriors. Different ceremonies mark the transition of Maasai girls into womanhood. In the Maasai culture, warriors are known as ***moran***. The *moran* are a special group of young men who have particular responsibilities. They are usually between the ages of fifteen

Competitive jumping can be part of the young Maasai warriors' rite of passage ceremonies.

and thirty-five and are traditionally responsible for protecting the community and for herding the cattle and other animals. Boys who become *moran* together form a special bond that continues throughout their lives. But first, a young man must survive his circumcision. For Tepilit, undergoing the circumcision ceremony was an intense and transformational experience:

> Three days before the ceremony my head was shaved and I discarded all of my belongings such as my necklaces, garments, spear, and sword. I even had to shave my pubic hair. Circumcision in many ways is similar to Christian baptism. You must put all the sins you have committed during childhood behind and embark as a new person with a different outlook on life.[1]

Tepilit describes the apprehension he felt as the day approached. The circumcision was important not just for him but for his entire family. His father and brothers warned him that he must not cry, scream, or kick the knife away when the circumciser removed his foreskin because that would embarrass his family. It could even jeopardize his future. Bravery is highly valued in the Maasai culture, and people would lose respect for Tepilit if he showed himself to be a coward. He would never be considered for a position of leadership if he became known as a "knife-kicker."

> The circumciser appeared, his knives at the ready. He spread my legs and said, "One cut," a pronouncement necessary to prevent an initiate from claiming that he had been taken by surprise. He splashed a white liquid, a ceremonial paint called *enturoto*, across my face. Almost immediately I felt a spark of pain under my belly as the knife cut through my penis's foreskin.[2]

Tepilit made it through the ceremony bravely, and his friends and family congratulated him. Two weeks later, his head was shaved again to mark his new status as a man and a warrior.

> As long as I live, I will never forget the day my head was shaved and I emerged a man, a Maasai warrior. I felt a sense of control over my destiny so great that no words can accurately describe it.[3]

Like the Maasai, most African cultures (and cultures everywhere) have rituals that mark the transition of young people into adulthood. Although details of the ceremonies vary from culture to culture, they share the public recognition that a young person has entered a new phase of life. Often, this new phase of life is understood through a religious worldview. In African religions, other phases of life are also marked through specific ceremonies. For example, birth marks the journey of an individual soul from the spirit world to the human world, and death is the transition back to the spirit world.

In this chapter, we will explore the indigenous, small-scale religious traditions of Africa. Although many Africans today are Muslims or Christians, we will concern ourselves here with religions that originated in Africa. Because North Africa (Egypt,

Libya, Algeria, Morocco, and Tunisia) has been predominantly Muslim for about 1,000 years, this chapter explores Africa south of the Sahara, where indigenous religions have remained more prominent until the present. This region is often referred to as "sub-Saharan Africa."

Today, well over 1 billion people live on the African continent. There are thousands of different African cultural, ethnic, and linguistic groups. This cultural diversity is reflected in the religious diversity of the continent. There is not one single "African culture" or "African religion." Because African religions are so numerous, we will not attempt to discuss them all in this chapter. Instead, we will explore examples from a few religions that reflect African cultural and geographic diversity. And although we address them together in a single chapter, it is important to remember that not all African religions are the same. Because of this diversity, it is not easy to generalize about them in a textbook chapter.

And yet, despite this diversity, it is possible to identify some common characteristics in the realms of practice, teaching and beliefs, and historical development. The story of Tepilit's initiation explores one of these characteristics: many African religions have specific ceremonies that mark the transition from one social state of being to another. Many African religions also share some elements of belief and worldview. For example, many share the belief in a supreme deity, or creator god. Also, many African religions are primarily concerned with life in the here and now, rather than with what comes after death.

African religions also share a great deal in terms of historical development. Many African

TIMELINE
Indigenous Religions of Africa

2000 BCE–1500 CE	Bantu migration from West Africa to the central, eastern, and southern regions of the continent.
100–600 CE	Kingdom of Axum thrives in northeast Africa.
700s	Arab Muslims extend control across North Africa.
1000s	Islam begins to spread throughout West Africa and coastal East Africa.
600–1100	The empire of Ghana rises.
800–1400	The rise of the great cities and empires of Mali.
1000–1400s	Great Zimbabwe thrives in southern Africa.
1500–1800s	Muslim Swahili city-states thrive on the East African coast.
1500s–1800s	Atlantic slave trade; African religions begin to spread to the Americas.
1884	Berlin Conference; European colonial powers divide Africa.
1800–1900s	European colonization and Christian missionary work in Africa.
1804–1809	Usman dan Fodio leads campaigns in northern Nigeria to rid Islamic practice of indigenous religious elements.
1905	Kinjiketele organizes Maji Maji revolt against German colonizers in Tanganyika (today's Tanzania).
Early 1900s	Several new African Christian churches are founded.
1920s	Josiah Oshitelu founds an independent Yoruba Christian church, known as the Aladura Church.
1950s–1990s	Decolonization: sub-Saharan African countries gain independence.
1962–1965	Vatican II permits local church leaders around the world to be more accepting of local practices.

religions originated in small-scale communities and thus may be connected intimately with a particular culture in a particular place. And although some followers of African religions live in small-scale societies today, many more have been incorporated into large political systems and market economies in the modern, global era.

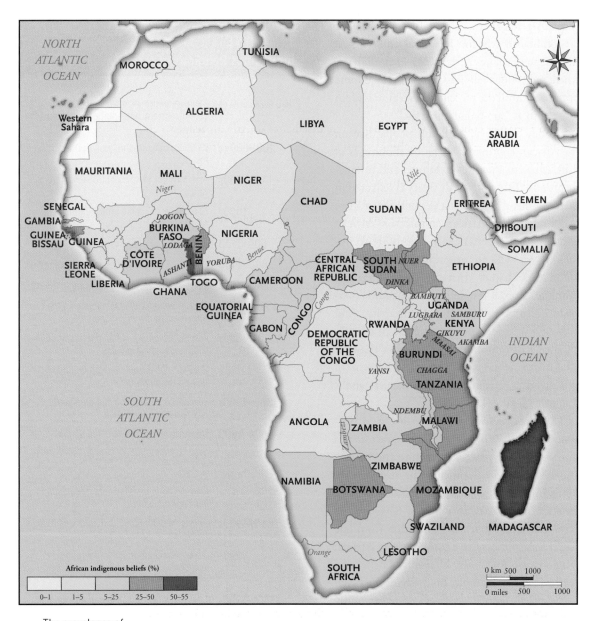

The prevalence of indigenous African religions today, with peoples and cultures that are discussed in this chapter (in red).

Furthermore, in the nineteenth and twentieth centuries, African religions faced the reality of widespread European colonialism on the continent. In addition, the influence of African religions has spread far beyond their places of origin. This was primarily a result of the Atlantic slave trade, which lasted from the 1500s to the 1800s. As we will learn in this chapter, certain religions of the Americas, such as **Vodou** and **Santería**, were derived from and share a great deal with African religions.

3.1 The Teachings of Indigenous Religions of Africa: Sacred Narratives

For followers of indigenous African religions, "religion" is not considered to be separate from everyday existence. Religious practice is not relegated to particular times, places, or spaces. Instead, religious beliefs and practices infuse and inform daily life and everyday concerns. We will begin our discussion of African religions by considering their beliefs and teachings. Although the religions of Africa differ significantly, certain ideas about the supernatural, the natural world, and humanity's place within it are common to many of the continent's religions.

We find the beliefs of African religions primarily in mythic narratives, which contain essential teachings. All religions, as we learned in Chapter 1, have a mythic component. African religions are no exception, and most have a very rich mythic heritage. Myths are not falsehoods; rather, they are narratives that humans tell about human origins, the way of being human, and the nature of the world and the cosmos. In religions the world over, myths relate compelling stories about gods, spirits, heroic figures, or human ancestors. Because of these intriguing narratives, myths have the ability to teach the listener about the origins of humanity, about supernatural beings, and about morality and ethics in a powerful and memorable way.

In most African religions, myths have been part of an oral tradition and have been passed from one generation to the next through the spoken word. Today, however, many myths also exist in written form. In many African cultures, elders or religious leaders are responsible for maintaining and disseminating the teachings of myths to others. Although all members of a culture may be familiar with basic mythic narratives, elders and religious specialists often know more details and deeper meanings.

The myths of many African religions are most often concerned with this world—the world of humanity—rather than the greater universe. Myths most often tell stories about the origins of the Earth and of human beings and about human social life and social organization. Myths often convey moral lessons. When African myths contain stories of gods and other supernatural beings, the stories frequently focus on the way in which these beings interact with or relate to humanity.

Among the Dogon people of Mali and Burkina Faso, in West Africa, myth has been part of the oral tradition for generations. The Dogon are primarily farmers, and although some Dogon are Christians or Muslims, most still follow Dogon religion. Dogon religious experts know far more about myths than the average person and are therefore responsible for preserving, understanding, and passing on the myths. Dogon mythology is intimately related to religious and social life. It involves complex explanations of the origins of the world and human beings and the way in which human beings should live on Earth, such as explanations for farming practices. Throughout this section of the chapter, we will consider various myths from different African religions, including the Dogon, as we learn about the beliefs and teachings of African religions.

Supernatural Beings: Gods and Spirits

Many African religions teach that everyday human life is influenced or even controlled by gods or other supernatural beings. African religions are therefore *theistic*, a term you will recall from Chapter 1. Most also share the belief in a supreme deity, or High God. African religions often teach that the High God is all knowing, all powerful, and the creator of the world and of humanity. This supreme deity is frequently associated with the sky and may be specifically connected to the sun or the rain because both the sun and rain have life-giving powers. Most African religions regard the High God as eternal. And although the High God is generally not thought to be human-like, the supreme deity may be described as having human-like attributes, such as mercy, goodness, and a concern for justice.

Many African religions consider the High God to be transcendent and thus removed from the lives of humans. As a result, there are rarely temples, churches, or shrines devoted to the High God, and most religious practice focuses on communicating with spirits or lesser gods. In the religion of the Dogon, the High God **Amma** is an example of a deity who is distant from the lives of ordinary humans. The Dogon creation myth tells that Amma made Earth out of mud and clay. Although he was active in creation, Amma eventually retired from the world and left lesser deities to manage earthly affairs and attend to human interests. Other African mythologies explain the transcendence of the High God as the result of a transgression committed by humans or animals that upset the High God, who then left this world for a supernatural realm. We will examine some of these myths later in this chapter.

In some African religions, the High God is associated with the qualities of both a father and a mother. In others, the High God has no gender. The Samburu people of Kenya believe that God, known as Nkai, is flexible in gender and in form. In the Samburu language, the word *Nkai* is feminine. God is associated with procreation and is considered to have many female characteristics. Interestingly, some Samburu people who claim to have been taken to the divine home of Nkai have reported that the deity is not one individual but rather a family group.[4]

VOICES: Interviews with Sammy Letoole and Festus Ogunbitan

Sammy Letoole, a young Samburu man from Kenya, studied at the Friends Theological College in Kaimosi, Kenya. Although he studied Christianity, he was raised in the Samburu religion and finds that it does not conflict with his Christian faith. The Samburu people live in northern Kenya, and Samburu culture and religion share some elements with Maasai culture and religion. Festus Ogunbitan is a scholar of religion from Nigeria whose ancestry is Yoruban. Festus was raised in a Christian home, but he explored his ancestral religion as he matured. An author, he has written several books on Yoruba religion.

What is your religious background?

Sammy: My religious background is Samburu and now I am a Christian. I was raised in a pure Samburu family who believed in traditional Samburu religion. Every day, my father woke up very early in the morning to go out and pray for everything—including the animals and the children. As a result, my faith in God became very strong because I saw my dad praying without stopping. And this makes my Christian foundation strong.

Festus: I am from the Yoruba nation of the southwestern part of Nigeria. I was born into a Christian family who were biased about the values and virtues of their ancestors' culture. This happened to many Africans, since Christianity and Islam declared their religion as the universal religion. When I grew up, I started to read books about the religion of my ancestors, and I discovered that religion is a social process—it is like a plant growing up to bring forth fruits. Therefore, my Yoruba religion does not need to be suppressed by any foreign religion.

Sammy Letoole.

Sammy, you don't seem to see much conflict between Christianity and Samburu religion. Could you explain their similarities and differences? How does your religious practice draw on both traditions?

The Samburu religion and Christianity have a similar conception of God. In both traditions, God is a creator, provider, and protector and is caring and loving. The Samburu people believe that God is found in the mountains, so they name their gods after those big mountains. During the time of the Old Testament, Moses climbed Mount Sinai to pray, and he was given the commandments; similarly, the Samburu pray to their God to give them direction.

There are many things that the Samburu religion shares with the Bible, especially the Old Testament. During that time, the Israelites were not supposed to eat animals without divided hooves and who did not chew the cud. Even now, the Samburu do not eat those animals. Also, the people in the time of the Old Testament offered sacrifices to their God; the Samburu also offer sacrifices to their God.

Festus, could you explain your view of the nature of the world and humanity's place in it and how this developed through learning about the religion of your ancestors?

I believe that the universe is created by God, and the universe is part of God through nature. I believe in the ancient Yoruban concept of God which says that nature is part of God—plants, animals, outer space, and human nature. As a result, they worship nature and human nature by reinforcing them with praise singing. I believe that nature is divine, and a sincere and ingenious person is divine, and we should respect them. If we treat nature and creativity in humans as divine, we shall be able to get lots of good things from them—such as the invention of products and services for the needs of mankind.

Festus Ogunbitan.

Could you both describe your worship and religious practice?

Sammy: My worshiping styles and praises are influenced by Samburu religion. Samburu prayers and Christian prayers differ because the Samburu believe that God is found in mountains, rivers, and good springs. Therefore, when performing prayers, a person must face a certain mountain like Mount Kenya or Mount Nyiro. Christians forward their prayers to God through Jesus Christ, our savior. Although people pray to God in different ways, they all seek protection, guidance, love, and satisfaction.

Festus: I am not a Christian, and I don't really practice Yoruba traditional religion in a shrine. But I have faith in the religion of my ancestors, most especially Ogun—the Yoruba god of Iron—which is half of the pronunciation of my last name. My last name, Ogunbitan, means "a child through whom Ogun the god of Iron shall create history." By writing a book called *Lyric Poems on Creation Story of the Yorubas*, I have fulfilled this promise.

In addition to the belief in a High God, most African religions also recognize other supernatural beings that are lower in status than the High God but are still powerful. As you learned in Chapter 1, a belief system in which many supernatural beings (including gods and spirits) are recognized but in which one of these beings is elevated to a higher status is known as henotheism. In African religions, gods or spirits interact with human beings and are sometimes thought to be mutually interdependent with humans. Accordingly, much religious practice focuses on these beings. Therefore, unlike the High God, these lesser gods and spirits often have temples, shrines, and rituals devoted to them.

In many African religions, including the Dogon, the Ashanti, and the Igbo, Earth is an important female deity. She is often understood to be the consort or daughter of the High God, who is typically associated with the sky, the sun, or the heavens in general. In Dogon mythology, Amma created Earth and then forcibly took her as his mate. A jackal was born from this union. The Dogon consider the birth of the jackal to be unfavorable because it was a single birth, not a twin. In Dogon culture, twin birth is considered ideal. This misfortune of the jackal's birth is attributed to Amma's unjust rape of Earth.[5]

Dogon religion provides another example of lesser deities. Although the original union of Amma and Earth was problematic, Dogon myths tell of a second union. This union was favorable and produced twins—an ideal birth. The twins took the form of another supernatural being—a lesser god called the Nummo. The Nummo twins represent the balance of male and female elements. The Nummo plays an important role in Dogon myths about the origins of humans and the development of human social structure. The Nummo is active in the affairs of humans, while Amma is not.

Some African religions have a large and complex **pantheon** or group of deities. One example of a pantheon is in the religion of the Yoruba people, a large ethnic group in West Africa. Although many Yoruba have converted to Islam and Christianity, indigenous beliefs are still prominent, even among the converts. In Yoruba religion, the High God, known as Olodumare, is accompanied by other categories of deities. One such category is the **Odu**, who were the original prophets gifted with the ability to look into the future. Another category is the **orisha**, who are believed to inhabit an otherworldly realm called *orun*. The orisha live in a hierarchical social order that closely reflects Yoruba social organization. Yoruba mythology teaches that the hundreds of orisha were the first inhabitants of the world. The High God sent the orisha to Earth to create land from the water and gave each a specific duty. Yoruba people believe that the High God ultimately determines their destiny, although they serve different orisha as their personal deities.

One of the foremost orisha is a goddess known as **Oshun**. Oshun is merciful, beautiful, and loving, and she is associated with fertility and the life-giving properties of water. Yoruba people may therefore call on her to help them with matters pertaining to childbirth and family. She is also known as the "hair-braider" or "hair-plaiter" and has the power to make people beautiful. In Yoruba mythology, Oshun was present at the time of creation,

This picture of a Nuer homestead was taken by anthropologist E. E. Evans-Pritchard in the 1930s.

but she was the only female, and the *Odu* ignored her. However, Olodumare reproached them and explained how important Oshun was. The following passage from a Yoruba myth relates how the *Odu* appealed to Oshun for forgiveness. In the myth, Oshun eventually bears a son who joins the other *Odu*.

> They returned to Oshun
> And addressed her: "Mother, the pre-eminent hair-plaiter with the coral
>   beaded comb.
> We have been to the Creator
> And it was discovered that all Odu were derived from you.
> And that our suffering in the world would continue
> If we failed to recognize and obey you."
> So, on their return to earth from the Creator,
> All the remaining Odu wanted to pacify and please Oshun.[6]

In some African religions, such as that of the Nuer people of Sudan, the High God may manifest as multiple deities. The anthropologist E. E. Evans-Pritchard (1902–1973) lived with the Nuer in the 1930s and made a detailed study of their religion.[7] He argued that the Nuer belief system should be considered both monotheistic *and* polytheistic because the different deities recognized were simply reflections of the High God. Although many Nuer people are Christian today, some elements of Nuer religion remain important. The Ashanti people of West Africa similarly regard the many gods in their belief system as the way in which the High God manifests.

In African religions, spirits are often considered to be a part of God's creation, like humanity. Most often, spirits are thought to live alongside human beings in a shared world. As a result, in many African cultures, spirits are a part of normal daily life. Spirits are commonly believed to be immortal and invisible. Many African religions associate spirits with elements of the natural world, such as mountains and trees, and forces of the natural world, such as rain and lightning. However, they are able to interact with human beings in various ways. Like human beings, spirits are neither entirely good nor entirely evil. They are typically thought to be more powerful than human beings, but humans can learn to interact with and even manipulate them to some degree. Religious experts or leaders may even call upon the spirits to act as messengers between humans and God.

Spirits of the Dead

Spirits of the Dead　In many African religions, the spirits of deceased humans are very important. In fact, most African religions do not regard death as a final state of oblivion. Instead, death is seen as a change to another spiritual state. As birth is believed to be a transition from the world of the spirits to the world of the living, death is a transition back to the spirit world. This belief often has a basis in mythology. In Dogon myths, the original human ancestors became spirits, who then paved the way for later generations to enter the spirit realm after their death. Although the spirits of the dead are sometimes called "ancestor spirits," scholars of African religions argue that this term is not very accurate. This is because the category includes the spirits of many people who have died—not just those who bore children and have living descendants to whom they are ancestors.[8] Therefore, children or people who died childless can also become spirits.

The spirits of the dead are often active in the lives of their relatives and descendants for several generations. These spirits may also be concerned with upholding cultural values and family unity from beyond the grave. They are also frequently believed to be the most effective intermediaries between the High God and humans. Consequently, living people engage in specific practices to maintain positive relations with these spirits. And the spirits depend to some extent on humans. The living may symbolically care for the spirits by offering food and drink or by making sacrifices to them. Like other supernatural beings of African religions, ancestor spirits are not necessarily good or bad, and they can both help and hurt their living relatives. If spirits are neglected, they may become angry and cause problems for the living. It is therefore very important for the living to respect their elderly relatives, who are close to transitioning to the spirit world. It is also essential to remember to pay respect to the deceased.

The Gikuyu people of Kenya (also known as the Kikuyu) recognize several categories of spirits of the dead. One category consists of deceased members of the immediate family, and another category includes the deceased members of the extended family group, or clan. The former are active in the day-to-day life of the living immediate family, and the latter spirits maintain an interest in the welfare of the clan. Living people may consult with the spirits of the dead for advice or guidance in their own affairs.[9] Therefore, in African cultures such as the Gikuyu, a person's family is considered to include not just his living relatives but also those who have passed on. The Gikuyu believe that if the spirits of the dead are neglected, they can harm the living as a form of punishment for such bad behavior. They may cause illnesses or bring about other misfortunes on their negligent descendants. Usually, the living make an effort to care for the spirits of the dead until the last person who knew the deceased during his life has died. At this point, the deceased moves into a different spiritual category in which he will have less active involvement in the lives of the living, or none at all.[10]

3.2 The Teachings of Indigenous Religions of Africa: Humanity

Most African religions are anthropocentric, which means that they recognize humanity as the center of the cosmos.[11] Because of this, African belief systems understand the cosmos and elements within it, like supernatural beings, in terms of their relationship to humanity. Unlike many other religions, most African religions do not teach about the possibility of salvation or punishment in an afterlife. Rather, teachings generally focus on the importance of the present world.

Human Origins and the Human Condition

This anthropocentrism is reflected in the many African mythologies that begin with the creation of human beings instead of the creation of the world. As we have seen, a High God is often the creator of human beings. In many African myths, God creates humanity from clay or mud. The Dogon creation narrative tells that after the birth of the Nummo twins, Amma decided to create eight human beings from clay. The Dogon recognize these eight beings as the original human ancestors. In myths from other African traditions, God brings forth humanity from beneath the earth or out of a rock or tree. In still other myths, human beings come to this world from another one. The myths of the Chagga people of Tanzania explain that humanity descended to Earth from heaven by the gossamer thread of a spider's web.

In some creation narratives, lesser gods are responsible for creating human beings. In a Yoruba narrative, the deity Obatala, son of the High God, was assigned by his father to make human beings from clay. Once the beings were formed, the High God breathed life into them. One version of the myth tells that Obatala got very thirsty during his work of making humans. To quench his thirst, he started to drink beer. He became so drunk that he fashioned some people who were missing limbs, had crooked backs, or had other physical problems. When he sobered up, Obatala was so distraught at what he had done that he vowed to watch over the disabled people he had made. This myth accounts for people who are born with disabilities and for Obatala's special concern for them.

Many African religions teach that humans were created in a male–female pair as either husband and wife or (less often) as brother and sister. Dogon myths explain that the first eight humans each had a dual soul—they were both male and female. As a result, all humans are born with a dual soul. Circumcision reduces this dual soul to one soul—male or female. Other African cultures also regard humans as having a dual nature. Sometimes this is understood to be a physical body and an immaterial essence, like a spirit. The Lugbara people of Uganda believe that human beings have multiple souls. Each soul is associated with a different part of the body, like the heart or the lungs.

As we discussed earlier in this chapter, African religions often teach that the High God is removed from everyday human life. However, many teach that the High God was not always distant but originally lived with humans in a time of complete happiness, when God provided people with all they needed. However, God and humanity became separated. In some religions, this separation from God introduced death and toil into the lives of humans. These religions tend to emphasize the past—when humans coexisted with God—as an ideal, paradise-like existence.

In myths, the separation from the High God often was the result of humans breaking one of God's rules. In a myth of the Dinka people, who are cattle herders in southern Sudan, death is explained as the result of the anger of the first woman. In the beginning, the High God gave one grain of millet to the first woman and her husband. The woman was greedy and decided to plant more than a single grain. In her eagerness to plant, she hit God with her hoe. God was so angry that he withdrew from humanity and severed the rope that connected heaven and Earth. Because of her action, the Dinka believe that humans are doomed to work hard throughout life and then die. The myth also teaches an important moral lesson: humans should avoid being proud and greedy.

Sometimes, human mortality results from the actions of animals who deliberately or unintentionally betrayed humans. The religion of the Nuer people teaches that a rope originally connected Earth to heaven; this belief is similar to the Dinka myth. If someone climbed the rope to heaven, Kwoth, the High God, would make that person young again. One day, a hyena and a bird climbed the rope. Kwoth said they were not allowed to return to Earth because they would cause trouble there. However, they escaped and returned to Earth. Then the hyena cut the rope. As a result, humans could no longer get to heaven, and now they grow old and die.

Many African religions also teach that the High God created human social organization, customs, and rules of conduct. Ethical and moral teachings often focus on the importance of maintaining agreeable relationships within human society and the spirit world. Sometimes, this extends to the proper relationship between humanity and the Earth. Dogon mythology teaches that after they were created, the Nummo twins taught human beings how to farm. In many African cultures, farming is an important activity not only for subsistence but also in terms of religion. Dogon myths explain that the first child of the unfortunate union between Amma and the earth was a jackal. The jackal defiled its mother, the earth, by attempting to rape her. Humans, however, have the ability to correct this defilement and purify the earth through farming.

3.3 The History of Indigenous Religions of Africa: Religion in Early Civilizations and States

Just like large-scale world religions, religions in sub-Saharan Africa have developed historically and accommodated cultural changes. Individual African religious traditions have unique histories that would be impossible to explore fully in a single chapter. The task is made more difficult because, in many parts of Africa, there are few surviving written records documenting the histories of these religions before the modern period. However, we can identify some key events, people, and places that tell us something about African religions in the premodern period.

Human beings originated in Africa, and our earliest record of religions comes from Africa as well. Rock art from southern Africa dates as far back as at least about 30,000 years ago, and it was likely produced by early hunter-gatherers; recently, archaeologists identified a rock drawing in South Africa that is possibly over 70,000 years old. Anthropologists and archaeologists believe that early hunter-gatherers recognized an active spirit world, and that certain individuals had the ability to interact with spirits. Scholars think it likely that the complex, detailed images in rock art helped humans communicate with spirits or even enter the spirit world.[12]

The Bantu Migration was a major population movement from West Africa to central and southern Africa from around 2000 BCE until about 1500 CE. The movement of agriculturalist Bantu peoples spread their languages, technologies, political forms, and cultural practices to other African peoples, many of whom were hunter-gatherers. Although we do not know much about early Bantu religion, it is safe to assume that essential teachings and practices that we might term "religious" also moved with the Bantu Migration. Although Bantu peoples today and in the past are very diverse, it is possible that the migration led to the development of religious commonalities in many parts of western, central, and southern Africa, such as the recognition of complex spirit worlds that interact with the human realm.

In the Common Era, great city-states and powerful empires arose throughout sub-Saharan Africa. In the northeast, in what is today Ethiopia and Eritrea, the kingdom of Axum (also spelled Aksum) flourished from the first century to the eighth century CE. Axum was known for its impressive stone monuments called stelae, minted gold coins, and the written language known as Ge'ez (a precursor to modern Amharic). Prior to 350 CE, when Axumite King Ezana I converted to Christianity, Axumites practiced a polytheistic religion that held many similarities to religions elsewhere in northeastern Africa and the Arabian Peninsula. Axumites made offerings and sacrifices to a complex pantheon of gods that represented planets, the moon, warfare, and other aspects of the natural world and social life. Even after the adoption of Christianity by King Ezana, inscriptions on coins, stone tablets, and stelae marking burials suggest that many people continued to practice the indigenous religion for some time.

Further south in eastern Africa, dozens of prominent city-states arose in a narrow strip along the Swahili Coast (Kenya and Tanzania today) from the eighth century to the eighteenth century. City-states like Zanzibar, Mombasa, and Kilwa dominated trade between Africa and other Indian Ocean locales, and became particularly powerful from 1500 to 1800. The city-states were first populated by Bantu peoples but became increasingly diverse with the arrival of Arab and other Indian Ocean traders. This led to intermarriage and the emergence of the language and cultures known as Swahili. There was an early Islamic presence on the coast, and pre-Islamic religious ideas and practices were likely similar to farming and pastoralist communities further inland. Until the present day, the coastal region is home to both practitioners of indigenous religions and Islam, and many people incorporate elements of both into their lives.

In southern Africa, the city of Great Zimbabwe arose as a large urban center of as many as 20,000 Shona-speaking Bantu people. (The term *zimbabwe* refers to stone buildings, and the country of Zimbabwe takes its name from this city.) Great Zimbabwe was probably the center of a large state or kingdom, and it flourished as a major center of trade from around 1100 to 1500 CE, frequently trading with Swahili city-states. Great Zimbabwe was dominated by a central building complex that archaeologists believe was the religious and ritual center of the city. Although it is uncertain what forms of religious practice took place in the complex, some scholars think that people venerated their ancestors through offerings of various kinds. Numerous soapstone figurines of animals have been found on the site, which suggest a ritual function.

Several prominent states and empires arose in West Africa, including the Ghana Empire from 600 to 1100 CE and the Mali Empire from 800 to 1400 CE. Although the modern country of Ghana takes its name from the empire, the Ghana Empire was located farther north, in what is today Senegal, Mauritania, and Mali. The empire had a major role in trans-Saharan trade and became wealthy through controlling the gold trade. Although we do not know a great deal about religion in the Ghana kingdom, it seems evident that the wealthy and powerful kings were regarded as semidivine and were considered religious leaders of their people, who likely made offerings to them.

As the Ghana Empire began to decline, the Mali Empire arose and eclipsed it, growing incredibly powerful and wealthy. The first king of Mali was known as Son Jara (or Sundiata), who ruled from 1230 to 1255. Although Muslims were certainly present and influential in the region during his reign, oral tradition holds that Sundiata adhered to indigenous beliefs and practices. As with the kings of the Ghana Empire, it is likely that Son Jara was thought to have semidivine powers. A great narrative, known as the Epic of Son Jara, tells of his life, and attributes powerful magical abilities to him and his family. While later Malian kings were overtly Muslim, ordinary people probably held on to their indigenous religious practices and beliefs for some time.

Throughout the continent, indigenous African religions have faced common historical forces like the spread of Islam, and then later the spread of Christianity and the devastation of colonialism. However, as we have seen, even when merchants or kings become Christians or Muslims, the influence of indigenous religious traditions remained. This is true even until today, when about 90 percent of Africans identify as Christians or Muslims. Indigenous religious ideas, narratives, and practices coexist with Christianity and Islam, and Africans often combine elements of many religions in their own worldviews and practice, as will be discussed next.

3.4 The History of Indigenous Religions of Africa: The Spread of Islam and Christianity

In Africa today, Islam and Christianity are the dominant religions; about 60 percent of people in Africa are Christians, and about 30 percent are Muslims. Both religions have a very long history on the continent. Indeed, African Christian communities in northeastern Africa date back to the second century CE, and Islam has been present in Africa since the seventh century CE. In this section of the chapter, we will examine the spread and growth of Islam and Christianity through commerce, conquest, and colonization.

The Spread of Islam

By the eighth century, Arab Muslims controlled North Africa from Egypt to Morocco, and Islam has been the dominant religion in North Africa for several centuries. Islam spread more slowly throughout sub-Saharan Africa. The number of Muslims in sub-Saharan Africa increased as Islam spread throughout West Africa and along the East African coast from the eleventh century until the present. Powerful kingdoms in West Africa, like the Mali Empire, gradually became majority Muslim. At first, it was typically only the merchants and traders who were Muslim, and historians believe that many converted to Islam for strategic purposes, such as to secure trading relationships with Muslim leaders in North Africa. In the kingdom of Ghana around 1100, towns were divided: Muslim traders lived on one side, and practitioners of the indigenous religion, including the king, lived on the other. Along the Swahili Coast in eastern Africa, trade and conversion also went hand in hand, and most people were Muslim by about 1500. Today, in addition to North Africa, the populations of much of western Africa, northeastern Africa, and the easternAfrican coast are predominantly Muslim.

In most cases, Islam spread through trade and through the teachings of traveling scholars. Often, elite Africans adopted Islam as a means to facilitate trade connections because Muslim traders from North Africa were more likely to trade with other Muslims than with non-Muslims. As Africans became Muslims, they often retained elements of indigenous religious practice. For example, in northeastern and East Africa, the spirits known as *zar* are part of the religious worldview and practice of Muslims and Christians, as well as followers of indigenous religions. This is similar to the persistent belief in *bori* spirits in West Africa among Muslims and non-Muslims alike. The belief in possession by *zar* and *bori* spirits preexisted the arrival of Islam and has been incorporated into the religious practice of African Muslims. We will discuss possession in more detail later in the chapter.

Christianity and Colonialism

Christianity has been present in Africa for centuries and is widespread in Africa today. The Ethiopian Coptic Church is an indigenous African Christian church that dates to the fourth century CE, when King Ezana I of Axum converted to Christianity. As a result, northeastern Africa, particularly Ethiopia and Eritrea, has a Christian history that extends back nearly two millennia. However, Christianity did not become widespread outside of North and Northeast Africa until much more recently. In fact, much of African Christianity today is the result of missionary efforts and European imperialism in the nineteenth and twentieth centuries. Missionary movements and proselytizing often went hand in hand with imperialism, and almost all of Africa was colonized by European powers—primarily Britain, France, and Portugal. Ethiopia is a notable exception.

The colonial powers sent missionaries to convert Africans to Christianity, and the Christian Bible was translated into numerous African languages. Often, the process of converting Africans included cultural indoctrination. African people were taught not only that their indigenous religions were false but also that their cultures were inferior to Western ways of life. Therefore, when Africans became Christians, they sometimes left behind their own cultural practices and cultural identities. Often, the new Christians were incorporated into the colonial bureaucracies as government officials. African Christians were also sometimes put in charge of missions and were charged with furthering European aims by converting their own people.[13]

3.5 The History of Indigenous Religions of Africa: The Transatlantic Slave Trade and African Religions in the Americas

During the centuries of Atlantic slave trade (1500–1800s), the religions of the Yoruba and other West African peoples such as the Dahomey and the Fon spread far beyond the shores of their homelands. Most of the millions of African people who were enslaved and brought to the Americas followed indigenous religions. The religious traditions and practices of Africans were suppressed or even forbidden by enslavers, yet indigenous African beliefs survived and sometimes flourished in the Americas. Throughout the Americas today, many people of the African diaspora—and others—practice religions that have their roots in the African continent.

Candomblé and Santeriá

The recognition of Yoruba orisha persisted and until this day remains popular in some communities of African descent throughout the Americas. The religious tradition known as **Candomblé** owes much to the enslaved Yorubans who were brought to South America; Candomblé has been particularly prominent in northeastern Brazil. Enslaved Africans managed to keep worshiping Yoruba deities in the face of conversion pressure from the European slave master by cloaking the orisha in the guise of Catholic saints. Many of the divination practices of *Ifa* have been incorporated within Candomblé. Santería is a Cuban religion that bears similarity to Candomblé and also incorporates the orisha. The Cuban diaspora has spread the religion throughout the Caribbean region. Today, there are likely hundreds of thousands of practitioners of Santería in the United States alone.

Vodou

Another example from the Caribbean is the Vodou religion, which originated in Haiti and then spread elsewhere in the Caribbean and southern United States. Also spelled as *voodoo*, this religious tradition owes much to both Catholicism and religions of West Africa, especially the religions of the Yoruba, Fon, and Kongo peoples. The term *vodou* comes from the Fon word *vudon*, which means "spirit." Practitioners of Vodou recognize many different spirits. The spirits are called *loa* and have origins in West Africa. As in Santería and Candomblé, the spirits are also sometimes identified with Catholic saints. Today, the majority of Haitians claim Vodou as their primary religious affiliation, although earlier in the twentieth century the Catholic Church denounced it as heretical. Vodou is also common in the Haitian diaspora in the United States, Canada, and elsewhere.

3.6 The History of Indigenous Religions of Africa: Reform and Resistance

Both today and in the past, African Muslim and Christian communities have debated whether practices derived from indigenous religions are an appropriate or authentic part of Muslim or Christian religious practice. In some cases, disapproval of indigenous practices and customs has led to major reform movements. Such criticisms of indigenous religions have largely been based on the idea that the beliefs, teachings, and practices of indigenous religions are at best "primitive" deviations from Christianity or Islam and at worst heretical and sinful.

Beginning in 1804, Usman dan Fodio (1754–1817), a West African Muslim reformer and religious leader, waged a campaign in northern Nigeria to rid Islamic practice of what he thought were inappropriate indigenous elements. One practice that he specifically criticized was spirit possession by the *bori* spirits, which was widespread at the time among both Muslims and non-Muslims. For over two decades, Usman dan Fodio and his followers tried to rid Muslim religious practice of what they viewed as inappropriate "African" elements such as this. The teacher and scholar Nana Asma'u, a daughter of Usman dan Fodio, dedicated her life to encouraging the education of Muslim women. She taught that all women had a duty as Muslims to seek knowledge, and she is still a role model for Muslim women in Nigeria today.[14] Nana Asma'u is one example of prominent women's leadership in Muslim communities in Africa.

New Christian Churches

In the first decades of the twentieth century, African Christian leaders began to develop new Christian churches that spun off from the long-established mission churches, like the Anglican and Catholic churches. African Christian leaders were often frustrated with their inferior status in the mission churches. Their new churches aimed to make Christianity more accessible and appropriate for African cultural contexts. The new independent churches became very popular, and today there are thousands of such churches in Africa.

In the 1920s, a man called Josiah Oshitelu (1902–1966) founded an independent Yoruba Christian church known as the Aladura Church. As a young man, he thought witches plagued him. However, a Christian healer explained that it was God testing him and that if he prayed, he could chase away the evil. Oshitelu began praying. He received visions, and he tried to convince others that the old African religions were disappearing and that they should all become Christians. His teachings focused on the power of prayer and fasting to influence the will of God. Interestingly, many indigenous Yoruba religious beliefs and practices held relevance for Aladura Christians. For example, most of the practitioners maintained beliefs in witchcraft and powerful spirits. The emphasis on prayer is also reminiscent of Yoruba ideas of harnessing spiritual power. Furthermore, the Aladura Church focused on improving life in this world in much the same way as Yoruba religion.[15]

Women have had important roles in the historical development of religions in Africa. Some scholars have argued that women's active role in spirit possession, as we will discuss later in this chapter, has led to their prominence in new religious movements. Because mission churches such as the Anglican and Catholic churches most often prohibited women from holding leadership roles, women were highly influential in the development of the new African Independent Christian churches, and women founded new churches throughout Africa.[16] For example, a woman called Grace Tani founded the Church of the Twelve Apostles in Ghana in 1914. Tani was regarded as a prophet, and like many other influential women leaders, she incorporated many local traditions into her Christian practice.[17] Although many of these new churches are now headed by men, women have often maintained important roles in preaching, leadership, and healing in the churches. The Aladura Church, for example, has separate male and female leadership structures.[18]

The Maji Maji Revolt

Throughout Africa, religious groups spearheaded anticolonial movements, and indigenous religious leaders were at the forefront of some of the most important of these movements. In 1905, a religious leader called **Kinjiketele** organized a rebellion against the German colonizers in Tanganyika (later called Tanzania). The revolt was known as the **Maji Maji** (Water Water) rebellion. Kinjiketele was believed to receive communications from the spirit world. One well-known story about him reports that a spirit took him into a pool in the Rufiji River. Later, he miraculously emerged completely dry. Kijiketele carried a message to his people that all of their dead ancestors would come back. Many people came to see him and to take the sacred water, which they believed would make them impervious to the bullets of the Europeans. In another version of the narrative, the miracle water was said to have the power to turn German bullets into water.

Kinjiketele attracted a large multiethnic following that supported his call for rebellion against the German colonizers. His message was compelling because it drew on indigenous religious beliefs in the power of spirits and the power of sacred waters. (The revolt takes its name from this sacred water.) Eventually, a group of Kinjiketele's followers, impatient with waiting for him to signal the proper time, began the revolt against the Germans without him. The uprising lasted two years and was eventually defeated by the Germans. Early in the uprising in 1905, the German colonial government hanged Kinjiketele for treason; in the two years that followed, German forces killed tens of thousands of his followers.[19]

A Benzedeira, or Brazilian traditional healer, tends to an altar in the temple that is also her home.

3.7 Indigenous Religions of Africa as a Way of Life: Observance

For followers of African religions, religion is something that infuses everyday life. It is not reserved for just one day of the week or for certain times of the year. Instead, religious practice is a daily activity. As we have learned, most African religions do not focus on reward or punishment in the afterlife, so religious practice does not normally center on preparing for life after death. Instead, rituals and ceremonies focus on improving life in this world. Thus, religious practice might address vital material needs, such as a good harvest, or social needs, such as a harmonious family life. Also, because the High God is often believed to be remote from day-to-day human life, most African religions do not emphasize worshiping a supreme deity. Instead, religious practice normally focuses on communication with other supernatural beings.

Communicating with the Spirit World

Many African religions believe that the world of spirits and the world of humans are closely intertwined. Spirits live near human beings in the same communities and often exist in a reciprocal relationship with them. Because spirits can interact

VISUAL GUIDE
African Religions

Among the Dogon, the *dama* is a rite of passage for young men, which also helps the recently deceased enter the state of being ancestors. The rite happens only once every several years, and masked participants dance to usher the recently deceased into the world of the spirits. The masks prepared for the *dama* are elaborately carved and represent animals and the mythical ancestors.

This early twentieth-century wooden tray is used to determine future events with the *Ifa* divination system, a part of Yoruba religion.

These nineteenth-century Yoruba sculptures from Nigeria commemorate twins who died. Twins are of great significance in many African religions, as among the Dogon, discussed in this chapter.

and interfere with the lives of humans, religious rituals and ceremonies often focus on communicating with spirits or accessing their power. People may ask spirits to intervene with God on their behalf or to assist with particular problems in family or work life. In this section, we will discuss three practices associated with communicating with the spirit world: sacrifice, divination, and spirit possession.

Sacrifice   In many religions the world over, the dedication of something valuable to a spirit—a sacrifice—has the power to influence that spirit. In African religions, people communicate with supernatural beings primarily through sacrifice. A sacrifice can be relatively small, like a prayer or a portion of one's daily food or drink. In some religions, such as the Yoruba, individuals may have a special relationship with one or more spirits or gods, and they might make these small offerings every day to maintain their goodwill. Yoruba families often have household shrines at which they make similar offerings to the spirits of the dead.

In other African contexts, larger sacrifices, such as an animal, are necessary. In some religions, there has traditionally been a close relationship between practices of healing and sacrifice. Illnesses may be attributed to a spirit's punishment of a person's bad behavior. In such cases, an animal may be sacrificed as a form of repentance and as a request for forgiveness from the aggrieved spirit. The Nuer, for example, typically sacrificed animals as a substitute for the person who was afflicted with an illness. The animal was offered to the spirits in exchange for the health of the person. However, in recent years, as Nuer people have begun attributing illness to biological causes instead of angry spirits and as more have adopted Christianity, the use of animal sacrifice in healing has diminished.[20]

Divination   In some African religions, people use a practice called **divination** to communicate with spirits. Divination is the attempt to predict the future through supernatural agents or powers. The Yoruba use a divination system called **Ifa** to communicate with the spirit world. A person called a diviner performs the divination. Yoruba religion teaches that *Ifa* was developed when the High God removed himself from

Palm nuts with a blue cloth bag, used by the Yoruba people for divination.

the earthly world. His children remained behind, and he gave them a divinatory system to communicate with him. They shared this system with human beings. Through *Ifa*, humans are able to communicate with and make requests of the gods and the spirits of the dead.

Yoruba diviners also use *Ifa* to predict the destinies and future of individuals. The diviners use a special collection of poetic verses and palm nuts to foresee future events and converse with supernatural beings. Most of the verses are from sacred Yoruba texts, and they tell of the time of the gods and ancestors. Diviners select specific verses because they contain the solution to problems that faced the ancestors and are thus helpful in solving current problems.

Spirit Possession Another way people communicate with the spirit world is through spirit possession. A belief in spirit possession is prevalent throughout Africa, and in many places this sort of interaction with spirits is a normal part of daily life. People communicate with spirits through a **medium**—an individual who can become possessed. The possessed individual is called a medium because she *mediates* between the human world and the spirit world. The spirit takes over the medium's body, and the medium then acts according to the will of the spirit while she is possessed. Because spirit possession usually takes place in public, many people can witness the possession and interact with the spirit through the medium. When a spirit possesses a person, she enters a state of trance. Others may then talk to or make requests of the spirit through her.

Throughout Africa, people ascribe different meanings to possession. Some traditions view possession negatively. It might cause illness or cause the medium to harm others. In such cases, a spiritual healer may be called upon to drive the spirit away. Elsewhere, people may encourage possession in order to communicate with the spirit world. Individuals may use special dancing, music, and drumming to entice a spirit. In such contexts, some people may be more prone to spirit possession than others. Sometimes, people who have the ability to become possessed achieve a special religious status.

In West Africa, there is a widespread belief in spirits known as **bori** who have the power to possess people. There are many different *bori*, and they have individual personalities. Among the Mawri people of Niger, spirits such as Maria, a flirtatious young prostitute, regularly possess mediums.[21] In northeastern Africa, the **zar** spirits are similar to the *bori* and are prominent throughout the region. Possession

Two Orixás, or orishas, who possess the women, dance in their finery at a Candomblé festival in Brazil held in their honor.

beliefs are also prevalent among Muslims and Christians in Africa. As these religions gained adherents in sub-Saharan Africa, many elements of preexisting religious practice remained. For example, Mawri people began converting to Islam in the mid-twentieth century, but the *bori* spirits remain. The *zar* spirits possess both Muslims and Christians.

Why do people become possessed? What does it mean for those who become possessed? Many scholars have tried to answer these questions. Some have argued that spirit possession is therapeutic for those who have mental or physical illness. Others suggest that spirit possession is a way for people to deal with rapid cultural change and the problems of modernity. For example, when the spirit Maria possesses Mawri women, they might be expressing an internal conflict between their desire to be traditional wives and mothers and the temptations of urban life and consumer culture, which Maria loves.[22]

Women often play a prominent role in possession complexes, and throughout Africa women are often more likely to become possessed than men. When possessed, a woman becomes a powerful representative of the spirit world. Some scholars have argued that this allows women to achieve a temporarily high status in male-dominated societies and in religions in which men control mainstream religious practice.[23] However, women's spirit possession practices are frequently at the center of religious life, not relegated to the margins. In Nigeria, Edo women participate in the worship of the god Olokun, who is at the heart of Edo religion. In Edo cosmology, Olokun is a very important god who has authority over fertility and wealth. By participating in the possession cult, Edo women gain permanent high status in the community. And although women who serve Olokun as priestesses do not have political authority in the same way men do, they can exert a great deal of power by settling disputes and acting as medical advisors.[24]

Using Supernatural Powers

Practitioners of African religions believe that some people have the ability to manipulate the supernatural for their own ends. Western scholars have traditionally used the term **witchcraft** to explain the use of supernatural powers to cause illness or other misfortune. (It is important to note that in other religions, such as Wicca, the term *witchcraft* does not have negative connotations. For more on Wicca, see Chapter 14.) In African languages, many different terms are used to denote witchcraft, although the idea that one can use supernatural powers to cause harm is fairly widespread. Often, witchcraft pervades everyday life and is understood as a normal part of existence. However, the use of witchcraft is not always thought to be intentional. In fact, in some cultures, people may be "witches" without even knowing it. As a result, they may cause harm to others unintentionally.

One of the most well-known examples of witchcraft is from the Azande, who live in South Sudan and the Central African Republic. The Azande believe that witchcraft is a physical substance that is present in some people's bodies. Evans-Pritchard, who conducted research among the Azande in the 1930s, showed that witchcraft beliefs were part of the Azande theory of causation. Witchcraft is a way of explaining why certain things happen to certain people. For example, if a man happened to be killed because he was sitting under a granary when it collapsed, the Azande would attribute this to witchcraft. Even if the granary collapsed because termites had destroyed the supporting wooden posts, the question of *why* it collapsed when a particular individual was sitting underneath it remained. The Azande would argue that this was an instance of witchcraft: the termites explained *how* it collapsed, but this explanation did not answer the question of *why* it collapsed when it did and killed the man sitting under it. Only witchcraft could answer the "why" question.[25]

Sometimes, people use supernatural powers or call on supernatural beings to facilitate healing. Healers may use special divination methods to determine what has caused an illness. Although illness might be attributed to biomedical causes, a healer normally looks for an ultimate cause, which might be witchcraft or the malicious actions of spirits. Then the healer can take special ritual action to try to cure it. A cure may involve repairing damaged social relationships that have caused jealousy. Or a cure may involve a sacrifice to appease an angry spirit that caused the illness. Among the Ndembu of Zambia, in southern Africa, some illnesses are believed to be caused by a particular spirit that is attracted to social conflicts. The spirit eats at the flesh of quarreling people with a sharp "tooth." To get rid of the spirit, Ndembu religious priests encourage the afflicted people to air their grievances against one another. During this discussion, the priest will use a special cup to extract the "tooth" that has been causing the illness.[26]

3.8 Indigenous Religions of Africa as a Way of Life: The Life Cycle

Most African religions emphasize important stages in the life cycle. Celebrations and ceremonies that mark the transitions from one phase of existence to another are an significant part of religious practice. These ceremonies define individuals as new members of the human community, as adults with full responsibilities and privileges of adulthood, or as having departed the living for the world of the spirits. African religions frequently believe that the life cycle begins before birth and continues after death. Rituals (Chapter 1) are formal religious practice. They are repetitive and rule-bound, and people often enact them with a specific goal in mind.

The goal could be to please a deity, encourage a good crop, or smooth the transition between phases of the life cycle. As you learned in Chapter 2, rituals that facilitate this transition are called **rites of passage**. These rituals may be performed after a birth, during the transition from childhood to adulthood, or at death, when the deceased transitions to the world of the spirits.

Birth: The Transition to the Human World

In many African religions, birth is the first important spiritual transition in a person's life. It is the moment a new individual enters the living community of humans. Preparing for a birth and welcoming a child are part of a process that often begins long before the child is born. Among the Bambuti people of the central African rainforest, a pregnant woman will offer food to a god as thanks for the pregnancy. In other African cultures, a pregnant woman is expected to observe certain rules and restrictions as a means of protecting herself and the child. For example, a woman may avoid certain foods or sexual relations with her husband while pregnant.

Practices surrounding the birth of a child vary tremendously from culture to culture in Africa. However, there are some common beliefs surrounding birth. One of these is the belief that birth marks the transition of the newborn from the world of spirits to the world of the living. Ceremonies after birth designate the child as belonging to the entire community, not just the mother. In many cultures, the placenta symbolizes the link between the child and its mother in its dependent state in the womb, and special care may be taken with its disposal after the child is born. The disposal of the placenta can symbolize the necessary separation of the child from its mother. The Yansi people of the Democratic Republic of Congo throw the placenta into a river. This act symbolizes that the child no longer belongs only to his or her mother but now belongs to the entire community.[27] The Gikuyu of Kenya practice a rite with a similar meaning. After she has given birth, a mother's head is shaved. This represents the severing of the exclusive tie between her and the child and also represents renewal: the mother is now ready to bear another child. Like the Yansi, the Gikuyu then recognize the child as a member of the wider society.[28]

Many African cultures have special naming ceremonies for

Bambuti woman and children in Uganda.

children to mark their transition from the spirit world to the human world. The Akamba people of Kenya name a child on the third day after he or she is born. The next day, the child's father presents him or her with a special necklace, and the parents have ritual intercourse. Together, these events mark the transition of the child from the spirit world to the world of living humans.[29] The Yoruba name their children after a special birth ritual called "stepping into the world." The ritual teaches parents how to raise their new child. At the request of the new parents, a diviner uses the *Ifa* divination system (discussed earlier in this chapter) to determine the baby's future. Using special tools, foods, and texts, the Yoruba diviner will try to determine the nature of the infant and will select a name based on what is divined. In one of the most important parts of the ritual, the diviner holds the baby's feet in the center of a special divination tray, which represents the entire world. This act places the baby symbolically in the center of the world and lets the diviner understand the baby's nature.[30]

The Transition to Adulthood

Rites of passage marking the transition from childhood to adulthood are extremely important in African religious traditions. Although they differ significantly in the details, rites of passage focus on successfully initiating a young person into adulthood and setting him or her on the path to becoming a complete member of the community. The new adult will have new privileges and responsibilities and will be expected to behave with maturity and wisdom appropriate to this new status. Often, it is rites of passage at adolescence that create a fully gendered adult. In many cultures, young people are able to marry only if they have been initiated. Sometimes, young people acquire special religious knowledge during initiation. Rites of passage also form important bonds for young people who go through them together. Among the Ndembu people of Zambia, for example, boys going through initiation are secluded for circumcision rites. Their mothers bring them food, which all the boys share. The boys spend all their time together and develop close friendships, which are intended to last their entire lives.

Young Maasai men (like Tepilit, whose story begins this chapter) become warriors when they go through initiation. Much later, when men are in their thirties, they will be initiated as elders and be allowed to marry. Maasai girls are also circumcised when they reach adolescence. However, they do not transition into an intermediate warrior stage but become ready for marriage. Young women change the way they dress, and they create beautifully beaded necklaces and head ornaments to wear. Many of these young women marry soon after they are circumcised,

Maasai women often wear intricately beaded necklaces.

and they most often move away from their homes to the villages of their husbands. As with the young men, girls become fully socially mature when they transition through these important rituals. For both, the coming of age rituals express important community values, such as strength, responsibility, and maturity.

In recent years, much controversy has surrounded female circumcision. In some communities, it is understood to have a religious basis, sometimes to maintain the sexual purity of women. In Africa, followers of many different religions practice female circumcision. This includes Christians and Muslims, in addition to followers of indigenous religions. Circumcision can take many forms. It can range from a simple incision on the clitoris to draw blood to what is known as infibulation. In infibulation, most of the external female genitalia are removed, and the incision is then sewn together. Because the more extensive types of circumcision such as infibulation can endanger the health of young girls, many people have called for an end to the practice. Some countries, such as Uganda, have banned it. However, reaction to these calls is mixed. Many women in Africa argue that circumcision is an essential part of their cultural identity.[31] They stress that a girl would never be considered a marriageable adult without undergoing the procedure during initiation. Others resent what they see as a movement led by Western activists, who remain silent about male circumcision because it is also prevalent in the West. Still others have succeeded in replacing circumcision with different kinds of rituals to mark the transition from girlhood to adulthood.

Gender Identity: The Igbo Ekwe

Initiation rites also mark other transitions in the life cycle, some of which are gendered in important ways. For example, until the colonial period, among the Igbo of Nigeria, certain women who achieved a great deal of wealth and economic independence were chosen by the goddess Idemili to receive the title of *Ekwe*. The scholar Ifi Amadiume researched this phenomenon extensively in her hometown of Nnobi. Amadiume tells us that Idemili was thought to have the ability to possess a woman and give her wealth. When Idemili chose a woman to receive the title of Ekwe, rituals involving the distribution of food and feasting marked this transition to a new status. The entire process took several months to complete, and the final ritual included wives in the Ekwe's extended family crawling through her legs to show their recognition of her high status. The new Ekwe would wear her hair combed out instead of braided and cease performing manual labor. She would then become a female "husband" and take one or more wives, who worked for the Ekwe and bore children in her name. This relationship did not necessarily include a sexual component, yet it indicates that, historically, some African communities recognized gender identities beyond the male-female binary. Among the Igbo, women had the potential to achieve a very high economic and religious status as Ekwe. However, colonial administrators actively discouraged or prohibited expressions and practices of gender beyond the male-female binary, and with Christianization and British colonialism, the Ekwe title was eventually banned in Nigeria.[32]

Death: The Transition to the Spirit World

Many African religions understand death not as an end to existence but as the transition to the spirit world. Funerals and other rituals surrounding death are important because they have the ability to ease the transition of the deceased from one state of being to another. In many cultures, the spirits of the dead cannot make the transition to the spirit world without the proper rituals. Normally, the living relatives of the deceased must facilitate the performance of these rituals. The LoDagaa people of Ghana hold complex funeral rites to facilitate this transition. The LoDagaa carve a special tree branch that represents the deceased. Ideally, a son cares for the branch as a representation of his late parent. While the symbolic branch is being cared for, the soul of the dead person is believed to travel to the world of the dead. The ritual is very important. If the living relatives do not perform it properly, then the soul of the deceased will be trapped in his or her village instead of moving to the realm of the dead.[33]

Among the Dogon, a rite of passage for young men also helps the recently deceased enter the state of being ancestors. This rite is known as the **dama**, and the basis for it is laid out in myths. In the *dama*, which happens only once every several years, masked participants dance to usher the recently deceased into the world of the spirits. The masks prepared for the *dama* are elaborately carved and represent animals and the mythical ancestors. The *dama* is also important for the living. If the dead do not enter the world of the spirits, they can cause problems for the living. Therefore, a successful *dama* frees the living from misfortune caused by the spirits of the dead and restores the normal balance of life and death. Today, these masked dances are used not only for ritual purposes but are also performed to entertain tourists; versions of the masks are produced for the tourist trade.

The rituals surrounding death are not always sad; they may even be joyful. Among the Yoruba, for example, if a person over forty years of age dies of natural causes, then the death is regarded as an important and happy transition to the world of the spirits and gods. This world is called *orun*, and the spirit of the deceased person will remain there and be called upon to assist in the affairs of her living relatives. However, if someone is under the age of forty at the time of death or dies of unnatural causes, the Yoruba consider it to be a great tragedy. Their spirits cannot enter *orun* but are rather doomed to wander the Earth unhappily forever.[34]

A Dogon masked dancer.

3.9 Indigenous Religions of Africa as a Way of Life: Engaging with the World

Today, approximately 10 percent of the population of Africa practices only indigenous religions. The challenges of colonialism and expanding world religions in the last few centuries have vastly increased the number of Africans following such large-scale religions as Islam and Christianity. Although the majority of Africans today profess one of these two faiths, their prevalence has certainly not eradicated indigenous African religions. We can assume that African religions will continue to change and adapt to wider social environments both in Africa and in the African diaspora. Although their forms and modes of practice will change from one generation to the next, this development only continues processes of change that are common to all religions. African religions are not relics of the past; rather, they are meaningful living traditions that will continue to thrive in the future.

People throughout Africa have incorporated beliefs and practices from indigenous religions into large-scale religions. As a result, Islam and Christianity have taken on distinctly African forms and have essentially *become* indigenous African religions. African religions tend to focus on the present, and much African religious practice looks for ways to improve one's immediate circumstances. These concerns have remained meaningful to many people in Africa, even when they become followers of salvation-oriented religions such as Christianity and Islam.

Reforming Initiation Rites

The status of indigenous rites has also been contested in some Christian and Muslim communities. Christian and Muslim religious leaders have often targeted initiation rites, such as those discussed earlier in this chapter. The rites have sometimes been described as "backward," "un-Christian," and "un-Islamic" or have simply been condemned as relics of a past best left behind. In some cases, Muslims and Christians have been receptive to the criticism and have stopped performing initiation rites or have replaced them with ceremonies that are deemed more appropriate by Muslim and Christian religious leaders. However, elsewhere, Muslims and Christians have continued to participate in the rites, despite the condemnation. Advocates argue that the rites are important means of achieving adulthood and are not in conflict with Christianity or Islam.

Occasionally, religious leaders who criticized the rites in the past changed their approach. For example, at one time the Catholic Church in Zambia strongly restricted female initiation rites in some Zambian cultures. However, in the 1960s, Vatican II (a historic meeting of Roman Catholic Church leaders to address issues facing the church at the time) permitted church leaders to be more accepting of local practices. As a result, Zambian Catholic leaders changed their point of view. They argued that the initiation rites could be used to instill Catholic teachings about marriage and family in young women.[35]

Engaging with the Environment

African indigenous religions frequently designate elements of the natural world as sacred, and many creation narratives explain the ideal relationship between the earth and humanity. The African continent is suffering the effects of climate change. Some parts of Africa are experiencing increasing droughts, while coastal areas face damaging flooding. Africa is one of the areas that will suffer most from climate change, but it has produced far less damaging carbon dioxide than other parts of the world. Considering this, it behooves us to ask what African religions teach about humanity's relationship with the natural world.

Earth is often depicted as female and, as we saw in Dogon mythic narratives, humans are sometimes instructed to maintain the earth through activities like farming, which can be construed as a religious activity that maintains the High God's creation: Earth. Jacob Olupona, a prominent scholar of African religions, has written about the significance of water in many African religions.[36] Throughout the continent, African rivers are regarded as sacred. As you read earlier in this chapter, the early twentieth-century religious leader Kinjiketele and his followers bathed in the sacred waters of the Rufiji River in Tanzania in hopes of securing protection from the colonizers' bullets. In Yoruba religion, the large bodies of water in Nigeria, including the Atlantic Ocean, are depicted as goddesses. Water is the source of wealth and fertility, and Aje, the goddess of wealth and banking, is believed to derive her wealth from the ocean. In numerous African cultures, a religious expert known as a rainmaker has authority over rituals designed to promote and enhance rainfall, and shrines may be built to honor rain deities. Among the Chewa people of Malawi, a priestess known as a "spirit wife" is responsible for calling the rain and for maintaining the natural world around her. Similarly, the Lovedu culture of South Africa recognizes that only the queen has the power to control the rain.[37] In Yoruba religion, the concept of purity is connected to ideas about humanity's responsibility to live in balance with the natural environment—particularly women's responsibility. By maintaining the cleanliness and purity of the home and family, Yoruba women are also responsible for maintaining the natural environment and the cycle of seasons and fertility.[38]

SEEKING ANSWERS

What Is Ultimate Reality?

Most African traditions understand the world to have been created by a High God. The natural world, the supernatural world, and the social world of human beings are not separate and distinct realms but are often considered to be interlinked. Most African religions are *anthropocentric*, or human-centered; they teach that God created humans and that creation and the universe revolve around humanity. Often, it is believed that humans and God once coexisted

(continued)

SEEKING ANSWERS *(Continued)*

in an idealized past, but that something happened to separate humanity from God. African religions differ in terms of how ultimate reality is revealed to human beings: humans communicate with the divine through possession, sacrifice, and divination.

How Should We Live in This World?

Many African religions emphasize the importance of caring for and respecting the living and deceased members of one's family, the necessity of maintaining beneficial relationships with the beings of the spirit world, and the importance of harmony with the natural world. Because most African religions do not focus on reward or punishment in the afterlife,

religious practice does not normally center on preparing for an afterlife. Instead, rituals and ceremonies focus on improving life in this world.

What Is Our Ultimate Purpose?

Most African religions do not tend to focus on salvation or the goal of transcending the human condition but, rather, seek to emulate an idealized past in this life. However, many traditions hold that after death, people may transition to a spiritual state and may continue to interact with living humans. There are some exceptions to this. The Dogon and the Yoruba, for example, conceive of the possibility of a grand afterlife.

REVIEW QUESTIONS

For Review

1. What is the relationship between humanity and gods in African religions? Give specific examples from religions.
2. Describe the spirits of the dead. What role do they have in the lives of the living in particular religions? How are the beliefs about the dead reflected in religious practice?
3. What are the three main ways African religions communicate with the supernatural? Describe each.
4. What influence have African religions had on American religions? How did this happen?

For Further Reflection

1. Do you see any similarities between the religions of Africa and the religions of Native America? How do conceptions of the supernatural differ? Do they share similarities?
2. What parallels can you draw between Native American and African religious resistance movements?
3. What motivated these movements, and how were they carried out?

GLOSSARY

Amma (ah'muh; Dogon) The High God of the Dogon people.

bori (boh-ree'; various languages) A term for West African spirits.

Candomblé New World religion with roots in West Africa—particularly Yoruba culture—which is prominent in Brazil.

dama (dah'mah; Dogon) A Dogon rite of passage marking the transition to adulthood and to the afterlife.

divination The attempt to learn about events that will happen in the future through supernatural means.

Ifa (ee'fah; Yoruba) The divination system of the Yoruba religion, believed to be revealed to humanity by the gods.

Kinjiketele (kin-jee-ke-te'le) The leader of the Maji Maji rebellion in Tanganyika (today's Tanzania).

Maji Maji (mah-jee mah-jee; Swahili) A 1905 rebellion against German colonizers in Tanganyika (today's Tanzania).

medium A person who is possessed by a spirit and thus mediates between the human and spirit worlds.

moran (mor-an; Samburu and Maasai) A young man in Samburu or Maasai culture who has been circumcised and thus has special cultural and religious duties.

Odu (oh-doo; Yoruba) The original prophets in Yoruba religion.

orisha (aw-ree-shah'; Yoruba) Lesser deities in Yoruba religion.

Oshun (oh'shoon; Yoruba) A Yoruba goddess.

pantheon A group of deities or spirits.

rites of passage Rituals that mark the transition from one life stage or social stage to another.

Santería (sahn-teh-ree'ah; Spanish) New World religion with roots in West Africa; prominent in Cuba.

Vodou (vo-doo'; Fon and French) New World religion with roots in West Africa; prominent in Haiti and the Haitian diaspora.

witchcraft A contested term used by Western scholars to describe the use of supernatural powers to harm others.

zar (zahr; various languages) A term for spirits in East Africa.

SUGGESTIONS FOR FURTHER READING

Abimbola, Wande. *Ifa: An Exposition of Ifa Literary Corpus.* Ibadan, Nigeria: Oxford University Press, 1976. Scholarly look at Yoruba religious texts and beliefs.

Amadiume, Ifi. *Male Daughters and Female Husbands: Gender and Sex in an African Society.* London: Zed Books, 1987. Readable ethnographic account of gender, economics, and religion in an Igbo community in Nigeria.

Bongmba, Elias Kifon. *The Wiley-Blackwell Companion to African Religions.* London: Wiley-Blackwell, 2012. Extensive resource with interdisciplinary readings on numerous aspects of African religions and religion in Africa.

Evans-Pritchard, Edward E. *Witchcraft, Oracles, and Magic among the Azande.* New York: Oxford University Press, 1976. Classic anthropological account of beliefs about witchcraft and magic among the Azande people of southern Sudan.

Griaule, Marcel. *Conversations with Ogotemmeli.* London: Oxford University Press, 1965. A first-hand description of Dogon cosmology based on conversations between an anthropologist and a Dogon elder.

Mbiti, John S. *Introduction to African Religion.* 2nd ed. Long Grove, IL: Waveland Press, 2015. Useful introduction to African belief systems and religions.

McCarthy Brown, Karen. *Mama Lola: A Vodou Priestess in Brooklyn.* 3rd ed. Berkeley: University of California Press, 2011. Engrossing ethnographic account of a modern-day Vodou priestess.

Olupona, Jacob K. *African Religions: A Very Short Introduction.* New York: Oxford University Press, 2014. Useful look at African religions in the present day.

Olupona, Jacob K., and Rowland O. Abiodun. *Ifá Divination, Knowledge, Power, and Performance.* Bloomington: Indiana University Press, 2016. Interdisciplinary look at *Ifa* divination as expressive culture.

Ray, Benjamin C. *African Religions: Symbol, Ritual, and Community.* Upper Saddle River, NJ: Prentice Hall, 2000. Introduction to African religions aimed at students and focusing on religious practice.

ONLINE RESOURCES

National Museum of African Art
The National Museum of African Art, part of the Smithsonian Institution, offers abundant useful resources for African religion and material culture.

African Voices
The Smithsonian's "African Voices" site explores the diversity of African cultures and their connections to the global world.

Hinduism

4

Chapter Outline

4.1   Summarize Hindu beliefs about divine reality.

4.2   Explain Hindu teachings regarding the individual's quest for liberation.

4.3   Describe the relationship for Hinduism of the individual and society.

4.4   Identify the core texts of Hinduism and their purposes.

4.5   Differentiate the main varieties of Hinduism.

4.6   Describe the emergence and establishment of Hinduism through the Vedic period.

4.7   Summarize the development of Hinduism from the classical period through the nineteenth century.

4.8   Describe the significant Hindu figures and events of the past 100 years.

4.9   Identify primary forms of Hindu rituals and observance.

4.10 Summarize key aspects of the relationship between Hinduism and politics and of Hindu perspectives on gender roles and environmentalism.

THE SKIES OVER MUMBAI are clearing and the sun is poking through the clouds, shedding rays of light on the throng of worshipers that crowd to behold the Lalbaugcha Raja sculpture of Ganesha, the elephant god. It is the last day of Ganesh Chaturthi, the ten-day festival celebrated across India in honor of Ganesha's birthday. Most of those gathered had already performed **puja**, or worship, in their homes this morning, praying before temporarily installed clay idols of the god. There and in the presence of the Lalbaugcha Raja Ganesha sculpture and many other sculptures located around the city, all having been specially prepared for the festival, Ganesha is offered his favorite foods.

At this unique temporary shrine, an exquisite idol of the god, created by a master sculptor especially for this year's festival, is colorfully painted and

A Ganesha sculpture is about to be submerged at the seashore in Mumbai on the tenth and final day of Ganesh Chaturthi, a celebration of the elephant god's birthday.

TIMELINE
Hinduism

2600–1700 BCE	Indus Valley Civilization.
2000–1300 BCE	Migration of Indo-Aryans into northwestern India.
c. 1200 BCE	Rig Veda.
c. 1200–900 BCE	Later Vedas.
c. 900–200 BCE	Upanishads.
400 BCE–400 CE	*Mahabharata*.
200 BCE–200 CE	*Ramayana*.
c. First century CE	*Bhagavad Gita*.
100–500 CE	Expansion of Hinduism into Southeast Asia.
c. 320–540	Gupta Dynasty; rise of Hindu temple culture.
300–500	Earliest Puranas; Hindu law books.
700	Flourishing of bhakti in the south.
999–1226	Mahmud of Ghazi; repeated raids of India.
Fifteenth century	Bhakti movement begins in northern India.
c. 1398–1518	Kabir, bhakti poet.
1526–1757	Mughal rule in India.
1651	The East India Company opens first factory on the Hugli River in Bengal.
1786	Sir William Jones lectures on the common ancestry of Sanskrit and many European languages.
1828	Brahmo Samaj founded by Ram Mohan Roy.
1834–1886	Sri Ramakrishna.
1869–1948	Mohandas (Mahatma) Gandhi.
1875	Arya Samaj founded by Swami Dayananda Saraswati.
1893	Swami Vivekananda at the World's Parliament of Religions, Chicago.
1925	RSS (Rashtriya Swayamsevak Sangh) founded.
1947	India gains independence; partition with newly established nation of Pakistan.
1964	VHP (Vishwa Hindu Parishad) founded.
1992	Destruction of Babri Masjid and widespread riots.
2014	BJP (Bharatiya Janata Party) wins Indian elections by a landslide.

adorned with flowers. *Bhajan* and *kirtan*, sacred devotional songs, are performed in the god's honor. The shrine is alive with the music and the vibrant colors that seem to adorn most everything, including the worshipers. The entire city of Mumbai teems with life during Ganesh Chaturthi, one of India's most popular celebrations. Neighborhoods like Lalbaugcha sponsor their own production of Ganesha sculptures, competing with each other over the best artistic creation.

With his elephant head and human body, Ganesha is one of Hinduism's most easily recognized deities. As the patron deity of arts and sciences and the god of wisdom, new beginnings, and commerce, he is especially venerated by students, writers, travelers, and businessmen. He is worshiped at the beginning of every new undertaking, and he is the first deity invoked in almost any Hindu ritual context. Ganesha, known as the Remover of Obstacles, is often depicted as carrying objects in his four arms (including an axe, a noose, and an elephant goad) that he uses to destroy, subdue, or control the obstacles of life. He also often holds a bowl of sweets, symbolizing his benevolent and loving nature.

Later this afternoon, at the conclusion of Ganesh Chaturthi, the shrine's clay idol will be carried in a procession to the seashore and, to the accompaniment of music, will be submerged in the ocean where it will soon dissolve, becoming one with the natural world and thereby nourishing it. The worshipers celebrate this event, as Ganesha is believed now to return home to his parents, Shiva and Parvati, who live on Mount Kailash high in the Himalayas.

Unlike many other religions discussed in this book, Hinduism has neither a single founder nor a single sacred book. There is no single historical event that marks its birth. The history of Hinduism embodies both continuity and change. Having never had a sole central authority, Hinduism's fluid character has always allowed it to adapt to a variety of social and cultural contexts. This diversity has led many scholars to argue that Hinduism is not one religion at all but a constellation of many religious sects that share some common aspects. Others see enough by way of common beliefs and practices to regard Hinduism as a single religious tradition. In this chapter, we will explore Hinduism's variety of sects, beliefs, and practices and seek to understand what unites a tradition that is the religion of over 1 billion of the world's people.

4.1 The Teachings of Hinduism: Beliefs about Divine Reality

Prior to the nineteenth century, the word *Hinduism* did not exist. Most Hindus identified themselves by their sectarian orientation and their communal or caste affiliations. The word *Hindu* was initially used by the ancient Persians to describe the people who lived beyond the Indus River in the northwestern corner of the Indian subcontinent. When, by 325 BCE, Alexander the Great had crossed the Indus, Greeks adopted the Persian convention of calling the river the "Indos" and the land beyond it "India." In the centuries that followed, the term *Indu* or *Hindu* became a territorial, as well as a racial, social, and cultural, designation for the people of India. Beginning in the seventeenth century CE, the word appeared occasionally in Indian literature to distinguish "Hindus" from Muslims or other "foreigners." Although the "-ism" was added to "Hindu" in the early 1800s, only toward the end of the nineteenth century did the word *Hinduism* become widely used by Hindus themselves.

Some Hindus look to the authority of a group of texts known as the **Vedas**, India's oldest scriptures, and may rely on **brahmin** priests to officiate at various rituals. Others reject the centrality of the Vedas and brahmins. Some Hindus join organizations devoted to saints or sages. Others seek solitude to practice contemplation, meditation, or yoga. Some Hindus believe that God is a divine person with identifiable attributes. Others say that divine reality is so expansive as to be beyond all description.

Despite Hinduism's diversity, it is possible to identify common core concepts in which most every Hindu believes. For instance, the law of **karma** determines the nature of one's incarnations in **samsara**, the continuing cycle of death and rebirth. At the end of this cycle is **moksha**, or liberation, the final release from the trials and tribulations of samsara.

For the sake of simplicity, in this chapter we have organized our investigation of Hindu teachings around five

A photograph taken of a Hindu temple in Trinidad in 1931. The presence of Hindus in the Caribbean and South America can be traced back to the nineteenth century, when Hindus came as indentured workers on sugar cane plantations.

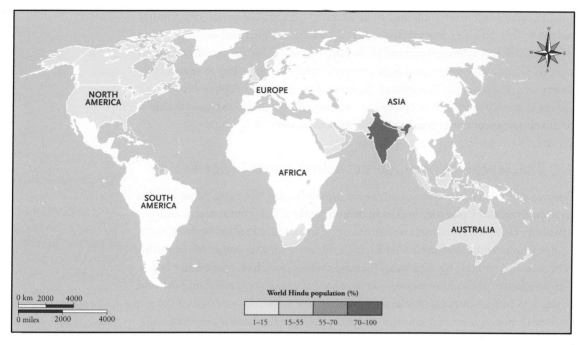

World Hindu population (%)

1–15   15–55   55–70   70–100

World Hindu population.

main topics: beliefs about divine reality; the individual's quest for liberation and the primary means of making this quest; the place of the individual within society; Hindu sacred texts; and Hinduism's main sects.

In keeping with Hinduism's general diversity, Hindu beliefs about divine reality are wide ranging. Indeed, one of the most fundamental differences in Hinduism is the split between monistic and dualistic or devotional viewpoints. Monism, as explained in this book's introductory chapter, is the doctrine that all reality is ultimately one. It is nondualistic in that there is no distinction between the divine reality and the rest of reality. The Hindu dualistic viewpoint, in contrast, understands divine reality as God, a personal being separate from the rest of reality. This means that God is separate from the individual, and therefore devotion to God is natural. Devotional practice of this sort is a primary religious activity of Hindus who hold this dualistic viewpoint. The majority of Hindus understand divine reality in this dualistic manner.

Names of the Divine Reality

Hindus refer to divine reality in a variety of ways. In this chapter, in order to maintain clarity between references to the monistic and the dualistic viewpoints, we use two distinct terms. When referencing monism, we use the term **Brahman** (Sanskrit, "expansive") to denote the divine reality, which monistic Hindus believe is the supreme, unitary reality that is the source of all being and all knowing. When referencing dualistic or devotional Hinduism, we use either "God" or the name of the specific deity under consideration.

In actual Hindu practice, conventions of naming the divine are often not so simple as our chapter's use of these two distinct terms might imply. Sometimes monistic Hindus, for example, refer to Brahman as "God." Many dualistic Hindus use "God" to denote a universal being that encompasses all the various deities worshiped in Hinduism, and sometimes they use "Brahman." When dualistic Hindus refer to a particular deity, they often use the specific name, such as Krishna, Rama, or Shiva. Devotees of the goddess traditions refer to God using terms such as Devi ("goddess") or Mahadevi ("great goddess").

One Divine Reality, Many Gods

The monistic viewpoint does not preclude belief in gods and goddesses. In a famous passage from the **Upanishads** (a collection of early philosophical texts), a sage is asked how many gods there are. Initially, he says there are "three hundred and three, and three thousand and three," but, upon reflection, he ultimately concludes that there is only one.[1] The sage explains that the various powers of the divine manifest as countless deities. In later times, the traditional number grew to 330 million. The passage from the Upanishads concludes with the sage giving the name of the one god: Brahman, which is the supreme, unitary reality, the ground of all being.

Although Brahman is the true nature of all that exists, including ourselves, it is virtually indescribable from the ordinary human perspective. Brahman can be described only by way of some general attributes: infinite being (*sat*), infinite awareness (*chit*), and infinite bliss (*ananda*). A passage from the Upanishads states that Brahman is *neti, neti*: "not this, not this."[2] When all of the identifiable particulars of the universe are subtracted away, what remains is Brahman, the essential substratum of all existence. This is monism, the belief that all reality is ultimately one.

These passages from the Upanishads influence how later monistic Hinduism forms its understanding of the mystery and majesty of being. Many monistic Hindus believe that the divine reality is simultaneously one—as Brahman, the ground of all being—and many. Given the worship of many deities, along with affirmation of the ultimate singularity of the divine, and indeed of *all* reality, this form of Hinduism can be described as both polytheistic and monistic. Unlike polytheistic religions that see the various gods as limited, Hinduism regards each god as a manifestation of Brahman.

Divine Reality as Sound and Image

The primordial sound **OM** (or, per the literal spelling, *AUM*) is constituted of three sounds of the Sanskrit language: *A* (the first vowel), *U* (the final vowel), and *M* (the final consonant). OM therefore encompasses all words and all things they represent. OM is the sound through which the universe is manifested and thus is the very expression of Brahman. Some Upanishads also identify it with four states of consciousness: *A* is waking consciousness, *U* is dreaming consciousness, *M* is deep sleep without dreaming consciousness, and *AUM* in its entirety is the fourth and

Shiva as Lord of the Dance (Nataraja) performs his Five Activities: creation, represented by the drum in his upper right hand; preservation, signified by the positions of his lower right and left hands; destruction, symbolized by the fire in his upraised left hand; illusion, personified by the Demon of Forgetfulness crushed beneath his right leg; and liberation, offered by surrendering to his upraised left foot. Chola period, c. eleventh century. India, Tamil Nadu.

final state, oneness with Brahman. In later Hinduism, the sounds are identified with the gods Brahma, Vishnu, and Shiva and their functions of creating, preserving, and dissolving the universe.

Paradoxically, given the difficulty of comprehending the nature of divine reality, Hinduism is an intensely imagistic religious tradition. This is especially true of dualistic Hinduism, as imagistic representations of God are naturally well suited for devotional practices.

Images of supernatural beings and mythical beasts decorate Hindu temples, as well as Hindu homes. These images can be richly adorned stationary icons enshrined in temples or beautifully crafted bronze icons carried in religious processions. Today, some Hindus revere print and online images of the divine. This love for the divine form emerges from Hindu notions of the simultaneous immanence and transcendence of God. An image of a deity is a symbolic representation meant to aid devotees in contemplating the deity's divine attributes, but the image is also believed to be suffused with divine presence, as we saw in the opening narrative about the Ganesha festival and temple. Thus, Hindus believe that God becomes accessible to devotees through images. For Hindus, an image of a god *is* God.

The Divine in Nature

If Brahman is everywhere and everything, it follows that the natural world is an expression of the divine. This belief is held by most Hindus, whether inclined toward the monistic or the dualistic viewpoint. The worship of such natural entities as rivers, the earth, mountains, and the sun, as well as a reverence for certain trees and animals, can be traced back to the roots of Hinduism.

Many sacred sites arose in conjunction with the worship of rivers and mountains. Rivers in particular are worshiped as embodying the creative energy that generates the universe, as well as being powerful places of crossing between the divine and terrestrial worlds. It is for all of these reasons that many Hindus bathe in rivers—of which the Ganges in India is the most important—believing that they wash away one's sins. For centuries, the awe-inspiring peaks of the Himalayas have attracted monks, yogis, and pilgrims seeking an experience of the divine. Mount Kailash, believed to be the home of the god Shiva, draws devotees who perform a ritual circumambulation of the mountain over the course of several days, reaching elevations of greater than 18,000 feet on the trek. Hindu mythology portrays the sun, planets, and other celestial bodies as gods.

For Hindus, all living things are sacred, and some especially so. For example, the type of fig tree under which Gautama the Buddha attained enlightenment (Chapter 5) is sacred to the god Vishnu. As is well known, Hindu society gives a special place to the cow, a practice that has deep historical roots in the pastoral, cattle-tending communities found throughout India. Because a child, once weaned from its mother's breast, is frequently given cow's milk, Hindus revere the cow as a second mother. Cows are worshiped on the first day of the important Hindu festival of Diwali, as well as on the first day of a harvest festival observed in southern India. For Hindus, the worship of cows is an expression of respect for creatures that help humanity.

Although Hinduism has a long history of reverence for natural entities, this has not always translated into ecological awareness and activism. The worship of rivers does not mean that India's sacred waterways are pristine. Because rivers are divine, they are said to be able to absorb the sins of worshipers and still remain unaffected. Thus, for many Hindus, rivers remain pure even if they are polluted by waste. In recent years, Hindu environmental activists have begun to challenge these assumptions by employing Hindu beliefs about the divinity of the natural world to promote more informed ecological awareness.

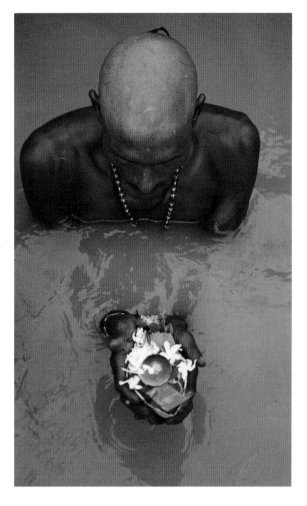

God Comes Down: Avatars

Two of the most popular deities in Hinduism are Krishna and Rama. Each is an **avatar**, a "descent" (Sanskrit, *avatara*) of God to earth in a physical form with the specific goal of aiding the world. Like most avatars, they are manifestations of Vishnu, whose primary function is the preservation of order in the world. Vishnu is believed to have ten such forms, of which nine have already appeared. As noted, the most popular of the avatars are Rama, Vishnu's seventh form, and Krishna, his eighth. It is said that Vishnu's final avatar, Kalki, will arrive at the end of the present age to usher in an era of peace.

We have seen that Hindus often use the names of particular gods as a way of referring to divine reality. This is the case with avatars. For example, Hinduism's best-known sacred text, the *Bhagavad Gita* ("The Song of the Lord"), presents Krishna as a manifestation of the supreme being.

A Hindu devotee performs rituals as he takes a holy dip in Allahabad, India, at the confluence of the Ganges and Yamuna rivers, one of Hinduism's important centers.

In the *Bhagavad Gita*, Krishna asserts the principle that although God's essential nature is unchangeable, God chooses to descend into the world in the form of an avatar when intervention is necessary to reinstate peace and harmony. Krishna says (4.6–8):

> Though myself unborn, undying,
> the lord of creatures, I fashion nature,
> which is mine, and I come into being
> through my own magic.
> Whenever sacred duty decays
> and chaos prevails,
> then, I create
> myself, Arjuna.
> To protect men of virtue
> and destroy men who do evil,
> to set the standard of sacred duty,
> I appear in age after age.[3]

We will learn more about the *Bhagavad Gita* later in this chapter.

4.2 The Teachings of Hinduism: The Individual and the Quest for Liberation

Having explored Hindu perspectives on divine reality, we turn now to basic concepts that form the framework of the Hindu outlook on the individual and the quest for liberation. Some of these concepts, such as samsara and karma, are also significant for other religions with Indian origins (Buddhism, Jainism, and Sikhism).

The Human Condition: Challenges and Ideals

Atman   All Hindus believe in an undying soul or self, the **atman**, whose nature is neither limited by the physical body nor defined by its relationship to the world. It is the atman that moves from body to body through successive incarnations.

The task of recognizing the true nature of the essential self is understood to be arduous and rarely achieved. Most Hindus assume that this will require many lifetimes. One's life ordinarily revolves around a sense of selfhood that is limited, constrained by desires and by ignorance of the true nature of atman. Therefore, life ordinarily is lived by the egoistic "self" that is by nature selfish and stuck with false identification of the self with the physical body. This leads to suffering, as the body undergoes painful changes brought on by disease, old age, and death.

Monistic Hinduism, true to its basic premise that all reality is ultimately one, teaches that the atman *is* Brahman. Another famous passage from the Upanishads conveys this idea through the story of a young man named Svetaketu, who receives instruction from his father on the true nature of the atman. Using a number of analogies, the father explains that despite the appearance of multiplicity, all reality is one. The father emphatically declares: *Tat tvam asi svetakato iti* ("*You* are that, Svetaketu!").[4] Atman *is* Brahman.

Karma
The course of the atman through successive incarnations is determined by karma. In its original, most basic sense, *karma* means "action," but for Hindus it means the consequences of action as well. Karma functions in accordance with the law of cause and effect: good actions produce good effects; bad actions produce bad effects. Karma encompasses all kinds of action, physical as well as mental. A person's situation in any given moment has been shaped by all previous actions. Similarly, the karmic forces that we set in motion in our present lives will determine the nature of our future incarnations. To ensure that the future will be good, our actions now must be good—and that means living in conformity with dharma.

Dharma
For Hinduism, the term **dharma** can mean law, duty, righteousness, or even religion, all of which have to do with living in a way that upholds cosmic and social order. Dharma is traditionally believed to have been divinely revealed to the *rishis*, the poet–sages who composed the Vedas.

Through the centuries, Hindu texts have set forth ritual and social obligations that define a good life. The *Laws of Manu*, for example, a classic juridical text from the period 200 BCE to 200 CE, contains detailed prescriptions for correct behavior in all aspects of life. The two ancient and enormously influential Indian epic poems, the *Ramayana* and the *Mahabharata*, depict the simultaneous particularity and universality of dharma. As we will consider in more detail in a later section, both poems present epic heroes who must resolve conflicts between social or family obligations and their own personal sense of what duty demands from them.

Samsara
Hindus use the term *samsara* in two closely related ways. Samsara is the continuing cycle of birth, death, and rebirth. It is also the worldly realm in which birth, death, and rebirth recur. When the physical body dies, the eternal self or soul, the atman, moves on to another body. This process continues until the true nature of the atman is recognized. As noted previously, the nature of each rebirth is determined by karma. Virtuous acts of kindness and generosity over lifetimes ensure favorable rebirths, perhaps even in the blissful heavens of the gods. Selfish action and meanness lead to undesirable rebirths.

Hindus believe in a multitude of heavens and hells, as well as other regions in between. A rebirth in a heaven or hell could last thousands of years but is still only temporary. The most desirable rebirth of all is as a human being in a situation that offers the greatest opportunity for realizing liberation from samsara; for example, as a sage or an ascetic.

The concept of samsara presents some basic questions. What gives rise to samsara? And why are human beings so prone to remain stuck in this samsaric realm?

A sannyasi, or Hindu ascetic. His sectarian affiliation is indicated by his forehead marking, which demonstrates that he is a worshipper of Vishnu.

Through the ages, Hindus have offered various answers to these questions. Some of these answers have involved the concept of **maya**, which in the Vedas refers to the magical power the gods used to create this world. Is the world an illusion, as is often the case with magic, or real? Hindus are divided on this issue. In either case, they agree that human beings are powerfully attracted to this world, with its many particulars—our egoistic selves, our relationships, our possessions, and the seemingly countless objects of our desires. Our attachment to such things in all that we think and do and the karma it generates steer us after each lifetime back into the samsaric realm of particulars.

All of this leads to another basic question: Why should anyone *want* to escape from samsara? After all, the prospect of a future filled with numerous lifetimes would seem to be appealing. Hinduism's answer is simple: beyond the samsaric realm lies something inexpressibly better.

Moksha   Freedom from the bondage of samsara is achieved through moksha, "release" or "liberation." Having overcome attachments to this world, the atman realizes its true nature. For monistic Hindus, moksha is the realization of the union of the atman and Brahman, such that no sense of individuality any longer exists. For dualistic or devotional Hindus, for whom the divine reality is identified with their supreme God (be it Vishnu, Shiva, or another), moksha involves the eternal existence of the atman in the company of God. Hindus also have differing opinions on whether moksha can occur for a living person or whether it must await death of the physical body. For all Hindus, however, moksha marks the end of the samsaric cycle of rebirth and the end of the effects of karma. Like Brahman, moksha is virtually impossible to describe, beyond being characterized—also like Brahman—as infinite awareness and eternal bliss.

The quest for moksha, for liberating oneself from samsara even while constrained by the limits of this world, is extremely challenging. Hinduism offers three main paths to moksha, each of which provides the means of eradicating ignorance and egoistic attachment and thus freeing the atman.

Three Paths to Liberation

Typical of the diverse nature of Hinduism, there are a variety of approaches to the goal of liberation. Traditionally, they have been categorized as three paths, or margas (also called yogas), each one featuring its own set of practices and being suited to certain personality traits and life situations. **Karma marga**, for those engaged in the activities of family and career, emphasizes ritual and ethical works. **Bhakti marga**, for the vast majority of Hindus who regularly worship in temples and in their homes, is devotion to a deity. **Jnana marga**, for those privileged to devote time and energy on study and contemplation, focuses on spiritual insight. The paths are by no means exclusive of one another: Hindus commonly engage in more than one. Almost all Hindus, for example, practice some form of bhakti marga, and karma marga is a natural way to approach life's everyday tasks. All three margas function to diminish the ignorance, attachment, and false identification of the self with the physical body that characterizes life in the samsaric realm.

The *Bhagavad Gita*, which was composed in about the first century of the Common Era, sets forth all three margas, explaining characteristics common to all three and making clear their mutual compatibility. Of fundamental concern is the need to eradicate the ignorance and attachment born of an egoistic sense of selfhood. One passage puts it this way: "He who abandons all desires and acts free from longing, without any sense of mineness or egotism—he attains to peace."[5]

Karma Marga   As noted previously, all Hindus are required to act in conformity with dharma, the duty to live in a manner that upholds the cosmic and social order. Karma marga combines focus on dharma with an attitude of detachment with regard to acting and to the results, or "fruit," of action. In the words of the *Bhagavad Gita* (5.11–12):

> Relinquishing attachment,
> men of discipline perform action
> with body, mind, understanding, and senses
> for the purification of the self.
> Relinquishing the fruit of action
> the disciplined man attains perfect peace;
> the undisciplined man is in bondage,
> attached to the fruit of desire.[6]

When the self, or atman, is devoid of attachment to the results of action, the problems of egotism and the suffering brought about by birth, disease, old age, and death are resolved.

Bhakti Marga   The path of devotion, bhakti marga, is the most widely practiced of the three paths to liberation. This chapter's survey of the history of Hinduism includes a section detailing the rise of the bhakti tradition. In an important manner, the tradition is grounded in the *Bhagavad Gita*, which, along with prescribing the other two margas, gives pride of place to bhakti. In the *Bhagavad Gita*, the featured deity is Krishna. Bhakti, however, can be directed toward whatever deity one chooses. The deity is perceived as the supreme divine reality, as is clearly shown with regard to Krishna in the *Bhagavad Gita*. Hindus typically worship more than one deity, depending on personal preference and on the occasion. For instance, during the festival in honor of Saraswati, goddess of education, Hindu schoolchildren offer devotion to her. There are numerous such festivals of the gods in the Hindu year.

In the *Bhagavad Gita* (12.6–8), Krishna makes clear to his devotee Arjuna the great benefits of bhakti:

> But men intent on me
> renounce all actions to me
> and worship me, meditating
> with singular discipline.
> When they entrust reason to me,
> Arjuna, I soon arise
> to rescue them from the ocean
> of death and rebirth.
> Focus your mind on me,
> let your understanding enter me;
> then you will dwell
> in me without doubt.[7]

Like karma marga and jnana marga, bhakti marga functions to eradicate egotism, ignorance, and attachment to the objects of desire. By devoting one's time and energy to a deity rather than to one's individualistic yearnings and concerns, ultimately the true nature of reality can be realized, the effects of karma neutralized, and liberation from samsara achieved.

Jnana Marga

Generally agreed to be the steepest ascent to liberation, jnana ("knowledge") marga requires disciplined study of sacred texts and intensive contemplation, typically through the practice of meditation. In the words of the *Bhagavad Gita* (4.38–39),

> No purifier equals knowledge,
> and in time
> the man of perfect discipline
> discovers this in his own spirit.
> Faithful, intent, his senses
> subdued, he gains knowledge;
> gaining knowledge,
> he soon finds perfect peace.[8]

The knowledge gained through jnana marga is wisdom or insight of a special kind. To attain this wisdom is to become aware of the true nature of atman. For monistic Hindus, this is to become aware that the atman is none other than Brahman, the ultimate, unitary reality.

We now turn our attention to the two most prominent forms of jnana marga and of Hinduism's six philosophical schools: Vedanta and Yoga. The Yoga school, which teaches specific physical and mental exercises designed to promote jnana, is so distinctive and historically significant that some Hindus classify it as a fourth marga. With its meditative practices often performed in the lotus position, Yoga is commonly envisioned by non-Hindus when pondering the spiritual life of India. The Vedanta school has been even more influential in the history of Hindu thought.

Vedanta: The Predominant School of Hindu Philosophy

The philosophical system that emerged out of the Upanishads is called **Vedanta**, which in Sanskrit means "the end of the Vedas"—"end" not only as conclusion but also as culmination. The Vedanta school asserts that the Upanishads reveal the truth about the fundamental questions of existence. The Upanishads are both profound and challenging and are open to a variety of interpretations. Following the composition of the early Upanishads, philosophy became a very important part of Hinduism. Predictably, there even arose a number of different schools within Vedanta. Each school of Vedanta sought to understand the precise nature of the relationships between Brahman, atman, and the world.

The impact of Vedanta on the development of Hinduism cannot be overestimated. As different Hindu sects emerged, their distinctive understandings of Vedanta shaped their philosophical orientations. Of the many schools of Vedanta, the three most important are *Advaita*, *Vishishta-Advaita*, and *Dvaita*.

Advaita Vedanta   Known as Hinduism's uncompromisingly monistic school of philosophy, *Advaita* ("Non-dualist") Vedanta teaches that the atman is identical to Brahman and denies any distinction whatsoever between Brahman and everything else. This school of thought grew directly out of the Upanishads but was further developed in the eighth century CE by Shankara, its most famous proponent. Shankara posited that the world is maya, "illusion." Earlier in this chapter we noted that the Vedas present maya as the magical power the gods used to create this world. For Shankara, maya veils the mind, such that it does not discern the true nature of the self (atman). According to Shankara, it is this lack of discernment, or ignorance, manifesting as attachment and desire, that keeps one bound to the cycle of death and rebirth (samsara). When one uses wisdom and discernment, one can cut through ignorance and recognize the inherent unity of all things, including the oneness of Brahman and atman. This in turn results in moksha and the complete dissolution of one's sense of individual selfhood.

Vishishta-Advaita Vedanta   Many of the sects that worship Vishnu, which we consider later in the section "Vaishnavism," differ on the subtler aspects of the relationship between Brahman and atman. For Vaishnavas, Brahman is identified with Vishnu. The school of *Vishishta-Advaita* Vedanta, founded by the twelfth-century CE

A Hindu ascetic sits in the lotus position, a prominent bodily posture for the practice of yoga.

philosopher Ramanuja, declared that all is Brahman and that the material world and individual souls also are real. The world is not illusion (maya); rather, it is the body of God. All beings are a part of God, eternally connected to Vishnu but not the same as him. We are more like cells in the divine body. Unlike Shankara, Ramanuja interpreted the ignorance that obscures true knowledge as forgetfulness—in particular, the devotee's forgetfulness of our eternal relationship with Vishnu. In this manner, Ramanuja's Vedanta marries philosophy to the devotional, sectarian traditions of Vaishnavism.

Dvaita Vedanta   The school of *Dvaita* ("Dualist") Vedanta, founded by the thirteenth-century theologian Madhva, advocates a complete distinction between Brahman and atman. It posits that there are five acknowledged aspects of complete separateness or difference: between the atman and Brahman, between Brahman and matter, between the various souls, between the souls and matter, and between various forms of matter. This philosophical strain, too, is associated with the worship of Vishnu, particularly in his avatar as Krishna.

Yoga

Yoga in its most basic sense means a "yoking" or "uniting." In religious discourse, it refers to the uniting of the self with God. Most of us are familiar with hatha yoga, which makes use of physical exercises to promote the health of the body. As a form of jnana marga, Yoga—often called Raja ("Royal") Yoga—employs both physical and mental techniques in order to make liberation from samsara possible.

By the fourth century CE, the principles and techniques of Raja Yoga had been systematized in the *Yoga Sutras* of Patanjali. The *Yoga Sutras* consist of 196 instructional sayings about the moral, physical, and mental conditions and techniques that can enable the individual to achieve moksha. These are evident in the eight steps through which practitioners move in their quest for liberation. The first two steps have to do with moral preparation. Prohibitions against harming other beings, lying, stealing, sexual irresponsibility, and greed must be observed. In addition, the five virtues of cleanliness, contentment, discipline, studiousness, and devotion to a god must be practiced. The next three steps involve preparation of the body. The practitioner learns postures (especially the lotus position) that promote comfort and alertness and the ability to breathe in rhythmic patterns that calm the body. Once these ends have been achieved, it becomes possible to withdraw the senses so that they no longer demand the mind's attention. The next two steps prepare the mind for liberation. By focusing its attention on a single thing, all other particulars fade away. All that remains is to remove this single object of attention from the mind's awareness. This brings the practitioner to the eighth step, which is also the ultimate goal: samadhi, a state in which one's awareness is of the self as Brahman.

4.3 The Teachings of Hinduism: The Individual and Society

The Hindu individual's quest for liberation is determined by such factors as gender, caste, status, and age. Like all aspects of the religion, the rules governing these factors admit to diversity even while conforming to basic patterns that have persisted through the centuries. Collectively, these rules are known as *varnashrama dharma*: the religious law regulating caste (*varna*) and stage of life (ashrama). Traditionally, all Hindus are required to comply with *varnashrama dharma*.

The Caste System

The Sanskrit term ***varna*** ("color"), commonly translated as "caste," refers to a system of hierarchical social organization. A more accurate way of expressing the meaning of *varna* in this context is through the English term *class*. There are four main classes in Hindu society: brahmin, the priestly class; **kshatriya**, the warrior and administrator class; **vaishya**, the producer class (farmers and merchants); and **shudra**, the servant class. *Varna* is determined by birth and is propagated through endogamy, or marriage only within a particular group.

The caste system, and *varnashrama dharma* generally, has traditionally been most important for males of the three higher classes, the so-called twice-born castes.

We encounter the first mention of *varna* in a poem known as the *Purusha Sukta*, an early Sanskrit poem found in the tenth book of the Rig Veda (c. 1200 BCE). The poem, which describes the primordial sacrifice of the cosmic man, ascribes a mythical origin to the *varna* system. From the various parts of the cosmic man emerge the component parts of the universe—the sun, the moon, the breath, and fire among them. At the very end, people emerge. From his mouth emerge the brahmins, from his arms the kshatriyas, from his thighs the vaishyas, and from his feet the shudras.

The *varnas* are organized along a continuum of purity and pollution. A person's state of purity or pollution is determined by the degree of contact with substances that are considered polluting (corpses, for example). Although it might appear from the *varna* system and from the *Purusha Sukta* that brahmins are at the top of the hierarchy, we know that from the earliest period brahmins and kshatriyas (and to some extent vaishyas as well) existed in close, mutually dependent relationships. The brahmins,

The Hampi Bazaar in the southwestern Indian state of Karnataka. Hampi, home to an important archaeological site, is a sacred town where doorsteps and houses are decorated by ritual protective drawings.

with their ritual knowledge, gave legitimacy to kings and ambitious chieftains who might come to power. In turn, kings supported the priestly class with gifts of wealth and land, while merchants and landlords paid taxes and sponsored priestly activities.

A fifth group below the shudras, called the "untouchables" or "outcastes," was added. Today, this lowest group constitutes nearly 20 percent of the population of India. During the Indian Independence movement of the early twentieth century, Mohandas (Mahatma) Gandhi (whom we will discuss later in the chapter) sought to uplift this class socially, referring to them as Harijans, "Children of God." Many people of this class now refer to themselves as *dalit*, a word that means "oppressed." In modern India, educational institutions and government jobs have been opened to the *dalits* and have helped many with social and economic mobility. Nevertheless, *dalits* continue to suffer terrible oppression, especially in rural communities in India.

The caste system is further classified through thousands of subcastes called *jatis*. *Jati* literally means "birth group." Usually, a *jati* is composed of an endogamous group. One can marry within *jati* communities that are equal in social and ritual status, but not into a *jati* above or below one's own position. Marriage across *jatis* is usually undertaken to widen communal alliances. Over time, the *jati* system has made social hierarchy more fluid.

In modern times, the strictures of caste have broken down. Many Hindus have embraced a more egalitarian outlook formulated by nineteenth-century Hindu reformers. These reformers regarded intercaste marriage as essential to bringing about social equality and the development of the Indian nation. In urban areas, caste status has often given way to a modern class-based system in which one's marriageability is based on education, current employment, and financial status, rather than solely on caste. But caste remains a challenging issue for many Hindus, particularly those living in rural settings.

The Four Stages of Life

Another main aspect of the *varnashrama dharma* system involves the ashrama, or "stage of life." Traditional Hinduism describes four ashramas:

1. The student
2. The householder
3. The forest-dwelling hermit
4. The renouncer (the sannyasi)

As affirmed by the *Laws of Manu*, the repository of dharma discussed earlier, fulfilling the duties of these stages is said to repay the following three debts of life:

1. To the ancient seers (by studying the revealed texts known as the Vedas)
2. To the gods (by making offerings as a householder)
3. To the ancestors (by having a son—again, as a householder—who will continue to perform ancestral rites)

The specific regulations pertaining to each stage of life are meticulously spelled out in Hindu texts. For example, the *Laws of Manu* prescribes the ritual of initiation for boys who are about to enter the student stage:

> In the eighth year after conception, one should perform the initiation (*upanāyana*) of a *brāhmin*, in the eleventh [year] after conception (that) of a *kṣatriya*, but in the twelfth that of a *vaiśya*.[9]

The student's main duty is to acquire a sufficient understanding of the Vedas. Upon getting married, a Hindu enters the stage of the householder, whose duties include supporting those in the other three stages of life. Hindus in the last two stages focus primarily on seeking moksha or liberation, first by detaching themselves from the worldly concerns of the householder and then, once this detachment has been achieved, by entering the fourth stage of the renouncer, or **sannyasi**.

Renunciation is understood to be the most effective life situation for working to achieve moksha. As we have seen, attachment to objects of desire binds one to samsara. Renouncing, or no longer clinging to, such objects is empowering. By not indulging one's desires for the impermanent things of this world, the true nature of the self (the atman) can be realized. Most renouncers are ascetics, celibate wanderers who engage in meditation and yoga. Some take formal vows and join a monastic order. Although estimates of the number of sannyasis vary, there may be as many as 15 million in India.

The four stages define the ideal life for men. Women participate primarily in vaguely defined supporting roles through the last three stages and thereby assist in repaying the three debts. Some Hindu texts, including the *Laws of Manu*, emphasize that women hold a place of honor because of these roles. In general, however, Hindu society has been highly patriarchal. (The place of women in Hinduism is explored in more detail in a later section of this chapter.)

The Four Aims of Life

Whereas the four stages of life describe an individual's social and familial responsibilities from birth to death, the four aims of life set forth Hinduism's primary spiritual purposes and goals. The four aims are dharma, duty or righteousness; kama, sensual enjoyment; *artha*, material wealth and social prestige; and moksha, liberation. A Hindu is meant to diligently pursue all four of these goals.

As we have seen, dharma applies throughout life. Along with taking care to observe regulations governing everyday routines, some Hindus may take vows to practice nonviolence, perhaps maintaining a vegetarian diet as part of that goal. Others have strict rules for maintaining ritual purity or they observe a complex ritual regimen each day to ensure the harmony and well-being of their household and family members.

The next two aims of life—kama and *artha*—apply especially to the second stage of life, that of the householder. Kama is directed at the fulfillment of desire.

It encourages Hindus to enjoy the human experience and celebrate the sensual aspects of life. *Artha*, the pursuit of wealth and social prestige, is also encouraged. It is a Hindu's duty not only to provide security for loved ones but also to savor and share life's bounty. Of course, kama and *artha* must conform to dharma.

Moksha, the ultimate aim of human existence, is the special focus of the last two stages of life (the forest-dwelling hermit and the renouncer). Having fulfilled the duties and obligations of student and householder, one is ready to turn inward, to contemplate the nature of the atman.

The four stages and the four aims of life represent traditional ideals intended primarily for upper-caste men. We do not know the extent to which the prescriptions of the stages and aims have been followed in the long history of Hinduism. These ideals, though to some extent impractical in today's contemporary society, still inform the beliefs and practices of many Hindus.

VOICES: An Interview with Jayashree Venkatesan

Jayashree Venkatesan is a wife, a mother, and a retired accountant who lives in Chennai, India. She is a devotee of the goddess Sharada (a form of Saraswati, goddess of wisdom), whose most important temple is in the town of Shringeri in southern India.

As a Hindu, what is the most important part of human existence? What should Hindus do or focus on in life?

As a Hindu, I believe that God is in all things, in every aspect of creation and in every aspect of life. Consequently, one must practice compassion and nonviolence towards all things. It is how we learn to see and experience the divine presence all around us. I also believe in the tenet that work is worship. It is an act of surrender. You don't shirk your responsibilities, whatever they may be—whether as a mother, a student, a professional—but do not cling to the fruits of work. As a Hindu, I trust that when you surrender fully, God will provide you with the solution and guide you through both the happy and difficult moments of life.

What aspect of your day-to-day life as a Hindu would you characterize as being most spiritually gratifying?

Every morning and evening, I light an oil lamp in my puja room (home shrine) before the image of the Supreme Mother, Sharada Ambal. I see Sringeri Sharada Ambal as my mother, as one who takes care of everyone in this world. In these moments of quiet peace, I feel her presence and her guidance. I begin my day by surrendering myself into her loving care.

What is your favorite Hindu holiday, and why?

I would not say I have a favorite Hindu festival. I like them all, as they are all so different. However, one of the most important festivals for me is Navaratri, which celebrates the Great Goddess. The festival falls sometime between September

Jayashree Venkatesan.

and October. We worship the goddess in her three forms as Durga, Lakshmi, and Saraswati over nine nights and ten days. During this festival, I recite the *Lalita Sahasranama*, the one thousand names of Devi, several times a day. I do more elaborate puja (home rituals) to the goddess. Most importantly, it gives me the opportunity to invite several women of all ages to my home to feed them and give them clothes as I honor them as aspects of the Great Goddess.

4.4 The Teachings of Hinduism: Sacred Texts

The great diversity within Hinduism is reflected in its astonishing array of texts, composed in many different languages over the course of centuries. Down to present times, Hindu texts have facilitated the asserting of new ideas, the overturning of old ones, and the reasserting of the dominance of fading traditions. In this next section, we undertake a brief survey of Hinduism's main texts and their continued relevance.

The Vedas

The term *Veda* ("knowledge") is used in two ways when categorizing Hindu texts. In the broader sense, "the Vedas" refers to all of Vedic literature. These texts are regarded by most Hindus as revealed. That is, they are believed not to have been composed by man but rather "heard" by the *rishis*, the poet–sages of ancient times who were divinely inspired. Vedic literature thus belongs to the category of Hindu texts known as **shruti** ("that which is heard"), as opposed to the other category, **smriti** ("tradition").

In the more narrow sense of the term, "the Vedas" refers to four collections (Sanskrit, "samhitas") of texts. Composed in Sanskrit between 1200 and 900 BCE and drawing on centuries of oral tradition, these are the earliest Hindu texts and are generally considered to be the world's oldest scriptures. The four Vedas are the Rig Veda, a collection of hymns to the gods; the Sama Veda, melodic renditions of hymns from the Rig Veda; the Yajur Veda, ritual formulas; and the Atharva Veda, hymns, spells, and incantations.

Following upon the four samhitas, the *Brahmanas* set forth instructions for brahmin priests. The next collection of texts, the *Aranyakas* (or "forest treatises," so-named because they record esoteric teachings conveyed to students in secret), form a bridge from the samhitas to the Upanishads by exploring the hidden meanings of rituals. The Upanishads are speculations with regard to the deeper truths of the samhitas, especially the Rig Veda.

The 1,028 hymns of the Rig Veda, the oldest and by far the most important of the samhitas, praise the gods and ask for their blessings. The gods include Indra, god of lightning, thunder, and rain and king of the gods; Agni, god of fire and messenger of the gods; and Varuna, god of law and order (who later becomes god of the sea). New deities emerged in the later portions of the Rig Veda. One deity that has enduring influence is the *Purusha*, who is praised and described in the famous Vedic hymn known as the *Purusha Sukta*, which was discussed earlier in connection with the caste system. This later Vedic hymn is also significant for the ways in which it asserts the centrality of sacrifice, and it continues to be recited in Hindu rituals even today. The *Purusha Sukta* describes the sacrifice of a primordial, cosmic man out of whose body the universe is created. As a creation myth, it has parallels in numerous Indo-European traditions. As we have seen, the *Purusha Sukta* not only details the first sacrifice but also delineates the structuring of society.

The Upanishads (900–200 BCE)

The Upanishads, also known as Vedanta ("end of the Vedas"), are so distinctive from the earlier Vedic texts and so important as to deserve their own treatment here. The term *Upanishad* means "sitting down near [a teacher]." The term *Vedanta*, while identifying these texts as the concluding portion of Vedic literature, implies for some Hindus—for example, followers of the Vedanta philosophical school—that the Upanishads contain the culmination of the wisdom of the Vedas.

Departing from the Vedic focus on ritual, and especially sacrifice, the Upanishads feature philosophical speculation on the nature of the divine, the self, the world, and the relationships between them. These texts signal a significant shift away from emphasis on the external performance of sacrifice characteristic of the Vedic era. The Upanishads also mark a new stage in the development of religious texts, having been composed in part by people of nonbrahmin backgrounds.

HINDU SACRED TEXTS

SHRUTI ("THAT WHICH IS HEARD")	SMRITI ("TRADITION")
Samhitas ("Collections")	*Dharma Shastras* (including *Laws of Manu*)
	Epics and Puranas
Rig Veda	
Yajur Veda	*Ramayana*
Sama Veda	*Mahabharata* (includes the *Bhagavad Gita*)
Atharva Veda	*Bhagavata Purana*
	Markandeya Purana
Brahmanas	
Aranyakas	*Darshanas* (treatises of the philosophical schools)
Upanishads	Tantras (scriptures of the various sects)
	Writings of Hindu gurus

The newfound emphasis on philosophical speculation, no longer the sole domain of the brahmin class, had an enormous impact on the development of Hinduism. It propelled the development of the contemplative disciplines of yoga and meditation and influenced the philosophical concepts found later in the *Bhagavad Gita.*

The Upanishads are also significant for describing for the first time the concepts of karma, samsara, reincarnation of the soul, and the soul's immortality, which were initially closely guarded secrets. We had occasion earlier in the chapter, when discussing Brahman and the monistic concept that atman is Brahman, to draw from the *Brhadaranyaka* and *Chandogya Upanishads.* They are two among the thirteen so-called principal Upanishads (some scholars set this number at ten). Traditionally, there are 108 Upanishads, although the term has been applied to some 200 texts, some of which were written in recent times.

Epic Poems

Ramayana　For most Hindus, belief and practice are informed by and disseminated through storytelling traditions and narrative texts. Two of the most significant of these texts are the Sanskrit epics the *Ramayana* and the *Mahabharata*, both of which are categorized as smriti rather than shruti—although this in no way diminishes their relevance as Hindu sacred texts. Both epics are among the most important sources of Hindu notions of duty, or dharma.

The *Ramayana* ("The Journey of Rama"), composed between 200 BCE and 200 CE, is a compelling tale of political intrigue, romance, and philosophical speculation. It tells the story of a ten-headed demon king named Ravana, who was rewarded for his austerities with the granting of a wish by Brahma. Ravana asks for protection from gods, celestial beings, and other members of his own demon race. Protected in this way, he and his demon hordes dominate the Earth and eventually enslave the gods of heaven. But in his arrogance, Ravana neglects to ask for protection from humans and animals.

In the meantime, King Dasharatha of Ayodhya and his three queens, desiring an heir, perform a sacrifice in hopes that the gods will grant their wish. The king is blessed with four sons— Rama, Lakshmana, Bharata, and Shatrughna. Rama, as we have noted earlier, is an avatar of Vishnu. Rama eventually marries a princess, Sita. As Rama is beloved for his righteousness and

Hindu priests perform *arati*, waving a lamp of burning camphor before an image of Hanuman (the monkey god of the *Ramayana*) at a temple in Kuala Lumpur, Malaysia, during the festival of Diwali.

virtue, King Dasharatha, wishing to step down from the throne, announces that Rama's coronation will soon be held. Then Kaikeyi, Dasharatha's favorite wife, suddenly calls in two wishes that the king had once granted her. She demands that Rama be banished to the forest for fourteen years and that her own son, Bharata, ascend to the throne of Ayodhya instead. Distraught, King Dasharatha grants Kaikeyi's wish but dies of a broken heart.

Rama accepts his exile without protest and is accompanied by his wife Sita and his brother Lakshmana into the forest, where they spend many years, until one day Ravana kidnaps Sita and carries her off to the island of Lanka.

A despairing Rama and Lakshmana wander in search of Sita. They eventually meet Hanuman, a messenger from a kingdom of monkeys. Hanuman helps to search for Sita. At the citadel of Ravana on Lanka, Hanuman finds Sita held prisoner in a garden. He tells her not to lose hope, promising that Rama will soon come to free her.

Upon hearing Hanuman's news, Rama and his army march to Lanka. During the battle that ensues, Rama kills Ravana and is reunited with Sita. However, after spending a year in another man's house, Sita must publicly prove her chastity through a trial by fire. With the fire-god Agni as her witness, she passes through the flames and into Rama's embrace. Their exile concluded, Rama, Sita, and Lakshmana return to Ayodhya, where Rama is reinstated as the rightful king. All are happy for a time, but later, because of rumors circulating about Sita's chastity, Rama is compelled to abandon Sita in the forest. He doesn't know she is pregnant with their two sons, who are raised by the hermit Valmiki. Valmiki, who, while meditating, has seen all that has come to pass, composes the *Ramayana* and teaches it to the two boys, who eventually sing it before their father. Rama dies shortly thereafter, sadly pining for Sita.

Rama and Lakshmana, with their army of monkeys and bears, are camped outside the palace of the demon-king Ravana on the isle of Lanka, while the demons try to rouse Kumbhakarna, the giant brother of Ravana. India, Mughal period, c. 1595–1605.

For many Hindus, the characters in the *Ramayana* serve as exemplary social role models. Sita is the faithful wife, Rama is the ideal man and perfect king, Lakshmana is the loyal brother, and Hanuman is the selfless devotee. The text grapples with issues involving dharma, both in the public, political realm and in the private, familial realm. The characters of the *Ramayana*, however, are also understood to be divine. Thus, the *Ramayana* is as much a text that imparts religious and ethical knowledge as a text that reinforces Hindu beliefs about the accessibility and immanence of God.

Mahabharata   The other great Hindu epic, the *Mahabharata*, is composed of over 100,000 verses and is the world's longest epic poem. Like the *Ramayana*, this work is deeply concerned with issues of dharma. The epic also introduces Krishna, the beloved avatar of Vishnu.

The main storyline of the *Mahabharata* concerns a dynastic conflict between two groups of royal cousins. These are the *Pandavas* (the five sons of King Pandu), the heroes of the epic who are all descendants of the gods, and their antagonists, the *Kauravas* (the hundred sons of the blind king, Dhritarashtra). Their dispute ultimately results in a terrible war that marks the end of an epoch for humanity.

On the eve of the battle, the great Pandava warrior Arjuna experiences crippling doubt. When Arjuna asks his charioteer, Krishna (an avatar of Vishnu), to pull the chariot into the middle of the battlefield, he sees his friends and relatives on both sides clamoring for war. Not wanting to commit the sin of killing his kinsmen and overcome with sorrow, he refuses to fight. It is at this key point in the story that the profound philosophical discourse known as the *Bhagavad Gita* begins. Many Hindus regard this conversation between Krishna and Arjuna as the most significant philosophical work in Hinduism.

The *Bhagavad Gita* (The Song of the Lord)

The *Bhagavad Gita*, the conversation between Krishna and Arjuna, was probably composed around the first century CE. The text, which seeks to reconcile the tension between renunciation and worldly life, also presents radical new ideas about the pursuit of moksha, including the three margas or paths to liberation that we explored in an earlier section.

The *Gita* begins with Arjuna refusing to act on his dharma, as is demanded of a member of the kshatriya, or warrior class, out of fear of the consequences of killing his kinsmen. Krishna responds to his dilemma by revealing that one does not need to give up action to achieve moksha. Rather, as we noted earlier, one gives up the *fruit* of action. That is, one cultivates "desireless action," or acting without attachment to the fruit or benefit of the action.

Arjuna must honor his dharma as a warrior and fight his own kinsmen. But he transcends the karmic repercussions of this act by relinquishing personal attachment and realizing that Krishna is the primary cause leading all the individual actors toward this inevitable outcome.

As you have seen in the earlier section on bhakti marga, the *Gita* emphasizes the path of devotion, which later comes to dominate Hindu practice and belief. The *Gita* also teaches that it is possible to achieve moksha by being active in the world, provided that, through selfless devotion, one surrenders attachment to the expectation of any particular result. This contrasts with earlier teachings that advocated complete detachment through renunciation as the primary means of escaping samsara.

Krishna, in the guise of Arjuna's charioteer, counsels the warrior on the verge of battle against his kinsmen. The battle scene in the *Mahabharata* is the setting of the *Bhagavad Gita*.

Puranas

In addition to the rich storehouse of narrative material in the epics, there are equally important collections of mythic stories known as **Puranas** (Sanskrit *purana*, "ancient"). Like the epics, the Puranas existed in oral form before being committed to writing—in this case, between the fourth and sixteenth centuries. The Puranas contain useful historical data, such as the genealogies of regional kings, but they also reflect the rise of dualistic or devotional Hinduism. This is evident primarily in their narrations of the deeds of the great deities such as Shiva, Vishnu, and Devi. They also consider the genealogies of gods, rules governing the proper worship of the gods, the construction of temples, the observance of festivals, the undertaking of pilgrimages, and similar topics.

There are eighteen major Puranas, two of the most influential of which are the *Bhagavata Purana* and the *Markandeya Purana*. The *Bhagavata Purana* focuses on Vishnu and his incarnations, most especially Krishna. It is one of the most widely recited, performed, and studied texts in contemporary Hinduism. The tenth book, which serves as the primary source for Krishna's life story, is particularly important. The *Markandeya Purana* includes the *Devi Mahatmya*, which is an important text of Shaktism, one among various Hindu sects that we explore in the next section.

4.5 The Teachings of Hinduism: Varieties

The most prevalent devotional sects in Hinduism are Vaishnavism, Shaivism, and Shaktism. Each features veneration of one of the major deities at the center of Hindu cosmology. The devotees of these sects are called **Vaishnavas** (devotees of Vishnu and his avatars), **Shaivas** (devotees of Shiva), and **Shaktas** (devotees of the Great Goddess, Devi). Within each of these sects are numerous individual orders that differ in the sacred texts and saints they revere, their modes of worship, and their philosophical orientation.

Vaishnavism

Vaishnavas worship Vishnu and his consort (wife) Lakshmi as supreme. Vishnu mercifully intervenes in the world through his avatars (such as Rama in the *Ramayana* and Krishna in the *Mahabharata*) and is inseparable from his beloved Lakshmi, who is the goddess of auspiciousness and good fortune. For Vaishnavas, Vishnu is the source of all existence. These ideas about Vishnu's fundamental nature are expressed in myths and poems that invoke him as the lord who created the universe.

Hindus worship Vishnu in a number of different forms. He is often depicted reclining with Lakshmi on a thousand-headed serpent that floats on the cosmic ocean. From his navel rises a lotus, upon which Brahma the creator god is seated. Visually, this image asserts that the world is born from Vishnu and that he is its sole originator and sustainer. Brahma, Vishnu, and Shiva constitute a triad of gods whose roles are, respectively, to create, preserve, and dissolve the universe as it moves through cycles. For Vaishnavas, Vishnu is not just the preserver but the supreme God who performs all three roles.

In Hindu sacred art, Vishnu typically is shown holding objects in his four hands that symbolize his powers and characteristics. In his upper right hand, he holds a flaming discus (symbolizing the sun and omniscience); his upper left hand bears a white conch shell (the moon and creativity). In his lower right hand, he holds a mace (power), and in his lower left hand, he holds a lotus (purity). Most Vaishnavas have special devotion for Vishnu's avatars, Rama and Krishna.

Shaivism

Shiva is the destroyer and at the same time a benefactor. He embodies both the ideal of ascetic renunciation and sensual participation in the material world. Beyond being the god of spiritual insight and of yogis and ascetics, Shiva is also the god who destroys the universe at the end of time before a new cycle of creation can begin. Most Shaivas worship Shiva as a god with no beginning or end who transcends time but also presides over its endless cycles. Some Shaivas emphasize that Shiva is also a family man, to be venerated with his divine queen Parvati and their two sons, the divine princes Ganesha and Skanda.

Shiva is usually depicted sitting in deep meditation on Mount Kailasha in the Himalayas, with a tiger skin wrapped about his waist and wearing serpents for jewelry. His third eye is turned inward in meditative contemplation, and he wears the crescent moon and the holy river Ganges in his matted hair. A common symbol of Shiva is the linga, an abstract phallic symbol that represents his creative potential. His consort Parvati is also believed by Shaivas to represent the creative energy of the universe.

Shaktism

The cults of the Great Goddess venerate her as the supreme cause and end of the universe. Although she has many names and many forms, the Great Goddess is most often referred to as Devi, Mahadevi, or Shakti. Devotees of the goddess are referred to as Shaktas.

The primacy of Devi is definitively asserted in the fifth century CE. Sanskrit text called the *Devi Mahatmya* ("The Greatness of Devi"), which, as noted previously, is part of the *Markandeya Purana*, posits that the supreme cause of the universe is feminine. The text argues for Devi's greatness through three main myths, the most important

Accompanied by a legion of other goddesses and fierce creatures and riding a lion, Devi, in the form of the goddess Durga, protects the world by battling the buffalo demon Mahishasura. (The buffalo is associated with Yama, the god of death.) Pallava period, seventh century, Mahishasura Mardini Cave, Mamallapuram Tamil Nadu, India.

of which tells how she killed the buffalo-headed demon, Mahisha, who threatened the world and whom even the gods Vishnu and Shiva were not able to vanquish.

To Shaktas the goddess is all-powerful and pervades the entire universe. She is the one who creates, preserves, and destroys the universe in harmony with the rhythms of cosmic time. The *Devi Mahatmya* teaches that the goddess is eternal and that she manifests herself over and over again in order to protect the universe as a mother would her child.

Shaivas and Shaktas have much in common, as Shiva and Devi (also called Parvati) are believed by both sects to be married to each other. So the difference between Shaivism and Shaktism is a matter of emphasis regarding the importance of each of these two primal forces. For Shaivas, Shiva is pure consciousness that pervades all existence, and Devi is his creative (but subordinate) power. In contrast, Shaktas believe that Shiva is entirely passive and that Shakti is the creative energy that constitutes and governs the whole of existence. Thus, the Shaktas say that "Shiva without Shakti is *shava*" (Sanskrit, "a corpse"), an idea that is iconographically represented in the form of the goddess Kali dancing upon the inert body of Shiva.

Gurus, Saints, and Sages

Entire sects of Hinduism are constantly forming around the veneration of gurus, saints, and ascetics. In the words of one scholar, "saints still remain . . . as they have always been, the generating centers of Hindu religion."[10] The fully enlightened are

A modern painting of the goddess Kali, whose name means both "Black" and "Time," dancing on the body of Shiva. From the Indian state of Odisha.

regarded as being the most immediate means of accessing the divine reality directly, either to obtain material and mundane blessings or to receive spiritual teaching to quicken one's own journey toward moksha. Some saints are venerated as embodiments of God, others for being humble and perfectly surrendered devotees.

Gurus are sometimes powerful religious authorities who preside over well-established institutions in which the divine authority of a guru has been passed down to his senior disciple in an unbroken lineage for many generations. Certain important gurus and saints have been responsible for the formulation of the specific philosophical orientation of various sects and monastic orders, making interpretation of sacred texts and belief more systematic and consistent. We have noted, for example, the founding roles of Shankara, Ramanuja, and Madhva in, respectively, the Vedanta schools of Advaita, Vishishta-Advaita, and Dvaita. The roles of guru as founder and authority are characteristic of Hindu movements outside of India, such as the International Society for Krishna Consciousness (commonly known as the Hare Krishna movement) and Transcendental Meditation—both of which are explored in Chapter 14.

4.6 The History of Hinduism: Origins

Hinduism is a vibrant tradition that has exhibited dynamic change and a willingness to embrace innovations in thought and practice. At the same time, Hinduism has preserved many of its most ancient elements to the present day, cherishing some traditions that go back more than 3,000 years.

The history of Hinduism can be traced back to the Indus Valley Civilization (c. 2600–1700 BCE) and to the Indo-Aryan peoples who composed the Vedas (c. 1200–900 BCE).

The Indus Valley Civilization

As its name suggests, the Indus Valley Civilization developed along the Indus River, which flows through modern Pakistan. It reached its developmental peak between 2300 and 2000 BCE, when its thriving cities, such as Harappa and Mohenjo-Daro,

Significant sites in the history of Hinduism.

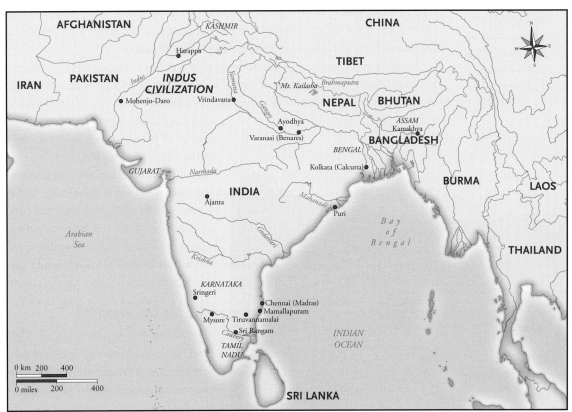

The Proto-Shiva seal. The male figure, sometimes called the "Lord of the Animals," is surrounded by various totemic animals, such as an elephant, a tiger, a rhinoceros, a water buffalo, and two antelopes or deer.

enjoyed a high standard of living. Archaeological excavations at Indus Valley sites have yielded evidence of trade with regions as far away as Mesopotamia and impressive skill in metallurgy, handicrafts, and urban planning. The archaeological finds include a vast number of stone seals that were perhaps used to stamp products for trade. These are decorated with depictions of animals and people and with a script that has not yet been deciphered.

Some scholars believe that in the Indus Valley seals we can detect very early elements of Hinduism. For example, the most famous seal has been called the Proto-Shiva seal because its central image may be an archaic form of Shiva. The male figure is seated in a yoga posture, wears a buffalo-horned headdress, is surrounded by animals, and appears to have three faces. Later images of Shiva often show him meditating in a yoga posture, being in the company of animals, and having three faces. Of course, without a decipherment of the script it is difficult to understand fully this and other images depicted on the seals.

Archaeologists working in the Indus Valley have also discovered a number of terracotta figures depicting women. Some scholars have identified these as representations of a mother goddess. It may be that the widespread worship of goddesses in later Hinduism originated in the veneration of female deities in the ancient Indus Valley Civilization.

During the eighteenth century BCE, there was a sudden decline in the Indus Valley Civilization. Scholars are uncertain as to what caused the decline, although climate change that disrupted agriculture is cited as a likely contributing factor.

Who Are the Aryans?

The English linguist Sir William "Oriental" Jones (1746–1794) described how Sanskrit, Latin, Greek, and several other ancient languages shared a common linguistic ancestor. These languages are

The great bath can be seen amid the ruins of the ancient cityscape of Mohenjo-Daro, an important city of the Indus Valley Civilization. A towering granary can be viewed in the distance.

referred to as "Indo-European" and probably stem from a lost language we call "Proto Indo-European." Jones's discoveries astounded Europeans, who soon learned that Sanskrit was closest to the original language spoken by the earliest Indo-Europeans.

The ancient speakers of Sanskrit who moved into the Indian subcontinent around 1500 BCE referred to themselves as the *Arya*—that is, those who are "noble," "cultivated," and "civilized." Today, we call them *Indo-Aryans* or, more simply, *Aryans*—although this use of the term is more specific (and accurate) than the general label "Aryan race" as used by the Nazi Party in the twentieth century. Skilled in handling the horse and chariot, the Aryans were a warlike and nomadic people who were well prepared to make themselves the dominant elite soon after they entered the Indian subcontinent.

Like other Indo-European peoples, the Aryans revered the horse, placed special importance on sacrifice, and organized their society into a three-part structure. For the Aryans, sacrifice was a means to maintain order in the universe. The priests (brahmins) who conducted sacrificial rituals occupied the top rung of the social order because of the religious power they wielded. The rulers and warriors (kshatriyas) were equally important. Last were the traders and farmers (vaishyas). As the Aryans did not place a great deal of emphasis on agriculture, one can see why the vaishyas would occupy a lower social position. The servant class (shudras) probably derived from the indigenous people at the time of the Aryan immigration. This social structure has remained fundamental to Indian society until today.

The Aryans, who eventually settled across northern India, have left us a body of texts composed in Sanskrit, of which the earliest example is the Vedas. It is to the era of these texts that we now turn.

The Vedic Period

Ritual was of ultimate importance in Vedic times, as rites of sacrifice were performed to sustain the cosmic order and please the gods. Much of ritual sacrifice involved the pouring of offerings into a sacrificial fire as Vedic hymns were recited. Although the construction of their fire altars became quite elaborate, Indians of the Vedic period inherited from their nomadic ancestors a very "portable" religion with no fixed buildings or icons and with sacred knowledge maintained by priests.

A *yajna* or fire sacrifice, one of the most archaic of Hindu rites, is performed by priests before an image of Durga during the Durga Puja festival in Kolkata, India.

In Vedic times, as today, fire was considered a god. Known as Agni, he was the mouth of the gods and the gateway to the celestial realms, so offerings were magically transported through Agni to whichever god was invoked.

In Vedic mythology it is Indra, god of lightning, thunder, and rain, and the virile god of fertility itself, who, as the most powerful, is king of the gods. More hymns in the Vedas are addressed to Indra than to any other god, but in later Hindu tradition and mythology he is somewhat comical: haughty, proud, and often drunk. Many of the Vedic gods continue to play a part in the later Hindu pantheon but endure only in a subordinate status.

In the later Vedic period, philosophical innovations began to supplant the older Vedic emphasis on sacrifice. It is in hymns from the later period that Vedic religion begins to take a decisive turn, shifting away from an emphasis on myth, cosmology, and sacrifice to a keener interest in philosophy and introspection. In these hymns, the perception of the nature of existence emerges as being more important than upholding the cosmic order through sacrifice. Late Vedic hymns mark a transition toward what would be the philosophical revolution of the speculative texts known as the Upanishads.

During the time of the Upanishads (c. 900–200 BCE), contemplative and philosophical reflection became more widespread. Many philosophers moved from urban areas to the forest in order to lead simpler lives. Some lived as hermits, some lived in colonies of contemplatives, and others practiced strict ascetic disciplines in the solitude of the jungle. Still others became wanderers, going from town to town begging for food and engaging in lively philosophical debates.

4.7 The History of Hinduism: Development

By the end of the Vedic period, foundational components of Hinduism as it is still known and practiced today had been established. These components notably include the Upanishads and the epic poems, the *Ramayana* and the *Mahabharata*, the latter, as we have seen, containing the *Bhagavad Gita*. Hindu culture would continue to flourish in the early centuries of the Common Era, achieving especially impressive innovations during the age of the Guptas.

The Age of the Guptas

Most scholars characterize the time of the Gupta Empire (c. 320–540 CE) as a period of remarkable creativity. The Guptas, who ruled much of northern India, patronized the arts, sciences, religion, and literature. Their reign was an era of relative peace and prosperity, often described as "the Golden Age of India."

The Gupta rulers practiced religious tolerance and sponsored groups and institutions associated with Buddhism, Jainism, and other religions. The Guptas, who were themselves Hindus, promoted Hinduism and sought to organize society in accordance with Hindu beliefs. Thanks in part to Gupta patronage, the worship of

Vishnu and Shiva became increasingly popular during this period, which also saw a shift from worship at open-air sacrificial altars to worship in temples. As temple institutions arose, so did special forms of temple art and architecture. These developments quickened the spread of bhakti and the emerging devotional sects.

A very significant religious development during the age of the Guptas was the rise of devotional Hinduism. The two great Sanskrit epics, the *Ramayana* and the *Mahabharata*, had been completed and were well established by this time. As we have seen, these epics are concerned with political problems, dynastic successions, duty, and obligations. But they also feature the exploits of the gods and have much to tell us about popular deities and avatars and forms of devotion to them. Composition of the Puranas commenced during this period, indicating the growing popularity of devotional Hinduism.

The Development of Bhakti

The devotional aspects of Hinduism became increasingly popular under the Guptas, but they took on new life in southern India between the sixth and ninth centuries CE through an ecstatic form called bhakti marga, the path of devotion. This movement eventually spread all over India, changing and adapting to new regional and linguistic circumstances. Devotion now came to be expressed through poetry, art, architecture, and temple building. Bhakti was instrumental in the development of the various sectarian orientations of Hinduism and in its vibrant temple cultures.

By the late fifth century CE, Buddhism (Chapter 5) and Jainism (Chapter 6) were deeply entrenched in southern India. Bhakti arose as a challenge to these traditions. Over the next four centuries, wandering poets roamed the countryside and converted royalty and commoners alike to the devotional ethos of bhakti. Royal patronage for Jainism and Buddhism waned, and kings sought legitimacy through poets' songs that praised the kings as the representatives of the gods Shiva and Vishnu. The religious networks forged by the itinerant poets sometimes developed into political networks and strengthened alliances between religion and politics.

By the twelfth century, the bhakti movement had transformed once again, becoming an adversary of caste and gender prejudice. In this new transformation, practitioners of bhakti often rejected ritual and temple-based worship, insisting that the body is itself a temple and that God dwells in every individual. Many scholars argue that the bhakti movement had such a far-reaching impact because it was egalitarian, revolutionary, and frequently anti-brahmin. Bhakti poet–saints represented a variety of caste backgrounds. Furthermore, rather than using Sanskrit, the language of the Vedas and of priestly authority, the bhakti poets used vernacular languages such as Tamil, Kannada, Marathi, and an early form of Hindi. The bhakti poets asserted that caste and other circumstances of one's birth did not determine one's access to God. Rather, it was the quality of one's surrender to God that mattered.

Tantra

Bhakti was not the only revolutionary new development to challenge the strictures of gender and caste. **Tantra**, another new system, emerged alongside it. Making use of symbols, rituals, yogic postures, breathing techniques, mantras, and other spiritual practices—sometimes in shocking or forbidden ways—Tantra offered the possibility of sudden liberation from samsara. Likely having arisen among mystics in the northern Indian region of Kashmir and perhaps also in eastern India, by the seventh century Tantra had come to influence not only Hinduism but Buddhism and Jainism as well.

Tantra (Sanskrit, "loom") assumes the interweaving and interconnectedness of all things. These include pure consciousness, which is identified with Brahman or Shiva, and material reality in its most basic state, which is identified with Shakti. Similarly, samsara and moksha are understood not as two different things but as aspects of a single continuum of being. For practitioners of Tantra, the material world is a manifestation of the divine energy associated with pure consciousness. Their spiritual practices are said to give them the ability to manipulate or channel that energy in order to gain liberation. Unlike the ascetics who renounced the material world and its sensual pleasures, practitioners of Tantra made use of material things and the senses as the means by which to transcend them. For them, moksha could be found in the midst of everyday experience.

Tantric practitioners taught that the ritual transgression of social boundaries could create ideal conditions for transcending the egocentric self and achieving instantaneous moksha. Recognizing that people's egos are embedded in caste identity and in taboos regarding purity and pollution, practitioners of Tantra performed rituals in which they identified their bodies as deities, ritually consumed meat, fish, and wine, and engaged in ritual sex with low-caste partners.

As Tantra increased in popularity, it also became increasingly secretive. While many were attracted by the promise of achieving liberation in this life, others alleged that some practitioners exercised seductive magical powers and that others suffered mental breakdown. For these reasons, along with disapproval of rituals that violated social conventions, Tantra for the most part remained hidden during its later development.

Hindus and Muslims During the Mughal Dynasty

One of the first sustained encounters between Hindus and Muslims in India was initiated by the raids of Mahmud of Ghazni (Afghanistan) early in the eleventh century CE. Mahmud repeatedly raided the subcontinent, annexed states headed by Hindu, Buddhist, and Jain kings, and made the kings his vassals. His most famous incursion involved the looting and destruction of the great temple of Shiva in Somnath (1025). According to Muslim sources, more than 50,000 defenders of the temple were killed, and its immense wealth was taken back to Ghazni. These Muslim accounts also speak of the forced conversions of Hindus to Islam.

Contemporary Hindu nationalists often point to this early encounter with Islam as the beginning of centuries of oppression and persecution under Muslim rule.

The Mughal Dynasty was established in India in 1526, by which time Islam already had a strong foothold there, particularly in the northern regions. The Mughals were Muslim rulers of Turkic-Mongol origin. The Mughal Dynasty endured until 1857, although it reached its apex of power in the eighteenth century, declining thereafter with the rise of British influence. Under the Mughals, a complex relationship existed between Hinduism and Islam. Some Mughal emperors were hostile to religions other than their own and to Hinduism and Jainism in particular. Others, such as Akbar (1542–1605), were open to them. Akbar encouraged dialogue with representatives of different religions at a weekly salon. He even invented his own religion, the "Divine Faith" (in Arabic, *Din-I-Ilahi*), which incorporated elements of various religious traditions including Hinduism, Islam, and Zoroastrianism. Akbar was a clever political strategist who understood non-Muslims as subjects rather than infidels, counted Hindu kings among his closest advisors, and married the daughters of Hindu kings to cement political alliances with them. Good relationships between Mughal emperors and high-ranking Hindus helped to produce a vibrant pluralistic culture.

Under the Mughals, the conversions of Hindus to Islam do not appear to have been forced. Instead, Hindus converted for a variety of reasons, the most common one being improved economic and social standing and sincere belief in the teachings of Islam. There were also conversions of Muslims to Hinduism, especially when Muslims married into Hindu families.

Some of the greatest Hindu thinkers, poets, and philosophers lived during the time of the Mughals. The influential poet–saint Tulsidas (1532–1623), a member of Akbar's court and a devotee of Rama, wrote the *Ramcharitmanas*, an epic retelling in Hindi of the original Sanskrit *Ramayana*. The Muslim weaver-mystic Kabir (c. 1440–1518) was inspired by a Hindu teacher and composed poetry that seamlessly combined Hindu and Islamic philosophical ideas, while at the same time critiquing the social policies of Hindu and Muslim rulers.

Colonial Critique and the Hindu Reformers

When employees of the British East India Company established an imperial presence in India in the late eighteenth century, they initially adapted themselves to local customs and practices. They learned regional languages, married into local families, and even embraced local religious beliefs. One particularly colorful example is Charles Stuart (1758–1828), an Irish general in the Bengal Army ("Bengal" in this case refers to the area of eastern India between the Bay of Bengal and the Himalayas). Stuart was such an avid admirer of Hinduism that his colleagues nicknamed him "Hindoo Stuart." His book, *Vindication of the Hindoos* (1808), was intended to discourage the ever-growing support for British missionaries who sought to convert Hindus to Christianity. When these missionaries tried to embarrass Stuart

by calling attention to aspects of Hindu mythology that seemed strange to Westerners, he eloquently wrote in response: "Whenever I look around me in the vast region of Hindoo Mythology, I discover piety in the garb of allegory: and I see Morality, at every turn, blended with every tale; and, as far as I can rely on my own judgment, it appears the most complete and ample system of Moral allegory that the world has ever produced."[11]

But not everyone involved with the British East India Company admired Hindu beliefs and customs. Many felt that the "primitive backwardness" of Hindu belief was enough to warrant colonial intervention. By the middle of the nineteenth century, and certainly after the 1857 Indian Uprising (referred to as the "Mutiny" by British chroniclers, but as the "First War of Independence" by many Indian historians), the attraction to Hinduism and Indian culture represented by figures such as "Hindoo" Stuart and the linguist William "Oriental" Jones (whom we met earlier in this section) began to fade. As the commercial and administrative presence of the British East India Company gave way to the colonial control of the British Crown, critiques of Hinduism became an increasingly important means of exerting political power over the subcontinent.

One of the major effects of the British presence on Hinduism was a shift to English as the common language of religious written discourse (although Sanskrit retained its role as the primary priestly language). Other major effects on Hinduism resulted from the prevalence of Christianity and its Bible.

Temple volunteers unveil a statue of Swami Vivekananda at the Hindu Temple of Greater Chicago, Saturday, July 11, 1998, in Lemont, Illinois. The statue honors Vivekananda as "the first man to bring Hindu religion and the practice of yoga to America."

In the nineteenth century, Hindus began to reassert the place of the Vedic texts, especially the Upanishads, as the authoritative foundation of their religion. This trend toward a more book-based religion continued, although by the early twentieth century, it was the *Bhagavad Gita* rather than the Upanishads that emerged as the most popular text of Hinduism. To this day, Hindus tend to regard the *Bhagavad Gita* much as Jews and Christians regard the Bible.

By the mid-nineteenth century, amid the movement to reassert the authority of the Vedic texts, English-educated Hindus took up the work of reform as a response to colonial critiques of Hinduism. They, too, began deriding Hinduism's many gods, erotic symbolism, temple worship, and rituals as crass corruptions of the purity of the authentic Hinduism embodied in the Vedas and Upanishads. They sought to transform Hinduism from within.

One of these reformers was Ram Mohan Roy (1774–1833), a member of a wealthy Bengali brahmin community who in 1828 established the Brahmo Samaj (Community of Brahman Worshipers) as a neo-Hindu religious organization open to all, regardless of religious orientation. Roy believed that British rule offered India considerable opportunities for progress, and he devoted his life to religious, social, and educational reform. He was particularly concerned with issues involving the protection of women, such as child marriage, polygamy, dowry, and the practice of sati, an upper-caste practice in which a widow immolated herself on her husband's funeral pyre. This ritual suicide was believed to bring great honor to the family and to raise the status of the dead widow to that of a goddess. Roy campaigned for the abolition of sati, arguing that there was no scriptural basis in the Vedas for this practice. Finally, in 1829, sati was made illegal in Bengal. Roy was among the first members of the Indian upper classes to visit Europe, traveling there in 1830 to ensure that the British would not overturn the sati law. He died in 1833 and was buried in Bristol.

Another influential reformer was Dayananda Saraswati (1824–1883). Having become a wandering monk early in life, Dayananda studied under a blind sage who urged him to campaign for a return to what he considered the pure and original Vedic religion. Following his advice, Dayananda rejected the epics and Puranas as departures from the purity of the Vedas and spoke out against all aspects of temple tradition, image worship, and pilgrimage. In 1875, he founded the Arya Samaj (the Noble Community) as a "Vedic" religious organization whose social reform platform condemned child marriage and untouchability while promoting the equality of women. Dayananda rejected social hierarchies based on *jati*; rather, he believed, caste status should be based on one's character, which the organization would determine in a public examination. Although Dayananda Saraswati, like Ram Mohan Roy, favored a return to Vedic religion, his Arya Samaj distinguished itself from Roy's Brahmo Samaj in its encouragement of Hindu nationalism, anticipating the more extreme Hindu nationalist groups that would appear in the early twentieth century.

Other figures, less influenced by colonial and Christian critiques of Hinduism, were not as concerned as Ram Mohan Roy and Dayananda Saraswati with reforming Hinduism in ways that would appeal to the West. One of these figures was the enormously popular Bengali mystic, Ramakrishna (1836–1886). A devotee and temple priest of the goddess Kali, Ramakrishna devoted himself to spiritual exercises drawn from different religious traditions, including Vaishnavism, Advaita Vedanta, Tantrism, and even Islamic Sufism and Roman Catholicism. These served as the basis for his teaching that all religions are directed toward the experience of a God who creates religions to suit the spiritual needs and tastes of different peoples. Seen in this way, Hinduism could claim the same legitimacy as any other religion.

Among Ramakrishna's disciples was Narendranath Datta (1863–1902), a former law student who took monastic vows during Ramakrishna's last days and was thereafter known as Swami Vivekananda. In 1886, shortly after the death of Ramakrishna, he oversaw the founding of what would become the Ramakrishna Math, an order of monks devoted to the teachings of Ramakrishna. Swami Vivekananda had an enormous impact on the representation of Hinduism in the West, particularly in the United States. In 1893, he visited the United States to speak on behalf of Hinduism at the World's Parliament of Religions in Chicago. Quoting from the *Bhagavad Gita*, he represented Hinduism as a tolerant and universal religion. Like his teacher, Ramakrishna, Vivekananda asserted that all religions are true. His stirring speech proved a milestone in changing Western attitudes toward Hinduism. It also ensured his fame in America, and he went on to establish the Vedanta Society of New York. Today, Vedanta Societies throughout the world are dedicated to the study, practice, and promotion of Hinduism.

4.8 The History of Hinduism: The Modern Age

Momentous developments of the twentieth century, most notably the establishment of India as an independent nation-state, were to have significant effects on Hinduism. The central figure in these developments was Mohandas (Mahatma) Gandhi.

Gandhi and the Struggle for Indian Independence

Mohandas Karamchand Gandhi (1869–1948), a towering religious, political, and social reformer in India, recast many Hindu ideas in the service of the fight for Indian independence. Born into a middle-class family of merchants, Gandhi was an English-educated lawyer and a deeply religious man. As a law student in England, he had read the *Bhagavad Gita*, and it had a profound impact on him.

Gandhi's political career began in South Africa, where he worked as a lawyer. It was here, in a struggle against racial discrimination, that he began to develop his political philosophy of nonviolent resistance. He characterized nonviolent resistance as *satyagraha* (Sanskrit, "grasping the truth") and explained that its strength lay in converting wrongdoers to justice rather than striving to coerce them.

Gandhi returned to India in 1915 to join the fledgling Indian independence movement, which sought to free India from British colonial rule. Deeply influenced by the American writer Henry David Thoreau (1817–1862), especially his thoughts on civil disobedience, Gandhi established an ashram (a place of religious seclusion) to train freedom fighters. The ashram chose as its motto a statement from the Upanishads: *satyameva jayate*, "the truth alone will prevail." Like his Upanishadic forebears, Gandhi believed that truth could be sought only through selfless service and humility, which could in turn be achieved by disciplining the body through fasting and celibacy.

Gandhi did not hesitate to criticize certain Hindu beliefs and practices, particularly that of *varnashrama dharma*, the ancient system by which society was ordered into various classes or castes. He worked tirelessly to abolish untouchability, calling the untouchables Harijans ("Children of God"), thereby seeking to increase their respectability. Gandhi also strove to improve the status of women.

Gandhi's charisma and influence were so great that even in his lifetime he was revered as a saint or Mahatma (Sanskrit, "Great Soul"). A lifelong Hindu, Gandhi also advocated the universality and truth of all religions and sought throughout his life to reconcile Hinduism and Islam. Tragically, on January 30, 1948, he was assassinated by Nathuram Godse, a Hindu nationalist who thought Gandhi was too accommodating of Muslims. Godse was later executed for the crime despite the pleas of Gandhi's two sons and Jawaharlal Nehru (1889–1964), India's first prime minister, who believed that violence would dishonor everything Gandhi represented. After decades of struggle, Gandhi had lived to enjoy just five months of freedom after Great Britain had partitioned colonial India into the independent states of India and Pakistan in mid-1947.

Hindutva and Hindu Nationalism

Whereas reformers such as Ram Mohan Roy, Vivekananda, and Gandhi sought to build bridges with the West through calling attention to the commonalities between Hinduism and other religions, other figures, such as V. D. Savarkar (1883–1966), insisted on the distinctiveness of Hinduism. Savarkar called this concept ***hindutva*** (Sanskrit, "Hindu-ness"), a term he coined in a 1923 pamphlet. For Savarkar, *hindutva* was a force to unite Hindus in repelling all dangerous foreign influences. As president of the Hindu Mahasabha, a Hindu nationalist political party that embraced this concept, Savarkar argued that India was an exclusively "Hindu Nation."

In 1925, the Rashtriya Swayamsevak Sangh (RSS; National Volunteer Corps) was founded. Although it has presented itself as a Hindu cultural organization, its members have a long history of political actions that have intensified communal tensions, precipitated violence, and propagated religious intolerance. The founder of the RSS, K. B. Hedgewar (1889–1940), was himself inspired by V. D. Savarkar's concept of *hindutva*. The RSS was meant to be a training ground for the self-empowerment of Hindu youth who were committed to defending a Hindu nation from the perceived threat posed by the Muslim world. Gaining independence from oppressive foreign rule can often rob nationalist movements of their momentum, but this was not the case in India after 1947. Hindu nationalists continued to be a major force in that country. The political backlash following Gandhi's assassination led many Mahasabha members to leave the party and ally themselves instead with a new political organization, the Bharatiya Jana Sangh (Indian People's Alliance), which was founded in 1951. Its founder, Syama Prasad Mookerjee (1901–1953), had been a member of both the Mahasabha and the RSS. Bharatiya Jana Sangh was a Hindu nationalist party specifically created to oppose the Indian National Congress, the more moderate party of Jawaharlal Nehru and Mahatma Gandhi.

VISUAL GUIDE
Hinduism

In Hinduism, folding one's hands and offering salutations by saying "Namaste" (nom-us-tay) is a simple way of giving a respectful greeting, as well as saying, "I bow to the divine in you."

Hindu forehead markings: bindi, *tripundra*, and *namam*. Bindi (drop) is a decorative mark on the forehead signifying auspiciousness. An additional "dot" is often applied by married women to the top of the head where the hair is parted. The mark between the eyes signifies the "third eye" (perception beyond ordinary sight). Some forehead markings denote sectarian affiliation, such as the three horizontal lines worn by worshippers of Shiva and the vertical "V" of the worshippers of Vishnu. The red "drop" in the middle represents Lakshmi, the goddess of fortune.

The mandala (Sanskrit, "circle") is a sacred device that varies in form and function: to map cosmology, to embody deities, to serve as talismans, or to facilitate meditative contemplation.

Hinduism in the Twenty-First Century

There are nearly 1.2 billion Hindus in the world today, which makes Hinduism the world's third largest religion, behind only Christianity and Islam.[12] More than 1 billion Hindus live in India, where Hindus comprise about 80 percent of the population. There are nearly 29 million Hindus in Nepal, where with about 81 percent of the population, Hinduism is also by far the majority religion. Other countries with large Hindu populations include (all figures are approximate) Bangladesh (13 million), Indonesia (4.2 million), Pakistan (4 million), and Sri Lanka (3 million). There are about 2.5 million Hindus in the United States, making it the country with the seventh largest Hindu population.[13]

4.9 Hinduism as a Way of Life: Rituals and Observances

Hindus often insist that Hinduism is more a "way of life" than a system of beliefs. Indeed, Hinduism does place greater emphasis on what one *does* rather than on what one *believes*. The emphasis on doing rather than believing might explain the disconnection between textual injunction and actual practice that one often encounters in Hinduism. For example, the *Laws of Manu*, as we have seen, provide prescriptions for how to live based on the *varnashrama dharma* system, but these do not always translate into actual lived practice. In this section, we will explore Hinduism as a way of life.

Temples and Icons

Hinduism encourages a sensory religious experience in its adherents. This experiential aspect is nowhere more evident than when a Hindu goes to a temple. As religion scholar Diana Eck observes, the devotee doesn't say, "I am going for worship." Rather, the devotee asserts, "I am going for darshan." The Sanskrit word **darshan** means "to see," but in the Hindu context it refers specifically to the interlocking gaze shared by the deity and the devotee. That is, darshan is the intimate act of both seeing the deity and being looked upon by the divine, an act that establishes a loving relationship between devotee and God.[14]

As we learned earlier in this chapter, the image of a god in a temple or a personal shrine at home is not just a representation of the deity; rather, it is imbued with the divine presence. Thus, devotees believe that to see an image of a deity is to see the deity itself. In turn, the gaze of the deity's image is believed to confer blessings on every person who comes into its presence. In many ways, the act of darshan is often the most meaningful experience for Hindus.

Today, most Hindus go to a local temple or on pilgrimage to a sacred site for darshan. For this reason, the temple is a central religious and cultural institution in Hindu religious practice.

Temples generally house two different kinds of icons. The first type is the main image (or images), which resides at the center of the temple. These images are usually made of stone and are permanently fixed in the shrine. The second type of icon is the processional image, typically cast from an amalgam of five metals. Smaller and more mobile than fixed images, processional images are brought out of temples on special platforms or chariots for temple festivals and are usually adorned in elaborate costumes and jewels. Hindus gather for a darshan in the presence of the divine form embodied in these mobile images. Although both types of icons are made by human hands and are constituted of material substances, while the icon is being worshiped it is understood not to be *merely* stone or metal but the very body of God.

In temple rites, deities are treated as royal guests. Temple worship usually involves sixteen different offerings. Of these, the most significant is the eighth offering, which involves pouring auspicious substances over the icon. These substances might include scented water, milk, and sandalwood paste. After the ritual, the deity is adorned in ornaments, textiles, and flowers. The temple rituals end with a waving of lamps before the image. For Hindus, this is the ideal moment for darshan.

Divine images can also directly convey religious teachings. For instance, Nataraja, Lord of the Dance, is one of the most iconic forms of Shiva (see the photo in the earlier section, "Divine Reality as Sound and Image"). In his dance, Nataraja represents what Shaivas call the Five Activities of Shiva, which can also be understood as the five principal manifestations of divine energy: creation, preservation, destruction, illusion, and liberation.

Forms of Worship

The Sanskrit word *puja* is commonly used to describe worship in Hinduism. In its simplest form, puja involves making some offering to the deity (such as fruit, incense, or flowers). The deity is then believed to partake of the devotion inherent in the offering. The material aspect of the offerings left behind is thought to be infused with the deity's blessing.

Clouds of incense billow from a censer as devotees pray before a multiarmed clay icon of Durga (upper center), Ganesha (lower left), and other deities. This is the final opportunity for darshan, as the icon is about to be dissolved by immersion into the Ganges River at the conclusion of the festival of Durga Puja. Kolkata, India.

Puja can be simple or elaborate. Along with material items, offerings can consist of washing or clothing the image of the deity, greeting it, prostrating oneself before it, and similar gestures. Puja can be offered almost anywhere—before a home shrine, at a temple, at pilgrimage sites, by sacred trees or rivers, at roadside shrines, or within temporary structures specially made for a specific rite. Rituals may be carried out as an expression of love for the deity, in a rite of passage, in celebration of a holiday or festival, when asking for blessings, in order to create an atmosphere of peace and harmony, or in propitiation of the gods in times of trouble. Ritual occasions are ideal for maintaining and strengthening community ties.

Certain forms of Hindu worship are so popular as to deserve special attention, especially *arati*, mantras, and sacrifice.

Arati   A common form of puja, **arati** involves an offering of light. *Arati* is so common that some Hindus use the term *arati* rather than puja to refer to worship generally. A lamp fueled with ghee (clarified butter) or camphor is lit and waved in a clockwise direction in front of the deity. The five flames used in *arati* symbolize the five elements (earth, water, fire, air, and ether), as well as the totality of the universe. This waving of the lamp is thought to remove evil influences and to return the object or recipient of the offering to an auspicious state, regardless of any negative thoughts or desires that might have been projected onto it. At the end of the ritual, participants wave their hands over the flame and touch them to their foreheads, taking the divine light of the deity into their innermost being.

Mantras   Nearly all rituals in Hinduism are accompanied by the recitation of **mantras**. These are ritual formulas used to produce a spiritual effect. Mantras can be used for a variety of reasons: to heighten awareness of God, to enhance the efficacy of an offering, to aid the practice of meditation, or to produce some magical effect. Mantras are usually—but not always—in Sanskrit.

The mantra that we have considered previously, OM, is prominent throughout Hinduism. The intonation of OM, the sound through which the universe is manifested, is thought to attune the mind to the essence of reality. Various Hindu sects use specific mantras especially suited to them. For example, the most important mantra for Vaishnavas is *Om Namo Narayanaya*, which means "obeisance to Narayana" (another name for Vishnu). For Vaishnavas, this mantra articulates the relationship between God and the devotee while also asserting the unity of Vishnu. Reciting and contemplating the mantra is an act of devotion that brings the devotee closer to Vishnu.

Sacrifice Fire sacrifice has been an essential component of Hinduism since the Vedic period. Sacrifice usually involves building an altar, kindling a fire, feeding it with ghee, and casting offerings (milk, cereals, fruits, flowers, etc.) into the fire while chanting mantras. Although fire sacrifice is usually performed by a brahmin priest, these rites can be performed by any married upper-caste man. A fire sacrifice is a crucial component of life-cycle and temple rituals.

Although sacrifice has persisted as an important feature of Hindu worship through the centuries, perspectives on the relevance and meaning of sacrifice have varied. In the Vedic period, sacrifice was seen as essential to maintaining cosmic order. This is the reason that one of the most important Vedic myths describes the universe as being born from the sacrifice of the cosmic man. The Upanishads, however, tend to diminish the relevance of sacrifice as an effective means of liberation from samsara. These texts argue that the true sacrifice takes place internally, with the breath itself fueling an inner sacrificial fire that awakens one to knowledge. The *Bhagavad Gita* follows in this line of interpretation, asserting that it is the surrender of the fruit of action that is the true meaning and purpose of sacrifice.

In the earliest period, the sacrifice of animals was an important aspect of Hindu ritual. However, over time (and particularly under the influence of Jainism and Buddhism), animal sacrifice ceased to play a role in upper-caste sacrificial rituals. In such sacrifices, coconuts and pumpkins came to act as substitutes for the animals. Animal sacrifice continues to play a significant role in folk Hinduism.

The majestic gate of a Shiva temple in southern India is reflected in one of the two ritual bathing tanks found within its precincts. These towers are erected in the four directions and are often covered in sculptural imagery that refers to the sacred myths of the gods venerated within. Arunachaleswar Temple, Tiruvannamalai, India, eleventh century.

Rites of Passage

Hindu rites of passage are intended to invoke blessings and divine favor during important times of transition. In addition, they help socialize individuals, assisting them as they move into new roles and stages of life. Some rites of passage occur very early in life. These include the naming ceremony of a child, typically held on the tenth or twelfth day after birth; a child's first haircut, usually performed between the first and third years of life; and ear piercing, which is typically done for both boys and girls before age five. The following are also major rites of passage.

Initiation Rituals   Boys of the brahmin, kshatriya, and vaishya classes traditionally underwent initiation by means of the *upanayana*, or sacred thread ceremony. Today, it is performed almost exclusively for brahmin boys at about the age of eight, giving them permission to perform certain religious functions. Beginning with a fire sacrifice, the ritual culminates in the promotion of the initiate to the category of "twice-born." The initiate is given a sacred thread that symbolizes a kind of umbilical cord linking the boy to the sun, the source of all light and knowledge. The sacred thread consists of three cotton threads, each composed of three strands, which are joined together by a single knot. It lies across the chest, resting over the left shoulder and under the right arm, thus being a highly visible sign of caste status.

Girls from all castes undergo initiation at the onset of the first menstrual period, which marks the transition from childhood to adulthood. Sometimes in these ritual observances the girl will spend the first three days of her first period secluded, although friends can visit. Now considered a young woman, she takes a ritual bath on the fourth day, and a feast is held in her honor. This transition is a public affair because it announces her availability for marriage. Often the young woman is taken to the local temple to receive a special blessing from an older married woman in her community, who will perform an *arati* ceremony to honor her new potential to bear children. Her life radically changes afterward, and, for many communities, her freedom to have unsupervised interaction with boys may be greatly curtailed.

Marriage   Marriage is a very important rite of passage. It is through marriage that one enters the householder ashrama, which provides the main support for society as a whole. In the past, marriage was traditionally arranged by the parents between a bride and groom of the same *jati* after consulting an astrologer, who determined the couple's compatibility. In the last few decades, caste strictures have eased somewhat. As a result, marriages for love have become more commonplace.

The marriage ceremony is sanctified through a fire sacrifice in which the gods are asked for blessings and offerings are poured into the fire. A thread is tied around the bride's wrist, and she is asked to step three times on a grinding stone from the groom's family as a demonstration of her fidelity to the new household she is joining. At the high point of the rite, the bride and groom walk together seven times around the sacred fire. The bride's family then provides a sumptuous meal for all guests. After the last day of celebration, the bride goes to the home of her husband.

Death   Hindus most often cremate the dead. The cremation pyre is likened to a fire sacrifice so that the funerary ritual is regarded as "the last sacrifice." Cremation usually takes place on the same day as death. The body is washed, smeared with sandalwood paste, wrapped in a cloth, and then carried on a litter by male relatives, who chant a holy name or phrase as they bear the body to the cremation ground.

It is usually the duty of the eldest son of the deceased to conduct the last rites and light the pyre. An ancient practice that is still often observed requires him to also crack the skull of the deceased in order to release the soul from the body.

Although cremation is the typical means of disposing of the body, there are exceptions. Earth burial is practiced for babies and among some low-caste communities. Saints, yogis, and ascetics are also buried. Their bodies are placed in special tombs, around which shrines are sometimes erected and worship is performed.

Following the funeral ceremony, the family and home of the deceased are considered to be polluted for a period of about ten days. The bereaved are expected to keep to themselves until the rites of ancestral offerings are completed. During this period, the deceased is offered balls of rice with which he or she is believed to construct a body in the spirit world or intermediate realm. This rite, which reflects the gestation of a human embryo for ten lunar months, may very well predate the formulation of a belief in reincarnation that was developed by the time of the Upanishads.

Pilgrimage

In Hinduism, sacred pilgrimage sites are believed to lie at the border between this world and that of the divine. Many of the earliest pilgrimage sites were located at sacred rivers and pools, and pilgrimage specifically involved ritual bathing as a means of purification. Some revered sites, marked by a shrine or temple, commemorate a sacred event or the life of a holy person. For pilgrims, these sites allow immediate, tangible access to the sacred.

One of the most important Hindu pilgrimage sites is the sacred city of Varanasi (Benares) on the banks of the Ganges. Many Hindus believe that to die in Varanasi is to be immediately released from samsara. For this reason, many old and sick people travel to Varanasi to die. However, because the Ganges is held to be the most sacred river in India, people who are unable to go to Varanasi to die arrange to have their ashes scattered in the river. In this way, the sacred river is believed to carry the dead from this life into the divine realm.

The largest pilgrimage in India is to the sacred city of Allahabad (Prayag), where the Ganges and Yamuna rivers (as well as the Sarasvati, a now-vanished river mentioned in sacred texts) come together. To bathe at the confluence of these three rivers is considered especially auspicious. Every twelve years, the Kumbha Mela festival takes place at Allahabad. During the Kumbha Mela, the largest gathering of humans on Earth takes place as pilgrims converge to bathe in the holy waters in the hope that all their sins will be washed away.

There are many other important pilgrimage sites in India. Some are dedicated to the goddess Devi and are referred to as *Shakti Peethas* ("Seats of Power"). Still others, like the city of Vrindavan in northern India, attract devotees of Krishna, who believe that it is not only the site of the god's birth and childhood but also where he continues to live.

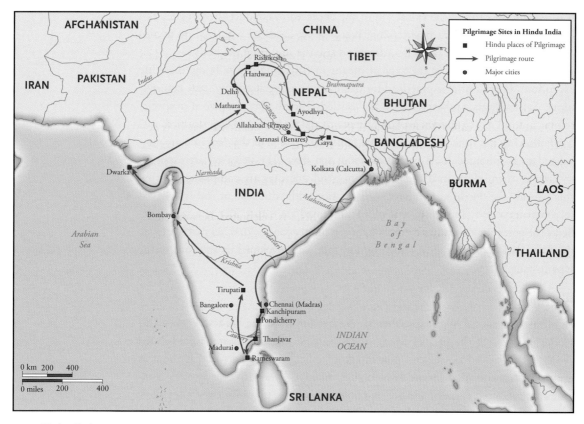

Hindu pilgrimage
routes in India.

Festivals and Holidays

Hindus make use of both solar and lunar calendars, as well as a calendar based on twenty-seven different constellations. All three calendars are consulted to determine when festivals and holidays will be observed. Many Hindu festivals link mythic events to the agricultural cycle. There are also innumerable holidays and observances that commemorate saints and sages, historical events, and sacred sites of regional interest.

Three popular Hindu festivals that are celebrated with many regional variations serve to illustrate the diversity of observances in Hinduism.

Navaratri and Dussehra

Navaratri (Sanskrit, "nine nights") is a holiday cycle celebrating the end of the monsoon season in India. In some regions, Navaratri also commemorates the conclusion of a great war between Rama and the demon-king, Ravana. In other regions, such as southern India and in Bengal, the festival celebrates Devi's battle against the buffalo-demon, Mahisha. To commemorate this conquest, altars are set up with images of the Goddess. For the first three days of the festival, devotees worship Devi in her manifestation as Durga. They then turn their attention to worshiping her as Lakshmi. On the concluding three days, she is worshiped as Sarasvati, the embodiment of knowledge. In Bengal, the eighth day is especially important, as it celebrates Durga slaying Mahisha and is marked with the sacrifice either of black goats or a substitute sacrifice of pumpkins. The festival culminates with street processions of large painted clay icons of Durga that are later dissolved in the nearby river or the sea.

Dussehra, also called Vijayadashami (Sanskrit, "victorious tenth day"), is celebrated on the day after Navarati throughout India as Rama's final victory over the demon Ravana. Dussehra occurs annually on the day of the full moon in the Hindu month of Ashvin (and so, this also determines the calendar dates of Navaratri).

Diwali   Diwali, the five-day "Festival of Lights," is celebrated between mid-October and mid-November (like Dussehra and Navaratri, the dates of Diwali are determined on the basis of the lunar calendar). For many Hindus, it commemorates Rama's rescue of Sita and their heroic return to Ayodhya. Other myths are invoked as an explanation for the festival in different regions of India. During Diwali, oil lamps are set out on doorsteps and window ledges, and floating lamps are placed as offerings in rivers and reservoirs to signify the triumph of good over evil. Fireworks are lit on the night of the new moon, when Lakshmi is worshiped. The third day of Diwali marks the end of the harvest season, and Lakshmi Puja is performed to thank the goddess for the abundance that she has given. New clothes are worn and gifts are exchanged. Diwali is also celebrated by Sikhs and Jains.

Holi   The spring festival of Holi, always celebrated at the vernal equinox, is Hinduism's most colorful holiday. Celebrated in late February or early March (commencing on the full moon day of this period), its festivities take place over two days. On the first night, bonfires are lit, and coconuts are offered as a sacrifice. The following day is a carnival celebration during which social and gender hierarchies are temporarily inverted, as crowds of young and old alike frolic in the streets, spraying colored water and staining one another with brightly colored powders.

Performance Traditions

There is a multitude of performance traditions in Hinduism, many of which cross over into the realm of ritual. Even the act of publicly reciting the *Ramayana* is believed to transform the performance site into sacred space. Hindu sacred performance traditions include many different genres: theater, puppetry, dance, music, storytelling, processions, and street festivals.

Ram Lila   The *Ram Lila* ("The Play of Rama") is one of Hinduism's most popular performance traditions. During the month of September, northern Indian villages and cities host *Ram Lila* festivals to coincide with the festival of Dussehra. These festivals, lasting anywhere from ten days to a month, are costume dramas based on the

Ramayana. The most famous and elaborate *Ram Lila* is sponsored by the Maharaja (the hereditary ruler) of Ramnagar, a city located across the Ganges from Varanasi. The Ramnagar *Ram Lila* attracts pilgrims from all over northern India who come not only to participate in this annual festival but also to have darshan of Rama. The roles of Rama, Lakshmana, and Sita (the three principal characters of the *Ramayana*) are played by young upper-caste boys. For the duration of the *Ram Lila*, these boys are worshiped as the embodiments of divinity. Every evening, a priest waves a lamp, illuminating the principal characters who give darshan to the assembled pilgrims and devotees. Just as in a temple, where God is actively present in the icon, here, too, the very act of performing the *Ramayana* enables the young boys to embody divinity.

Fun and frolic characterize the spring festival of Holi, as participants mischievously smear colored powders or spray colored water on each other.

Sacred Songs: *Bhajan* and *Kirtan*

The term *bhajan* refers specifically to devotional songs in Hinduism and Sikhism. The *bhajan* helps the gathered community to contemplate the divine. This is usually achieved through repetition of key phrases and lines and also through a call-and-response format of singing. Often, profound mystical concepts are presented in simple language that everyone may understand.

Bhajan may be contrasted with *kirtan*, which is not formal in either form or structure, nor is it constrained by setting. *Kirtan* may be performed in lively sing-along processionals that roam the streets. Instruments are not necessary for *kirtan* performance, although they are often used. There are two different types of *kirtan* performances: in one type, the *kirtan* leader and the chorus alternate singing the divine name; and in the other, a hymn is communally recited. *Kirtan* continues to be popular today, especially for the Vaishnava sect. As explained in Chapter 7, *kirtan* is also a vital component of Sikh worship.

Storytelling

An important way in which Hindus learn about the content of their religion is through storytelling. Even today, as in centuries past, professional storytellers continue to travel particular routes throughout India to visit local festivals, where they sing the epics and other myths in all-night performances.

Modern Hindus enjoy sacred narratives through new and equally vibrant media, such as movies, television, and even comic books. Throughout the history of Hinduism, there have been numerous versions of sacred narratives, the *Ramayana* being perhaps the most obvious example. In recent decades, sacred narratives have been invigorated through print, radio, and television, as well as the Internet, with new and imaginative retellings of these ancient stories.

4.10 Hinduism as a Way of Life: Engaging with the World

For the most part, Hinduism developed in a rural setting, in small villages, and

A performance in Mumbai, India, of *Ram Lila*, the very popular enactment of the *Ramayana*.

even in forests. In such rural settings, the hold of centuries-old traditional ways of being Hindu has been very strong. In recent decades, however, there has been a pronounced shift in population from rural to urban settings. Furthermore, India, the world's second largest country in population and its largest democracy, has become a leader in high-tech industries, with cities like Bangalore and Mumbai now epicenters of international corporations. Hinduism, in the face of significant challenges brought on by modernization and the accompanying phenomenon of globalization, is constantly being reshaped. In this final section, we explore how Hindus engage with cultural issues that highlight some recent aspects of such reshaping: religious involvement with politics, personal identity and gender roles, and environmentalism.

Hinduism and Political Forces

In the earlier discussion of Hinduism in the modern period, we noted the Bharatiya Janata Party (BJP) and the Indian National Congress are the two major parties in India's political system, and that in 2014, the BJP won a landslide victory in India's national election. In the years leading up to the 2024 election, the BJP and Prime Minister Narendra Modi became all the more powerful, with consequences involving notable effects on Hinduism and on India's treatment of other religions.

That earlier discussion also considered *hindutva* (Sanskrit, "Hindu-ness") that was introduced by V. D. Savarkar (1883–1966), and insisted on the distinctiveness of Hinduism. Arguing that India was an exclusively "Hindu Nation," Savarakar intended *hindutva* to be a force to unite Hindus in repelling all dangerous foreign influences. Today, Savarakar's *hindutva* ideology has come under an umbrella group called the Sangh Parivar (Family of Associations). The RSS is the cultural wing, the BJP is the political wing, and the Vishwa Hindu Parishad (VHP; World Hindu Council) is the religious wing of the Sangh Parivar. The RSS continues to attract mostly lower-middle-class male youth, who feel empowered by the strong sense of cultural identity that it advocates. The RSS has awakened a deep sense of cultural pride among Hindu youth, but in recent years some of its members have been leading participants in sectarian violence against Muslims.

The BJP has employed aggressive strategies in its campaign to create a thoroughly Hindu India. In 1991, the BJP led a pilgrimage around India gathering bricks to build a temple to Rama in Ayodhya, India. This was to be no ordinary temple. The pilgrims claimed that a fifteenth-century CE Islamic mosque called the Babri Masjid had been erected over an older Hindu temple that marked the exact birthplace of Rama. Their purpose was to tear down the mosque and build a grand Rama temple in its place. Members of Sangh Parivar rallied around the cause, which culminated in 1992 with more than 200,000 participants converging on Ayodhya and demolishing the mosque with their bare hands. RSS youth then targeted the local Muslim community, destroying other mosques, ransacking Muslim homes, raping Muslim women, and murdering Muslim men. The backlash of these events echoed throughout India and Bangladesh, resulting in more than a thousand incidents of riots and communal violence perpetrated by both Hindus and Muslims. By the time calm had been restored, more than 4,000 people had been injured and at least 1,100 had lost their lives. In a highly significant new stage in the ongoing saga, in August 2020 Prime Minister Narendra Modi initiated construction of a new Hindu temple at the Ayodha site. Opponents regard this, and many other moves on the part of the prime minister and his BJP party, as dangerously inflammatory and unfair to the Muslim majority, who also face the prospect of being legally declared of less stature in terms of Indian citizenship than Hindus and members of other religious traditions.

Among other measures, the BJP in the 1980s and 1990s attempted to rewrite Indian history by distributing new school textbooks throughout India, a trend that continues to the present day. These textbooks have reflected the BJP's vision of India as a Hindu nation and Hinduism as a unified, monolithic tradition. Most important, and dangerously, this historical revisionism has minimized Muslim contributions to the development of India and has described India's Muslim rulers as foreign invaders. The RSS also has a strong presence in the Hindu diaspora communities in Europe and North America. Many Hindu emigrants send their children to RSS youth camps to give them a sense of their Hindu identity and cultural pride.

At the current juncture, the future of Hinduism in India seems more than ever inextricably tied to politics and, in particular, to the fortunes of the BJP. Encouraged by the BJP and other nationalist groups and political parties, some of today's Hindus see Hinduism as monolithic, homogeneous, and impermeable, closed off from what they perceive as the corrupting influences of the West and foreign religions.

Personal Identity and Gender Roles

Hinduism's diversity and inclusivity are reflected in the variety of gender identities and roles in Hindu society. The hijras—persons who identify as neither male nor female, and who recently have attained through a major decision by India's Supreme

Court the designation of a third gender—exemplify this diversity. Having in the past served as eunuch overseers of Mughal harems, hijras today occupy various positions in society and enjoy newfound rights, although most work in the sex industry and are under the control of "gurus," themselves older hijras. Many, but not all, are males by birth who have undergone castration or sex change. The fact that hijras are highly visible and, although often forced to endure some degree of harassment and social alienation, legally recognized in Indian society attests to modern Hinduism's generally inclusive stance on gender identity. The same attitude holds, again in general, for Hinduism's perspective on homosexuality.

With regard to the roles of men and women, Hindu tradition has tended to be patriarchal, both subordinating and marginalizing women, while affording men far easier access to positions of authority. Some evidence in the Vedic literature suggests that some women participated in early philosophical movements or dialogues. But for the most part, throughout the history of Hinduism the public roles of women have been secondary to those of men. In the domestic sphere, however, Hindu women have played a significant role.

The *Laws of Manu*, in the course of its extensive coverage of *varnashrama dharma*, includes some statements that confer upon women a relatively high place; for example: "Where women are honoured, there the gods are pleased; but where they are not honoured, no sacred rite yields rewards."[15] At the same time, numerous passages in the *Laws of Manu* and other classical texts subordinate and marginalize women, clearly asserting the predominance of father, husband, and even sons.

The bhakti movements enabled women to overturn social hierarchies. Women poets and saints such as Meera, who lived during the fifteenth century in Rajasthan, rejected marriage, devoted themselves to a spiritual life, and challenged the limits of gender, class, and caste. Today, Hindu women are increasingly assuming leadership roles in India and in the Indian diaspora. Women sometimes act as priests and are beginning to wield influence as spiritual teachers, monastics, and theologians. One of the most important contemporary female gurus is Mata Amritanandamayi Devi (b. 1953). Known to her followers as Ammachi ("Mother") and popularly referred to as "the hugging saint," she is believed by her devotees to be the embodiment of Devi, the divine mother.

In contemporary South Asian and Southeast Asian Hindu society, women are regarded as the custodians of traditional beliefs and ritual for the family. Generally, the social roles of men and women are expressed through clothing and other outward signs. While men wear contemporary slacks, dress shirts, and ties, women prefer traditional modes of dress. Although many men eschew sectarian forehead markings except on ritual occasions, most Hindu women, especially those who are married, adorn their foreheads with the bindi. In addition to performing puja at the home shrine, observing festivals, and encouraging regular temple visits for the family, women also perform pujas for the spiritual welfare of their husbands and children on certain holidays. They also commonly take vows—*vratas*—which we now consider.

Vrata A *vrata* is a vow of temporary self-denial usually undertaken by a woman. This generally involves a short period of fasting, but a *vrata* can also be a vow of silence or a short-term renunciation of anything to which one is attached. A woman usually undertakes a *vrata* for a specific purpose, such as to ensure the health and well-being of her husband and family. There are many special *vratas* observed at specific times throughout the calendar year. One of the most popular, observed by married women throughout southern India, always falls on a Friday in early August. This *vrata* involves a period of purification and fasting, after which the woman invites the goddess Lakshmi into her home. The hope is that Lakshmi, goddess of wealth and good fortune, will bring these things to the home. All *vratas* are vows taken by women on special festival days.

Hindu Environmentalism

In an earlier section of this chapter ("The Divine in Nature"), we noted that, although Hinduism has a long history of reverence for natural entities, this has not always translated into ecological awareness and activism. Recently, a new emphasis on Hindu environmentalism has emerged. True to the wide variety of ways of being Hindu, such activism takes various forms. Here we consider two, both aligned with prominent religious approaches: the ascetic approach of renunciation, and the path of devotion, or bhakti marga.

As we have seen, renunciation, which characterizes the fourth stage of life, that of the sannyasi, is understood to be the most effective life situation for achieving moksha. In a manner similar to that of the Jain ascetics and their focus on ahimsa, or nonviolence (see Chapter 6), the ways of the sannyasi also are extremely environmentally friendly. Hindu renouncers practice environmentalism through denying themselves the various enjoyments in life that threaten in one way or another the ecological well-being of the world. For example, far beyond merely restricting themselves to a vegetarian diet, Hindu ascetics eat hardly anything at all and, it might be said, "tread lightly" through life, thus avoiding inflicting harm on the natural world. To borrow from modern parlance, the carbon footprint of the Hindu renouncer is virtually zero.

Bhakti marga, the Hindu path of devotion, to which the *Bhagavad Gita* gives a certain pride of place, has also contributed to the modern upsurge of interest in Hindu environmentalism. In fact, teachings set forth in the *Bhagavad Gita* contain foundational tenets on which this environmentalism is based.[16] In the *Gita*, Krishna reveals himself as being Brahman, the supreme, unitary reality and ground of all existence. The natural world is both completely dependent upon and permeated by Brahman—reverence for which naturally involves reverence for the natural world. As we have observed, Hindus revere specific natural entities—rivers, mountains, the earth, the sun, and certain trees and animals—as manifestations of Brahman. Means of revering these entities amount to acts of love and adoration—in other words, again in modern parlance, environmental activism.

SEEKING ANSWERS

What Is Ultimate Reality?

Monistic Hindus believe that Brahman is the supreme, unitary reality, the ground of all being. Understood as undifferentiated and without attributes, Brahman manifests itself as the world, in all its particular forms. Thus, all things are inherently divine. Humans are unable to apprehend this ultimate reality because of attachment, delusion, and identification with the limited ego-self. For dualistic or devotional Hindus, ultimate reality is typically understood to be fully embodied in a deity, such as Vishnu or Shiva.

How Should We Live in This World?

Powerfully attracted to the samsaric realm of particulars—our egoistic selves, our relationships, our possessions, and the seemingly countless objects of our desires—we are caught up in the continual cycle of death and rebirth. Hinduism prescribes living in a manner that moves the self toward liberation from samsara. Three paths (margas or yogas) lead to moksha: karma (action), jnana (knowledge), and bhakti (devotion). All the while, Hindus are required to live in conformity with dharma, upholding the cosmic and social order.

What Is Our Ultimate Purpose?

Moksha is liberation from samsara—the continuous cycle of death and rebirth, and the this-worldly realm in which this cycle recurs. Impossible fully to describe from the perspective of this world, the experience of moksha is said to be one of infinite awareness and eternal bliss. For monistic Hindus, moksha involves the full realization of the identity of the self with Brahman rather than with the world. For dualistic or devotional Hindus, moksha is the complete realization of the soul's perpetual and deep loving relationship with God.

REVIEW QUESTIONS

For Review

1. What were the essential features of Vedic religion? How was it different from Hinduism as it is practiced by most Hindus today?
2. In what ways do Hindus seek an experience of the divine?
3. What is the relationship between the ideas of karma, samsara, and dharma?
4. Describe the three margas, or paths, to liberation.
5. Describe the Vedas, Upanishads, epics, and Puranas. What are the most important features of each?

For Further Reflection

1. What are the various ways in which Hindus understand divine reality? How do these compare with those of other religions?
2. What is an avatar? How does the concept of avatar compare with the ways in which other religions speak of God on Earth?
3. How does the traditional system of *varnashrama dharma* compare to systems of social organization with which you are familiar?
4. How were Hindus and Hinduism affected by British colonialism?
5. What are the most important turning points or milestones in the history of Hinduism?

GLOSSARY

arati (ah-rah'tee; Sanskrit) Worship with light, involving the waving of a lamp in front of the deity.

atman (aht'-muhn; Sanskrit) The eternal self or soul that is successively reincarnated until released from samsara through moksha.

avatar (a'vuh-tahr; from Sanskrit *avatara*, "descent") A "descent" of God (usually Vishnu) to Earth in a physical form with the specific goal of aiding the world.

bhakti marga (bhuhk'tee mahr'guh; Sanskrit) The path of devotion.

Brahman (brah'muhn; Sanskrit, "expansive") For monistic Hinduism, the supreme, unitary reality, the ground of all being; for dualistic Hinduism, Brahman can refer to the supreme God (e.g., Vishnu).

brahmin (brah'min; Sanskrit) A member of the priestly class of the *varna* or caste system.

dalit (dah'lit; Sanskrit, "oppressed"; Marathi, "broken") Self-designation of people who had traditionally been classified as untouchables or outcastes.

darshan (duhr'shuhn; from Sanskrit *darshana*, "to see") Worship through simultaneously seeing and being seen by a deity in the presence of its image.

dharma (dahr'muh; Sanskrit) Duty, righteousness, "religion"; basis for living in a way that upholds the cosmic and social order.

hindutva (hin-doot'vuh; Sanskrit, "Hindu-ness") A modern term that encompasses the ideology of Hindu nationalism.

jati (jah'tee; Sanskrit, "birth group") One of thousands of endogamous groups or subcastes, each equal in social and ritual status.

jnana marga (juh-nah'nuh mahr'guh) The path of knowledge.

karma (kahr'muh; Sanskrit, "action") Action; also the consequences of action.

karma marga (kahr'muh mahr'guh) The path of ethical and ritual works, or "action."

kshatriya (ksha'-tree-uh; Sanskrit) A member of the warrior and administrator class of the *varna* or caste system.

mantra (mahn'truh; Sanskrit, "sacred utterance") A ritual formula recited to produce a spiritual effect.

maya (mah'yah; Sanskrit, "magic" or "illusion") In the Vedas, the magical power the gods used to create this world; in Vedanta philosophy, illusion that veils the mind.

moksha (mohk'shuh; Sanskrit, "release") Liberation, the final release from samsara.

OM (ohm; from three Sanskrit letters: *A-U-M*) The primordial sound through which the universe is manifested.

puja (pooh'jah; Sanskrit, "worship") Generally, worship; usually the offering before an image of the deity of fruit, incense, or flowers.

Purana (poo-rah'nuh; Sanskrit, "ancient") A compendium of myth, usually with a sectarian emphasis.

samsara (sahm-sah'ruh; Sanskrit) The continuing cycle of birth, death, and rebirth; also the this-worldly realm in which the cycle recurs.

sannyasi (suhn-yah'see; Sanskrit) Renouncer in the fourth stage (ashrama) of life.

Shaiva (shai'vuh; Sanskrit) A devotee of Shiva.

Shakta (shahk'-tah; Sanskrit) A devotee of the Great Goddess, Devi.

shruti (shroo'tee; Sanskrit, "that which is heard") Term denoting the category of Vedic literature accepted by orthodox Hindus as revealed truth.

shudra (shooh'druh; Sanskrit) A member of the servant class of the *varna* or caste system.

smriti (smree'tee; Sanskrit, "tradition") Term denoting the vast category of Hindu sacred texts that is not shruti.

Tantra (tuhn'truh; Sanskrit, "loom") System of ideas and practices that potentiate sudden liberation from samsara; also a form of sacred text detailing the ideas and practices.

Upanishads (oo-pah'nee-shuhds; Sanskrit, "sitting down near [a teacher]") Philosophical texts from the later period of Vedic literature, also called Vedanta ("end of the Vedas").

Vaishnava (vaish'nuh-vuh; Sanskrit) A devotee of Vishnu and his avatars.

vaishya (vaish'yuh; Sanskrit) A member of the producer (farmer and merchant) class of the *varna* or caste system.

varna (vahr'nuh; Sanskrit, "color") Caste or class; the four main classes form the basis of the traditional hierarchical organization of Hindu society.

Vedanta (vay-dahn'tuh; Sanskrit, "end of the Vedas") Synonym for Upanishads; prominent Hindu philosophical school.

Vedas (vay'duhz; from Sanskrit *veda*, "knowledge") Broadly, all Vedic literature; narrowly, four ancient collections (samhitas) of hymns and other religious material.

yoga (yoh'guh; Sanskrit, "yoking" or "uniting") Generally, uniting of the self with God; sometimes used as an alternative to marga when referring to the three main paths to liberation; also (normally capitalized: Yoga) one of the six philosophical schools, focusing on moral, physical, and spiritual practices leading to liberation.

SUGGESTIONS FOR FURTHER READING

Eck, Diana. *Darsan: Seeing the Divine Image in India.* New York: Columbia University Press, 1998. An excellent discussion on the significance of darshan and traditions of Hindu temple worship.

Flood, Gavin. *An Introduction to Hinduism.* Cambridge: Cambridge University Press, 1996. A concise and in-depth study of Hinduism.

Flood, Gavin, ed. *The Blackwell Companion to Hinduism.* Oxford: Blackwell, 2003. A presentation on select special topics that are key to understanding Hindu belief and practice.

Hawley, John Stratton, and Mark Juergensmeyer. *Songs of the Saints of India.* Oxford: Oxford University Press, 2006. A survey of the lives of medieval *bhakti* saints, with excellent translation of some of their poetry.

Hawley, John Stratton, and Vasudha Narayanan, eds. *The Life of Hinduism.* Berkeley: University of California Press, 2006. Special topical articles that explore personal voices and perspectives on Hindu life experience.

Klostermaier, Klaus K. *Hindu Writings: A Short Introduction to the Major Sources.* Oxford: One World Publications, 2000. A keen survey of excerpts from many of the important textual sources that inform Hindu belief.

Knipe, David M. *Hinduism: Experiments in the Sacred.* New York: HarperCollins, 1991. A dependable and clear study organized based on the history of the tradition; includes a helpful timeline and glossaries.

ONLINE RESOURCES

"Hinduism," The Pluralism Project, Harvard University
Harvard University's Pluralism Project, a valuable source in general for the study of the world's religions, provides extensive and reliable information on Hinduism, including Hinduism in North America.

Internet Sacred Text Archive (Hinduism)
The Internet Sacred Text Archive provides an excellent array of the many genres of Hindu sacred texts with multiple public domain translations of key works.

The Sri Vaishnava Home Page
The Sri Vaishnava homepage is designed primarily for adherents to this important sect of Hinduism, yet it is accessible and informative for outsiders.

The Shaivam.org Site
The Shaivam.org site, self-described as the "Abode of God Shiva on the Internet," is designed primarily for devotees but is also useful for academic study.

Buddhism

Chapter Outline

5.1   Describe the teachings of the Buddha about the nature of things, suffering, and how suffering can be brought to an end.

5.2   Identify the essential features of Theravada Buddhism.

5.3   Describe the teachings of Mahayana Buddhism about the nature of reality, buddhas, and bodhisattvas.

5.4   Identify the distinctive features of the Pure Land, Tiantai, Nichiren, Zen, and Vajrayana forms of Mahayana Buddhism.

5.5   Describe how Theravada and Mahayana Buddhism came to parts of Asia beyond India and where each became predominant.

5.6   Describe when and how Buddhism came to the West and the nature of Buddhism in the West today.

5.7   Describe how Buddhist practices reflect the teachings of Buddhism.

5.8   Explain how Buddhist principles are evident in Buddhist engagement with issues related to identity, gender, inclusion, and the environment.

TODAY IS VESAK. Here in Chiang Mai, northern Thailand's largest city, throngs of Thais and tourists crowd the streets and fill the city's 300 Buddhist temples. This is a day to honor the **Buddha**, the Awakened One, who learned great truths about the cause and cure for human suffering and taught them to the world. It is also a day for expressing gratitude to the order of Buddhist monks who have preserved the **Dharma**—the teachings of the Buddha—for twenty-five centuries. More than 1,500 monks will receive gifts of food and drink from thousands of laypeople during this celebration in Chiang Mai.

Vesak commemorates the birth, awakening, and death of the Buddha. According to tradition, all three occurred miraculously on the same day of the year, the full moon day of the lunar month of Visakha. On the Western calendar, this places Vesak sometime in May or, less frequently, in June.

Vesak is a time when Buddhists everywhere make a special effort to observe the ethical teachings of the Buddha. Many visit temples to hear sermons

Buddhists offer alms to monks during a celebration of Vesak in Chiang Mai, Thailand.

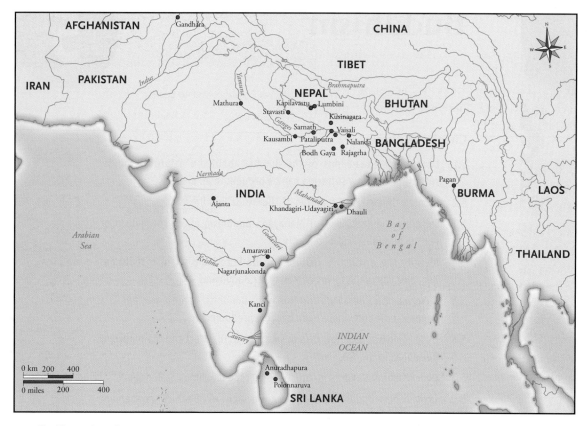

Significant sites of
Early Buddhism.

given by monks and leave offerings of flowers and candles. In Chiang Mai there is a special way of expressing devotion to the Buddha. At sunset on the day before Vesak, devotees
light candles inside paper lanterns and set out on a nine-mile trek to the summit of a nearby
mountain. Their destination is Wat Phrathart Doi Suthep, a famous temple that holds relics
of the Buddha. Once there, they circle three times around the temple's Bhote chapel holding incense sticks and lotus buds. Then, at dawn, they make offerings for the support of the
temple's monks.

According to an ancient story, as the Buddha lay dying, he told his disciples there was no
reason to weep; his death would be in accordance with the impermanence of all things. They
were welcome to honor him with offerings and devotions when he was gone, he said, but it
would be more important for them to honor the Dharma and strive to follow its teachings.
Like the Buddha's disciples, those who understand the meaning of Vesak today honor the
Buddha with simple expressions of devotion and their commitment to follow his teachings.

There are nearly 500 million Buddhists in the world today, about 7 percent
of the global population.[1] They belong to a vast number of Buddhist
groups. These differ in important ways, but all trace their origins back

to the Buddha, our point of departure in this chapter. After examining the Buddha's life and teachings, we will explore the teachings of Buddhism's Theravada and Mahayana traditions, survey the history of Buddhism, and then review some important features of the Buddhist way of life.

5.1 The Teachings of Buddhism: The Life and Teachings of the Buddha

The Buddha lived in northern India nearly 2,500 years ago. It was the Buddha who set in motion the "Wheel of the Dharma," the body of teachings about the cause and end of suffering that lies at the heart of Buddhism.

The Life of the Buddha

Written primarily in Sanskrit and Pali, two languages of ancient India, our earliest texts about the Buddha were composed long after he lived. None is a biography of the Buddha; however, some describe events in the Buddha's life. Although their accounts are sometimes in conflict, their many points of agreement have served for centuries as elements of the traditional story of the Buddha's life. This is the story we will tell here.

The Early Life of the Buddha   Most scholars believe that Siddhartha Gautama, who was to become the Buddha, lived and taught c. 485–405 BCE. According to tradition, Siddhartha's father was the ruler of a small kingdom that straddled part of what is now the border of India and Nepal.

Siddhartha's father was determined that his son would follow in his footsteps. Fearing that Siddhartha would be drawn to the spiritual life if he became aware of suffering in the world, he tried to shield his son from the harsh realities of life. And so Siddhartha grew up living a sheltered and luxurious life with no hint of pain. In time, he married a princess, Yasodhara, with whom he had a son. There were many reasons for Siddhartha to find happiness and satisfaction in life, and yet he grew restless.

TIMELINE
Buddhism

c. 485–405 BCE	Life of the Buddha.
c. 405 BCE	First Buddhist Council.
c. 305 BCE	Second Buddhist Council.
c. 272–231 BCE	Emperor Ashoka promotes Buddhism in India.
c. 250 BCE	Third Buddhist Council.
c. 247 BCE	Mahinda, a monk and son of Ashoka, brings Buddhism to Sri Lanka.
c. 25 BCE	First written text of Pali Canon produced in Sri Lanka.
c. 1–100 CE	Buddhism arrives in Central Asia and China.
1–200	Beginning of Mahayana Buddhism in India; composition of *Lotus Sutra*.
300–400	Buddhism arrives in Korea.
300–500	Beginning of Vajrayana Buddhism in India.
c. 320–550	Gupta Dynasty promotes Buddhism in India.
400–450	Beginning of Chan (Zen) Buddhism, in China.
552	Buddhism arrives in Japan.
600–800	Buddhism arrives in Tibet.
c. 1100	Construction of Angkor Wat in Cambodia.
c. 1200	Muslim conquest brings virtual end to Buddhism in India.
c. 1800	Western scholars begin to study Buddhism.
1890–1921	T. W. Rhys Davids translates Buddhist texts into English.
1893	Buddhist leaders speak at The World's Parliament of Religions in Chicago.
1959	Tibet's Dalai Lama flees to India.
1970	Development of Engaged Buddhism.

Siddhartha cuts his hair. Mural depicting the life of Buddha, Jogyesa Temple, Seoul, South Korea.

At the age of twenty-nine, Siddhartha ventured outside the protected world of the palace. Accompanied by his charioteer, he saw things that changed his life. Buddhists call these the Four Sights. The first was a frail old man. Siddhartha, who had never seen old age, asked if he, too, would become old and feeble. He was dismayed when his charioteer assured him that he would. The second sight was a man afflicted by disease. Sickness, said the charioteer, is also a part of human life. The third sight, a corpse being carried off to cremation, was terrifying. Death, too, said the charioteer, is something no one can escape. Siddhartha now saw through the illusion his father had created and was filled with despair at the inescapable truths of old age, sickness, and death and the suffering they bring. It was not until he witnessed the fourth sight that he found some reason to hope. Sitting by the side of a road, he saw a wandering ascetic, homeless and without possessions, who seemed to be content.

The Great Going Forth   For Siddhartha, the ascetic pointed the way. To return to life within the palace would be to hide from the truth. He resolved instead to face it. He would renounce the life he had lived, become an ascetic, and search for the truth about suffering. Was it inevitable, or could something be done about it? One night, Siddhartha kissed his sleeping wife and son good-bye and silently slipped away. As soon as he was alone in the forest, he took off his expensive clothing and cut off his hair, symbolically severing the bonds that tied him to his old life.

At first, Siddhartha turned to ascetic sages renowned for their wisdom, becoming a disciple first of one, then another. They taught him meditation techniques and yogic disciplines, but these left him unsatisfied. He then committed himself to extreme asceticism. After a time of wandering, he found a grove of trees by a river. Joined there by five other ascetics who wished to follow his example, he began to practice severe austerities in the hope they would clarify his thought. For five years, Siddhartha wore rags and did not bathe. He slept on thorns and in cremation grounds strewn with bones and ash. According to some accounts, he ate as little as a single grain of rice a day. But he did not gain the knowledge he sought.

One day, Siddhartha overheard a music teacher explaining to his student that a string wound too tightly will break, whereas one that is too loose makes no sound at all. To make music, said the teacher, one must find the midpoint between these extremes. These words brought Siddhartha to the realization that neither sensual indulgence nor self-denial is helpful in the quest for liberation from suffering. Because both weaken the body and the mind, the best path lies between them.

This principle of the **Middle Way** was to become foundational in Buddhism. According to tradition, it was at this moment that a woman came to Siddhartha with a bowl of porridge. He ate it, bathed himself, and then returned to his companions, but they left him when he told them he would no longer practice asceticism.

Awakening Siddhartha's resolve was now unshakable. At a village in northern India now known as Bodh Gaya, he sat beneath a fig tree and vowed to remain there in meditation until he gained the understanding he sought. One night, as he sat under a full moon, Siddhartha's mind moved through progressively deeper states of meditation in which his awareness brightened and expanded. As his vision sharpened, he began to see reality with extraordinary clarity. At first, he saw his countless thousands of past lives and the past lives of all other beings. He then saw how karma, the law of causes and effects, had been at work throughout time, conditioning the existence of all beings as they took form and then passed away. He saw the truth about suffering, the cause of suffering, and the path that leads to the end of suffering. Finally, Siddhartha saw through and eliminated the last traces of ignorance in his mind so that his awareness was perfected. He had awakened.

"Calling the Earth to Witness." According to tradition, the demon Mara afflicted the Buddha with powerful temptations to give up his quest for understanding. Ignoring them, the Buddha touched his hand to the ground, thereby calling upon the Earth to testify to his unshakable resolve, demonstrated throughout his many past lives, to achieve awakening.

According to Buddhist tradition, Siddhartha was not the first to attain awakening. Buddhists believe that others before and after him became, and will become, buddhas. But it is from *this* buddha that they have received the Dharma, and so for them he is *the* Buddha, the Awakened One. The Buddha's awakening brought an end to the desire that causes suffering. It also brought him freedom from rebirth, which results from attachment to the world. Freed from the disturbances caused by attachment, his mind came to rest in its natural state, and he was filled with joy. He had attained **nirvana** (Sanskrit; Pali, nibbana), the "extinguishing" of unwholesome desire and the suffering it brings. For many days the Buddha remained close to the site of his awakening. Then, moved by compassion for others, he set out to teach what he had learned.

Beginning of the Buddhist Community The Buddha went first to a deer park at Sarnath, near modern Varanasi, where the five ascetics who had abandoned him were still practicing harsh austerities. Seeing that he had broken through to some new understanding, they gathered around the Buddha, who began to teach them. In his first sermon, which came to be known as the Sermon in the Deer Park, he told them of the Middle Way and set forth the Four Noble Truths and the Noble

Rock-cut reclining statue of the Buddha preparing to enter *parinirvana*, in a cave shrine at Ajanta, Maharashtra State, India. Fifth century CE.

Eightfold Path, which describe the cause and cure of suffering. The ascetics became the first followers of the Buddha and the first members of the **sangha** (Sanskrit, "community"), the community of Buddhist monks and nuns.

It was not long before others joined the sangha. Among them were Rahula, the Buddha's son, and Ananda, a cousin who became his most devoted disciple. The Buddha wandered across northern India for more than four decades, teaching, ordaining monks and nuns, and accepting lay followers.

The Parinirvana of the Buddha The earthly existence of the Buddha came to an end in his eightieth year, forty-five years after his awakening. He and Ananda had stopped at the village of Kushinagara and eaten at the home of a blacksmith. Something in the meal was tainted, causing the Buddha to become ill. In a grove just outside the village, Ananda made a bed for him between two trees. His monks soon began to gather at the scene, frantically seeking a final bit of the Buddha's wisdom. When they asked what they would do without him to teach them, he responded that the Dharma would always be their guide. Not long after this the Buddha closed his eyes, went deep into meditation, and left this world. Without attachments to the world, and unbound by karmic forces that would have drawn him into another incarnation, he passed into **parinirvana**, the complete and final entry into nirvana.

What the Buddha Taught

In his awakening, the Buddha learned great truths about the cause of suffering and the means for ending it. These truths constitute the core of the Dharma. We saw in Chapter 4 that in Hindu usage the Sanskrit word *dharma* has a wide range of meanings, including "law," "duty," and "righteousness." In Buddhist contexts, Dharma generally refers to the teachings of the Buddha.

Interdependent Origination

We will begin our investigation of the Buddha's teaching with his doctrine of **interdependent origination**, also known as dependent origination, because so much of the Dharma is based on it.

To most of us, the world seems to be a composite system consisting of different and separate things. The chair you are sitting in certainly appears to exist on its own, apart from all other things in the room. And it is likely that you see yourself as existing independently of everyone and everything around you.

Probing deeply into the nature of reality, the Buddha saw things very differently. He taught that reality is a complex of interrelated and interdependent phenomena in which nothing exists apart from anything else. Instead, all things depend on all other things for their coming-into-existence—that is, for their origination. Of course, everyone recognizes at some level that this is the case. Someone built your chair, for example, and your parents had something to do with you. But the Buddha's teaching goes far beyond this in explaining that the coming-into-existence of every phenomenon depends on other phenomena which are themselves dependent upon still other phenomena, and so on. All things originate in a state of dependence on all other things.

Of course, things also *remain* in existence after their origination—or at least they *seem* to. How can this be explained? And what *are* things, really? Here, again, the Buddha taught that all things are interdependent—so much so, in fact, that they have no existence whatsoever *in and of themselves*. Once again, take your chair as an example. Probing deeply, you will find that it consists of different elements: height, width, wood, legs, texture, firmness, color, and so on. But you will not find "chair." Instead, your chair exists only as a complex of "not chair" elements, and only for as long as these constituent parts remain together. And so it is with all things. Each thing exists only as a collection of other elements, having no independent existence of its own.

Impermanence   The Buddha's teaching about impermanence holds that all things are always changing. Nothing remains the same, even for a moment. All things are always in a state of *becoming*. For example, imagine a blade of grass. It may seem static even if we observe it for hours, but the truth is that it is growing and becoming a different blade of grass in every moment.

Suffering   The Buddha's teaching about suffering is central to the Dharma. He once said, "I have taught one thing and one thing only, suffering and the cessation of suffering." The Buddha taught that suffering is caused by *tanha*, a Pali word often translated as "desire" that can also mean "craving," "clinging," or "thirsting." All work well is describing our wanting to hold on to things. Of course, in a world in which all things are always changing nothing can be held. Sadly, we are ignorant of this fact, and so we form attachments to things we want in our lives and aversions to things we don't want. These three mental states of ignorance, attachment, and aversion are known as the Three Poisons and are the root causes of suffering.

The Buddha understood suffering as a "dissatisfactoriness"—a sense that something is "off" somehow or that things are "not quite right"—that is present throughout our lives. This is the meaning of **dukkha**, the Pali word found in early Buddhist texts. Understood in this way, we can see that suffering can take innumerable forms. Wanting something you don't have causes suffering. Fearing that something you have might be lost causes suffering. Believing that you cannot be happy unless you have something causes suffering. Being averse to something causes suffering. Wanting things to stay the same causes suffering. Wanting things to be different causes suffering. Stress and worry cause suffering. Envy and jealousy cause suffering. Anger, hatred, grief, loneliness, and frustration cause suffering. Finally, the unhealthy influences these mental phenomena have on the body cause suffering.

No-self The Buddha taught that there is no unchanging self or identity in things, including ourselves. This is the essence of the Buddha's teaching about no-self (Sanskrit, **anatman**; Pali, anatta). Of course, the doctrine of no-self does not suggest that you do not exist. Clearly, you do. But just as there is nothing we could call "chair" among the many elements of the chair we described earlier, there is no solid and unchanging "you" among the fundamental components of your own existence. The Buddha referred to these fundamental components as **skandhas** (Sanskrit, "bundles"), five ever-changing phenomena that give rise to our sense of self: our material form, our feelings, our perceptions, our mental constructions, and our awareness. Because these are always in flux, we are as well. Each of us has an existence that is always changing in response to changes happening throughout the great web of interdependent and impermanent phenomena that make up reality.

It can be difficult to accept this idea. After all, we are attached to our individual identities and expect to keep them for as long as we live—and, perhaps, even after we die. No-self might seem to imply a destruction or annihilation of something we like very much—ourselves. But this is not the case. Instead, the Buddha taught that what we call the self is not concrete, permanent, or independent of other things. The great benefit he saw in this truth is that it opens the way to living without the suffering that arises fro\m a false notion of self. The Buddha found the full realization of this ideal in his awakening and in the bliss of nirvana.

The Four Noble Truths and the Noble Eightfold Path We saw earlier that the Buddha first taught the **Four Noble Truths** and the **Noble Eightfold Path** in his Sermon in the Deer Park. Now that we have investigated his teachings about the nature of reality, we are in a good position to understand these central features of the Dharma.

THE FOUR NOBLE TRUTHS

1. Suffering is inherent in life.
2. The cause of suffering is desire.
3. There is a way to put an end to desire and suffering.
4. The way is the Noble Eightfold Path.

The First Noble Truth acknowledges that suffering is a part of human existence. The Second Noble Truth identifies desire as the cause of suffering. The good news is that there is a way to end desire and the suffering it causes. This is the message of the Third Noble Truth. The Fourth Noble Truth tells us that the solution to the problem of desire and suffering is the Noble Eightfold Path.

Treading the Noble Eightfold Path, we follow in the footsteps of the Buddha in eradicating ignorance, attachment, and aversion, the causes of suffering. Moving beyond ignorance to an understanding of the true nature of things—that they are impermanent and interdependent, with no thing having its own existence or identity—we no longer desire them, for we know they are not at all what we once imagined them to be. The suffering caused by attachment and aversion subsides and is replaced by equanimity, a peace of mind that is perfected in nirvana, as the Buddha discovered.

The eight aspects of the Noble Eightfold Path are sometimes divided into three divisions, each with its own goal. The first includes Right View and Right Intention. Here, the aim is to ensure that one understands and accepts the Buddha's teachings about impermanence, suffering, and no-self and is committed to striving for goals consistent with them. The second division has the purpose of cultivating ethical conduct through Right Speech, Right Action, and Right Livelihood. The Buddha taught that unethical conduct is an obstacle to mental clarity. For this reason, destructive speech, immoral behavior, and making a living in a way that is harmful to oneself or others are to be avoided. The third division promotes concentration. Through Right Effort, one seeks to eliminate all qualities of the mind that give rise to unwholesome thought and action and to encourage those that produce more positive effects. Right Mindfulness is the observation of thoughts, feelings, and all

THE NOBLE EIGHTFOLD PATH

1. **Right View**: seeing things as they are, in accordance with the Buddha's teachings.
2. **Right Intention**: making a commitment to tread the path to awakening in accordance with the Buddha's teachings.
3. **Right Speech**: addressing others with kindness, while abstaining from lying, divisive or abusive speech, and idle chatter.
4. **Right Action**: abstaining from killing, stealing, and sexual misconduct.
5. **Right Livelihood**: making a living in a way that harms no one and benefits all.
6. **Right Effort**: striving to abandon all thought and action that is harmful to oneself or others and to cultivate virtues that benefit oneself and others.
7. **Right Mindfulness**: focused awareness of the body and mind and the phenomena arising within and affecting each.
8. **Right Concentration**: cultivating concentration that leads to equanimity beyond pleasure and pain.

other phenomena that occur in the body and mind. Finally, Right Concentration involves progress through four stages of concentration until one achieves a state of nonattachment and equanimity.

Karma and Rebirth

In the West, **karma** (Sanskrit, "action") is often understood as a force that shapes our lives in good and bad ways in accordance with the good and bad things we do. Although there is some truth in this, the Buddha's teaching is not so simple. The Buddha taught that karma has as much to do with the intentions that precede our actions as with the consequences of our actions. For this reason, we can understand karma as "intentional action." When our intentions arise from the Three Poisons of ignorance, attachment, and aversion—the primary causes of suffering—our lives are shaped in ways that make them more difficult. However, when our intentions are consistent with the ideals of wisdom, nonattachment, and nonaversion, our lives are shaped in ways that make them more pleasant and allow us to make progress to nirvana and an end to suffering.

According to the Buddha's doctrine of no-self, our current sense of self arises from the interrelationship of the five skandhas. Death brings a separation of the skandhas and an end to this sense of self. The Buddha taught that nothing permanent or substantial remains, nothing that might pass from one life to another. And yet there is a connection between one life and the next, for the last moment of consciousness in one life sparks the first moment of consciousness in the next within the same mental continuum. It is in this sense that there is a kind of rebirth.

Nirvana

The ultimate goal of Buddhist practice, nirvana is an "extinguishing" or "blowing out" of desire that leads to suffering and a liberation from rebirth in **samsara**. Because this is utterly unlike anything one might experience with ordinary awareness, no comparison is possible. For this reason, the Buddha said very little about nirvana.

VOICES: An Interview with Reverend Bob O.

Reverend Bob O., known to many as RB, served for many years as a priest in a Jodo Shinshu temple. Jodo Shinshu is a Japanese form of Pure Land Buddhism.

How has Buddhism contributed to your sense of purpose or goals in life?

When I was about twenty, I asked my mentor, Dr. Mokusen Miyuki, "What is the goal of Buddhism?" He responded gently, "To become a true human being of no rank." This was a goal I thought worthy of pursuing in my life. Years later, I was a priest in a temple that served 800 families. One evening, some college-bound students who were considering their own goals in life asked me about mine. I told them that many years earlier I had decided not to seek great accomplishments or wealth. Instead, my goal was to live in such a way that I could let go of life at any time with no regret. To me, this is a very Buddhistic goal, for with the clear awareness that everything is impermanent we try to live mindfully, simply cherishing every moment. Also, Buddhism's essential teaching about the fundamental oneness of things awakens kindness in our hearts. In feeling our shared oneness, our sense of "self" begins to fade and we begin to understand that in the realm of oneness there is no "rank" that separates us. For me, trying to live as "a true human being of no rank" is both my goal and my fulfillment.

How do the teachings and values of Buddhism shape your life, especially when you make major life decisions involving such things as education, career, and marriage or partnership?

Reverend Bob O.

Dogen Zenji once said, "To pursue Buddhism is to know the self." Everything is constantly changing, so self-awareness is a lifelong, ongoing process. Being in touch with our ever-changing selves helps us to make decisions that may well shape our lives. I smile looking back on a much younger me when my girlfriend told me she wanted to break up. When I asked why, she said, "You have much potential but no ambition." I felt like she had held up a mirror. I responded, "That's true. I have little ambition. But I feel a great sense of purpose." I was sad, of course, but I knew that we were not a good match and I remain grateful to her for helping me to better see the person I was becoming. I still have very little ambition. But I do have a clear sense of purpose in seeking to become a true human being of no rank.

How does Buddhism help you when you experience a significant loss or disappointment in life?

Buddhism teaches that all things are impermanent and interdependent. Nothing lasts forever, yet all things are interconnected and one in the vast karmic fabric of the universe. These two teachings have grounded me when I have experienced difficult losses of loved ones.

Buddhism did not take away the deep pain of loss. But its teaching regarding the impermanence of all things helped me to accept it. And its teaching of interdependence helped me to see, with Wisdom Eyes, that although someone has died, we are never separated, for all things are interwoven in the karmic fabric of reality. Impermanence and interdependence are two teachings that help us to see things as they are. With awareness that nothing is forever, we begin to live with an ever-deepening gratitude. In understanding that all things are interconnected and one, kindness and caring flow naturally from our hearts.

5.2 The Teachings of Buddhism: Theravada Buddhism

Now that we are familiar with the life and teachings of the Buddha, we are ready to turn to Buddhism itself. In this section, we will see how monks sought to define early Buddhism at a series of councils and how these gave rise to Theravada Buddhism. We will also briefly survey the essential teachings and texts of Theravada Buddhism.

The Buddhist Councils

According to early Buddhist accounts, not long after the parinirvana of the Buddha a council of monks was convened at the town of Rajagriha in northeast India. This was the first in a series of councils that defined Buddhism by addressing key doctrinal and practical issues as they arose at particular times and places in its early history.

The First and Second Buddhist Councils

The First Buddhist Council was convened c. 405 BCE. According to an ancient tradition, this was an assembly of 500 monks who had been disciples of the Buddha. Recalling that the Buddha had urged them to look to the Dharma as their guide after his death, they established an oral canon of his teachings. In this way, the First Council established the Dharma as the primary authority in the sangha.

Although monks dominated the proceedings at this and later councils, early Buddhist literature attests to the influence of women in the earliest years of Buddhism's history. For example, spiritual poems written by nuns were preserved along with those of monks in the *Therigatha* and *Theragatha* (*Poems of Elder Nuns* and *Poems of Elder Monks*).

The Second Buddhist Council (c. 305 BCE) was convened at Vaisali in northern India after monks in that region began to relax monastic rules that had been in place since the time of the Buddha. These included prohibitions of the handling of money and eating after midday as well as protocols for monastic assemblies. When the Second Buddhist Council ruled that there should be no relaxation of monastic rules, the defeated minority withdrew and formed a separate school. Scholars point to this event as the first split in the Buddhist community.

Ashoka and the Third Buddhist Council

While early Buddhist monks were working out their differences, the political situation in India was changing dramatically. In the third century BCE, a ruler came to power who was the first great champion of Buddhism. This was Ashoka (r. c. 272–231 BCE), the renowned emperor of India's Mauryan Dynasty who brought nearly all of the Indian subcontinent under his rule.

Despite his success as a conqueror, Ashoka came to regret the violence and suffering he had imposed on others. Abandoning his expansionist policies, he committed himself to peace, became a Buddhist, and embarked on a program of social reform grounded in Buddhist ethics. In order to improve the welfare of his subjects, Ashoka published edicts endorsing Buddhist ideals such as moral purity, self-awareness, nonviolence, and respect for all religions. Inscribed on stone pillars set up throughout his empire, Ashoka's "rock edicts" are our earliest evidence for the widespread promotion of Buddhism.

According to tradition, it was Ashoka who convened the Third Buddhist Council at Pataliputra in northern India c. 250 BCE. Attended by 1,000 monks, the council sent missionaries to lands beyond India and addressed disputes concerning the interpretation of the Dharma. It appears that it also recognized one sect, which eventually gave rise to Theravada Buddhism, as having most faithfully preserved the teachings of the Buddha.

Theravada Buddhism

Theravada Buddhism views itself as representing the original and authentic teaching of the Buddha. Today, Theravada (Sanskrit, "Way of the Elders") is the predominant Buddhist tradition in Sri Lanka, Thailand, Cambodia, Laos, and Myanmar (Burma).

Theravada Buddhism emphasizes the pursuit of nirvana solely through one's own effort. The Buddha is understood as a human being who attained nirvana and taught the Dharma to humanity so that others might find freedom from suffering and attain nirvana themselves. Theravada Buddhists revere the Buddha but believe he is no longer available to assist his followers. For this reason, Theravada emphasizes the Buddha's admonition in his last words to his disciples: "Work out your own salvation with diligence."

One of many marble slabs containing text and commentary from the *Tipitaka* or Pali Canon, Kuthodaw Pagoda, Mandalay, Myanmar (Burma).

Theravada's heroes are the **arhats**, "worthy ones" who have attained awakening through their diligence in following the Noble Eightfold Path. In most cases, arhats have been monks and nuns who devoted themselves to study and meditation within monastic communities. In Theravada countries, these communities have always played a central role in society. Monks, in particular, have been responsible for safeguarding the Dharma by preserving and teaching the texts in which it is found. They perform rituals during festivals and at ceremonies marking births, marriages, deaths, and other important occasions. Monks have also served as advisors to government officials. In return for the contributions monastic communities make to society, lay communities give them financial and material support.

Theravada Texts   Theravada claims to follow the original teachings of the Buddha as found in an early collection of Pali texts known as the **Pali Canon**, or *Tipitaka*. According to tradition, four centuries after the Buddha's death a group of 500 monks met in Sri Lanka to commit his teachings to writing for the first time. As there were already significant differences in oral reports of what the Buddha had said, these monks were intent on ensuring that the most accurate account of the Buddha's teachings was preserved in written form. The name *Tipitaka* (Pali, "three baskets") reflects the ancient practice of storing manuscripts in baskets.

The first of the three baskets, the *Vinaya Pitaka* ("Discipline Basket"), contains rules for monastic life prescribed by the Buddha. The second basket, the *Sutta*

Pitaka ("Discourse Basket"), consists of *suttas* (Sanskrit, **sutras**), texts that contain the discourses and sermons of the Buddha. The third basket is the *Abhidhamma Pitaka* ("Basket of Texts about the Dharma"). These texts systemize and analyze the teachings found in the *Sutta Pitaka*, exploring topics such as psychology, cosmology, and meditation.

The opening verses of the *Dhammapada*, an early collection of sayings of the Buddha found in the Pali Canon, present one of the key concepts in Theravada Buddhism: we are responsible for our own happiness:

> What we are today comes from our thoughts of yesterday, and our present thoughts build our life of tomorrow: our life is the creation of our mind.
>
> If a man speaks or acts with an impure mind, suffering follows him as the wheel of the cart follows the beast that draws the cart.
>
> What we are today comes from our thoughts of yesterday, and our present thoughts build our life of tomorrow: our life is the creation of our mind.
>
> If a man speaks or acts with a pure mind, joy follows him as his own shadow.[2]

5.3   The Teachings of Buddhism: Mahayana Buddhism

Mahayana Buddhism is the largest of the Buddhist traditions. This is suggested by its name—Sanskrit *mahayana* means "great vehicle"—as well as by the many schools and sects that make Mahayana a large and accommodating tradition with room for Buddhists of all kinds. Mahayana is the dominant form of Buddhism in China, Tibet, Mongolia, Japan, South Korea, Vietnam, Indonesia, Malaysia, and Taiwan.

Mahayana differs from Theravada in emphasizing the ability of laypeople to make progress toward awakening and an end to suffering even while engaged in family and social life. And unlike Theravada, which says we can attain nirvana only through our own effort, Mahayana teaches that there are buddhas and bodhisattvas who can help us along the way.

The *Trikaya* Doctrine

The two traditions also differ in their understanding of the Buddha. As we have seen, Theravada Buddhism understands the Buddha as a human being, albeit an extraordinary human being. Mahayana Buddhism's teaching about the Buddha is more complex.

According to the Mahayana doctrine of ***trikaya*** (Sanskrit, "three bodies"), there are three "bodies" or modes of being in which the Buddha is known. At the lowest level is the *nirmanakaya* or "emanation body" in which the Buddha can be seen and heard in the everyday world by ordinary people. This is the body of the historical Buddha who taught the Dharma as he traveled across northern India.

It is also the body, in various forms, of all other buddhas who appear in this world. More subtle and existing at a higher level is the *sambhogakaya* or "enjoyment body" of the Buddha. This is the Buddha to whom Mahayana Buddhists direct their devotion, the Buddha who is described as teaching higher doctrines in Mahayana sutras, and the Buddha who is said to dwell in countless universes and pure lands from which he reaches out to bring others to liberation. The highest body of the Buddha is the *dharmakaya* or "truth body." This is ultimate reality as it truly is and as it is experienced by awakened minds. It is the source of the *nirmanakaya* and *sambhogakaya*, which emanate from it. It is the true nature of the Buddha.

The concept of **buddha nature** is an important feature of Mahayana Buddhism, which teaches that the awakened awareness of the Buddha is found within all sentient beings. Thus, awakening is not an experience of something outside of us that we must strive to acquire. Instead, it is already present *within* us. The experience of awakening is ours if we will only uncover it by sweeping away all of the false notions about reality that cloud our vision.

Bodhisattvas and Buddhas

One of the most distinctive features of Mahayana Buddhism is its emphasis on compassion. Whereas the heroic figure in Theravada Buddhism is the arhat, who attains awakening for his own sake, the Mahayana ideal is the compassionate **bodhisattva** who is devoted to helping others attain awakening.

THE MAHAYANA *TRIKAYA* DOCTRINE

According to the *trikaya* doctrine, there are three "bodies" or modes of being in which the Buddha is known.

The true nature of the Buddha is the *dharmakaya* or "truth body," which is ultimate reality itself. Empty of any distinguishing qualities and beyond rational comprehension or description, this is reality as it truly is and as it is perceived by awakened minds. All phenomena are emanations of the *dharmakaya*.

The *sambhogakaya* or "enjoyment body" is a manifestation of the Buddha at a level that is supramundane yet still within space and time. The five buddhas pictured here—Vairochana, Amitabha, Akshobya, Ratnasambhava, and Amoghasiddi—represent aspects of the *dharmakaya*. Sometimes called "buddhas of the five families," they preside over pure lands in the directions they face and "families" of deities that surround them. There are countless other buddhas as well. Although they exist as *dharmakaya* after their *parinirvana*, for the sake of others they manifest as *sambhogakaya* and create their own pure lands where they teach the Dharma surrounded by crowds of bodhisattvas. Among these are great bodhisattvas such as Maitreya, a future buddha, and Avalokiteshvara, the bodhisattva of compassion.

The *nirmanakaya* or "emanation body," the lowest manifestation of the Buddha, is the body of buddhas who appear in the material world. These include buddhas of the past—such as Gautama Buddha and Dipankara, who is said to have attained awakening eons before Gautama Buddha—and buddhas still to come.

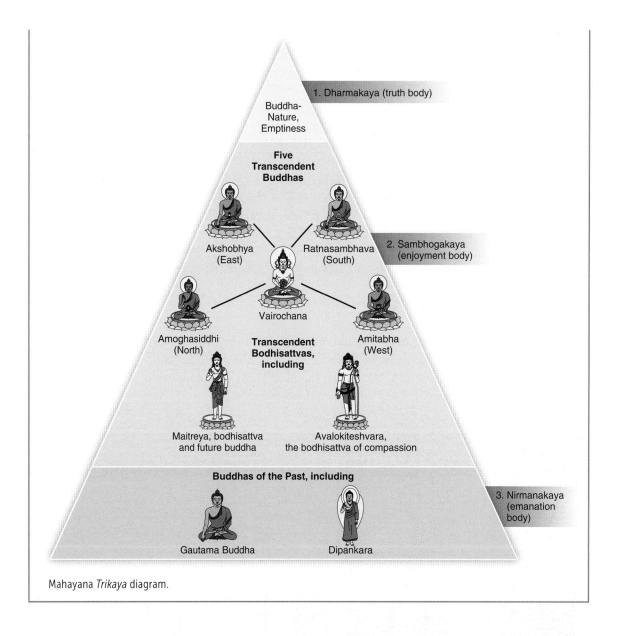

Mahayana *Trikaya* diagram.

Originally, the term "bodhisattva" (Sanskrit, "one who aspires to awakening") was used to describe the Buddha in lives he lived prior to his awakening. But Mahayana Buddhism gives this term a new interpretation. In the Mahayana view, a bodhisattva is anyone who takes a "bodhisattva vow" to strive for awakening for the sake of all other beings.

But *how* do bodhisattvas work for the awakening of others? By cultivating virtues such as the Six Perfections (generosity, morality, patience, energy, meditation, and wisdom), bodhisattvas accumulate merit. Mahayana Buddhists think of merit as a beneficent force that brings positive developments in one's present and future lives and contributes to one's progress to awakening. In East Asia, many believe that merit can be transferred to others by means of wishes, intentions, and rituals and without any depletion of one's own accumulation. For example, a daughter might transfer merit to her deceased father in the hope of giving him a good rebirth—and without diminishing her own store of merit.

Many bodhisattvas are ordinary people who have taken a bodhisattva vow. Your best friend, the person who sits next to you in class, the checker at the grocery store—any of these might be a bodhisattva. But there are also bodhisattvas who manifest in *sambhogakaya* pure lands. With limitless stores of merit, infinite wisdom and compassion, and miraculous powers, they have the ability to alleviate the suffering of others and help them along the path to awakening.

The most widely venerated of these bodhisattvas is Avalokiteshvara, the bodhisattva of infinite compassion. A male figure in South Asia, in East Asia this

Gilded bronze sitting Maitreya icon. Maitreya ("Loving-kindness") is the future Buddha. Like Rodin's *Thinker*, he is seated on his throne in deep contemplation with his hand touching his chin. Three Kingdoms period, seventh century. National Museum, Seoul, Korea.

"Manjushri, Bodhisattva of Wisdom" appearing with the flaming sword of discrimination and a copy of the *Prajnaparamita Sutras* in the blooming lotus of awakening. Kopan monastery, Kathmandu, Nepal.

"The Laughing Buddha." This form of Maitreya is popular in China, where his fatness symbolizes prosperity and joy. It is customary for Buddhists to rub his belly for good luck. Here, people try to improve their luck by touching an image of Maitreya during the New Year fair at the Huayan Temple on the Laoshan Mountain in Qingdao, China.

bodhisattva is female. Known as Guanyin in Chinese, she is a compassionate goddess of mercy who uses her supernatural powers to assist those who call upon her for help. Another popular bodhisattva is Manjushri, who symbolizes supreme wisdom. Manjushri has manifested himself in many ways in this world—in dreams, as a pilgrim, as a monk, and even as the emperor of China—in order to work for the liberation of others from suffering.

In addition to its bodhisattvas, Mahayana Buddhism recognizes a multitude of buddhas. Some have preceded Gautama Buddha in this world. Others have yet to come. The most prominent of future buddhas is Maitreya. Existing now as a bodhisattva, he will appear on Earth at a time when the teachings of Gautama Buddha are no longer followed, become a buddha, and then restore the pure Dharma to the world. There are also many buddhas who manifest in the *sambhogakaya* realm. Among them are five buddhas, sometimes called the "buddhas of the five families," who represent aspects of the *dharmakaya*: Vairochana, Amitabha, Amoghasiddi, Akshobhya, and Ratnasambhava. These are said to have manifested themselves at various times as earthly buddhas and bodhisattvas. They have also created pure lands or buddha-fields to which they bring those who call upon them for salvation from suffering. In these ideal realms the pure Dharma is taught and one can make greater progress toward awakening.

Skillful Means

Early Buddhist texts describe the Buddha as a teacher who employed **skillful means**. Drawing upon his compassion and wisdom, the Buddha skillfully adapted his words and actions to the particular needs and capacity for understanding of the many different kinds of people he sought to guide along the path to awakening. When explaining his teachings to Indian Brahmins, for example, the Buddha made skillful use of their doctrines, using them as helpful points of comparison with his own. On another occasion, he described the bodhisattva Avalokiteshvara as employing skillful means in taking the form of a student to help students and that of a monk to assist monks.

In Mahayana Buddhism, skillful means is more than a guiding principle for those who wish to help others. It also explains and justifies the existence of Buddhism's various schools and sects. The Buddha illustrated both functions in a famous parable about a father who discovers a fire spreading quickly through his house. He calls to his children, begging them to flee, but they are absorbed in playing with their toys and pay no attention to him. Realizing there is no time for him to pick them up and carry them to safety, the father skillfully exploits his children's love of toys in devising a means for saving their lives. He tells them he has toys they have always wanted—little carts drawn by goats, deer, and oxen—waiting for them. In doing so, he succeeds in persuading his children to run outside. Once there, they do not find the little carts their father had promised. Instead, they find something far better: a magnificent cart covered in jewels and drawn by white oxen. Commenting on his parable, the Buddha explained that just as the little carts are skillful means for saving the children from the fire, Buddhism's different "vehicles" or paths to awakening are skillful means of saving people from suffering. The magnificent cart given to the children represents the *Lotus Sutra*, the Mahayana text said to enable those who follow it to attain awakening. Although the carts in the parable are effective, they are not worthy of attachment. Like rafts used to cross some great sea, they are meant to be abandoned when we reach the distant shore and find something far beyond our imagination: nirvana.

Emptiness

We have seen that in his doctrine of interdependent origination the Buddha taught that things do not exist in their own right. Instead, all things depend on all other things for their existence. Reflecting on the meaning of this teaching, a third-century Indian monk named Nagarjuna, perhaps the greatest of all Buddhist philosophers, formulated a doctrine of **emptiness** or **shunyata** (from Sanskrit *shunya*, "empty") that became a foundational feature of Mahayana Buddhism. According to this doctrine, all things are empty of self-existence. This is not to say they do not exist at all. They do exist, but only as transitory phenomena that are in every way dependent upon all other things. The ultimate nature of things—*all* things—is emptiness, the absence of anything solid, essential, intrinsic, independent, or enduring.

Mahayana Texts

Mahayana Buddhism makes use of many texts, including those found in the Pali Canon. Some investigate profound states of awareness reached in meditation. Others elaborate on the implications of doctrines such as interdependent origination and emptiness. Still others describe the qualities of bodhisattvas and explain the benefits of calling upon various buddhas. All are said to be grounded in the teachings of the Buddha, whose implications they identify and explain.

Among the earliest Mahayana texts are the *Perfection of Wisdom Sutras*. Written between 100 and 600 CE, these texts represent the Buddha in dialogue with others on themes related to the acquisition of wisdom, understood here as a perfected understanding of the nature of reality. The most important of these texts are the *Diamond Sutra* and the *Heart Sutra*. Both emphasize concepts that were to become

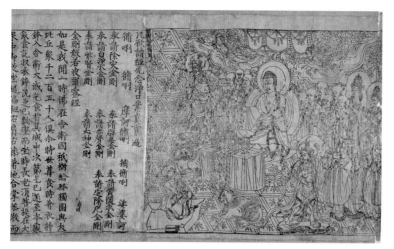

Frontispiece of the *Diamond Sutra* of Dunhuang, 868 CE. This manuscript is the oldest known printed book in the world; it appeared 587 years before the Gutenberg Bible.

essential features of Mahayana thought, including the bodhisattva ideal, no-self, and emptiness.

Another influential Mahayana text is the *Lotus Sutra*. Written in the second century CE, it represents the Buddha as giving his final and ultimate teaching to thousands of monks, nuns, and bodhisattvas. Making frequent use of parables, the Buddha describes the doctrine of skillful means, teaches that all beings have the potential to become buddhas, and states that the bodhisattva ideal is greater than that of the arhat. The *Lotus Sutra* also describes the Buddha as far more than a merely historical personality. Instead, he is a glorious figure whose existence is beyond time.

Mahayana Buddhism's ideal of compassion is emphasized in the Pure Land sutras, and especially in the *Longer Sukhavativyuha Sutra*, the *Amitayurdhyana Sutra*, and the *Shorter Sukhavativyuha Sutra*. Appearing as early as the second century CE, these texts focus on Amitabha, "the Buddha of Boundless Light," a compassionate figure who brings those who call upon him to rebirth in his pure land and works through Avalokiteshvara, the bodhisattva of infinite compassion, to alleviate the suffering of all beings.

5.4 The Teachings of Buddhism: Five Mahayana Schools

We noted earlier that Mahayana Buddhism is a "great vehicle" with room for Buddhists of all kinds. This is especially evident in the great number of Mahayana schools and sects, all of which are seen as skillful means of presenting the Dharma. The five major Mahayana schools we will investigate here illustrate the range of Mahayana beliefs and practices.

Pure Land Buddhism

Pure Land Buddhism is one of the most widely practiced forms of Mahayana Buddhism and is the dominant form in China and Japan. It emphasizes devotion to Amitabha Buddha and faith that he will bring his devotees to a blissful rebirth in his own pure land, the Western Pure Land known as Sukhavati.

According to the Pure Land sutras, conditions in this world obstruct the teaching and practice of the Dharma. In order to save suffering beings, Amitabha Buddha created his pure land as a place of respite. Those who are reborn there live comfortably and receive instruction from Amitabha Buddha and his many bodhisattvas until they are ready to attain awakening. In order to be reborn in Amitabha Buddha's pure land, one must strive to keep the thought of him always in mind. This is most commonly done by reciting the phrase "Praise to Amitabha Buddha" throughout each day. Ideally, one will also look to Amitabha at the moment of death, when the process leading to rebirth begins.

Pure Land Buddhism has been called "the easy path" because it requires no commitment to the rigors of monastic life. One need only have faith that the compassionate Amitabha Buddha will smooth the way to a happy rebirth and subsequent awakening in his pure land and express it by making the thought of him a feature of everyday life. For this reason, Pure Land Buddhism has always had immense appeal for laypeople.

Tiantai Buddhism

Tiantai Buddhism takes its name from Tiantai Mountain in southeastern China, where its founders lived and taught. It later spread to Japan, where it is known as Tendai, and to Korea and Vietnam.

By the time of Tiantai's early development, hundreds of sutras attributed to the Buddha had been brought from India to China, many of them with different interpretations of the Dharma. Tiantai began as an effort to harmonize these in a single unified system of Buddhist thought. It asserted that the Buddha always taught the same truths but at different levels of difficulty intended for different audiences. It also claimed that the highest form of Buddhist teaching is found in the *Lotus Sutra*, which is the basis for all Tiantai doctrine.

Tiantai is an elastic form of Buddhism that has absorbed features of other Buddhist schools and makes room for both monastics and laypeople. Many adherents follow the Pure Land practice of reciting the name of Amitabha Buddha, some practice forms of meditation, others focus on study of the *Lotus Sutra*, and still others look to ceremonies and rituals for a heightened sense of the buddha nature that lies within themselves and throughout the natural world.

Nichiren Buddhism

Nichiren Buddhism is a Japanese school founded by Nichiren, a thirteenth-century monk who left the Tendai movement when he became convinced that the *Lotus Sutra* is the supreme manifestation of Buddhist wisdom and a source of spiritual power that can transform individual lives and society as a whole. In Nichiren's view, no other sutra was worthy of attention. Believing that neglect of the *Lotus Sutra* was the cause of Japan's troubles in his time, Nichiren became an activist who fiercely condemned corruption and called upon government officials, monastics, and laypeople to make the *Lotus Sutra* the basis of Japanese national life. He enjoined his followers to venerate the *Lotus Sutra* by reciting the *daimoku*, a phrase (*Namu myoho renge kyo*) that means "Homage to the Scripture of the Lotus of the Good Teaching."

A Nichiren Buddhist performs her devotions.

Some Nichiren Buddhists regard Nichiren as a master teacher, others as a bodhisattva, and still others as an incarnation of the Buddha. Their tradition teaches that veneration of the *Lotus Sutra* and its title, as found in the *daimoku*, is sufficient for the attainment of awakening. They typically express their devotion to the *Lotus Sutra* each morning and evening, reverently chanting the words of the *daimoku*. As they chant, they direct their devotion to the *Gohonzon*, a replica of an inscription once carved by Nichiren that features the *daimoku* along with symbols of the *trikaya* and various buddhas and bodhisattvas. This practice is said to activate the buddha nature within oneself, bringing positive change and, ultimately, awakening. Nichiren Buddhism also preserves its tradition of political and social activism that reaches back to Nichiren himself. Its Soka Gakkai ("Value Creation Society") sect is influential in Japanese politics and in social and environmental causes throughout the West, where its adherents are growing in number.

Zen Buddhism

Zen Buddhism traces its unique teachings back to the Buddha and credits Bodhidharma, a legendary Indian monk, with bringing them to China in the fifth century. From China, where it is known as **Chan Buddhism**, Zen spread to Japan, where Chan, which means "meditation," is pronounced as Zen, and to the rest of East Asia.

Zen teaches that doctrines, sutras, good works, and faith in buddhas are of little help in awakening. Instead, it emphasizes meditation as a means of looking into one's own nature and becoming aware that it is identical with buddha nature. As we have seen, buddha nature—the pure and essential nature of reality—is empty of independent phenomena. And yet our minds seem to insist that independent phenomena do exist, always forming attachments to and making distinctions between you and I, this and that, having and not having, and so forth.

How can meditation help us to get past this tendency of the mind? In Zen, meditation is not a matter of "doing" or "achieving" something. It is not a striving either to empty the mind or to concentrate on anything. Instead, Zen practitioners often refer to meditation as "just sitting." Dogen, the thirteenth-century Japanese founder of the Soto school of Zen, described "just sitting" as sitting in a state of alert awareness in which the mind, as it lets go of attachments to the objects of its attention, settles into a joyous awareness of its own true nature.

Both the Soto and Rinzai schools of Zen make use of koans, paradoxical riddles designed to astound the mind with some problem it cannot solve by means of rational analysis or reference to reality as it is commonly understood. Presented with a koan such as "What is the sound of one hand clapping?" or "How did my face appear before my parents were born?" the rational mind falters, allowing awareness to settle into a deeper, intuitive experience of one's own nature as buddha nature. According to the Rinzai school, this can sometimes happen suddenly in a flash of insight, but in most cases practitioners follow a lengthy and highly structured path in which they are given numerous and increasingly difficult koans.

Today, Zen is known worldwide and has become especially popular among lay practitioners in the West. In fact, Zen has a long history of attracting laypeople. Dogen himself is said to have taught meditation to both men and women and to people of all social classes. Today, many laypeople combine meditation at home with meditation at weekly meetings of local Zen groups.

Vajrayana Buddhism

Vajrayana Buddhism began in India, but much of its early development occurred in Tibet. Today, it is the most prominent form of Buddhism in Tibet, Nepal, Bhutan, and Mongolia and also has a presence in Japan, China, Indonesia, and the Philippines. Vajrayana is also known as the Thunderbolt Vehicle and the Diamond Vehicle, both of which translate the Sanskrit *vajrayana*. These suggest Vajrayana's power to smash or cut through false notions about reality.

Vajrayana is Buddhist Tantra. We saw in Chapter 4 that Tantra was a religious movement in India that took both Buddhist and Hindu forms. Buddhist Tantrists made use of secret knowledge and practiced special forms of meditation and magic rituals in order to break through delusion into awakened awareness. With this in mind, one scholar has described Tantra as "a technique for magically storming the gates of Buddhahood."[3]

Tibetan Vajrayana Buddhism sees the material world as a manifestation of divine energy it identifies with buddhas, advanced bodhisattvas, and gods and goddesses from Tibetan folk religion. Making use of the esoteric knowledge found in Tantric texts and practicing the rituals they prescribe, adherents seek to gain control of this energy and channel it in ways that allow them to shatter the illusion of self. The most fundamental practice in Vajrayana Buddhism is "deity yoga." This exercise, which involves visualizing oneself as a buddha in the form of a deity, brings a heightened understanding of the true nature of reality. In "guru yoga," the practitioner seeks to unite his mind with that of his teacher and experience his higher level of awareness. Other Vajrayana practices take advantage of states in which the mind is more attuned than usual to the true nature of reality and

The Dalai Lama.

capable of awakening suddenly. These states occur in meditation, while dreaming, and during sex and death.

Mantras and Mandalas

Mantras and mandalas play a central role in the Vajrayana tradition. **Mantras** are words and sounds thought to have spiritual power. The chanting of mantras can bring a heightened awareness of the true nature of reality and protect the mind from disturbing influences. The most popular Tibetan mantra is the Sanskrit phrase, *Om mani padme hum!* Found everywhere—on walls, rocks, and prayer flags—it combines the sacred sound *Om* found in Indian religions (in Hindu usage, see Chapter 4 on OM) with the words for jewel (*mani*) and the lotus flower (*padma*), a symbol of purity and spiritual awakening, and *hum*, a mystical syllable that denotes wisdom and awakening. There is no commonly accepted translation, but tradition says the mantra represents the whole of Buddhist teaching in just six syllables.

Just as mantras express the true nature of reality in sound, **mandalas** describe reality visually. Usually painted on cloth, mandalas are diagrams of the universe filled with colorful images of buddhas, bodhisattvas, rainbows, flames, clouds, mountains, and charnel grounds where bodies of the dead are left to decay. Each symbolic element illustrates some dimension or element of the *trikaya* universe. Mandalas are used in public rituals and in forms of meditation such as deity yoga where, as representations of the true nature of reality—that is, of buddha nature or buddhahood—they guide the meditator along the path to awakening.

Tibetan Monasticism and Lamas
Monasticism is the most visible feature of Tibetan Buddhism. There are four major schools of Tibetan Buddhism, each with its own monasteries and monastic orders. With room for hundreds of monks, Tibet's greatest monasteries are immense and have massive walls that offer protection from extreme winter cold. Some seem to dominate peaks of the Himalayas and defy their most frightening cliffs. The lives of monks and nuns are focused on meditation, study, chanting of sutras, and participation in rituals. Although celibacy is common, it is not universal.

Tibet's spiritual leaders are **lamas**, the Tibetan equivalent of "gurus." Although this title was once reserved for heads of monasteries and spiritual masters, in recent years it has been extended to monks, nuns, and laypeople whose achievements have earned them recognition as authoritative teachers. The most prestigious lamas are *tulkus*, individuals said to be reincarnations of earlier lamas and other figures. During the last six centuries the most important of Tibet's lamas have been the Dalai Lamas. Believed to be incarnations of Avalokiteshvara, the bodhisattva of compassion, they served as Tibet's temporal as well as spiritual leaders until 1959 when conflict with the People's Republic of China forced the current Dalai Lama, Tenzin Gyatso, to flee his country. Living since then as a refugee in India, he has continued to have great influence on the practice of Tibetan Buddhism and has become a globally recognized figure by virtue of his many publications and public teachings on Buddhism and his advocacy for peace and the cause of Tibetan freedom.

The Potala Palace in Lhasa, Tibet, was the winter home of the Dalai Lamas from 1649 until 1959.

Vajrayana Texts   The textual foundation of Vajrayana Buddhism consists of major Mahayana sutras and a large body of Buddhist Tantras. It is these Tantric texts that give Vajrayana its most distinctive features. Some Tantras offer highly detailed descriptions of buddhas and bodhisattvas, others focus on the roles of mantras and mandalas in the quest for awakening, and still others explain how alcohol, sex, and other things often associated with unwholesome desire can offer the mind opportunities to transcend it and attain awakening.

In addition, Tibetan Buddhism honors hidden texts attributed to Padmasambhava, a legendary Tantric master who is said to have brought Vajrayana Buddhism from India to Tibet. According to tradition, Padmasambhava hid these texts with the intention that each would be found at the proper time. The "treasure finders" who discover them do so only when Padmasambhava's "time-lock spells" unravel—always at a time when the world is ready for a new revelation.

The most famous of Vajrayana texts is the *Bardo Thodol* or *Liberation Through Hearing in the Intermediate State*. Commonly known in the West as the *Tibetan Book of the Dead*, it is traditionally attributed to Padmasambhava. The *Bardo Thodol* is a guide to the experience of dying. It describes the intermediate state (*bardo*) between death and rebirth, the phenomena one experiences after death, and how these phenomena offer opportunities for a good rebirth or, ideally, the attainment of awakening and an end to the samsaric cycle of birth-death-rebirth.

COMPARISON OF THERAVADA AND MAHAYANA BUDDHISM

SCRIPTURES

THERAVADA: The Pali Canon, or *Tipitaka*

MAHAYANA: Foundational Mahayana sutras include the *Lotus Sutra* and the *Prajnaparamita Sutras* (*Perfection of Wisdom Sutras*), which include the *Heart Sutra* and the *Diamond Sutra*. There is no single and exclusive Mahayana canon acknowledged by all Mahayana groups.

REALITY

THERAVADA: Reality is a system in which all things are in constant flux. All phenomena are interdependent and interrelated. Nothing exists on its own.

MAHAYANA: Reality is a system in which all things are in constant flux. All phenomena are interdependent and interrelated. The Mahayana doctrine of emptiness states that phenomena are absolutely devoid of fixed identities and qualities.

THE BUDDHA

THERAVADA: Acknowledges the historical Buddha, Siddhartha Gautama, as a man whose teachings have been of great benefit to others. The Buddha is a model to be emulated and venerated.

MAHAYANA: According to the *trikaya* doctrine, the Buddha exists as *dharmakaya* and manifests for the sake of others as *sambhogakaya* and *nirmanakaya*. The Buddha, in all forms of the *trikaya*, is to be worshiped.

BODHISATTVAS

THERAVADA: The Buddha in his previous lives is considered a bodhisattva, as is Maitreya, a buddha who is still to come.

MAHAYANA: Bodhisattvas are those who take a "bodhisattva vow" to attain awakening for the sake of others. Advanced bodhisattvas make use of their vast stores of accumulated merit to help those who call upon them, often in miraculous ways.

ULTIMATE GOAL

THERAVADA: The attainment of awakening and nirvana solely through one's own effort.

MAHAYANA: The attainment of awakening for all beings. In accordance with the bodhisattva ideal, which emphasizes compassion for others, their entry into nirvana should precede one's own. Reliance on the compassion of others is emphasized.

PRACTICES

THERAVADA: Taking the Three Refuges, making offerings on altars to honor the Buddha, meditation, chanting sutras, observing holidays, participating in rituals that mark important life events, and making pilgrimages.

MAHAYANA: In addition to Theravada practices: chanting mantras and the name of the Buddha; honoring buddhas and bodhisattvas in devotional practices; taking the bodhisattva vow; and proclaiming faith in and seeking the saving power of the Buddha and the bodhisattvas.

5.5 The History of Buddhism: Asia

Buddhism's future beyond India was ensured by monks and laypeople who spread the Dharma throughout Asia along two lines of transmission: a Southern Transmission into Sri Lanka and Southeast Asia and a Northern Transmission into Central and East Asia. As we will see in the next section, a more recent Western Transmission has brought Buddhism to the West.

Buddhism in India

As we have seen, the Mauryan emperor Ashoka promoted Buddhism throughout India in the third century BCE. The years that followed saw the early development of the Theravada and Mahayana traditions. Theravada had a short history in India; instead, its future lay in Sri Lanka and Southeast Asia, where it had been taken by Ashoka's missionaries. For a time, Mahayana continued its development in India, but it ultimately found new geographical centers in Central and East Asia.

The Mahayana tradition was fortunate in receiving financial and political support from the Gupta Dynasty (c. 320–550 CE), which ruled much of India. During this period, Indian monasteries adopted Mahayana beliefs and practices and enjoyed the widespread support of laypeople. The vibrancy of Mahayana in India is also attested by the fact that from the fifth century onward East Asian monks regularly traveled there to study and bring home Mahayana texts. Buddhism's greatest institutions in India were the monastic universities at Nalanda and Vikramashila, where thousands of students studied astronomy, medicine, logic, and philosophy as well as Buddhist sutras.

Despite its initial success, Buddhism did not survive in India. Its decline was brought about by the fall of the Gupta Empire; a resurgence of Hinduism; and invasions by Huns, Mongols, and Islamic Turks and Persians who persecuted Buddhists and destroyed their monasteries. The destruction of the Buddhist universities at Nalanda and Vikramasila c. 1200 delivered the final blow. When the Tibetan Buddhist monk Dharmasvamin described his journey to India in the thirteenth century, he despaired that almost no one there claimed to be a Buddhist. Indian Buddhism never recovered. Today, less than 1 percent of the population of India is Buddhist.

Buddhism Beyond India: The Southern Transmission

One of the first lands to adopt Buddhism was Sri Lanka, an island off the southern tip of India. Ancient accounts say that Ashoka's son, Mahinda, brought the Dharma there in the third century BCE and that King Devanampiyatissa, his first convert, built a huge monastery complex in his capital at Anuradhapura. It is said that Ashoka's daughter, Sanghamitta, also came to the island, planted a sapling from the Buddha's Bodhi tree, and established an order of Sri Lankan nuns. From the beginning, monastic institutions were strong in Sri Lanka, nourishing a society devoted to the Dharma and making the island a bastion of Theravada Buddhism.

Buddhism may have arrived in Southeast Asia as early as the third century BCE. For centuries, the Theravada and Mahayana traditions existed alongside each other there. A pivotal moment came in the eleventh century with the creation of a Burmese Empire (1057–1287) and its adoption of Theravada Buddhism as its state religion. In time, Theravada became the predominant form of Buddhism in Cambodia, Thailand,

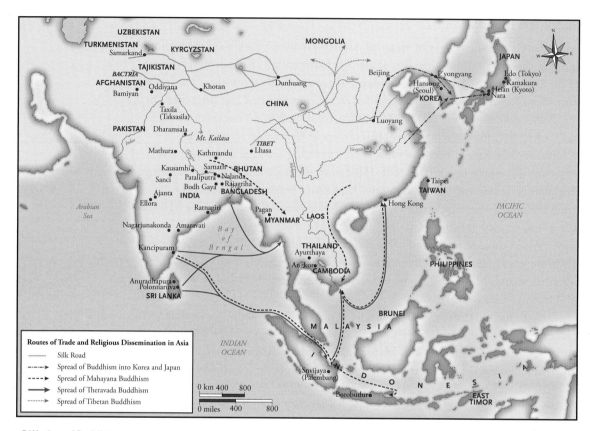

Diffusion of Buddhism
across Asia.

Indonesia, and Laos as well. Mahayana Buddhism prevailed in Vietnam, largely because of its close cultural relationship with China, its northern neighbor, where Mahayana had great influence.

Buddhist beliefs and ideals have been preserved in some of Southeast Asia's greatest sacred sites. Covering more than 400 acres, Cambodia's Angkor Wat ("City of Temples") is the largest religious monument in the world. This vast temple complex was originally dedicated to the Hindu god Vishnu but was later transformed into a Buddhist temple whose architecture expresses aspects of both Theravada and Mahayana Buddhism. These include relief sculptures of the bodhisattva Avalokiteshvara and the high central tower, which represents Mount Meru, the center of the universe in Buddhist cosmology. Another great monument is the Borobudur Temple on the island of Java in Indonesia.

Built in the ninth century, this gigantic Mahayana temple contains 504 Buddha statues, some of them hidden within perforated screens of stone. For centuries, pilgrims have ascended to its summit through three levels that correspond to the three Buddha "bodies" or modes of existence of the Buddha described in the *trikaya* doctrine. Along the way, they pass through endless corridors and stairways lined with 1,460 relief sculpture panels that depict the life of the Buddha and describe his teachings.

Buddhism Beyond India: The Northern Transmission

According to tradition, Ashoka sent missionaries northward into Central Asia as well as southward to Sri Lanka and Southeast Asia. For a time, Buddhism established a presence in regions known today as Iran, Afghanistan, Pakistan, Kazakhstan, Kyrgyzstan, Tajikistan, Turkmenistan, and Uzbekistan. In some places it flourished as a state religion; for example, in the Kushan Empire (c. 30–350) and the Kingdom of Khotan (56–1001). But the Muslim conquest of Central Asia that began in the eighth century brought a virtual end to Buddhism there. Its future in East Asia was to be much brighter.

According to legend, Buddhism came to China after the emperor Ming of the Han Dynasty (r. 57–75 CE) dreamed of the Buddha, who appeared to him as a golden-robed figure flying before his palace. Intrigued, he sent envoys to India who returned with Buddhist monks and two white horses laden with Buddhist scriptures and images of the Buddha. Scholars regard this story as more fiction than fact, but most agree that Buddhism did come to China in the first century.

China was not eager to embrace the Theravada form of Buddhism that was first to arrive there. Its emphasis on monasticism seemed incompatible with the Chinese ideals of achieving material success in the world and the importance of family life. Mahayana Buddhism, which came to China in the second century, received a more favorable response. Its many buddhas and bodhisattvas were reminiscent of the Chinese pantheon of gods and goddesses, and its teaching that laypeople as well as monks and nuns can attain awakening made it more appealing than Theravada. In addition, Mahayana

Borobudur Temple, Java, Indonesia, c. 800 CE. Here, one of the Buddha statues is revealed. In order to see others, pilgrims would have to peer through holes in bell-shaped stupas, such as those visible in the background.

The Angkor Wat temple complex, Cambodia.

The earliest known image of the Buddha appears on the reverse of a coin minted by the second-century Kushan king, Kanishka I. Previously, the Buddha was depicted more as an absence than a presence, symbolized with images such as footprints or an empty chair.

Avalokiteshvara peers out in all directions from the temple towers at Angkor Wat.

Buddhism easily accommodated Chinese ethical values, such as filial piety and submission to rulers. It also addressed the issues of death and the afterlife, largely ignored by native Confucianism and Daoism, in teachings about rebirth in accordance with one's karma.

By the sixth century, Mahayana had established itself as the predominant form of Buddhism in China, hundreds of sutras had been translated into Chinese, monasteries had appeared everywhere, and Buddhism had taken its place alongside Confucianism and Daoism as one of China's three great religions. For the most part, these have coexisted peacefully throughout China's history, sometimes coalescing as their common features were identified and explored. Each has passed through periods of favor and disfavor tied to the preferences and policies of China's rulers. In the case of Buddhism, such a change in fortune happened early in its history in China. Its golden age under the Tang Dynasty (618–907), when it was promoted by notable rulers such as the empress Wu Zetian, came to a sudden end in 845 when the emperor Wu launched a major persecution in which monks and nuns were forced to leave their monasteries and thousands of temples were destroyed. Despite occasional setbacks, Buddhism flourished in China. Schools with origins in India thrived, and new Chinese schools appeared. The most influential schools have been Chan (Zen), Jingtu (Pure Land), Tiantai, and Huayan, a philosophical school noted for its teachings about the fundamental unity of all things.

Buddhism came to Korea from China in the fourth century CE. It soon won support from the rulers of the peninsula's three kingdoms and formed a symbiotic relationship with its indigenous nature religion. Buddhist monks performed shamanistic rituals, and Buddhist temples served as centers for the veneration of Korean mountain spirits as well as the Buddha. Several Mahayana schools made their way to Korea, including Tiantai, Pure Land, and Chan. Known as Seon in Korea, Chan has long been the predominant form of Buddhism there.

Buddhism arrived in Japan in 552 CE in the form of sutras and images of the Buddha—gifts from a Korean king to the ruler of Japan. Not long thereafter, Prince Shotoku (574–622), a prominent member of Japan's ruling family, incorporated both Buddhist and Confucian ideals in a constitution he created for the newly institutionalized Japanese state. Buddhism became Japan's predominant religion in the Nara period (710–784) and has remained an essential feature of Japanese culture ever since, always existing peacefully alongside Japan's indigenous Shinto religion. Mahayana has always been the dominant form of Buddhism in Japan. Most of its schools were imported from China. A few, such as Nichiren, are native to Japan. Historically, the most influential forms of Buddhism in Japan have been Pure Land, Zen, Nichiren, and Shingon, a Japanese form of Vajrayana.

5.6 The History of Buddhism: The West

Buddhism was little known in the West until the nineteenth century. Unlike the earlier Southern and Northern Transmissions, in which monks were the prime agents in transmitting the Dharma, the Western Transmission has been carried out primarily by laypeople, including travelers, scholars, and immigrants, as well as by monks.

Many of the West's earliest contacts with Buddhism resulted from its colonization of Asia. European colonials who traveled there returned with Buddhist texts and accounts of Buddhist cultures that generated great interest in the West. One very influential example is *The Light of Asia*, a narrative poem about the life and teachings of the Buddha by Sir Edwin Arnold, an English poet who had been a school principal in India in the 1850s. Arnold's sympathetic account of the Buddha offered many Europeans their first encounter with Buddhism. Published in 1879, *The Light of Asia* quickly became an international best-seller and was translated into more than thirty languages. At that time, Western scholars were beginning to translate Buddhist literature into Western languages, making the Dharma available to wider audiences. One of the most influential scholars was T. W. Rhys Davids (1843–1922), a British colonial administrator who became fascinated by Buddhism while stationed in Sri Lanka. His translations of Buddhist texts attracted the attention of thousands of Westerners, many of whom came to see Buddhism as a practical philosophy whose teachings could be tested through personal experience and did not require faith in truths that could not be verified by reason and observation.

Waves of Asian immigrants also played an important role in the Western Transmission. Chinese immigrants who came to the United States, Canada, Australia, and New Zealand in the nineteenth century brought Buddhism with them, as have more recent immigrants, many of them refugees from Southeast Asia and Tibet. An important event in the history of Western Buddhism was the 1893 World's Parliament of Religions in Chicago, where leading Buddhists from Japan, Sri Lanka, and other Asian countries gave stirring speeches that made a lasting impression on Western religious thought. This was followed by the arrival of twentieth-century Buddhist teachers such as D. T. Suzuki (1870–1966), a Japanese proponent of Zen Buddhism; Ajahn Chah (1918–1992), a Thai monk who popularized Theravada Buddhism in Europe and North America; and Thich Nhat Hanh (1926–2022), a Vietnamese monk who founded monasteries in France, Germany, and the United States and published more than one 100 books in English teaching a blend of Theravada and Mahayana Buddhism. Perhaps the most influential of all recent teachers has been Tibet's fourteenth Dalai Lama, Tenzin Gyatso. The recipient of the Nobel Peace Prize in 1989, he has traveled widely in the West and published many books on Buddhism.

The Character of Emerging Western Buddhism

Although Western Buddhism is still in its infancy, it is already exhibiting its own distinctive features. In the West, most regions with significant populations are home to a variety of Buddhist groups representing both Theravada and Mahayana Buddhism. Members often call their local groups sanghas, expanding the application of a term that has traditionally referred to monastic communities. In a city of modest size, you might find meditation centers (often called Dharma centers) with roots in Theravada Buddhism thriving alongside Mahayana Buddhism represented by a Tibetan Buddhism sangha, a Jodo Shinshu temple, and a Zen center. This is a departure from the situation in Asia, where entire countries have traditionally been identifiable as either Theravada or Mahayana. Western Buddhist groups tend to be more democratic in their organization and give greater authority to laypeople and women than their counterparts in Asia. Finally, the focus of some sanghas is primarily on meditation and instruction in the Dharma. Others make ample room for aspects of traditional Buddhist cultures as well.

In meditation centers, usually located in buildings with no distinctively Buddhist features, sanghas are typically made up primarily of non-Asian converts to Buddhism. Members meet in a large room and sit on chairs or meditation cushions on the floor. At the front of the room there is usually a simple altar with a small Buddha statue. There might be a few decorative touches in the room, perhaps a mandala or an image of the Dharma wheel, the symbol of the Noble Eightfold Path, but little more. Gatherings of sangha members often begin with announcements followed by a brief "dharma talk" by one of the sangha's leaders. This is followed by group meditation lasting thirty to forty-five minutes. Most members of meditation centers see meditation and living in accordance with Buddhist ethical principles as more important than the religious and cultural aspects of Buddhism, which they honor but do not emphasize.

More traditional sanghas seek to maintain a connection with their religious and cultural foundations in Asia. In a typical Jodo Shinshu temple, for example, the designs of both the exterior and interior of the building are likely to reflect Jodo Shinshu's origins in Japan. Many members of the sangha will be of Japanese ancestry; of course, others are always welcome. The altar at the front of the temple's interior will often be large, elaborate, and Japanese in style. The weekly Dharma service begins with announcements followed by an opening *gatha*, or song, a congregational reading from a Buddhist text, and a chanting of sutras in Japanese. Members of the sangha then *oshoko* (offer incense). After a reading from another Buddhist text, the sangha's leader offers a Dharma message. The service concludes with a *gatha* and a final *oshoko*.

Now that Buddhism is becoming increasingly popular in the West, we might ask: What will Western Buddhism look like in fifty or a hundred years from now? Will it preserve its many forms or will these combine somehow into some form of blended Buddhism? Of course, we will have to wait to see what the future holds. But today's Buddhist leaders agree that wisdom and compassion are certain to lie at the heart of Western Buddhism. Buddhists have always prized these two virtues: wisdom grounded in an understanding of the true nature of reality and a compassion for all beings that arises from awareness of the interconnectedness of all things.

Buddhism in the Twenty-First Century

There are approximately half a billion Buddhists in the world today. About 62 percent are Mahayana Buddhists and 38 percent are Theravadins. More than 98 percent of Buddhists live in Asia, half of them in China.

Buddhism's position in Asia varies from country to country. It is the state religion and receives government support in Thailand, Cambodia, and Bhutan. Buddhist minorities are persecuted in Afghanistan and Pakistan. In China, Mongolia, Vietnam, and Laos, Buddhism was suppressed early in the communist era but is making a comeback now. In Japan and South Korea, Buddhism continues to be a central feature of traditional culture. In North Korea, it is discouraged by an authoritarian government that has reduced it to a cultural relic.

Buddhism's recent growth in Europe, the Americas, and Oceania has made it a global religion. In the United Kingdom the number of Buddhist organizations increased from seventy-four to 400 between 1979 and 2000. In Germany, the number of organizations grew from approximately forty in 1975 to 600 in 2005. As of 2010, there were 280,000 Buddhists in the United Kingdom and 210,000 in Germany. Similar growth is evident elsewhere in Europe and in Australia, where Buddhism is the fastest-growing religion in terms of percentage increase. There are also clear indications of growing interest in Buddhism in South America. With nearly 250,000 Buddhists, Brazil has the largest Buddhist population in Latin America. In the United States, Buddhists make up 1.2 percent of the population. Of these, the majority live in Hawaii and on the West Coast.

The importance of Buddhism in Asian cultures has always been well-attested in their classical art forms. With a very short history in the West, Buddhism is largely absent from its arts. But Buddhism does have a considerable presence in contemporary popular culture, a globally shared culture made possible by technology. Today, Buddhists throughout the world listen to Dharma teachings on podcasts and use apps that allow them to time meditation sessions, read sutras, and keep up with the Dalai Lama's teachings and travels. The lives of buddhas and bodhisattvas are featured in Japanese and Chinese anime. *Buddha*, a multivolume story of the Buddha drawn by Osamu Tezuka, "the god of manga," has been translated into numerous Asian and Western languages. Western films with Buddhist themes include the *Star Wars* saga, *Kundun*, *Little Buddha*, and *Seven Years in Tibet*, and contemporary music with Buddhist connections is available on YouTube and other websites. American comic book heroes such as Xorn of the X-Men are Buddhists. Even Batman is said to have received instruction in Buddhism in Tibet. Those who wish to learn more about Buddhism can visit websites such as *Buddha-Net* and its online magazine *BuddhaZine*.[4]

World Buddhist populations.

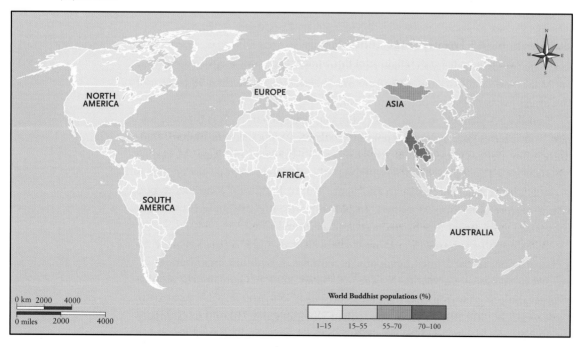

5.7 Buddhism as a Way of Life: Practices

Buddhists practice the teachings of the Buddha in many ways. Seeking to observe the ethical principles he taught, they aspire to proper conduct in daily life. Those who seek to observe the workings of the mind and to see reality more clearly practice meditation. Some become members of monastic orders. Most Buddhists participate in rituals that celebrate important events in the history of Buddhism and mark important transitions in human lives. In this part of our investigation, we will look at Buddhist practices to gain an understanding of the meaning they have for followers of the Buddha.

Who Is a Buddhist?

You will recall that the Budda preached his first sermon, the Sermon in the Deer Park, to the five ascetics who had once practiced severe austerities with him. Convinced that he had found what they had been seeking, they became the first members of the sangha by making three affirmations known as the **Three Refuges**:

> I take refuge in the Buddha.
> I take refuge in the Dharma.
> I take refuge in the Sangha.

Since then, followers of the Buddha have affirmed their Buddhist identity by reciting this formula, Buddhism's most fundamental ritual. To take refuge in the Buddha is to acknowledge him as the supreme example of one who has fully realized the potential of human life. To take refuge in the Dharma is to recognize it as the path to awakening and an end to suffering. To take refuge in the sangha is to acknowledge one's reliance on the order of Buddhist monks, which has been the custodian of the Dharma and responsible for teaching and preserving it.

Monks, Nuns, and Monastic Life

From the beginning, monasticism has been Buddhism's most important institution. Monks and nuns have been responsible for teaching and preserving the Dharma and for living lives that model Buddhist values.

The foundation of Buddhist monastic life is the *Vinaya*, a collection of texts in the Pali Canon that contains rules governing the lives of monks and nuns. These require the cultivation of good moral character, nonattachment to material things, and abstention from sexual activity and other forms of inappropriate contact with others.

In Theravada countries, a monk's day begins at daybreak. He rises, washes himself, and spends time in meditation. He then joins his fellow monks in going from house to house asking for food. This provides monks with the nourishment they need and offers laypeople an opportunity to gain merit. Returning to the

A Cambodian monk at work on his computer.

monastery, the monk eats a vegetarian breakfast with his companions and then sits with them in an assembly hall for a time of chanting and instruction. Because monks are not permitted to eat after noon, there is an opportunity for a second meal just before noon. Spending the afternoon in his room, a monk typically devotes his time to study and meditation. At sundown, he sweeps his room and lights a lamp. Later, he returns to the assembly hall for instruction and meditation and then retires to his room for the night.

The lives of monks in the Mahayana tradition resemble those of Theravada monks in their emphasis on simplicity and meditation but can vary in significant ways. In Tibet, where extreme cold makes the usual vegetarian diet impractical, monks eat meat. Some East Asian monks and nuns are allowed to marry. In China, Japan, and Korea, where begging is not socially acceptable, monks and nuns prepare food donated by their local communities or grown in their own gardens.

Early Buddhist texts say that the order of nuns was established by the Buddha at the request of his aunt, Mahapajapati, who became the first Buddhist nun. The Buddha's initial hesitation in agreeing to Mahapajapati's request may reflect contemporary attitudes toward women, and these must also have influenced the *Vinaya*, which contains many more rules for nuns than it does for monks. The order of nuns has always been subordinate to the order of monks, but fully ordained nuns may teach, perform rituals, and officiate at ceremonies, just as fully ordained monks do.

Ethics

Like most religions, Buddhism includes a body of teachings on ethics, the principles that define moral behavior. The Buddha taught that ethical behavior alleviates suffering, the great problem that afflicts all beings, and brings compassion to others. Unethical behavior causes suffering and seeks to benefit oneself in ways that are inconsistent with the Buddha's teaching that there really is no essential self.

Buddhists recognize the Ten Precepts as basic guidelines for ethical behavior. These require abstention from (1) killing or harming other beings; (2) taking anything not freely given; (3) sexual misconduct; (4) false speech; (5) using intoxicants; (6) eating after noon; (7) dancing, singing, and foolish entertainments; (8) adorning the body with scents and jewelry; (9) sleeping in luxurious beds; and (10) handling money. Ideally, the first five of these, the Five Precepts, are to be followed by all Buddhists. In practice, however, most lay Buddhists are selective in their observance of the precepts. For example, many eat meat or drink alcohol. Monks and nuns observe all of the Ten Precepts and the rules of the *Vinaya* as well.

Buddhism sees wisdom and compassion as more helpful than absolute standards of right and wrong in matters of ethics. Absolute standards dictate that certain actions are *always* right or wrong regardless of circumstances. As we saw earlier in our discussion of skillful means, wisdom and compassion allow us to adapt our actions to circumstances in order to achieve the highest good—even if this means setting aside normal standards. The untruth told by the father in the Buddha's parable of the burning house is a good example.

Pema Chodron is an American-born Buddhist nun whose books describe skillful ways of dealing with everyday suffering.

Meditation

The Buddha encouraged his followers to practice meditation, which enables practitioners to identify and eliminate patterns of thought that perpetuate desire and suffering. Of course, most of the Buddha's followers were monks and nuns who devoted themselves entirely to meditation and other monastic practices. With families to care for, most of the Buddha's lay followers contented themselves with supporting monastic communities and doing their best to practice the other virtues which, together with meditation, are aspects of the Noble Eightfold Path. This has remained the case for most of Buddhism's history. It is only in recent years that large numbers of lay Buddhists have begun to make meditation a part of their daily lives.

Samatha and Vipassana Meditation   From the beginning, Buddhists have practiced two basic and complementary forms of meditation: samatha, which calms the mind, and vipassana, in which one gains insight into the workings of the mind.

Samatha meditation calms the mind by allowing awareness to rest lightly on just one thing. For most meditators, this is the breath. By simply following their breath, letting each inhalation and exhalation fill their awareness, they allow the mind to settle into a state of greater calm and stability.

The object of vipassana meditation is to gain insight into the nature of the mind and of reality as a whole. Also known as insight meditation and mindfulness meditation, vipassana begins with calming and stabilizing the mind. The meditator then observes how thoughts, feelings, and sensations arise and learns how to let them pass without becoming caught up in them. Gradually, it becomes clear how attachment and aversion to these and all other phenomena cause suffering and that letting go of attachment and aversion brings greater calmness of mind. With each new insight, the meditator takes a step, however small, on the path that led the Buddha to awakening and an end to suffering.

Other Forms of Meditation

As Buddhism grew, new forms of meditation developed, each suited to the tradition in which it developed.

Some Buddhists practice meditation while walking, one of the techniques taught by the Buddha. Chinese Tiantai Buddhism builds its meditation practice on samatha and vipassana and takes a special interest in correct and incorrect forms of breathing. In Tendai, the Japanese form of Tiantai, meditation practices are influenced by Vajrayana as well as Tiantai and include the chanting of mantras and the use of mudras, symbolic gestures made with the hands and fingers. In Pure Land Buddhism, meditation is focused on repetition of the name of Amitabha Buddha who has promised to bring all who call upon him to rebirth in his Western Pure Land. Some practitioners repeat the name constantly, devoting themselves to Amitabha throughout each day. Others visualize Amitabha, the bodhisattvas who surround him, and his pure land while meditating. Chan meditation emphasizes correct posture. It is important to sit straight with the head held high and hands resting one upon the other in the lap. To calm the mind, awareness is allowed to settle on the breath. As in vipassana, the meditator observes as thoughts and sensations arise and then pass away without becoming entangled in them. Some schools of Chan/Zen favor awareness of the totality of *all* phenomena rather than the breath or some other object. Others make use of koans, paradoxical riddles that confound the mind and move it to a deeper awareness of the true nature of reality. As we have seen, Tibetan Buddhism makes use of Tantric meditation practices. These include deity yoga, in which meditators focus on a mental image of a buddha or bodhisattva. Another form of Tibetan meditation involves seeing through thoughts and sensations that arise in the mind in order to experience the ultimate nature of mind itself, which is identical with buddha nature. Finally, Buddhists of many kinds practice loving-kindness meditation. This is the cultivation of boundless compassion for oneself and for all other beings.

A large contemporary image of the Walking Buddha in Thailand. Thai images often stylistically craft his right arm to represent the graceful swaying trunk of an elephant.

Chanting

Chanting is practiced in all forms of Buddhism and is commonly heard in monasteries, temples, and meditation centers. Often accompanied by the sounds of gongs and drums, it is used as a form of meditation, in devotional liturgies, and in public rituals.

Some chants are recitations of sutras. For Buddhists, chanting sutras brings greater insight into the Buddha's awakened awareness. Other chants are mantras said to transform the mind through repetition. Still others are mantras in Pali and Sanskrit thought to have a protective and healing influence and to generate merit for chanters. Among the most common Theravada chants are the Three Refuges and the Five Precepts. Pure Land Buddhists chant the name of Amitabha Buddha using various formulas, such as the *Nianfo* (Chinese) and the *Nembutsu* (Japanese). Nichiren Buddhists, who believe the *Lotus Sutra* is the supreme expression of the Buddha's wisdom, honor it by chanting the *daimoku*: "Homage to the Scripture of the Lotus of the Good Teaching." The *Lotus Sutra*, *Heart Sutra*, and *Diamond Sutra* are commonly chanted by Mahayana Buddhists.

Sacred Spaces and Objects

Like adherents of other religions, Buddhists recognize some places and objects as having a sacred character that sets them apart from the many other things they encounter in everyday life.

The most sacred sites in Buddhism are the Buddha's birthplace at Lumbini in Nepal and, in India, Bodh Gaya, where the Buddha attained awakening; Sarnath, where he preached his Sermon in the Deer Park; and Kushinagara, where the Buddha died and passed into *parinirvana*. Hundreds of thousands of pilgrims visit these and other sites every year, most made sacred by relics or connections with events in the lives of the Buddha and other Buddhist figures.

Temples are sacred spaces where Buddhists venerate the Buddha and gather for rituals and ceremonies. Temples vary in outward appearance in accordance with regional architectural styles, but most share common interior features. These include an altar with a small statue of the Buddha and room for an incense bowl and offerings of fruit and flowers; a main hall; a library of sutras and other texts; a space for meditation; and rooms for resident monks.

For Buddhists, the most sacred of all objects are relics of the Buddha. According to tradition, the Buddha's

Buddhists visiting the site of the Bodhi tree under which the Buddha is said to have attained awakening. This tree is likely a descendant of the original Bodhi tree. Bodh Gaya, India.

followers collected the ashes, teeth, bits of bone, and other relics that remained after his cremation. These were later divided into 84,000 portions by Ashoka, who ordered them enclosed in caskets and placed in earthen reliquary mounds called **stupas**. Today, most stupas are impressive hemispherical structures whose shapes are reminiscent of the original mounds built on the sites where they stand. The relics they preserve have a powerful and inspiring effect on those who venerate them.

Because the Buddha said that his teaching would serve as his "Dharma body" after his death, many Buddhists venerate the sacred texts in which the Dharma is preserved. Some Mahayana groups place manuscripts of sutras within images of the Buddha, making them objects especially worthy of veneration. For others, the titles of sutras, inscribed on stone, wood, or paper, are also objects of reverent devotion.

Artistic representations of the Buddha also have a sacred quality. Early Buddhist art tended not to represent the Buddha in human form. Instead, he was depicted in other ways; for example, as an empty chair, a pair of footprints, or the Bodhi tree he sat under at the time of his awakening. By the first century CE, Buddhists began to make extensive use of anthropomorphic images to represent more vividly the physical forms of Gautama Buddha and other buddhas and bodhisattvas. Many of these images make use of subtle iconographic cues such as mudras to represent the powers and functions of the buddhas and bodhisattvas they represent. Objects associated with important events in the life of the Buddha and aspects of his teaching are also sacred. Fig trees are revered, for it was in the shade of a fig tree that the Buddha attained awakening. Another commonly venerated symbol is the wheel. With eight spokes representing the eight aspects of the Noble Eightfold Path, the Dharmachakra, or Dharma wheel, is a universally recognized symbol of Buddhism. Prayer wheels, which have become a symbol of Vajrayana Buddhism, are almost as well known. Hand-held or mounted on posts, these hollow cylinders contain tightly wound scrolls on which mantras are written, in some cases more than a thousand times. Because one turning of the wheel is thought to generate as much merit as reciting the mantra as many times as it appears on the scroll, a few swipes of the hand on a prayer wheel can bring significant benefits for oneself and others.

The Great Stupa of Sanchi, India. Early Andhra Dynasty, first century BCE.

Holidays and Festivals

The Buddhist year is filled with holidays, festivals, and other special observances. In most countries, their dates are determined by the lunar calendar and therefore fall on different days each year. The most important occasions are commemorations of key events in the life of the Buddha, but there are also celebrations of the birthdays of bodhisattvas, commemorations of historical events, and seasonal observances that have taken on a religious significance.

Vesak The most important of Buddhist holidays is Vesak. In Theravada and Tibetan Buddhism, Vesak is a commemoration of the Buddha's birth, awakening, and *parinirvana* that occurs on the day of the first full moon in the lunar month of Vesakha, usually in May. Celebrants decorate local shrines and light lamps to symbolize the Buddha's awakening and the spreading of his wisdom throughout the world. Some stay up all night in meditation as the Buddha did on the night of his awakening. In most Mahayana countries, the celebration of the Buddha's birth is known as Buddha Day and usually occurs at the traditional time of Vesak. Celebrations of the Buddha's awakening (Bohdi Day) and *parinirvana* (Paranirvana Day) are separate and occur at other times of the year.

Other Festivals The Buddhist calendar makes room for many other special days. Mahayana Buddhists make New Year's Day an important occasion, some beginning their celebration on December 31 and others waiting until the first full moon in January. Traditions vary but often include visits to temples, good food, and fireworks. Asalha Puja, a Theravada festival known in the West as Dharma Day, recalls "the first turning of the wheel of the Dharma"—that is, the Buddha's first teaching of the Dharma in his Sermon in the Deer Park—and is traditionally celebrated during the full moon in July. Kathina, another Theravada festival, is usually celebrated in October. On this occasion, laypeople express their gratitude to monks by bringing them new robes and gifts to support their monasteries. During the late summer Hungry Ghosts Festival in China, known in Japan as the Feast of the Dead, the spirits of ancestors are placated with offerings of food, and monks are called upon to recite sutras in order to aid the departed in securing a favorable rebirth.

Father and child bathe an image of the Buddha as a baby during a celebration of the Buddha's birth in Taiwan.

Death

When the death of a Buddhist approaches, family and friends will often sit in the dying person's room to offer comfort. Knowing that it is best to die with a mind that is calm and pure, they might chant sutras, recite the name of Amitabha Buddha, or simply offer assurances that death is a natural part of the human experience.

When death has come, family members generally follow the dictates of tradition. Theravada Buddhists dress the deceased person in white clothing, which represents virtue, and lay the body out in the home so that visitors might come to say goodbye. Much the same pattern is followed in Chan Buddhism. In the Pure Land tradition, friends and family chant the name of Amitabha Buddha before and after a death in order to help the deceased person find the way to his Pure Land. The body is not disturbed in any way for up to an entire day so that the journey will not be made more difficult. In Tibetan Buddhism families keep vigil over the body of the deceased for four to nine days. During this time, a monk guides the deceased person to a good rebirth, or possibly awakening and freedom from rebirth, by reading from the *Tibetan Book of the Dead*.

Buddhists practice both cremation and burial. Funeral services may be held either before these events or, in the form of a memorial service, after them. Whatever form a funeral takes, it is always a solemn affair. A photograph or some other image of the deceased is usually set upon an altar at the front of the room in which the service is held, as are flowers provided by family and friends. When entering the room, mourners approach the altar, bow with their hands pressed together in a prayerful manner, spend a moment in quiet reflection, and then take their seats. It is customary for monks, family, and friends to speak, offering eulogies to honor the deceased. In most cases monks or family members lead those in attendance in the chanting of sutras.

5.8 Buddhism as a Way of Life: Engaging with the World

Buddhism urges its followers to put the principles it teaches into practice in the many ways in which they are involved in the world we live in. Of these principles, the most important is a compassion for all other beings. In this concluding section of our survey of Buddhism, we'll look briefly at three examples of Buddhists' engagement with the world.

Buddhism, Concord, and Conflict

Seeking to put the Buddha's teachings about wisdom and compassion into practice, committed Buddhists are working alongside others to make the world a better place for everyone. Buddhists practicing Engaged Buddhism, a term coined by Thich Nhat Hanh in the 1970s, are alleviating social, political, and economic suffering through organizations that include the Buddhist Peace Fellowship, Buddhist Global Relief, Zen Peacemakers, the International Network of Engaged Buddhists, and the Order of Interbeing founded by Thich Nhat Hanh. Engaged Buddhists feed the hungry, operate schools and orphanages, educate the public, and advocate for positive change in government policies.

Although Buddhism has a well-deserved reputation as a religion that promotes peace, we would be mistaken in assuming that Buddhists never lose sight of this ideal. Recent events in Myanmar and Sri Lanka demonstrate that when ethnic and religious identities become more important than peaceful coexistence, the results can be disastrous.

Myanmar, formerly known as Burma, is a Buddhist country in Southeast Asia with a long history of social strife. Between 1962 and 2011 its military government persecuted ethnic and religious minorities. Its most visible victims were the Rohingya people, Muslims who were denied citizenship and suffered killings, house burnings, and the displacement of thousands. Persecution continued between 2011 and 2021 when Myanmar's government was in the hands of the National League for Democracy whose leader, Aung San Suu Kyi, had been awarded the Nobel Peace Prize in 1991. Repression of the Rohingya and other minority groups has persisted in Myanmar since the military returned to power in 2021.

Ethnic and religious conflict has also plagued Sri Lanka, a small island country southeast of India. Here, the majority Sinhalese, who are Buddhists, fought Hindu Tamils in a civil war (1983–2009) in which more than 80,000 were killed. More recently, there has been violence against Muslims, much of it incited by Bodu Bala Sena (BBS; Buddhist Power Force). An organization led by monks, BBS sees Islam as a threat to Sri Lanka's Buddhist culture. It makes effective use of public rallies and social media to attract supporters.

Buddhism, Gender, and Inclusion

Early Buddhist texts express both positive and negative views of women. Some say the Buddha's doctrine of no-self leaves no room for meaningful distinctions between genders, that women can attain awakening just as readily as men, and that it was in a past life as a woman that the Buddha first resolved to attain awakening. Others say that women should aspire to rebirth as men, that no woman could ever become a buddha, and that even if a woman were to attain buddhahood, she would not be qualified for leadership in a Buddhist community.

To provide women with the opportunity to attain awakening, the Buddha established the order of nuns. Like monks, nuns live in monastic communities and in accordance with the rules for monastic life found in the *Vinaya*. Most of their time is devoted to study, meditation, and service. Nuns pass through two levels of training before they are fully ordained. Because fully ordained nuns are required to place themselves under the

Buddhist women with begging bowls.

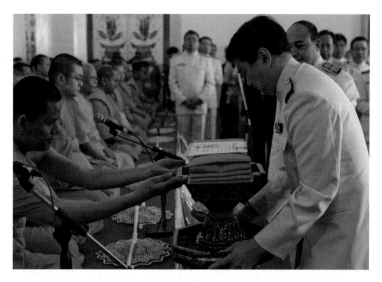

Prime Minister Abhisit offers Kathina robes to monks at a 2010 Kathina ceremony in Bangkok, Thailand.

authority of senior monks, monks are ultimately in control of the order of nuns. Seeking greater freedom, some religious women in Asia live as if they were nuns but choose not to take vows. Living outside of the traditional order of nuns, they determine what their spiritual practice will be. But there is a price to be paid for their independence. Because of their unofficial status, they do not have the community support enjoyed by traditional nuns and often fall into poverty and homelessness.

Traditionally, women have had roles secondary to those of men in Buddhist institutions. This situation is beginning to change, especially in the West where liberal values are shaping the development of new and inclusive Buddhist institutions. For example, laywomen are on a par with men in teaching and governance at Western meditation centers. And many prominent Buddhist writers and retreat leaders are women.

The issue of inclusion is also of concern to those who identify as LGBTQ. Although one can find evidence of resistance and hostility toward those who identify as such in Buddhist history and literature, these attitudes have been informed more by cultural traditions than Buddhist teaching. For the most part, Buddhists have refrained from making sexuality and sexual identity moral issues. What does matter is how one behaves sexually. For monks and nuns, who are celibate, all forms of sexual activity are prohibited. For laypeople, the general rule is that any kind of sexual behavior that harms others is immoral. Early Buddhist literature generally speaks about queer individuals without judgment. Recording examples of what some today might call gender fluidity, some texts even describe people who experienced changes in gender in a single lifetime due to karmic influences. Today, and especially in the West, Buddhist communities are increasingly welcoming

The Buddha achieved awakening while seated beneath a fig tree that came to be known as the Bodhi tree ("awakening tree"). Here, monks gather at Bodh Gaya in India, the site of the Buddha's awakening.

to people who identify as LGBTQ, many of whom are assuming positions of leadership.

Buddhism and the Environment

Although the Buddha did not teach about the environment itself, his foundational teachings do provide a basis for Buddhist environmentalism. His doctrine of interdependent origination, for example, states that all things exist as aspects of a single, all-inclusive web of interdependent phenomena. Because we exist in a state of interdependence with all other things, Buddhist environmentalists believe that in taking good care of the world we take good care of ourselves. Conversely, in harming the world we harm ourselves. They also believe that the virtues of compassion and nonviolence should be extended to all of nature in both its animate and inanimate forms.

At a major conference held in Assisi, Italy, in 1986, representatives of the world's religions made declarations about their commitment to the health of the environment. According to the Buddhist declaration, Buddhism's emphases on compassion and nonviolence make it a religion that "attaches great importance to wildlife and the protection of the environment on which every being in this world depends for survival."[5] Several months prior to the 2015 United Nations Climate Change Conference in Paris, the Dalai Lama, Thich Nhat Hanh, and other Buddhist leaders signed a "Buddhist Climate Change Statement to World Leaders" in which they urged world leaders to use wisdom and compassion to come to an agreement on actions that will preserve a healthy environment.

In order to work with others in achieving this goal, Buddhists have created numerous environmental organizations. These include One Earth Sangha, Dharma Action Network

Before the Buddha himself was first depicted in works of art, Buddhists venerated his footprints, which symbolized his path into nirvana. The convention of venerating his footprints continues today.

Buddhists of all sects demonstrate their reverence for the Buddha by bowing and prostrating themselves. Some show reverence while walking to a sacred site by bowing or prostrating themselves every step of the way.

As in Hinduism and Jainism, the lotus in Buddhism is a symbol of both purity and awakened awareness.

In Vajrayana Buddhism, monks spend weeks constructing sand mandalas such as the Avalokiteshvara Mandala shown here. The sacred image will then be swept toward the center and destroyed as a reminder of the impermanence of all things.

SEEKING ANSWERS

What Is Ultimate Reality?

According to the doctrine of interdependent origination, reality is a web of interrelated and interdependent phenomena in which nothing comes into existence independently of other things. Instead, the origination or coming-into-existence of things depends on all other things. All things are constituted of elements of other things. Nothing exists in and of itself. Further, according to the Buddha's doctrine of impermanence, all things are in a constant state of flux and without any underlying or enduring essence or identity.

How Should We Live in This World?

Believing that there is stability and permanence in the world, we desire to possess what we want and to avoid what we do not want. Our inability to do so results in suffering that arises from our ignorance of the true nature of reality. Accordingly, the Buddha's guide to life, the Noble Eightfold Path, begins with the acceptance of reality as it truly is. By striving for goals consistent with the Buddha's teaching about reality and living in accordance with the ethical principles he taught, we build lives that bring happiness and satisfaction.

What Is Our Ultimate Purpose?

For Buddhists, our ultimate purpose is to achieve the end of suffering that is found in nirvana. But Buddhists also recognize that suffering is a condition that afflicts all sentient beings. Moved by compassion for others, they seek to live in a way that encourages them to follow the path that will lead to their own awakening and liberation from suffering.

for Climate Engagement, Global Buddhist Climate Action, the International Network of Engaged Buddhists, and the Green Sangha. In addition, talks and programs sponsored by Buddhist temples, meditation centers, and other groups are encouraging their members to take an active role in addressing threats to the environment.

REVIEW QUESTIONS

For Review

1. Describe two ideas or practices that give Vajrayana Buddhism its distinctive character.
2. Why does the Buddha's doctrine of interdependent origination require us to think of ourselves and reality as a whole in a new way?
3. What is the Buddha's doctrine of no-self? How does it relate to the Buddha's teachings about interdependent origination and impermanence?
4. How does Zen differ from Pure Land Buddhism?

5. What did the Buddha mean by "suffering" (*dukkha*)? How does following the Noble Eightfold Path bring an end to suffering?

For Further Reflection

1. It is sometimes said that Buddhism is a philosophy rather than a religion. Do you agree?
2. How do the teachings of the Buddha differ from those of Hinduism? In what ways are they similar?

3. In what ways do the teachings of Mahayana Buddhism elaborate on those of early Buddhism?

4. Why is the principle of the Middle Way essential to Buddhism?

5. To what extent are the Buddha's teachings about the nature of reality in agreement with those of modern science?

6. Would you find it difficult to accept the Buddha's doctrine of no-self? Why or why not?

GLOSSARY

anatman (ahn-aht'muhn, Sanskrit; anatta, ahnaht'tah, Pali) "No-self." The Buddha's doctrine that there is no independent and eternal self or soul underlying personal existence.

arhat (ahr'huht; Sanskrit, "one who is worthy") In Theravada Buddhism, one who has attained nirvana and is not subject to rebirth.

bodhisattva (boh-dee-saht'vah; Sanskrit) "One who aspires to awakening."

Buddha (booh'duh; Sanskrit) An "awakened one" or "enlightened one."

buddha nature In Mahayana teaching, the awakened awareness of the Buddha, which is the true nature of the Buddha and, in fact, the true nature of all reality.

Chan Buddhism See **Zen Buddhism**.

Dharma (dahr'muh; Sanskrit) In Buddhism, the teachings of the Buddha.

dukkha (dook'kuh; Pali) Usually translated as "suffering," *dukkha* can also be understood as anxiety, unease, or dissatisfaction caused by the ignorance, attachment, and aversion that lead to unwholesome desire.

emptiness A Mahayana doctrine according to which all things are empty of any inherent existence. Also known as **shunyata** (shoon'yuh-tah; Sanskrit, "emptiness").

Four Noble Truths The four truths that are the basis of the Dharma in Buddhism: suffering is inherent in human life, suffering is caused by desire, there can be an end to desire, and the way to end desire is the Noble Eightfold Path.

interdependent origination The Buddha's teaching that reality is a complex of interdependent phenomena in which the origin or coming-into-existence of all things depends on all other things.

karma (kahr'muh; Sanskrit, "action") Because Buddhism emphasizes the intentions that precede actions, karma can be understood as "intentional action" and its consequences.

lama (lahm'ah; Tibetan, "guru" or "teacher") In Tibetan Buddhism, an authoritative teacher.

Mahayana Buddhism (mah-hah-yah'nah; Sanskrit, "Great Vehicle") The form of Buddhism most prominent in China, Tibet, Mongolia, Japan, South Korea, Vietnam, Indonesia, Malaysia, and Taiwan.

mandala (mahn'duh-luh; Sanskrit, "disk") A geometric figure, usually a circle, that makes use of elaborate symbolism to represent buddhahood.

mantra (mahn'truh; Sanskrit, "sacred utterance") A word or sound thought to have spiritual power.

Middle Way In the teaching of the Buddha, the path to awakening between the extremes of asceticism and self-indulgence.

Nichiren Buddhism (nee-chee-ren) A form of Mahayana Buddhism with origins in Japan.

nirvana (neer-vah'nuh, Sanskrit; Pali, nibbana). The ultimate goal of Buddhist practice, nirvana is the extinguishing of unwholesome desire and suffering.

Noble Eightfold Path The Buddha's prescription for a way of life that leads to awakening, it consists of the practice of eight ideals.

Pali Canon Also known as the *Tipitaka*, the Theravada canon of Buddhist texts consisting of three "baskets" of sutras.

parinirvana (pah'ree-neer-vah'nuh; Sanskrit) The full entry into nirvana at death of one who has attained nirvana, *parinirvana* brings release from samsara and rebirth.

Pure Land Buddhism A form of Mahayana Buddhism that emphasizes devotion to Amitabha Buddha.

samsara (sahm-sah'ruh; Sanskrit) The continuing cycle of birth, death, and rebirth; also, the this-worldly realm in which the cycle recurs.

sangha (sahn'guh; Sanskrit, "community") The community of Buddhist monks and nuns. Sangha can also denote individual communities of Buddhists or the worldwide community of Buddhists.

shunyata (shoon'yuh-tah; Sanskrit) A Mahayana doctrine according to which all things are empty of any inherent existence. Also known as **emptiness**.

skandhas (skahn'duhs; Sanskrit, "bundles" or "heaps") In Buddhism, transitory phenomena (material form, feelings, perceptions, mental constructions, and awareness) that give rise to a sense of self.

skillful means The Mahayana doctrine that in teaching or demonstrating the Dharma one should adapt one's words and actions to the needs of one's audience.

stupas (stooh'puhs; Sanskrit) Reliquary mounds or other structures in which the relics of the Buddha are preserved and venerated.

sutra (sooh'truh, Sanskrit; *sutta*, Pali) A text containing a discourse or sermon of the Buddha.

Theravada Buddhism (thai-ruh-vah'duh) The form of Buddhism that is most prominent in Sri Lanka, Thailand, Cambodia, Myanmar (Burma), and Laos.

Three Refuges Also known as the Three Jewels. Buddhists proclaim their identification as such by saying that they take refuge in, or place their trust in, the Buddha, the Dharma, and the Sangha.

Tiantai Buddhism (tyen-tai, Chinese; ten-dai, Japanese) Known as Tendai in Japan, Tiantai is a form of Mahayana Buddhism with origins in China.

Tipitaka (ti-pee'tah-kah; Pali, "three baskets") The Pali Canon of Buddhist texts.

trikaya (treh-kai'ya; Sanskrit, "three bodies") The Mahayana doctrine of the three "bodies" or modes of existence of the Buddha.

Vajrayana Buddhism (vuhj-ruh-yah'nuh; Sanskrit, "Thunderbolt Vehicle" or "Diamond Vehicle") The most prominent form of Mahayana Buddhism in Tibet, Nepal, Bhutan, and Mongolia.

Zen Buddhism The Japanese and (the Chinese name is Chan) for a Mahayana school that emphasizes meditation over doctrine.

SUGGESTIONS FOR FURTHER READING

Lopez, Donald. *The Story of Buddhism: A Concise Guide to Its History and Teachings*. New York: Harper, 2001. An excellent introduction to the history of Buddhism and Buddhist thought and practice.

Prebish, Charles, and Damien Keown. *Introducing Buddhism*. 2nd ed. London: Routledge, 2010. An authoritative introduction recommended as the first text to be consulted by those who are new to the study of Buddhism.

Skilton, Andrew. *A Concise History of Buddhism*. Birmingham, UK: Windhorse Publications, 1994. An excellent and accessible history of Buddhism.

Suzuki, Shunryu. *Zen Mind, Beginner's Mind*. New York: Weatherhill, 1997. An excellent introduction to meditation practice.

Williams, Paul. *Mahayana Buddhism: The Doctrinal Foundations*. 2nd ed. New York: Routledge, 2008. A history of Mahayana that places emphasis on the veneration of certain Buddhist texts.

ONLINE RESOURCES

The Wikipedia Buddhism Portal
Collection of articles in the Wikipedia Buddhism series that is generally quite reliable and extensive in scope.

Access to Insight: Readings in Theravada Buddhism
Readings that include helpful summaries and substantial translated portions of the Pali Canon.

The Berzin Archives
An excellent collection of translations, teaching, and scholarship on the Vajrayana tradition.

Jainism

6

Chapter Outline

6.1 Explain how the tirthankaras, especially Mahavira, exemplify Jain teachings.

6.2 Summarize the key beliefs central to an understanding of Jainism.

6.3 Explain the historical development of Jainism.

6.4 Differentiate the main varieties of Jainism.

6.5 Identify main practices and observances of Jain ascetics and laity.

6.6 Explain Jainism's engagement with social issues such as gender roles and environmentalism both in the Indian homeland and in the diaspora.

IN A SMALL VILLAGE in the southern Indian state of Karnataka, a middle-aged man stands silently in the main room of the home of Mr. and Mrs. Chandra, lifelong residents of the village and followers of the Jain religious tradition. Mr. Chandra carefully places small amounts of food in the cupped hands of his visitor. Other family members look on reverently, respectful and admiring both of the man who is receiving the food and of all that he represents—even though they have just met him for the first time. These morsels of food—thirty-two altogether—and the small amount of water to follow are the only things he will ingest on this or any other day. His sole possessions consist of a gourd for drinking water and a broom for sweeping the path before him as he walks, lest he accidentally destroy a living being even as small as an ant. As a monk of the **Digambara** (Sanskrit, "sky-clad") sect of Jainism, this visitor does not even possess clothing. He stands naked before the Chandra family and, during his annual eight-month period of wandering about the land, goes naked before the elements.

Along with illustrating the austerities of the Jain monastic life, this ritual of giving, known as *dana*, indicates certain distinctions between ascetics (that is, both monks and nuns) and laypeople. The Chandras and the other laypeople who have gathered to participate in this *dana* represent the great majority of Jains in the world today. As members of the laity, their religious duties differ from those of the ascetics, who exemplify Jainism's highest ideals of nonviolence

Jains worship in a temple at Ranakpur, India. Splendid marble temples such as this are a common feature of the Jain tradition.

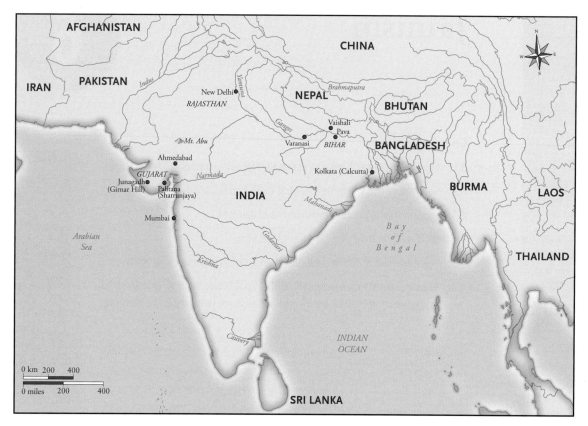

Significant sites in the development of Jainism.

and self-denial. The layperson depends on the ascetic for spiritual nourishment. But this in no way diminishes the sanctity or relevance of the lay religious life. The reverence shown by the roomful of admirers is as true to Jainism as is the monk's extraordinary self-discipline as he follows the ascetic path. Through such acts as *dana*, the lay participants can positively affect their **karma** ("action") and its consequences that determine prospects for a good rebirth. At the same time, the ascetic depends on laypeople like the Chandras for physical nourishment and support.

Viewing the scene from a more distant perspective, we can note other features of Jainism. For one thing, Mr. and Mrs. Chandra painstakingly prepared the food and carefully strained the water in preparation of the ritual, in order to avoid harming any living organism such as a tiny plant or insect in the water. They had invited the monk to partake of the food, for it would not befit one so venerated as a Digambara monk actually to have to beg for his food. The monk's accepting of the offerings was not a foregone conclusion. Had he for any reason found the circumstances objectionable and refused, the Chandras' reputation would have been damaged. In other words, the ritual of *dana* is played out within an interwoven network of religious and social ideas and forces. The fact that the monk stands naked with cupped hands is proof that he is a member of the Digambara sect, the more prevalent sect in southern India. In any number of households across India on this very morning, we could find similar scenes, but with some variations. Members of Jainism's **Shvetambara** sect, for example, don white robes and hold alms bowls for receiving their food. Or the ascetic could be a nun, in which case she would be clothed, even if she belonged to the Digambara sect.

Stepping back even further as we view this ritual of *dana*, we can observe a number of correlations with other South Asian religions. A nonviolent ethical stance, the ascetic path, karma, rebirth, and *dana* are also prominent aspects of Hinduism and Buddhism. Compared with those two religions, Jainism is a very small one, with just over 5 million adherents, the great majority of whom live in India. Because it rejects the authority of the Vedas (Chapter 4), Jainism (along with Buddhism) is considered to be distinctive relative to the Hindu traditions. Through the centuries, Jainism has earned a special reputation for having exemplified the ideal of nonviolence.

This chapter sheds light on the main elements of Jainism, with regard to both the ascetics and the laity—and the interplay between the two groups. For the most part, we focus on the traditional form of Jainism—what we might call the "orthodox" form, as it is lived to this day in India. We have already identified some central Jain teachings that are embraced by all Jains in India and beyond: nonviolence, the need for an ascetic lifestyle, and the ultimate need to attain perfect knowledge. In the following section, we explore in more detail these central elements and how they relate to the Jain understanding of the nature of the universe, the human condition, and the quest for spiritual deliverance. But first we will look to the distant past, to the foundational figures whom all Jains revere as the **jinas** (Sanskrit, "conquerors"), those the Jains believe have shown the way to spiritual deliverance.

TIMELINE
Jainism

c. Eighth century BCE	Probable period of Parshva, the twenty-third tirthankara.
Sixth or fifth centuries BCE	Probable period of Mahavira (Shvetambara traditional dates).
599–527 BCE	Digambaras date Mahavira's death at 510 BCE; current scholarly opinion holds that he died c. 425 BCE.
	(From antiquity through the medieval period, there is scant evidence for historical events, though there is much evidence for the Jains' general involvement in the cultural life of India, through the building of temples and monuments, founding of schools and sects, and interaction with other religions.)
1313 CE	Pillaging of Mount Shatrunjaya by Turkish invaders.
Fifteenth century	Period of Lonka, precursor of Sthanakvasi and Terapanthi sects.
1526	Founding of the Mughal Empire.
1556–1605	Akbar the Great (Mughal emperor who maintained good relations with Jain leaders).
Seventeenth century	Period of the founding of the Sthanakvasi sect.
1726–1803	Acarya Bhikshu, founder of the Terapanthi sect.
1867–1901	Shrimad Rajacandra (also spelled Rajchandra), teacher and mystic, friend of Mohandas (Mahatma) Gandhi.
1893	Lecture on Jainism delivered by Virchand Gandhi at the World's Parliament of Religions at Chicago.
1900–2000	Period of geographical expansion of sizable Jain communities outside of India.

6.1 The Teachings of Jainism: Mahavira and the Tirthankaras

Most of the world's religions look to a glorious founding figure, who is typically regarded both as an exemplar of the religious life and as the revealer of the religion's most significant teachings; the Buddha, Confucius, Jesus, and Muhammad are examples of such founding figures. Jainism looks not to just one but to a series of founding figures, the **tirthankaras**, "makers of the ford (or river crossing)." Each is considered to be a jina, "conqueror"—whence comes the name Jainism. Through having conquered the realm of samsara, the continuing cycle of death and rebirth (a concept that is also prominent in Hinduism and Buddhism), the tirthankara has, metaphorically, successfully crossed the river from the worldly realm to the beyond—the realm of the liberated.

The most recent of the tirthankaras, Mahavira, is especially significant. We begin this section by considering his captivating and highly influential life story.

Mahavira, the Twenty-Fourth and Last Tirthankara of This World Cycle

Nataputta Vardhamana, popularly known as Mahavira ("great hero"), was probably born near Vaishali (located in the northern Indian state of Bihar). He lived, according to the Shvetambara sect, from 599 to 527 BCE, although the Digambaras date his death at 510 BCE (and scholars tend to date it later still, to sometime in the second half of the fifth century BCE). The earliest biography of Mahavira is from the ninth century CE (the Sanskrit work *Vardhamanacharita*, by the poet Asaga), and so it is not possible to determine with historical certainty the details of his life. All, however, agree on one detail: Mahavira was a contemporary or near-contemporary of Gautama the Buddha, who lived in the same area of northern India and preached his last sermon at Vaishali. There is no record of the two having met, but their legendary biographies are strikingly similar.

Vardhamana is said to have been born into the ruling class (the kshatriyas), the second son of a rajah or local ruler who was also a pious Jain. Vardhamana grew up amid the luxuries of the palace, eventually marrying a princess named Yashoda (although the Digambara sect denies that he married), with whom he had a daughter. Eventually, however, he yearned for more than his princely life could offer, and so at age thirty he asked for permission to leave and become a monk. He joined a group of Jain ascetics who were followers of Parshva, the last tirthankara to have lived prior to Mahavira.

Vardhamana soon set off from the other ascetics and wandered about for over twelve years, naked and exposed. Fasting, going for long periods without sleep, withstanding the verbal and physical abuse of human opponents, and enduring the bites of insects rather than doing them harm, Vardhamana exemplified the ideals of nonviolence and asceticism, thereby earning his epithet "great hero," Mahavira.

In the thirteenth year of his ascetic wanderings, Mahavira is believed by Jains to have attained the state of *kevala*, or omniscience, the complete and perfect knowledge that leads at the time of death to liberation from the realm of samsara. The tradition recounts that Mahavira attained this enlightenment after spending two and a half days fasting in the heat of the sun, squatting near a tree but out of its shade. With these acts of extreme asceticism, his steadfastly nonviolent approach to life, and his supreme spiritual achievement of attaining *kevala*, Mahavira exemplifies Jainism's central ideals.

Now perfectly enlightened, Mahavira set about preaching the tenets of Jainism. His followers included eleven *ganadharas*, or disciples, who had been Hindu brahmins before hearing Mahavira's message. All of them eventually attained *kevala*, ending with Jambu, who is regarded as the last human being ever to attain *kevala* in this world cycle.

Mahavira preached for some thirty years until, at the age of seventy-two, he died in the town of Pava (like Vaishali, located in the northern Indian state of Bihar). Now liberated from his body, Mahavira's perfected soul is said to have ascended to the top of the universe in a state of eternal bliss.

Sculpture of Mahavira in the cave temples of Ellora, India.

It is helpful at this point to recall the similarities between the Buddhist accounts of Gautama's path to enlightenment (Chapter 5) and Mahavira's path to *kevala*. Both men practiced severe austerities. But whereas Mahavira continued on the path of strict asceticism to the very end of his life, Gautama, at the time of his enlightenment, rejected strict asceticism and instead embraced the Middle Way, which calls for moderation in the treatment of one's body. The distinction is highlighted during the climactic moments of each story, for while Gautama is said to have sat underneath the Bodhi tree when he experienced enlightenment, Mahavira is said to have squatted in the scorching heat of the sun, near a tree but apparently intentionally avoiding its shade.

Whatever the historical accuracy of these accounts, clearly the two traditions diverged over the question of the degree of ascetic rigor. Indeed, Buddhists typically held Jains in contempt for their extraordinary rigor, which for Jains has always been the hallmark of their religion and a mark of honor. And so, even though Buddhism and Jainism have a considerable amount in common doctrinally and in terms of practice and of artistic representations of their founding figures, who are typically shown in meditative trance, the two traditions seem not to have engaged much with each other. Apparently, it was this way from the beginning, for while Mahavira and Gautama the Buddha seem to have been at least near-contemporaries, none of the texts claim that they ever met.

An Eternal Succession of Tirthankaras

Jainism, like Hinduism and Buddhism, is categorized by scholars as an "eternal" religion in the sense that it subscribes to an ongoing succession of world cycles, without beginning or end. Jains believe that twenty-four tirthankaras, or jinas, have appeared in this current world cycle. Mahavira is the latest in an infinite line of previous tirthankaras, but he is not expected to be the last.

All twenty-four tirthankaras of this world cycle are known by name and by their specific symbols: Mahavira by the lion, for example, and Parshva—of whom there are more sculptures in India than of any other tirthankara—by the serpent. Along with Parshva and Mahavira, however, the only additional jinas who play a prominent role in the scriptures and in the tradition generally are the first, Rishabha (symbolized by the bull), and the twenty-second, Nemi (symbolized by the conch shell). Rishabha, who is clearly legendary and not historical, is believed to have been the father of Bharata, whom Jains regard as the first world emperor of this world cycle. Nemi, in addition to being the predecessor to Parshva, is traditionally thought to be a relative of Krishna, whom many Hindus revere as an avatar (human incarnation) of the god Vishnu (Chapter 4). The nineteenth tirthankara, Malli (symbolized by the jar), is also especially notable, for according to the Shvetambara sect, Malli was a woman. The Digambaras, who in general are more conservative, deny this assertion, regarding this tirthankara as a man by the name of Mallinatha.

Sandstone sculpture of Parshva, the tirthankara most commonly depicted in Jain art.

6.2 The Teachings of Jainism: Central Precepts

Jainism and Hinduism

Throughout the centuries, Jainism has coexisted with Hinduism. The list of interesting and relevant points of contact between the two religious traditions is almost endless. Here we shall make note of just a few of them, in order to shed some light on the cultural interplay.

Jains commonly worship deities of the Hindu pantheon, and they tend to think of them in similar ways. There are, however, certain glaring exceptions. For example, Hindus would probably be surprised to learn from one popular Jain text that Rama and Krishna were both pious Jains. Also, the various Jain renditions of the *Mahabharata*, the great epic poem that, in its more standard form, is regarded with devotion by almost every Hindu, transform Krishna into a devious trickster. As for Hinduism's part in this cultural interplay, devotees of the god Vishnu have at times adopted the tirthankara Rishabha as being an avatar of their god. These few examples suffice at least to indicate the extensive interaction between Jain and Hindu religious and other cultural aspects.

Cultural interaction and similarities notwithstanding, Jainism is very much its own tradition. Among its more distinctive features is the very special status assigned to the tirthankaras. Jains believe them to be human—not gods or avatars of gods—but nevertheless to deserve the highest degree of veneration.

Jain reverence for twenty-four tirthankaras, as opposed to focusing on just one founding figure, is instructive with regard to some basic elements of the religion. Why, you might wonder, would more than one jina be needed? Human nature, Jainism would answer, is depraved to the point of needing repeated assistance from these spiritual masters. In a related manner, Mahavira is the last jina of the present world cycle because human nature has become continually *more* depraved. In the present state of affairs, *kevala* is no longer a possibility in this world, having been attained for the last time by Jambu, the disciple of Mahavira.

So, the next logical question is, what hope do human beings have if they are confined to this realm of samsara? What needs to happen before a tirthankara once again appears to show humanity how to cross the river from this shore to the beyond, the eternal realm of complete freedom and perfect bliss? Answers to such questions call for an analysis of Jain teachings.

We will now turn to a brief survey of Jain scriptures, the main source of Jain teachings. All Jains agree that, originally, there were fifty-eight books of scripture based on the preaching of Mahavira, who in turn based his views on the earlier tirthankaras. These books are divided into three categories: *Purva*, *Anga*, and *Angabahya*. But much is believed to have been lost. The Digambaras believe that only excerpts from one of the books of *Purva* survive; these excerpts, together with later commentaries written about them, constitute Digambara scripture. The Shvetambara sect, however, officially rejects the Digambara texts and follows instead eleven books of *Anga* and thirty-four books of *Angabahya*.

Ahimsa and Asceticism: Jainism's Ideals

We have observed how, in the ritual of *dana* ("giving") and in the ascetic practices of Mahavira, the principle of nonviolence functions as a basic ethical norm in Jainism. This principle, commonly known by its Sanskrit name **ahimsa**, is prevalent throughout the traditional religions of India. Hindus and Buddhists, for instance, all tend to favor vegetarianism because of its relative nonviolence. Jainism emphasizes the place of ahimsa, the "pure, unchangeable, eternal law" in this well-known passage from the *Acharanga Sutra*, the first book of the *Angas*:

> All breathing, existing, living, sentient creatures should not be slain, nor treated with violence, nor abused, nor tormented, nor driven away. This is the pure, unchangeable, eternal law which the clever ones, who understand the world, have proclaimed.[1]

All aspects of life are set in the context of avoiding injury toward "sentient creatures," an extensive category that includes not only human beings and animals but also plant life. Jain ascetics expand the category nearly to its logical extreme, striving even to avoid harming the atomic particles believed to pervade the natural elements.

The most distinctive characteristic of Jain doctrine, then, is ahimsa, the avoidance of doing injury to any life form. As this striving to avoid violence becomes more intense, an ascetic lifestyle emerges naturally. Denying the body anything beyond what is necessary to sustain life lessens the risk of injuring other forms of life. Restricting one's diet to vegetables, for example, avoids doing violence to animals. On a more subtle level, straining one's water before drinking it (as we saw in this chapter's opening account of the Chandra household) and, indeed, drinking only as much water as is absolutely necessary further decreases violence, in this case to the small organisms that live undetected in drinking water.

Interrelated aspects of ahimsa are helpfully set forth by two other Jain concepts: *anekantavada* ("nonabsolutism") and *aparigraha* ("nonpossessiveness"). As stated in the introductory section of *Jain Way of Life*, a publication of the Federation of Jain Associations of North America, these three concepts—AAA—set forth the foundations of Jain teachings:

> Jains have three core practices: Non-Violence, Non-Absolutism, and Non-Possessiveness (Ahimsa, Anekantvad, and Aparigraha—AAA).
>
> *Non-Violence* is compassion and forgiveness in thoughts, words, and deeds toward all living beings. For this reason, Jains are vegetarians.
>
> *Non-Absolutism* is respecting views of others. Jains encourage dialog and harmony with other faiths.
>
> *Non-Possessiveness* is the balancing of needs and desires, while staying detached from our possessions.[2]

Another basic doctrine of Jainism is the need to diminish karma through limiting one's actions. In order to understand karma and Jain beliefs regarding spiritual fulfillment, it is best first to consider Jain cosmology, or its theory of the universe.

Theory of the Universe

According to tradition, Mahavira taught extensively and in detail about the nature of the universe, its makeup, and its functioning. He did so not merely as an intellectual exercise, but because, as he saw it, understanding the universe had sweeping implications for the spiritual quest. Thus, to understand Jain doctrine, one must understand Jain cosmology. We begin with considering the Jain concept of time, which incorporates the notion of eternally recurring cosmic or world cycles. Then we examine the makeup of the universe and all that exists within it.

Cosmic Cycles of Generation and Degeneration   In keeping with the general Indian notion of samsara, Jainism conceives of time as cyclical and envisions the cycles as upward and downward turnings of a wheel. During the upward turning of the wheel (which proceeds through six spokes, or ages), the world is in a state of ascendancy, with all aspects of existence, notably including the moral propensity of human beings, in the process of improvement. The three upper spokes are

considered to be a golden age of goodness and prosperity. Once passing the top of the wheel and entering into its downward turning, however, things begin gradually to decline, until the end of the age of the sixth spoke, at which point the universe reaches utter moral deprivation. Then the wheel once again begins its turn upward. And so it continues, eternally.

The traditional length of each of the six ages is 21,000 years. The world currently is in the age of the fifth spoke of the downward turning, called *Kali Yuga*, to be followed by the sixth, final period of degeneration. In this sixth age, the theory goes, people are more prone to immorality, and they become physically smaller. The consequences for the spiritual quest are pronounced, for human beings can no longer hope to attain *kevala* in this world until the wheel has once again begun its upward turning. Mahavira is the last of the tirthankaras of the turning of the wheel in which we now live, and his eleven *ganadharas*, ending with Jambu, are the last people to achieve liberation during this cycle. The wheel will need to advance considerably into its upward motion before anyone else can hope again to attain *kevala* in this world.

Notably, Rishabha, the first tirthankara of this downward turning of the world cycle, is believed to have appeared during the third spoke. Before that, the world was so healthy morally and spiritually that human beings did not need a jina to show them the way to liberation. Rishabha and the other early tirthankaras are understood to have been of greater physical stature than their successors.

The concept of *Kali Yuga* and the continuing downward turning of the wheel gives rise to a fundamental and serious question. If indeed *kevala* is no longer a possibility, what purpose is there in continuing to pursue the religious life? Thinking again of the *dana* ritual, why should laypeople like the Chandras go to the effort of giving so conscientiously to monks? And why would anyone opt to undergo the physical hardships of the ascetic life? Part of the answer depends on the nature of karma, which we will address next. Another part of the answer is provided through consideration of the composition of the universe, which Jains call the **loka** and regard as containing within it three distinct lands inhabited by human beings.

The *Loka*   The *loka* is understood to be vast almost beyond description. Over the centuries, Jains have speculated as to just how vast the *loka* is, deriving a unit of measure known as the "rope," which is strikingly similar to the "light-year" of modern astrophysics. According to one account, the *loka* is fourteen ropes from top to bottom. This means, according to traditional Jain calculations, that it would take a god, flying at the speed of 10 million miles per second, seven years to traverse its full span. These attempts at specifying the size of the universe are probably to be taken figuratively rather than literally. Still, a tendency toward something like scientific understanding is in keeping with the Jain belief that perfect and complete knowledge is attainable and indeed has been attained—namely, by Mahavira, his disciples, and the countless numbers of those who have achieved enlightenment before them.

The *loka*, then, is a vast and yet a finite space, within which all beings dwell. Beyond the *loka* there is nothing but strong winds. The *loka*, together with everything in it, has always existed and will continue to exist eternally. Jainism thus does not believe in a creator god.

Jains sometimes depict the *loka* as a diagram in the shape of a giant man, the *purusha*. Across the midsection runs a relatively small band known as the Middle Realm, which contains a series of oceans and continents, three of which together form the region inhabited by human beings. This region is further divided into various lands, one of which is India and another of which, Mahavideha, is not affected by the corruption of this world cycle and therefore continues to be the home of tirthankaras and of human beings who still can attain *kevala*. This notion is crucial when considering the quest for spiritual liberation that takes place in this corrupt world. As we shall discuss in more detail shortly, living a good life that is true to Jain ideals leads to a good rebirth, perhaps even in a land like Mahavideha, where tirthankaras currently reside and where *kevala* is a possibility.

Below the Middle Realm is a series of progressively darker hells, whose denizens suffer agonizing torments. At the very bottom of the *loka*, below the lowest hell, there are only clouds. Above the Middle Realm is a series of progressively brighter heavens, inhabited by deities who enjoy pleasures not unlike those of earthly rulers. For both the denizens of hell and the deities, their stays in those realms are only temporary, as they will eventually be reborn in another realm. In other words, just as in Hinduism and Buddhism, the realm of samsara extends well beyond the human domain. Because only humans can ever attain *kevala*, however, the Jains believe that even being reborn as a deity in one of the brightest heavens is ultimately not as fortunate as it might seem. The best rebirth is as a human being, so that the quest for spiritual fulfillment can be continued.

At the top of the *loka*, in the crown of the head of *purusha*, is a roof that is described as having the shape of an umbrella. Called the "slightly curved place," this is the eternal home of the souls that have been liberated from the realm of samsara.

Categories of Existence: Jiva and Ajiva

Jain scriptures spell out the categories of existing things in meticulous detail (in keeping with the belief in the omniscience of Mahavira and others who have attained *kevala*). The categories of existence can be said to begin with a simple distinction: that between the living, which is termed **jiva**, and the non-living, **ajiva**. The non-living is further divided into four: motion, rest, atoms, and space. These four basic entities plus the jiva are the five building blocks of all that exists in the universe. The entities interact but forever maintain their individual existence. This view contrasts with the main form of Hindu cosmology, which envisions an ultimate union of all being. Furthermore, Jainism holds that the universe has an infinite number of atoms, forever distinct from one another, along with an infinite number of jivas, or souls.

Each jiva ("soul") is eternal, completely without form, and yet capable of inter-acting with the atoms of the body it inhabits in such a way that it can control the body's mechanisms. While avoiding the notion that the jiva is in any way dependent upon the body, Jainism does posit a complex integration of soul with body. Thus, while bodies do act, it is the soul that wills actions and therefore is held responsible for their moral quality.

All jivas are essentially equal, regardless of the bodies they inhabit. For example, the jiva of an insect is considered to be of identical quality to that of a large animal or a human being. This belief has significant implications with regard to the doctrine of ahimsa, as it encourages equal treatment of all living beings.

The great variety of bodies inhabited by the jivas produces many different life forms. Jainism's detailed classification of these life forms is among its most fascinating features, and one that shows remarkable similarities to the modern field of zoology. A simple twofold approach distinguishes life forms that are stationary, such as plants, from those that are moving. Another approach categorizes life forms based on the number of senses they have. In the words of one text:

> Up to the vegetable-bodied ones, selves have one sense [i.e., touch].
>   Worms, ants, bumblebees, and men each have one more than the one preceding.[3]

Human beings are thus categorized with life forms having five senses: deities, denizens of hell, and most animals aside from insects. Flying insects (bumblebees and the like) are thought to lack the sense of hearing, while most that crawl on legs also lack sight. Along with such insects as worms, shellfish are thought to have only the senses of touch and taste. Plants and "microbes" (a large category of the most basic life forms) are devoid of all sensations but touch.

More elaborate systems of classification abound in Jain scriptures. This fascination with the intricacies of life forms supports the religion's general concern for their welfare and for maintaining the attitude and practices that secure this welfare as best possible. To some extent, the attitude and practices of the religious life are expected of nonhuman life forms as well. Lions, for example, are said to be able to learn to fast. Even plants and the simplest microbes are believed to have some basic religious capacity that they can apply toward spiritual advancement. Ultimately, however, all jivas must be reborn as human beings before they have any chance of attaining *kevala* and release from the realm of samsara.

Liberation and Salvation

Many religions typically emphasize teachings concerning salvation or liberation, and Jainism is no exception. As our account will make clear, salvation depends on understanding the challenges of samsara and how to overcome them.

To begin, salvation in no way depends on the power of a deity. Just as Jainism has no creator god, neither does it have one to assist with the all-important quest for liberation. Some would thus label Jainism an atheistic religion, but this is not quite accurate. We have seen that in the Jain cosmology, deities inhabit the various heavens. Many of their names would be recognizable to the student of Hinduism, for the pantheons are similar. Thus, Jainism might best be labeled *transtheistic*[4] in the sense that there are gods (in fact, a great variety of gods), but ultimately the religion moves beyond them when it comes to the truly crucial issues of salvation. To understand why this is so, let us first examine Jainism's concept of karma.

Karma and the Human Condition

Notwithstanding the intricate categories of existence, so far as the human condition is concerned, Jainism is best understood in terms of two categories: soul (jiva) and matter (ajiva). As noted earlier, the jiva is essentially pure and formless. And yet, for reasons that defy explanation, souls have become entwined with impure matter, causing them to be weighed down and bound to samsara. Human beings are born into this state. The religious life strives to clean away the dirt that tarnishes the jiva, returning it to its original state of pristine purity and releasing it from samsara, so it can ascend upward to the "umbrella" ceiling of the *loka*, the realm of liberated souls.

For Jains, the term *karma* refers to the process in which matter dirties the soul. In both Hinduism and Buddhism, karma is commonly understood as involving the law of cause and effect. This general notion applies to Jainism as well, but here the term's more literal meaning of "action" is stressed. Because all actions encumber the jiva with matter, whenever the soul wills an action, it risks tarnishing itself. Immoral actions, those that violate the principle of ahimsa or other Jain ethical teachings, are especially damaging because they dirty the jiva with heavier impurities. Highly virtuous actions, in contrast, bring about only small quantities of light matter that neither cling to the soul nor weigh it down.

Along with this emphasis on the material aspects of karma, Jainism also emphasizes the intentions behind one's actions. That is, the immorality that tarnishes the soul with heavy matter lies mainly in the evil intention, not in the consequence of the action. Similarly, an action that might appear to have evil consequence could be considered moral if good was intended. For example, the accidental killing of microbes, provided proper means were taken to avoid it, would generally not be immoral and thus would not lead to the dirtying of the jiva.

Kevala: Omniscience That Leads to Liberation

Kevala, best translated as "omniscience," is knowledge of everything: the nature of one's inner self, of one's past lives, and of the external world and all things, including fellow living beings (and their past lives and future lives) that inhabit it. Little wonder that Jainism so boldly sets forth cosmological explanations, based as they are on the omniscience of Mahavira and the other tirthankaras. One who has attained this state is a *kevalin*.

The most significant feature of *kevala* is that it frees the jiva completely from the tarnishing effects of karma so that it may be liberated. The final experience of liberation or release is known as moksha (as it is in Hinduism). Moksha and *kevala* are distinguishable in that one who has attained *kevala* normally goes on living in the physical body, confined to the realm of samsara, while one who achieves moksha is liberated from the body. Mahavira, like the jinas before him, passed many years as an enlightened one (sometimes referred to in Jainism, as in Buddhism, as arhat) before experiencing moksha at the time of his death, which finally freed him completely from any impurities that would bind him to the material world.

You might ask at this point, does omniscience lead to the purity of the soul, or does purification of the soul bring about omniscience? A Jain would respond by asserting that the two work together harmoniously. This notion of religious impulses working in harmony is embodied in the Jain concept of the Three Jewels of the religion: right faith (*darshana*), right knowledge (*jnana*), and right practice (*charitra*). All three are integral to the religious quest. Right faith, which for Jainism involves a proper outlook or mindset, the correct way of "seeing" (which is the root meaning of *darshana*), nurtures right knowledge and practice. Likewise for the other Jewels; they function together like three legs of a stool.

The Quest for a Heavenly Rebirth

We have noted that Jambu, the last of Mahavira's eleven disciples to attain *kevala*, is believed to be the last person of this world in the current cycle ever to achieve liberation. But this does not imply that for Jains living since Jambu's time it is meaningless to seek liberation. Every living being remains destined for rebirth, and the nature of rebirth depends on karmic status. A good rebirth, into the delights of one of the heavens or back into the human realm, therefore requires living a good life.

In contrast to the beliefs of most Hindus (and some Buddhists), Jainism understands rebirth as occurring immediately after death. This has various implications that set Jainism apart from Hinduism, especially in regard to the need to perform rituals on behalf of the dead. For Jains, such rituals are deemed superfluous—which is not to say that Jains forgo mourning rituals or that they fail to honor their deceased loved ones. But the most crucial thing, the destiny of the deceased's soul, is determined as soon as the person dies. In fact, the soul is believed immediately to begin animating another life form.

Having examined the primary teachings of Jainism, we now turn our attention to the various ways these teachings have been manifested in Jain society and rituals.

6.3 The History of Jainism

In the previous section, we focused on Jain teachings. Turning now to a study of Jain history, we begin by considering the general place of Jainism in the context of Indian religions.

The Indian Historical Context

Earlier in this chapter we learned about the traditional understanding of Jainism's founding figures: the tirthankaras of this world cycle, most notably Mahavira. Here, our attention shifts to the scholarly understanding of Jainism's historical foundations, so we can observe some features of Indian religious culture that help situate the stories of the tirthankaras within a broader context.

Jains themselves do not regard Mahavira as having founded their religion. Historians, too, tend to agree with the traditional view that Mahavira himself followed an already established form of Jainism—possibly that of Parshva, the twenty-third tirthankara of this world cycle. Scholars situate Parshva's lifetime in the eighth century BCE. As noted previously, there are more sculptures in India of this tirthankara than of any other, Mahavira included, indicating his great popularity as an object of Jain devotion.

In the eighth century BCE, the probable period of Parshva, Indian civilization was beginning an important transition. The Vedic period, named for the Sanskrit texts that form the scriptural foundation of Hinduism, was ending, as was the domination of the priestly leadership of the brahmin caste (Chapter 4). Now began a period of religious diversity that included philosophical speculation on the Upanishads (themselves, technically, the last section of the Vedic corpus) and religious movements that eventually gave rise to Buddhism and the devotional forms of Hinduism that continue today. Parshva, and Mahavira after him, fit into a general category of religious movements that emphasized asceticism as a means of spiritual development.

Perhaps because of Jainism's belief in a never-ending succession of world cycles, Jains have not kept a detailed historical record of their own tradition. As we have seen, the dates for the lifespan of Mahavira are a matter of dispute, and so, too, is the place of his birth. The texts that contain the accounts were written hundreds of years after the fact. Similarly, much of the story of Jainism through its early centuries does not lend itself to precise historical reckoning. With the religious changes of the period around 1000 CE, the historical record begins to become clearer.

The Legacy of the Tirthankaras: Jainism through the Centuries

In the ninth century CE, about the time that the influence of Buddhists was severely diminishing in India, the country's religious landscape was undergoing a rather sudden shift with the influx of Islam. Muslim rule was established in 1192 in the form of the Delhi Sultanate, which was succeeded in 1526 by the Mughal Empire. During the early centuries of Muslim rule, relations between Muslims and Jains were not always friendly. There are accounts of large-scale destruction of sacred Jain sites, for example, the Muslims' pillaging of Mount Shatrunjaya, a major Jain pilgrimage site in the western state of Gujarat, in 1313. But during the period of Mughal rule, and especially at its apex during the reign of Akbar the Great (1556–1605), remarkably close relations developed. Akbar himself was the close friend of a Jain leader,

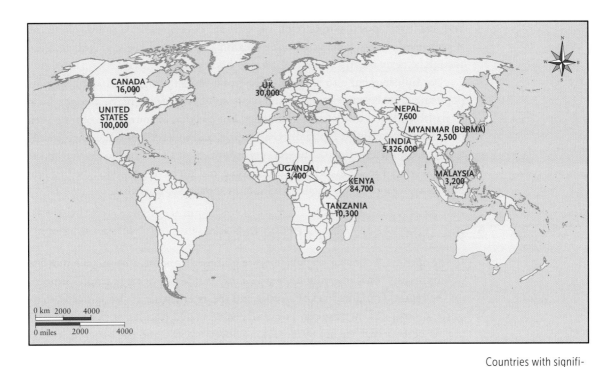

and he issued several decrees promoting the protection of animals, motivated apparently by learning about the Jain emphasis on ahimsa.

During the eighteenth and nineteenth centuries, Jainism became somewhat more diverse through establishment of the Sthanakvasi and Terapanthi sects. In the twentieth century, immigration led to the establishment of Jain communities in various places around the globe.

Countries with significant Jain populations (all figures are approximate, as estimates vary widely).

Recent Developments in the Jain Tradition

Given that there are fewer than 6 million Jains in India, living alongside over 1 billion Hindus, the Jain influence on contemporary Indian culture is quite remarkable. To some extent, this influence can be measured in financial terms. For centuries, Jains have been very successful in business, perhaps because of their religiously motivated focus on trade as opposed to agriculture. Also, the Jain community is highly respected for its charitable giving. In keeping with their profound emphasis on ahimsa, Jains commonly take in and care for animals that are maltreated or are targeted for slaughter. Although they generally do not actively seek converts to their religion, Jains tend to be outspoken advocates of universal vegetarianism, and so they have exercised wide influence in this regard.

Among Jains of recent times, Shrimad Rajacandra (1867–1901; also spelled Rajchandra) is especially known outside of India because of his connection to Mohandas (Mahatma) Gandhi. Both from the state of Gujarat, they met in 1891, and according to Gandhi's autobiography, Rajacandra made a strong impression and had a very positive impact on his spiritual development. Gandhi, of course, is perhaps the most famous advocate of ahimsa the world has ever known, even though he never overtly adopted Jainism as his religion.

Jain influence has also reached well beyond India through the Indian diaspora population. Their centuries-old focus on business has made life in the modern world a relatively natural thing for the Jain laity. For ascetics, of course, life outside their traditional homeland is especially challenging; and indeed, it is quite rare, as only the Sthanakvasi and Terapanthi sects even allow monks and nuns to journey in the world at large. The Terapanthis are responsible, too, for having founded the first Jain university, recently established at Ladnum in the state of Rajasthan.

6.4 Jainism as a Way of Life: Varieties

In the opening section of this chapter, we glimpsed a moment in the religious life of Jainism, the ritual of giving known as *dana*. While this ritual illustrates concern for the central Jain principles of ahimsa and the ascetic path, it also indicates some of the diversity of the religion. For example, we noted features of the Digambara version of *dana* that are not found among Shvetambaras, and the basic distinction between the ascetics and the Jain laity was evident. In this section, we examine in greater detail these varieties of Jainism.

Digambaras and Shvetambaras

Before highlighting those features that distinguish the Digambaras from the Shvetambaras, it is important to acknowledge the many things they share in common, including a general heritage of teachings and similar forms of practice. Still, the differences are interesting and instructive, helping to illustrate Jainism's rich diversity.

We have noted some differences at earlier points in the chapter. The two sects posit differing dates for the death of Mahavira (527 BCE for Shvetambaras, 510 BCE for Digambaras). The Digambaras deny that Mahavira ever married. In keeping with their generally more conservative views, Digambaras do not agree that the nineteenth tirthankara, whom the Shvetambaras know as Malli and the Digambaras as Mallinatha, was a woman.

The most obvious issue differentiating the two sects involves clothing. Digambara (or "sky-clad") monks, as their name infers (and as we have witnessed in the *dana* ceremony), go about naked; Digambara nuns do not, donning simple white garments as do their counterparts in other

Jain ascetics and impressive religious monuments, such as this nun on pilgrimage at Shravanabelagola, are common sights in India. Through its diaspora population of some 275,000 people, Jainism also has a significant presence outside of India.

Jain sects. From the Digambara perspective, wearing clothes puts monks back into the ordinary category of the laity. Nuns are not esteemed quite as highly as monks, and in general, Digambara doctrine is more severe than the other sects when it comes to spiritual deliverance of men versus women. In short, women (including nuns, even though they perform the same ascetic practices as monks) are deemed incapable of attaining *kevala*; they must await rebirth in a male body in order to reach the potential of final deliverance.

VOICES: An Interview with Girish Shah

Girish Shah was born in the Indian state of Gujarat, which is home to many Jains and to important pilgrimage destinations. He attended college in Mumbai and then left India to attend graduate school in the United States, where he now lives. A founding member and director of the Jain Center of Northern California and the Federation of Jain Associations in North America, Mr. Shah is dedicated to educating people about his religion.

What do you consider to be the most important reason for living a proper Jain religious life?

The goal is to become free of karma. To make your soul and its properties of infinite knowledge, infinite vision, infinite strength, and infinite capacity to character "clean," you have to get rid of all the karmas that are polluting it. For one to live a religious life it is important to achieve that. . . . But for me, the more important part of living the proper religious life is that it is the way you will support each other, it is the way you will serve each other. You are helping each other grow, and you are reciprocating, giving back. We need to have empathy toward everyone. Forgiveness is not for those who have done nothing to you; forgiveness is for someone who has hurt you.

Girish Shah.

Do you consider Jainism to be an atheistic religion?

I think the question is what you mean by "atheistic religion." If you mean by atheistic religion god the creator and god the controller and god the sustainer; that there is an entity that created the world, that controls the world, that sustains the world, and that judges everybody, then no. We do not believe in god in that sense, but we do believe in the quality of the soul, which is godliness. Infinite compassion—that is the characteristic of soul. The knowledge, the vision, and working with and relating to everybody, comes from infinite compassion. And that has the power, that has the godlike characteristics. It doesn't control anything. Even our enlightened or tirthankaras cannot make me achieve moksha. They can show me the path, but cannot say, such as the gods will say, "I bless you." There is no blessing. There is no divine grace that anyone can give. Forgiveness has to be done by you, by your own action. The burden is on you completely, but you can achieve it. Jainism is the religion that says: "I am god" (if we call the tirthankara "god," which is the common word that we use). No other religion tells you that you can become god. But Jainism says everyone can become god.

How important to you are vegetarianism and other forms of ahimsa?

Very important. The idea is to minimize the amount of *himsa* that you are doing, and so you give up some of these things—at least for the important religious days, if not all the time. Some people will take vows to give up this or that for their entire lifetime. Increasingly I am becoming vegan, knowing that there is so much *himsa* in dairy. I have not become fully vegan, but hopefully someday I'll get there. Traditionally, milk was okay, because of the way cows were treated before. Now things have changed, and so we have to evolve and look at it. It's just sensitivity to it. Here is another example. I ask myself: "Why am I wasting natural resources?" I have a nice home. I have never felt the need to go beyond. This is my first house and my last house. I have no attachment to the house. People say, "Girish, you should be living in a beautiful big home," and I say, "What beautiful big home? Why do I need one?" It's all internalizing. I don't have the need. I have a four-bedroom house; it's big enough. That's plenty of space, 1,800 square feet. Why do I need a 7,000-square-foot house, why do I need a 10,000-square-foot house? Just because I can afford it doesn't mean that I should have it. . . . This is all part of ahimsa. It's all part of ahimsa because then you are not wasting your resources. Charity is a form of ahimsa because you are now using money that you made for the benefit of others, for their growth, their progress, their betterment of life. People need to have betterment of life beyond their basic needs in order for them to spiritually think. If you don't have enough even to eat and to think, you're not going to have spirituality.

You immigrated to the United States from India. What do you consider to be the most notable differences between being a Jain in India and being a Jain in the United States?

For Jains in India, things are taken for granted, whereas being a Jain here, you have to put up with a lot of issues. Every time I go shopping, it takes a half hour reading the ingredients to see how many animal products are in it. There is no green mark on food packaging here like we have in India, where you can look at it and say, green—it is vegetarian. Also, I can't walk to places here. In India, you walk to places. You don't have to use the car. To go shopping, to go to the temple, you walk. Here in California you have to drive, particularly when you drive here in summer, your car windshield is filled with all those butterflies that you're killing on the way. And so my wife refuses to travel at night. You're going to get up in the morning and go. You're not going to kill all those butterflies, just to get there at night.

Another identifying feature of the Digambara sect involves the ascetics' avoidance of alms bowls as a means of collecting food, using instead only their cupped hands. The reasoning is based in the principle of ahimsa: washing of bowls presumably would bring about greater harm by injuring tiny insects or microbes in the water. The same reasoning supports the "sky-clad" practice of monks, for the washing of dirty clothes causes harm. Finally, as previously noted, the Digambaras have their own official collection of scriptures.

A sizable majority of Jains are Shvetambaras. Since about the thirteenth century CE, they have followed their set of forty-five sacred texts as authoritative. Unlike the

Digambaras, they use alms bowls when begging for food; they accept the possibility of a woman attaining *kevala*; and, of course, they wear clothing (monks and nuns alike), consisting of upper and lower white garments.

Interestingly, even Shvetambara texts make clear that Mahavira and his early male followers went about naked. Gradually, the opinion arose among Shvetambaras that the wearing of clothes was an option. One text from the second or third century CE designates three specific factors making this permissible: embarrassment; causing others to feel disgust; and inability to endure hardships caused by nakedness.[5]

Sthanakvasis and Terapanthis

Within Shvetambara Jainism, two distinctive sects, the Sthanakvasi and the Terapanthi, have features that distinguish them somewhat from their parent. Most significantly, both reject the worship of images, which is a common religious practice among the majority of Shvetambaras. Ascetics of both sects constantly wear the *muhpatti* ("mouth shield"), a cloth that protects insects from accidentally being inhaled as the monks and nuns traverse the land. And both sects allow monks and nuns to travel abroad.

The Sthanakvasis trace their origins to the seventeenth century, the Terapanthis to the late eighteenth century. The Sthanakvasis are relatively liberal with regard to the role of women. For instance, of the over 3,000 Sthanakvasi ascetics today, about five-sixths are nuns, and nuns are allowed to travel unaccompanied by monks.

Jain emblem. The emblem's outline represents the *loka*, or universe. The swastika (a Sanskrit term implying "well-being") is an ancient and common symbol in various religious traditions, Jainism among them; its four arms represent the four realms of life (heavens, human realm, animal realm, and hells). The hand represents ahimsa.

Tirthankara. Sculptures of tirthankaras, like this one of Rishabha, whom Jains revere as the first of the current world cycle, are objects of Jain worship.

Whisk. Shown here with a book of Jain scripture, the whisk is used by ascetics to clear away, and thus to protect, insect life. It symbolizes ahimsa.

6.5 Jainism as a Way of Life: Practices and Observances

Along with aspects of Jain life that distinguish various sects, distinctive practices and observances apply to Jain ascetics, on one hand, and Jain laypeople, on the other, as was demonstrated in the chapter's opening with regard to *dana*, ritual

A Jain monk wearing the *muhpatti* in order to prevent unnecessary harm to airborne insects.

giving. In this section, we explore these practices and observances in greater detail.

The Ascetic Life

Through their biographies and teachings, the tirthankaras, "makers of the river crossing," show the way to liberation to all Jains. However, as neither the tirthankaras nor any Jain deities can bestow salvation, all individuals must make their own spiritual progress and eventually attain their own deliverance. Moreover, as noted, Jains believe that the ascetic life offers the spiritual path that best replicates the lives and follows the teachings of the jinas. Still, no one expects the average Jain to enter upon this arduous path. Simply having entered into the human realm does not imply that one is ready for the ascetic life. A Jain takes this life on gradually, after having become an accomplished layperson who fulfills all religious duties successfully and with a pure disposition. When the circumstances are right, whether in this lifetime or in a future lifetime, the decision to renounce the lay life and become an ascetic is made.

The decision of renunciation is not to be made lightly. The initiation ritual, *diksha*, marks the point at which the individual becomes completely committed to the ascetic life. Through the centuries, minimum age requirements have been imposed—young adulthood for the Digambara sect, younger for the Shvetambaras (historically, as young as age six, although today only the Terapanthi sect permits the initiation of young children). The ceremony includes a symbolic removal of hair (via the traditional method of being pulled out tuft by tuft) and presentation to the initiate of the whisk and other implements of the ascetic life, such as the alms bowl for Shvetambaras. *Diksha* is overseen by a teacher, who typically continues to provide guidance to the new ascetic. The ritual marks the symbolic rupturing of the participant's past and future lifestyles, usually involving total separation from one's family, although Shvetambara nuns are on occasion allowed to interact with family members.

Ascetics depend on the almsgiving of the Jain laity, and sometimes of Hindus, in order to eat. Usually wandering in groups, they spend eight months of the year traversing the land, and then four months, during the rainy season, with lay communities. By remaining settled during this wet period, the ascetics do not jeopardize the well-being of life forms, which tend to be on the roads in greater numbers because of the rains. So, once again, the principle of ahimsa underlies Jain practice.

The Five Great Vows   All ascetics commit to five "Great Vows" that serve as the doctrinal groundwork of both their inner purity of intention and their outer purity of action:

1. Avoid inflicting violence (ahimsa) on other life forms.
2. Abstain from lying.
3. Do not take what has not been given.
4. Renounce sexual activity.
5. Renounce possessions.

Jain texts expand on these vows in great detail, elaborating on the subtleties of their content and means of satisfactorily fulfilling them. As you might expect, most attention is devoted to the first vow, as ahimsa is understood to be the foundation of the entire ethical outlook of Jainism. Each of the other four vows is interrelated to ahimsa. For example, the third vow (not to take what is not given) is interpreted to mean, in its most profound sense, not to take a life. The fifth vow is understood also to imply avoidance of violence, for to renounce possessions is to deflect the passion that arises through attachments to them. Passion is thought to be a primary cause of violence.

Ascetic Practices   The basic impulse toward asceticism, so pervasive throughout the history of Jainism, is grounded in two objectives: the avoidance of further dirtying of the jiva with karmic matter and the eventual burning off of the matter that has already tainted it. Specific practices are prescribed in Jain texts, notably the Six Obligatory Duties, which for the Shvetambara sect are enumerated as follows (the Digambara list differs only slightly):

1. Equanimity, achieved through meditation
2. Praise of the tirthankaras
3. Veneration of teachers
4. Repentance
5. Laying down the body (standing or sitting motionless for varying periods of time)
6. Abandonment (renunciation of specific foods or activities for a certain period of time)

The Six Obligatory Duties are to be performed by all ascetics and, ideally, by laypeople as well. The specifics of each duty are developed in the texts. The duty of repentance, for example, involves acknowledging wrongdoings before one's teacher twice daily and ends with the recitation of a passage well known to Jains: "I ask pardon from all living creatures. May all creatures pardon me. May I have friendship for all creatures and enmity towards none."[6]

Perhaps the most startling Jain ascetic practice in the view of outsiders is *salle-khana*, the intentional fasting of oneself to death. Although this practice was quite

The Dilwara Temple on Mount Abu in the state of Rajasthan is famous for its exquisite, delicate carvings and architectural design.

common in earlier times and is believed to have been the form of dying adopted by Mahavira and other great ascetics of the past, today it is rare. Insistent that *sallekhana* is in no way suicidal, Jains argue that, because the act of eating generally involves the risk of harming other life forms, fasting even to the point of ending one's own life is a highly effective means of warding off karma. In general, an individual's mindset at the moment of death is considered to be a significant factor for the prospects of rebirth, and so *sallekhana*, lacking the passion and violence that regularly accompanies suicide and instead fostering a tranquil and meditative state, is thought to provide an ideal means of dying.

The Religious Life of the Jain Laity

Although Jainism is best known for its asceticism, a balanced understanding of the religion demands a careful look at the role of the laity. For one thing, lay adherents constitute the great majority of Jains. Also, even as the laity looks to the monks and nuns as exemplars of Jain ideals, the ascetics themselves depend on the lay community for their livelihood and support. In other words, these two components function hand in hand. The worship activities of the Jain laity are rich and diverse and have been a vital part of the religious life of India for centuries.

Jain worship occurs on two separate levels. At the more mundane level, the objects of worship are various gods who, as we have noted, tend to be the same as those worshiped by Hindus. While having nothing to do with the ultimate religious pursuit of liberation, the gods are believed to respond to material needs, such as providing weather favorable for agriculture and cures for health maladies.

On a more sublime level, Jains worship the tirthankaras—even though they, like the gods, are unable actively to assist a worshiper in achieving salvation. Nevertheless, worship of the tirthankaras nurtures a properly devout religious attitude; its net effect is to burn off the dirtying karma that weighs down the soul. It is this second level of worship that warrants our consideration here.

Religious Places   In its most visible form, Jain worship concentrates on images of the tirthankaras, although, as we have observed, the Sthanakvasis and Terapanthis shun this. Most of this worship takes place in temples, some of which rank among India's most impressive architectural achievements. For example, the Dharna Vihara at Ranakpur in the state of Rajasthan, which is dedicated to the tirthankara Rishabha, is remarkable for its unique four-directional design, four-faced image of the tirthankara, and 1,400 carved columns. Along with such spectacular temples as the Dharna Vihara, many temples co-exist with shops and offices on city streets, indistinguishable from the neighboring buildings.

Jain sacred places also include various sites in the countryside, such as Mount Shatrunjaya in Gujarat in western India, one of five sacred mountains for Shvetambara Jains. Hundreds of shrines are located at Mount Shatrunjaya, and one textual tradition predicts that nineteen future tirthankaras will spend time preaching there.

Shatrunjaya, a hill near the town of Palitana, India, and for centuries an important Jain pilgrimage site, features 863 temples of various sizes and styles.

Pilgrimages to places like Mount Shatrunjaya constitute an important aspect of lay worship. Every Jain strives to make at least one pilgrimage in his or her lifetime. Typically undertaken at considerable expense, the pilgrimage offers each lay individual an opportunity to experience, through the interruption of normal life and the rigors of journeying to the site, an ascetic lifestyle for a temporary period. This experience allows for the concentration of effort in gaining karmic merit. Traditionally, pilgrimages were made on foot, which is still the mode of transportation for ascetics. Today, laypeople often travel by train or other modern means. Sometimes the expenses for entire groups of pilgrims are paid for by one person, who is thought to gain much karmic merit through this act of benevolence.

Rituals and Observances
In addition to the relatively rigorous periods of pilgrimage, the religious life of the Jain laity overlaps with that of the ascetics in some everyday aspects. All Jains are careful with regard to their eating habits. They are diligently vegetarian, and they go well beyond abstaining from meat by avoiding foods such as eggs, vegetables, and fruits with a large number of seeds in order not to destroy life forms unnecessarily. Fasting, a common practice among ascetics, also is quite common among the laity, especially, as we have seen, among women.

These similarities notwithstanding, it is easy to observe that in almost every way, the ascetics' religious life demands significantly more by way of exertion and endurance of physical hardships than does the religious life of most laypeople, who strive mainly to behave morally in order to ebb the flow of harmful karma and thus to foster a good rebirth. As we observed at the outset of this chapter, the ritual of *dana* (the giving of food to monks and nuns) provides one opportunity to be a good Jain layperson and to enhance one's karmic status. A somewhat similar practice involves bidding for the right to sponsor rituals, with any extra money being donated to charitable causes and the winning bidder gaining in social esteem. Whenever a new image of a tirthankara is erected or installed in a temple, for example, rituals are performed to celebrate each of the "five auspicious events" of a tirthankara's life: conception, birth, renunciation, attainment of *kevala*, and moksha. The person who sponsors the building of such an image and funds the rituals is said to acquire positive karmic merit, so that the person likely will be born into a world blessed with a living tirthankara.[7]

A formalized system of religious observance features the Twelve Vows for the layperson. The first of the Vows, for instance, makes clear that it is the intentionality, rather than the specific action, that most matters with regard to ahimsa. Proper intentionality is involved, for example, in choosing the right profession, one that would not likely result in violence toward sentient life forms. As a result, through the centuries Jains have tended to engage in trade and other forms of business. Obviously, harmful occupations such as hunting and fishing are strictly prohibited; farming is acceptable because it can be done without *intentionally* harming life forms. Trade and business, however, are generally considered optimal because they can be done without causing any harm at all.

6.6 Jainism as a Way of Life: Engaging with the World

In this closing section, we focus on Jainism's perspectives on gender roles and environmental issues, and on how Jainism has accommodated its increasingly global reach.

Gender Roles in Jainism

We have observed that among Jain ascetics the places and roles of women and men vary considerably. The relatively conservative Digambaras allow only monks, not nuns, to go about naked, and they deny that women can attain *kevala*. They, unlike the Shvetambaras, also insist that the nineteenth tirthankara was a man. In general, there tend to be fewer distinctions between monks and nuns among Shvetambara Jains. The Sthanakvasi subsect, in which nuns outnumber monks by about five to one, can be said to be relatively liberal, even among Shvetambaras. One Sthanakvasi group has recently taken the unprecedented step of promoting a nun, Candanaji, to the rank of *aharya*, a general term in Jainism for a "leader" of a group of ascetics.

The long history of Jainism reveals some diversity with regard to the places and roles of women and men. One ancient text states that the original group of Mahavira's followers, both the laity and the ascetics, was composed mostly of women. It also states that during Mahavira's lifetime 1,400 women, as opposed to 700 men, attained *kevala*.[8]

For most of Jain history, however, women have tended to be regarded as less spiritually capable than men, even among the Shvetambaras. Recently, attitudes have begun to shift. For example, the long-standing assumption that women are prone to lead men away from virtuous lives by tempting them and arousing passions has gradually subsided. Today, the moral fortitude of the chaste Jain woman provides a role model for the proper behavior of women and men alike.

Jain laywomen occupy vital roles within the family and community, roles that, especially until recently, have tended to differ from those of men, but that have been vital nonetheless. In the chapter's opening vignette, we entered the home of the Chandras and observed the ritual of giving known as *dana*. It is difficult to imagine such a scene without the presence of the wife, who takes a leading role in managing household affairs and raising the children. The fact that women tend to be less involved than men in business and other professional concerns means that they tend to have more time and energy to devote to the important lay religious practice of fasting.

Jainism and the Natural World

Several points have already been made that indicate Jainism's inherent concern for the natural world. The principle of ahimsa, of course, demands care for all living beings, starting but by no means ending with vegetarianism. Elaborate "zoological" categorization of life forms attests the ambitious and meticulous approach to this care. That all jivas are believed to be essentially equal means that the natural world is permeated with life; regard for the sanctity of life therefore implies regard for the sanctity of nature itself. When Jain ascetics drink only as much water as absolutely necessary so as not to harm small organisms, water is preserved.

How does this ecological ethos fit with the doctrine of samsara, which maintains that the world is currently in a process of degeneration and destined for final dissolution, after which a new world will arise? The Jain response to this question involves the quest for liberation, which requires that one avoid negatively affecting karma, which in turn depends on perfect moral behavior, achieved through diligent practice of ahimsa and its related principles.

Ahimsa demands not only avoiding violence but also constant striving toward friendship with all fellow living creatures. "The Jain Declaration on Nature," an essay written in 1990 by L. M. Singhvi on the occasion of Jainism's participation in the World Wildlife Fund Network on Conservation and Religion, celebrates this ideal. It concludes with the assertion that Jain teachings "offer the world today a time-tested anchor of moral imperatives and a viable route plan for humanity's common pilgrimage for holistic environmental protection, peace and harmony in the universe."[9]

In 2019, with climate change at the forefront of environmental concerns, the Federation of Jain Associations in North America (JAINA) issued its Declaration on the Climate Crisis.[10] Backed by scientific evidence on emissions caused by fossil fuels and common agricultural practices, the Declaration calls for a wide variety of actions, including opposing the beef and dairy industries insofar as they practice conventional means of production, avoiding use of chemical fertilizers and pesticides, and opting for renewable energy sources. The Declaration also notes the Jain principle of *aparigraha*, or nonpossessiveness. One implication of *aparigraha* is that Jains should own relatively small houses, as they tend to leave a smaller carbon footprint.

Jainism as a Global Religion

One of the world's oldest traditions, Jainism today remains relatively small, with only about 5.6 million adherents, and also relatively confined to its place of origin, with the great majority of Jains living in India. This tendency for the tradition to maintain itself demographically and geographically is natural for Jains, who do not actively seek converts to Jainism and, even when living outside of India, tend to maintain strong ties to the motherland.

Until the late nineteenth century, virtually all Jains lived in India, and very few people outside of India took much notice of them or their religion. In 1893, at the World's Parliament of Religions in Chicago, Virchand Gandhi, a Jain layman, delivered a lecture on Jainism that, for the first time, conveyed to Westerners Jainism's relevance with regard to such modern issues as peace and tolerance for others. At about this same time, the first significant emigration of Jains from India was taking place, to East Africa. In the late 1960s, Jains began to emigrate from Africa and from India to Great Britain, the United States, and Canada. Today there are also sizeable Jain communities in various Asian countries aside from India, including Nepal, Myanmar (Burma), and Malaysia. All told, there are about 275,000 Jains outside of India.

Jainism in the diaspora tends to be less orthodox than Jainism in its traditional Indian homeland. To some extent, orthodox teachings—for instance, the prohibition held by all but the Sthanakvasi and Terapanthi sects against monks and nuns ever leaving India—themselves serve to impede an orthodox form of Jainism in the diaspora. The main factors, though, that foster a less traditional mode involve the challenges of living in nontraditional situations and the pressures to conform to modern ideals.

The specific example of the Jain community in Singapore serves to demonstrate some ways of being Jain in the diaspora. Numbering about 700, the community, organized as the Singapore Jain Religious Society (SJRS), maintains a website and a main place of worship that offers regular prayer meetings, classes, and celebrations of religious festivals. Its youth group, Young Jains of Singapore, was formed to help Jains of age thirteen to twenty-five years organize communal events and activities benefitting Singaporean society. About 95 percent of Singaporean Jains have roots in the Indian state of Gujarat. Whereas in the traditional homeland of India distinctions between Jain sects are more noticeable, the SJRS center encourages participation by Jains of various sects. Indeed, its constitution insists on Jain unity. The SJSR worship space features side-by-side sculptures favored, on the one hand, by Shvetambaras and, on the other, by Digambaras. Established in 1972, the

SJRS has since managed to make Jainism one among the ten members of the Inter-Religious Organisation Singapore, which actively supports interreligious dialogue and educational events aimed at enhancing understanding across traditions.

Like every religion in the world today, Jainism has become diverse, as indicated by the differences between the sects and varieties of practices in locales around the world. Some aspects of the religion are more adaptable to modernization, pluralism, and other contemporary forces, and some are less so. In this regard, Jainism as a whole can perhaps best be summed up as a tradition that is both eternally constant and constantly evolving. At one extreme, a group of monks and nuns wandering the countryside, sweeping ahead of their bare feet with their whisks, hardly fit into the picture of the modern world. Paradoxically, these same ascetics carry on a tradition of cosmology that appears remarkably modern relative to most traditionally religious points of view. Moreover, the conscientiousness of Jains with regard to social justice issues—expressed in their advocacy of vegetarianism and other forms of nonviolence—is in step with many who are concerned about the state of the world, the environment, and humanity's plight.

SEEKING ANSWERS

What Is Ultimate Reality?

Like Hinduism and Buddhism, Jainism maintains belief in samsara, the wheel of life. Time is conceived of as being cyclical, such that this world is but one in an eternal sequence of worlds that have come to be. The Jain perspective on space features the *loka*, a vast expanse that includes three realms inhabited by human beings. Jainism does not emphasize the importance of deities, even to the point of appearing atheistic; it can be considered a transtheistic religion. Souls (jivas) and matter (ajiva) are believed to exist eternally. Ultimate reality for Jainism might best be identified as *kevala*, the supreme state in which the eternal soul is perfectly pure.

How Should We Live in This World?

Jainism bases its ethical teachings on the principle of ahimsa (nonviolence) and on the accompanying value of asceticism. Both are exemplified by Mahavira and the other tirthankaras, and Jain monks

and nuns continue to act as exemplars. Jainism understands human beings—like every other sentient being—to be made up of a soul (jiva) combined with bodily matter (ajiva). This matter is believed to contaminate the soul and thus to weigh it down and to prevent it from attaining spiritual perfection. Jains explain this through their doctrine of karma, understanding the term in its literal sense as "action."

What Is Our Ultimate Purpose?

Jains believe that eventually every soul will become perfectly pure, allowing it to rise to the top of the *loka* in the transcendent state of *kevala*, the Jain equivalent of Buddhist nirvana or Hindu moksha. Jains also believe that the soul that does not experience *kevala* is destined for rebirth, which is understood to occur immediately after death and is determined by the adequacy of one's spiritual and moral life in this world. Death, then, does not "end it," and mortality for Jains involves the prospect of a good rebirth.

REVIEW QUESTIONS

For Review

1. What is the role of Mahavira as one of Jainism's tirthankaras?
2. How do Jain practices of asceticism promote the cause of ahimsa?
3. What is the *loka*?
4. Identify and briefly describe the various Jain sects.
5. Differentiate the main religious duties of the Jain laity from those of the ascetics and explain what religious advantages a monk or nun might have over members of the laity.

For Further Reflection

1. Compare the biographies of Nataputta Vardhamana (Mahavira) and Siddhartha Gautama (the Buddha), focusing especially on the episodes of attaining enlightenment.
2. What is the relationship between Jain cosmology and the Jain perspective on spiritual liberation? Consider especially the classification of reality into ajiva and jiva and how this relates to the quest for spiritual liberation.
3. What is *kevala?* How does it compare to Buddhist nirvana? To Hindu moksha?

GLOSSARY

ahimsa (ah-him'suh; Sanskrit, "nonviolence," "not desiring to harm") Both the avoidance of violence toward other life forms and an active sense of compassion toward them; a basic principle of Jainism, Hinduism, and Buddhism.

ajiva (uh-jee'vuh; Sanskrit, "nonsoul") Nonliving components of the Jain universe: space, time, motion, rest, and all forms of matter.

dana (dah'nuh; Sanskrit, Pali, "giving") Ritual of giving.

Digambara (di'guhm-buh-ruh; Sanskrit, "those whose garment is the sky") The second largest Jain sect, whose monks go about naked so as to help abolish any ties to society; generally more conservative than the Shvetambara sect.

jinas (ji'nuh; Sanskrit, "conquerors") Jain title for those who have "conquered" samsara; synonymous with tirthankaras.

jiva (jee'vuh; Sanskrit, "soul") The finite and eternal soul; also the category of living, as opposed to nonliving, entities of the universe.

karma (kahr'muh; Sanskrit, "action") "Action" and the consequences of action; determines the nature of one's reincarnation; in Jainism, all activity is believed to involve various forms of matter that weigh down the soul (jiva) and thus hinder the quest for liberation.

kevala (kay'vuh-luh; shortened form of Sanskrit *kevalajnana*, "isolated knowledge" or "absolute knowledge") The perfect and complete knowledge or omniscience that is Jain enlightenment; marks the point at which one is free from the damaging effects of karma and is liberated from samsara.

loka (loh'kah; Sanskrit, "world") The Jain universe, often depicted as having the shape of a giant man.

Shvetambara (shvayt-ahm'buh-ruh; Sanskrit, "those whose garment is white") The largest Jain sect, whose monks and nuns wear white robes; generally more liberal than the Digambara sect.

tirthankaras (teer-tuhn'kuhr-uhs; Sanskrit, "makers of the river crossing") The Jain spiritual heroes, such as Parshva and Mahavira, who have shown the way to salvation; synonymous with jinas.

SUGGESTIONS FOR FURTHER READING

Dundas, Paul. *The Jains*. 2nd ed. London: Routledge, 2002. A thorough and scholarly study that has become a standard reference work for students and academics alike.

Jain, Satish Kumar, and Kamal Chand Sogani, eds. *Perspectives in Jaina Philosophy and Culture*. New Delhi: Ahimsa International, 1985. Helpful insights from within the Jain tradition.

Jaini, Padmanabh S. *The Jaini Path of Purification.* 2nd ed. Columbia, MO: South Asia Books, 2001. The first comprehensive work in English that offers a sympathetic study of the religion, this modern-day classic has been revised and updated.

Lopez, Donald S., Jr., ed. *Religions of India in Practice.* Princeton, NJ: Princeton University Press, 1995. Offering some translations for the first time, this anthology presents a wide range of texts well beyond the usual collections of sacred writings.

Radhakrishnan, Sarvepalli, and Charles A. Moore, eds. *A Sourcebook in Indian Philosophy.* Princeton, NJ: Princeton University Press, 1957. A standard anthology of sacred texts in English translations.

ONLINE RESOURCES

Internet Sacred Text Archive (Jainism)

A repository of Jain scriptures.

The Wabash Center

The Wabash Center, a trusted resource for all aspects of the academic study of religion, offers links to a wide variety of dependable internet resources on Jainism.

JAINA: Federation of Jain Associations of North America

The JAINA website is especially useful for studies of Jainism in North America.

The Forum on Religion and Ecology at Yale (Jainism Introduction)

This site presents Christopher Key Chapple's "Introduction" to the book *Jainism and Ecology.* The site also presents Chapple's excellent overview article on Jain environmentalism and provides easy access to the Forum's richly informative homepage of the Forum on Religion and Ecology.

Sikhism

Chapter Outline

7.1   Describe the life of Guru Nanak and the emergence of Sikhism.

7.2   Identify the core texts of Sikhism and their purposes.

7.3   Summarize the key beliefs central to an understanding of Sikhism.

7.4   Summarize the development of Sikhism through the time of Guru Gobind Singh, the tenth and final historical Guru.

7.5   Describe the challenges faced by the Sikh community in the modern age.

7.6   Describe the methods and purpose of Sikh devotional practices.

7.7   Associate specific Sikh traditions and rituals with stages in the life cycle.

7.8   Identify key aspects of Sikh practices focused on ethics and identity.

MANJIT KAUR, a sixteen-year-old girl, and Sandeep Singh, a fourteen-year-old boy, stand in the **gurdwara**, the place of Sikh worship, in their small village in northwestern India. Here in the region known as the Punjab, Sikhism's ancestral homeland, Manjit and Sandeep are members of the majority religion, and gurdwaras are common sights in the farming villages that dot the land. Most of the village has gathered together to witness the proceedings, and Sandeep and Manjit have spent the morning preparing for this momentous event—their initiation into the Sikh **Khalsa**, or community of "Pure Ones." They have both bathed and washed their long hair carefully and have dressed especially for the occasion. Most notably, they both don the five articles of faith, known as the Five Ks: uncut hair, a comb, a steel wristlet, a short sword, and a pair of shorts. (For more detail on the Five Ks, see the section "Teachings of Guru Gobind Singh and the Khalsa.")

Manjit and Sandeep join a group of five older villagers who also don the Five Ks and who for this ceremony play the part of the *Panj Piare*, or "Beloved Five." They are established members of the Khalsa and will oversee the initiation.

The five Sikh men who participate in the *Amrit Sanchar* represent the original "Beloved Five" in commemoration of the founding of the Khalsa.

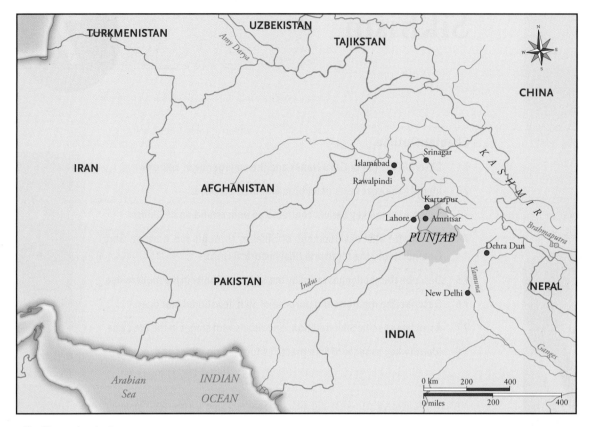

Significant sites in the history of Sikhism.

The grouping of five recalls the founding of the Khalsa centuries ago, when Guru Gobind Singh (1675–1708 CE), the tenth in a line of Gurus going back to Guru Nanak (1469–1539 CE), chose five original initiates who had distinguished themselves for their loyalty to the Guru and for their commitment to Sikh ideals. On this day of *Amrit Sanchar*, the Khalsa initiation ceremony, the stirring memory of these founding figures and the ideals they embody is palpably felt. But the most vital presence of all is a large book, lying open on a special platform. It is Sri Guru Granth Sahib, or the **Adi Granth**, the sacred scripture of Sikhism, and the Sikhs' **Guru**, or spiritual teacher, from the time of Guru Gobind Singh forward.

Sandeep and Manjit stand before the *Panj Piare*, one of whom explains the basic principles of Sikhism. They agree to accept these principles by nodding, the ritual action that makes the initiation official. Sandeep and Manjit are then served **amrit** ("immortalizing fluid"), a special drink made from water and sugar crystals, which the *Panj Piare* have mixed in an iron bowl and stirred with a two-edged sword. Meanwhile, hymns from the Adi Granth are sung by the congregation. The amrit is drunk and sprinkled on the eyes and heads of the initiates, who recite the **Mul Mantra**, the summary of Sikh doctrine that comprises the opening lines of the Adi Granth. The *Panj Piare* then instruct Manjit and Sandeep about the ethical requirements of the Khalsa. These include prohibitions against the cutting of one's hair, the eating of meat that has been improperly slaughtered, extramarital sexual relations, and the use of tobacco.

The initiates are also told that all Sikhs are brothers and sisters and that there should not be any distinctions made on the basis of caste.

Manjit and Sandeep are among a minority of Sikhs, approximately 15 percent, who undergo the traditional ceremony of initiation into the Khalsa. Some 70 percent of the approximately 25 million Sikhs in the world, however, are popularly considered to be members of the Khalsa, insofar as they observe the Five Ks, or at least the one that is generally deemed most important: not cutting one's hair.[1] And regardless of percentages or degrees of membership, the traditional ways of the Khalsa greatly influence the practices and customs of the entire **Panth**, or Sikh community. We can thus glimpse in this ceremony, with its powerful ties to tradition and its rich symbolism, key aspects that are at the heart of Sikhism.

I n this chapter, we will study these and other key aspects, attending in turn to the founding of Sikhism and its primary doctrines, its historical development, and its most prevalent rituals, worship practices, and teachings regarding ethics and Sikh identity. By virtue of its size alone, Sikhism is among the major religions of the world. Theologically, Sikhism's intermixing of concepts that are common to some Hindu traditions, on the one hand, and to Islam, on the other, make it a very interesting subject for the comparative study of religion. And with about 2 million Sikhs living outside of India,[2] and Sikh communities being found today in most of the large cities of the West, Sikhism clearly is a global tradition that has a significant impact on the world.

TIMELINE
Sikhism

1469 CE Birth of Guru Nanak, founder of Sikhism.

1520s Establishment by Guru Nanak of the township of Kartarpur, the first Sikh community.

1539 Death of Guru Nanak.

1606 Death (execution?) of Guru Arjan, under Mughal emperor Jahangir.

1675 Execution of Guru Tegh Bahadur, under Mughal emperor Aurangzeb.

1699 Founding of the Khalsa by Guru Gobind Singh.

1708 Death of Guru Gobind Singh and establishment of the Adi Granth as Guru.

1799 Establishment of independent Sikh kingdom by Ranjit Singh.

1849 Annexation of Sikh kingdom by the British.

1947 Partition of Punjab with the establishment of India's independence.

1984 Indian army attacks and occupies Sikh holy sites, including the Darbar Sahib (or Golden Temple).

1999 The Panth celebrates the third centennial of the establishment of the Khalsa.

2004 Manmohan Singh elected prime minister of India, the first Sikh to attain this office.

7.1 The Teachings of Sikhism: The Life of Guru Nanak

The term *Sikh* is derived from an ancient Sanskrit term that means "disciple." Sikhs are thus disciples, specifically of the ten Gurus, beginning with Guru Nanak and ending with Guru Gobind Singh, founder of the Khalsa.

By the time Guru Nanak had come on the scene, the important role of the guru had long been established within Hindu traditions of northern India. A guru is a spiritual teacher. *Guru* is actually used in three slightly different ways in Sikhism. Along with being the title of Guru Nanak and his successors and of the sacred text (Sri Guru Granth Sahib), it is used as a name for God. In fact, *Waheguru*, "Praise to the Guru"—pronounced Va'hee-gooh'rooh—is the most common name for God used by Sikhs today. In each case, the guru functions as the teacher of God's will. As Sikhs believe that God lovingly reveals the divine will to humans, God, too, thus functions as Guru.

We now consider the career of the guru of northern India whose extraordinary life experiences and bold spiritual leadership were to have such a profound impact that a new religion would arise.

The Early Life of Guru Nanak

Nanak was born in 1469 CE in the small village of Talvandi (modern-day Nankan Sahib, located near Lahore, Pakistan). He was born to Hindu parents of a mercantile caste who probably were worshipers of Vishnu (for more information about the caste system and the worship of Vishnu, see Chapter 4). His parents arranged for him to marry early, when he was still in his teens, as was customary at the time. Nanak and his wife, Sulakhani, moved to Sultanpur, where Nanak's older sister Nanaki lived. Soon Nanak and Sulakhani had two sons.

Sultanpur, located on the main road between Lahore and Delhi, was a religiously diverse community, with residents and visitors who practiced varieties of Hinduism and Islam. Nanak, who is said to have been dissatisfied with traditional forms of religion, gravitated toward a religious outlook similar to Hindu bhakti, the path of devotion (see Chapter 4). Nanak believed in the oneness of God and in the need to move closer to God. This could best be accomplished, he believed, through meditation and singing hymns in praise of God. Eventually, Nanak began composing his own hymns. With his friend Mardana, a Muslim musician, accompanying him on the rebab (a stringed instrument), Nanak sang his hymns at communal worship gatherings. These hymns are included in the Adi Granth and are sung in Sikh services today.

Sikhs pay homage to Guru Nanak, the founder of Sikhism, in a crowded room in Lahore, Pakistan.

According to tradition, Nanak became recognized as a spiritual leader early in his life. He would rise before dawn and bathe in the river, meditate, and then lead others in singing hymns of praise. When Nanak was about thirty years old, he underwent a crucial experience that led to the origin of the Sikh tradition.

Receiving God's Revelation

One morning while Nanak was bathing in the river, he did not resurface from the water. He was presumed drowned, and yet his body was not found. Three days and three nights later, however, Nanak emerged from the river, and, returning to the village, he proclaimed: "There is neither Hindu nor Muslim so whose path shall I follow? I shall follow God's path. God is neither Hindu nor Muslim and the path which I follow is God's."[3]

When he explained what had happened, Nanak said that he had been escorted to the court of God, who gave him a cup of amrit (the same drink that is used in the Khalsa initiation ceremony) and said to him:

> This is the cup of the adoration of God's name. Drink it. I am with you. I bless you and raise you up. Whoever remembers you will enjoy my favor. Go, rejoice in my name and teach others to do so. I have bestowed the gift of my name upon you. Let this be your calling.[4]

This experience dramatically changed Nanak's life, causing him to cease participation in the civic life of Sultanpur, to send his wife and sons back to his parents' home, and to embark on the next major stage of his life.

The Journeys of Guru Nanak

Deeply moved by this revelation, Guru Nanak spent the next two decades of his life, from age thirty to about age fifty, traveling far and wide and learning about a variety of religious customs, including Hindu, Muslim, and Jain. He is said to have undertaken four long journeys: eastward to Assan; southward to Sri Lanka; northward to the Himalayas; and westward, reaching as far as Mecca and Baghdad. He visited holy sites and encountered a wide variety of religious people. He also proclaimed and practiced his own teachings, sometimes to hostile audiences.

Several incidents during Guru Nanak's travels illuminate the new message he proclaimed. On one occasion, while visiting a Hindu shrine in Haridwar, India, he found himself among brahmins throwing water toward the rising sun as an offering to their dead ancestors. Nanak turned and threw water the other way, explaining, "If you can send water to your dead ancestors in heaven, surely I can send it to my fields in the Punjab."[5] On another occasion, Nanak was awakened from sleep by an angry Muslim who chastised him for sleeping with his feet pointing toward the Ka'ba in Mecca, the most sacred site in Islam. (Many Muslims consider showing the soles of one's feet to be a grave insult.) Nanak responded: "Then turn my feet in some other direction where God does not exist."[6]

Such stories as these illustrate a general theme of Nanak's religious outlook. He consistently rejected traditional rituals and "proper" religious protocol, whether Hindu or Muslim.

Founding the Sikh Community

Drawing from his revelation experience and years of journeying, Nanak continued proclaiming his own religious ideals, among them monotheism; lack of distinctions based on gender, caste, or creed (for example, whether Hindu or Muslim); and performance of good deeds. Nanak attracted a large following. At about the age of fifty, he established a new settlement called Kartarpur ("abode of the creator") in what is now Pakistan. Here he and his followers formed the first Sikh community and instituted the lifestyle that has characterized Sikh society to this day.

Guru Nanak erected a special building, a *dharamsala* ("abode of faith"), for worship. In so doing, he provided the prototype of the gurdwara, which today is the central structure of any particular Sikh community. (The term *dharamsala* gradually was replaced in the eighteenth century with *gurdwara* to designate the Sikh place of worship.) Nanak welcomed people from all segments of society to reside in Kartarpur and to work together to maintain it. Nanak himself joined in the work, which was primarily agrarian. Nanak also saw to the providing of food through a community kitchen known as the **langar**. This would become a standard feature of gurdwaras down through the centuries to the present day. Though in most respects a regular member of the community, Nanak sat on a special seat when addressing the congregation. Followers recognized the nature of the Guru as merely human and yet also as spiritually very advanced.

On September 22, 1539, after leading the Kartarpur community for about twenty years, Guru Nanak died. According to the traditional account, the Guru (here referred to as "Baba Nanak"), aware of his approaching death, settled a dispute regarding the proper disposal of his body.

> Hindus and Muslims who had put their faith in the divine Name began to debate what should be done with the Guru's corpse. "We shall bury him," said the Muslims. "No, let us cremate his body," said the Hindus. "Place flowers on both sides of my body," said Baba Nanak, "flowers from the Hindus on the right side and flowers from the Muslims on the left. If tomorrow the Hindus' flowers are still fresh let my body be burned, and if the Muslims' flowers are still fresh let it be buried."
>
> Baba Nanak then commanded the congregation to sing. They sang *Kirtan Sohila* and *Arati*. . . . Baba Nanak then covered himself with a sheet and passed away. Those who had gathered around him prostrated themselves, and when the sheet was removed they found that there was nothing under it. The flowers on both sides remained fresh, and both Hindus and Muslims took their respective shares. All who were gathered there prostrated themselves again.[7]

Even with his death, Guru Nanak encouraged Hindus and Muslims to transcend their differences and to let peace prevail.

Guru Nanak's example powerfully informs the beliefs and practices of Sikhs up to the present day. We will next turn our attention briefly to Sikh scripture, the collection of texts that contains the doctrinal position as set forth by Guru Nanak and his successor Gurus.

7.2 The Teachings of Sikhism: Sacred Texts

We have previously identified the Adi Granth, commonly known as Sri Guru Granth Sahib, as Sikhism's most important sacred text. This is without question true for all Sikhs today. There are, however, other texts that most Sikhs would classify as scripture, the most important being the Dasam Granth and the Rahit, both of which we consider here. In addition, works by two disciples of the Gurus are granted sufficient status to be recited in the gurdwara: Bhai Gurda (disciple of Guru Arjan and Guru Hargobind) and Nand Lal (disciple of Guru Gobind Singh). A collection of stories about the life of Guru Nanak, called the *Janam-sakhi*, also deserves mention. The account of Guru Nanak's death cited in the previous section is from the *Janam-sakhi*.

The Adi Granth

Compiled by Guru Arjan in 1603–1604, the Adi Granth contains the works of his four predecessors, along with his own hymns and various works by poets, such as Kabir (c. 1440–1518). Through the centuries, the Adi Granth

A Sikh reads from Sri Guru Granth Sahib, here occupying its customary place on a cushion within a gurdwara.

has occupied a central place in Sikhism. Whereas the Gurus once sat on a special seat amid Sikh disciples, since the time of the tenth and last historical Guru, Gobind Singh, the Adi Granth has occupied the same type of seat in the middle of any place of worship. And whereas the Gurus were once the authorities on religious matters, now Sikhs consult the Adi Granth.

The name "Adi Granth" ("the Original Volume" or "the First Book") is standard among scholars. Sikhs commonly express their reverence for the scripture by referring to it as Sri Guru Granth Sahib ("sahib" is a title of respect). Every copy is identical in both script and page number; there are 1,430 pages in every copy. It was composed using the Gurmukhi script and a variety of languages that were used in northern India at the time, most prevalently Punjabi. It also contains some words in Arabic, Persian, Prakrit, and Sanskrit. All of these factors render the Adi Granth somewhat difficult to read, as well as difficult to translate. Today, English and French translations are available. Many Sikh families have at least a condensed version of the Adi Granth containing all of the works used in daily prayers, including Guru Nanak's *Japji*, which is the only portion of the entire Adi Granth that is chanted rather than sung. For Sikhs, the Adi Granth rings with brilliance when it is set to music and proclaimed in its original language. In the words of one commentator: "The poetic excellence, the spiritual content, and the haunting, lilting melodies of the hymns of the Adi Granth are Sikhism's greatest attraction to this day."[8]

The Dasam Granth

The composition of the Dasam Granth ("Volume of the Tenth Master") has been traditionally attributed to Guru Gobind Singh, although many Sikhs today believe that only some parts were authored by the Guru. The first compilation of works into the Dasam Granth is thought to have taken place in 1734 (twenty-six years after the death of Guru Gobind Singh), although in the ensuing decades variant versions appeared. In 1902, the version that is used today was officially authorized.

During the eighteenth century, the Dasam Granth was considered to be Guru alongside the Adi Granth. Today, however, only one group of Sikhs, the Nihangs, bestow equal honor on the Dasam Granth. Nevertheless, the sections of the text that all Sikhs attribute to Guru Gobind Singh can safely be categorized as Sikh scripture. These sections include the well-known *Jap Sahib* and the *Ten Savayyas*; both are recited daily in morning prayers.

The Rahit

In the chapter's opening, we observed that the *Amrit Sanchar*, the Khalsa initiation ceremony, is undertaken only by a minority of Sikhs, even though the Khalsa continues to exemplify the ideals of Sikhism. These ideals are spelled out in written form in *rahit-namas*, texts composed over the centuries and collectively referred to as the **Rahit**. Traditionally, the contents of the Rahit are believed to stem from the teachings of Guru Gobind Singh himself. In both this section on Sikh doctrinal teachings and the following section on Sikh religious life, we shall draw frequently from the contents of the Rahit.

7.3 The Teachings of Sikhism: Core Precepts

More than anything else, Sikhism is a religious path to spiritual liberation through devotional praise of God, most especially by way of meditation on the divine Name. This meditation is often done through prayerful recitation of sacred words. In this section, we take up in more detail three main aspects of Sikh teachings that will shed light on this religious path: the nature of God and the "divine Name"; the nature of the human condition and its need, through the aid of the Guru, to move from darkness to enlightenment; and the nature of liberation, which is release from samsara, the cycle of death and rebirth that is also a foundational concept for Hinduism, Buddhism, and Jainism.

God: Formless One, Creator, True Guru

Guru Nanak's understanding of the nature of God is the center from which all Sikh teachings emerge. It is fitting that the Adi Granth begins with a concise summary of Sikh theology. This summary is known as the *Mul Mantra*, the passage recited by initiates to the Khalsa (as we noted in the beginning of the chapter) and by most Sikhs daily as part of their morning prayers.

> There is one Supreme Being, the Eternal Reality, the Creator, without fear and devoid of enmity, immortal, never incarnated, self-existent, known by grace through the Guru.
>
> The Eternal One, from the beginning, through all time, present now, the Everlasting Reality.[9]

As this description suggests, Sikhism is similar theologically to the monotheistic religions Zoroastrianism, Judaism, Christianity, and Islam. God is one, eternal, self-existent, and "Creator." The Punjabi term that the Gurus used for God is *Akal Purakh*, "The One Beyond Time." Guru Nanak sometimes used the name *Nirankar*, "Without Form." For Sikhs, then, God is without form and beyond all attributes that humans use to describe reality. God is without gender and is referred to as "he" in Sikhism only begrudgingly and when grammatically necessary because of the limitations of language; there is no neuter pronoun in Punjabi. Sikhs actively strive to avoid assigning such human attributes to God.

For reasons beyond the grasp of human comprehension, God decided to create the world and all that is in it, including human beings. Akal Purakh (we'll use this traditional name, although as we have noted earlier, modern Sikhs commonly refer to God as *Waheguru*, "Praise to the Guru"; note that Akal-Ustat Singh sets forth this name in his interview, later in this chapter), in addition to being the Creator, is also the Preserver and the Destroyer. Sikhism here draws from the important Hindu triad of gods and their respective functions: Brahma (Creator), Vishnu (Preserver), and Shiva (Destroyer). All Sikhs, though, insist that their God is one. These three functions are thus different aspects of the one God. For Hindu Vaishnavas, Vishnu similarly incorporates all three functions within his own being (Chapter 4).

In God's primary state, to which Guru Nanak referred when he used the name *Nirankar* ("Without Form"), God is distinct from his creation in much the same way that an artist remains distinct from her or his artwork. And yet God dwells within creation—within nature and within human beings. God is thus said to be immanent, or indwelling (as opposed to transcendent or beyond creation). In this state of immanence, Akal Purakh is personal and approachable through loving devotion. Because of God's immanence in creation, it is possible for humans to make contact with God and to come to know God. To extend our analogy, one can know something of an artist by seeing the artist's works. So, too, can one come to know Akal Purakh through experiencing God's creation. Indeed, part of the ongoing purpose of creation is that God, through loving grace, might reveal the divine self to human beings. It is in this capacity that God is referred to as Guru, for in this manner God delivers humans from darkness to enlightenment.

The Human Condition: Self-Centered and Bound to Samsara

Human beings are especially near to Akal Purakh. Though Sikhism advocates kindness to living things, it also holds that other creatures are here to provide for us. (Unlike most Hindus and all Jains, therefore, Sikhs are not opposed to eating meat—although many prefer vegetarianism.) More importantly, Akal Purakh is believed to dwell within all human beings and is actively concerned about their spiritual welfare. Humans, however, tend to neglect the need to center their lives on God.

Rather than being God-centered, humans are inclined to be self-centered and to depend on the powers of the mind. The Sikh term for this self-centeredness is **haumai**, which causes one to resist submitting to Akal Purakh. When life is dominated by *haumai*, its five accompanying vices—lust, anger, greed, attachment, and pride—tend to run rampant. *Haumai* and its vices increase the distance between the person and God and at the same time cause attachment to the charms of the world.

As long as *haumai* and its accompanying vices persist, humans are destined to remain in samsara, the ongoing cycle of death and rebirth.

Spiritual Liberation through Union with God

Sikhism teaches that the ultimate purpose of life is to attain **mukti**, spiritual liberation. This liberation is similar to Hindu moksha, "release" from samsara, the cycle of death and rebirth. This release is believed to bring about an experience of being in the presence of God, a state of eternal bliss. The quest for mukti is a constant struggle between *haumai*, the self-centeredness to which humans are naturally inclined, and the call to live in accordance with the will of God. Akal Purakh plays an essential role in determining the outcome of this struggle. God is immanent in creation through **hukam**, the divine order. It is through *hukam* that Akal Purakh asserts the divine will and communicates truth. Through humbling oneself, thus denying the normally dominating powers of *haumai*, a person is opened to the power of God's grace. Having received God's grace, the task is to respond in loving devotion through meditation on the nature of God. The term most often used in the Adi Granth to denote the nature of God is *nam*, the "divine Name." Meditation on the *nam* or recitation of the *nam* is prescribed repeatedly as the path to spiritual liberation. A chapter of the *Japji* sets forth these points:

> The Eternal One whose Name is Truth speaks to us in infinite love. Insistently we beg for the gifts which are by grace bestowed. What can we offer in return for all this goodness? What gift will gain

Gurbaj Singh Multani (right) wears a ceremonial dagger, known as a kirpan, after a news conference on Parliament Hill in Ottawa on March 2, 2006. Multiculturalism and religious freedom trumped safety concerns in a Canadian Supreme Court decision that allows orthodox Sikh students to carry traditional daggers to school.

entrance to the hallowed Court? What words can we utter to attract this love? At the ambrosial hour of fragrant dawn meditate on the grandeur of the one true Name. Past actions determine the nature of our birth, but grace alone reveals the door to liberation. See the Divine Spirit, Nanak, dwelling immanent in all. Know the Divine Spirit as the One, the eternal, the changeless Truth.[10]

The significance of the *nam* for Guru Nanak, and thus for the entire Sikh tradition, can hardly be overstated. In the words of one modern commentator, "Anything that may be affirmed concerning Akal Purakh constitutes an aspect of the divine Name, and a sufficient understanding of the divine Name provides the essential means to deliverance."[11]

Mukti brings about the eternal, infinitely blissful state of being in the presence of God. This is not dependent in any way on one's caste status or gender. Also, the focus is on inward meditation and piety rather than on outward forms of worship, such as festivals or pilgrimages—although Sikhism is not entirely without such forms of worship, as we shall consider shortly. But before we move on from this section on Sikh teachings, we next consider elements introduced with the foundation in 1699 of the Khalsa, the community of "Pure Ones," and take up the crucial question of the relationship of the Khalsa to the Panth or Sikh community at large.

VOICES: An Interview with Akal-Ustat Singh

Akal-Ustat Singh is a California-born university student at California State University, Sacramento. As this interview attests, the Sikh path—*Sikhi*—plays a central role in his life, providing the basis for seeking happiness, relating to others, and facing challenges brought on by loss or disappointment. Although he regards himself as still a traveler on this path, and by no means a final authority, he is honored to share *Sikhi* as it has impacted his life.

Akal-Ustat Singh.

How does Sikhism help you in your personal quest for happiness or fulfillment?

Gurbani (the "word of the Guru") describes life with the duality between the *Manmukh* and the *Gurmukh*. The *Manmukh* ("mind follower") is bound by *haumai* (literally "me, me"); their world revolves around themselves—in their relations, actions, and belief. This is the root of unhappiness, because other people are not bound to our wishes and unexpected things happen. But the path of the *Gurmukh*, who follows the Guru, rejects this self-worship. Instead, they give up their cleverness and live earnestly and contentedly. This is *Sikhi*, the Sikh path.

This *Bachittar Natak* ("wonderous play") is at once directed and acted by the Creator, whose light illuminates life: somewhere, a king and a beggar, and elsewhere an ant—even me. Happiness is all in the light within me. The bliss of life is finding it and sharing it with others; as stated on the 522nd *Ang*, or page, of the Sri Guru Granth Sahib: "Laughing, playing, eating, and dressing, [the *Gurmukhs*] are liberated."

How does Sikhism influence how you regard and relate to other people?

The Sikh philosophy is to love. Life is a game of love with the Creator, and the Creator is imbued in every atom. Even a small act of kindness expresses this love—bringing water to my exhausted parents, giving freely, even smiling. The mantra is *Sarbat Da Bhalla* ("good for all"). Everyone should have their needs met, freedom from oppression, and opportunity to reach their potential. For my part, I have the small, daily acts of kindness and service to offer.

How does Sikhism help you when you experience a significant loss or disappointment in life?

Above all, *Sikhi* helps me to accept loss and disappointment. When a loved one passes, I cherish the time I spent with them. I miss them. And then, I continue their legacy on by adopting their virtues in my life. When I fail or something unexpected happens, I acknowledge that failing is human. I always have the choice to try again; while I still breathe, I have a chance, and beyond this life, I have the next—after all, death is merely a transformation. *Sikhi* encourages steady progress, at my pace. It's not a race: one day, we'll all reach the same destination: *Waheguru*.

Teachings of Guru Gobind Singh and the Khalsa

The teachings that Guru Gobind Singh proclaimed to the *Panj Piare*, the "Beloved Five" who became the first initiates into the Khalsa, are believed by Sikhs to make up the Rahit, the regulatory code that spells out correct belief and behavior for members of the Khalsa.

The Rahit contains vital teachings pertaining to the religious life. As we observed in the opening of the chapter, Manjit and Sandeep, as part of their initiation into the Khalsa, were taught certain norms of behavior, all of which are contained in the Rahit. Among the teachings are four cardinal prohibitions (*kurahit*): cutting one's hair, eating meat that has been improperly slaughtered, engaging in extramarital sex, and using tobacco. Along with these and other prohibitions, the Rahit also sets forth requirements, including the requirement to don the Five Ks, so named because all five of the items begin in Punjabi with the letter "k." The Five Ks are as follows:

- *Kes*, uncut hair, symbolizing the Sikh belief that one should not interfere with natural, God-given form
- *Kangha*, a small comb worn in the hair, a reminder of cleanliness
- *Kara*, a steel wristlet, affirming constant connectedness with God
- *Kirpan*, a sword, a sign of devotion to truth and to the defense of just causes
- *Kachh*, a pair of shorts tied with a drawstring, symbolizing chastity

To some extent, both the meaning and the practical implications of the Five Ks have varied somewhat through the centuries. At the time the Khalsa was founded, for example, the wearing of a sword would have suggested true preparedness to fight.

Today, the kirpan is usually only five to eight inches long and often is concealed underneath clothing in order not to appear threatening.

Study of Sikh teachings has led us naturally to a consideration of some historical aspects of the Sikh tradition. In the next section, we take up in more detail significant events from the time of Guru Nanak to the present.

7.4 The History of Sikhism: Development

Although Guru Nanak has remained the most prominent and revered of the ten Gurus of the Sikhs, his nine successors contributed significantly to development of the religion. Young Sikhs like Manjit and Sandeep learn about all of them as a natural part of their upbringing, celebrating their heroic life stories.

Guru Nanak's Successors

All ten Gurus are considered to have been revealers of truth and to have been linked to one another through sharing the same divine essence. This made them spiritually more adept than ordinary people. They were not, however, thought to be divine incarnations of God. The Gurus thus are not to be worshiped by Sikhs, though they are greatly revered. Guru Nanak constantly stressed his human limitations, humbly referring to himself as God's slave. All the Gurus were revered for their spiritual gifts and acquired much worldly prestige as well. The Mughal (therefore, Muslim) emperors who ruled northern India knew the Gurus personally and tended to respect them, in some cases developing strong friendships with them.

Nanak's successors are responsible for a wide variety of impressive accomplishments that gradually transformed the Sikh community. Arjan, the Fifth Guru (from 1581 to 1606), deserves special mention. For one thing, he compiled the scripture that would come to be known as the Adi Granth ("the Original Volume," distinguishing it from the later Dasam Granth), thus giving the Sikhs their most important sacred scripture. By traditional count, he included 2,312 of his own compositions, beautifully melodic hymns that are considered to be among Sikhism's most impressive musical accomplishments. Arjan also constructed at the city of Amritsar the Hari Mandar ("Temple of God"), now called Darbar Sahib ("Court of the Lord") or the Golden Temple. This provided the Sikhs with a geographical center.

The Darbar Sahib remains one of the world's most impressive and important religious buildings. Along with being architecturally magnificent, it is rich in symbolic meaning, beginning

A woman prays at the Golden Temple in Amritsar, India.

with the building process itself. At Arjan's invitation, Mian Mir, a Muslim Sufi saint, laid the foundation stone. Even as the Sikh community was gaining independence from its Muslim and Hindu neighbors, Sikhism served as a bridge between religions. In contrast to Hindu temples, which typically have only one door, Arjan designed the Darbar Sahib with four doors. Traditionally, this is interpreted as representing Sikhism's openness to all people—to adherents of all four of northwestern India's major religious traditions of the time (Hinduism, Islam, Buddhism, and Sikhism); to people of all four classes of the prevalent Hindu caste system; and to people of the north, south, east, and west.

Guru Gobind Singh and the Khalsa

The tenth Guru, Gobind Singh, who was born in 1666 and died in 1708, is revered as the greatest Guru after Nanak. His strength of character and spiritual adeptness made him a successful and memorable leader. By the time he became Guru at the age of nine, he had already begun training in the art of warfare and hunting, along with the ways of religion. A modern history of the Sikhs makes note of the enduring impression made by the Guru's appearance:

> Every description of Guru Gobind Singh's person delineates him as a very handsome, sharp-featured, tall and wiry man, immaculately and richly dressed as a prince. Decked with a crest upon his lofty, cone-shaped turban with a plume suspended behind from the top, he was ever armed with various weapons, including a bow and a quiver of arrows, a sword, a discus, a shield and a spear. His choice steed was of bluish-grey color and on his left hand always perched a white hawk when he sat on the throne or went out hunting.[12]

Whereas Guru Nanak is traditionally depicted as being contemplative and the master of things spiritual, Guru Gobind Singh is portrayed as a worldly prince, ever ready for battle.

Guru Gobind Singh contributed significantly to the growth of Sikh militarism and engaged in many armed conflicts during a period when revolts against the Mughals, which had been occurring periodically for about a century, were common. Because of his success in consolidating and strengthening the Panth, the Sikhs had a realistic possibility of establishing independent rule. Most notably, Guru Gobind Singh brought about two innovations that forever changed the structure of Sikhism. As we have already noted, he instituted the Khalsa, which would redefine the Panth, and he installed the Adi Granth, the sacred scripture, as Guru, which radically altered the nature of leadership.

Founding the Khalsa
The traditional story of this momentous event is set forth in this account by twentieth-century Sikh historians Teja Singh and Ganda Singh. Note the story's emphasis on the virtues of loyalty and unity of the Sikh community, with its details concerning various castes and livelihoods.

On the Baisakhi day, March 30 of 1699, [Guru Gobind Singh] called a big meeting at Anandpur. When all were seated, he drew out his sword and cried, "Is there
anyone here who would lay down his life for dharma?" At this the whole assembly was thrown into consternation; but the Guru went on repeating his demand.
At the third call, Daya Ram, a Khatri of Lahore, rose from his seat and offered
himself. The Guru took him into an adjoining enclosure, where a few goats were
kept tied, and seating him there cut off a goat's head. He came out with the dripping weapon and flourishing it before the multitude asked again, "Is there any
other Sikh here who will offer himself as a sacrifice?" At this Dharam Das, a Jat of
Delhi, came forward and was taken into the enclosure, where another goat was
killed. In the same way three other men stood up one after another and offered
themselves for the sacrifice. One was Muhkam Chand, a washerman of Dwarka;
another was Himmat, a cook of Jagannath; and the third was Sahib Chand, a
barber of Bedar. The Guru after dressing the five in handsome clothes brought
them before the assembly. He baptized them with sweetened water [i.e., amrit]
stirred with a dagger and called them his Beloved Ones.[13]

Guru Gobind Singh, after preaching to the crowd about the unity of the Sikh community, asked the *Panj Piare*, the "Beloved Ones" (or "Beloved Five"), to baptize
him—a surprising request given the traditional elevated standing of the Guru. The
five baptized the Guru, thus forming the original Khalsa, the community of "Pure
Ones" (as we noted in the chapter's opening description of the initiation ceremony).
Over the course of the next few days, some 80,000 were baptized. All the men were
given the additional name Singh, which means "lion," and all the women were named
Kaur, which means "princess." To this day, these names indicate a family's affiliation
with the Khalsa (although they no longer imply that one has undergone initiation).

By the time of his death in 1708, Guru Gobind Singh had managed to befriend
the Mughal rulership and to ease tensions between the peoples, although his own
death came at the hands of a Mughal assas-
sin. Before dying, he is said to have declared
that he was to be succeeded, not by another
individual, but by the Adi Granth and by the
Panth, to both of which he assigned the title
"Guru."

Manmohan Singh, who
served as India's prime
minister from 2004
to 2014, the first Sikh
to do so, joins a cel-
ebration of the 350th
birth anniversary of
Guru Gobind Singh on
December 24, 2017, in
Ananadpur, India.

7.5 The History of Sikhism: The Modern Age

Over the centuries, the Punjab has tended to
be a volatile region, marked by political and
military strife. In the century following the
death of Guru Gobind Singh in 1708, the
Sikhs struggled through a period of especially

violent confrontations with the Mughal Empire, eventually managing to establish independent rule.

Sikhs in Conflict and in Search of Nationhood

Under the leadership of Ranjit Singh (1780–1839), who ascended to the throne in 1792, the Sikh community thrived as a sovereign kingdom in the Punjab. In 1849, the kingdom was annexed by the British, who had established control over India and had commenced the period known as the British Raj.

When India gained independence from the British in 1947, the Punjab was divided, with India gaining control of the east and Pakistan gaining control of the west. Most Sikhs living in the western region migrated eastward, favoring the Hindu-dominated India over the Muslim-dominated Pakistan. These Sikhs left behind their traditional homeland and many significant sites, including Nanak's birthplace.

In recent times, a new nationalist movement for independence, commonly called "Khalistan," has involved the Sikhs in conflict, both within and outside the Sikh community. The most violent tragedy of all took place in 1984 when, in an attempt to control the more radical aspects of the independence movement, the Indian government launched Operation Blue Star. This action culminated in the occupation of Sikh holy sites, most notably the Darbar Sahib (or Golden Temple), by Indian forces and the death of as many as 10,000 Sikhs. (Estimates of the death count vary widely, with various sources citing from 500 to 10,000.) This led to the assassination of Indian Prime Minister Indira Gandhi by two of her Sikh body-guards on October 31, 1984. Today, the Khalistan movement is not nearly as prevalent as it was in the 1980s. The fact that in 2004 a Sikh, Manmohan Singh, for the first time became India's prime minister perhaps signals a new degree of assimilation of Sikhism within Indian society.

Sikhism in the Twenty-First Century

There are approximately 25 million Sikhs in the world, more than 90 percent of whom live in India, and the great majority of those Sikhs live in the Indian state of Punjab, which is located in Sikhism's traditional homeland (also called the Punjab).

Since the early twentieth century, what might be called orthodox Sikhism has been defined by the Khalsa; prior to that time, Sikhism tended to be more diverse. Today, a great majority of Sikhs conform to this orthodox model, although there are a number of sects that to some extent do not exactly fit the Khalsa norm. One such sect is the Nihangs, mentioned earlier in this chapter as the only group of Sikhs who regard the Dasam Granth as of equal stature with the Adi Granth. Another sect, relatively popular in the United States, is the Sikh Dharma of the Western Hemisphere, or the 3HO (Healthy, Happy, Holy Organization) Sikhs. Members of this organization, which was founded in 1971 by Yogi Bhajan, rigorously practice mediation and a special form of yoga. The fact that most Khalsa Sikhs tend to be

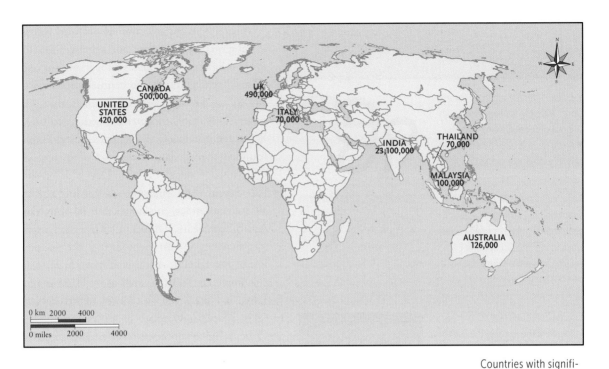

CANADA
500,000

UNITED
STATES
420,000

UK
490,000

ITALY
70,000

INDIA
23,100,000

THAILAND
70,000

MALAYSIA
100,000

AUSTRALIA
126,000

0 km 2000 4000
0 miles 2000 4000

Countries with significant Sikh populations (all figures are approximate, as estimates vary widely).

perplexed by these practitioners indicates the diversity among those who regard themselves as Sikhs in today's world.[14]

The approximately 2 million Sikhs who live outside of India typically conform to the orthodox mold as established by the Khalsa. As many as 650,000 Sikhs live in Canada, and 500,000 in the United States, although some estimates are significantly lower. Sikhs began to immigrate to North America in 1903, first to British Columbia and soon thereafter to other destinations. In 1912, the first gurdwara in the United States was established in Stockton, California. Regions in the United States with large Sikh populations today include New York and California, especially in the Central Valley. Yuba City, located just north of Sacramento, is home to an annual Nagar Kirtan parade that draws more than 100,000 people to share in the celebration. Much more ominously, Sikhism in North American in the twenty-first century, in the wake of the World Trade Center attacks of September 11, 2001, has been forced to confront the threat of extreme violence, including the murders of six in Oak Creek, Wisconsin and two in Elk Grove, California.

7.6 Sikhism as a Way of Life: Devotional Practices

One aspect of Guru Nanak's teachings was the rejection of the outward forms of religion that he found troubling in the Islam and Hinduism of his day. Focused as he was on seeking the indwelling God through meditation on the divine Name, Guru Nanak regarded the external forms of religion as useless.

VISUAL GUIDE
Sikhism

Ik Onkar. Literally meaning "one God," *Ik Onkar* is the primary Sikh symbol of monotheism. The *Mul Mantra*, recited daily by most Sikhs, begins with these words.

Five Ks. Objects symbolizing membership in the Khalsa: *kes*, uncut hair; *kangha*, a small comb worn in the hair; *kara*, a steel wristlet; kirpan, a sword; *kachh*, a pair of shorts tied with a drawstring.

Golden Temple. Located in Amritsar in the Punjab, the Darbar Sahib ("Court of the Lord") or Golden Temple, was built by Guru Arjan in about 1600 CE, providing Sikhs to this day with a geographical center.

Composed (from the center outward) of a double-edged sword, the circular *Chakar*, and two kirpans, the *khanda* symbolizes the balanced unity of Sikh spiritual and worldly life.

Guru Nanak's rejection of outward forms of religion, however, has not led the Sikhs to avoid religious observances altogether. For one thing, Sikhs through the centuries have continued to celebrate annual festivals that are generally features of northern Indian culture. We noted previously that Guru Gobind Singh founded the Khalsa on the day of an important annual festival, Baisakhi Day, which is the first day of the Indian year (according to the Western calendar, this day occurs in March or April). For Sikhs, Baisakhi Day has the special significance of commemorating the founding of the Khalsa. Another important festival celebrated by Sikhs, as well as by Hindus and Jains, is Divali, the Festival of Lights (which takes place in October or early November). Other religious observations were instituted by the Sikh Gurus, most notably by Guru Gobind Singh, and are unique to Sikhism.

Daily Devotional Practices

Guru Nanak emphasized the importance of *nam simaran*, "remembrance of the Name." This can be done simply by repeating one of the names used to refer to God. Recall that Guru Nanak composed many hymns; *kirtan*, the singing of hymns, is another form of *nam simaran*. A third form involves meditation practices designed to contemplate the divine Name and ultimately to bring one into perfect harmony with God.

Daily prayers are another form of devotional practice that can (and should) be done by every Sikh. The Khalsa Rahit, which spells out the ideal regimen for much of the religious life, gives the following instructions:

A Sikh should rise early (3 A.M. to 6 A.M.) and having bathed he should observe *nam japan* by meditating on God. Each day a Sikh should read or recite the order known as the "Daily Rule" (*nit-nem*). The Daily Rule comprises the following portions of scripture: Early morning (3 A.M.–6 A.M.): *Japji, Jap*, and the *Ten Savayyas*. . . . In the evening at sunset: *Sodar Rahiras*. . . . At night before retiring: *Sohila*. At the conclusion of the selections set down for early morning and evening (*Sodar Rahiras*) the prayer known as *Ardas* must be recited.[15]

To follow such a regimen requires much diligence and much time: altogether, these prayers cover about twenty pages in English translation. Whereas some Sikhs, especially those more advanced in age, commonly do this on a regular basis, the majority do not.

Sikh Worship in the Gurdwara

Gurdwara means "doorway of the Guru" (a variant translation is "by means of the Guru's [grace]"). Any building that contains a copy of the Adi Granth is, technically speaking, a gurdwara, a Sikh house of worship. There is at least one gurdwara in virtually every village in the Punjab. Most gurdwaras have a characteristic Sikh style, with minarets and chalk-white paint. Aside from the presence of the Adi Granth, which usually sits atop cushions and under a canopy, there are no specific requirements regarding the interior.

The gurdwara serves mainly as a place for Sikh men, women, and children to congregate for worship. This they do frequently, on no particular day of the week. Worship usually takes place in the evening, though the early morning is also a popular time. Worship in the gurdwara is preceded by bathing and consists of singing the Gurus' hymns, reading from the Adi Granth, or telling a story about one of the Gurus. No formal requirements govern the exact nature of worship. It generally ends, though, with a sharing of a special pudding made of wheat flour, sugar, and ghee (clarified butter), known as *karah prasad*. This act is symbolic of the unity of the Panth.

As we have seen, since the times of Guru Nanak the sharing of food is an important feature of Sikhism. Each gurdwara typically has within it the *langar*, where Sikhs gather at various times to share in the preparation and consumption of a meal. The food served in the *langar* is strictly vegetarian; even eggs are not allowed. Again, this sharing of food symbolizes the equality of all. It also provides food for the needy.

Volunteers prepare food for the *langar* meal at the Golden Temple in Amritsar. Many thousands of people share meals together here daily, at no cost to the visitor.

7.7 Sikhism as a Way of Life: The Life Cycle

In the chapter's opening description of the *Amrit Sanchar*, the Khalsa initiation ceremony, we witnessed an example of a Sikh

ritual that marks a certain point in the individual's life and does so through detailed actions and rich symbolism that are steeped in tradition. Having already considered the Khalsa initiation ceremony in some detail (and bearing in mind that only about 15 percent of Sikhs undergo initiation), we now turn to considering other important rituals of the life cycle.

Birth and Naming

On the birth of a child, Khalsa Sikhs can choose to undertake a ritual that resembles an aspect of the initiation ceremony. A sweet drink is made by stirring water and sweets with a kirpan (the short sword, one of the Five Ks), while reciting from the *Japji*. A few drops are given to the baby, and the rest is drunk by the mother.

A short time after giving birth, the parents and child proceed to the gurdwara, where hymns are sung and the Adi Granth is opened randomly. The child's first name is chosen based on the first letter that appears on the left-hand page of the Adi Granth, the letter with which the name is to begin. If the child is a girl, she is also given the name Kaur; if male, he is given the name Singh. The names Singh or Kaur normally correspond to an English last name. No distinction is made between girls' and boys' first names. The "last name" of Kaur or Singh serves to make this distinction.

Tying a Turban

When a boy reaches the age of ten or eleven, Sikh families often undertake a ceremonial tying of his first turban. This act symbolizes the great respect that Sikhs hold for the turban. Even though wearing the turban is not technically required, it is regarded as a natural corollary of *kes*, not cutting one's hair (one of the Five Ks). Indeed, because one's hair is typically kept inside the turban, it is really the turban, not the hair, that is the most visible sign that one is a Sikh.

Traditionally, the turban is tied in a specific way that is both easy to do (once one has learned how) and effective, keeping the turban securely on the head. The style and color of the turban may sometimes indicate regional, political, or religious affiliation. The turban is generally considered to be highly practical, providing protection both from the summer sun and from the cold of winter. Women rarely wear turbans; instead, they traditionally wear a scarf or veil that can be used to cover the head.

Marriage

Proper Sikh marriage, according to the traditions established by the Khalsa, is arranged by the parents of a child of marriageable age through the assistance of a relative, who seeks out a suitable spouse and sets up meetings with the families. The parents thus can become acquainted with their child's potential bride or groom. The same type of meeting takes place with the other set of parents. Once both families have agreed on a match, the marriage ceremony is planned. According to the Rahit, a Sikh woman is only to be married to a Sikh, but no account whatsoever is to be taken of caste status. In actual practice, however, there are many exceptions. Caste status commonly dictates the choice of marriage partners, and Sikhs (men more commonly than women) sometimes marry outside the tradition. As we have remarked previously, common practice by no means always complies with Khalsa ideals.

The ceremony takes place at the gurdwara, with Sri Guru Granth Sahib the central focal point, just as it is in everyday worship. First seated before the Adi Granth during the singing of hymns, the couple then stands and receives instruction in the teachings of the Gurus on marriage, nodding their assent to the Adi Granth, and afterward walking around it. This focus on the scripture exemplifies the central role that the Adi Granth is to play in the life of the married couple. The ceremony concludes, like other worship services in the gurdwara, with the distribution of *karah prasad*, the special pudding made of wheat flour, sugar, and ghee.

Death

Traditional Sikh mourning rituals center on the process of cremation. The body is washed and dressed in clean clothing and adorned with the Five Ks. A hymn is recited, and the body is carried to the cremation grounds, which women do not enter. The funeral pyre is lit by a son or other male relative or friend, while the other mourners sing funeral hymns. The *Kirtan Sohila*, the prayer that is recited daily when retiring for the evening, is then sung.

Once the fire has burned out, the ashes are recovered and are either buried there at the cremation site or immersed in running water. Then the entire Adi Granth is read, within a period of ten days if possible. (The Rahit specifies that a full reading takes forty-eight hours, if done without interruption.) Such traditional practices are modified today in places where laws prohibit outdoor cremations.

7.8 Sikhism as a Way of Life: Engaging with the World

Like every global religion, Sikhism is continually in contact with people of other traditions. In this chapter, we have seen how Guru Nanak inspired followers who were both Muslims and Hindus. Although the common notion that Sikhism somehow resulted from the mixing of Islam and Hinduism is not an accurate one, clearly Guru Nanak and Sikhs after him helped to bridge differences among these two major religions of India. Sikhism has generally maintained peaceful relations with other religions and with other peoples, both in their homeland and abroad.

Worship, Work, and Charity

Sikhs have a well-deserved reputation for reaching out to achieve social justice and helping to improve their communities. From its beginnings, Sikhism has been on the side of religious freedom and justice for oppressed people. Justice is carried out partly through the regular donation of one-tenth of one's income to charitable causes.

Three guiding principles of Sikh life are worship, work, and charity, as embodied in the popular Punjabi proverb, *nam japo, kirat karo, vand chhako*: "Repeat the

The *langar* meal is shared at the conclusion of the annual Sikh Day Parade in New York City.

divine Name, work, and give a share [of your earnings to the less fortunate]."[16] An outsider need only pay a visit to a Sikh gurdwara and witness the worship and afterward partake of the carefully prepared food in the *langar* to experience these guiding principles in action. Sikh communities across North America tend to emphasize the importance of the gurdwara as a social as well as a religious gathering place, with the *langar* and its weekly meals—served to anyone attending—being especially important.

Sikhism and the Natural World   The Sikh emphasis on monotheism, on one God who created all things, human beings and the natural world alike, leads naturally to concern for the environment. In fact, caring for the natural world is one means of living in accordance with *hukam*, the divine order that allows for God to be immanent in creation. Not to treat the environment properly, as stewards of God's creation, is to succumb to *haumai*, self-centeredness. God is Creator, and yet Sikhism does not set forth a creation story. It emphasizes instead the task of sustaining creation, and of achieving harmony with the natural world—and thereby, with God. To attempt to use nature for selfish advantage is, again, to succumb to *haumai*.

One among various Sikh organizations that promotes environmentalism is EcoSikh; its vision statement captures Sikhism's ecological ideals:

> We honor our Gurus' wisdom by believing that all humans have an intrinsic sensitivity to the natural world, and that a sustainable, more just society is possible, where water, air, land, forests, and biodiversity remain vibrant, living systems for our generation and future generations.[17]

Bandana Kaur, an EcoSikh Ambassador, has written eloquently about the ideal of harmony of God and creation:

> The Divine permeates all life, and is inherent in the manifest creation around us, from the wind that blows across land and skies, to the water that flows through rivers and seas, to the forests and fields that humans rely on for food and shelter, as well as all the creatures of land and sea that depend on the earth for sustenance. The Sikh Gurus teach that there is no duality between that which makes a flower grow and the petals we are able to touch and sense with our fingers.[18]

A variety of specific actions are prescribed and being carried out in the name of Sikh environmentalism. As we might expect, given the traditional and enduring lifestyle of most Sikhs in their homeland of the Punjab, to some extent they are focused on agriculture. Actions include sharing and recycling natural resources, and in general limiting as much as possible the use of resources. Regarding the natural world as sacred and as a manifestation of *hukam* means not to pollute or in other ways destroy it.

Sikh Identity

This chapter has consistently used a rather flexible definition of who is a Sikh. On one end of the spectrum, we have considered the rigorous regimen of observance as spelled out in the Rahit, which calls for the recitation of some twenty pages of prayer every morning before six o'clock. At the other end of the spectrum are those who cut their hair, and yet one cannot deny that they are Sikhs.

This flexible definition is in keeping with the Sikh perspective. Every religious tradition sets forth ideals that are not necessarily put into practice by all of its followers. Sikhism openly acknowledges this reality. It is also important to recognize that the label "Sikh" can refer broadly to an ethnic group, without necessarily implying adherence to the religion of Sikhism. For centuries, Sikhs maintained a society in the Punjab that was quite distinctive, and the vast majority of today's Sikhs are themselves descendants of Punjabi Sikhs. Thus, being Sikh has both a societal and a hereditary aspect, neither of which necessarily involves the explicitly religious aspects of belief or conduct.

Gender Roles in Sikhism   Sikhism, like every religion, has both its ideals and its practical realities. Such is the case with the relative roles of men and women over the centuries. Certain ideals regarding the status of women are set forth straightforwardly, for instance in these words by Guru Nanak:

> From women born, shaped in the womb, to women betrothed and wed, We
> are bound to women by ties of affection; on women man's future depends.
> If a woman dies he seeks another, source of society's order and strength.
> Why then should one speak evil of women, they who give birth to kings?
> Women also are born from women, as are all who have life and breath.[19]

Sikhism has always maintained this ideal of gender equality with regard to the crucial issue of spiritual liberation (mukti). Sikh teachings from the beginning rejected practices such as female infanticide, which were common in the Punjab in Guru Nanak's time. The Rahit emphasizes that women are to participate fully in the religious life. But teachings alone do not always ensure equality in society, even in religious society. Men have predominated; notably, the ten Gurus were all men.

Sikh society, through the centuries and up to the present day, has tended to be quite patriarchal, with positions of institutional power occupied by men. The wedding ceremony that we have considered suggests a certain patriarchal tendency with its prescribed vows. The groom promises to be "protector" of the bride and her honor; the bride promises to accept her husband as "master of all love and respect."

Yet the social history of Sikhism includes many examples of equal participation by women in religious matters and of women who serve as role models. Sulakhani, the wife of Guru Nanak, certainly is portrayed as a role model—not only in the domestic domain of the household but also as a confidant and advisor to her husband. There is evidence that wives of other Gurus participated to some degree in administration of the Panth.

As is the case with all of the world's major religions, the degree of gender equality in Sikhism varies from circumstance to circumstance. Generally speaking, modern times have brought changes. In 1977, a wedding ceremony took place in a small town in the Punjab in which the bride led the groom in the final walk around the Adi Granth—a surprising incident, but no one was able to find anything in Sikh scripture to provide an objection based on doctrinal grounds. In another example of changing times, in the late 1990s women began to take on the traditionally male practice of ritual washing of the Golden Temple at midnight.[20]

The rapid growth of the Sikh diaspora in places where gender equality is held up as an ideal suggests that such changes will bring new opportunities for women to occupy roles of power in Sikh religion and society. With regard to the issue of gender equality, too, the Panth will need to continue to make adjustments as it orients its way as a global religion.

Sikh Identity in the Diaspora

About 2 million Sikhs now live in the diaspora (that is, outside of the Punjab and of India).[21] For these Sikhs, many of the traditional practices taken for granted in the Punjab simply are not feasible—or, in some cases, even legal—in other lands. Consider, for example, Sikh funeral rituals. According to the Rahit, and in keeping with long-standing tradition, the body of the deceased is to be borne to the pyre on a bier, not in a coffin, and the fire is to be lit by a close relative or friend. In countries such as the United States, such a practice is not permitted; as a result, adjustments are made. The ceremonial departure for the cremation site is replaced by placing the coffin into a hearse, which then proceeds to a crematorium. (Alternatively, the ceremony is held at a funeral home that is equipped with a crematorium.) The lighting of the pyre is replaced by the chosen person pushing the button that conveys the coffin into the cremation furnace.

Other challenging situations for Sikhs in the diaspora involve the Five Ks. Wearing the turban, for example, which is based on the requirement of *kes*, not cutting one's hair, is almost universal among male Sikhs in their traditional homeland and is an important symbol of Sikh identity. But in many places in the diaspora, wearing a turban is not so easily done. In the United States, for example, there are laws in most states requiring that helmets be worn when driving a motorcycle. An innovative adaption relating to *kes* is the use of the *patka*, a smaller version of the turban that is often worn by Sikh boys and young men in North America. One Sikh website offers *patkas* for sale in four different sizes, ranging from eighteen inches square to twenty-seven inches square—still much smaller than the traditional turban, which is several feet long. Khalsa Sikhs who wish to don the kirpan (the sword or knife, another of the Five Ks) when traveling by plane must be prepared for varying rules governing security practices at airport screenings.

In some cases, governments have attempted to accommodate Sikhs. In the United Kingdom and in California, for example, motorcycle helmet laws have been modified. But in many situations, such traditional practices as wearing the turban have led at least to inconvenience and sometimes even to tragedy. In the aftermath of the attacks on the World Trade Center and the Pentagon of September 11, 2001, Sikhs have been mistaken (presumably because of the wearing of the turban) for Muslims and have become targets of hate crimes, including murder.

For Sikhs living in the diaspora, this issue of identity needs to be weighed against practical concerns, sometimes even involving one's safety. Whereas most Sikhs in the Punjab continue to follow the injunction not to cut their hair, most living in Western countries do not. The Panth, as a global religious community, must contend with this complex mix of issues and concerns.

SEEKING ANSWERS

What Is Ultimate Reality?

Sikhism is strictly monotheistic, emphasizing the oneness of God, while also teaching that God dwells within creation. For reasons that human beings cannot understand, God created the world. Knowing the divine nature can be considered analogous to knowing the nature of an artist through contemplation of her artwork. Sikhism holds that the world is good, that God is immanent in the world, and that the world is permeated with divine order, called *hukam*. If this divine order can be recognized, it stands to reason that human beings can come to know God.

How Should We Live in This World?

Sikhs believe that God dwells within everyone. Humans tend, however, to be self-centered, rather than God-centered, a concept known as *haumai*, the self-reliance or pride that poses the primary obstacle to spiritual fulfillment. Sikhs further believe that the world is permeated with *hukam*, or divine order. To live in accord with *hukam* naturally requires proper ethical conduct. The Khalsa, though technically made up of only a minority of Sikhs, continues to be the authoritative source for ideals on the right way to live.

What Is Our Ultimate Purpose?

Immanent in creation, God is knowable to human beings. The flaws of *haumai* can be overcome through attention to the presence of the divine, most effectively through meditation on *nam*, the Name of God. As the term suggests, liberation (mukti), which for Sikhism is being in the presence of God, is the complete overcoming of the human condition. Sikhism teaches that the ultimate purpose of life is to attain spiritual liberation, and thereby release from samsara, the cycle of death and rebirth.

Sikhism today is a global religion, as vital in such places as Toronto, Canada, and the Central Valley of California as it is in its ancestral homeland of the Punjab. As it continues to draw upon the richness of its eventful historical tradition, Sikhism shows every sign of continuing to adapt to modernity in the various places across the globe that it has come to call home.

REVIEW QUESTIONS

For Review

1. What is the meaning of the term *guru*?
2. Identify at least three of the names for God in Sikhism. What is the relationship of the names to each other?
3. Compare the contributions of Guru Nanak and Guru Gobind Singh for the development of Sikhism.
4. What is the Khalsa? What is its ongoing relevance for Sikhism?
5. How do the Five Ks of Sikhism serve to strengthen Sikh identity?

For Further Reflection

1. What aspects of the Sikh God would Jews, Christians, or Muslims find familiar?
2. Describe mukti, spiritual liberation. How does this compare to forms of spiritual liberation in other religions—for example, to Hindu moksha or Buddhist nirvana?
3. Compare Sikh worship in the gurdwara with the forms of worship in religions with which you are familiar, either through studies or through personal experience. What are the notable similarities and differences? What do these comparative points regarding worship suggest about the nature of the religions, in general?

GLOSSARY

Adi Granth (ah'dee gruhnth; Punjabi, "first book") Sikhism's most important sacred text and, since the death of Guru Gobind Singh in 1708, Sikhism's primary earthly authority; traditionally known as Sri Guru Granth Sahib.

amrit (am'rit; Punjabi, "immortalizing fluid") A special drink made from water and sugar crystals, used in the Khalsa initiation ceremony.

gurdwara (goor'dwah-ruh; Punjabi, "doorway of the Guru" or "by means of the Guru's [grace]") A building for Sikh worship that houses a copy of the Adi Granth; the central structure of any Sikh community.

guru (gooh'rooh; Sanskrit, "venerable person") A spiritual teacher and revealer of truth, common to Hinduism, Sikhism, and some forms of Buddhism. When the word *Guru* is capitalized, it refers to the ten historical leaders of Sikhism, to the sacred text (Sri Guru Granth Sahib, or Adi Granth), and to God (often as True Guru).

haumai (how-mai; Punjabi, "self-centeredness") The human inclination toward being self-centered rather than God-centered, which increases the distance between the individual and God.

hukam (hooh'kahm; Punjabi, "order") The divine order of the universe.

Khalsa (khal'sah; Punjabi, "pure ones") An order within Sikhism to which the majority of Sikhs belong, founded by Guru Gobind Singh in 1699.

langar A gurdwara's community kitchen that is used to prepare meals for anyone who visits, regardless of religious or caste identity.

mukti (mook'tee; Punjabi, "liberation") Spiritual liberation bringing on the eternal and infinitely blissful state of being in the presence of God; sometimes the Sanskrit term *moksha* is used instead.

Mul Mantra (mool mahn'truh) The summary of Sikh doctrine that comprises the opening lines of the *Japji*, Guru Nanak's composition that in turn comprises the opening section of the Adi Granth. (See p. 245 for an English translation of the full text.)

Panth (puhnth; Sanskrit, "path") The Sikh community. In lower case, *panth* ("path") is a term applied to any number of Indian (primarily Hindu) religious traditions.

Rahit (rah-hit'; Punjabi) The *rahit-nama*, a collection of scripture that specifies ideals of belief and conduct for members of the Khalsa and, by extension, for Sikhism generally.

SUGGESTIONS FOR FURTHER READING

Cole, W. Owen, and Piara Singh Sambhi. *The Sikhs: Their Religious Beliefs and Practices*. 2nd rev. ed. Brighton, UK: Sussex Academic Press, 1995. A highly readable and informative account, organized to make the main figures and ideas easily accessible.

Mann, Gurinder Singh. *Sikhism*. Upper Saddle River, NJ: Prentice Hall, 2004. A clear and up-to-date overview, with focus on modern times.

McLeod, Hew. *Sikhism*. London: Penguin Books, 1997. A detailed yet accessible overview of the religion, with a helpful appendix of primary source material.

McLeod, W. H., ed. and trans. *Textual Sources for the Study of Sikhism*. Totowa, NJ: Barnes & Noble Books, 1984. A helpful collection of source material that goes well beyond the Adi Granth and presents texts in such a way as to clarify the identity of authors.

Singh, Khushwant. *A History of the Sikhs*. 2 vols. Princeton, NJ: Princeton University Press, 1963–1966. A detailed and authoritative resource.

ONLINE RESOURCES

Sikhs.org: Philosophy & Scriptures

Provides access to the Sri Guru Granth Sahib, along with other scriptures, in English translation. More generally, the website sets forth a wide array of helpful information from a Sikh's insider's perspective.

SikhNet

Like Sikhs.org, SikhNet offers an extensive insider's perspective on Sikhism, with information on many aspects of the religion.

The Pluralism Project at Harvard University: Sikhism

Thorough and dependable coverage of Sikhism in the United States.

Chinese Religions: Confucianism and Daoism

8

Chapter Outline

8.1 Describe the content of Chinese religion prior to Confucianism and Daoism.

8.2 Describe the teachings of Confucius and his early followers.

8.3 Identify the essential teachings of Daoism.

8.4 Describe the historical development of the Confucian tradition.

8.5 Describe the historical development of the Daoist tradition.

8.6 Explain how Confucianism and Daoism are practiced.

8.7 Explain how Confucianism and Daoism engage with significant issues in the contemporary world.

TODAY IS *QINGMING*, a "pure and bright" day (the literal meaning of this Chinese compound word) that arrives once a year, 105 days after the winter solstice. It is a day for all Chinese families to remember their dead relatives and ancestors by visiting their graves. Spring is definitely in the air. The days have been getting longer and warmer. The rice seedlings, standing in neat rows in ankle-deep water in the paddy fields, wave gracefully in the gentle breeze. Their luxuriant greenness is most pleasing to the eyes of Chen Liang, a peasant from southern China in his early fifties. He and his two sons have been working hard in the past couple of months to plow and flood the paddy fields, seed the nursery plots, and then transplant the young seedlings one at a time into their current location.

But today there will be no work in the fields. *Qingming* marks the return of spring. It also celebrates the rekindling of the kitchen fire. Two days earlier the old fire had been put out, so only cold food had been eaten at the Chen household. Chen Liang and his wife get up today at the crack of dawn to light

Woman making offerings in front of her ancestor's tomb.

Important Confucian and Daoist sites in China.

a new fire in the kitchen. Leftovers from the previous days' cold meals are wrapped in rice pancakes and fried, making "spring rolls" that many Chinese restaurants the world over serve regularly on their appetizer menu. They prepare for an important family gathering at the ancestral graves of the Chen clan. During this annual spring event (another one occurs in the fall on the ninth day of the ninth lunar month), family members gather at and sweep the graves of their relatives and ancestors to renew their kinship ties with both the dead and the living. Plates of fruits, freshly steamed chickens, a whole roasted pig, bottles of rice wine, bundles of incense sticks and bright-red candles, and strings of firecrackers, as well as piles of fake paper money and paper clothing for the dead, are all ready to be carried to the lineage burial ground just outside the village.

At the gravesite, where several generations of the Chen clan are buried, Chen Liang meets up with his three brothers, his five cousins, and their families. The children, numbering more than twenty, are all dressed in brightly colored clothing, giggling and playing. They help remove overgrown weeds, clean the tombstones, and arrange food in front of the tombstones. Then, by generation and birth order, all members of the Chen clan bow before their ancestors, address them in silent prayers, offer them wine and food, send them clothing and stacks of underworld money by burning their paper imitations, and set off firecrackers to scare off wandering ghosts unrelated to the family.

TIMELINE
Confucianism and Daoism

Era in Chinese History	Confucianism	Daoism
Shang-Zhou dynasties (c. 1600–256 BCE*)	Ancient Chinese religion Beginning of *ru* tradition	Ancient Chinese religion Shamans
Spring and Autumn (c. 722–481 BCE)	Confucius (551–479 BCE*)	World-escaping recluses and hermits
Warring States (c. 480–221 BCE)	Mencius (371–289 BCE*), Xunzi (c. 310–238 BCE*)	Zhuangzi (365–290 BCE*), *Daodejing* (earliest extant ed. c. 300 BCE)
Early Han Dynasty (206 BCE–9 CE)	Confucianism declared orthodox (136 CE); Five Classics designated	Worship of Xiwangmu (Queen Mother of the West)
Later Han Dynasty (25–220 CE)	Confucian classical commentaries and Scholasticism	Laozi deified as Taishang Laojun. Tianshi ("Celestial Master") movement founded by Zhang Daoling (142 CE), *Laozi bianhua jing* (Classic of Laozi's Transformations) (170s*)
Period of Disunion (221–589)	Confucian texts introduced to Korea and subsequently to Japan	Shangqing (Highest Clarity) movement (fourth century), Lingbao (Numinous Treasure) movement (fourth century)
Tang Dynasty (618–907)	First stirring of Neo-Confucianism	First attempt at compiling canon State patronage of Daoism Daoism merged with Chinese folk religion
Song Dynasty (907–1279)	Neo-Confucianism: Zhu Xi (1130–1200)	Quanzhen (Complete Perfection) movement founded by Wang Zhe (1113–1170)
Yuan Dynasty (1279–1368)	Four Books designated as civil service examination curriculum (1313)	
Ming Dynasty (1368–1644)	Wang Yangming (1472–1529), an alternative Neo-Confucian view to Zhu Xi's Confucianism became state orthodoxy in Joseon Dynasty (1392–1897) Korea Confucianism also became state ideology in Tokugawa Japan (1600–1868)	*Daozang* compiled (1445) Daoist sacrificial rituals and notions of health influenced both elites and commoners in Korea, Japan, and Southeast Asia
Qing Dynasty (1644–1911)	Civil service examination abolished (1905) Confucianism became dominant ideology in Nguyen Dynasty Vietnam (1802–1945)	
Early twentieth century	Chinese intellectuals rejected Confucianism as feudalistic and reactionary	Chinese intellectuals criticized Daoism as superstition
Chinese Republic (1949–present)	Cultural Revolution (1966–1976) devastated Confucianism. Confucianism gradually recovering since 1980s	Cultural Revolution (1966–1976) devastated Daoism Daoism gradually recovering since 1980s

Note: Asterisks indicate contested or approximate dates.

Afterward a picture is taken of the entire gathering in front of the graves. The families divide up the fruits and the meats to be consumed later back at their respective homes. The men linger to talk about the weather and the crops, the women catch up on family news, and the children play.

Gatherings similar to that of the Chen extended family are replicated millions of times throughout China in observance of *qingming*. It is through this activity of remembering the ancestors and reaffirming kinship relations that the Chinese act out some of their most basic religious beliefs. At the core of this ritual is the Confucian notion of filial piety (honoring parents and ancestors) and familial cohesiveness. Equally on display is the Daoist (Taoist) attentiveness to changes in season and in nature, as well as the practice of warding off unwelcome ghosts through thunderous explosives. From this single family gathering we see that Confucianism and Daoism can coexist quite harmoniously among the Chinese, with no sense of incompatibility or mutual exclusivity.

In this chapter you are invited to appreciate the religious nature of these two Chinese traditions. (Even though Buddhism is the third main religious tradition in China, we only give passing notice to it in light of its alien origin and its totally different worldviews; see Chapter 5 for a complete treatment of Buddhism.) In addition, you will see that these two traditions, while sharing a common source, end up with very different views and practices. They compete with and complement each other in remarkable ways. Importantly as well, you will see that both have gone well beyond the national boundary of China and are indeed world religions.

8.1 The Teachings of Chinese Religions: Before Confucianism and Daoism

Before Confucianism and Daoism arose, an ancient religion had already been in existence in China for over a thousand years. Both Confucianism and Daoism may be regarded as two divergent outgrowths of this ancient Chinese religion, with Confucianism focusing on interhuman relationship, while Daoism emphasizes the relationship between humans and nature. To understand Confucianism and Daoism, then, this ancient Chinese religion needs to be examined first.

Ancient Chinese Religious Views

The *Book of Changes*, the *Yijing* (traditionally spelled *I Ching*, believed to have been compiled by the end of the second millennium BCE), represents the earliest expression of the Chinese religious mindset. It conveys a worldview that has been described as "organismic," meaning that every single component of the cosmos belongs to an organic whole and that all the component parts interact with one another continuously. Unlike the foundational or sacred texts of most religions, the *Book of Changes* does not include a creation myth, nor is it regarded as divinely revealed. This absence of a creation myth may be attributed to the practice of honoring ancestors in China since antiquity. When worship of ancestors, who are former human beings who share the same attributes as the living, dominates the religious activities of the ancient Chinese, the sense of mystery and "otherness" of a creator being may be difficult to envision. Instead, the *Yijing* posits that from an original state of "undifferentiated chaos,"[1] two polar yet complementary energies known as **qi** ("breath," "energy," or "force") emerged. One is called **yang** (literally the south-facing, sunny side of a mountain) and the other **yin** (the north-facing, shady side of a mountain). Representing all binary entities and concepts (such as day and night, male and female, hot and cold), yang and yin interact and alternate ceaselessly to form a continuum or spectrum, generating the myriad things in the process.

The yin-yang symbol best represents the Chinese religious mentality. This worldview recognizes differences but also complementarity between the differences.

In this kind of a worldview, nothing exists outside the cosmos. This absence of a "wholly other" transcendent creator in the early Chinese cosmological myth has significant implications. This organismic view uses the metaphor of procreation or giving birth, not creation or fashioning something out of nothing, for the beginning of the universe. In this ancient Chinese understanding, the idea of an almighty god preceding and existing outside of creation is simply nonexistent. Correspondingly, the notion of an active evil dedicated to undermining the plans of a supposedly benevolent creator is also absent. In other words, there is no frighteningly personified devil dueling with a benign god until the latter triumphs over the former, with humans caught in between. In this world without sin (at least sin as understood by the Abrahamic faiths of Judaism, Christianity, and Islam), humanity is released from an acute sense of guilt when it follows the lure of the evil one. Instead, harmony and balance between yin and yang are good and preferable, while disharmony and imbalance between the two are not.

As the diagram illustrates, the two halves of the circle are not perfectly divided right down the middle. Instead, they are interlocked and mutually penetrating. Each half also contains the seed of the other. Thus, the entire cosmos is involved in a ceaseless flow of shift and change. Ultimately, like the swinging of the pendulum, what drives this dynamic process is the principle of alternation and reversal: when one extreme is reached, it reverts back to the other. Such is the way the cosmos operates.

Human Body and Soul

As fundamental energies of the cosmos that constantly interact with each other, yin and yang form solid matter when they coalesce and become immaterial when diffused. Their interplay can manifest in concrete and materialistic things, as well as in subtle and spiritual entities. It is in this context that the constitution of human beings can be understood.

All humans have a physical body, the physical manifestation of the interplay between yin and yang. But all humans also have an immaterial aspect, subdivided into *hun* and *po*. *Hun* reflects the yang component, being light, pure, and upward-rising, whereas *Po* indicates yin, being heavy, turgid, and downward-sinking. *Hun* and *po*, introduced into the physical body when the fetus is gestating, together make up the spiritual aspect of the individual. For lack of a better term, they constitute the "soul matter" of the individual. As long as they stay with the human body, with only short and temporary absences during the dream state or when in a coma, the individual remains alive. At death, however, *hun* departs from the body permanently, rising skyward, and *po* settles down on Earth alongside the interred and decomposing body. Both *hun* and *po* eventually dissipate and become reconfigured in different proportions to form future beings.

The Spiritual World of Gods and Ghosts

After death, as long as *hun* and *po* remain intact—though in most cases only for a while, the spirit of the deceased lingers. On very rare occasions, the spirit of one who has accomplished particularly meritorious feats in life and who is well remembered by a grateful community and/or the state may become ***shen***, a benevolent power that protects and brings benefit to the living. By contrast, the spirit of one who suffers great injustice in life and dies a tragic death will become ***gui***, a vengeful and malevolent ghost who haunts and frightens people with ill-will. *Shen* is a generic term for all benevolent deities and gods whose power and efficacy are sought to fulfill people's wishes for health, wealth, progeny, and status. Conversely, *gui* refers to all spiteful ghouls, demons, and ogres who wreak havoc in people's lives. Motivated both by longing and fear, the Chinese from ancient times to the present strive to cultivate good relations with both *shen* and *gui*. This is perhaps the underpinning reason for the Chinese worship and commemoration of ancestors.

Political Implications of Ancient Chinese Religious Beliefs

During the Shang Dynasty, the earliest verifiable historic period in China to date, whose traditional dates are 1600–1046 BCE, the spirits of the ancestors were sometimes asked to carry messages to a higher deity for decision and response. This higher, more authoritative deity was **Shangdi**, the Lord on High, who was the most powerful deity in the Shang spiritual world and who also happened to be the ancient ancestor of the Shang imperial house. This Lord on High was the controlling power in the cosmos, but by no means its creator. Along with the spirits of the ancestors, Shangdi monitored the behavior of the royal descendants, dispensing rewards and meting out punishments as appropriate. It was precisely for this reason that the Shang rulers needed to maintain close contact and good relationship with Shangdi and the other ancestral spirits, for they were their source of kingly power. This power was termed ***de***, commonly translated as "virtue" but more accurately as "potency," the charismatic power the king supposedly possessed. With *de* the Shang king ruled with authority and legitimacy.

But sometime near the end of the second millennium BCE, a former minister of the court staged a rebellion that overthrew the Shang Dynasty and founded the next regime, the Zhou (1122–256 BCE). This power shift was rationalized brilliantly in religious terms. The defeat of the Shang, as the victorious Zhou founders explained it, was in fact sanctioned by Shangdi, who now had a different name and was in fact a different kind of deity. Shangdi was now known as **Tian**, literally, "the sky," but more properly "the force above." (Regrettably, most books and articles written in English on Chinese religion and philosophy translate *Tian* as "Heaven," which is both inaccurate and misleading. In this chapter, we continue to use the term *Tian* rather than any English equivalent in order to avoid any mistaken notion of *Tian* being a paradise-like location.)

Tian was believed to be the source of all things in the universe (not as a creator, but rather as a procreator), as well as the ultimate divine entity that provided order throughout the cosmos. More significantly, *Tian* was also a "will" that would support only the morally deserving individual as king. This made *Tian* radically different from the former Shangdi, who was understood to be partial to the Shang kings and amenable to their "bribery" through offerings. *Tian* was not swayed by asserted blood ties or sacrificial offerings; instead, it insisted on moral uprightness as the only condition for its bestowal of political authority and legitimacy, which was labeled **ming**, or **Tianming**. This was the "mandate" or "charge" given by *Tian* to the person and the imperial line to rule the known world on *Tian*'s behalf. More significantly, this *ming* was understood as only a conditional gift, as it could be revoked and transferred to another person or family any time its provisional holder was found unworthy to exercise it. This withdrawal of the mandate was labeled "*geming*" (the revocation of the "*ming*"). It sanctions and justifies revolution—the toppling of the current regime. Shang's last ruler, who, according to the Zhou founders, was a corrupt and immoral individual, was no longer fit to be ruler, hence his removal from power. To this day, this Chinese term means a violent overthrow of the existing government or a radical rejection of the prevailing norm (as in literary styles, artistic tastes, or scientific rules).

According to the religious mindset of the Zhou, *Tian*'s operation in nature and in the human world is its **Dao**, its "way" or "path." It is the Dao of *Tian* that provides order and regularity in nature and in human society. By following and obeying this Dao, both the natural and the human worlds would operate smoothly and would reach their optimal potential. This implementation of the Dao of *Tian* is the duty and obligation of the human ruler. As the chosen deputy of *Tian* in the human world, the Zhou king (and all subsequent imperial rulers in China) called himself *Tianzi* ("Son of *Tian*"), the person who had been entrusted with the power to rule *Tianxia* ("domain under *Tian*," that is, the entire known world). The king was therefore not just a political leader exercising power over both land and people; he was also a religious figure who served as *Tian*'s deputy to interact with the human and natural worlds. To fulfill his roles as both king and priest, the Zhou ruler had to observe a set of behavioral practices collectively referred to as **li** ("rituals" or "rites"). It was the correct and sincere performance of *li* that would demonstrate the ruler's moral worth, ensure *Tian*'s continuous favor, and guarantee the ruler's power through his *de*, his "potency." *Li* covered every aspect of kingly behavior—from matters of state, to relationships with ancestors, to conduct on important familial occasions such as marriage and funerals, and even to launch military campaigns. It would in time govern all the ritual conduct of the king's ministers as well, as their proper behavior would also contribute to the stability and longevity of the regime.

Other Ancient Chinese Texts

Such prescribed rites for the king and his ministers would later be codified into a text known as the *Record of Rites* (*Liji*). However, the people's reaction to kingly power, as well as the record of government conduct, is fully addressed in two other texts: the *Book of Odes* (*Shijing*) and the *Book of History* (*Shujing*). The *Book of Odes* is an anthology of poems and ballads expressing the sentiments of both elites and commoners, whereas the *Book of History* consists primarily of recorded activities and pronouncements of kings and nobles. Added to them is the previously mentioned *Book of Changes* (*Yijing*), which outlines the early Chinese views of cosmology and the supernatural. Collectively, these texts, which existed in some form after the founding of the Zhou regime, provide most of the information on the ancient Chinese religion from which Confucianism and Daoism would evolve. The Confucians, in particular, would revere them as canonical, foundational texts. The four just mentioned, along with the *Spring and Autumn Annals* (*Chunqiu*), purportedly compiled by Confucius himself, would in time be designated as the Confucian **Five Classics**. The Daoists, while fully aware of the authority of these texts, especially the *Book of Changes*, would create their own corpus of scriptural works focusing more on the constitution of the human body, the basic elements of nature and the cosmos, and the interaction between humans and deities, as you shall see in later sections.

8.2 The Teachings of Chinese Religions: Confucianism

In this chapter, the term *Confucianism* is used with reservation. The Chinese refer to this tradition as the "Teachings of the ***Ru***" (scholars and ritualists), whose function in the Zhou Dynasty will be discussed later in this chapter. Even though Confucius has been rightfully credited with giving this tradition prominence and profound religious meaning, he is by no means its founder, nor is he worshiped as a supernatural savior figure like Jesus Christ in Christianity or the Buddha in Mahayana Buddhism. Therefore, *Confucianism* is quite a problematic term. In fact, the name *Confucius* is likewise used here with some misgivings, as it is actually a Latinized way of representing the Chinese reference to "Kong Fu Zi," the honorific way of addressing "Master Kong." Master Kong's full name is Kong Qiu (Kong being the family name), whose dates are conventionally given as 551–479 BCE. He is only one of two Chinese religious and philosophical figures with a non-Chinese sounding name in Western writings. When the Jesuit missionaries arrived in China in the sixteenth century, they showed their admiration for him and a latter-day follower of his by making them the equivalent of Greek and Roman philosophers. You will get a closer look at his life and times later in this chapter; here, we first examine his teachings.

The *Analects* of Confucius

Confucius inherited the entire corpus of ancient Chinese religious views discussed in the preceding pages. This is made clear in the single most important work that contains his main teachings, the *Lunyu*. Literally meaning "comments and sayings" but customarily translated as the *Analects*, this text is believed to have been compiled by Confucius's leading disciples after his death. It serves as a record of statements he had made, exchanges with students he had conducted, and even remarks some of the students had offered. As such, it is an authoritative source for Confucius's teachings. Despite the possibility of later interpolations and the apparent lack of organization, the extant twenty "Books" of the *Analects*, taken as a whole, reflect a coherent picture of Confucius's major beliefs and aspirations. A careful analysis of the content of the *Analects* shows that, while accepting many of the preexisting cosmological concepts and religious beliefs of ancient China, Confucius and his immediate followers offered many new insights and creative interpretations regarding them. In the end, these "comments and sayings" contributed to the formation of a distinct tradition with unique views on humanity and its relation to the ultimate reality. The following are some of the most notable topics addressed in the *Analects*.

The Primacy of *Tian* Confucius lived during the last centuries of the Zhou dynasty, a period of manifest decline. The likely impending revocation of *Tianming* from the Zhou ruler was on the minds of the elite members of society. What Confucius takes up in the *Analects* is a fresh and innovative understanding of *Tian*, *Tianming*, and their relationship to the moral elites of the time.

The *Tian* of early Zhou, as we have seen, was an august and aloof divine power whose interaction with human beings was largely confined to the ruler, who alone could be in direct contact with it. By contrast, the *Tian* of Confucius was a far more intimate religious and ethical entity. It had a conscious will that no longer reached out to the corrupt Zhou rulers (as it had done in the past), but now to moral and noble men of diverse backgrounds so that they might revive a moral order that was in obvious decline. Confucius saw himself, and encouraged his followers to become, the vanguard of this moral "crusade."

Tian's communication with the moral elite is not verbal or revelatory. Unlike the biblical God or the Qur'anic Allah, *Tian* silently manifests itself in the course of the seasons and in the records of human events to allow perceptive individuals to take notice of its command. Once the individual moral person firmly understands that imperative, he becomes the new recipient of the *ming* of *Tian*. He is now an obedient messenger through whom *Tian*'s moral injunctions will be delivered and implemented, resulting, hopefully, in the improvement of society. Various passages in the *Analects* attest to this faith in the primacy of *Tian* in Confucius's life and teachings. The following are particularly illustrative.

> A border official from the town of Yi requested an audience with the Master. . . . After emerging from the audience, he remarked [to the Master's disciples], "The world has long been without the ideal Way. *Tian* intends to use your Master like a wooden clapper for a bell [to awaken the world]."
>
> —*Analects 3:24*

> When Huan Tui, the Minister of War of the feudal state of Song, tried to kill Confucius (who was visiting), Confucius exclaimed, "It is *Tian* who has endowed me with virtue. What harm can Huan Tui do to me?"
>
> —*Analects 7:23*

> When under siege in the feudal state of Kuang, the Master declared, "With King Wen (founder of Zhou Dynasty) dead, does not civilization rest now on me? If *Tian* intends to have civilization destroyed, those who come after me will have nothing. But if *Tian* does not intend to have civilization destroyed, then what can the men of Kuang do to me?"
>
> —*Analects 9:5*

> The Master lamented, "Alas, there is no one who understands me." Zigong (one of his disciples) said, "How is it that no one understands you?" The Master continued, "I do not complain against *Tian*, nor do I blame my fellow men. I study what is mundane to reach what is transcendent. If there is anyone who understands me, it is *Tian*!"
>
> —*Analects 14:35*

What these passages show collectively is the centrality of *Tian* in Confucius's thinking. *Tian* is clearly the highest religious authority, as well as ultimate reality, in the *Analects*. The *Analects* suggests a conscious *Tian* who has a blueprint for a perfect human and natural order, and who reaches out to a few noble individuals to implement it. This is *Tian*'s mandate or imperative (*ming*). For Confucius, *Tianming* is no longer a bestowal of dynastic power to the political rulers, but instead a call to moral action by the spiritual elite.

Some scholars of Confucian studies have noted a "prophetic voice" in Confucius and his followers. To be sure, unlike Moses or Muhammad, Confucius did not see himself as the messenger of a personal God. Nevertheless, he railed against the moral failings of the political leaders of his time and condemned their departure from *Tian*'s ethical injunctions. He presented himself as someone who, at *Tian*'s command (*Tianming*), had been called to sound the warnings. In effect, Confucius changed the very nature of *Tianming*. It became the self-ascribed duty of the moral individual to serve as mouthpiece to a *Tian* that did not speak itself, to be inspired and motivated by the sense of mission, indeed of commission, by *Tian*. The men of virtue, the *Analects* insists, must be "strong and resolute, for their burden of responsibility is heavy and the journey is long. Taking upon themselves the burden of humaneness, is that not heavy? Stopping only at death, is that not long?" (*Analects* 8:7). *Tian* in the *Analects* spurned the power holders of a decadent age, but instead entrusted the awesome responsibility of protecting the ideals of the human order to a commoner like Confucius—in a way similar to the prophets in the monotheistic traditions covered in other chapters in this volume.

The Content of *Tian*'s Imperative—The Dao

Just what is this message that *Tian* seeks to convey through the spiritual elite? It is the Dao, the Way. Confucius often complains in the *Analects* that the "Dao is no longer in practice" (*Analects* 5:7) or that the "Dao no longer prevails in the world" (*Analects* 16:2). Notice that this Dao is not the former "natural order" in the Zhou understanding of the term. What Confucius means by the Dao is the entire normative social-political-ethical order with the prescriptions for proper ritual behavior publicly, as well as moral rectitude privately. However, when men in power are incapable or unwilling to uphold this order, as Confucius sees it, men of virtue and uprightness must take it upon themselves to fulfill this obligation, or civilization will be doomed. It is for this reason that Confucius regards the search for and implementation of the Dao to be the ultimate, paramount task in his life. He proclaims: "If I can hear the Dao in the morning, I will die contented that evening!" (*Analects* 4:8).

As Dao represents the entire normative human order, Confucius focuses on certain key aspects for detailed discussion: *ren* and *li*.

Ren

Perhaps the single most important concept articulated by Confucius is **ren** (benevolence, humaneness, virtue)—the kernel of humanity that exists intrinsically in all human beings, and in them alone. Mentioned more than 100 times in the *Analects* (far more than any other term), it is described as the germ of moral consciousness present in all human beings that equips them to be ethical individually and empowers them to create a perfect human order collectively. Etymologically, it points to the interrelatedness among humans, for in writing it is a combination of the character for person (人) and the character for the number two (二), signaling that it is in a "state of person-to-person" that *ren* (仁) can be enacted. Throughout the *Analects*, the centrality of *ren* in Confucius's teachings is evident. Many of his leading disciples ask him about it, and he gives various answers to drive home the idea that *ren* is all-rounded and multifaceted. Indeed, *ren* is so fundamental a concept that Confucius allows the giving up of one's life in order to preserve it (*Analects* 15:9), implying that a life without acting on *ren* is meaningless.

All people are born with *ren*, but only those who can preserve and develop their *ren* can be entrusted to carry out the imperative of *Tian*. "When the root is firmly established, the Dao will grow. Filial piety and deference among siblings, are they not the basis of *ren?*" (*Analects* 1:2). It is the cultivation and nurturing of this root of moral propensity by the individual within the familial setting that starts the process for the actualization of the Dao. Note that Confucius here is not asserting the perfection of all human beings. Rather, he is advocating their perfectibility through self-effort. This inner moral disposition needs to be expanded and developed before it can result in the full implementation of the Dao. What is remarkable about this view is the belief that this moral potentiality is not a monopoly of either the political elite or those of high social status, but is in fact possessed by all humans, irrespective of wealth, education, or age.

Furthermore, this goodness is exemplified by filial piety (**xiao**) and deference among siblings, as well as by a sense of dutifulness (*zhong*) and reciprocity (*shu*). Filial piety stresses one's indebtedness to the family elders and to the parents, and deference among siblings acknowledges their mutual obligations to one another. Thus, it is within the family that humans first undergo their moral cultivation. Outside the family, one should exert one's utmost effort in interacting with others in society. This effort arises from one's sense of dutifulness and "not doing unto others what one does not want done unto oneself" (*Analects* 15:24), which is the height of reciprocity. *Ren* is thus this intrinsic human moral capacity, which, when developed and enacted, will produce harmony in the human world and in the relationship that humans maintain with *Tian*.

Li   *Ren* alone, however, is not enough to enable one to enact and revive the Dao. This inner potentiality for goodness and benevolence has to be manifested by an external performance of prescribed behavior within the family, the community, the entire human society, and the spiritual world beyond. This is referred to as *li* (rites, rituals, normative behavior) in the *Analects*, a word that in ancient China meant only the sacrificial and behavioral rituals of the kings and the nobles. The ideograph for *li* shows a sacred ritual vessel, indicating that the etymological origin of the word has something to do with sacrifice to the spirits or the ancestors (禮). In Confucius's understanding of the term, *li* encompasses the entirety of proper human conduct vis-à-vis other human beings, dead ancestors, and the spirits. *Li* cultivates a learned pattern of behavior that, when combined with the moral propensity present in each individual, will produce a magical transformation in inter-human relationships, as well as in relations with the spirits. Once a ritual gesture is initiated in the proper ceremonial context and performed with grace and sincerity, goodwill, trust, and harmony will follow. This is the irresistible and invisible power of ritual itself.

The *Analects* is most optimistic about the efficacy of *li*. In a famous response to his favorite student's question about *ren*, Confucius states: "Restraining oneself and returning to *li*, this is *ren*" (*Analects* 12:1). Only through ritualized interaction with others and with the spirits can one realize one's full potential as a human being. The mastery and performance of *li*, then, is in fact a "process of humanization."[2]

Li is the external enactment of *ren*. Conversely, *ren* is the inner source of *li*. This is why Confucius asks rhetorically: "A man who is not *ren*, what has he to do with *li?*" (*Analects* 3:3).

Junzi   Confucius uses the term **junzi** (the noble man, the man of virtue, and the superior man) for the noble *ru* on whose shoulders rests the burden of reviving the Dao. This is Confucius at his most creative and radical in the usage of traditional terminology. Originally used to refer to the scions of feudal rulers, *junzi* in Confucius's refashioning comes to mean men of moral rectitude. From someone highborn, *junzi* becomes for Confucius someone high-minded. From those of noble birth, *junzi* now means those of noble worth. They are the prophet-like individuals who, though holding no political office or having no privileged positions, nevertheless receive *Tian*'s call. They undertake the most arduous task of implementing *Tian*'s Dao in the human world. The *Analects* puts the issue most plainly: "Without knowing the imperative of *Tian* (*Tianming*), one cannot be a *junzi*" (20:3).

The self-cultivation of the *junzi* will earn them a power (*de*) similar to that possessed by the ancient sage rulers. It is a charismatic, noncoercive, potent influence that both inspires and persuades, and coaxes and shames, people into doing what is right. In the *Analects*, Confucius confidently declares: "The *de* of the *junzi* is like wind, while that of the common people is like grass. When the wind blows over the grass, the grass cannot help but bend in the direction of the wind" (*Analects* 12:19). The epitome of the *junzi* is the sage (**shengren** or simply **sheng** 聖), the rarest of human beings who are perfect in their moral standing and kingly in their worldly accomplishments. The traditional Chinese character for sage contains three components: ear, mouth, and ruler (耳, 口, 王). The sage is someone who hears or listens to the Way of *Tian*, conveys it to others through the mouth, and acts in the capacity of the ancient ruler whose job it is to link up the three realms of Heaven, Earth, and Humankind. Thus the sage is decidedly a religious figure, a saintly person who is at once a messenger of *Tian* to the human world and an exemplar of human perfection in the eyes of *Tian*.

The Religious Vision of the *Analects*

Taken as a whole, the vision of the *Analects* offers an amazingly clear picture of Confucius's religious concern, in the sense that it is ultimately a discourse on the "transcendent," as Bruce Lincoln has designated as one domain of religion (see Chapter 1 in this volume). It has been accurately pointed out that, unlike some other religious figures, Confucius envisaged no escape from the world and society, nor did he insist on ascetic self-denial as a precondition for spiritual progress. Moreover, Confucius did not consider concern with the afterlife or with the spirits to be of primary importance. The following exchange between him and his student Zilu on that subject is famous: "Zilu asked about serving ghosts and spirits. The Master said, 'When we are not yet able to serve fellow humans, why worry about serving the ghosts and spirits?' 'What about death?' [Zilu persisted]. 'When we do not yet know enough about life, why worry about death?' [the Master replied]" (*Analects* 11:12).

In summary, then, you have been shown that Confucius has an abiding faith in the transcendent ultimate *Tian*. He feels an intimate relationship with it. He has a keen awareness of its command (*ming*) given to the moral and spiritual elites (*junzi*) to create the ideal human order (Dao). He firmly believes in the *Tian*-endowed human capacity for perfection and genuine humanity (*ren*) through self-cultivation, and enthusiastically participates in sacrificial rituals and familial and social rites (*li*). These are all components of his religious outlook. To be sure, this religiosity does not express itself in faith in a personal God and the need for salvation through divine grace. Rather, it distinguishes itself as a form of "this-worldly transcendentalism." It treats the "secular as sacred,"[3] and it imparts deeply religious meaning to participation in the mundane. Thus, it expresses a different mode of religiousness. For this reason, it has been paradoxically labeled a "humanistic religion" as well as a "religious humanism."[4] To be truly human is to be ultimately divine.

Admittedly, this religiousness of the Confucian *Analects* has been largely overshadowed by its familial, social, and political messages throughout the course of Chinese imperial history, so much so that Confucianism as a religion is not readily recognized. However, the discussion that follows should further confirm the intrinsic religiosity of the Confucian tradition as it unfolded.

The *Mencius*

The second most important figure in the Confucian tradition is Mencius (a Latinized rendition of "Master Meng," whose full name was Meng Ke, 371–289 BCE?), who was born a full century after Confucius's death. Along with Confucius, he is the only other Chinese religious and philosophical figure who has a non-Chinese sounding name in Western writings. Claiming to be the rightful intellectual successor to Confucius, Mencius reaffirmed moral cultivation as a religious calling. Mencius also made one lasting contribution to the Confucian belief system with his insistence on the basic goodness of human beings, thus upholding Confucianism's optimistic view of human perfectibility, but not human perfection.

Next to the *Analects*, the *Mencius* (an eponymous work compiled by some of Mencius's leading disciples) is significant as a Confucian foundational text. Unlike Confucius, who does not regard himself as a sage—a title he reserves only for the few legendary sage rulers in ancient China—Mencius not only boldly declares his predecessor's sagehood but also asserts his own. Indeed, he considers every human being a potential sage, as he believes that each possesses all the innate qualities to become one. It is on the basis of that assumption that he proclaims the intrinsic goodness of human nature, which he compares to the natural tendency of water to flow downward (*Mencius* 6A, 2:2). This is Mencius's fundamental article of faith.

Identifying four "sprouts of morality" in all humans—the inborn sentiments of commiseration (inability to watch the suffering of others), shame, deference and yielding, and the sense of right and wrong—Mencius proclaims them to be the roots of benevolence (*ren*), righteousness (*yi*), propriety (*li*), and wisdom (*zhi*), respectively. With this belief as his religious premise, he constructs a logical progression from moral cultivation to the ultimate attainment of divine spirituality. He states,

> That which is sought after is called "good." To have it in oneself is called "true." To possess it fully is called "beautiful," while making it shine forth with brilliance is called "great." To be great and be able to transform others is called "sage." To be sage and be beyond understanding by others is called "spiritually divine." (*Mencius* 7B, 25)

Through our moral progress, Mencius suggests, we can become not only good, true, beautiful and great, but also sagely and ultimately divine. With utter conviction, then, he maintains, "Probing one's heart/mind to the utmost, one will know one's nature. Knowing one's nature, one will know *Tian*. To preserve one's heart/mind and nurture one's nature is to put one in the service of *Tian*" (*Mencius* 7A, 1:1). Once one has embodied the moral imperatives of *Tian*, Mencius reasons, one will find all other concerns secondary. In one of his most celebrated statements, Mencius declares: "I like fish, and I also like bear's paw [as gourmet food]. If I cannot have both, I will give up fish and keep the bear's paw. Life is what I desire, but so is righteousness. If I cannot have both, I will give up life but cling to righteousness" (*Mencius* 6A, 10:1). With morality as his ultimate concern, Mencius is willing to sacrifice his own life in order to preserve it. This is certainly reminiscent of Confucius's commitment to benevolence (*ren*), for the preservation of which he, too, is willing to suffer death. It is clear here that Mencius puts righteousness (*yi*) on an equal footing with benevolence (*ren*)—his major contribution to the Confucian discourse. It exhibits a spirit of the martyr and a deeply held religious commitment.

The *Great Learning* and the *Doctrine of the Mean*

The remaining two texts of the **Four Books**, completing the Confucian scriptural corpus designated by the Neo-Confucian scholar Zhu Xi in the twelfth century (discussed later in this chapter), are the *Great Learning* and the *Doctrine of the Mean*, purportedly compiled by two of Confucius's prominent students. Both are chapters from the *Book of Rites* that have been excerpted as independent texts because of their canonical significance. The *Great Learning* refers to learning about what is of primary importance. It prescribes a practical step-by-step roadmap for self-cultivation. Listing eight steps in the process of learning—investigating things, extending knowledge, making sincere the will, rectifying the mind, cultivating the self, unifying the family, administering the state, and keeping peace of all under *Tian*, the *Great Learning* outlines a sequence of individual and social effort made to manifest "illustrious virtue," "love the people," and reach the "ultimate good," which is nothing short of the *Tian*-ordained perfect world order. Thus, learning involves far more than the acquisition of knowledge, but is actually an ethical-religious program of personal and societal improvement toward perfection.

The *Doctrine of the Mean* begins with a bold declaration: "What *Tian* has ordained is called human nature. Following this nature is called the Dao. Cultivating the Dao is called teaching" (*Doctrine of the Mean* 1:1). These three statements articulate the fundamental Confucian articles of faith, representing what Confucianism regards as self-evidently true. The text asserts that humans are born with a benign nature imparted by *Tian*, the ultimate religious authority. This nature provides them with the inner strength to reach their fullest potential as perfect beings. Furthermore, when extended beyond the individual, this human nature can bring about an ideal social-political-ethical order, the actualization of which is the purpose of education. The text further maintains that the real possibility for achieving perfect goodness exists because of the special relationship between human beings and *Tian*. There is a logical progression from self-generating moral effort to the perfection of the practitioners and the world around them: "The *junzi* [noble person] cannot avoid cultivating his person. Thinking of cultivating his person, he cannot neglect serving his parents. Thinking of serving his parents, he may not avoid knowing other humans. Thinking of knowing other humans, he cannot ignore knowledge of *Tian*" (*Doctrine of the Mean* 20:7). It is clear that to actualize their genuine humanity and divine potential, human beings must fully engage with others.

There are five cardinal human relations for such interaction: three within the family and two outside of the family: that between father and son, husband and wife, elder and younger brothers, ruler and subject, and friends. All these relations obligate individuals to perform their respective roles in society. In other words, the father has to be kind, while the son is respectful; the husband has to be caring, while the wife is submissive; brothers need to be mutually deferential; the ruler needs to have the people's welfare in mind, while the subjects need to be obedient; and friends must maintain fidelity toward one another. It is therefore the entire human community that provides the setting for the Confucian religious quest. The *Doctrine of the Mean* offers a climactic conclusion to the process of self-cultivation:

> Only the most authentic and genuine person can fully develop his nature. Able to fully develop his nature, he can then thoroughly understand the nature of other people. Able to fully understand the nature of other people, he can develop the nature of things. Able to fully develop the nature of things, he can assist in the transforming and nourishing process of *Tian* and *Di* (earth, counterpart to *Tian*). When he assists in the transforming and nourishing process of *Tian* and *Di*, he forms a trinity with them!
>
> *—Doctrine of the Mean 22:1*

This euphoric assurance of the final outcome of human moral cultivation is breathtaking in its grandeur. Not only does the person who realizes his own nature to the full become a paradigm of genuine humanity, he actually becomes a "coequal" with *Tian* and *Di* through his participation in their nurture and sustenance of the myriad things. Forming a trinity with the ultimate divine entity in the cosmos is the highest accomplishment for any religious seeker in the Confucian tradition.

In the preceding paragraphs, we have analyzed the content and religiosity of the Four Books. These four texts neatly annotate the later Neo-Confucian goal of **neisheng waiwang**—inner moral cultivation and external skillful management of society and state, as we will consider later. This is believed to reflect Confucius's original vision, namely, to pursue a personal relationship with the ultimate reality through moral cultivation, culminating in an ordering of society and state in accordance with the Way ordained by *Tian*. This religious mission is best expressed by the famous Neo-Confucian scholar Zhang Zai (1020–1077) who declares his lifelong goals:

> To establish the mind of *Tian* and *Di* (Earth),
> To inculcate an understanding of [*Tian*'s] command
>   (*ming*) for the multitudes,
> To revive and perpetuate the teachings of the sages
>   of the past, [and]
> To provide peace and stability for all future generations.

This is a succinct summary of a four-point program for spiritual self-actualization and social-political improvement—an inner search for dialog with the divine, an outer effort to benefit society, a backward revisit with the wisdom of past sages, and a forward look to bring about peace and prosperity for future generations. It is an eloquent declaration of both the secular and the sacred aspirations of the Confucian teachings.

8.3 The Teachings of Chinese Religions: Daoism

As asserted earlier, Daoism evolved out of the same ancient Chinese religious mindset as Confucianism did. But instead of regarding *Tian* as the Absolute Ultimate, as the Confucians do, Daoists from the beginning hold Dao to be supreme. It should be recalled that the Dao is also central to the Confucian tradition. However, the Daoists articulate a very different understanding of the Dao. It is this alternative apprehension of the Dao that serves as the point of departure for their entirely different mode of religious experience from that of the Confucians.

Laozi riding on the back of a water buffalo as he retires into the realm of the immortals.

Laozi and Zhuangzi

For much of Chinese history, the best known and earliest identifiable Daoists were Laozi (Master Lao, traditionally spelled Lao-tzu) and Zhuangzi (Master Zhuang, traditionally spelled Chuang-tzu). Laozi, believed to be a mystical teacher of lost rituals from whom Confucius had sought instruction, was in fact more of a composite figure than an actual person and was the reputed author of the **Daodejing** (traditionally spelled *Tao-te Ching*; The Scripture of the Way and Its Potent Manifestation), alternatively known as the *Laozi*. Zhuangzi was an obscure individual reportedly active in the late fourth century BCE who was credited with authorship of the second most influential Daoist text, the *Zhuangzi*. Both texts are more representative of certain modes of thinking than of individual thinkers, as they are in effect anthologies containing different strands of thought rather than coherent and logical teachings of single authors. One point, however, is clear: they are self-consciously anti-Confucian in that they express a decidedly alternative understanding of the Dao and of ideal human action. In addition, both the *Daodejing* and the *Zhuangzi* contain descriptions of perfected human beings who possess amazing powers of magic and immortality, a subject that Confucian texts never touch upon. Both texts suggest that, through intense inner psychic journeying and mystical conditioning of the human body, individuals can acquire impressive powers of transformation and invulnerability to the decaying agents in nature.

The *Daodejing*

The eighty-one-chapter *Daodejing*, categorized into two sections labeled respectively as "Dao" and "De," is the most translated and most popular Chinese book in the West. Virtually all the different schools and sectarian lineages within the Daoist movement regard this work as foundational in importance.

In contrast to the Confucian Dao, which, as you may recall, is the ideal ethical-social-political order ordained by *Tian* for human beings, the Dao of the *Daodejing* antedates *Tian* and acts as the root of the natural order. Here Dao is the primordial entity that exists in an undifferentiated state prior to the appearance of the myriad things, including *Tian* and *Di*, which now stand for nothing more than nature itself. The lofty primacy of the Confucian *Tian* is supplanted by the nebulous Dao of the *Daodejing*, as indicated by the following celebrated passage:

> There was something undifferentiated and yet complete, which existed before
> *Tian* and *Di*
> Soundless and formless, it depends on nothing and does not change
> It operates everywhere and does not stop
> It may be regarded as the "Mother of the world"
> I do not know its name; I call it Dao.

—Daodejing, Chap. 25

In one broad stroke, the entire Confucian cosmological scheme is turned upside down here. It is Dao, not *Tian*, that gives birth, like a mother, to the myriad things. It is Dao, not *Tian*, that serves as the primal source of the cosmos. Echoing the cosmogonic (concerning the origin of the cosmos) view of the *Book of Changes*, the *Daodejing* gives an even terser summary of the generating process of the cosmos:

> The Dao gives birth to the One [Being, Existence]
> The One brings forth the Two [Yin and Yang]
> The Two give rise to the Three [*Tian, Di*, and Humans]
> The Three engender the Ten Thousand Things [world of multiplicity and diversity]
>
> —*Daodejing, Chap. 42*

Again, the primacy of the Dao as the procreator of the entire universe and everything in it is unequivocally asserted here. As the ground of all beings, this Dao is compared to a "mysterious female," "water," "infant," and "uncarved block." However, unlike the Confucian Dao, which requires superior human beings (the *junzi* [men of virtue] and the *shengren* [sages]) to actualize its ideal design, the Dao of the *Daodejing* can only maintain its pristine form when humans are not involved and are wise enough to leave it alone. Thus, the ideal course of action for insightful and wise human beings is to observe **wuwei** (actions without intention) and ***ziran*** (natural spontaneity) to allow the Dao to maintain a spontaneous order and optimal state. These two ideal approaches to life are indicative of the *Daodejing*'s belief in the innate perfection and completeness of the Dao. Wuwei calls for a minimalist and noninterventionist attitude in human action, whereas *ziran* rejects any artificiality and contrived undertaking as detrimental to the well-being of humans and nature. Ultimately, the Dao in the *Daodejing* is indescribable and ineffable, for it defies verbalization and precise definition. "The Dao that can be [verbally] expressed is not the constant Dao," insists the *Daodejing* in its first verse.

Yet the transcendent Dao is, at the same time, manifested in the myriad things through its presence in them as *de*—the very "potent manifestation" of each thing. In contrast to the *de* of the Confucians, which is the charismatic power of the moral elite—and morality itself, the *de* of the *Daodejing* points to the concrete expression of the Dao in all things. *De* is the "thingness" of a thing—that which makes a thing what it is. The combination of Dao and *de*, then, helps to bridge the gap between the transcendent and the immanent in the *Daodejing*. The Dao is the transcendent ground of being; yet through its expression in the *de* of the myriad concrete things, it is also fully immanent.

The *Zhuangzi*

The extant version of the *Zhuangzi* consists of thirty-three chapters divided into three sections—"Inner," "Outer," and "Miscellaneous." The first seven, or Inner, chapters are generally believed to be the authentic writings of Zhuang Zhou, the putative author. Yet as in the case of the *Daodejing*, we have only a vague biographical account of the purported author of this text, and little of substance is known about him.

The *Zhuangzi* is overall a different kind of text from the *Daodejing*. Whereas the *Daodejing* is terse and aphoristic in language, the *Zhuangzi* is effusive and vividly narrative. The *Daodejing* idealizes the feminine and regards the Dao as mother, but the *Zhuangzi* refuses to show any preference for the female. The *Daodejing* gives much emphasis to politics and the techniques of rulership; the *Zhuangzi* is deliberately dismissive of all political involvement. The *Zhuangzi* tells stories with a witty, playful, irreverent tone that is totally absent in the *Daodejing*. In terms of basic worldview and cosmological assumptions, however, the *Zhuangzi* shares much in common with the *Daodejing*, hence their grouping together by later historians and bibliographers as representatives of the "School of the Dao."

In the *Zhuangzi*, the Dao is not only the ineffable transcendent entity that gives rise to all things but also the immanent core that exists in all things, from the loftiest perfected beings to the lowliest broken pieces of tile and even excrement. It is therefore omnipresent, making all things ultimately equal. As such, the Dao transcends all polarities, dichotomies, and dualities that the human mind is inclined to create. Hence the use of the human cognitive and rational approach to apprehend the Dao is futile and even harmful, as it can only be realized intuitively through the abandonment of the intellect. The mind must be able to be free from all conventional distinctions and established views, hence the advocacy of "carefree wandering" in the *Zhuangzi*. In this connection, the discussion of "fasting the mind/heart" (**xinzhai**) and "sitting and forgetting" (**zuowang**) becomes pertinent, as both practices dispense with rationality and deliberative cognition in order to arrive at the perfect intuitive understanding of the Dao.

Physical Invulnerability in the *Daodejing* and the *Zhuangzi*

Although both the *Daodejing* and the *Zhuangzi* are best known (in China and in the West) for their sophisticated philosophical discussions of the Dao, much less known—but more relevant to the religious nature of these two texts—is their commentary on the physical prowess of the Daoist adepts. They hint at bodily invulnerability, longevity, and even immortality—the very promises of a Daoist religious movement that began no later than the second century CE.

We next explore the impact the two texts have had on Daoism as a religion. The following passages from both are highly suggestive:

> He who does not lose his proper place lasts long
> He who dies but does not perish has longevity.

> —*Daodejing, Chap. 33*

I have heard that people who are good at preserving their lives will not encounter wild bulls or tigers when traveling on land, and will not need to protect themselves with armor when in the army. Wild bulls will find nowhere to thrust their horns, tigers will have no place to sink their claws, and weapons will find no point to insert their cutting blades. And why is that? Because in them there is no room for death.

—*Daodejing, Chap. 50*

He who is richly endowed with *de* is comparable to a newborn baby: poisonous insects will not sting him, ferocious beasts will not seize him in their claws, and birds of prey will not snatch him with their talons.

—*Daodejing, Chap. 55*

Far away on Mt. Guye there dwells a divine person whose skin is like ice and snow, and who is gentle and shy like a young girl. He does not eat the five grains; but [only] inhales the wind and drinks the dew. He ascends the clouds, mounts flying dragons, and wanders beyond the four seas. His spirit is focused, thus he saves creatures from sickness and plagues, and guarantees bountiful harvests.

—*Zhuangzi, Chap. 1*

The ultimate person is spirit-like. Though the great marshes are set ablaze, they will not make him hot. Though the rivers and streams freeze up, they cannot chill him. Though violent thunder splits the mountains and howling gales churn the ocean, they will not frighten him. A man like this rides the clouds and mist, mounts the sun and moon, and goes beyond the four seas. Death and life have no effect on him, how much less will profit and loss?

—*Zhuangzi, Chap. 2*

The perfected individuals of old . . . could go up to high places without getting frightened, enter water without getting wet, and go into fire without feeling hot. Only those whose knowledge ascends the height of the Dao can be like this. . . .. The perfected breathe with their heels, while the ordinary men breathe with their throat.

—*Zhuangzi, Chap. 6*

Blowing and breathing, exhaling the old and inhaling the new, [imitating the postures of] bear strides and bird stretches—these are all undertaken for the purpose of longevity. They are pursued with fondness by people who practice gymnastic calisthenics and body nourishments in hope of [matching] Patriarch Peng's longevity.

—*Zhuangzi, Chap. 15*

It is clear these two texts suggest that potent (that is, healthy and long-living) individuals embody the Dao (the holy), and that physical longevity and holiness are closely linked. As described by the *Daodejing* and *Zhuangzi*, the early practitioners of the Dao were people who, through the use of various bodily techniques, acquired powers that enabled them to defy death and to embody the divine. These techniques and powers would very much become the concern of later Daoists.

Other Foundational Daoist Teachings

In addition to those set forth in the *Daodejing* and the *Zhuangzi*, there are other concepts that contributed to the formulation of the Daoist tradition. The most significant of these are immortality, the related concept of alchemy, and Daoist deities.

Immortality and Alchemy
Long before the appearance of the *Daodejing* and the *Zhuangzi* texts, there had been shamans who practiced austerities and world-denying habits that they claimed would earn them magical prowess, physical potency, and longevity. They are equally foundational—like the legendary Laozi and the more historical Zhuangzi—in the sense that they constitute another major feature of the Daoist movement. One Daoist preoccupation is with the notion of **xian** (immortals or "transcendents"), long a folk religious fascination dating back to at least the fourth century BCE. People with the right recipe, formula, or prescription (**fangshi**) would teach these esoteric techniques and provide ready-made elixirs to those who had the financial resources and the necessary devotion to secure their services. But the full and eloquent articulation of *xian* is found in the *Baopuzi* (*Master Who Embraces Simplicity*), a text authored by the Daoist advocate Ge Hong (283–343 CE). Central to this concept is the conviction that bodily transformation, good health, longevity, and ultimately immortality can be acquired through proper diet, physical exercise, and drugs.

Inherent in the belief in immortality are the ancient Chinese assumptions about the human body and the measures that can be taken to keep it healthy and even immortal. As you may remember from our earlier discussion, the ancient Chinese believed that the human body is the microcosm that reflects the macrocosm of the cosmos. In other words, there is a direct correspondence and parallel between the human body and nature. All the myriad things in the universe are produced by the interaction of the vital energies (qi) of yin and yang. This belief was retained and developed prominently by Daoism and Chinese folk religion. According to this view, there are three central nodal points in the human body called **dantian** (locations for the concoction of *dan*—pill of immortality)—in the head, the chest, and

A Daoist immortal flying through the clouds, 1750. Portrayed is the sage mother of Dongling, who studied the Way and could cure illnesses. One day, amid a throng wishing to thank her, she ascended to the clouds.

the abdomen—connected by meridian circuits through which the qi flows. And because the body is the cosmos writ small, just as there are gods and deities inhabiting the physical world outside, there are also numerous spiritual beings residing in various organs of the human body.

Based on this whole series of assumptions, the techniques of **yangsheng** (nourishing life) are developed. First mentioned in the *Zhuangzi*, *yangsheng* has the goal of refining the body so that it can overcome its earthly limitations and be in perfect harmony with the Dao, making it last as long as the universe. It involves an entire menu of exercises, including deep meditation, controlled breathing, therapeutic gymnastics, dietary regimens, even sexual techniques. All these measures of nourishing life have been practiced by Daoists since the second century CE and are grouped under the general heading of **neidan** (internal alchemical regimens) that result in immortality.

While these *yangsheng* techniques aim at the regeneration and reinforcement of the human body by making use of what the body intrinsically possesses, some practicing Daoists also focus on the compounding and refining of elixirs with substances (herbal and mineral) from nature. References to "refining gold" and transmuting cinnabar (mercury sulphate) in some later Daoist texts indicate a growing practice of alchemy for the purpose of attaining longevity and immortality. This pursuit of alchemical manufacturing of **dan** with minerals and plants would eventually lead to the **waidan** (external alchemical regimens that result in immortality) tradition in Daoism.

All the internal and external alchemical techniques discussed here are intended to produce a new body that grows within the old so that, in time, the old self will be replaced by the new in the same way that cicadas and snakes regenerate themselves.

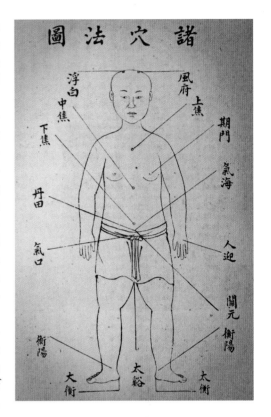

A Daoist view of the vital points in the human body through which the qi flows.

Daoist Deities

As the Daoist tradition matured, the most exalted god in the Daoist pantheon is believed to be the *Yuanshi tianzun* (Celestial Venerable of Primordial Beginning), who is in turn head of a trinity of deities known as the Three Purities. Below them are innumerable divinities of both genders who fill up various ranks in a mindboggling celestial bureaucracy that loosely corresponds to its human counterpart.

The lowliest among the spiritual bureaucrats is the local earth god, while the head of the celestial government is the Jade Emperor. Many of them have divine origins, but many are also former humans whose merits earn them their promotion to godly status. Some of the deities have national appeal, such as Lord Zhenwu (Perfect Martiality) of Mount Wudang, whereas others are more local in influence,

Figurine of Lord Guan as seen in many Chinese restaurants.

including the stove god in each household. One ubiquitous Daoist deity, Lord Guan, is honored by business owners as their protector and benefactor. A human-turned-god, Lord Guan can be seen in the form of a striking figure with a red face and a cascading black beard, sporting a long robe and holding a long blade. An altar or alcove containing a figurine of him can be found in most Chinese restaurants in North America, where he is worshiped as a patron deity.

Daoist deities not only reside in the heavens, on Earth, in the underworld, and in the homes but also inside the human body. They are supposed to protect all the major internal organs from the decaying effect of unwholesome food and old age. The entire pantheon of Daoist deities can be accessed and appealed to through ritual performance for assistance in warding off evil, improving health, guaranteeing harmony in family and community, and attaining immortality.

8.4 The History of Chinese Religions: Confucianism

As you may recall, the earliest time in Chinese history for which we have both written records and archaeological evidence is the Shang Dynasty, whose traditional dates are 1600–1046 BCE. The head of the Shang spiritual world was Shangdi, the ultimate benefactor of the royal house. Eventually, around the end of the second millennium BCE, the Shang Dynasty was toppled by the Zhou. The Zhou founders replaced Shangdi with *Tian* as the overarching spiritual authority. They claimed their victory as a mandate they received from *Tian*, ostensibly because of their moral worthiness. Early Zhou society was idealized as well ordered and harmonious, presided over by men of virtue.

At the time of Confucius's birth, the entire political system and moral framework put in place by the early Zhou kings was in disarray. Powerful feudal lords jockeyed to replace the current Zhou king and to become the next *Tianzi*, the son of *Tian*. The more capable and ambitious among them actively sought the service of talented men outside the hereditary aristocratic circles, thereby creating upward social mobility for some among the commoners. Conversely, powerful lords could become commoners overnight as a result of their defeat by their rivals, creating a downward social spiral as well.

In the midst of such social and intellectual turmoil, experts and specialists known as **shi** (men of service) made their appearance. Drawn from lower aristocratic or commoner backgrounds, they entered the employ of feudal lords and imperial rulers. The *shi* performed two major categories of duties: military and civil. The military men of service were referred to as *wushi*, whereas their civilian counterparts, the scholars and ritualists, were known as *rushi*, or simply *ru*. *Ru* were scribes and record keepers, masters of religious ceremonies, as well as diviners and spiritual professionals. To perform their duties well, *ru* had to acquire mastery of history, poetry, religious rites, divination, dance, and music. Confucius was just such a *ru*.

Confucius—The Man and His Life

Confucius was born into a family of former aristocrats in the feudal domain of Lu (located in present-day Shandong Province in north China). His father died when he was still an infant, so he had to do menial work as a young man to support himself, his sickly older brother, and his widowed mother. He apparently had an extraordinarily inquisitive mind and a voracious appetite for study, especially of the ancient texts of history, rituals, and poetry. By the age of thirty, he gained respect as an expert *ru*. His service in government was limited to a number of minor posts, but his greatest accomplishment was in his vocation as a teacher.

A Chinese oracle bone made of tortoise shell.

After age fifty, as he realized that the feudal lord of his native Lu did not value his service, Confucius left with a number of trusted disciples in tow and headed for other feudal domains. His hope was that other lords would embrace his ideas and would implement his political blueprint for restoring order to the world. For the next thirteen years he travelled all across northern China, but he was met with disappointment everywhere, at times suffering much indignity, deprivation, and even physical danger. In the twilight years of his life, he returned to his home state of Lu with his political ambition unfulfilled. He devoted the remainder of his life to teaching, writing, and editing the ancient texts. Confucius died in his early seventies.

Toward the end of his long life, Confucius gave a telling summary and assessment of his intellectual and spiritual journey over seven decades, as recorded in the *Analects*:

> At fifteen I set my mind on learning
> At thirty I had become established [as a *ru*]
> At forty I was free from doubts
> At fifty I knew the command of *Tian* (*Tianming*)
> At sixty my ears became attuned [to what I heard from *Tian*]
> At seventy I could follow my heart's desires without transgressing what was right

—*Analects* 2:4

This intellectual and spiritual autobiography of Confucius illustrates the trajectory of his development from scholar to spiritual figure. His biography shows that

Statue of Confucius at the entrance to the Confucian Academy in Beijing, China.

he was a fully human figure with no claim to supernatural origin or power, and he was the consummate representative of the *ru* tradition and an exemplary teacher. Eventually, however, Confucius would be honored as a sage and the founder of China's most important philosophical and religious tradition.

Later Major Contributors to the Confucian Tradition

After Confucius's death, the Chinese world took a turn for the worse. Warfare among the feudal states became more frequent and brutal. The centuries between Confucius's death in 479 and 221 BCE are known as the Warring States period in Chinese history. During this time, Confucius's original vision of moral cultivation and benevolent government seemed impractical and quixotic. Internally, the Confucian tradition was rocked by self-doubt and resignation, as his *ru* followers became mere functionaries for the feudal lords, enjoying little influence or self-esteem. Externally, rival traditions such as Daoism and other more pragmatic schools competed for attention and attacked many of the Confucian ideas.

Into this picture came Mencius (371–289 BCE?), the second most important figure in the Confucian tradition. As the self-declared ardent defender of the faith, he articulated views that would be revered as definitive interpretations of Confucius's teachings, as we have discussed them earlier. His ideas would become orthodox for most later Confucians.

A younger contemporary of Mencius was Xun Qing (310–238 BCE?), or Master Xun (Xunzi), who initially and for the following several centuries exerted far greater influence on the Confucian movement than Mencius did. Xun Qing's rationalism and pragmatic approach to rituals and learning had given a decisively secular and worldly bent to the Confucian tradition, resulting in a noticeable eclipse of its religious nature. His view of human nature as evil also contradicted that held by Mencius. Nevertheless, Xun Qing shared with Mencius an abiding faith in the transformative influence of moral cultivation and the perfectibility of humanity through self-effort. Eventually, however, later Confucians rejected Xun Qing as heterodox, and the text bearing his name was never recognized as a Confucian classic.

Confucianism as Orthodoxy

When China was unified by the Qin (traditionally spelled Ch'in) state in 221 BCE, the Confucian tradition became a target of state persecution. Its call for benevolent government and individual moral autonomy was rejected by the First Emperor of

Qin as dangerous and subversive. But the Qin Dynasty soon fell, succeeded by the Han (206 BCE–220 CE), a much more hospitable regime for the Confucians. By the middle of the second century BCE, the Confucian tradition had triumphed over all its competitors by becoming the state-designated orthodoxy, in recognition of its usefulness in fostering effective governance and enhancing social cohesiveness. Yet its orthodox status also necessitated fundamental changes in its orientation. From a teaching that called for high-minded personal moral cultivation and benevolent government, Confucianism in the Han Dynasty became a scholastic tradition, a means to bureaucratic advancement, and a tool for state control and patriarchal authoritarianism. In fulfilling these roles, Confucius was showered with grandiose titles by subsequent generations of Chinese rulers who scrambled to outdo one another in showing their adoration of him, culminating in the breathtakingly exuberant title of "Ultimate Sage of Greatest Accomplishment, King of Manifest Culture" given to him by an emperor in 1308. "Temples" dedicated to Confucius were built throughout the empire. Nevertheless, they served more as memorials, such as those dedicated to Thomas Jefferson or Abraham Lincoln in the United States, than as places of worship, and Confucius himself remained by and large an exemplary human figure worthy of veneration, rather than as a god promising salvation.

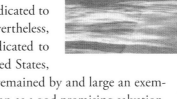

The Apricot Platform (Xingtan) is traditionally identified to be the location where Confucius held discussions with his students.

The Neo-Confucian Tradition

Although Confucianism served nominally as China's orthodoxy from the second century BCE to the beginning of the twentieth century CE, a span of over 2,000 years, it coexisted with Daoism and Buddhism during that entire period and at times was even overshadowed by them. Its refusal to address issues pertaining to the supernatural and its neglect of matters in the afterlife made it less appealing to the people in a tumultuous and uncertain age. The vacuum was conveniently filled by Daoism and Buddhism, with the former promising good health and longevity, and the latter rebirth or heavenly bliss. Since the twelfth century CE, however, through a revitalization movement known in the West as Neo-Confucianism, it regained the initiative over its Daoist and Buddhist rivals through the embracing of their metaphysical and cosmological assumptions, and became the predominant religious tradition in China until modern era. Indeed, as advocated by its most influential representative, the scholar Zhu Xi (1130–1200), the Four Books, composed of the *Analects*, the *Mencius*, the *Great Learning*, and the *Doctrine of the Mean*, would constitute the main curriculum upon which the civil service examination of late imperial China for entry into officialdom would be based. Between 1313 and 1905, all aspiring scholars and government officials in China were examined on their mastery of this set of canonical works. Others within the Neo-Confucian movement would challenge Zhu Xi's interpretations, both during his lifetime and beyond, notably Wang Yangming (1472–1529) three centuries later. These scholars differed primarily in what they viewed as the best way to attain the same Neo-Confucian goal of "inner moral cultivation and external skillful management of society and state" (*neisheng waiwang*). However, personal moral perfection and universal transformation of the human community remained the shared religious quest of all Neo-Confucians.

Confucianism in the Modern Age

Beginning in the fourteenth century, as China entered the late imperial period, the Confucian tradition became fossilized and rigid. The examinations were mere formulaic wordplays instead of genuine expressions of moral insight or sound administrative proposals. The entire Confucian tradition was turned into a useful tool of state control and social patronage. Political autocracy, patriarchal authoritarianism, and social exploitation were all carried out in its name. But it was since the mid-nineteenth century that Confucianism suffered its most precipitous decline. This process began after the Opium War of 1839–1842, in which China was handily defeated by Great Britain. Other foreign powers quickly followed suit to demand enormous concessions from a weakened and disgraced China. For China's patriotic young generation of intellectual elite, this humiliating development exposed what they regarded as fatal shortcomings of their Confucian heritage. Confucianism was blamed for China's political, social, and economic backwardness. As a result, the New Culture movement that began in the second decade of the twentieth century made Confucianism their main target of assault. "Down with Confucius and sons!" was now the popular call for rebellion against the tradition. Indeed, the birth of the Chinese communist movement was in part attributable to this rebellious mode of thinking. From the perspective of the radical revolutionaries, Confucianism was a reactionary ideology of the ruling elite in China's feudal past that should be cast into the dustbin of history.

But the obituary for Confucianism appears to have been written prematurely. Despite repeated and sometimes violent attempts to rid China of the harmful influence of Confucianism, the "anti-Confucius" campaign of the Cultural Revolution period (1966–1976) on mainland China being the most glaring example, the tradition has survived. As the opening vignette demonstrates, Confucianism as a religious tradition is still very much alive in contemporary China. The central importance of the family, the persistence of ancestral remembrance, and the value placed on education and self-improvement are evidence of the resilience of the Confucian ethos among many Chinese and other East Asians. Some argue that the financial and industrial progress of the "Four Dragons" of Taiwan, South Korea, Hong Kong, and Singapore since the 1980s, and an even more spectacular economic development in China as well, might have been brought about by this Confucian heritage.

At the same time, an emergent group of "New Confucians," both inside and outside China, has been active as advocates for the revival of the Confucian teaching in the contemporary world. This group finds a new relevance for the Confucian tradition in postmodern society on the ground that it expresses values of universal significance. These new defenders of the Confucian faith seek to rearticulate Confucianism for our time in the same way Confucians of the past had rearticulated it for theirs. Their reinvigorated advocacy has brought about genuine interest in the universal relevance of Confucian ethics and religiosity among some Western scholars. One notable group is the "Boston Confucians,"[5] who argue that Confucian teachings should be an integral part of the dialogue on contemporary social, political, and moral issues.

Equally notable is the new popularity enjoyed by Confucianism in China in recent decades, largely promoted by the Chinese government. Academies devoted to the study of the Confucian tradition have been established, instruction on and the memorization of the *Analects* for school-age children are widely promoted, and even TV programs dedicated to highlight the relevance of Confucian teachings to contemporary Chinese society are eagerly viewed by a huge audience. And ceremonies commemorating the birthday of Confucius are now led by high-level central and local government officials. When China hosts major international athletic meets, such as the 2008 Beijing Olympics, Confucian themes are featured prominently to showcase Confucianism as the quintessential core of Chinese culture and identity. Confucianism has become a convenient tool for the government to promote patriotic sentiments and cultural pride. Additionally, "Confucius Institutes" have been sponsored and funded by the Chinese government at universities in many Western countries to export China's "soft power" and to enhance China's positive image abroad.

Confucianism as Pan-Asiatic Tradition

Confucian texts had found their way beyond China no later than the turn of the Common Era, along with China's outward expansion both culturally and militarily. But it was in the form of Neo-Confucianism that this religious and philosophical tradition had exerted its most significant impact on China's neighbors. Thanks to the dynamic influence of Zhu Xi and his intellectual successors, Confucianism became the dominant philosophy and state orthodoxy, beginning with the Joseon Dynasty in Korea (fourteenth century), the Tokugawa Shogunate in Japan (seventeenth century), and the Nguyen Dynasty in Vietnam (nineteenth century).

The Xuankong (Hanging) Temple near the City of Datong in China's Shaanxi Province. Built more than 1,400 years ago, it hangs on a mountain cliff hundreds of feet above the ground through the use of crossbeams inserted deep into the vertical rock surface. Honoring Confucius, Laozi, and the Shakyamuni Buddha, the Temple exemplifies the harmonious co-existence of the three prominent religions of China: Confucianism, Daoism, and Buddhism.

Confucian influence to the rest of Southeast Asia was brought about through Chinese emigration there since the eighteenth century. The social organizations, bureaucratic cultures, and religious assumptions of these Asian neighbors of China echoed much of what existed in China during its late imperial period.

8.5 The History of Chinese Religions: Daoism

As you have learned earlier, Laozi and Zhuangzi, traditionally considered founders of Daoism, were shadowy figures whose books bearing their names were in fact anthologies containing divergent strands of thought, including the cultivation of magical powers and attainment of longevity. Alongside them were mysterious shamans who claimed that they had secret formulas for dietary regimens and alchemical concoctions that would bring about impressive health benefits and even immortality. In addition, numerous other early commentators of the Dao, focusing on healing techniques and combatting body-decaying elements, further contributed to the formation of a "Daoist school" or "Daoist tradition" no later than the second century BCE.

The Deification of Laozi

A crucial development that led to the rise of Daoism as an organized religion was the deification of Laozi. Sometime between the second century BCE and the second century CE, Laozi came to be revered as a human incarnation of the Dao. Remarkably, a belief arose that the Dao could now intervene in human affairs by directly and personally imparting teaching to save the world through its human form. As the Dao incarnate, Laozi was the object of worship. In a text entitled *Laozi bianhua jing* (*Scripture of the Transformations of Laozi*), compiled around the middle of the second century CE, the various incarnations of Laozi over time were recounted. One such incarnation was in the form of a messianic figure dedicated to the salvation of the world; the title Laozi assumed in this case was Taishang Laojun, the Venerable Lord of the Most High.

Even more significantly, Laozi as Taishang Laojun could give instructions to selected individuals on the esoteric secrets of the Dao as part of his scheme to save the world. This deified and messianic Laozi thus turned the Daoist teaching into a divine revelation on salvation, which has since become a major tenet of organized Daoism. Once Laozi was venerated as the Dao incarnate, as well as the dispenser of redemptive instructions, Daoism became a salvational faith. A whole pantheon of gods and spirits, both in nature and within the human body, came to be worshiped as physical manifestations of the Dao and as agents of deliverance.

Beginning in the middle of the second century CE, Daoism became an organized and large-scale movement among the common people. In the year 142 CE, a man by the name of Zhang Ling (or Zhang Daoling) allegedly had a fateful encounter with the deified Laozi, who indicated to him that the world was in great trouble

Confucian influence in East Asia.

and that he, Zhang Ling, would be taught the right knowledge and proper practice to save it. Zhang Ling was to adopt the title of **Tianshi** ("Celestial Master"), and the teaching he was to transmit would be called Orthodox Unity.

Zhang Ling supposedly transferred the Tianshi title to his descendants down through the ages until the present day (in Taiwan). The movement would be known variously as "Celestial Master," "Orthodox Unity," or "Five Bushels of Rice," the last derived from the size of contributions members were expected to make to the organization at their initiation. During the second half of the second century CE, the movement acted as a theocratic shadow government, providing material aid and physical healing services to its membership, in addition to offering a vague hope of messianic salvation. A contemporary and parallel movement, alternatively known as "Great Peace" (*Taiping*) and "Yellow Turbans" (*Huangjin*), took the messianic message more seriously and rebelled against the government in an attempt to usher in a new age. This movement was ruthlessly suppressed, even though the dream of *Taiping* would live on among many Daoists.

Later Daoist Historical Development

The Celestial Masters made an arrangement with the government in 215 CE whereby it abandoned its theocratic base in southwestern China and migrated closer to the political center in the north. But soon the Han Dynasty fell, and the subsequent short-lived regimes failed to maintain their power in the face of devastating invasions by nomadic non-Chinese groups such as the Huns, forcing the political and cultural elite to flee south toward the Yangzi River basin. The Celestial Masters followed this southward migration and became popular there as well, setting up its headquarters on the Dragon and Tiger Mountain (Mount Longhu) in Jiangxi Province in southeast China. During the ensuing Period of Disunion, three centuries when China was politically divided between north and south, Daoism entered a most creative period.

First, both the *Daodejing* and the *Zhuangzi* were given new philosophical interpretations that downplayed, if not totally ignored, the discussions on meditative transformations and magical physical transmutations in the two texts. Then someone who was much more closely related to the Celestial Masters, the aforementioned Ge Hong (283–343 CE), author of the *Baopuzi* (*Master Who Embraces Simplicity*), vigorously asserted the possibility of attaining physical perfection in the form of immortality through various alchemical techniques.

But the most significant development in Daoism was in the area of brand-new textual revelations and ritual reforms. Responding both to the competition offered by a rapidly expanding Buddhism and to the need to distinguish itself from the "uncouth" and "coarse" practices of popular religion, Daoist leaders from aristocratic families created new texts and devised new rituals that they claimed were revealed to them through ecstatic encounters with an ever-growing number of Daoist deities.

In the south, the Shangqing (Highest Clarity) and the Lingbao (Numinous Treasure) set of texts and rituals began to emerge almost simultaneously in the fourth century CE. While the Shangqing emphasized individual experiences of spiritual fulfilment through meditation and mental visualization, the Lingbao focused on ritual precision and use of talismans for the purpose of universal salvation, though the two overlapped considerably as well. In the north, similarly intense and creative activities also took place under the claim of new revelations from *Taishang Laojun*, the deified Laozi. A Tuoba (a people outside of the Great Wall) ruler, Emperor Taiwu of the Northern Wei Dynasty, was touted by his Daoist minister as the "Perfect Lord of Great Peace" who would usher in the ideal world. This was a deliberate effort made to reclaim the aspiration of *taiping* proposed by the Yellow Turbans in the second century CE.

Common among the various Daoist groups of this period was the belief in and anticipation of an impending cataclysmic disaster that would radically transform the existing world. There was an anxious, yet exciting, expectation of the imminent arrival of a savior-like figure who would protect the devout followers from harm and ensure them a safe journey to the world to come—a perfect world populated by the faithful alone. This eschatological (vision of the end of time) and apocalyptic (revelation of a secret divine design) feature of the Daoist movement resembles many millennial traditions in other cultures.

Because of the proliferation of revelatory texts and the diverse array of rituals, the Period of Disunion also witnessed the first attempts made to classify and standardize them. The texts on revelations and rituals were organized into "three caverns" (a conscious imitation of the *Tripitaka* canon of Buddhism) and "four supplements." This form of classification would constitute the framework of the ultimate Daoist canon, known as the **Daozang** (Treasury of the Dao). The most complete version of this work was printed in 1445 CE in 480 sections, 1,120 titles, and over 5,300 volumes.

During China's medieval period, lasting from the seventh to the fourteenth centuries, organized Daoism enjoyed imperial patronage and became very much a part of the cultural life of the elite. Along with a popular Buddhism and the nominal state ideology of Confucianism, it was one of the "three teachings" of the realm. Its emphasis on nature and a free spirit informed much of the art and literature of the time. The highly valued monochrome landscape paintings and cursive calligraphic art of the elite scholars of this time reflected central Daoist values.

Several new orders also gained prominence during this time, the most influential among them being the Quanzhen sect (Complete Perfection). Founded by a man named Wang Zhe (1113–1170 CE), this school of Daoism embraced elements from both Confucianism and Buddhism. From Confucianism it took moral values, and from Buddhism it adopted monasticism and clerical celibacy. In addition to the *Daodejing*, the Confucian *Classic of Filial Piety* and the Buddhist *Heart Sutra* were given the highest prominence by this tradition. Quanzhen Daoism is one of the only two Daoist groups that are still active today, with its headquarters located in the White Cloud Shrine in Beijing. The other group is the Celestial Masters, with its current leader residing in Taiwan.

Daoism in the Modern Period

During the late imperial period in Chinese history (fourteenth to nineteenth centuries), Daoism was put on the defensive by the triumphant Neo-Confucians. Its clergy was tightly controlled by the state through the highly regulated issuance of ordination certificates. Although the Confucian elite grudgingly acknowledged the "philosophic" brilliance of the *Daodejing* and the *Zhuangzi*, they regarded organized Daoist

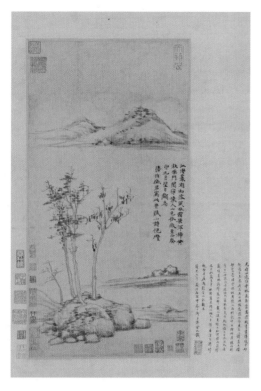

This painting, *Wind among the Trees on the Riverbank* by Ni Zan (1306–1374), is best known for the quietude and balance in nature it expresses. China, Yuan Dynasty (1271–1368), dated 1363.

groups as nothing more than a corrupted form of pristine, original Daoism. Organized Daoism was marginalized as superstition, unworthy of elite attention. This contempt for Daoism continued beyond the imperial period, was intensified in the early twentieth century, and was adopted as official policy under the communist regime in 1949.

The New Culture movement of the 1910s and 1920s regarded both Daoism and Confucianism as unwanted vestiges of China's feudal past. The Cultural Revolution (1966–1976) that did so much damage to Confucianism also proved devastating to Daoism. Many historic Daoist shrines and sites were destroyed or sacrilegiously damaged, and all performances of Daoist rituals and liturgies were banned. For all intents and purposes, Daoism as an organized religion ceased to exist in mainland China. Yet the tradition survived amid China's nebulous folk religion. It also continued to exist, often robustly, outside China among Chinese communities in Taiwan, Hong Kong, and Southeast Asia.

Since the late 1970s, however, a Daoist revival of sorts has begun. The death of Chairman Mao ended the period of fervent anti-traditionalism among the Chinese intellectuals since the beginning of the twentieth century. Daoist ceremonies are once again openly observed in China, and a new generation of Daoist priests has been trained to carry on the tradition and to rebuild the shrines. Academic study of Daoism, primarily by Japanese and French scholars at the beginning, and now joined by Americans and Chinese themselves, has created new understanding of the tradition from the point of view of both doctrine and practice. Some of the scholars have actually become ordained Daoist priests of either the Celestial Master or the Quanzhen tradition to access more accurate and authoritative interpretations of Daoism.

As in the case in its promotion of Confucianism to a worldwide audience, the Chinese government has also established the "World Federation of Daoism" in September 2023 with an inaugural forum attended by five hundred delegates from nineteen countries and regions. The goal of the Federation is to apply Daoist teachings to the understanding and solution of the many social, political, environmental, and healthcare challenges the contemporary world is facing.

Daoism as a Pan-Asiatic Tradition

Like its Confucian rival, Daoism is not confined to the Chinese mainland. The foundational texts *Daodejing* and *Zhuangzi* had certainly reached Korea no later than the Three Kingdoms Period (first century BCE to tenth century CE). It gained significant popularity during the Goryeo period (918–1392), even though Buddhism was the dominant faith of the time. By the ensuing Joseon Dynasty (1392–1897), when Confucianism was the state orthodoxy, Daoism in the form of shamanism, mountain worship, and immortality practices had become an integral part of Korean folk religion. Even today, the national flag of South Korea contains the Taegeuk symbol of yin-yang complementarity and four of the eight divinatory trigrams. Similarly, in Japan, Daoist practitioners have combined with certain Buddhist groups and indigenous Shinto cults to form specific folk religious traditions since Japan's exposure to continental influence. Specifically, the Shugendo (shamanistic mountain ascetics) and the Koshin religious practice of controlling the decaying agents of the human body to

This painting of the poet Li Bo (Li Bai, 701–762) shows him as a Daoist immortal.

prevent them from shortening the human lifespan display unmistakable Daoist influences. The Onmyodo (The Way of Yin and Yang), with prominent Daoist roots, had a dominant influence in Japanese society because of its divinatory and magical practices, and its practitioners have been featured in popular Japanese manga and films. In Southeast Asia as well, Daoism has found its way into the beliefs of the Xiantian Dao (Way of Prior Heaven) of Malaysia and the Caodai (High Power) tradition in Vietnam. Both are movements promising deliverance from the current age of decadence and corruption.

8.6 Chinese Religions as a Way of Life: Rituals and Observances

The two Chinese religions discussed in this chapter are not just collections of philosophical precepts and religious beliefs developed over a long history. More importantly, they are lived and practiced traditions. It is in the living and practicing of the two traditions that their true meaning and value can be gauged.

The Temple of *Tian* (*Tiantan*), where the Chinese emperor prayed to *Tian* on behalf of his subjects and in his capacity as "Son of *Tian*," is now a popular park in Beijing.

Confucian Rituals

From the very beginning, the Confucian tradition has put great emphasis on ritual as a crucial expression of humanity. As "moral behavior," rituals teach people to conduct themselves with dignity and decorum, making them authentically human. As "holy rites," rituals enable humans to communicate effectively with the spiritual powers and to interact harmoniously with one another. It is in the latter more overtly religious sense that Confucian ritual is addressed in this section.

In addition to the mundane rituals of familial and social interaction with other human beings in accordance with the prescribed rules outlined in the classic texts, the most important aspect of Confucian religious ritual in in the premodern period was the sacrificial presentation. These presentation rituals were performed at different levels—the state, the community, and the family. The grandest of the rituals were, of course, conducted at the state level. And chief among the state rituals were those connected with sacrifices to *Tian* and *Di*—and to Confucius once his teachings were exalted to orthodoxy.

The Hall of Praying for an Abundant Harvest (*Qi'nian dian*), Temple of *Tian* (*Tiantan*), Beijing. The whole complex was built in 1420 under Emperor Yongle and restored in 1530 and 1751. Here the emperor celebrated the sacrifice to *Tian* for a good harvest. The decorated ramp between the two stairways was reserved for the emperor's palanquin.

Sacrifice to Tian and Di

Tian, you should recall, had been the source of legitimate political power since the Zhou Dynasty. As son of *Tian*, the Chinese ruler carried out *Tian*'s mandate to exercise his imperial prerogatives over the entire realm under *Tian*. The worship of *Tian* thus became the ruler's exclusive privilege and obligation. Later, with Confucianism imbued with yin-yang cosmological ideas in the Han Dynasty, *Tian*, the yang element, was paired up with *Di* (earth), the yin element, and worship of *Di* was added, though with much less pomp and ostentation.

In late imperial China, the worship of *Tian* and *Di* took place annually. On the day of the summer solstice, the

VOICES: An Interview with Jason Ch'ui-hsiao Tseng

Jason Ch'ui-hsiao Tseng is from Taiwan with a master's degree from an American university. He engages in educational exchange for Chinese students wishing to study in the United States.

Do you consider yourself a Confucian or a Daoist?

I do not consider myself exclusively as one or the other. Both have influenced me deeply, and I regard their teachings as equally valid and complementary.

How is that possible, as their teachings often conflict with each other?

They are not in conflict. They merely represent the polar opposite of the other. They complete each other. For most Chinese, there is no necessity to choose one or the other. We think of them as the two sides of a coin—without both there is no coin. The two together constitute our native Chinese religious outlook. As a matter of fact, we also consider Buddhist teaching a third way of guiding our religious life. These teachings are generally not jealous of one another. They do not demand total exclusive devotion. They provide meaning to different aspects of our lives. There is religious pluralism for most Chinese.

How is that so?

We do not believe that one teaching alone corners the market. As a respectful son and an upright citizen, I embrace Confucian values. They teach me to put family and society ahead of myself and to value education as the most important undertaking to improve myself. In my views on how my body works, how my health can be maintained, how different ingredients should be used to achieve balance in my food, and how I can relate to the spirits in the invisible world, I follow the Daoist teaching. And Buddhism gives me hope for a good afterlife. Together they make me a complete person.

Jason Ch'ui-hsiao Tseng.

emperor made a sacrifice to *Tian* at the Temple of *Tian* (*Tiantan*) located in Beijing's south side. Correspondingly, on the day of the winter solstice, worship of *Di* was conducted at the Temple of *Di* (*Ditan*) located at the northern end of the capital. The rituals involved nine steps, including purification of the participants, performance of dance and music, reading of prayer documents, and offering of sacrifices.

Sacrifice to Confucius

The state cult of Confucius began in the Han Dynasty with the elevation of Confucianism as orthodoxy. The descendants of Confucius were first given a hereditary fief, and later the Master himself was given increasingly laudatory titles and ducal honors. "Temples" commemorating Confucius were ordered to be built in every county and major city throughout the empire. In time, wooden tablets commemorating some of his prominent students, as well as those of successive generations of Confucian worthies such as Mencius and Zhu Xi,

Confucius serves as an object of veneration and commemoration. He is the "Utmost Sage and Late Teacher," as the tablet in front of his statue declares.

were installed in these temples. Although the frequency and elaborateness of the sacrificial rites conducted at these temples varied with time and locale, the traditional birthday of Confucius (the twenty-eighth day of the ninth month) was generally observed. These rites involved dance and music accompanied by drums and bells, proclamations and didactic lectures given by local dignitaries and government officials, and offerings of incense and animals.

The most magnificent Temple of Confucius is located in his native Qufu, not far from Mount Tai in present-day Shandong Province. This Qufu Confucian Temple has a main building with a palatial design supported by dragon-decorated pillars, all meant to accord the Master the highest honor comparable to that of a ruler. Stone steles are engraved with the calligraphy or essays of various emperors in Chinese history, all lauding the moral and cultural accomplishments of the sage. This Confucian Temple in Qufu was a pilgrimage site for generations of scholars and aspiring literati and is still popular among tourists today.

Family Rituals   The custom of commemorating and honoring ancestors in China goes back to the dawn of recorded Chinese history. But Confucianism, with its focus on *xiao* (filial piety), lent further theoretical support to the practice. The Confucian teaching maintains that one's filial obligation to parents and ancestors is the core of one's humanity. Thus, while the state monopolized the worship of *Tian/ Di* and the educated elites controlled the sacrifice to Confucius, all people could participate in the family ritual of honoring parents and ancestors. Sacrifice to the ancestors is especially important because it gives the descendants a sense of belonging and continuity and thereby a religious appreciation of the chain of life that links them to their forebears as well as their descendants.

In the *Family Rituals*, compiled by the Neo-Confucian scholar Zhu Xi, detailed step-by-step liturgies are provided for ceremonies associated with ancestor worship. Chapters describe daily "looking in" on the ancestors; more elaborate semi-monthly "visits," "reports" on major family events such as births, weddings, and deaths; and formal "offerings" on festival days and seasonal sacrifices. The following is a summarized version of Zhu Xi's instructions for the rites of making seasonal offerings to the ancestors:

In the preparatory phase, the date for the sacrifice is selected by divination performed in front of the ancestral shrine in the preceding month. Then, three days before the event, the designated leading man and woman will each lead family members of their respective gender to perform purification rituals in their designated quarters, men in the outer and women in the inner. The men also make the main hall sparkling clean and arrange the place settings for each generation properly. The women will set the incense burner and incense box, as well as prepare wine racks and containers, along with meat plates for the ancestors.

On the day of the event, when the sun is fully up, the wooden tablets containing the names of the different generations of ancestors, separated by gender, are moved to their proper places in the main hall. Then the spirits of the ancestors are greeted, and food is offered to them three times. The ancestors are invited to eat the food and are given privacy to do so, with everyone from the presiding man on down exiting the main hall, and the door is closed. After a suitable interval, the master of ceremony coughs three times to announce his intention to reenter; then he opens the door, and everyone else comes back in. Tea is offered to the ancestors for the rinsing of their mouths. Then the presiding man receives the sacrificed food from the master of ceremony. With reverence, the presiding man bows and prostrates himself to taste the food and drink the wine. Then the entire group takes leave of the ancestral spirits, returns their tablets to their original locations, and clears away the offering tables. The presiding man supervises the division of the sacrificial food to be consumed by all the family members later that day. This brings an end to the ritual of the ancestral sacrifice.[6]

Confucius's tombstone boldly declares that he is the "Ultimate Sage of Greatest Accomplishment, King of Manifest Culture."

Daoist Practices

The Daoist goal of promoting communal harmony, maintaining good health, and attaining actual immortality involves a whole spectrum of ritual undertakings and practices.

Daoist Communal Festivals and Liturgies

To ordinary practitioners—those who have no hope of going through the rigor and expenses of pursuing immortality—the Daoist religion as practiced by the Celestial Master sect offers the promise of health, long life, even collective salvation. Participation in collective rituals called *zhai* (fasts) is a major undertaking in this tradition. Lasting several days each, these fasts involve abstinence from food, public performance of penance for past moral transgressions, submission of written memorials to request pardon from the deities, and communal prayers for the salvation of the faithful.

The Fast of Mud and Soot in China's medieval period reflected the general tone of *zhai* rituals. With hair disheveled and face smeared with soot, believers prostrated themselves before a raised altar to ask for forgiveness from the gods. Consumed by their agitated emotions, many fell to the ground and rolled about amid loud wailings. Such public acts of penance were performed to earn pardon and spiritual merit. Another liturgical ritual was the Fast of the Yellow Register, during which the participants performed penitence for their ancestors going back seven or nine generations. The names of deceased ancestors, entered in registers, were read by the officiating priests and were then considered to have gained postmortem immortality. In this way, the filial obligation of the faithful was ritually expressed.

Another communal ceremony, the **_jiao_** (offering), is popular also in the present day. This public liturgy is usually performed by Daoist priests on behalf of the entire community to petition the gods to bestow good fortune, health, and prosperity on all. Sometimes labeled as a rite of cosmic renewal, the _jiao_ brings together the community to participate collectively in a religious ritual that is loud, colorful, and dramatic. Depending on the needs of the community, a _jiao_ is conducted at periodic intervals (ranging from once a year for the affluent communities to once every several decades for the less financially endowed communities) or as special thanks to the deities for having successfully protected the entire community by, for example, warding off an epidemic.[7]

A _jiao_ ceremony usually lasts several days. The dates are chosen for their astrological auspiciousness. Daoist priests are contracted to perform the ritual with efficacy and precision. Prior to the official dates of the ceremony, the priests submit "memorials" to the celestial bureaucracy of the gods to give notice of the scheduled _jiao_. Then the location at which the liturgy takes place, usually both the inside and the outside of the largest local temple or shrine, is marked off by hoisted lanterns to signal the enclosure of the sacred space. Afterward, the local deities are invited to take their honored seats within the enclosure; their

VISUAL GUIDE
Confucianism and Daoism

This is an iconic image of Confucius as a learned scholar and an exemplar of human moral accomplishment. Traditionally, the Chinese did not see religion as a separate realm of activity. Hence, the pursuit of scholarship and the conduct of moral behavior within the family and community were very much part of their religious experience.

This yin-yang symbol surrounded by the eight trigrams reflects the Chinese belief in the complementarity of opposites and the harmonious unity of the cosmos. More than any other visual symbol, it represents Chinese religiousness.

Family cohesion and respect for elders are central Confucian values. A daughter and her husband pay a visit to her parents on Chinese New Year's Day to renew her kinship tie with her natal family.

Statue of Laozi carved out of a huge rock in Fujian Province, China. This legendary founder of Daoism symbolizes wisdom and irreverence for conventional thinking. He is understood as the yin to Confucius's yang, and the image of passive acceptance of what nature has ordained to Confucius's active attempt at improving society.

statues or wooden tablets are carried there by community elders. The procession of the deities through the community is accompanied by lion or dragon dances, made even more boisterous with lots of firecrackers. Then the ritual proper begins in earnest.

Reenacting the beginning of the cosmos in a ritual called *fendeng* (distributing the lamp), the chief Daoist priest, in full vestment, blows on a buffalo horn and rings his "thunder" bell, to the accompaniment of an entire music ensemble, and repeats the forty-second chapter of the *Daodejing* by announcing that "the Dao gives birth to the One [Being, Existence]; the One brings forth the Two [Yin and Yang]; the Two give rise to the Three [*Tian, Di*, and Humans]; and the Three engender the Ten Thousand Things [world of multiplicity and diversity]." Entering a meditation-induced trance, the priest transforms his body into the body of the Dao. He takes prescribed steps

Chinese taiji (commonly spelled "tai chi") exercise is perhaps the most representative expression of Daoist beliefs in the human body as a microcosm of the universe. Through harnessing the qi of nature and bringing it into the body for attaining balance and improving health, the taiji master demonstrates the intimate relationship between humans and the cosmos.

Acupuncture is a good expression of the Daoist belief in the circulation of qi in the human body. By inserting the needles into critical nodal points in the qi circuitry, pain can be diverted and the rejuvenating energy of the body can heal the ailing parts.

that are dancelike, spins on himself, and sanctifies the ritual enclosure by requesting the dispatch of heavenly troops to guard the place. At the same time, to placate the wandering ghosts in the neighborhood and to warn them against intrusion into the sacred ground, he provides a feast for them while lecturing them on the reasons for their suffering.

At some point during the ceremony, the names of every member of the community will be posted on a roster and read aloud by the priests to signal their financial and spiritual support of this elaborate and expensive event, as well as to ensure that they will receive their share of the benediction of the gods. There is great interest among the community members in checking the posted name list to make sure that the names are written accurately and that they have not been inadvertently left out.

The climax of the ceremony occurs when the highest of the Daoist deities, the Three Purities and the Jade Emperor, are invited to take part in the ceremony. Piercing prepared talismans with his sword, the chief Daoist priest burns them with great dramatic effect to appeal to the august deities. Once the gods are properly seated, a blanket pardon of every immoral act committed by every member of the community between the last *jiao* and the present one is announced. In grateful response, the community performs a public charitable act of "releasing life"—setting cages of captured birds free and returning buckets of live fish to a stream. On the last night of the ceremony, a grand feast for all ghosts trapped in hell is hosted by the

A group of Daoist priests perform a ritual service for a member of the community.

community. Once again, the Daoist priests exhort the ghosts to behave themselves and to refrain from wreaking havoc in the lives of the living. Balance is restored among the worlds of humans, gods, and ghosts. The rite concludes with sending off the celestial gods and the local deities, distributing food and buns to the spectators, and performing operas for the entertainment of all.

8.7 Chinese Religions as a Way of Life: Engaging with the World

It is worth noting that, with the exception of diehard partisans, Confucianism and Daoism have displayed a uniquely nonsectarian posture toward each other, as well as toward other religions. It is not at all unusual to find Confucian-Daoists, Daoist-Confucians, or, for that matter, Confucian-Daoist-Buddhists. Similarly, it is conceivable that one can be a Christian-Confucian or a Jewish-Daoist. Neither Confucianism nor Daoism has initiation rites or member registers to reflect a reliable number of their respective adherents. There are few "card-carrying" and "self-identifying" pure Confucians or Daoists. For this very reason, any attempt to gauge even an approximate number of Confucians or Daoists can only be speculative. Nevertheless, no matter how imprecise the population figures for Confucianism and Daoism are, there is evidence that interest in Confucianism and Daoism, both as intellectual traditions and as practiced faiths, remains strong. Both religions continue to be resilient and appealing to all who search for meaning and purpose in their spiritual lives.

Chinese Religions and the Environment

Early in this chapter, we discussed the cosmological foundations of the ancient Chinese religious tradition, which subsequently gave rise to both Confucianism and Daoism. Fundamental to this cosmology is the notion of qi, the all-pervasive energy-matter that is the building block of all the myriad things in the universe. In this belief, everything that exists is made up of the same "stuff," only in different configurations and manifestations. The human body is a microcosm of the environment, while nature is a macrocosm of the human body. There is a porous fluidity that flows between the two. Hence the well-being of the environment is equated with the health of the human body, and vice versa. There is therefore a natural and logical inclination within the two Chinese religious traditions toward environmentalism, as no one desires ill health. To be sure, China in the modern period, thanks to full-throttled industrialization, rapid economic growth, and unrestrained urbanization, coupled with a deliberate rejection of its traditional religious values, has experienced a devastating environmental degradation evidenced by air and water pollution, as well as toxic contamination of nature. Yet there is nothing in Confucian and Daoist beliefs that regards the environment as something to be dominated and exploited, or as an entity pitted against the human body and external to its welfare. The Confucian notion of the moral elite taking on the responsibility to improve human society and its harmonious relation with nature has been noted. The Daoist love of nature as the highest form of embodying the Dao has also been observed. There is in fact a growing awareness among Chinese leaders that traditional Chinese religious views can be forged with environmental concerns as China moves forward in the twenty-first century. China's full recognition of the perils of climate change, together with its development of renewable energy projects such as wind turbines and solar panels, exemplifies this recognition.[8]

Chinese Religions' Perspectives on Gender and Identity

It is indisputable that traditional China was patriarchal, paternalistic, sexist, and authoritarian, as were most other traditional civilizations and countries. Despite its lofty religious teaching, Confucianism has often been criticized for its dismissive and negative attitude toward women. The single most notorious statement made by Confucius regarding women is truly incriminating: "Women and the petty men are alike, in that they are both hard to deal with" (*Analects* 17:23). In addition, one of the most prominent features of Confucianism during the Han Dynasty (206 BCE–220 BCE) and beyond is the oppression of the female by the male. Cleverly manipulating the traditional yin-yang belief into an argument for the superiority of yang over yin, hence the male over the female, Han Confucians and their successors in later dynasties insisted that women submit to their fathers when young, their husbands when married, and their sons when old and widowed. This aspect of Confucianism in imperial China became a major cause of its criticism in the modern period. Since the beginning of the twentieth century, Confucianism has been portrayed as a sexist, patriarchal ideology responsible for the oppression of women in China. The insidious Chinese practices of foot binding (the crushing of the feet of young girls with long binding cloth to make walking difficult and painful, but supposedly feminine and seductive), concubinage (the keeping of multiple wives by one man), disallowance of women-initiated divorce, prohibition against widow remarriage, and encouragement of widow suicide have all been blamed on Confucianism.

This view of Confucianism may, however, be too broad-stroked in characterizing the 2,000 years of Chinese gender history. It makes no distinction between theory and practice, as well as wishful normative values versus actual, living experiences. The oppression of women by Confucian men during China's imperial periods, admittedly real and widespread, should not result in an outright denial of the intellectual and religious dynamism of Confucianism as a teaching of human improvement and self-cultivation with no gender specificity. Just as any petty man can become a sage, potentially, so can a woman. Hence there is nothing in Confucian teaching that denies women's parity with men. Some contemporary scholars have taken note of the parallels between Confucian and feminist ethics. Confucianism as an ethical and religious teaching, with its emphasis on mutual care, empathy, responsible government, and communal welfare, shares many similarities with feminist care ethics.[9]

The Daoist view of the feminine is far more positive than the traditional Confucian one. The Dao is exemplified by the female in the *Daodejing*, and the Daoist pantheon is populated by many female deities. Daoist priestesses performed purifying rituals alongside their male counterparts, even though they are much smaller in number.

So how do these two traditions fare on the issue of gender in the contemporary world? It should be remembered that foundational to Chinese religions is the concept of yin-yang—the two qi that pervade all the myriad things. Yin and yang are understood to be symbiotic and mutually penetrative. Moreover, they are complementary instead of antagonistic or mutually exclusive. Gender identity, whether it is male, female, or LGBTQ+, is understood to be the result of the variegated configurations of yin and yang in an individual. Male identity does not mean the sole and exclusive presence of yang, for yang does not, and cannot, exist in the absence of yin. Similarly, a female identity does not mean the sole and exclusive presence of yin either, for the exact same reason. And LBGTQ+ identities reflect the innumerable proportional combinations of yin and yang in the individuals involved. Hence the range of gender identities does not automatically suggest superiority or inferiority, conventional views of society notwithstanding.

Chinese society has also long been unapologetically unequal and oppressively hierarchical. Yet when the beliefs of its two indigenous religious traditions are examined with no preconceived bias—as we have tried to do in this chapter—a strong sense of justice and equity can be detected. To be sure, the Confucian tradition does not assert equality in social status, as it is essentially elitist in its orientation. Yet this elitism is based on moral standing, not on birth, wealth, or social-political status.

The emphasis is on equality of opportunity and personal improvement through moral education. No one is deemed incapable of becoming a *junzi*, or assured of being one automatically. Likewise, Daoism promises equity in the apprehension of the Dao and the achievement of spiritual and physical health, with no consideration given to gender or status.

Furthermore, both traditions insist that there is an overarching authority that oversees human behavior to ensure ultimate justice. For the Confucians, *Tian* is an active will that calls on all to be personally righteous and to work toward the general improvement of the human community. For the Daoists, whether they are members of an organized movement or mere participants in communal rituals, the Dao in the form of an entire pantheon of deities rewards the just and metes out punishment to the wicked. Together, the two traditions inspire much proverbial wisdom among the Chinese, as shown in the following: "People do things, but *Tian* is watching," "*Tian* casts its net wide; though the meshes seem wide and loose, they let nothing slip through," "People do not complain about the inadequacy of resources, they find fault with the inequity in their distribution," and "There are gods and spirits hovering three feet above our heads [keeping watch over our thoughts and deeds]."

Chinese Religions and Feng Shui, Herbal Medicine, and Martial Arts

There are two popular worldwide practices that can be attributed to the influence of Chinese religions: the New Age art of building-siting and interior design, known by the Chinese name "feng shui," and martial arts practiced for their promised benefits in health, mental sharpness, and self-defense. Feng shui, meaning "wind and water," is based on the belief in the efficacy of qi to allow humans to live and thrive in their natural environment.

By siting a house, a tomb, or a business in an auspicious spot where positive qi is deemed to flow unobstructed, feng shui practitioners believe they will enjoy good fortune and good health. Conversely, they also consider rearranging furniture, mirrors, and doorways in certain directions, or changing the interior partitions of one's dwellings to be effective in warding off evil influences and averting disasters. Hong Kong Disneyland is known to have moved its main gate by 12 degrees to accommodate the feng shui sensitivities of the local theme park attendants.

Chinese herbal medicine, significantly informed by Daoist theories, is gaining respect in the medical community as a complement to synthetic drugs and surgery in keeping and improving people's health. The therapeutic qualities of many plants and herbs, the palliative effect of the acupuncture needles, and the soothing, relaxing results of whole body massage are all part of the repertoire of Daoist healthcare that have become widely acceptable to health professionals worldwide.

Similarly, Chinese martial art forms such as taiji (traditionally spelled "tai chi"), Wudang fists, and qigong (cultivation of qi) call for the harnessing of qi in reducing stress, calming the mind, and protecting oneself from illnesses. The popularity of Chinese martial arts in movies and in exercise gyms, particularly when they feature

In Paris, France, people gather to practice qigong and taiji exercises.

themes of the soft overcoming the hard, the yielding winning over the aggressive, can be attributed to the global acceptance of the Daoist teachings of the Dao as passive and nonassertive. Bruce Lee, who captivated a worldwide audience through his several classic movies exemplifying the grace and power of Chinese martial arts, summed up his philosophical outlook with the words "Be water," a very Daoist metaphor. Similarly, the dance-like movements of taiji and the subtle strength of qigong meditational steps have attracted a global following as well.

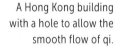

A Hong Kong building with a hole to allow the smooth flow of qi.

The Enduring Significance of Chinese Religions

In this chapter, we have invited you to explore the religious world of the Chinese through a study of their two native religious traditions—Confucianism and Daoism. We have argued that Confucianism is not just a teaching of ethics and good government, but is in fact informed by a deep religious faith in an ultimate Absolute—*Tian*. Moreover, this faith mandates dedicated human effort to transform the individual and the world. Also documented is the historical unfolding of this tradition over the course of more than 2,000 years. At the same time, the ritual dimensions of this tradition have been described, ranging from the elaborate and solemn state observations of the past to the simple familial ceremonies that are still practiced today.

As for Daoism, we have also shown that it is not confined to the metaphysical discussions of the *Daodejing* and the *Zhuangzi*, but rather is richly informed by a sophisticated belief in the cosmological importance of the human body, a salvational message of communal redemption, and an abiding yearning for physical well-being and perfection. Moreover, we have examined the historical progression of this tradition as it meandered through the different periods in China. We have also documented the colorful ritual performance of Daoism in the community.

Both Confucianism and Daoism (along with a Chinese version of Buddhism and a syncretized amalgamation of the three teachings in the form of folk religion) have contributed to the shaping of the Chinese religious mindset. Both have experienced ups and downs in their respective history, at times being the dominant ideology of the realm and at times being eclipsed by other traditions. Nevertheless, both have maintained their central importance to the Chinese people. Despite suffering a brutal critique and rejection in the twentieth century by the modern Chinese intellectual elite, both have remained resilient among the populace. In fact, there are clear signs of their revival and rejuvenation at the dawn of the twenty-first century. Confucian values continue to inform Chinese familial ethics and social and political behavior, and Daoist concerns for the well-being of the human body and harmonious relationship with the spiritual world shape contemporary Chinese attitudes toward health, medicine, cuisine, and the environment. Indeed, these values and concerns have gone beyond the Chinese world to attain worldwide relevance.

As a final point, we have attempted to justify the inclusion of both Confucianism and Daoism in the study of world religions. Confucianism treats the fulfilment of the human potential as an ultimate aspiration. The tenacity with which Confucianism exhorts people to strive for human perfection in our mundane lives as a form of divine calling—thereby making the secular sacred—demonstrates an interesting type of religiosity. In addition, its assertion of human coequality with the divine offers an intriguing contrast with other religious traditions. Daoism is similarly a significant world religion. Its perception of the divine Absolute as a life-generating, feminine entity; its call for a harmonious coexistence between humans and nature; its emphasis on healthy improvement of the human body as a religious mission; and its promotion of communal cohesiveness through ritual participation make it all the more relevant in a postindustrial world. Both traditions fit the definition of religion suggested by Bruce Lincoln and discussed in Chapter 1 of this text. Both possess the four "domains" of discourse, practice, community, and institution.

SEEKING ANSWERS

What Is Ultimate Reality?

Confucianism and Daoism share the same cosmological myth they inherited from ancient China. The natural world is not in a fallen state. There is no almighty creator, nor is there a demonic counterpart. There is no definite beginning of the world, and there is no predicted end. Instead, the world unfolds cyclically and operates like a pendulum, arcing between two extremes and alternating between two polar but complementing opposites. Human beings are not caught in a tug of war between good and evil, and the side they choose does not result in a permanent fate in paradise or hell. Emphasis is placed on balance, coexistence, and harmony.

(continued)

SEEKING ANSWERS (Continued)

How Should We Live in This World?

In both Confucianism and Daoism, there is an absence of the notion of sin. However, this does not mean that human beings are already perfect and need no improvement from their current state. A yawning gap still exists between human beings as they are and human beings as they should or can become. For the Confucians, the right way to live is to live ethically, in accordance with the moral dictates of *Tian*. In concentric circles extending outward from the individual, moral behavior will transform the family, the community, and the world at large. "Do not do unto others what you do not want done to you" is the minimal moral guide for correct living in Confucianism. For the Daoists, the right way to live is to live healthily. To be sure, ethical behavior is part of desirable living, but Daoists also emphasize the human body as a microcosm reflecting perfectly the macrocosm of the cosmos. Thus, taking care of one's body through both internal and external "alchemical" means is a way of living life properly in accordance with the Dao—indeed, it is the way of approaching the holy.

What Is Our Ultimate Purpose?

Confucians and Daoists differ in their answers to this question. For the Confucians, humans are potentially perfect and inclined toward the good. Yet this potentiality and inclination need to be rigorously nurtured and developed through scholastic learning, moral introspection, and ethical behavior. Learning to be authentically human, to enact the "way" of *Tian*, is the way to improve the human condition and to perfect it. The highest achievement of human endeavor is to become the coequal of the divine ultimate—*Tian*.

Daoists regard humans on the same level as all the myriad things—they are all concrete expressions of the Dao, the ultimate Absolute. With no meddling from humans, the Dao maintains a spontaneous and perfect order. However, through their ignorance or negligence, humans meddle with nature and dissipate their primordial endowment of the vital energy, the qi, resulting in disharmony with nature and their vulnerability to disease and death. Consequently, the Daoist prescription for improving the human condition is to engage in exercises and rituals designed to replenish the body and the spirit, restoring their harmony with nature and making them as immortal as the Dao. Confucians and Daoists also diverge in their beliefs about what happens at the end of life. Confucius himself famously brushed aside a student's inquiry on death. He just did not consider it an issue worthy of exploration. His priority was to pay exclusive attention to life and how to improve it. This "prejudice" has affected all subsequent Confucians, none of whom showed any strong interest in addressing death or its religious meaning. Even the Confucian practice of ancestor worship and respecting the dead can be explained as a way of bypassing the issue, as dead ancestors are treated very much as living members of the lineage and the family. Daoists, by contrast, confront the topic of mortality by emphasizing the possibility and desirability of immortality. Even with the appearance of death as inevitable, Daoists explain it as a stage of transformation to a higher plane of existence, a way of attaining true immortality. Thus, Daoists equally ignore the deeper meaning of death.

REVIEW QUESTIONS

For Review

1. Why should the term *Confucianism* be used with caution? In what way may it be a misnomer?
2. How do Confucianism and Daoism define such terms as *Tian*, *Dao*, and *de* differently?
3. Why is Daoism more than the teachings of the *Daodejing* and the *Zhuangzi*?
4. Why is Confucianism a religious tradition despite its lack of concern for the afterlife?

For Further Reflection

1. In what ways do Confucianism and Daoism complement each other, and in what ways do they oppose each other?
2. Compare and contrast the Confucian notion of *Tian* with the Christian concept of God.
3. Compare and contrast the Daoist notion of Dao with the Hindu concept of Brahman.
4. Having examined Confucianism and Daoism, have you arrived at any conclusion regarding Chinese religiosity? How does it differ from that of other religious traditions?

GLOSSARY

dan (dahn) Literally a pill, but understood as the essence of immortality.

dantian (dahn'tee-an) "Fields for the refinement of the immortal pill"; major nodal points in the human body where the "pill" of immortality can be refined through alchemical means.

Dao (dow) A fundamental concept in Chinese religion, literally meaning the "path" or the "way." In Confucianism, it specifically refers to the entire ideal human order ordained by the Absolute, *Tian*. In Daoism, it is the primary source of the cosmos, the very ground of all beings.

Daodejing (dow-duh-jing) Foundational Daoist text, lit. "The Scripture of the Way and Its Potent Manifestation"; also known as the Book of *Laozi*, the name of its purported author.

Daozang (dow'dzahng) Literally "Treasury of the Dao," this is the Daoist Canon that contains the entire corpus of Daoist texts. The most complete version, still in use today, was first published in 1445.

de (duh) Another fundamental concept in Chinese religions, meaning "virtue" or "potency." In Confucianism, it is the charismatic power of the ruler or the man of virtue, while in Daoism it means the concrete manifestation of the Dao.

fangshi (fahng-shuhr) "Magicians" who allegedly possessed the recipe for immortality.

Five Classics The five canonical works of Confucianism designated in the Han Dynasty. They are the *Book of Odes*, *Book of History*, *Book of Changes*, *Record of Rites*, and *Spring and Autumn Annals*.

Four Books The four texts identified by the Neo-Confucian Zhu Xi as fundamental in understanding the Confucian teaching. Between 1313 and 1905, they made up the curriculum for the civil service examination. They are *Analects*, *Mencius*, *Great Learning*, and *Doctrine of the Mean*.

gui (gwee) Ghosts and demons; malevolent spirits.

jiao (jee-ow') Daoist communal sacrificial offerings to signal cosmic renewal and collective cohesion.

junzi (joon'zee) The personality ideal in Confucianism; the noble person.

li (lee) Etiquette and proper manners; rituals and holy rites.

ming See *Tianming*.

neidan (nay-dahn) Daoist "internal" alchemical regimens designed to attain immortality through meditation, breath control, gymnastics, diet, and massage.

neisheng waiwang (nay-sheng wai'wahng) Neo-Confucian ideal of "inner moral cultivation and external skillful management of society and state."

qi (chee) Breath, force, power, material energy.

ren (ruhn) Human-heartedness, benevolence; the unique moral inclination of humans.

ru (rooh) Scribes and ritual performers of the Zhou period; later used exclusively to refer to followers and practitioners of Confucius's teachings.

Shangdi (shahng-dee) The August Lord on High of the Shang period.

shen (shen) Gods and deities; benevolent spirits.

shengren (sheng-ren) (or *sheng*) The Confucian sage, the epitome of humanity.

shi (shir) Men of service; lower-ranking civil and military officials in the Zhou period.

Tian (tee-yahn') The Ultimate Absolute in Confucian teaching; the conscious Will that regulates the cosmos and intervenes in human affairs; in Daoist usage, it means nature itself; conventionally but misleadingly translated as "Heaven."

Tianming The mandate or command of *Tian* that confers political legitimacy to the ruler; also understood by Confucians as the calling to morally improve oneself and to transform the world.

Tianshi (tee-yahn'shir) "Celestial Master"; reference to a Daoist salvational figure, as well as an organized movement.

waidan (wai'dahn) Daoist "external" alchemical regimens involving refining of "pills" with herbs and minerals for ingestion so that immortality can be attained.

wuwei (wooh-way) Daoist notion of action without intention; actionless action.

xian (shee-ahn') Daoist immortals and perfected individuals.

xiao (shee-ow') Filial piety; respect and care for parents and ancestors.

xinzhai (shin'jai) "Fasting of the Mind" in the *Zhuangzi*.

yang (yahng) Lit. the south-facing side of a mountain, representing the energy that is bright, warm, dry, and masculine.

yangsheng (yahng-sheng) Daoist techniques of nourishing life and attaining immortality.

yin Lit. the north-facing side of a mountain, representing the energy that is dark, cold, wet, and feminine.

zhai (jai) Daoist "fasts" designed to seek redemption of transgressions by the gods.

ziran (zee'rahn) Daoist notion of natural spontaneity.

zuowang (zoh'wahng) Practice of "sitting and forgetting" in the *Zhuangzi*.

SUGGESTIONS FOR FURTHER READING

de Bary, William Theodore. *The Trouble with Confucianism*. Cambridge, MA: Harvard University Press, 1991. A thought-provoking discussion of the "prophetic voice" in Confucianism.

Fingarette, Herbert. *Confucius: The Secular as Sacred*. New York: Harper Torchbooks, 1972. A creative interpretation of the Confucian notion of li as holy rites.

Gardner, Daniel K. *Confucianism: A Very Short Introduction*. New York: Oxford University Press, 2014. A pocket-size introduction to the Confucian tradition for beginners.

Gardner, Daniel K., trans. *The Four Books: The Basic Teachings of the Later Confucian Tradition*. Indianapolis, IN: Hackett, 2007. A handy translation of important excerpts from the textual corpus of Confucianism.

Kirkland, Russell. *Taoism: The Enduring Tradition*. London: Routledge, 2004. An impassioned monograph by a specialist to correct many of the misconceptions regarding Daoism and its history.

Kohn, Livia, ed. *Daoism Handbook*. Leiden, The Netherlands: Brill, 2000. A magisterial and encyclopedic collection of essays on various aspects of Daoism, ranging from history to schools to texts.

Schipper, Kristofer. *The Taoist Body*. Berkeley: University of California Press, 1993. An authoritative discourse by an ordained Daoist priest on the rituals and practices of Daoism as they relate to the texts and teachings.

Sun, Anna. *Confucianism as a World Religion*. Princeton, NJ: Princeton University Press, 2013. An authoritative monograph on the issue of Confucianism's religious content.

Taylor, Rodney L. *The Religious Dimensions of Confucianism*. Albany: State University of New York Press, 1986. A convenient collection of mostly previously published essays by the author to argue for the religiousness of Confucianism.

Yao, Xinzhong. *An Introduction to Confucianism*. Cambridge: Cambridge University Press, 2000. An authoritative basic text on the entire Confucian tradition.

ONLINE RESOURCES

Research Centre for Confucian Studies

This useful website for Confucian studies is maintained by the Research Center for Confucian Studies, Chinese University of Hong Kong. It contains a rich resource guide for Confucian studies.

The Daoist Foundation

The Daoist Foundation was created by two American academics who, having studied and practiced Daoism for many years, "are committed to fostering the flourishing of authentic and tradition-based Daoist practice, community, and culture with attentiveness to the needs and concerns of Western students."

Center for Daoist Studies

This useful website is the education and research branch of the Daoist Foundation.

Religion for Breakfast

This YouTube channel is hosted by Andrew Mark Henry, who provides to the nonacademic audience a very informative introduction to various religious traditions. The episodes on Confucianism and Daoism are useful.

Shinto

9

Chapter Outline

9.1 Describe the teachings of Shinto through an examination of its foundational texts.

9.2 Examine the historical development of Shinto.

9.3 Describe how Shinto shapes the devotional practices of people who subscribe to its teachings.

9.4 Examine how Shinto addresses some of the significant contemporary global issues.

IT IS THE LAST DAY of the three-day Sanja Festival in Asakusa, a historic precinct in Tokyo. The climax of the festival is the wild parading of *mikoshi*, portable shrines carrying the "essence" of the patron deities of the various neighborhoods and merchant groups. As one of the most popular annual events in Tokyo, the Sanja Festival attracts upward of half a million spectators and participants during the three-day festivities.

At 5 a.m. on the third Sunday in May, Satoshi Tanaka, a young grocery clerk in his twenties, is waiting expectantly outside the Asakusa Shrine. Along with hundreds of other young men (and some equally enthusiastic young women), he has signed up months in advance to be a member of a team of shrine carriers sponsored by a local merchant group. Though ordinarily preferring to sleep late on Sundays, Satoshi finds himself excited and alert this morning. Dressed in a colorful shirt and shorts with matching headbands, he waits with others to receive their purification by the Shinto priests so that he will be considered spiritually clean and ready for the sacred task ahead. Even though he does not see himself as a seriously religious person, Satoshi feels perfectly comfortable in being a shrine carrier at this Shinto festival. It is his way of being Japanese and participating in the activities of his community.

The job of these carriers is to carry the *mikoshi* through the streets of Asakusa so that all in attendance can share a moment of communal solidarity

Throngs of portable shrine carriers with their respective *mikoshi* outside the Asakusa Shrine in Tokyo.

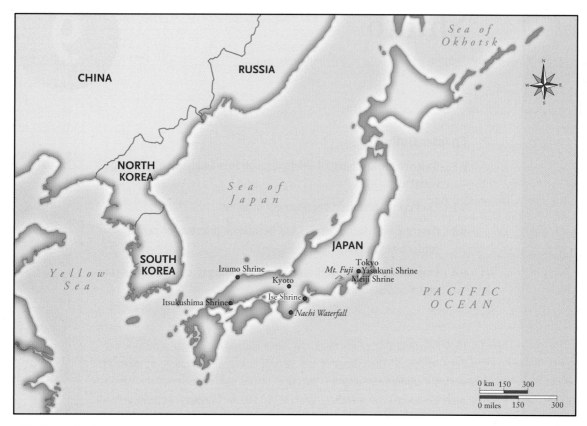

Significant sites in the history of Shinto.

as well as intimacy with the deities temporarily housed in these portable shrines. These ornately decorated *mikoshi* rest on poles that are carried on the shoulders of the carriers. Shouting and grunting in unison, to the accompaniment of much drumming, cymbal clanging, and loud cheers from the crowd, the carriers attempt to move the portable shrines along. But because no one among them is in total control of the direction of the *mikoshi*, all the carriers move back and forth or sideways more or less involuntarily. The movement of the portable shrines can thus be wild and unpredictable, subject to the unconscious collective will of the entire group of carriers (or, as many of those in attendance believe, that of the deities inside). This cumbersome and potentially dangerous parade lumbers down narrow streets and broad boulevards amid large crowds.

Quite frequently, one shrine will cross paths with another, resulting in great commotion and competition for attention from the throngs of spectators. Sweating profusely and hoarse from too much shouting and chanting, individual shrine carriers drop out and are quickly replaced by others without disrupting the progress of the shrines. Thirsty and hungry, the temporarily retired carriers sit or lie on the ground in total exhaustion. Meanwhile, the spectators watch, take pictures, applaud, cheer, visit the main shrine, purchase the sundry food, drink, and souvenirs offered by enterprising street vendors, and make a day of it.

The preceding scene is typical of a *matsuri*, centuries-old Shinto festivals in Japan that help to create religious awareness and social solidarity within the entire community. The *matsuri* is both a religious and a social occasion. Though the oldest surviving religion in Japan, Shinto has, by and large, coexisted with and been profoundly influenced by Buddhism and Confucianism since the sixth century CE. The two latter traditions were introduced into the country from China by way of Korea. Although the three religions have been rivals and competitors over the centuries, they have also experienced accommodation and mutual acceptance. There is an observation about Japanese religious behavior that describes perfectly the eclectic attitude of the Japanese. It says that the Japanese are born and wed in Shinto, die Buddhist, and live in accordance with Confucian ethical principles. In other words, most Japanese do not see the three religions as mutually exclusive or incompatible. Rather, they regard them as mutually reinforcing and relevant in separate aspects and stages of their lives. For this reason, it is impossible—and meaningless, to have an accurate count of Shinto believers in Japan or worldwide. We therefore do not provide a map showing global distribution of Shinto adherents in this chapter. We simply invite you to get acquainted with the beliefs, history, and ritual practices of this Shinto tradition as it intersects with the Confucian and Buddhist traditions.

TIMELINE
Shinto

10,000–300 BCE*	Jomon period.
300 BCE–300 CE*	Yayoi period.
300–500 CE*	Kofun period.
538*	Introduction of Buddhism and Confucianism, also Daoism, to Japan.
604	Prince Shotoku promulgates "Seventeen Articles Constitution."
712	*Kojiki* (Record of Ancient Matters) completed.
720	*Nihon-shoki* or *Nihongi* (Chronicles of Japan) completed.
794	Heiankyo (present-day Kyoto) becomes the capital until 1868.
1185	Beginning of samurai rule in Japan.
1339	Kitabatake Chikafusa publishes the *Jinno shotoki*.
From 1750s*	Rise of *Kokugaku* (National Learning, Neo-Shinto).
From 1780s*	Birth of founders of New Religions.
1868	Meiji Restoration begins; creation of State Shinto.
1937	Beginning of Pacific War, fought in the name of Emperor Hirohito.
1945	Japan surrenders to Allies; State Shinto ended.
1946	Emperor Hirohito renounces his divinity. Shinto is categorized as one of several religions in Japan, receiving no special government support.

Note: Asterisks indicate contested or approximate dates.

9.1 The Teachings of Shinto

The term **Shinto** is a relatively late but elegant reference to the longest existing religious tradition in Japan. "Shin" is the Japanized pronunciation of the Chinese word *shen*, which refers to gods and deities (see Chapter 8). "To," alternatively "do," is the Japanese pronunciation of the Chinese word *Dao*, which suggests the "way." Hence, Shinto literally means "the way of the gods." The term *Shinto* did not come into existence until the Japanese used it to distinguish their preexisting religion from

Buddhism, which, when first introduced into the country, was known as *Butsudo*, "the way of the Buddha." In more colloquial form, Shinto is known as kami-no-michi, "the way of the **kami**," as Shinto is essentially a ritual tradition that focuses on the existence and veneration of kami, a broad term that suggests a whole range of meanings that will be discussed later in this chapter.

To begin with, Shinto has no precise or even approximate beginning date, no identifiable founder, and does not have a sacred book similar to the Bible or the Qu'ran. Rather, it is based on a set of highly revered texts, dating back to the eighth and ninth centuries CE. The **Kojiki** (*Record of Ancient Matters*, completed in 712 CE) and the **Nihon shoki** (alternatively known as *Nihongi, Chronicles of [the Land Where] the Sun Originates*, compiled in 720 CE) are the two foundational texts for our understanding of ancient Shinto; but they are not regularly read as creedal authorities of the religion by either priests or practitioners. They do, however, represent the broad outlines of kami belief and worship at the time of their compilation. The following narrative is based primarily on the *Kojiki*.

Creation Myth in the *Kojiki*

The *Kojiki* begins with several generations of invisible divinities at the beginning of time, all of whom have titles that end with the word *kami*, until the primordial pair, **Izanagi** and his wife **Izanami**, appears. The couple is credited with bringing the world out of its original chaos. Standing on the Heavenly Floating Bridge, they lower a jeweled spear to stir the ocean below. When they lift up the spear, the brine dripping down from its tip forms an island—a thinly veiled reference to a sex act that results in conception and birth. In like manner, "the grand eight islands" of the Japanese archipelago are created. This figurative sexual union of the divine couple has brought forth the sacred Japanese islands as well as the various nature deities that inhabit them.

Izanami is burned to death while giving birth to her last child, the fire god. Izanagi follows his wife to Yomi, the realm of the dead, where, upon seeing her putrefied and decomposing body, he is horrified and makes a hasty retreat. After his return to the world of the living, Izanagi washes himself in a stream—the first act of purification on which later Shinto cleansing rituals are based. From his eyes are born the sun goddess **Amaterasu** (The Kami Who Shines in the Sky) and the lunar god Tsukiyomi. From Izanagi's nose comes the violent and ill-tempered storm god Susa-no-o.

When the *Kojiki* continues, the focus shifts to the relationship between Amaterasu and her brother Susa-no-o. Petulant and mischievous, Susa-no-o gives much grief to his sister. He ravages her heavenly domain, destroys her rice fields, and desecrates her house. Annoyed and frightened, Amaterasu retreats into a cave, thereby plunging the world into darkness. The other deities try to lure her back out with all sorts of tricks, but to no avail, until a goddess by the name of Ame-no-Uzume performs a lewd dance that causes so much raucous laughter among the gods that the curious Amaterasu is finally enticed to emerge from her hiding. (This is an ingenious Shinto attempt to explain solar eclipse.) Susa-no-o is forced to apologize to his sister and is banished to Izumo, a region facing the Japan Sea (alternatively referred to as the East Sea) on the other side of the main island from Ise, the future home of Amaterasu's grand shrine. Having battled and subdued a huge serpent in Izumo, Susano-o settles down and locates a sword, which he presents to Amaterasu as a token of his apology and goodwill. The sword will later become one of the "three imperial regalia" Amaterasu bestows on her descendants who will occupy the Japanese throne.

The final cycle of the narrative in the *Kojiki* focuses on the successors of Susano-o and the descendants of Amaterasu. Ninigi, grandson of Amaterasu, is instructed by her to rule all of Japan. But his mission is thwarted by Susa-no-o's descendants in Izumo, who refuse to yield to the Amaterasu line until she promises to honor her young brother by building him a grand shrine there. After this initial accommodation between the storm god and the sun goddess groups, the descendants of all the other deities fall in line, and Ninigi's own grandson, the Emperor Jimmu, becomes the first human ruler to claim imperial authority over all of Japan. He is provided with the three imperial regalia of a sword, a mirror, and a crescent-moon-shaped jewel as symbols of his power, which he exercised in the Yamato region near present-day Nara. According to tradition, this momentous event took place in 660 BCE, and the imperial line has supposedly continued uninterrupted to the present day.

From the *Kojiki* story just outlined, major themes of Shinto belief can be identified: the divine origin of Japan, the centrality of fertility and purification, the prominence of the feminine, the absence of ethical teachings and a corresponding lack of absolute good or radical evil, and, finally, a profound intertwining of divinity with imperial power.

Japan as a Divine Creation
The core belief of Shinto centers on the kami and Japan's unique relationship with them. Representative of the Shinto notion of the sacred or the holy, kami are mysterious and tremendous powers in nature and in the human world. They pervade the natural world. Illustrious objects in the sky such as the sun and the moon, majestic mountains such as Fuji, serene waterfalls such as the Nachi, and strange-shaped rocks are all kami. In the human world, clan ancestors, rulers, and people with extraordinary accomplishments are revered as kami as well. Most kami are believed to be the source of blessing and protection; hence, worship of them is understood either as thanksgiving or as pleading for more divine gifts. But some kami are ill-tempered and even ill-intentioned, so worship of them is a necessary and prudent act for preventing

The Meoto-iwa (Wedded Rocks) in Mie Prefecture is an iconic landmark in Japan that symbolizes the union between Izanagi and Izanami.

The Nachi Waterfalls in Kumano, Japan. Like Mount Fuji, the Nachi Falls is an iconic Shinto symbol long revered in Japan. Also considered a kami, it is a popular site for Shinto pilgrims who appreciate not only its purifying power but also its scenic beauty.

disaster. According to this Shinto creation myth, then, Japan is the land of kami, created and populated by them. Nature, with its awesome power and captivating beauty, is the very expression of divine presence. Human beings, who can trace their origins back to the same divine forces, therefore have the duty to respond in celebration and adoration to the gifts and blessings of the kami.

Fertility, Fear of Pollution, and Purification

Shinto, from its earliest beginning down to the present day, is centrally concerned with fertility. In the *Kojiki* cosmogonic (explanation of how the cosmos came about) myth, the main function of the primeval pair of kami is to "fertilize" the land and to procreate the other gods. This procreative power of the original divine couple continues even after the death of Izanami, when Izanagi, on his own, manages to bring forth more deities through ritual washing. At the same time, this mythic story highlights the Shinto fear of contamination and defilement, as well as its emphasis on purification. Despite the love that he has for his wife, Izanagi is so horrified and repulsed by Izanami's decomposing form after her death that he abandons her in the netherworld and hurries back to the world of the living. Death, disease, and blood are seen as polluting; persons connected to them are considered spiritually impure and must be ritually purified before they can approach the kami. The arrangement of the typical Shinto shrine and the main ritual responsibility of the Shinto priests illustrate well this vital aspect of Shinto belief, as you shall see later in this chapter.

The Feminine in Shinto

It is highly noteworthy that in the Shinto myth, the sun, the most illustrious object in the sky, is portrayed as female, despite the later patriarchal (male-dominated) nature of Japanese society. It is equally significant that the sun goddess Amaterasu is also the ancestress of the Japanese royal family and that, at least up through the tenth century CE, some of the imperial rulers were women. Also prominent in early Shinto is the role of the shamanic figure, often a female. The ecstatic dance of the goddess Ame-no-Uzume to lure Amaterasu out of hiding, thereby saving the world from perpetual darkness caused by solar eclipse, is indicative of the power of the female shamanic dancer. In addition, both the *Kojiki* and the *Nihongi* mention the mother of Emperor Jimmu, the first human ruler of Japan, whose name is Tamayori-hime. This name suggests her role as a female shaman, as it literally means "a princess (*hime*) in whom dwells (*yori*) the spirit (*tama*) of the kami."

The high prestige of female shamans in ancient Japan is further attested by the story of Empress Jingu, also recorded in the *Nihongi*. Jingu is a capable shamanic diviner for her husband, Emperor Chuai, after whose death she personally leads an armada to invade Korea because of the oracle of assured victory she receives from the gods. It is the extension of Japanese political control over Korea that paves the way for the powerful reign of her son, Emperor Ojin. Together with him and her husband, Jingu would be worshiped as the kami Hachiman, the god of war and protector of all warriors. (The issue of women in Shinto will be further addressed later in this chapter.)

Ethics, Good, and Evil

Conspicuously absent in early Shinto belief is any specific reference to ethics and moral code. Although much emphasis is placed on fertility and purity, *Kojiki*'s cosmogonic story does not address the issue of morality at all. The fire god, though causing the death of his mother Izanami, is not depicted as a villain. Izanagi, though abandoning his wife in the eternally dark and terrifying underworld, is not portrayed as a heartless spouse. Susa-no-o, though causing much distress to his sister Amaterasu with his destructive and willful behavior, is not stigmatized as an evil culprit. Likewise, the explicitly lewd behavior of the kami in drawing Amaterasu out of her hiding is not described as immoral. In other words, the early Shinto account of creation and the relationship between the gods places no emphasis on proper ethical conduct. There is no supreme god giving moral instructions and laws. Nor is there any hint of a cosmic struggle between good and evil. Whether in the primeval divine realm of the gods, in the natural world, or within the human community that comes into being afterward, Shinto beliefs make no reference to a radical evil entity bent on subverting the will and handiwork of a benevolent creator god. Divine and human actions are judged only as fertile or infertile, pure or impure, desirable or undesirable. Wayward behavior can be remedied, and impurities can be removed. What are most offensive to the gods are not sin and guilt, but pollution and defilement.

This notable absence of ethical concerns in early Shinto myth by no means suggests that the Japanese are not governed by moral principles in their behavior. What it does mean is that Japanese ethics came largely from non-Shinto sources, primarily Buddhism and Confucianism. The introduction of these two alien traditions in the history of Shinto will be discussed later in this chapter.

Shinto and Imperial Authority

Shinto's tie to the imperial state and the emperor is a crucial aspect of this tradition. Early Shinto texts clearly attempt to establish the divine origin of the imperial family and the august nature of the emperor. As descendant of the sun goddess Amaterasu, the Japanese ruler (both male and, occasionally, female—at least up to the tenth century CE)

The legendary Empress Jingu, center, leading a military campaign. Japanese silk painting, Edo period.

traditionally wielded both political and religious power. As a matter of fact, government affairs and government in general were originally referred to as *matsurigoto*, "matters relating to rites, rituals, and festivals." There was no concept of the separation between religion and politics, and the relation between Shinto and state, or kami and the Japanese throne, would become a major issue, as we examine State Shinto later in this chapter.

9.2 The History of Shinto

The history of the Shinto tradition can be divided roughly into three periods: ancient, medieval, and modern. The ancient period lasted from prehistoric times to the unification of the country by the Yamato leaders (purportedly the descendants of the sun goddess Amaterasu) sometime prior to the sixth century CE. The medieval period spanned the sixth to the thirteenth centuries when Shinto undertook a process of interaction and accommodation with the two alien traditions of Confucianism and Buddhism. Finally, the modern period witnessed Shinto's reassertion of its uniqueness and relevance to the Japanese nation, the elevation of Shinto as a state cult, and its adjustment to a pluralistic religious landscape after the conclusion of World War II.

Ancient Shinto

Shinto probably began with nature worship and clan identities going back to prehistoric times. There was no name or label attached to a growing set of attitudes and practices that focused on the potency of impressive objects in nature and leaders within clan groups. Generically known as "kami," these objects and personages were revered, and their supposed powers were recognized. In time, a loosely knit set of beliefs developed to define the relationship between humans and nature, as well as among humans. It came to be known as the "way of the kami," whose major tenets have been discussed earlier in this chapter.

Medieval Shinto

By the time the *Kojiki* and *Nihongi* had been compiled, the broad outlines of ancient Shinto belief had been formed, and the second (medieval) stage of its development had begun. This stage was marked by the new religious and political challenge that came from the continental culture of China by way of Korea. In the year 538 CE, Confucianism and Buddhism were formally introduced into Japan by the Yamato leaders, who had consolidated their power over all the other rival clans. This was an accomplishment confirmed by the mythological accounts that describe the submission of the various kami (who were believed to be the founding ancestors of these clans) to Amaterasu, the ancestress of the Yamato rulers.

Confucianism and Buddhism gave a great jolt to this "way of the kami," addressing issues it had ignored or had no interest in. Confucianism (see Chapter 8) provided an ethical framework for state, society, and family, and Buddhism (see Chapter 5) addressed the important issues of suffering and death. The clearest evidence of the influence of the two alien traditions can be seen in the "Seventeen Articles Constitution" promulgated in 604 CE by Prince Shotoku, de facto ruler of the Yamato court at the time. More a vision statement than a constitution in the modern sense, the document clearly acknowledges the strengths of Confucianism and Buddhism in giving guidance to harmonious living and purpose in life. Article One declares the primacy of Confucian morality and harmony as the operating principles of both government and society, while Article Two professes adherence to the Buddhist Three Treasures: the Buddha, his teachings, and the community of monks he created.

In the face of strong challenge from such potent rivals, Shinto reacted with accommodation and adaptation. With no clear inherent ethical orientation (as noted earlier), Shinto embraced Confucian moral principles with little resistance. With respect to Buddhism, the Shinto reaction was more complicated. Initially, some of the elites within the Yamato court rejected the Buddha as an alien challenger to the prevailing religious system of which they were the power holders. In time, however, when Buddhism began its successful conversion of the imperial court during the Nara period (710–784 CE), Shinto kami became guardians and protectors of the Buddha and his various manifestations. Sometime later, with the table turned, Buddhas and bodhisattvas became saviors of the kami. It was common for Buddhist scriptures to be recited before the sanctuaries of the kami, and for Buddhist monks to be put in charge of Shinto shrines. At the end, though, Shinto and Buddhism became nearly merged, when Shinto kami were worshiped as Buddhas or bodhisattvas, and the alien Buddhist deities were in return regarded as Japanese kami. Using the Todaiji temple in Nara as an example, the Vairocana Buddha housed there is known as Dainichi Nyorai, the "Great Sun Tathagata [Buddha]," reflecting a conscious effort to conflate him with Amaterasu the sun goddess. By the Heian period (794–1191 CE), Shinto and Buddhism had become quite accommodating with each other.

One interesting form of this Shinto-Buddhist merger at the folk level was the emergence of a lay Buddhist and occult Shinto group known as Shugendo ("The Way of Cultivating Magical Power"). To this day, practitioners of this faith usually undergo austere training in the mountains to acquire mysterious powers of healing, divination, and exorcism. Shugendo practitioners are ascetics with no formal affiliation with either established Shinto or Buddhism but are revered as shamanic healers and exorcists, as well as guides for pilgrims making their way to remote sacred sites.

The convergence of Shinto, Buddhism, and Confucianism in Japan can be discerned in the samurai ("sword-wielding warriors") code of conduct that began in medieval Japan. Known formally as Bushido ("way of the warrior"), this

The Dainichi, or "Great Sun," Tathagata [Buddha] at Todaiji temple in Nara, Japan.

samurai ethic emphasizes purity of the heart and soul, contempt for pain and death, and undying loyalty to the emperor himself. As mentioned earlier, the Shinto deity Hachiman is worshiped as the principal god for the warriors and the divine protector of Japan and the imperial house. The samurai stress on spiritual purity and its support of the imperial claim of divine origin are evidence of Shinto influence. Equally present in the Bushido is the Buddhist teaching on the acceptance of pain and suffering, as well as the wish for a better rebirth.

The Modern Period

The modern period of Shinto history began with its attempt to recover its pristine past and its claim of superiority over the non-native traditions. Stirrings of this sentiment can be detected after the unsuccessful Mongol invasions of Japan in 1274 and 1281. The near disasters aroused in the Japanese a strong sense of national consciousness, resulting in a reinvigorated subscription to their native beliefs. Sentiments showing strong advocacy of Japan's special position and the emperors' sacred nature based on Shinto beliefs were expressed by nationalists and royalists from the fourteenth century on. In a work entitled *Jinno shotoki* (*Direct Succession of Gods and Sovereigns*), published in 1339 by Kitabatake Chikafusa (1293–1354), the superiority of Japan and the divine status of the emperors were forcefully asserted: "Great Japan is the divine land (*shinkoku*). The heavenly progenitor founded it, and the sun goddess bequeathed it to her descendants to rule eternally. Only in our country is this true; there are no similar examples in other countries."

With the rise of the *Kokugaku* (National Learning) movement in the eighteenth century, a call was made for Japan to return to the original beliefs and practices of ancient times before the introduction of "inferior" alien traditions such as Buddhism and Confucianism had contaminated Japanese culture. These concepts were advanced in the writings of Motoori Norinaga (1730–1801) and Hirata Atsutane (1776–1843).

> Our country's Imperial Line, which casts its light over this world, represents the descendants of the Sky-Shining Goddess [Amaterasu]. And in accordance with that Goddess' mandate of reigning "forever and ever, coeval with Heaven and Earth," the Imperial Line is destined to rule the nation for eons until the end of time and as long as the universe exists. That is the very basis of our Way. That our history has not deviated from the instructions of the divine mandate bears testimony to the infallibility of our ancient tradition. It can also be seen why foreign countries cannot match ours and what is meant by the special dispensation of our country.[1]
>
> —*Motoori Norinaga*

> [A]s a special mark of favor from the heavenly gods, they gave birth to our country, and thus there is so immense a difference between Japan and all the other countries of the world as to defy comparison. Ours is a splendid

and blessed country, the Land of the Gods beyond any doubt, and we, down to the most humble man and woman, are the descendants of the gods.... Japanese differ completely from and are superior to the peoples of China, India ... and all other countries of the world, and for us to have called our country the Land of the Gods was not mere vanity.... This is a matter of universal belief and is quite beyond dispute.[2]

—Hirata Atsutane

Meanwhile, with redoubled effort, the priests of the Grand Shrines at Ise actively promoted pilgrimage there by groups from all over Japan. This helped create a sense of national unity, binding all Japanese together under one common Shinto faith.

Radical Nationalism and Imperialism

These efforts became a prime motivating force that eventually brought down the last feudal military government and ushered in a restoration of imperial rule in 1868. With the help of Shinto nationalism and deep respect for the imperial line, the fifteen-year-old Meiji emperor emerged from the shadow of centuries of domination of the royal family by military commanders to reclaim his divine right to rule. In 1870, the Meiji government proclaimed that "the way of the kami" would be the guiding principle of the nation. Reversing the previous Tokugawa military regime's practice of requiring all households to register in Buddhist temples, the new government mandated every household to enroll in the shrine of the local kami. The newly promulgated Rescript on Education required all Japanese to attend shrine gatherings and rituals, as well as bows to the emperor's portrait. The government also encouraged Shinto funeral rites in a deliberate effort to deprive Buddhism of its monopoly in conducting funeral services. Indeed, Buddhism was forcefully separated from Shinto, and Buddhist monks who had been affiliated with Shinto shrines were ordered to return to secular life.

But it was the Meiji government's promotion of the emperor cult that constituted the core of State Shinto. The emperor was venerated as a "living kami"—a god in flesh and blood. During the Meiji reign, a special shrine was built in Tokyo (formerly known as Edo), the seat of power of the just-toppled military regime, now the new capital. The shrine, named Yasukuni Jinja ("Shrine for the Pacification of the Nation"), was dedicated to those who had sacrificed their lives for the royalist cause in toppling the last feudal regime and the restoration of imperial authority in 1868. All of them had been elevated to kami status, as would others who were subsequently enshrined there after each of Japan's foreign wars in the twentieth century, including the Russo-Japanese War of 1904–1905 and World War II. Because of its close association with State Shinto and the emperor cult, both of which have been blamed for Japan's imperialistic expansion in Asia (the colonization of Taiwan and Korea in 1895 and 1910, respectively; the occupation of Manchuria in the 1930s; and the outright invasion of China and Southeast Asia during the Pacific Wars of 1937–1945), the Yasukuni Shrine has become a controversial symbol. That it also houses the remains of some of the most notorious wartime government leaders and commanders makes matters even more sensitive. Japan's neighbors (China and Korea, in particular), who were victims of Japan's imperialistic expansion, invariably file official complaints whenever prominent Japanese political figures (such as the prime minister) pay formal visits to the Yasukuni Shrine.

But the best illustration of the emperor cult in State Shinto was the building of the Meiji Shrine that began in 1915 and was completed in 1920. Constructed to enshrine the kami spirits of the late Meiji emperor and his wife, the shrine was a tremendous undertaking funded by the government. Located in the heart of Tokyo, the Meiji Shrine covers close to 200 acres of prime real estate, surrounded by elaborate gardens and wooded areas. It remains to this day a popular site for New Year's celebrations and other festivals.

State Shinto has also been blamed for the fanatical nationalism among many Japanese, particularly among the rank and file of the military, during World War II. Japanese soldiers ravaged much of Asia in the name of their imperial ruler, Emperor Hirohito (r. 1926–1989). They considered their foreign aggression a divine mission, to be carried out with brutality and wanton cruelty. Even when Japanese defeat appeared inevitable by the early 1940s, the military commanders sent suicide pilots to plunge their planes into Allied battleships in a desperate attempt to reverse the fortune of the war. Calling the pilots kamikaze ("divine storm"), they tried to evoke the memory of the Japanese defeat of the invading Mongol troops in 1274 and 1281 when allegedly the kami sent a storm (*kaze*) to destroy the Mongol navy, thereby protecting the nation. State Shinto's hold on Japan during those war years was gripping and overwhelming.

Japanese lawmakers from several political parties visit the Yasukuni Shrine in April 2017.

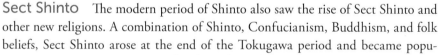

Sect Shinto

The modern period of Shinto also saw the rise of Sect Shinto and other new religions. A combination of Shinto, Confucianism, Buddhism, and folk beliefs, Sect Shinto arose at the end of the Tokugawa period and became popular throughout the Meiji period. Initially thirteen such sects had been given official recognition, but after the end of World War II, the number was increased to seventy-five. Grouped with other eclectic religious organizations that arose in the 1920s and 1930s under the general category of "New Religions," they include such influential sects as Tenrikyo ("Teaching of Heavenly Principles"), Konkokyo ("Teaching of Golden Light"), and Kurozumikyo ("Teaching of the founder, Kurozumi Munetada" [1780–1850]).

Although different in doctrine and practice, these religious groups share a number of common features. Their founders were charismatic individuals steeped in the shamanic tradition of Shinto,

the esoteric teachings of Buddhism, and a whole host of other folk beliefs. A noticeable number of them were women. Mostly of farming origin, they appealed to the anxiety and unease experienced by the lower classes during a time of rapid social change and political upheaval. Explaining that calamity and disaster emanate from disturbances in people's mind and spirit, they offered their shamanic powers to bring peace, harmony, health, and prosperity to their followers. The emphasis on worldly benefits was often accompanied by the promise of the impending arrival of a new age and a new world. To impress the faithful and the larger society around them, they have built imposing headquarters and even whole cities of great beauty. Their teachings generally stress clean living, hard work, moral conduct, familial cohesion, and social solidarity. The sectarian nature of these groups has made their believers more fervent than members of the established traditions of Shinto and Buddhism.

After Japan's surrender to the Allied Forces in 1945, the new Japanese Constitution maintains a strict separation between religion and state. Shinto is no longer the state religion, nor is the emperor any longer a kami. Today, the vast majority of Japan's Shinto shrines are members of a voluntary organization named the Association of Shinto Shrines (Jinja Honcho) with no direct government sponsorship. The Grand Shrines at Ise, however, remain the ancestral shrine of the imperial family. Some Japanese blame Shinto for its support of the imperial cult that gave rise to Japan's nationalistic militarism which resulted in the country's defeat and devastation in 1945. Nevertheless, the imperial family continues to enjoy great affection from the majority of the Japanese people. Public reference to members of the emperor's family, even children, has to be couched in honorific language, and great throngs of people visit the grounds of the Imperial Palace on New Year's Day to greet the imperial family.

As the opening vignette involving the young man Satoshi Tanaka illustrates, most Japanese still live their lives very much shaped by Shinto beliefs and practices. Shinto continues to give the Japanese people their sense of identity and aesthetics, as well as providing venues for communal activities and celebrations.

9.3 Shinto as a Way of Life: Rituals and Observances

Shinto is a tradition that puts more emphasis on ritual practices than doctrinal beliefs. Some scholars even argue that Shinto beliefs are "more acted out than thought out." Often, many Japanese perform some of the Shinto rituals and daily habits without full knowledge or consciousness of their doctrinal and theoretical underpinnings. It is certainly the rituals, both public and private, that enable Shinto practitioners to directly experience the presence of the divine kami and to recognize their bond with them, as well as with one another. The young shrine carrier Satoshi Tanaka, whom you met at the beginning of this chapter, is representative of this Shinto mindset. Although he does not consider himself a deeply religious man, he finds fun and meaning in his participation in the Sanja Festival. Instead of reciting dogma and creed, Shinto practitioners participate in *matsuri* processions, visit shrines, and perform purification rituals. Let us examine how the Shinto beliefs discussed earlier in this chapter are lived and acted out in the daily lives, as well as the ceremonial occasions, of its practitioners.

Fertility Rites

As you may recall, a major emphasis of Shinto is fertility, especially human reproductivity. In villages and towns across Japan, one can find phallic and vaginal symbols being paraded around much in the same way as the *mikoshi* on *matsuri* days are, with no embarrassment or modesty. To this day the Shinto ritual calendar gives prominence to ceremonies celebrating Earth's fertility and crop productivity. In early spring, the *kinensai* ("festival for praying for good harvest") is observed when the fertility-dispensing kami are believed to be physically present in their shrines. Processions of worshipers greet these deities, carry them into the fields in portable shrines, and dance to celebrate their divine powers while rice seedlings are being planted or transplanted. In the fall, the *niiname matsuri* ("harvest festival"), is observed, when the kami are honored and thanked with joyous and boisterous celebrations.

The harvest festival is also closely linked with the traditional Shinto belief in the divine nature of the Japanese rulers. Until 1945, the Japanese emperor, the *tenno* ("august heavenly ruler"), had both religious and political responsibilities, as he was regarded as a direct descendant of the sun goddess Amaterasu and was thereby entrusted to rule over the land. One such religious responsibility was the guarantee of fertility of the soil and bountiful harvest. This is consummated ritually each fall at the *niiname* festival, presided over by the emperor as high priest. The most spectacular expression of this divine power of the Japanese ruler is the *daijosai* ("the great food festival"), which is performed by a new emperor the year after his ascension to the throne. In an elaborate and ancient ritual, rice and rice wine (sake) from specially cultivated fields are presented by the new ruler to the deities in the middle of the night, a gesture that consecrates the emperor's religious power and political legitimacy. This rite, still performed as the climax of a royal accession in modern Japan, marks the distinctive religious foundation of the Japanese imperial institution, the disavowal of his own divinity by Emperor Hirohito at the end of World War II notwithstanding.

Rites Performed at the Shrine

The Shinto ritual event at the shrine generally involves a four-step sequence of purification, presentation, petition, and participation. The first three steps are performed by priests, and the last one involves the entire "congregation" in attendance. The rationale for the sequence is first to make the participants (both clergy and laity) physically and spiritually clean before their encounter with the kami. The second step is to present food offerings to the kami to show respect and good will and to pave the way for the third act of petitioning. This involves formally pleading with the kami, through beautiful and correct words intoned with reverence and awe by the chief priest, for the concrete benefits being sought. Finally, the last sequence of the ritual is to have the entire worshiping audience fully participate in the ceremony through the watching of performances, the sharing of ritual drinks, and the gift of shrine souvenirs.

Purification   The Japanese word for the purification ritual performed by the Shinto priest is **harae**, the purpose of which is to please and appease the kami. The ceremony is deemed necessary to prepare the faithful for their encounter with the deity or to remove the defilement from the mundane world. All sorts of occasions call for the performance of *harae*, many of which take place at the shrine; but sometimes the priest may go to the place where it is needed. It is common to call in the Shinto priest to perform the *harae* before moving into a new home, occupying a new office building, opening a new highway, driving a new car, or even purchasing a new cell phone. The priest, dressed in sacramental vestments, waves an *onusa* (the wand of stripped paper or an evergreen branch) over the person(s) or the object(s) to be purified, first on the left, then the right, and finally back to the left. Ritual bathing is another form of purification. In a practice known as **misogi**, ardent Shinto practitioners purify themselves by standing under a waterfall or immersing themselves in ocean water. Shrine visitors rinse their mouths and wash their hands at a fountain before approaching the shrines themselves.

Salt also plays an important role in the *harae*. Its snow-like appearance symbolizes purity, and its potency as a purifying agent is widely accepted in Japan. The Shinto priest often sprinkles salt over the place, the people, or the object to be purified. Sumo wrestling, a characteristic Japanese spectator sport, has strong Shinto connections. Each match begins with the wrestlers throwing salt into the ring to purify themselves and their opponents. This belief in salt as spiritual purifier also makes its way into many aspects of Japanese life. After attending a funeral service, people sprinkle salt in the doorway before reentering their homes so as not to carry the defilement of death inside. Shop owners also put small mounds of salt on either side of their storefronts to ward off evil spirits.

Presentation, Petition, and Participation   The presentation component involves the offering of rice, fish, fruit, rice wine, water, and salt to the kami. There is absolutely no blood sacrifice in the offerings, as blood is considered repulsive and polluting in Shinto. The petition takes the form of the priest reverently reciting the **norito** (prayers or "words spoken to the kami"), which is usually written in advance in very elegant and flowery language and read aloud with a rhythmical cadence, ending with a vowel that slides down an octave in pitch with the volume tapering off

Entry of the bridal procession at a Shinto wedding, walking through the shrine gate, led by *mikos*. Yasaka Shrine, Maruyama Park, Kyoto, Japan.

slowly. The worshipers' participation in the ritual event includes receiving purification by the priest, watching the dance of the **miko** (shrine maidens), listening to the performance of the musicians, and, when over, taking small sips of rice wine called *omiki*, as well as bringing home leafy sprigs of the native Japanese *sakaki* tree to complete their encounter with the divine. All of these activities are designed to create bonding between the worshipers and their kami, as well as among themselves.

The Shrine

The Shinto shrine is generally the location where Shinto rituals are carried out. It is referred to as the **jinja**, the "dwelling place of the kami." It is here that the kami can be approached and worshiped. In early Shinto and in some remote, isolated sacred locations today, a kami dwelling can be a tree, a waterfall, or an extraordinarily shaped rock, which local people believe to be a source of spiritual power. These kami dwellings are locations with awe-inspiring mystery and great natural beauty. They are often marked with nothing more than a pile of rocks, or sometimes an ornamental rope to suggest the approach to sacred space. Most modern-day *jinja*, however, are enclosed areas with a few simple structures. Entry into them requires a purified body and, ideally, a purified mind, as godliness in Shinto is synonymous with cleanliness. Thus, the shrine is a holy space, of which the visitor is immediately reminded by two guardian stone lions, one on each side of the entry approach. (In the case of the shrines of the grain goddess Inari, the stone lions are replaced by foxes, which are believed to be her preferred messengers.) The entry path then passes under the distinctive Shinto crossbar gateway, known as the **torii**, whose literal meaning is "bird dwelling," probably reflecting the earliest function of it as a roost for sacred birds.

In its most characteristic form, the torii of today is painted red and consists of two upright posts joined by one or two crossbeams, with the upper crossbeam either straight or gently curved in the middle toward the ground. This use of red paint and the curved line in the upper crossbeam indicates both Chinese and Buddhist influence and would not have been found in the early days of Shinto. The torii is not meant merely to be a decorative gateway. It is a symbolic protective device that guards the shrine against all impurities and contaminants. It is a gateway that leads one into a sacred space from the profane world outside. Sometimes visitors have to pass under multiple torii, and on occasion an extended series of them are set so close together that they form a veritable tunnel. (See the image of the Fushimi Inari Grand Shrine in Kyoto in this section.)

Once inside the shrine grounds, all visitors perform a simple purification ritual by

A family's new car receives a blessing from a Shinto priest at Minatogawa Shrine in Kobe, Japan.

approaching a basin or trough of purified water called ***temizuya*** (usually a natural stone basin filled with clear water from the mouth of a sculpted dragon) and, using a bamboo dipper, taking a ladleful of water to rinse their mouth and hands. They are now ready for communion with the kami. The *jinja* generally has two buildings—the *haiden* and the *honden*. The *haiden*, the "worship hall," is the more public of the two. As its name implies, it is where the faithful can approach and worship the kami. One very noticeable feature of the *haiden* is the ***shimenawa***, a huge rope made of rice straw that marks the boundaries of the building that has been purified or an area in which the kami might be present. Strips of paper called *shide* are hung from the rope.

Worshipers stand in front of the building, deposit money offerings (paper bills or coins) into a wooden chest, clap their hands twice, and ring a suspended bell to attract the attention of the kami. Then they bow their heads and, with hands clasped and sometimes eyes closed, silently utter their prayer of requests or thanksgiving. The *haiden* is also the place where the priests conduct their ceremonies on specific occasions on behalf of the community or the state but sometimes also on purely private matters for individuals or small groups.

In the courtyard facing the *haiden*, visitors display their interaction with the kami through two specific objects: the ***ema***, wooden tablets on which are written their pleadings with the kami for good marriage, safe childbirth, lucrative investment, even successful university entrance examinations; and the ***omikuji***, paper fortunes wrapped around tree branches as a form of divination to gauge the future outcome of an undertaking.

Beyond the *haiden* and more hidden from public view is the *honden* ("main sanctuary"), the place where the kami is believed to reside. It is generally raised higher than any other structure on the premises and has steep access stairs at the front. Only priests can enter this building, for it is regarded as the shelter of the ***shintai***, the "body of the deity" that is the very physical embodiment of the kami.

The Fushimi Inari Taisha Shrine in Kyoto, Japan, is dedicated to the god of rice and sake. Here, a tunnel of torii arches is guarded by a pair of foxes.

This *shintai* is the kernel of sacredness, the symbolic representation of the kami honored at the shrine. In and of itself the *shintai* has little intrinsic value. It may be a stone, a scroll, a mirror, a sword, or a small statue. Yet it is regarded with such awe and reverence that even the priests are prohibited from gazing upon it or handling it except on special occasions.

The Inner Shrine of the Grand Shrines at Ise, the main sanctuary of the sun goddess Amaterasu and the official shrine of the imperial family, deserves special mention in connection with this Shinto concern for purity and cleanliness. Though originally built more than thirteen centuries ago, it is completely

Top: The *shimenawa* marks off a sacred space at a Shinto shrine. Bottom: These prayer plaques express the hopes, aspirations, and requests for blessing of the shrine visitors.

torn down and rebuilt every twenty years in an adjacent lot. According to tradition, this practice was inaugurated in 690 CE by Empress Jito for the purpose of regular purification and renewal. The design, however, is meticulously replicated each time. The shrine we see today is supposedly an exact replica of the original one, and it was built in 2013.

Many carpenters for the Grand Shrines at Ise come from families that have been hereditarily entrusted to undertake the task. Only natural cypress wood is used for the main structures, and only hand tools are allowed to work on the wood. There are no metal braces or nails used in construction, and the different parts of the shrine are held together by complex and intricate wooden joints. The cypress wood is carefully selected years in advance of the rebuilding and is paraded through different communities throughout Japan to drum up interest in and support for the shrine rebuilding project. Thus, the Ise Shrine is simultaneously the oldest and the newest, as well as the most famous, shrine in Japan.

A shrine visit is a regular practice of most Japanese, even though many of them do not regard it as an overt or deliberate religious act.

The Family Shrine   In addition to worship at local, regional, and major national shrines, many Japanese also maintain miniature shrines at home for easy and ready access to the kami. Known as *kamidana* ("deity shelf" or family altar), it has many components of actual shrines. The home shrine is usually hung on a wall or placed on a shelf above eye level. The kami worshiped is often the deity of the local shrine or that of the householder's profession. Daily simple prayers are offered, as are fruit, water, and rice.

Religious Observances throughout the Year

Because of the diversity in Japanese religions, the yearly round of customary ritual observances is correspondingly diverse in religious affiliation. Excluding the various local festivals that pay tribute to particular Shinto kami and Buddhist feasts that honor the Buddha and specific bodhisattvas, the following are the most popularly observed annual ritual occasions.

New Year (Oshogatsu)

People prepare for the New Year each January 1 by cleaning their houses thoroughly to get rid of both physical and spiritual dirt. On New Year's Eve near midnight, they visit one of the major Shinto shrines such as the Meiji Shrine in Tokyo or a prominent Buddhist temple such as the Honganji in Kyoto to welcome in the New Year. Beginning on New Year's Day, they visit friends and relatives to offer their greetings and renew their relationship.

The Inner Shrine of Amaterasu at Ise.

The Turn of the Seasons (Setsubun)   This festival is observed, at most Shinto shrines, on February 3, the last day of the winter season. The entire family performs a special purification ritual that involves the throwing of roasted beans from the house into the yard, yelling *Oni wa soto!* (Demons get out!) and, from the yard into the house, calling out *Fuku wa uchi!* (Fortunes come in!). Various fruits and nuts are tossed from the balcony of shrine buildings by priests and local dignitaries for the throngs of worshippers to catch and to bring home.

Doll Festival (Hina Matsuri)   March 3 is devoted to the celebration of girls and daughters in the household. A notable feature of the observance of this special day is the prominent display of tiers of dolls with elaborate costumes that represent the styles of the court ladies of the ancient imperial period. These dolls are expensively made and serve as a reflection of the family's financial standing.

Boys' Day (Tango no Sekku)   This counterpart of the Doll Festival is celebrated on May 5. Dedicated to celebrating the healthy growth of boys, this festival is based on the traditional

An outdoor miniature Shinto shrine in the backyard of a restaurant in Kawagoe, Japan, includes a *hokora* (kami repository), fox statues; torii (gates), and offerings to the kami.

VISUAL GUIDE
Shinto

This image contains three major aspects of Japanese religiosity—the sun, the Shinto torii, and cherry blossoms. The sun is the chief deity responsible for the rise of the Japanese state, the torii (lit. "bird dwelling," hence the bird atop the arch) marks the sacred space of the Shinto shrine ground, and cherry blossoms convey the Japanese sense of fragile beauty and transience.

The iconic woodblock print titled *Great Wave off Kanagawa,* one of the *Thirty-six Views of Mt. Fuji,* by the artist Hokusai, produced in 1832.

The *shimenawa* in front of a Shinto shrine. A giant rope made of rice straw, the *shimenawa* marks off the sacred space within the shrine complex. Worshipers believe that beyond the line resides the spirit of the kami.

A Shinto priest at the Itsukushima Shrine in Miyajima, Japan. The priest acts as a bridge between the worshipers and the kami housed at the shrine. He makes presentation to the deity on behalf of the community, purifies the shrine visitors with prescribed rituals, and presides over community events.

annual court ceremony of warding off evil spirits for samurai boys, and was later embraced by the rest of Japanese society. It also involves the display of figurines of armored fighters and the flying of carp-shaped paper or fabric streamers on a tall pole.

Star Festival (Tanabata) This festival was introduced from China to commemorate the romantic story of two stars, Vega and Altair, personified respectively as a young weaver maiden and her lover the cowherd, who are allowed this one-time-a-year rendezvous in the heavens. Observed on July 7, it is a festival for young lovers and for unmarried girls who want to improve their chances of marriage by honing their skills in weaving, sewing, and embroidery or any arts and crafts requiring manual dexterity.

Ghost Festival (Obon) Though primarily Buddhist in origin, *Obon* has become an integral part of the Japanese ritual calendar. Unlike the other festivals listed here, the Ghost Festival's date each year is not determined by the solar calendar. Instead, it falls on the fourteenth day of the seventh month in the lunar calendar. This is the Japanese version of the *Yulanpen*, a Chinese Buddhist festival. *Bon* is the Japanese pronunciation of the Chinese word *pen* ("bowl of offerings"), and *o* is the honorific prefix. This festival welcomes the ancestral spirits to return home with food and offerings. Families clean the graves of their ancestors and wash the headstones. On the previous evening, people build a small fire outside the gate of their homes to greet the returning spirits. Sometimes Buddhist monks are invited to the house to recite sutras to soothe the souls of the deceased and comfort the living. Over the next two days, people participate in communal folk dances called *bon odori* to please the spirits and to enhance communal solidarity.

Harvest Festival (Niiname-sai) This giving of thanks by the community for the rice harvest occurs on November 23. In modern Japan, it has been renamed

"Labor Thanksgiving Day" and is designated a national holiday. Celebrating the harvest with the people, the Japanese emperor traditionally would taste the newly ripened rice and would offer it to the kami on behalf of his subjects. The festival also links all local shrines to the imperial court, as the emperor is believed to be the representative of the people to thank the kami for providing fertility and bountifulness.

VOICES: An Interview with Kaitlyn Ugoretz

Professor Ugoretz is Lecturer and Associate Editor at the Nanzan Institute for Religion and Culture, Nanzan University, Japan, and is host of the educational YouTube channel "Eat Pray Anime."

Kaitlyn Ugoretz.

How did you develop such a strong interest in Shinto?

I grew up as the daughter of a Presbyterian minister in the 90s. On Sundays we would go to church, and on Saturdays we would watch Saturday morning cartoons, and particularly anime such as Pokemon. So from a very early age I was interested in the Shinto mythology and the folklore that I saw in Japanese popular culture. I remember being particularly struck by seeing the different forest deities in Hayao Miyazaki's film *Princess Mononoke*, as well as all the fun supernatural creatures in *Spirited Away*. Through the lens of media, Japan and Shinto seemed almost magical to me as a child. As a non-Japanese academic, and as an anthropologist, I am fascinated by how this religious tradition that is often defined as indigenous or ethnic actually travels around the world. I am interested in how Shinto practitioners create transnational communities and how they navigate the particularities of their own situation and the fundamentals they see in Shinto.

You have studied Shinto's reach beyond Japan. What accounts for its global appeal and popularity?

In my view, Shinto has always been global, but Shinto practitioners outside of Japan today are attracted to the tradition for various reasons: some see it as a "green" or environmentally friendly religion. Others are impressed by its lack of a fixed dogma or doctrine, making it open to freer interpretations. Still others see it as more welcoming of people of diverse gender expression and sexual orientation. There is an active global LGBTQ+ Shinto community whose members connect with one another through the internet. There are also those who practice Shinto as a spiritual tradition and not as a religion per se. And of course anime, manga, and video games provide a visual and even virtual window into Shinto sites, practices, and mythologies that people outside of Japan don't see otherwise. In short, there are many gateways to Shinto.

One very interesting phenomenon in the spread of Shinto is "anime pilgrimage." Can you comment on that?

As many anime contain prominent Shinto themes, feature Shinto shrines as settings, and *miko* (shrine maidens) as wielders of magical power, locations where the anime takes place have become "meccas" for their fans. They visit to admire the surroundings, take pictures to prove their presence there and to brag to their friends, and write messages on the prayer plaques (ema) to communicate with their favorite anime characters, sometimes treating them as kami. The homes of the anime creators as well as the studios where the anime are produced have also become "power spots" for these self-styled "pilgrims" to organize tours to visit. There is a partnership between the media industry, shrines, and their surrounding communities, and local tourism boards all work together to promote such activities. It is a tide that lifts all boats.

9.4 Shinto as a Way of Life: Engaging with the World

In Japan, formal membership in organized Shinto is small. Most Japanese practice it informally simply through their participation in Japanese culture, in which Shinto's influence is present everywhere. Shinto belief in the ubiquitous presence of the kami, both in nature and in human society, informs Japanese views on nature and the human community. And Shinto's teachings on ethics and the afterlife, borrowed largely from Confucianism and Buddhism, respectively, have been a vital force in Japanese culture and society.

Shinto's continuing influence in Japan can be gauged in an entirely new phenomenon known as "anime pilgrimage," inspired probably by "shrine pilgrimage" or "temple pilgrimage" in the Shinto and Buddhist traditions respectively. In recent decades, due to the popularity of anime, principally among the younger generations (but also among some older folks as well), and both within Japan and across the world, some Shinto shrines have become hot spots for tourism for anime afficionados. The Washinomiya Shrine in Saitama Prefecture outside of Tokyo, for example, has become a mecca for devout fans of the popular anime series *Lucky Star*. The opening scene of the anime features the torii of this shrine, and two of the central characters are portrayed as sisters working as *miko* there. As a result, many loyal fans (mostly male) of the anime make pilgrimages there to take pictures of the spots where many of the actions take place and to offer prayer plaques (*ema*) to their favorite heroines. Likewise, the Taro Shrine in Okayama Prefecture is the setting for the hugely popular science-fiction anime series *Tenchi Muyo!* The central character is a high school student whose grandfather is a priest at the Taro Shrine. The shrine has also become a pilgrimage destination for fans of the anime series. To pique the interest of the pilgrims, the shrine sets up "Tenchi-bako (boxes)" whose doors can only be opened when trivia quizzes about the series are answered correctly. Fans can then leave messages and draw illustrations in the "Tenchi Notebooks" located inside. Two different Kamado Shrines in Kyushu have become favorite sites of worship and sightseeing by fans of the recently wildly popular manga series (and subsequently anime film) *Kimetsu no Yaiba* (Demon Slayer), whose principal protagonist is named Kamado Tanjiro. According to one survey, at least thirty shrines across Japan have become pilgrimage destinations after being featured in anime. Additionally, a "power spot boom" has swept across Japan in recent years. Power spots are believed to be sacred locations considered to possess a strong invisible energy that elevates the consciousness of their visitors to a higher plane. Various popular guidebooks on these sites have been published, and lavish tours have been organized to allow the faithful to travel to these places for spiritual transfusion and personal fulfillment.

Anime and Shinto

Despite its pervasive influence on Japanese thinking and behavior, Shinto is not a proselytizing religion. It makes little attempt to convert, whether inside or outside of Japan. Yet Shinto has attained a global reach, particularly among the young, in recent decades. This penetration of Shinto teachings and symbolism into a worldwide audience has been made possible by the internet and the popularity of Japanese films, video games, manga, and most notably, anime. Hayao Miyazaki's famously successful and critically acclaimed animation films *My Neighbor Totoro*, *Princess Mononoke*, and *Spirited Away*, all featuring the adventures of young characters, especially young girls, highlight the Shinto themes of the magic of the kami spirit world, health of the environment, and childlike purity of the human spirit. A popular PlayStation video game *Okami* ("Great August Spirit" or, a play on words, "Wolf") allows players to wield the powers of the Shinto gods such as Amaterasu and Susa-no-o in their battles with other deities.

But it is in manga and anime that many Shinto themes and beliefs are often expressed. The manga series *Urusei Yatsura* ("Shut up! Bro'") and *Susanoo the Brawler*, respectively, re-create the stories of Amaterasu the sun goddess hiding in the cave and her brother the storm god wreaking havoc. Similarly, the anime *Wanpaku Oji no Orochi taiji* (American title: *The Little Prince and the Eight-headed Dragon*) portrays Susa-no-o's adventures after his expulsion from Amaterasu's heavenly residence.

A significant number of anime in recent years focus on the adventures of teenage heroines who are shrine maidens (*miko*) with supernatural powers who valiantly combat demons and ogres to bring peace to and restore harmony in the world. Their exploits are set in the routines of Shinto shrine activities where they live and work. The following are representative titles that command a huge fan base worldwide: *Asagiri no Miko* (*Shrine Maiden of the Morning Mist*), *Gingitsune* (*Messenger Fox of the Gods*), and *Red Data Girl*. Collectively, they introduce Shinto concepts and practices to a global audience and create a positive and entertaining image for the religion.

It is clear that Shinto has gone beyond the confines of the Japanese archipelago. As discussed previously, the worldwide popularity of anime, manga, and video games, many of which contain overt Shinto themes, has also contributed to the spread of Shinto across the globe.

A woman dresses as Princess San, a character from Hayao Miyazaki's film *Princess Mononoke* that draws on Shinto beliefs and legends, at the 2017 MCM Comic Con in London.

A participant in the annual Sakura Matsuri festival in Washington, DC, dressed as an anime character.

Shinto torii gates, shrine maidens in their red pants, and priests waving their *onusa* to bless new buildings and new cars capture the imagination of many non-Japanese.

Shinto shrines can also be found outside Japan. There were shrines built in Korea and Taiwan when they were colonies of imperial Japan. There are shrines in Hawaii attended by mostly Americans of Japanese descent, and a couple of shrine communities in the continental United States. There are also shrines in Brazil and the Netherlands. It is noteworthy that a few non-Japanese Shinto priests currently serve at various shrines both inside and outside of Japan. At least one ordained non-Japanese priest was head of the Tsubaki Grand Shrine of America (a foreign branch of the main Tsubaki Shrine in Suzuka, Mie Prefecture, which is one of the oldest and most distinguished shrines in Japan). Regrettably it was abruptly closed down in June 2023. Also worth mentioning is that the head priest of the Shinto Shrine of Shusse Inari in America, located in Los Angeles, is female.

Japan's sentimental worship of the iconic Mt. Fuji, the Japanese people's habitual ritual viewing of cherry blossoms in the spring and maple leaves' color-changing in the fall, as well as the very prominent expression of environmentalism and love of nature in Miyazaki Hayao's animated films, are all indicative of Shinto influence. Shinto beliefs and practices have provided much rationale for Japan's environmentalist efforts and ecological programs.

Shinto and Gender Issues

We have pointed out that early Shinto has a strong emphasis on the feminine, its principal deity being the sun goddess Amaterasu. The imperial family, the most important lineage in Shinto Japan, claims an unbroken succession from generation to generation as descendants of Amaterasu. Some scholars maintain that Chinese historical records also confirm this female-dominant feature of the Yamato regime—the likely precursor to the imperial line—in the fourth century CE. They speculate that Empress Jingu's account (touched upon earlier in this chapter) is reminiscent of the story of Himiko in

Photo of a torii framing Mt. Fuji. This is a fitting illustration of the Japanese belief in Mt. Fuji as a kami, and the function of the torii as archway leading the faithful into the sacred ground where the kami is honored.

these Chinese historical records. They describe a female shamanic ruler of a region called Yamatai (suspected to be a variation of Yamato) in the country of Wa (Japan) whose bewitching control over the people is the source of her power. One interpretation of the name *Himiko* is "*miko* of the Sun (*hi*)." Now, **miko** in Shinto refers to unmarried women attendants at shrines who possess shamanic power to communicate with the kami through dance and other ritual performances. Practically all Shinto shrines have *miko* performing a variety of important, though subordinate, functions. Because of their believed access to the kami (or their possession by the kami spirit), they are entrusted to perform the sacred dance of *kagura* ("music of the kami") at festivals and other ritual occasions as an indispensable complement to the prayers and purifying acts of the priests. In addition, they serve as staff in shrine offices, sell amulets and other trinkets at shrine gift shops, and generally interact with the public by providing a feminine touch on behalf of the shrine.

It should also be noted that, though small in number (around 16% of the total number of credentialed Shinto priests according to 2020 Jinja Honcho records) and usually more junior in rank, female priests participate fully in all the Shinto rites performed by their male counterparts, though serving as chief ritualist remains rare. One reason for the junior role played by female priests can be attributed to the patriarchal mindset prevailing within the Shinto establishment. Another reason is menstruation, which disadvantages the female priests, as blood is considered a defilement in Shinto. A menstruating priestess may be deemed unfit to perform the purification rituals for the faithful. Some of them have managed to overcome this concern through various means, such as avoiding certain rituals or certain locations on shrine grounds, putting *sakaki* tree twigs or salt in a sack and wearing it on their sleeves or breast pockets, or taking menstrual leaves. However, it should also be noted that the most supreme religious figure at the Grand Shrine of Ise, the home of the sun goddess Amaterasu, is the *saio*, the priestess who is usually an unmarried member of the imperial family and who is ranked above even the chief priest there.

In the final analysis, whether Shinto can be considered "feminist" may remain a topic for debate. At the very least, however, it asserts a gender "complementarity" reminiscent of the Chinese yin-yang concept of mutual correspondence. Many kami come in husband/wife and sister/brother pairs, such as Izanagi and Izanami, the purported procreators of the Japanese islands. Some medieval *miko* and male ritualists also formed pairs.

Shinto and the Environment

It should be recalled that the core belief of Shinto is the kami, the animistic element that dwells

Prayer plaques offered to anime heroines at a Shinto shrine in Tokyo.

within certain objects in nature and certain people in the human world, which empowers them to be treated with awe and reverence. These kami are believed to be in possession of an overwhelming spiritual energy which inspires a deep sense of mystery, even fear. Kami worship therefore neatly meets the criterion of *mysterium tremendum* and *fascinans* described by Rudolf Otto and discussed in Chapter 1 in this volume. Many impressive objects in nature—trees, mountains, waterfalls—have been regarded as hallowed entities, and the space they occupy has been designated as sacrosanct. That is why many Shinto shrines are located in natural settings and often at sites of great beauty, approached only with pure minds and pure bodies. The Shinto practice of *harae* ("ritual purification") further solidifies the assertion that Shinto is a belief system centrally concerned with pristine cleanliness in nature.

The Enduring Significance of Shinto

In this chapter, we have pointed out that Shinto is the longest surviving religious tradition in Japan. It pervades much of Japanese life and informs much of Japanese behavior. It also provides a sense of identity and unity to the Japanese people. Shinto belief in the ubiquitous presence of the kami, both in nature and in human society, informs the Japanese view on nature and human community. Though originally lacking an ethical code and detailed understanding of the afterlife, Shinto, in conjunction with Confucianism and Buddhism, has been a vital force in Japanese culture and society. Shinto's adjustment to and enrichment of popular culture such as manga and anime have allowed it to cultivate a wider and younger audience worldwide. With the aid of the worldwide web and various online sites, many non-Japanese believers and practitioners of Shinto have formed global communities of the faith. Shinto's aesthetics, gender sensitivities, and nature loving attitudes make it a global religion with relevant answers to contemporary issues.

SEEKING ANSWERS

What Is Ultimate Reality?

According to Shinto, the world is a sanctified place divinely created by the kami. The kami reveal themselves in living and nonliving things, in nature and in the human world. They are responsible for the fertility of the world, and they prefer purity and cleanliness. Humans, some of whom are kami themselves, must pay constant attention to their relationship with the kami, for that is the only way that life can be fulfilled. Because the world is the creation of the kami, humanity is obligated to maintain the world's sanctity by acting as its guardian and caretaker. Shinto practitioners are extremely sentimental about nature and are easily moved by its beauty. Many Japanese literary compositions express this Shinto affirmation of the divine and sanctified nature of the world.

SEEKING ANSWERS (*Continued*)

How Should We Live in This World?

Original Shinto places little emphasis on morality or ethical living. There is no revealed moral code. Instead, it teaches right living primarily as fertile and pure living. The human condition is defined more in terms of purity and defilement. Death, blood, improper food, and improper behaviors are sources of contamination that make humans unfit to interact with the kami. However, these are temporary conditions. Constant attention to maintaining cleanliness and purity will ensure favor from the deities. As a result, Shinto practitioners meticulously perform rituals of purification and sanctification in order to seek good interaction with the kami.

What Is Our Ultimate Purpose?

Unlike several other religions, Shinto does not perceive the human condition as a fallen state or intrinsically tainted by sin. Humans are therefore not evil by nature; thus, there is no need for salvation or transcendence. At the same time, Shinto has no belief in an almighty benevolent God who has made humans in an initial state of perfection. Humans are therefore not good by nature either. Instead, humans are very much a part of nature, striving to live in harmony with it through interaction with its various spiritual manifestations, the kami.

REVIEW QUESTIONS

For Review

1. What is the Shinto version of creation?
2. Why is the concept of kami so central to Shinto beliefs?
3. How does Shinto view death?

For Further Reflection

1. If Shinto does not address ethics in its original outlook, what is the source of morality for the Japanese?

2. Discuss the role of women in Shinto.
3. What role did Shinto play in bolstering the nationalistic sentiments of the Japanese people?
4. Although there are rivalry and competition among the three major religions in Japan, there has been a conspicuous absence of religious wars based on doctrinal or theological differences. Please explain.

GLOSSARY

Amaterasu (ah-mah-teh-rah-sooh; Japanese, "deity that shines in the sky") The sun goddess in Shinto. Enshrined at Ise, Amaterasu is the kami of the imperial family. As the sun goddess, she is the most august of all deities. Her descendants are considered the only rightful rulers of Japan.

ema (e'mah) Wooden tablets expressing pleadings to kami for success in life.

harae (hah-rah'eh) Shinto purification.

Izanagi (ee-zah-nah-gee) The male kami who is the procreator of the Japanese islands as well as many other kami.

Izanami (ee-zah-nah-mee) The female kami who is the procreator of the Japanese islands as well as some of the kami.

jinja (jin'juh) Shinto shrine.

kami (kah-mee) Shinto deity and spirit with awe-inspiring power.

Kojiki (koh-jee-kee) *Record of Ancient Matters*, compiled in the eighth century CE.

matsuri (mah-tsooh-ree) Shinto religious festival.

miko (mee-koh) Unmarried female Shinto shrine attendants.

mikoshi (mee-koh-shee) Portable shrine temporarily housing a Shinto deity.

misogi (mee-soh-gee) Shinto ritual of purification with water.

Nihon shoki (nee-hohn shoh-kee) *Chronicles of [the Land Where] the Sun Originates,* eighth-century CE text.

norito (noh-ree-toh) Invocational prayer offered by Shinto priests to the kami.

omikuji (oh-mee'koo-jee) Paper fortunes found at shrines.

shimenawa (shee-meh-na-wah) Huge rope hung in front of the worship hall to mark sacred spaces and objects at a shrine.

shintai (shin-tai) The "body" of a kami housed in a public shrine, or temporarily in a *mikoshi.*

Shinto (shin-toh) "The way of the gods." Traditional Japanese religion that acknowledges the power of the kami.

temizuya (te-mee'zoo-yah) Purification fountain at a shrine.

torii (toh-ree-ee) Crossbar gateway leading up to the Shinto shrine.

SUGGESTIONS FOR FURTHER READING

Ambros, Barbara. *Women in Japanese Religions.* New York: New York University Press, 2015. A new and welcome historical study of Buddhist and Shinto women in Japan.

Ashkenazi, Michael. *Matsuri: Festivals of a Japanese Town.* Honolulu: University of Hawaii Press, 1993. An anthropological and sociological description of Shinto in practice at Yuzawa, a town in Japan's northern region.

Breen, John, and Mark Teeuwen. *A New History of Shinto.* Wiley-Blackwell Books on Religion. Hoboken, NJ: John Wiley, 2010. A new interpretative work on Shinto and its history.

Dougill, John, and Joseph Cali. *Guide to Shinto Shrines.* Honolulu: University of Hawaii Press, 2013. An authoritative guide to most of the famous shrines in Japan, with a good introduction to Shinto.

Earhart, H. Byron. *Religion in the Japanese Experience: Sources and Interpretations.* 2nd ed. Belmont, CA: Wadsworth, 1997. An informative collection of source materials on Japanese religion, arranged topically and with insightful comments.

Hardacre, Helen. *Shinto: A History.* New York: Oxford University Press, 2017. An authoritative work on the history of Shinto by a respected scholar.

Kasahara, Kazuo, ed. *A History of Japanese Religion.* Tokyo: Kosei, 2002. An English translation of a two-volume work in Japanese that contains chapters written by scholars on different stages in the historical development of Japanese religion.

Kitagawa, Joseph M. *Religion in Japanese History.* New York: Columbia University Press, 1990. A detailed historical narrative of the development of Japanese religions.

Nelson, John K. *A Year in the Life of a Shinto Shrine.* Seattle: University of Washington Press, 1996. An ethnographical description of the ritual cycle at the Suwa Shrine in Nagasaki.

Ogihara-Schuck, Eriko. *Miyazaki's Animism Abroad: The Reception of Japanese Religious Themes by American and German Audiences.* Jefferson, NC: MacFarland, 2014. An examination of Miyazaki Hayao's animated films and their challenge to the Western religious mindset.

Pye, Michael, ed., *Exploring Shinto.* Equinox, 2020. An illuminating collection of essays by different scholars on Shinto, its interaction with Buddhism, and its relation to new religions in Japan.

Swanson, Paul, and Clark Chilson, eds. *The Nanzan Guide to Japanese Religions.* Honolulu: University of Hawaii Press, 2006. An informative volume on Buddhism and Shinto in Japan.

Thomas, Jolyon Baraka. *Drawing on Traditions: Manga, Anime, and Religion in Contemporary Japan.* Honolulu: University of Hawaii Press, 2012. An insightful examination of the religious elements in popular manga and anime.

ONLINE RESOURCES

Encyclopedia of Shinto

This useful, English-language resource is maintained by Kokugakuin University in Japan. In addition to the *Encyclopedia of Shinto*, it includes various images and video clips of Shinto objects and rituals.

Green Shinto

A website maintained by John Dougill, who teaches in Kyoto, Japan. It is a Japanophile's work of love providing useful information about Shinto to an international audience.

Digital Shinto

The Digital Shinto Project, an interactive research website and hub for online Shinto resources run by Kaitlyn Ugoretz of UC Santa Barbara.

Eat Pray Anime

An educational YouTube channel that explores the religious and cultural elements behind Japanese pop culture hosted by Kaitlyn Ugoretz.

ReligionForBreakfast

An educational YouTube channel hosted by Andrew Mark Henry that introduces a nonacademic audience to various religious traditions. It provides good information in the series on Shinto written by Kaitlyn Ugoretz.

Zoroastrianism

10

Chapter Outline

10.1 Summarize the central teachings of Zoroastrianism.

10.2 Identify the core texts of Zoroastrianism and their purposes.

10.3 Describe the cultural milieu in which Zoroastrianism began and what Zoroastrians believe about Zarathushtra.

10.4 Describe the internal and external challenges faced by Zoroastrian communities through the centuries.

10.5 Describe the practices and purposes of Zoroastrian rituals and observance of holy days.

10.6 Describe what Zoroastrians believe about their social and ethical responsibilities.

TODAY IS A JOYFUL DAY for nine-year-old Yasmin and her family, who belong to the community of Zoroastrians, or Parsis, in the Indian city of Mumbai. They are celebrating Yasmin's initiation into the Zoroastrian religion in a ceremony that Parsis call **Navjote**. The Navjote is performed by Zoroastrians worldwide. Iranis, the Zoroastrians of Iran, where Zoroastrianism began, call it **Sedreh Pushi**—"putting on the *sedreh*"—which refers to a central feature of the ceremony.

Yasmin began preparing for her Navjote some time ago, learning the essential features of her religion and memorizing important prayers she would need to recite. Earlier today, she bathed in sacred water in a purification ritual. She then joined an assembly of her family and friends where, in the presence of a flame burning fragrant sandalwood and frankincense, she sat before the officiating priest, ready for the Navjote to begin.

The Navjote was a complicated ceremony with several essential parts. First, the priest led Yasmin in a prayer of repentance. This was followed by a declaration of faith in which Yasmin acknowledged Zoroastrianism as the true

Her kusti cord tied around her wrist, a young girl beams during her Navjote ceremony in Mumbai, India, as her proud parents look on.

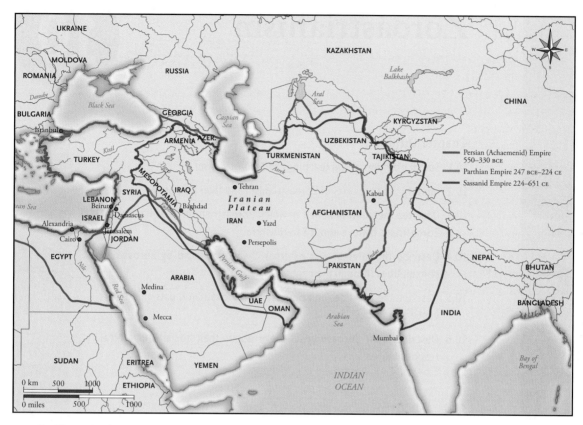

Significant sites in the development of Zoroastrianism.

and perfect religion given by God to the prophet **Zarathushtra**. The priest then invested, or "clothed," Yasmin with two sacred articles: The first was the *sedreh*, a white cotton vest, often called a "sacred shirt," that symbolizes the path of righteousness. From now on, Yasmin will make a practice of wearing this undergarment beneath her outer clothing. The second was the **kusti**, a sacred cord the priest tied around Yasmin's waist. Woven from seventy-two threads spun from lamb's wool—seventy-two also being the number of chapters in the *Yasna*, one of Zoroastrianism's most ancient sacred texts—the kusti had been carefully produced by women in Yasmin's community and then consecrated by a priest. From this day forward, the kusti will serve Yasmin as a visible symbol of her full membership in the Zoroastrian community. After her investiture with the *sedreh* and kusti, Yasmin recited a statement of faith in which she proclaimed her new identity as a Zoroastrian and her commitment to the Zoroastrian ethical ideals of good thoughts, good words, and good actions. The ceremony concluded with the priest's benediction, in which he asked God to bless Yasmin with health, long life, and piety.

Yasmin's Navjote has been a happy occasion for all involved. When the ceremony is over, she joins her family and friends in a celebration in which she is showered with gifts and congratulations. Everyone present is pleased to have witnessed the teachings of arguably the world's oldest living religion passed on to a new generation.

This chapter explores the teachings, history, and way of life of Zoroastrianism—also known as Mazdaism or Zarathushti *din*. Zoroastrianism has a very long history. Its founder, Zarathushtra (also spelled "Zarathustra," and often called "Zoroaster," as he was known by the ancient Greeks), may have lived as long ago as c. 1300 BCE, in which case Zoroastrianism is the world's oldest living religion. This introductory study, while acknowledging that Zoroastrianism has taken different forms throughout its history, presents the religion mainly as it is practiced today by the majority of Zoroastrians, who commonly refer to themselves as Zarathushtri or, especially in Mumbai, as Parsis ("Persians"). We begin by focusing on its principal teachings.

10.1 The Teachings of Zoroastrianism: Central Precepts

Through the centuries, Zoroastrians have lived in evolving cultural circumstances—most notably the rise of Islam in the seventh century CE and the subsequent migrations of Zoroastrians to India and other lands. In this chapter's section on the history of Zoroastrianism, we explore some of these circumstances in more detail, paying careful attention to Zoroastrian texts from different eras and how they reflect changing perspectives. Here, we describe in more general terms the central teachings of Zoroastrianism that have endured until today. Some of these teachings date from the religion's origins, whereas others have developed in much later periods.

The two most notable Zoroastrian teachings are monotheism and **dualism**—the ongoing opposition between the forces of order and chaos, of good and evil, understood to be played out on a cosmic level.

Monotheism and Dualism

Zoroastrians are monotheists, believing in one God, **Ahura Mazda**, who is perfectly good, all-powerful, and eternal. Like the scriptures of other monotheistic religions—such as Judaism, Christianity, and Islam—those of Zoroastrianism speak of other supernatural beings. We will discuss these later, but two must be mentioned briefly here: Spenta Mainyu, the "Holy Spirit" of Ahura Mazda, and Angra Mainyu, the

TIMELINE
Zoroastrianism

2000 BCE	Indo-Iranian tribes migrate to the Iranian Plateau.
1300–800 BCE	Most scholars place the life of Zarathushtra within this period.
1300–550 BCE	Composition of the Avesta.
550–330 BCE	Persian (Achaemenid) Empire. Most of the Achaemenid kings were Zoroastrians.
247 BCE–224 CE	Parthian Empire. Zoroastrianism loses its royal endorsement, existing as one of many religions.
224–651	Sassanid Empire. Sassanid kings declare Zoroastrianism to be the official state religion.
651	Arab invaders topple the Sassanid Dynasty. Islam begins to eclipse Zoroastrianism in Iran.
700–900	Composition of most chapters of the *Bundahishn*.
c. Ninth century	Iranian Zoroastrians flee to western India, where they are known as Parsis (Persian for "Persians").
900–1000	Composition of the *Denkard*.
1878	The first fire temple in the United States is built in Florence, Arizona.

"Foul Spirit." These "Twin Spirits" are emanations from Ahura Mazda and represent the realities of order and goodness, on one hand, and chaos and evil, on the other, that exist in countless oppositional forms; for example, life and death, growth and decay, and right and wrong. As we will see, Zoroastrians believe that Ahura Mazda is at work in history orchestrating the gradual process by which the cosmos will ultimately be purged of evil and chaos so that goodness and order will prevail.

Thus, there is an unmistakable dualism in Zoroastrianism. In fact, there are two forms of dualism. Interrelated with the dualism of order and chaos is the dualism of spirit and matter.

The Dualism of Spirit and Matter

Zoroastrianism teaches that reality is divisible into two realms: that of spirit and thought and that of matter and physicality. Everything in existence is the result of the incorporation of spirit within the realm of matter. Readers familiar with Platonic philosophy will recognize similarities with Zoroastrian spirit/matter dualism—and, indeed, Zoroastrianism might have influenced Plato. In turn, Greek philosophy, Platonic and also Aristotelian, might have influenced the ongoing development of Zoroastrian beliefs.

Human beings must orient themselves toward the spiritual realm in order to live righteously and in accordance with order and ultimately to achieve salvation. And yet Zoroastrianism teaches a healthy regard for the body and its enjoyments, within appropriate limits. The realm of spirit and thought is the true origin of human life, but embodiment is not a negative thing. In fact, as we will consider in more detail later in the chapter, it is a general religious duty for Zoroastrians to have children, thereby furthering the incorporation of the realm of spirit and thought within the realm of matter or body. And ultimately, the final triumph of good over evil depends on this incorporation. But in order to understand Zoroastrian teachings on this final triumph, we must first examine the dualism of good and evil and the opposing forces at work in the cosmos.

The Dualism of Order and Chaos

The Zoroastrian dualism of order and chaos involves two key concepts: **asha** ("order") and **druj** (the "lie"). *Asha* is the true, cosmic order that pervades both the natural and social spheres of reality, encompassing the moral and religious life of individuals. *Asha* is symbolized by light, and therefore by the sun and by fire. *Asha* is opposed by *druj*. Whereas *asha* gives rise to good thoughts, words, and deeds, *druj* produces evil thoughts, words, and deeds. The two are fundamentally incompatible and locked in a cosmic struggle. But *asha* is eternal and every bit as steadfast in truth and goodness as Ahura Mazda; in fact, ancient Zoroastrian texts portray the two as good friends. The ultimate outcome of this cosmic struggle is therefore never in doubt. In the meantime, though, human beings must engage in their own struggle between order and chaos, a topic we will soon explore. First, we investigate how this dualism divides the Zoroastrian pantheon of divine beings.

The Divine Realm

Zoroastrian teachings about a pantheon of supernatural beings are similar to the teachings of other monotheistic religions. The Bible, for example, makes many references to supernatural beings—seraphim, cherubim, angels—other than the one God of Judaism and of Christianity (Chapters 11 and 12). Similarly, the Qur'an, while strongly emphasizing belief in only one God, Allah, assumes the existence of other supernatural beings, namely, angels, devils, and jinn (Chapter 13). All three of these monotheistic religions acknowledge the existence of an Evil One, named Satan.

Ahura Mazda Zoroastrianism emerged from an earlier Iranian religious perspective that undoubtedly was polytheistic. Zarathushtra seems to have been responsible for declaring that one god is primary and qualitatively above all others: Ahura Mazda, the "Wise Lord" (*ahura* in ancient Iranian means "lord"; there is no other known ancient usage of the term *Mazda*). In later centuries, Zoroastrians came also to use the name Ohrmazd to refer to their God.

Zarathushtra worshiped Ahura Mazda as the only eternal deity, omniscient and omnipotent, and responsible for the creation of the world. This does not mean that Ahura Mazda is responsible for the creation of evil in the world. This could not be the world of a God who is the source of good, not evil. Rather, Zarathushtra taught that Ahura Mazda created this world ultimately to overcome evil. It is in this world that the embodied forces of order and good do battle against the embodied forces of chaos and evil. The final triumph will be accomplished through the forces of good aligned with Ahura Mazda.

Divine Forces of Good Especially prominent among the forces of good are the seven **Amesha Spentas**, the "Beneficial Immortals"—angels who help Ahura Mazda govern creation. Chief among them is **Spenta Mainyu**, Ahura Mazda's Holy Spirit. The *Amesha Spentas* function together as semi-independent powers, all of them in service of Ahura Mazda. Among them is Asha, the embodiment of the cosmic principle of order that we have already encountered ("Asha" is capitalized when referring to the *Amesha Spenta*). Each of the *Amesha Spentas* constitutes an element of the cosmos; Asha, for example (whose full name is Asha Vahishta, "Best Order"), constitutes fire.

The seven *Amesha Spentas* are assisted by a large number of beings called **yazatas**, "ones worthy of worship." Eventually, their number was fixed at

Integration of the dualism of spirit/matter and the dualism of order (good)/chaos (evil). The spirit of *asha*, personified in the *yazatas* ("ones worthy of worship"), is embodied in the physical world; so, too, is the spirit of *druj*, personified as the *daevas*, embodied in the physical world—the stage on which the cosmic struggle between good and evil is played out.

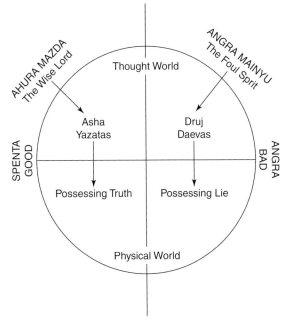

thirty, so that each day of the Zoroastrian month is represented by a different *yazata* (this includes the seven *Amesha Spentas*, who sometimes are classified along with the *yazatas*). One of the most important among them is Mithra, a god of light who works to keep human beings in harmony with *asha*. As we will see in the later section on the history of Zoroastrianism, Mithra was to become a very popular god in Roman culture, in the mystery religion of Mithras (his Greek and Latin name). Another *yazata* of particular note is Sraosha ("Obedience"), the caretaker of the souls of the dead who also plays an important role in overseeing ritual practices.

The "Lie" and Forces of Evil
From the beginning of time, Spenta Mainyu, Ahura Mazda's Holy Spirit, has battled against his adversary **Angra Mainyu**, the "Foul Spirit," who in later texts also is named Ahriman. This battle is at the basis of the cosmic dualism between order and chaos, also manifested in the struggle between *asha* and the "Lie," or *druj*. One of Zoroastrianism's earliest texts provides us with insight regarding the battle and its participants, chief among them being the twins Spenta Mainyu and Angra Mainyu:

> Truly there were two primal Spirits, twins renowned to be in conflict. In thought and word, in act they are two: the better and the bad. And those who act well have chosen rightly between these two, not so the evildoers. And when these two Spirits first came together they created life and not-life, and how at the end Worst Existence shall be for the wicked, but (the House of) Best Purpose for the just man. Of these two Spirits the Wicked One chose achieving the worst things. The Most Holy Spirit, who is clad in hardest stone, chose right, and (so do those) who shall satisfy Lord Mazda continually with rightful acts. The Daevas indeed did not choose rightly between these two, for the Deceiver approached them as they conferred. Because they chose worst purpose, they then rushed to Fury, with whom they have afflicted the world and mankind.
>
> —*Yasna 30.3–6, from the Gathas*[1]

The **daevas** mentioned here are the various demonic powers (*daevas* in ancient Iranian originally meant "gods," but eventually came to mean "demons"). Notably, as this text reports, the *daevas* came to be demonic because they *chose* "worst purpose." As we will see, this same opportunity for choice presents itself throughout the lifetime of each human being.

Creation and the Nature of the World

In Zoroastrian cosmology, or teachings on the nature of the world, there are three progressive phases: the creation of the physical world; the mixing in the physical world of the embodied spirits of evil forces with those of good forces; and the final transformation, in which the world will be cleansed of all evil.

According to Zoroastrianism's most prominent creation myth, in the beginning Ahura Mazda conceived a plan for creation and also secured the support of the **fravashis**, preexisting higher souls and guardian spirits of individual human beings. Distinct from the lower souls that exist together with human bodies, the fravashis were to descend into the material world once it was created, and to combat the forces of evil and gently guide human beings toward ethical lives and the realization of their true nature. After Ahura Mazda had taken these initial steps, he overcame Angra Mainyu, who fell into a kind of stupor for 3,000 years. He then created the seven *Amesha Spentas*. He also created *asha*, the cosmic order that underlies the universe, intended to serve as a bulwark against the destructive actions of Angra Mainyu.

The best-known symbol of Zoroastrianism, the Faravahar is believed to represent the fravashis. This example is from Yazd, Iran.

During this period of 3,000 years, as Angra Mainyu was incapacitated, Ahura Mazda and the *Amesha Spentas* created the physical world. As the primary textual account makes clear, the process of creation—the first of the three progressive cosmological phases—took place in seven stages:

> When the Evil Spirit was helpless in prostration, he lay prostrate for 3,000 years. During the helplessness of the Evil Spirit, Ohrmazd created the creation materially. First, He created the Sky as a defence; second, He created Water, to defeat the demon of thirst; third, He created the all-solid Earth; fourth, He created the Plant, to help the beneficent Animal [a bull]; fifth, He created the beneficent Animal, to help the Just Man; sixth, He created the Just Man [the first human being], to smite the Evil Spirit together with the devs [the *daevas*] and to make them powerless. And then He created Fire [the sun] and linked its brilliance to the Endless Light.
>
> —*Bundahishn 1a.1–4*[2]

According to the same account, the entire span of time between creation and the final triumph of good over evil will be 12,000 years. After the 3,000-year period during which the physical world was created comes the period of the Mixture, during which Angra Mainyu is again active and the evil spirit forces are mixed together with the spirit forces of good—hence the cosmic struggle that currently is ongoing. Angra Mainyu and the evil forces destroyed the primordial Plant, Animal (a bull), and Just Man. But these victories would prove to be only temporary.

Eventually, there will ensue the period leading up to the final triumph of good over evil. This will be achieved through separation of the evil from the good, culminating in complete purification. The ultimate purpose of human life is to help bring about this purification through leading virtuous lives according to Zoroastrian teachings.

Human Nature and Human Destiny

Dualism, the most significant feature of Zoroastrian teachings, lies at the heart of the religion's perspective on human nature and human destiny. For Zoroastrianism, the meaning of life rests in an ethical choice: whether to comply with Zarathushtra's revelations and live in accordance with *asha*, cosmic order, or to deviate from this and succumb to the evil ways of *druj*, the Lie.

Dualism in Human Life: Ethical Choice   Zoroastrianism teaches that human beings are free to choose to live in harmony with *asha*. This way of living involves making Ahura Mazda, the transcendent God, immanent in one's own being, a blessing made possible through Spenta Mainyu, the Holy Spirit of Ahura Mazda.

Zoroastrian teachings regarding human nature and destiny can be simplified by considering a few parallels involving the basic dualism of good and evil. *Asha* is opposed to *druj*. Spenta Mainyu and Angra Mainyu are, respectively, spirits of good and evil because of the choice they made. This choice is the prototype of the ethical choice confronting every individual.

Judgment of the Soul   The ethical choices made in life determine the fate of the soul in the afterlife. The outcome of these ethical choices is knowable by the individual's thoughts, words, and deeds. The goodness of these three must outweigh the evil if the individual is to be saved and to live for eternity in heaven. The alternative is eternal torment in hell.

Zoroastrian teachings on the judgment of the soul involve two aspects that are especially notable: the **Daena** and the **Chinvat Bridge**. The Daena is a feminine being who embodies the individual's ethical quality and who appears to the soul after death. If the individual has lived in harmony with *asha*, then the Daena appears as a beautiful young woman. To the soul of an evil individual, however, the Daena appears as an ugly old hag.

The Chinvat Bridge needs to be crossed by the soul in order to reach the afterlife. For the good individual, the Chinvat Bridge is wide and easy to cross. But for the evil, it is razor-thin, causing the soul to plummet down into hell.

The Final Triumph   The ultimate purpose of individual striving for righteousness transcends the salvation of the individual soul. The combined efforts of all individuals' strivings will eventually overcome evil, bringing about the purification of the world and the final triumph.

At some point (the date is uncertain), new teachings arose that elaborated on this doctrine of the final triumph. These teachings asserted that a messianic savior figure named Saoshyant, a son of Zarathushtra (whose semen is said to have been miraculously preserved in a lake), will appear to usher in the events that will transform the wicked world into the glorious and eternal kingdom of Ahura Mazda. The cosmic struggle will culminate in a battle between the *yazatas*, allied with righteous human beings, and the *daevas*, allied with evildoers, in which the good will emerge victorious. Then the dead will be resurrected, and all souls will be judged. The evil will be burned in molten metal while the righteous will be saved, to live forever in the presence of Ahura Mazda.

10.2 The Teachings of Zoroastrianism: Sacred Texts

The languages of several early Iranian peoples became the languages of Zoroastrianism. Avestan, spoken by tribes of northeastern Iran, is the language in which the earliest Zoroastrian text, the **Avesta**, is written. The development of the Avesta over time resulted in some parts being written in Old Avestan and others in Younger Avestan.

Developing alongside Avestan was Old Persian, a language from the southwestern region of Pars (also Parsa), from which "Persia" derives. Old Persian texts relating to Zoroastrianism are mostly cuneiform inscriptions written on clay tablets and seals between 600 and 300 BCE. A later form of Old Persian is Middle Persian, usually called Pahlavi in connection with Zoroastrian texts. Inscriptions in Pahlavi can be dated as early as the third century CE. Most of the Zoroastrian scriptures were written in Pahlavi in the eighth and ninth centuries CE after circulating orally for centuries.

The Avesta

The oldest and most important of the Zoroastrian scriptures is the Avesta, a collection of sacred texts that preserve the teachings given to Zarathushtra by Ahura Mazda and a great deal besides. The history of the Avesta is described in later texts written in Pahlavi. According to the tradition, the Avesta we have today is a remnant of a much larger collection of texts said to have been destroyed when Alexander the Great conquered the Persian Empire in the fourth century BCE.

The Avesta is organized into five parts. The *Yasna* consists of material recited by priests when performing their liturgical functions. At the core of the *Yasna* are the *Gathas*, hymns attributed to Zarathushtra. Written in a very ancient dialect, the *Gathas* are the part of the Avesta thought to most accurately reflect the life and thought of Zarathushtra. The *Visperad* is a collection of texts recited along with the *Yasna* in order to solemnize seasonal celebrations, such as the Zoroastrian New Year's Day. Unlike the *Yasna* and *Visperad*, which are liturgical collections, the primary purpose of the *Vendidad* is to describe the many ways in which the *daevas* work evil in the world and various means for confounding them. The *Vendidad* also contains stories about the creation of the world, the first human being, and the temptation of Zarathushtra by Angra Mainyu. The *Yashts* constitute a collection of hymns that venerate Zoroastrian virtues such as wisdom, truth, justice, and obedience and the angels associated with them. Originally, there were thirty *Yashts*, one dedicated to each day of the month. Only twenty-one survive today. The final part of the Avesta is the *Khordeh* Avesta. Sometimes called the "concise Avesta," it consists of selections from the rest of the Avesta that are used by laypeople in the course of their daily lives. These include *Yashts* and special prayers recited during the five parts of the day, before undertaking certain tasks, and before eating and drinking.

Pahlavi Texts

In addition to the Avesta, there are numerous later texts written in Pahlavi. Two of the most important are the *Denkard* and the *Bundahishn*. The *Denkard* is a compendium of materials relating to Zoroastrian beliefs and customs, some of them much older than the *Denkard* itself. It includes doctrines; instructions for ethical behavior; the writings of Zoroastrian sages; observations on the arts and sciences, as well as on philosophical and theological topics; a history of the world up to the time of Zarathushtra; and substantial material on Zarathushtra himself. The *Bundahishn* ("Primal Creation") is technically not scripture, though it elaborates on ideas found in the Avesta. Earlier in this chapter, we studied the myth of creation as presented in the *Bundahishn*.

10.3 The History of Zoroastrianism: Origins

Its roots reaching back 3,000 years to the ancient Iranian tribes, Zoroastrianism by the sixth century BCE had become the dominant religion in Iran. But the rise of Islam in the seventh century CE changed the religious culture of the Middle East, pushing Zoroastrians into corners of the world where their numbers have dwindled. Still, Zoroastrianism persists as a living religion, and its teachings and practices continue to fascinate scholars and other observers.

The Background of Zoroastrianism

The Indo-Iranians At some time about 2000 BCE, two nomadic peoples related by language and religion began moving southward from their ancestral home in Central Asia. One was the Indo-Aryans, who migrated to what are now Pakistan and western India. There, joining with the indigenous population, they produced Vedic culture and laid the foundations of Hinduism (Chapter 4). The other was the Indo-Iranians, who found a new homeland on the Iranian Plateau just east of Mesopotamia. Living apart from their cultural relatives, these ancient Iranians formed a religious tradition that was very different from Hinduism. And yet both retained vestiges of their common past. Consider, for instance, a linguistic example with clear religious implications: Iranian *daevas* and Indian *devas* both mean "gods" or "spirits."

Pre-Zoroastrian Religion Ancient texts tell us that early Iranian religion had marked similarities with early Hinduism as described in the Vedas (Chapter 4).

They describe worship of the *daevas* as widespread in Iran, just as devotion to the *devas* was common in India. The *daevas* were personifications of the aspects of nature on which all people depend: sky, sun, earth, fire, water, wind, and so forth. There was also a higher order of deities, known as *ahuras* ("lords"), responsible for maintaining order in the universe as a whole. These included Intar, a war god known as Indra in the Hindu Vedas; Mithra (Vedic Mitra), a god of light who gave cattle and children to the Iranians; and Yima (Vedic Yama), ruler of the dead. Finally, our sources describe belief in *asha*, an underlying natural and moral order that promoted goodness in all its forms—most notably light, truth, and justice. At times, order would be overcome by chaos in its many aspects—such as darkness, falsehood, and injustice—only to reestablish itself later. The universe was the setting for an unending struggle between order and chaos.

Human beings could support the forces of order through religious practices designed to strengthen them: sacrifices of cereal grains and, more commonly, animals; fire worship; and the preparation and consumption of **haoma**, a sacred drink made from the sour, milky juice of the soma plant (and similar to the soma drink described in the Vedas). In time, however, the violence involved in animal sacrifices, the cost of sacred rituals, and the power of the priests who conducted them became oppressive to many of the early Iranians. One of them was Zarathushtra.

Zarathushtra

Scholars cannot agree on where and when we should locate the life of Zarathushtra. Some scholars go so far as to argue that he was not a historical figure at all. Most plausibly, however, Zarathushtra was indeed a historical figure who lived in eastern Iran or in Central Asia at some point between 1300 and 800 BCE.

Legends preserved in Zoroastrianism's sacred texts say that Zarathushtra displayed religious inclinations even as a child and that at the age of twenty he left his wife and family in order to search for truth. Ten years later, he had a vision of Ahura Mazda, leader of the forces of *asha* (order). Lifted out of his material body, Zarathushtra was taken up into a heavenly court where he beheld Ahura Mazda, the "Wise Lord," attended by his angels. Calling upon Zarathushtra to be his prophet, Ahura Mazda revealed the grave threat posed by Angra Mainyu (the "foul spirit" and leader of the forces of chaos). In additional visions occurring over the next eight years, each of the six principal angels of Ahura Mazda appeared to Zarathushtra and elaborated on the content of the first vision. By the time the visions ended, Zarathushtra understood the message Ahura Mazda wanted him to proclaim to human beings: Ahura Mazda was the Supreme Being and the power on which order depended. Human beings could join in the struggle against Angra Mainyu by resolving to live lives of exemplary morality. Any other decision would establish them as allies of Angra Mainyu. At the end of time, every human being would be judged on the moral quality of his or her life and would be assigned to an eternity either in the paradise of Ahura Mazda or the hellish pits of Angra Mainyu.

Much in the revelations Zarathushtra had received was new. Ahura Mazda, formerly on equal terms with other *ahuras*, was now raised to a level far above them. Ethical conduct on the part of the individual now displaced sacrificial rituals performed by priests as the most significant form of human activity. Human beings were now understood as full participants and no longer as semiengaged bystanders in the cosmic struggle between order and chaos, good and evil.

The unfamiliarity of such ideas helps to explain the difficulty Zarathushtra encountered in finding converts to the new religion. It is also likely that many people resented certain reforms made by Zarathushtra, especially his prohibition of sacrifices to the *daevas*, whom he saw as agents of Angra Mainyu. It is said that he suffered through many years of discouragement and that Angra Mainyu himself urged him to give up. But then Zarathushtra came to the court of King Vishtaspa, whom legend describes as a good man surrounded by a class of wicked priests who profited from their bloody animal sacrifices and from popular belief that their magic could ensure good harvests and protection from the raids of nomadic tribes. These organized such great opposition to Zarathushtra that he was thrown into prison. But when Zarathushtra managed to perform a miraculous cure for Vishtaspa's favorite horse, the king took a stand against the priests and converted his kingdom to Zarathushtra's new religion. From this point on, Zarathushtra and his followers had great success in bringing it to other parts of Iran. According to Zoroastrian scripture, Zarathushtra died at the age of seventy-seven, killed by a nomadic raider in the city of Balkh (in modern Afghanistan) while performing a ritual at his fire altar.

10.4 The History of Zoroastrianism: From Ancient Times to the Present

The history of Zoroastrianism in the period immediately following the time of Zarathushtra is uncertain. The historical record begins in the sixth century BCE with the *Histories* of Herodotus, a Greek who lived a century later. Herodotus's interest in the Persian Empire—so called because the ancestral home of its Achaemenid Dynasty was Pars ("Persia") in southwestern Iran—can be explained by the fact that it invaded Greece twice in the early years of Herodotus's own century. Wanting to provide his countrymen with an account of the culture of the enemy, Herodotus included his observations on the religion of the Persians and its priests, the Magi.

Zoroastrianism in the Persian Empire (550–330 BCE)

The Magi appear to have been members of a powerful Zoroastrian priestly caste in the empire of the neighboring Medes, which was annexed to the newer Persian Empire by its founder, Cyrus the Great, in 550 BCE. Owing to the unwelcome political intrigues of the Magi, Cyrus and his son Cambyses II curtailed their influence and sometimes persecuted them. But Zoroastrianism began to gain momentum among the Persians with the accession of Darius I (r. 549–485 BCE), who credited

Ahura Mazda with bringing him to power. Thereafter, the religious culture of the Persian Empire became thoroughly Zoroastrian, and the role of the Magi as priests was secured. Surviving monuments and inscriptions testify to the influence of Zoroastrianism, as do many Avestan texts from this period.

Zoroastrianism in the Parthian Empire (247 BCE–224 CE)

Achaemenid Persia fell to the Greeks and Macedonians under Alexander the Great in 330 BCE. A century later, Iran made a resurgence under a new dynasty of rulers from the region of Parthia. At its height, the Parthian Empire encompassed Iran, Mesopotamia, and parts of the Arabian Peninsula and what is now Turkey. Its culture combined Iranian and Greek cultures along with features of many other cultures found within its borders. This can be seen, for example, in the Parthian tendency to equate Iranian and Greek deities. Thus, Ahura Mazda was identified with Zeus and Angra Mainyu with Hades.

Because the Parthian kings did not give Zoroastrianism the endorsement it had enjoyed under the Achaemenids, its status during this period was somewhat diminished. Still, there is evidence that some Parthian rulers built fire altars to honor Ahura Mazda and had Magi serve as priests in their courts. The Magi (sometimes translated "wise men") described in the Gospel of Matthew as coming to visit the infant Jesus would have begun their journey in Parthian Iran.

Zoroastrianism in the Sassanid Empire (224–651)

Much larger than the empire of the Parthians, the Sassanid Empire included all of today's Iran, Iraq, Armenia, and Afghanistan, as well as parts of Turkey, Syria, the Arabian Peninsula, and Central Asia. It was the last of the Iranian empires before the conquest of the Middle East by Muslim Arabs and the only one to formally adopt Zoroastrianism as the state religion. This, however, was a Zurvanite Zoroastrianism that differed from the traditional Mazdean form in teaching that Ahura Mazda (now known as Ohrmazd) and Angra Mainyu were twin brothers produced by Zurvan, a higher creator god. Thus, Zurvanism departed from orthodox Zoroastrianism in demoting Ahura Mazda from his status as the supreme being and in creating a link between good and evil that was denied by other Zoroastrians, who saw these two principles as being completely separate and absolutely opposed to each other. Sassanid Zoroastrianism also encouraged the worship of some of the old Iranian gods, such as Mithra, god of light, and Anahita, goddess of water and the moon.

The Sassanid rulers aggressively promoted their form of Zoroastrianism. With their support, the basic features of its rituals were established, and a priestly hierarchy was created, with the chief priests

This wall carving features a Faravahar, thought to represent the fravashis. The wall is located in Persepolis, the ancient ceremonial center of the Achaemenid Empire.

assigned to every region being supervised by a high priest. The most important duty assigned to priests was the tending of the sacred flame of Ahura Mazda in fire temples. Because fire, like water, was considered an agent of purity, great care was taken to avoid pollution; thus, Zoroastrian priests adopted the habit of wearing cloth masks that covered the mouth and nostrils to prevent any unclean element from coming into contact with the fire. Because the bodies of the dead had the potential to pollute fire, earth, and water, they were exposed on high places, such as mountaintops, where vultures and other scavenging animals would pick the bones clean before putrefaction could begin.

Zoroastrianism and Other Ancient Religions

One of the most striking features of Zoroastrianism is the number of features it shares with other ancient religions.

The number of points of similarity in the Zoroastrian, Jewish, and Christian scriptures is especially impressive. There are far too many to mention here, but a few good examples will make the point. Just as the Zoroastrian Ahura Mazda is an all-powerful, all-knowing, and eternal being who exercises his creative power in the world through his Spenta Mainyu (Holy Spirit), the God of Jews and Christians makes his presence known in the world through the Spirit of God (Judaism) or Holy Spirit (Christianity). All three religions imagine God, supported by angels, locked in a struggle with Evil, backed by demons. All three anticipate an end of the world that will involve the coming of a savior, the resurrection of the dead, judgment, the restoration of the world to a state of perfection, and everlasting life. All three describe God as intervening in human affairs in order to communicate his nature and will to human beings. The scriptures of all three religions describe human beings as descended from a single, primordial couple. Finally, not long after their creation, a great catastrophe destroys all of humanity except for a single righteous individual and his family; in Zoroastrianism (according to one Avestan text), it is a cataclysmic winter; in Judaism and Christianity, a great flood.

Although noting such similarities is easy, explaining them is difficult. As it is well known that Jews and Iranians were in close contact beginning in the sixth century BCE, most scholars believe that the religion of the Jews (and, through them, that of the Christians) was influenced by Zoroastrianism. Claims that Jews influenced Zoroastrians have not won significant support. A more successful argument has been that the shared beliefs of the two religions reached the forms they take in their respective scriptures at roughly the same time, and so their similarity can be explained as the result either of a collaborative creativity or of a parallel development nourished by a shared cultural milieu.

The matter of influence is much clearer with respect to Manichaeism, a religion that appeared shortly after the founding of the Sassanid Empire in the mid-third century. At that time Mani, an itinerant prophet, began preaching an extreme form of dualism that combined elements of Zoroastrianism with aspects of other Iranian religions and Christianity. Manichaeism enjoyed great success in the third through fifth centuries, when it was one of the most visible religions in the Roman Empire and was practiced as far east as China. Manichaeism's central teaching, that the world is divided by the struggle between the forces of light and darkness, clearly derives from Zoroastrianism. It is also true that Zoroastrian deities were included in its pantheon. But Mani's teaching that all matter is evil and only spirit is good cannot have come from Zoroastrianism, which teaches that spirit is indeed sometimes evil—most notably of course in the case of Angra Mainyu. Similarly, Mani's claim that all material reality is formed from the substance of Satan differs radically from the Zoroastrian teaching that matter was created by Ahura Mazda, the source of all good things.

The tauroctony (bull-slaying) was the universal symbol of Mithraism. The symbol includes several features drawn from ancient Iranian religion, including the slaying of a primordial bull and the figure of Mithras himself, known in Zoroastrianism as Mithra, one of the *yazatas* ("ones worthy of worship").

A final ancient religion with Zoroastrian associations is Mithraism. Based on devotion to the ancient Iranian god Mithra, known as Mithras in the West, Mithraism thrived in the Roman Empire in the second and third centuries CE. It was one of the mystery religions of the Greco-Roman world, so called because membership was limited to initiates (in this case, only men) into the secrets of their underlying myths. From Roman times until the late twentieth century, Mithraism was understood as an Iranian religion that had managed to make its way westward. But recent scholarship has shown that although Mithras and his iconography (such as his slaying of a divine bull) had their origins in ancient Iran, where Mithra was included in the Zoroastrian pantheon, the actual content of the religion was more closely related to the speculations of intellectuals in what is now southeastern Turkey about the stars and their relationship to human events. Still, the mere presence of Mithra in the West speaks to the influence and prestige of Zoroastrianism far from its Iranian homeland.

Zoroastrianism and Islam

In the seventh century, the Sassanid Empire was overthrown by the Arabs, converts to Islam who were then conquering much of the Middle East. Although the Zoroastrians of Iran were now living under an Islamic government, they managed at first to cope with their new circumstances because the Qur'an calls upon Muslims to be lenient in their treatment of non-Muslims to whom God had given a book of scripture. The Arab conquerors were satisfied that the Avesta, like the Jewish and Christian scriptures, qualified as just such a book. Zoroastrians were required to pay a special tax imposed on all non-Muslims, and there were occasional acts of violence against them, but there was security in the fact that they remained the majority in Iran.

But the position of Zoroastrians had deteriorated markedly within a century after the arrival of the Arabs. Zoroastrians were subjected to harassment and violence, priests were executed, fire temples were destroyed or turned into mosques, and books of scripture were burned. Worse, Zoroastrians lost their status as a "People of the Book" and the protections it offered. The dangers of their situation

Detail from *The School of Athens* by Raphael. The bearded figure in the center depicts Zarathushtra holding an astral globe, suggestive of the common association of Zoroastrians, especially the priestly Magi, with astrology. Raphael supposedly depicted himself as the man to Zarathushtra's left who looks to the viewer.

were enough to persuade many Zoroastrians to flee Iran. Of these, most found refuge in western India and eventually established a Zoroastrian community in Mumbai that still thrives today. Many of those who remained in Iran capitulated in the face of Arab persecution and converted to Islam. Conversion was made easier by a legend invented to link Shi'a Islam, the dominant form in Iran, with the Zoroastrian royalty of the Sassanid Empire. According to the story, the fourth Shi'a imam was the son of Husayn, Muhammad's grandson, and a Sassanid princess. The effect of these and other factors on Iran's Zoroastrians was dramatic. By the end of the eighth century, they had become a religious minority.

By the tenth century, Arab rule of Iran had come to an end. It was replaced by a series of Iranian dynasties, some with Turkish or Kurdish associations, that lasted until the overthrow of the Pahlavi Dynasty in 1979. Throughout this period, the number of Zoroastrians in Iran continued to decline steadily. Those who remained faithful to their religious traditions continued to suffer discrimination, periodic persecutions, and economic hardship.

Zoroastrianism in the West

Historically, the presence of Zoroastrians in the West has been minimal. Even today, in an age of large-scale patterns of immigration across the globe, there are still only very small populations of Zoroastrians in Europe and the Americas.

But the West has been fascinated by Zarathushtra for centuries. Early Christian theologians made reference to him, as did medieval and early modern writers. Since the sixteenth century, Zarathushtra has made appearances in well-known works of art, music, and literature, some of which make use of his image in ways he would certainly have found surprising.

In *The School of Athens* (1510), the Italian painter Raphael placed Zarathushtra in a gathering of ancient Greek philosophers, thereby acknowledging his cultural significance. Voltaire, an eighteenth-century leader of the French Enlightenment, misunderstood the teachings of Zarathushtra as a form of rational religion resembling the deism of his day. A leading character in Mozart's opera *The Magic Flute* (1791), "Sarastro," is a wise and benevolent ruler who triumphs over darkness and the Queen of the Night. In his philosophical work *Also Sprach Zarathustra* ("Thus Spake Zarathustra," 1885), the German philosopher Friedrich Nietzsche described a new Zarathushtra who condemns conventional morality and its conceptions of good and evil. Inspired by Nietzsche's work, the German composer Richard Strauss composed a tone poem also titled *Also Sprach Zarathustra* (1896). Its memorable fanfare ("Sunrise") became a best-selling recording and earned a place in American popular culture after being featured in Stanley Kubrick's 1968 science-fiction film *2001: A Space Odyssey*. More recently, some have suggested that the television series *Game of Thrones* incorporates teachings of Zarathushtra.

Zoroastrianism in the Twenty-First Century

A 2012 study sponsored by the Federation of Zoroastrian Associations of North America (FEZANA) places the world population of Zoroastrians at just over 111,000, while other worthy sources suggest closer to 200,000.[3] It is reasonable, therefore, to estimate the current number of Zoroastrians as somewhere within this rather broad range. The most significant populations are indicated in the map. Much smaller populations are found in various other countries. Overall, the FEZANA study reports a decline of just over 11 percent in the number of Zoroastrians world-wide between 2004 and 2012.

The largest community of Zoroastrians today is in western India, particularly in the area of Mumbai. Known as Parsis, they are the descendants of Zoroastrians who fled Iran to escape Muslim persecution in the early medieval period. Today, they are among the most affluent of India's ethnic groups and are highly regarded for their success as industrialists and their generosity as philanthropists.

The second largest group of contemporary Zoroastrians is in Iran. Known as Iranis and Zarathushtis, throughout most of the modern era they have been marginalized and persecuted. Like the Parsis, Iranis have tenaciously held on to traditional beliefs and rituals. Many still speak Dari, an Iranian language that is distinct from the Farsi (Persian) spoken by other Iranians. Because they are non-Muslims, Iran prohibits the election of Zoroastrians to any representative body in government except its parliament, the Islamic Consultative Assembly, which reserves a few seats for religious minorities. Zoroastrians have found greater acceptance among the general population of Iran because they represent a part of its pre-Islamic history in which Muslims as well as Zoroastrians take great pride.

Perhaps the greatest concern of Zoroastrians today is their dwindling numbers. One reason for this decline is that Zoroastrians do not seek converts to their religion. Another, mentioned in the opening to this chapter, is an ancient tradition that forbids marriage to non-Zoroastrians. In addition, some Zoroastrians choose to leave their religion because they find its strictures burdensome or its ancient teachings difficult to accept.

Because of the decline in their numbers, Zoroastrians are concerned about the future of their religion. Conservatives argue that adherence to tradition is the key to its survival. Liberal Zoroastrians remind conservatives that Zarathushtra himself was a reformer who broke with tradition. They find the essence of their religion in the *Gathas*, the Avestan hymns said to have been composed by Zarathushtra, and have less interest in the beliefs, doctrines, laws, and rituals that became a part of tradition after him and tend toward exclusivity.

Far from the oldest Zoroastrian communities in Iran and India, many of today's Zoroastrians live in a diaspora whose most significant populations are in the United States, Canada, Singapore, Hong Kong, and Australia. Zoroastrians in the diaspora are well aware that their populations are at risk. The greatest threat is posed by assimilation into surrounding non-Zoroastrian communities, primarily through intermarriage and conversion to other religions. Because Zoroastrianism teaches that every individual must choose to do what seems right, decisions that contribute to the decline in the number of Zoroastrians must be respected. The key to their survival is to promote cohesion, inclusion, and education among those who choose to remain fully involved in the Zoroastrian tradition.

10.5 Zoroastrianism as a Way of Life: Rituals, Holy Days, and Rites of Passage

Perhaps because of its status as a minority religion, the Zoroastrian way of life is rooted in a tightly knit sense of community and the routine practice of well-established customs. These customs can in turn be seen to reflect fundamental religious teachings. For example, Zoroastrian reverence for fire means that candle flames are not extinguished but rather allowed to burn out (although today birthday candles commonly are blown out). Reverence for fire relates generally to the deep-seated preference for light over darkness, which leads Zoroastrians to speak a blessing when a light is lit, and to cite a more specific example, to avoid killing roosters once they have begun to crow, for a rooster crowing signals the break of dawn and the return to daylight. Another fundamental Zoroastrian teaching, respect for life, is the basis for a general attitude of kindness toward animals. Custom dictates, for instance, that at mealtime dogs be fed prior to people.

As we turn to considering religious rituals, festivals, and rites of practice, we will observe how consistently these same fundamental teachings—reverence for fire, light, and life itself—tend to underlie many aspects of the Zoroastrian way of life.

Ritual Practices

Zarathushtra opposed many traditional Iranian rituals, especially animal sacrifice, but tradition says he established new rituals that were in accord with his teachings. To this day, Zoroastrianism is a tradition rich in ceremony and ritual, with regular activities carried out both within and without temples or other religious buildings. The most commonly practiced ritual activity is prayer.

Prayer and Purification   Zoroastrians pray five times daily, during five periods determined by the position of the sun: dawn until noon, noon until midafternoon, midafternoon until sunset, sunset until midnight, and midnight until dawn. For many Zoroastrians, this amounts to more than one hour of prayer per day. Zarathushtra himself is believed to have prescribed formal prayer. Its importance has endured throughout the centuries.

Daily prayers often coincide with the kusti ritual, which also should be performed several times per day. This ritual involves untying and tying the kusti cord while standing in a lighted space and reciting ritual texts. Recalling Yasmin's investiture ceremony described in this chapter's opening, we can see that the kusti ritual is a repetition in shorter form of this very important rite of passage.

The kusti ritual and the recitation of prayers require that the worshipper undergo ritual purification using water, washing the face, forearms, hands, and feet. Zoroastrians thus are expected to undergo rituals of purification on a daily basis. These ritual ablutions take only a few minutes. Longer, more elaborate rituals of purification are performed on special occasions. We have already seen, for example, that Yasmin took a sacred bath before her Navjote ceremony. This cleansing ritual, known as the *Nahn*, is also performed individually by men and women just before their wedding ceremonies. The *Barashnum* takes ten days and must be performed by a priest during the daylight hours and in rooms especially designated for this purpose. Special substances are consumed, including pomegranate leaves, ashes from a sacred fire, and consecrated bull's urine. The Barashnum is required in cases of severe pollution or as preparation for major ceremonial events, such as marriage or initiation into the priesthood.

VOICES: An Interview with Rustom Ghadiali

Rustom Ghadiali is a resident of Singapore, home to a community of about 200 Zoroastrians. This community was founded in the early twentieth century by Parsis who emigrated from India. Mr. Ghadiali is a Zoroastrian priest with a strong interest in the history and transformations of the tradition through time.

Zoroastrianism is an ancient religion. Has it taken steps to adapt to new conditions in the modern world?

The Zoroastrian religion has taken steps to adapt to new conditions in the modern world in some countries. In Iran, as it is difficult to get young boys to join religious orders and become priests, eighteen girls for the first time have become initiated as priests and carry out all rituals. Zoroastrians in India are still very orthodox and do not accept the same.

Rustom Ghadiali.

What are the greatest challenges faced by Zoroastrians and Zoroastrianism today?

The greatest challenge faced by Zoroastrians and Zoroastrianism is that their numbers are dwindling. This is because of late marriages, not having children, and not being allowed to marry outside the community.

What features of Zoroastrianism are most important to you in your daily life? Why?

Prayers are most important in our daily life, and thanking God for good health and happiness.

How common is the traditional Zoroastrian practice of exposing the bodies of the dead, and how is it carried out?

The practice of exposing the bodies of the dead to the birds is followed in India today, but it is slowly disappearing, as it is difficult to have vultures in urban settings. Also, vultures are dying as the bodies of sick Zoroastrians contain medicine which kills the vultures. The orthodox Zoroastrians in India are struggling to accept changes in traditional practices and to accept burial or cremation. It is only a matter of time when the practice of exposing the dead will disappear and burial or cremation will be accepted.

You are a Zoroastrian priest. What are your most important responsibilities in worship and in serving the Zoroastrian community?

The most important responsibilities of the priest are the carrying out of rituals and praying for any and all Zoroastrians. The religion as practiced in India and as practiced abroad has a lot of variance. If all were to follow the *Gathas*, the original verses of the Prophet, then there would be harmony. Scholars and the High Priest, however, enforce their own views. Also, the priests are not being looked after by the temples where they work and must depend on the community to pay them as they pray. They prefer to study and get educated in commercial subjects, so that they can earn and be independent.

Where Zoroastrians Worship   The strong emphasis on purity is evident in the designation of certain spaces as appropriate for worship. By definition, temples and other sacred precincts are set apart from the impurities of the world outside. Spaces such as private homes can be used for religious activities as long as they are pure in a religious sense. In India and Iran, this means that no non-Zoroastrians may be present (elsewhere, such as North America, non-Zoroastrians are not considered to have a polluting influence). Indeed, rituals often are performed in private homes, especially in India and Iran. Older homes are particularly suitable as they are believed to be inhabited by the spiritual presence of deceased ancestors— making these spaces desirable for rituals performed on the souls' behalf. In India, and especially in large cities like Mumbai, most religious activities occur in temples.

Temples include rooms and water wells specifically designed for purification rituals. All temples provide a source of clean water. Special kitchens are equipped for preparation of food, some to be used in rituals and some to be consumed in communal meals. Temples have various other rooms, including at least one meeting hall. The most important rooms are the ceremonial room and the fire chamber. In the ceremonial room, the floor is inscribed with grooves that demarcate a rectangular space 3.5 meters by 2 meters. The rituals performed within this space are of a special category and are named "inner liturgies."

Partially open to the sky, the fire chamber consists of a stone floor with a domed covering, vented in order to permit the fire to burn. This in turn is protected from rain and from the sun's rays by a partial roof.

Sacred Fire
Fire is of supreme significance in Zoroastrianism and plays a central role in ritual activities. A fire is consecrated through ritual practices. Once consecrated (and thereby sacred), the dying out of the fire is held to be a catastrophe. Sacred fires therefore are tended very carefully. The fire chamber in a temple is covered over in such a way as to prevent rain from falling on and extinguishing the fire, and fires generally are not extinguished but rather are allowed to burn out. Fires are protected from coming into contact with polluting objects, including corpses and the bodily fluids of the living, such as saliva. Fires are tended and fed with dried wood several times per day.

There are three main categories of sacred fires, the highest of which is the Atash Behram ("victorious fire"). India had over 100 Zoroastrian temples at the beginning of the twentieth century. Today, only eight of these fires exist. One of them is said to have been consecrated in the eighth century; others did not begin to burn until the early twentieth century. Consecration of the Atash Behram takes a group of priests nearly a full year to accomplish, involving intricate steps of purification.

Fire is employed in various ways in ritual practices. The most important of the inner liturgies, those that are performed within the specially marked rectangular space in a temple's ceremonial room, is Yasna, the sacrifice of the sacred drink haoma before a fire. The extensive preparations for Yasna include the preparation of the haoma, a mixture of water, pomegranate, ephedra, and goat's milk. During the three-hour ritual, the entire *Yasna*, the seventy-two-chapter portion of the Avesta, is recited while the sacred fire is fueled.

Priests
The Yasna liturgy and other ritual activities in the temples are orchestrated by priests, who also officiate at rituals outside the temple. As we have seen, Yasmin's Navjote ceremony was at her family's home, but such events can also be held in public places.

Priests have always occupied an important place in Zoroastrian society. As we have observed, in his description of Persia, the ancient Greek historian Herodotus emphasized the influence of Zoroastrian priests, whom he called Magi. The training and precise roles of priests and the organizational features of priesthoods

A Parsi priest tends the sacred fire within a temple in India.

have varied widely depending on cultural circumstances. Throughout the centuries, priesthoods have been made up of men.

Today, the nature of the priesthood varies somewhat between India and Iran. In India, training for initiation into the priesthood mainly involves memorization of sacred texts used in rituals. The training normally begins when the candidate for initiation is still a youth, and it takes several years. In Iran, where Zoroastrians are generally less insistent on maintaining traditional rituals, priests are not expected to be expert in the performance of rituals, and many work as priests in addition to having secular careers. Also in Iran, women have recently been allowed to become priests, while in India the priesthood is only open to men. It is normal for all Zoroastrian priests to marry and raise a family, although until the twentieth century priests were expected to marry within priestly families.

Holy Days and Rites of Passage

Most religions feature their own special calendar of holy days and periods. The Zoroastrian calendar is more elaborate than most, connecting days of the month and months of the year to various deities.

The Zoroastrian Calendar
Since ancient times, the Zoroastrian calendar has been based on twelve months of thirty days each, although during the Achaemenid period five days were added to the twelfth month. (Today, because of various attempts to align the calendar with the solar year, there are three Zoroastrian calendars, one or the other favored by each community.)

The first day of the month is named for (and dedicated to) Ahura Mazda. The next six days are named for the other six *Amesha Spentas*. The other days are named for various *yazatas*; for example, the sixteenth day is named for Mithra. The twelve months also bear names of divinities. Whenever one of the days aligns with the month, such that the same deity is honored for both, Zoroastrians celebrate a feast for that deity. And so, for example, the sixteenth day of the seventh month (September/October) is celebrated in honor of Mithra. To cite another example, the fifth day of the twelfth month (February/March) is celebrated in honor of Spenta Mainyu, the Holy Spirit of Ahura Mazda.

Annual Holy Days
Zoroastrians observe seven obligatory holy days, traditionally believed to have been established by Zarathushtra. Each of these holy days honors one of the *Amesha Spentas*, and each celebrates aspects related to its divine benefactor. For example, the holy day associated with Spenta Mainyu is named All Souls and celebrates, along with the Holy Spirit of Ahura Mazda, humankind, Ahura Mazda's primary creation.

Of the seven obligatory holy days, the one that is most popularly observed is **Nowruz** (or No Ruz), the Zoroastrian New Year's Day. Nowruz honors the *Amesha*

Spenta Asha Vahishta ("Righteousness"), who is associated with creation of the very special element, fire. Nowruz originally was celebrated at the time of the vernal (spring) equinox and still is by most Zoroastrians, regardless of which of the three calendars they use. Throughout western Asia, people of all religious and ethnic backgrounds celebrate New Year's Day at the time of the vernal equinox. Even for non-Zoroastrians, these New Year's celebrations tend to show vestiges of Zoroastrian influence, for example, the symbolic significance of fire.

For Zoroastrians, the spring equinox symbolizes the triumph of light over darkness. The holy day of Nowruz features a sense of renewal of personal commitment to righteousness and of communal ties. It is richly celebrated, with a special table on which seven treats are offered, all with names beginning with the same Persian letter: wine, sugar, milk, syrup, honey, candy, and rice pudding.

Death and Funeral Rites   In this chapter's opening, we witnessed the Navjote (investiture ceremony) of Yasmin, a nine-year-old Iranian girl. This is Zoroastrianism's primary rite of initiation, marking the passage from youth to adulthood. While other rites of passage (such as marriage) are observed through similarly elaborate rituals, the most elaborate religious activities signifying a rite of passage for Zoroastrians occur at death.

According to Zoroastrian teachings, death involves the separation of the soul, the spiritual element of the person, from the physical body. The soul is believed to undergo judgment by crossing the Chinvat Bridge, where it encounters the Daena, a feminine being who embodies the individual's ethical quality. Zoroastrian funeral rites are intended to free the soul for this journey, while also attending to the body in a manner that ensures as much purity as possible.

Because a corpse is considered to be polluting, it is away from water, fire, plants, and even fertile ground. This makes both cremation and burial problematic. This need to maintain purity explains the Zoroastrian practice of exposing corpses on dakhmas, or "Towers of Silence" (a British term from the colonial period), elevated circular structures with a platform at the top on which bodies would be left. Rather than cremating or burying their dead—as fire is holy and unfit for contact with a corpse, and the ground is sacred because it bears life—corpses are exposed to the elements, to be devoured by vultures and other scavengers. This is deemed to be the manner of disposal that best maintains purity. Today, in part because of laws prohibiting this practice, bodies are sometimes buried in burial vaults designed to prevent contact between the corpse and the Earth. A form of flameless electric cremation is also sometimes used.

The dakhma, or "Tower of Silence," provides a space for exposure of the dead body to vultures and to the sun. This dakhma is located in Yazd, Iran.

Zarathushtra. Copies of this painting of Zarathushtra are found in fire temples and Zoroastrian homes throughout the world. The original is found in the fire temple in Yazd, Iran.

Zoroastrian symbols—the sun, a fire, the moon, and the Faravahar—thought to represent the fravashis. These symbols adorn a Parsi temple in Ahmadabad in the state of Gujarat, India.

The Ateshkadeh Fire Temple in Yazd, in central Iran, is perhaps the most famous of the fire temples found worldwide in Zoroastrian communities. Although the structure itself was built in the twentieth century, the sacred flame inside is said to have burned continuously since 470 CE. Zoroastrians believe that fire is symbolic of purity and of Ahura Mazda.

10.6 Zoroastrianism as a Way of Life: Engaging with the World

Zoroastrians look to their religion as a source of instruction about their social and ethical responsibilities, gender roles, and care of the environment. We will briefly explore each of these in this concluding section.

Social and Ethical Responsibilities

At the outset of our investigation of the Zoroastrian way of life, we noted that it has always emphasized the importance of a tightly knit Zoroastrian community and the practice of traditional customs. As we have seen, these include communal observance of religious festivals such as Nowruz and other holy days as well as rites of passage such as the investiture ceremony. Zoroastrian communities take pride in the care of their temples and other religious buildings as well as in their social and cultural achievements. All Zoroastrians are expected to marry and to raise families, and responsibilities for caring for family members extend even beyond this life: individuals' moral behavior affects the fate of their deceased ancestors' souls.

Ethical responsibilities have always been a central feature of Zoroastrian life. Traditionally, even such daily activities as eating food have been regulated by prescribed rituals, for example, by the religious requirements to maintain purity. Zoroastrian texts from ancient times have spelled out specific ethical requirements. The early medieval text *Arda Viraz Namag* (*The Book of the Righteous Viraz*) is one notable example. Similar to Dante's *Divine Comedy* (and, in fact, this book was one of Dante's influences), the *Arda Viraz Namag* recounts a seven-day journey of the righteous Viraz through the afterlife, where he encounters the spirits of Ahura Mazda and Angra Mainyu and many instances of souls of the righteous enjoying heavenly rewards and souls of the evil suffering horrible torments in hell. In each instance, the specific virtue or vice is identified. The book strongly condemns such vices as lying, the breaking of contracts, greediness, and cruelty to animals—for example, beasts of burden must not be overworked; when animals are slaughtered, they must first be stunned; and young animals cannot be killed at all.

Concerns regarding ethical responsibility and social justice have, then, been featured components of Zoroastrianism for many centuries. And yet texts have also emphasized social hierarchies and obedience toward one's superiors, including that of women toward men. Accumulation of personal wealth, naturally resulting in situations of economic disparity, has been condoned, although dishonest means of gaining wealth have been condemned.

Today, although general ethical norms such as admonition against vices such as lying still guide behavior, many of the traditional rules and regulations tend to be overlooked. With regard to the once prevalent purification rituals—some of which are still very much in effect—a newfound emphasis on personal hygiene has become the equivalent of the older insistence on "purity." And rather than focusing on traditional lists of virtues and vices, a more basic ethical outlook has taken hold, based on the "motto" of the Zoroastrian religion: "good thoughts, good words, good deeds." Good deeds include supporting the poor and significant charitable efforts on the part of those who can afford such, including the establishment of schools and libraries. Along with aspiring to base their lives on these ideals, some Zoroastrians strive to practice confession of sins on a daily basis, mostly as a means of improving upon their moral behavior.

Gender Roles

The prevalent doctrine of dualism is reflected in Zoroastrianism's traditional tendency to maintain distinctive roles for men and women. Recently, there has been a general trend toward egalitarianism, but premodern texts tend to portray women that invoke images of chaos rather than order, which, the texts assert, is a relatively stronger characteristic in men.

This highly patriarchal perspective is apparent in texts such as the *Arda Viraz Namag*, which clearly asserts that women are to be subordinate to men. Even a woman who is virtuous in every other way but who has not been obedient to her husband is said to have no chance of crossing the Chinvat Bridge and proceeding to heaven. Next to obedience as a wife, the most important role for a woman is to be a caring mother. Despite the continuing influence of tradition, the declining number of Zoroastrians is bringing some significant changes. In Iran, for example, women have recently been allowed to enter the priesthood. In India, women still are not allowed to become priests. The gender roles and expectations of women are reflected in the female deities as portrayed in the Avesta, as chaste, motherly, and generally subordinate to male deities.

Special ethical norms and ritual practices apply to women, many of them stemming from Zoroastrianism's stance on menstruation as being polluting. The Avesta, for example, sets forth rules governing the conduct of a menstruating woman, including the need for them to stay at least fifteen steps away from water, fire, religious implements, and men. At the end of her period, the woman is to be cleansed with bull's urine, which was used as a disinfectant in ancient times.

Zoroastrian Centre in London. With 5,000 Zoroastrians, the United Kingdom is one of several countries across the world with sizable communities.

In the modern period, such rules as these have become largely obsolete. Most Zoroastrians today support a general attitude of egalitarianism, even if some limits are still imposed because of ritual regulations and other traditional aspects. The rationale for this attitude is not necessarily a modern invention. Although, as we have observed, premodern texts tend to present a strongly patriarchal perspective, the *Gathas* address women and men together, suggesting a type of equality in the time of Zarathushtra. As we have observed, girls undergo the investiture ceremony and become full members of the Zoroastrian community, thereafter wearing the kusti cord and partaking in the kusti ritual and daily prayers. Women have equal right of access to temples—unless they are menstruating, in which case still today they are not permitted to enter. In recent times, a category of rituals that can *only* be performed by women has become popular. Called *sofreh* rituals, after the cloth (*sofreh*) on which Iranian meals traditionally have been served, they involve the consumption of special foods and drinks. Overseen only by a select group of qualified women, the foods and drinks are consecrated through recitation of Zoroastrian miracle stories.

One notable sign of women lagging behind men in terms of participation involves positions of leadership. Women hold fewer seats than men on committees in Zoroastrian organizations, regardless of the location. Among the Parsis of India, women are not allowed to become priests. The degree to which Zoroastrianism will become fully egalitarian obviously remains to be seen.

Zoroastrianism and the Environment

Zoroastrians believe their religion teaches sound environmental principles that reach back to the prophet Zarathushtra himself. In fact, some claim that Zoroastrianism is the world's first "green religion." According to the Zoroastrian scriptures, nature consists of Ahura Mazda's Seven Bounteous Creations: sky, water, earth, plants, animals, fire, and humanity. Under the influence of evil, these have been corrupted. As Ahura Mazda's partners in the work of restoring all things to their original perfection, it is the responsibility of human beings to serve nature as well as its creator. In caring for the natural world, Zoroastrians believe they are acting in accordance with *asha*, the principle of cosmic order that pervades all of reality. They make the cleanliness of their bodies and their surroundings a priority and strive to maintain the purity of the land and water on which they and all others depend. In doing so, they hope to enjoy the benefits of good health, plentiful food, and other material rewards as well as the spiritual blessings that accrue from living in harmony with the will of Ahura Mazda.

These ancient principles remain at the heart of contemporary Zoroastrian thought. Representatives of Zoroastrianism at the 2015 Parliament of the World's Religions set forth these essential features of contemporary Zoroastrian teaching about the environment: The natural world is sacred because it is God's creation. God has made humanity stewards of the natural world. As such, human beings are

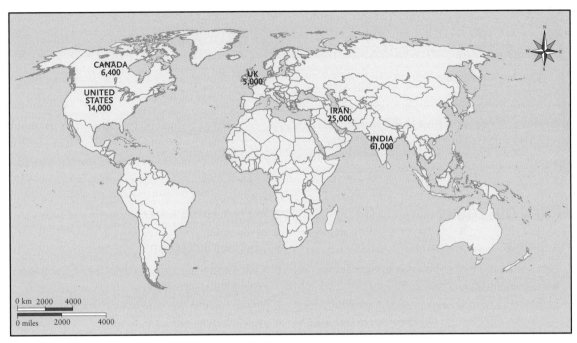

CANADA
6,400

UNITED
STATES
14,000

UK
5,000

IRAN
25,000

INDIA
61,000

0 km 2000 4000

0 miles 2000 4000

responsible for its protection and preservation. The present state of the environment cannot be improved until there is an increased awareness among human beings of their responsibility for the environment. Zoroastrians must work with others to bring about this necessary "change in the consciousness of individuals."

Countries with significant Zoroastrian populations (all figures are approximate, as estimates vary widely).

SEEKING ANSWERS

What Is Ultimate Reality?

Zoroastrians believe that Ahura Mazda, eternal and all-powerful, created the world and human beings. Ahura Mazda, allied with forces of order (*asha*) and good, continues to oversee the world. Also preexistent, however, is Angra Mainyu, the "Foul Spirit" who leads the forces of chaos and evil—those on the side of *druj*, the Lie. The cosmos is currently in a state of struggle between these opposing forces. This is cosmic dualism, which along with monotheism forms the basis of Zoroastrian teachings.

Zoroastrians believe, however, that in time good will triumph over evil.

How Should We Live in This World?

Human beings are constantly presented with a choice: to live righteously according to the cosmic order (*asha*) or to live according to the Lie (*druj*). Zoroastrian texts contain many specific ethical commands. Today, however, many Zoroastrians focus on the more general ethical ideals set forth in the motto: "good thoughts, good words, good deeds."

(*continued*)

SEEKING ANSWERS *(Continued)*

What Is Our Ultimate Purpose?

Human beings are believed to participate in the cosmic struggle currently ongoing, and therefore to play a part in the future triumph of good over evil. In the meantime, each individual strives for a heavenly afterlife, anticipating after death the judgment of the soul on the Chinvat Bridge through the soul's encounter with the Daena, a feminine being who embodies the person's ethical quality.

REVIEW QUESTIONS

For Review

1. Describe and distinguish between Zoroastrianism's two types of dualism.
2. Explain Zoroastrian teachings on creation and cosmology.
3. Summarize the historical relevance of Iran (or Persia) for Zoroastrianism.
4. Why is fire such an important symbol in Zoroastrianism? In what specific ways does fire play a part in the practice of the religion?
5. Describe Zoroastrian funeral rites, noting how Zoroastrian teachings relate to practices.

For Further Reflection

1. Many Zoroastrians today consider their religion to be monotheistic. Do you agree?
2. Why do you think Westerners find Zarathushtra such a fascinating figure?
3. Imagine a Zoroastrian student talking about religion with Jewish, Christian, and Muslim students who know nothing about Zoroastrianism. Assuming the student wants to point out teachings Zoroastrianism has in common with their religions, what do you think he or she would say?

GLOSSARY

Ahura Mazda (ah-hoo'reh maz'dah; Avestan, "Wise Lord") The God of Zoroastrianism; also known as Ohrmazd.

Amesha Spentas (ah-may'shah spen'taz; Avestan, "Beneficial Immortals") Seven angels—including Spenta Mainyu, the Holy Spirit of Ahura Mazda—who help Ahura Mazda govern creation.

Angra Mainyu (an'grah main'yoo; "Foul Spirit") Evil adversary of Ahura Mazda; also called Ahriman.

asha (ah'shuh) The true, cosmic order that pervades both the natural and social spheres of reality, encompassing the moral and religious life of individuals; opposed to *druj*. When capitalized, the term refers to the *Amesha Spenta* Asha Vahishta.

Avesta (a-ves'tuh) The oldest and most important of Zoroastrian scriptures, consisting of a collection of texts including the *Yasna* and *Gathas*.

Chinvat Bridge The bridge the soul needs to cross in order to reach the afterlife—wide and easy to cross for the good, razor-thin and impossible to cross for the evil.

Daena (dai'nuh) The feminine being who embodies the individual's ethical quality and who appears to the soul after death.

daevas (dai'vuhs) The various demonic powers aligned with Angra Mainyu.

druj (droohj; Avestan, "lie") Cosmic principle of chaos and evil, opposed to *asha*.

dualism In Zoroastrianism, of two types: cosmic dualism of order and chaos (or good and evil); dualism of spirit and matter (or thought and body).

fravashis (fruh-vah'sheez) Preexisting higher souls and guardian spirits of individual human beings.

haoma (how'meh) Sacred drink made in ancient times from the sour, milky juice of the soma plant; in modern times from water, pomegranate, ephedra, and goat's milk.

kusti (koo'stee) Sacred cord that is to be worn daily by Zoroastrians who have undergone the initiatory rite of the investiture ceremony.

Navjote (nahv'-yoht) For Parsis, the name of the ceremony of initiation into the community of Zoroastrians. See also **Sedreh Pushi**.

Nowruz (now-rooz') Zoroastrian New Year's Day coinciding with the vernal equinox, the most popularly observed annual holy day; celebrated in varying ways throughout western Asia by people of all religious and ethnic backgrounds.

sedreh (sed'reh) White cotton vest worn by Zoroastrians that symbolizes the path of righteousness.

Sedreh Pushi (sed'reh poo'shee) For Iranis, the name of the ceremony of initiation into the community of Zoroastrians. See also **Navjote**.

Spenta Mainyu (spen'tah mine'yoo) Ahura Mazda's Holy Spirit; one of the seven *Amesha Spentas*.

Yasna (yas'nuh) Seventy-two-chapter section of the Avesta containing material recited by priests in rituals; includes the *Gathas*. The Yasna liturgy, an important ritual, is the sacrifice of the sacred drink haoma before a fire.

yazatas (yah-zah'tahs; "ones worthy of worship") A large number, eventually fixed at thirty, of deities on the side of Ahura Mazda and order/good.

Zarathushtra (za-ruh-thoosh'truh) (Also spelled "Zarathustra") Called Zoroaster by the ancient Greeks; ancient Iranian prophet and poet, founder of the Zoroastrian religion; dates uncertain (between 1300 and 800 BCE).

SUGGESTIONS FOR FURTHER READING

Boyce, Mary. *Textual Sources for the Study of Zoroastrianism.* Manchester, UK: Manchester University Press, 1984. An anthology of Zoroastrian sacred texts, suitably thorough for an in-depth study of the religion, and with reliable translations and commentary.

Rose, Jenny. *Zoroastrianism: An Introduction.* London: I. B. Tauris, 2011. An engaging, dependable, and in-depth introductory study, organized by historical period and geographical locations.

Stausberg, Michael. *Zarathustra and Zoroastrianism: A Short Introduction.* Translated by Margret Preisler-Weller. Postscript by Anders Hultgård. London: Equinox, 2008. First published in German in 2005 (by Verlag C. H. Beck oHG), this slim volume provides a concise, yet remarkably informative, clearly written overview.

ONLINE RESOURCES

Religion Facts: Zoroastrianism
 A good resource for, as the site states, "just the facts."

Avesta: Zoroastrian Archives
 Provides links to an extensive set of Zoroastrian texts, including the complete Avesta, along with a variety of other useful information.

The Metropolitan Museum of Art Heilbrunn Timeline of History
 The site offers three essays with links to illustrations that are pertinent for studying the historical context of Zoroastrianism: "The Achaemenid Persian Empire," "The Parthian Empire," and "The Sasanian Empire."

The World Zoroastrian Organisation
 Created and maintained by Zoroastrians, a dependable resource that provides an insider's perspective on the religion.

Judaism

11

Chapter Outline

11.1 Describe Judaism's essential teachings about God, Torah, covenant, and Israel.

11.2 Describe Judaism's essential teachings about the Messiah, the afterlife, and Jewish mysticism.

11.3 Identify the most important developments in Judaism in the ancient, medieval, and premodern eras.

11.4 Identify the most important developments in Judaism in the modern era.

11.5 Describe Judaism's most important festivals and life-cycle events.

11.6 Explain the role of the dietary code and prayer in Judaism.

11.7 Explain how Judaism has engaged with the wider world in its Renewal movement, ecology, and Zionism.

IT IS A SATURDAY morning, and Seth is waiting to read from the Torah—the most ancient of Jewish Scriptures. Seth has spent the past ten months preparing for this moment, and he is about to become a **Bar Mitzvah** (Hebrew, "son of the commandment"). In late antiquity, a young Jewish male became a Bar Mitzvah simply by turning thirteen years old, but by the later Middle Ages a formal rite of passage had developed that signaled a young man's entry into religious manhood. By demonstrating that he can read directly from and comment on the Torah, Seth is proclaiming, before an entire congregation of worshipers, his intention to enter the Jewish community as a literate adult.

Moving a silver pointer shaped like an outstretched hand across the Torah scroll, Seth reads the passage assigned for that particular Sabbath morning. The sacred text before him is especially difficult to decipher because, as in ancient times, it is written in the ancient Hebrew language; however, Seth has reviewed this passage many times and has practically memorized it. After the service, Seth will be joined by friends and family who will celebrate his accomplishments with a party, gifts, and praise. This coming-of-age ritual has been

The Bar Mitzvah stands behind a lectern, facing an open Torah scroll, preparing to read his scriptural passage in Hebrew.

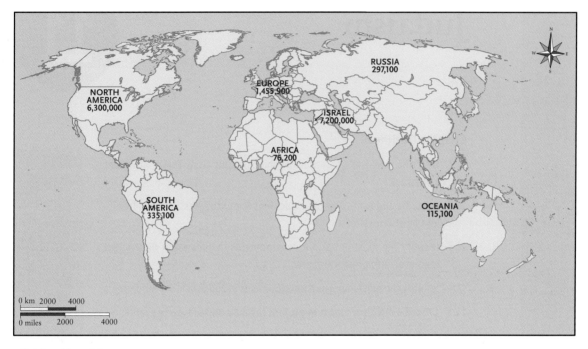

NORTH
AMERICA
6,300,000

SOUTH
AMERICA
335,100

EUROPE
1,455,900

RUSSIA
297,100

ISRAEL
7,200,000

AFRICA
76,200

OCEANIA
115,100

0 km 2000 4000

0 miles 2000 4000

Total number of Jews presently living in the world (all figures are approximate, as estimates vary widely).

enacted countless times over the centuries in Jewish communities throughout the world, but it is only since the 1920s that the privilege of participating in this ritual has been extended to young women (a **Bat Mitzvah**—a "daughter of the commandment"). Nevertheless, it has become quite common today for twelve- and thirteen-year-old Jewish girls to perform the same ritual acts that their male counterparts do and to receive the same recognition.

Of all of the life-cycle events in Judaism, the Bar and Bat Mitzvah rite reflects the most fundamental of Jewish beliefs. At the core of the Judaic belief system is the assumption that a very special historical and spiritual relationship—referred to, traditionally, as the **covenant**—exists between the one God of heaven and Earth and the people of Israel. By demonstrating both religious literacy and a willingness to freely embrace a life of sacred duties and obligations, adolescent Jewish boys and girls renew that covenant in a public and deliberate way.

The Bar or Bat Mitzvah ritual is not, however, a prerequisite for membership in the Jewish community. Historically, the only precondition of Jewish identity has been whether or not one has been born to a Jewish mother. Although Judaism has always accepted converts, the majority of the world's Jews have been persons whose ancestors were also Jewish. Nevertheless, this rite of passage has achieved its present popularity because it symbolizes a commitment to a communal religious life and to Judaism as the collective faith experience of the Jewish people.

Judaism is one of the world's oldest extant religions. In addition to examining the teachings and practices of the Jewish religion, we will also survey the historical context out of which they emerged and to which they responded. But first we present an overview of Judaism's teachings.

11.1 The Teachings of Judaism: God, Torah, Covenant, and Israel

Judaism has undergone many changes in its long history. For the purposes of our study, however, we will start by looking at those concepts and values that the majority of Jews living today would regard as enduring. We will then consider the diversity of belief that increasingly characterizes Judaism in the present age, beginning with Judaism's concept of God.

God

The Jewish religion is most commonly referred to as a type of **ethical monotheism**, as it assumes the existence of a Creator God whose benevolence and goodness are reflected in his love of humanity and who has imparted to the Jews ethical principles by which they (and the rest of the human race) are expected to live.

As Jewish philosophy developed over the centuries, an understanding of God's nature deepened, and additional qualities—such as **omniscience** and **omnipotence**—were added to the portrait of the deity. Most important for Judaism, however, is the concept of divine "oneness," which can be understood to mean that there is only one divine Being in the universe; this one Being is truly incomparable, and no human being (or anything we can possibly imagine) can be compared to this Being. Judaism's idea of divine **transcendence** presupposes that a fundamental difference in reality exists between God and the world he has brought into existence, and that this difference precludes the possibility of God's embodiment or incarnation in a particular human personality.

Yet for all its emphasis on God's "otherness," Judaism is not lacking a sense of God's nearness, or **immanence**. The very fact that Jews pray to God—and do so with the expectation that their prayers will be heard and that those prayers may move the deity to respond—suggests that there are limits to the distance between the divine reality and human consciousness. Moreover, the ancient liturgical tradition of addressing God through the use of masculine nouns and pronouns (still preserved in many prayer books today) suggests that, at the level of common speech, Jews have long thought of God in human terms. As we shall learn, contemporary feminist critics of traditional Judaism have challenged this practice, arguing that the attribution of gender subverts God's transcendent character. Other critics have also challenged this practice, arguing that any anthropomorphic imaging of the divine is a false representation of an unknowable reality. Such contending views constitute part of an ongoing conversation within modern Judaism over the nature of the one God Jews have long proclaimed.

One of the great constants in Jewish theology, however, has been its assumption that the Creator God was also the shaping force behind our universe and our human world. Judaism has never conceived of God as a deity who abandoned the universe once it was brought into being. On the contrary, Jews have always assumed that God is determined to see his creative purposes fulfilled in time. Judaism assumes, therefore, that God is moved to respond by every human act of goodness and contrition.

The Problem of Evil   How such a God can tolerate the continued existence of evil in a world that he has created is a question that has long troubled Jewish philosophers. The oldest Judaic response to this question—a question that philosophers today often refer to as the "problem of evil"—takes the form of an accusation: the people of Israel have sinned against God by violating his covenant, and therefore God has no alternative but to punish those who have rejected him and his laws.

However, the Nazi genocide against the Jews during World War II has prompted many Jewish theologians to reexamine this traditionalist argument and to reject this cause-and-effect pattern of thinking. For some, the spectacle of mass murder or, even worse, the possibility of global annihilation makes the biblical idea of a just, compassionate, and omnipotent Creator God insupportable. Indeed, according to this argument, such a God concept is no longer acceptable to post-Holocaust Judaism.[1] Still others, unwilling to embrace the agnosticism (or atheism) this argument inevitably leads to, insist on reviving the biblical idea of a divine "eclipse": the belief that God periodically conceals himself from human understanding, thereby creating a seeming void in which evil, for a time, may prevail.[2]

Nevertheless, according to this counterargument, even during this period of divine "absence," God remains present in many human hearts, and in time God will "return" to our world in the form of humanity's moral striving and severe self-judgment. This alternative view of God's role in the world holds that reconciliation with God, and a renewal of those divine values that reside within all enlightened human cultures, is still possible, and that one should never doubt God's continuing love for, and anguish over, the human race.

Torah

In addition to a commitment to monotheism, Judaism also claims to be a "revealed" religion in that its most basic teachings are believed to be the result of divine revelation. Most of the twenty-four books that make up the Hebrew Bible advance this claim. Furthermore, when Jews employ the Hebrew word *Torah* (Hebrew, "teaching") in its most inclusive sense, they are referring to the totality of God's revelation to the people of Israel. The very fact that Judaism possesses a sacred scripture presupposes a belief in divine–human communication, as well as a belief in the trustworthiness of those individuals—whether prophets or sages—who served as instruments of divine speech and understanding.

Torah, however, has additional meanings that are crucial to an understanding of Jewish faith. Thus, when reference is made to the scrolls of the Torah (which Seth read from at the beginning of this chapter), what is meant are the parchment copies of the first five books of the Hebrew Bible (known in English as Genesis, Exodus, Leviticus, Numbers, and Deuteronomy). Such scrolls can be found in any synagogue in the world. Jews view this portion of Judaism's ancient scriptures with particular reverence because these scrolls contain virtually all of the sacred legislation contained within the Hebrew Bible. Given the centrality of the idea of sacred law in traditional Judaism, the word *Torah* has often been translated as "the Law."

An even more expansive use of the word *Torah* can be found in the practice of referring to a comprehensive collection of commentaries on biblical law as the "Oral Torah." This multivolume anthology of interpretive and folkloristic writings, more commonly called the **Talmud**, represents the final extension in Jewish history of the idea of revelation. The teachers—known as rabbis—whose comments are preserved in these volumes claimed to be passing on the oral instructions of the biblical Moses, to whom God originally imparted his laws at Mount Sinai. Though not every community of Jews has accepted this claim as historically or theologically valid, the vast majority of the world's Jews have accorded to the Talmud a degree of sanctity and intellectual authority almost equal to that of the biblical Torah, thereby making the Talmud a virtual second scripture in Judaism. Much of the education of rabbis today consists of studying the Talmud, as well as a vast body of interpretive literature (commentaries on a commentary) that has grown up around the Talmud.

Mitzvot   At the core of the Torah tradition lies the concept of the **mitzvot** (Hebrew, "commandments"). Judaism can be described as a religion of "divine commandments." By the Rabbinic (or "Formative") Age, the number of such commandments that can be found in the first five books of the Hebrew Bible was fixed at 613, and each of these mitzvot was viewed as an essential link in a chain of religious laws that could not be broken. Today, at least half of these laws are no longer applicable, either to contemporary society or to a Judaism without a temple in Jerusalem, and therefore without a priesthood and a system of animal sacrifice. At the heart of this vast network of sacred laws lie the Ten Commandments, which can be found in two slightly different forms in the books of Exodus and Deuteronomy. For Jews everywhere, these ten pronouncements have served not only as the bedrock of their faith but also as the basis of their social and philosophical ideals.

However, just like the term *Torah*, the word *mitzvot* (singular, *mitzvah*) has taken on another, more informal meaning—that of "good deeds." In ordinary conversation, Jews routinely refer to any act of generosity or good will as a mitzvah. A glance at a traditional prayer book will reveal exactly which good deeds the rabbis expected every adult to feel especially bound by in everyday life. The list includes honoring one's parents, visiting the sick, outfitting a bride, and peacefully resolving quarrels between neighbors. But the greatest mitzvah, the rabbis go on to explain, is the study of Torah because it contains all the moral wisdom God has imparted to the Jewish people.

Nevertheless, there are practical limits to how far anyone can go in performing a good deed or fulfilling a divine commandment. Those limits are formally acknowledged in rabbinic law under the principle of "the preservation of life." Thus, the rabbis taught that whenever carrying out a mitzvah entails imminent risk to one's life or health, one is released from that obligation until the threat to life has passed. The only exceptions to this rule—and these exceptions became the basis for the concept of martyrdom in Judaism—are those situations in which a Jew is commanded to worship another god, to commit adultery, or to murder an innocent human being. In all other cases, the traditionalist view is that laws may be bent, but not permanently broken, to accommodate exigent circumstances.

Covenant and Election

Throughout its long history, Judaism has thought of God's relationship with the Jewish people as an intimate contractual relationship (rather like a marriage), freely granted by God and freely entered into by the biblical Israelites and all their remote descendants. In English, this type of relationship is referred to as a covenant.

THE TEN COMMANDMENTS

1. I the Lord am your God who brought you out of the land of Egypt.
2. You shall have no other gods besides Me. You shall not make for yourself a sculptured image, or any likeness of what is in the heavens above, or on the Earth below.
3. You shall not swear falsely by the name of the Lord your God.
4. Remember the Sabbath day and keep it holy.
5. Honor your father and your mother.
6. You shall not commit murder.
7. You shall not commit adultery.
8. You shall not steal.
9. You shall not bear false witness against your neighbor.
10. You shall not covet anything that is your neighbor's.

In the Hebrew Bible, Israel's covenant with God is often portrayed as a kind of treaty, with reciprocal obligations and expectations. On God's side, an unconditional promise is given to the patriarch Abraham that his descendants would be numerous and that they would inhabit the land God had given Abraham as a legacy. The people of Israel, however, are expected to live up to all of God's demands and to obey his mitzvot. The penalty for disobeying God is a temporary dissolution of the covenant connection, coupled with such punishments as famine, defeat in war, and ultimately exile from the very land first promised to Abraham and his heirs. Clearly, this later understanding of the covenant idea is conditional and even punitive in nature, and for many centuries it provided a theological rationale for the worldwide dispersion of Jews and their subsequent statelessness. Since the establishment of the State of Israel in 1948, contemporary Jewish theology has tended to deemphasize that theme and to stress, instead, the bond of enduring love, trust, and forgiveness that exists between Israel and God.

Much more problematic than the covenant idea, however, is the accompanying belief in Israel's **election**, or, as this idea is more commonly expressed, a belief that the Jewish people have been "chosen" by God to receive his laws and to live in his presence. No concept in Judaism has evoked more hostility and misunderstanding; yet, despite the controversy, it would be difficult to imagine a historically credible form of Judaism that completely lacked this concept. On one level, all that the idea of election in Judaism affirms—and all that the Hebrew Bible attests to—is God's decision to reveal himself to the people of Israel in a way that is qualitatively different from the way he has related to any other people on Earth.

On yet another level of understanding, however, the covenant demands that Israel actively serve God's purposes in history: first, by becoming a "holy nation," completely obedient to his will, and, second, by representing God to the peoples of the world who have no knowledge of his existence. This latter understanding of the doctrine of election is what the biblical prophet Isaiah had in mind when he spoke of Israel becoming a "light to the nations," and after long centuries of existence in a stateless Diaspora, Jews have come to see their "chosenness" as an obligation to serve both God and humanity, rather than as an assertion of moral or religious superiority.

Historically, Jews have thought of the covenant in ancestral terms, as most Jews are persons born to Jewish parents. Nevertheless, conversion to Judaism has long been open to any non-Jew who wishes to assume the responsibilities (and the hazards) that are part of membership in the covenant community. Those who enter Judaism by choice are required by tradition to prove their sincerity and to undertake a term of study to prepare for full participation in Jewish religious life. The final stage of conversion customarily entails circumcision for men who are not already circumcised and, for both men and women, immersion in a ritual pool (known as a **mikveh** in Hebrew). From that moment on, the convert is known as a "son" or "daughter" of Abraham, and no Jew by birth is permitted to treat such a convert as anything but a spiritual equal. Paradoxical as it may sound, therefore, it is possible for anyone to choose to become part of the "chosen people." Nevertheless, because Jewish religious identity is traditionally traced through the mother's line, the conversion of a prospective bride is critical to determining the Jewishness of her offspring. The Reform movement in the United States, however, has attempted to trace Jewish identity through the male line as well.

Israel

Since 1948, the word *Israel* has been used to identify the Middle Eastern nation-state that bears that name. But for many centuries, beginning with the Hebrew Bible, the word *Israel* connoted both a political and a spiritual community. In the latter sense, therefore, Israel is that covenant community to whom God imparted Torah and to whom he is bound by promise and affection. Like the idea of election, however, the notion of peoplehood implicit in the concept of Israel can still generate controversy today.

Biblical writers, however, had no difficulty reconciling ethnic identity and religious affiliation: God's covenant, they believed, was established with the "children of Israel" (that is, the lineal descendants of the patriarch Jacob)—and that contractual bond was thought to be unique and without precedent in history. As a consequence, Jews continued to think of themselves over the centuries as members of a single extended family *and* as a faith community held together by a common set of beliefs.

During the modern era, however, Jews found themselves faced with a political dilemma that soon took on religious implications: they could receive citizenship within the now largely secular nation-states of Europe, but only at the expense of their collective historical identity, and by denying all other "political" loyalties. For many Jews, eager to assimilate into modern society and determined to secure civil rights that had been denied them for centuries, the demand that Judaism redefine itself as a religious creed and nothing more seemed a small price to pay for political emancipation.

Traditionally minded Jews—notably those we will later identify as Orthodox—were generally suspicious of secular values and distrustful of the process of acculturation and viewed this new understanding of Jewish identity with alarm. In addition, by the end of the nineteenth century, a very different group of secular dissident Jewish intellectuals—early advocates of the political movement known as Zionism (and described later), such as Theodor Herzl—also rebelled, though for completely different reasons, against the notion that Jews had no claim to nationhood and were just another religious denomination among thousands in the world.

Today, many of those who practice Judaism are comfortable with their double identity as members of both a religious and an ethnic community, while at the same time recognizing the inevitable tension between these two perspectives. For those Jews who have chosen to immigrate to Israel and become citizens of a Jewish state, this tension almost disappears, though secular/nationalist and religious values continue to clash with one another in contemporary Israeli society. For those Jews who remain in the Diaspora—a majority of the world's Jewish population—the need to establish a balance between national and religious self-identification remains a challenge.

11.2 The Teachings of Judaism: The Messiah, the Afterlife, and Mysticism

In this section we will discuss Jewish thought about the Messiah and the afterlife. We will also discover that Judaism includes a tradition of mysticism, a way of experiencing God that transcends rational thought.

The Messiah and the Messianic Age

One idea that emerged from ancient Judaism that has had a profound impact on the Western world is the idea of a messiah (Hebrew, *maschiach*). At its root, *mashiach* means "anointed one" and refers to a person who was ceremonially anointed with oil in preparation for becoming a priest or a king. When most biblical writers used this term literally, that was all they had in mind.

Nevertheless, later prophets such as the Second Isaiah (c. late sixth century BCE) began to use this term metaphorically by applying it to either non-Israelite kings or to an unnamed future "prince" who would redeem his people from subjugation to foreign nations. As the beginning of the Common Era approached, the idea of a messiah continued to evolve. In works that lie outside of the Hebrew Bible, such as the first book of Enoch and the fourth book of Ezra, the term *mashiach* took on explicitly supernatural meanings, signifying a heavenly redeemer figure sent by God to rescue Israel and the world from evil. This more imaginative use of the messiah concept was linked in such books with end-of-the-world visions, complete with predictions of a new world order emerging from a final era of chaos and destruction. Such writers saw the Messiah as an instrument of divine power through whom God would accomplish both a final judgment and the ultimate renewal of life on Earth.

When Christianity identified Jesus of Nazareth with this redemptive-supernatural messiah tradition, it prompted the rabbis of the Talmud to reevaluate the very notion of a "messiah." What followed in their writings on this subject was a remarkably diverse collection of views, with some religious authorities identifying the biblical king Hezekiah (late eighth century BCE) as a "messiah," whereas others deferred the appearance of an equally human messiah (albeit one from the line of David) to the indefinite future. Despite this uncertainty over the Messiah's precise identity, a lively debate ensued over which tasks such a messiah might be expected to accomplish and whether his mission would be accomplished within the span of human history or only at the "end" of time. Although centuries of longing for the fulfillment of these messianic visions have produced a succession of "false" messiahs in Judaism, this belief and its advocacy among traditionalist communities have persisted within contemporary Judaism.

The Afterlife

Of all the basic beliefs of Judaism, belief in an afterlife or "world to come," along with accompanying beliefs in the resurrection of the dead and the immortality of the soul, are among the most elusive. Historically viewed, these beliefs are not fully articulated until the period of the Talmud. For most biblical writers, the death of the body entailed the passage of the soul into an underworld, where it would remain forever. Still, various biblical texts contain hints of a countertradition; for example, the second book of Kings depicts the prophet Elijah ascending directly into heaven on a fiery chariot (2 Kings 2:1–12). But such miraculous transitions from life to a mysterious afterlife are exceptional, and it is only in a very late biblical work, the book of Daniel, that we come upon an explicit reference to the dead rising again to life.

By the rabbinic era, however, mainstream Judaism had already embraced the idea of a postmortem existence in the "world to come" (Hebrew, *olam ha-bah*), though just what this belief entailed remained uncertain. Thus, questions such as whether the departed enter the world to come automatically upon death or only after some ultimate judgment has been passed upon that soul by God, or whether a general resurrection of humankind would precede or follow the Messianic Age, were left unanswered.

By the modern era, many reform-minded Jews concluded that any belief in an existence beyond this world was either an archaic folk belief or an insupportable, unscientific hypothesis. Yet despite such opposition, the classic conception of the afterlife, along with references to the resurrection of the dead, persists within most contemporary prayer books. In Orthodox communities, Jews continue to insist that these beliefs are an integral part of the Judaism they uphold.

Jewish Mysticism

The origins of mystical thinking in Judaism can be found in the Hebrew Bible, in which at least one prophet, the sixth-century figure of Ezekiel, recorded visionary trances in which God appeared to him as a figure of infinite mystery, seated upon a throne:

> Above the expanse . . . was the semblance of a throne, in appearance like sapphire; and on top, upon this semblance of a throne, there was the semblance of a human form. From what appeared as his loins up, I saw a gleam as of amber—what looked like fire encased in a frame; and from what appeared as his loins down, I saw what looked like fire. There was a radiance all about him. Like the appearance of the bow which shines in the clouds on a day of rain, such was the appearance of the surrounding radiance.
>
> —*Ezekiel 1:26–28*

Visionary passages like these testify to a tradition of ecstatic meditation in biblical Judaism in which a prophetic writer experiences the presence of God in a manner that is at once direct and mysterious. For centuries, Ezekiel's vision of the heavenly throne served as an inspiration to mystics who sought a comparable glimpse of God and of the heavenly beings who, according to biblical tradition, surround his throne.

Another popular biblical text that served as inspiration for Jewish mystics was the opening chapter of the book of Genesis, in which the creation of the world and of humankind is described. What distinguished this school of mystical writers—known as kabbalists—from other visionaries was a fascination with the mysterious process of world creation and a deep curiosity about the role of the Creator in this process. This type of mystical inquiry, referred to in Hebrew as Kabbalah (i.e., "received tradition"), is often accompanied by some form of esoteric biblical interpretation, and it often incorporates some of the boldest kinds of cosmological speculation Jewish writers have ever indulged in.

Key to the writings of the Kabbalah is one underlying cosmic metaphor, the image of the *Sephirot*. The *Sephirot* are ten in number, and they can be visualized as connected "spheres" of divine power, or as stages in a process of divine self-revelation. As such, they represent at least one of two things: the primary attributes of God and the dynamic emanations of his creative force.

However, the goal of mystical meditation in Kabbalah goes well beyond a desire to describe God or his relation to our world in quasi-mythological terms. The kabbalists were united in their desire to reconnect heaven and Earth through a process of contemplative prayer and restorative moral actions. Thus, every blessing that a Jew utters in praise of God, or every mitzvah that is performed in strict accordance with tradition, they taught, can now be invested with an almost magical power to "heal" the world (Hebrew, *tikkun olam*) and is directly related to the soul's longing to reunite with its Creator. The end goal of this longing, kabbalists believe, is *devekut*, or a "clinging" to God that represents the highest state in mystical Judaism of the covenant relationship.

The Lurianic system of Kabbalah, in particular, has had tremendous appeal. In the "beginning" before creation, Rabbi Isaac Luria taught, God (whom kabbalists refer to as the *Ein Sof*, or "Infinite One") withdrew into himself, thereby creating an empty space within which a material universe could take shape. Having performed this voluntary act of self-contraction (Hebrew, *tzimtzum*), the Creator then allowed rays of light to penetrate the void, resulting in a concentration of this creative force into ten spheres (the *Sephirot*). However, the ten "vessels" God had prepared to hold this *Sephirotic* light mysteriously shattered, leaving the

The traditional arrangement of the Sephirot is designed to evoke either the tree of life or the human body.

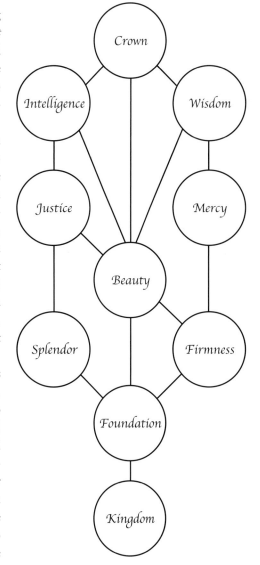

material universe in disarray. According to Luria, this cosmic event was the true origin of evil and disorder in the world, and this partly inexplicable catastrophe resulted in the scattering of divine "sparks" throughout the cosmos and within the human soul. Within each of us, therefore, is an intermingling of good and evil; even the worst human beings, he believed, retain some small portion of divine goodness. With the coming of the Messiah, all of these sparks would be reunited with God. Until that eschatological event transforms the world forever, each person has the potential to liberate that divine "spark" for himself or herself through a process of repentance and return to God (Hebrew, *teshuvah*).

Ideas and images derived from Kabbalah continue to exert some influence on contemporary Jewish thought, and particularly for those associated with the Jewish "Renewal" movement.[3] Admirers of Rabbi Abraham Joshua Heschel (1907–1972) and, more recently, followers of Rabbi Zalman Schachter-Shalomi (1924–2014)—who are determined to bring about a reinvigoration of Jewish spirituality—insist that such concepts as *teshuvah* and *tikkun olam* cannot be confined to the synagogue or to a life of conventional religious observance. For some, *teshuvah* entails a sincere and disciplined internalizing of our longing for God in the form of true piety, affecting every aspect of our behavior. For others, however, *tikkun olam* means, quite literally, actions that benefit humankind and promote peace in the world.

11.3 The History of Judaism: The Ancient, Medieval, and Premodern Eras

The earliest reference we have to the Jews—known variously as "Hebrews," "Israelites," and "Judeans" (depending on the era and the context)—dates from the late thirteenth century BCE. On a commemorative stone, inscribed at the request of the reigning Egyptian ruler, Pharaoh Merneptah (c. 1210 BCE), the following inscription appears: "Israel is laid waste, its seed is no more." No other reference to "Israel" or the "Israelites" appears in Egypt or anywhere else for centuries. Most of what we know about ancient Israel, as well as the beliefs and religious practices of the ancient Israelites, is derived from Jewish Scriptures, referred to in Hebrew as **Tanakh**. In English, we refer to these books as the Hebrew Bible, though Christians commonly refer to these books as the "Old Testament."

Dispersion, Assimilation, and Collective Identity

The composite portrait of ancient Israelite society and its faith that one finds in the books of the Hebrew Bible is one of seemingly endless conflicts and successive divine revelations. For the authors of the Hebrew Bible, the central conflict was over one issue: Would Israelites remain loyal to their one God (referred to, in Hebrew, by the consonants **YHWH**), or would they worship the deities of the nations that surrounded them? This was a politically relevant question, as well as a spiritual one, as the people of ancient Israel struggled to maintain their political and cultural

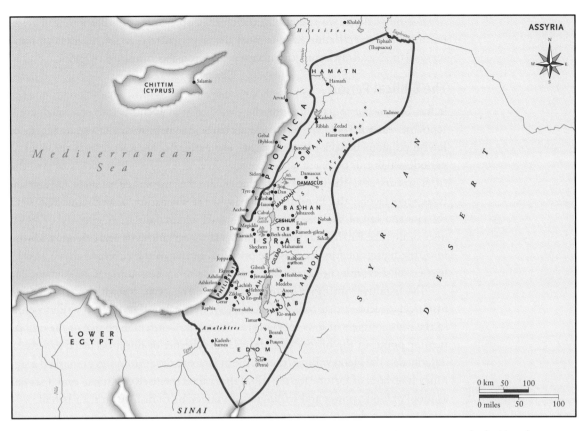

Ancient Israel.

independence for several centuries. Eventually, however, the tides of imperial Near Eastern politics swept over them, and after a series of devastating military defeats—first at the hands of the Assyrians in 722 BCE and later at the hands of the Babylonians in 587 BCE—the once-independent Israelite kingdoms of Israel and Judah were destroyed. Thousands of the Israelites were driven into exile or simply absorbed into the Assyrian and Babylonian empires.

Yet, despite this history of conquest and dispersion, the Israelites retained their national identity and their collective memory, and while living in exile they began to assemble a continuous history of their people and of their relationship with their God. Once completed, that history became part of their sacred scriptures. With the earliest copies of these books in hand, exiles from the kingdom of Judah began returning to their homeland after 538 BCE, believing that YHWH had at last forgiven them. Over the next few centuries, Jewish communities could be found not only in the historical land of Israel (which Greek and Roman geographers later named "Palestine") but also in Mesopotamia and throughout the Mediterranean. These communities were referred to as the Jewish **Diaspora**, and in the many centuries that followed, the number of Jews living outside of their historic homeland ultimately far exceeded those living within its borders.

For more than two millennia, therefore, dispersion, acculturation, and resistance to total assimilation have formed the larger pattern of Jewish life and must serve as the backdrop to any discussion of Judaism as a historical religion.

The Biblical Period

It has become customary to segment the history of Judaism into several discrete "epochs," each marked by certain key events that help to shape the direction of Jewish religious behavior and thought. The earliest of these epochs is the biblical period, which can be dated (speculatively) from the eighteenth century BCE to the sixth century BCE. The key events of this era are the rise of the Patriarchs (Abraham, Isaac, and Jacob); the **Exodus** from Egypt; the formation of the monarchy; and the rise and fall of the two kingdoms—Israel and Judah—that followed. Viewed historically, the Patriarchal period remains shrouded in myth and legend, with the towering figures of Abraham as the principal bearer of the covenant that YHWH first establishes with the people of "Israel."

The Exodus from Egypt remains a problematic event for which little credible historical evidence exists today. Nevertheless, in the minds of biblical writers—and in the consciousness of Jews for centuries thereafter—it remained one of the crucial turning points in the history of Judaism. For whether or not it occurred exactly as described in the Hebrew Bible, the escape of Israelite slaves from Egypt marked a significant reversal of fortune for the tribes that called themselves "Israel," and it served as proof of God's power and willingness to intervene in history on their behalf.

More than that, however, the Exodus also marked a decisive moment in Israel's history of divine revelation and lawgiving, for it was on a mountain peak in the Sinai Peninsula (variously identified as Mount Horeb or Mount Sinai) that divine instruction was provided to their leader **Moses**, who then imparted these teachings to the assembled Israelite masses. From this era on, "Israel" could no longer regard itself as a simple tribal society, cherishing memories of remote patriarchal leaders. The moment Israel encountered YHWH at Sinai it became a "confessional" community, bound together by a common faith in a Creator God and committed to his service. As for the land the Israelites were poised to invade, that was understood to be a gift from YHWH, as well as the fulfillment of promises made to their ancestor Abraham. But it was theirs only as long as they remained faithful to the God who had brought them into their "Promised Land" and true to the covenant he had established with them.

The Kingdoms of Israel and Judah   As a nation in the making, Israel began to emerge as a distinctive political entity only in the tenth century BCE, with the establishment of the dynasty of King David (c. 1000–961 BCE). For a time, David managed to unite a warring tribal society under his leadership, finally passing on the throne to his son Solomon (c. 961–922 BCE), whose even more exalted reign—at least in the eyes of biblical writers—brought a united monarchy to its height of power and fame.

The most important achievement of Solomon's reign, however, was not the extent of his legendary wealth and power, but rather the construction of the First Temple—a permanent sanctuary, designed to replace the portable tent (or "Tabernacle") of Moses's time, wherein prayers and animal sacrifices were offered to YHWH. By building this temple in the capital city of Jerusalem, Solomon ensured not only that the political and religious life of Israel would be geographically concentrated within one "holy" city but also that the Davidic monarchy would forever be associated with the most sacred site in Judaism.

Following Solomon's death, the northern tribes seceded to form a kingdom of their own, subsequently identified as the kingdom of Israel. The southern tribe of Judah remained loyal to the house of David and his descendants, and it bore the name of the kingdom of Judah. Both of these kingdoms, as we have noted, were relatively short-lived, and each in turn was overrun by the armies of more powerful empires. Of the two invasions, it was the second, by the Babylonians (587 BCE), that resonated most powerfully with Jews for centuries thereafter, if only because it was the occasion of the destruction of Solomon's Temple. In time, the loss of the First Temple and of the kingdom of Judah became the archetype of all later tragedies of displacement that the Jews were to endure and would be commemorated in both prayer and practice.

The Second Temple Period

The second great epoch in the history of Judaism, known as the Second Temple period, began with the gradual return of a relatively small band of Judean exiles from Babylonia, following the Persian conquest of the Babylonian Empire in 539 BCE. The rebuilding of the First Temple (c. 516 BCE), which the Babylonians had earlier destroyed during their siege of Jerusalem in 587 BCE, signaled the renewal of a centralized ritual life for Jews in what was formerly the kingdom of Judah, now merely a province within the Persian Empire. However, the movement of Jews between Babylonia and "Yehud" (as the Persians called Judah) not only provided for the repopulation of Jerusalem and its restoration as a center of religious life but also for the passage of ideas and literature from Mesopotamia to the land of Israel.

Even at the beginning of the Second Temple era, a "canon," or collection of sacred Jewish writings, was slowly taking shape. Thus, the formation of Tanakh can be dated most reliably from this period, and the persons most likely responsible for the gathering and editing of these books were scribes and priests. Using the historical and theological perspectives of earlier prophets as their guides, these priestly editors selected works that embodied a recurrent pattern of teachings about divine promise, judgment, and hoped-for restoration, binding together this diverse collection of sacred works with an archetypal vision of Israel's past and anticipated future.

Though politically turbulent, the Second Temple period saw both the growth of the Jewish Diaspora and an increase in the Jewish population of Palestine. In the absence of a Jewish nation-state, religious leadership within the Jewish community fell to the priesthood and to an intellectual class connected to the priesthood. These two groups are said to have formed a leadership "council," known as the "Men of the Great Assembly." Tradition assigns to this body the decision to "close" the canon of divinely revealed (or inspired) scripture. Scholars differ today on the probable period in which religious authorities—whether in Jerusalem or Babylonia—considered the period of prophecy (and therefore the process of revelation) to have ended. However, it is commonly assumed that by the third century BCE the writing and editing of the Torah had already reached a sufficient state of finality to allow Greek-speaking Jews to translate it from Hebrew into Greek. In time, additional portions of Tanakh were translated from available texts; this translation is referred to as the Septuagint, and it played a significant role in introducing Judaism to the larger Greek-speaking world. It was this version of Jewish Scriptures, rather than the Hebrew original, with which most early Christians were familiar.

Division and Revolt

One important development within the Second Temple period was the increasing tension within the Jewish community between those who favored social and intellectual assimilation into Greek (and, later, Roman) culture and those who resisted such assimilation in favor of preserving "traditional" values and religious practices. This struggle became openly violent during the Maccabean revolt of 167–164 BCE, as the leaders of the revolt found themselves fighting against not only Syrian-Greek armies but also their more assimilated countrymen who sided with the Syrian king, Antiochus IV (c. 215–164 BCE). Although this conflict finally resulted in the reestablishment of an autonomous Jewish state (c. 140–63 BCE), one result of this internal struggle was the gradual appearance of religious "parties" whose influence on Jewish belief and practice grew during the period of Roman domination and occupation of Palestine.

The first-century Jewish historian Josephus (37–c. 100 CE) identified the most important of these parties as the Pharisees, who appear to have commanded the attention and loyalty of the Jewish masses. Central to the Pharisees' form of Judaism was their belief in the "Oral Torah"—that is, a body of teachings imparted by God to Moses on Sinai (but never written down) and subsequently transmitted orally to later generations. For the Pharisees, these interpretive readings of scripture were an integral part of "scripture" itself, and therefore just as binding. Thus, the Pharisees taught that Torah—that is, the totality of divine revelation to the Jews—incorporated a belief in both the immortality of the soul and the resurrection of the dead. In the eyes of the common people, the Pharisees' knowledge of the biblical text and their familiarity with biblical law made them more reliable guides than the often corrupt and politically compromised priesthood. It is from the followers of the Pharisees that we derive our sense of what the dominant form of Judaism may have been like by the end of the first century CE.

A second group that Josephus identified was the Sadducees, whose influence on the Judaism of the time was much weaker. Drawing their constituents largely from priestly families, the Sadducees regarded the written Torah as exclusively sacred and authoritative and therefore rejected the very notion that an "Oral Torah" existed. Unlike the Pharisees, the Sadducees tended toward literalism in their understanding of scripture and therefore could find no warrant for believing in either immortality or resurrection. In politics, they tended to be sympathetic to—or at least accommodating of—Roman authority and therefore less likely than the Pharisees to favor revolutionary leaders.

The third, and most reclusive, community Josephus refers to is that of the Essenes, a general term designating groups of devout Jews who had withdrawn from society in protest against the moral and spiritual corruption of their contemporaries. These traditionalists viewed the temple priesthood with disgust and held the radical view of history that the "End Time" of divine judgment and global catastrophe was at hand. Such beliefs, which religious scholars refer to as **eschatological**, had become increasingly widespread during the late Second Temple era, particularly when coupled with a belief in a **messiah**. Although such beliefs were well known throughout the Jewish world, Essenes held to their faith in the imminence of the world's end with particular fervor, and they looked forward to a messianic age, when the Temple would at last be purified and the Romans defeated by armies of angels.

Many historians today associate the Essenes with a community of sectarian Jews who withdrew from Judean society and built a settlement near the northwestern shore of the Dead Sea, at a place called Khirbet Qumran, sometime during the second century BCE.[4] The religious literature written and preserved by this group was hidden away in caves near their settlement, and it was not until 1947–1956 that these ancient scrolls were discovered. Collectively, they are referred to as the **Dead Sea Scrolls**, and almost half of them are fragments of books from the Hebrew Bible. These copies of biblical texts are the oldest copies of the Jewish Scriptures known to exist today.

Last, and most transitory in their influence on Judaism, were those revolutionaries Josephus termed "the Zealots." Like the Pharisees and the Essenes, the Zealots were eager to see the Romans driven from the land of Israel and looked forward to a restoration of Israel's sovereignty and of its monarchy. However, believing that God would fight on their side, the Zealots sought to expel the Roman army through direct action, and Zealot agitation and rebellion were underlying causes of the First Jewish War against Rome (66–70 CE). Even after this war ended in the defeat of Jewish forces and in the destruction of the Second Temple, a group of Zealots continued to hold out against the Romans until 73 CE,

Masada was the last stronghold the Zealots held before taking their lives rather than yielding to the Roman army (73 CE).

The Touro Synagogue, built in Newport, Rhode Island, in 1759, is the oldest synagogue in the United States.

when their mountain fortress of Masada was besieged and overrun by the Roman army. Rather than surrender, the remnant of the Zealot fighters, along with their women and children, committed suicide (according to Josephus) rather than be taken alive by their enemy.

The Formative/Rabbinic Age

The fall of Jerusalem and of Masada, and the destruction of the Second Temple, signaled the end of the Second Temple era and the beginning of the third epoch of Judaism's history, known variously as the Rabbinic Age and the Formative Age (c. late first century through the sixth century). As long as the Temple stood, it served as both a treasured symbol of Israel's biblical past and the operational center of Jewish ritual life throughout the world. Once it lay in ruins, however, the Jewish people needed a new institutional center—a replacement sanctuary, until such time as the Temple could be rebuilt. The **synagogue**, whose remote origins can be traced back to the beginning of the Babylonian exile, provided just such a substitute, but unlike the Temple it was never a place of animal sacrifice, nor was it under the control of a priesthood. In all likelihood, the synagogue began simply as a place of assembly at which Judean exiles could meet and study together. With the Temple gone, however, Jews turned increasingly toward the synagogue as the place for religious leadership or for communal prayer.

Unlike the Temple, which could stand in only one place (namely, Jerusalem), a synagogue could be built anywhere. Moreover, almost anyone could build a synagogue or serve as a communal leader. Priests had no role to play in the ritual or social life of a synagogue, which made it a more democratic institution from the start.

The Rabbis
In time, the synagogue acquired a clerical leadership all its own, which brings us to the second major historical change that defines the Formative Age: the emergence of a class of religious intellectuals known as rabbis (*rabbi* in Hebrew means "my master"). The word was a term of honor conferred on someone whose piety and learning caused him to stand out among his contemporaries and whose teachings (or legal rulings) were sufficiently memorable that subsequent generations viewed him with respect and even reverence.

One such figure, who had come from Babylonia to study in Jerusalem, was Hillel (fl. 30 BCE–4 BCE), whose compassionate nature was as remarkable as his scholarship. According to legend, it was Hillel who, when asked (mockingly) by a pagan to teach him Torah while he stood on one foot, replied: "What is hateful to you, do not do to your neighbor; the rest is commentary"—a version of the so-called Golden Rule. Like Hillel, many of the early rabbis thought of themselves as more than just legal scholars whose expertise in biblical law allowed them to advise common folk on matters of correct observance. They also saw themselves as sages or wisdom teachers whose insights into human nature complemented their knowledge of divinely revealed law.

The Compilation of the Talmud   The signature accomplishment of the rabbinic scholar class during the Formative Age was the writing and compilation of the Talmud, a composite work that, in time, was seen as a second Torah or, at the very least, as an indispensable addendum to the Torah. On one level, the Talmud is a collection of expansive (and occasionally imaginative) interpretations of biblical law. The format of the Talmud is often dialogical (that is, a series of question-and-answer exchanges). Nearly every page consists of some portion of a rabbinic debate over the alternative ways in which a particular biblical statute can be understood or implemented. The practical objective of all these debates was the creation of an authoritative form of ritual behavior—referred to in Hebrew as **halacha**—that would enable the observant Jew to sanctify daily life and fulfill the commandments imparted to Moses on Sinai. God gave Torah to Israel, the rabbis believed, and now it was their responsibility to clarify its terms and relate them to daily life. In the section of this chapter on sacred practices, we will see how halacha informs the ways many Jews today live their faith.

The Babylonian version of the Talmud, compiled at the beginning of the sixth century CE, consists of sixty-three separate volumes covering a wide range of legal issues. The historical process by which these volumes came into being, however, can be studied in two stages: the earlier stage, known as the Mishnah (Hebrew, "repetition"), is written in Hebrew and consists of economical formulations of halacha, often accompanied by the attribution of specific legal opinions to particular rabbinic scholars; the later stage, referred to as the Gemara (Hebrew, "completion"), is written in Aramaic (a Semitic language, very close to Hebrew), and the rabbinic debates recorded there often take up where the Mishnah leaves off.

This process of recording and summarizing rabbinic debates continued, in both Palestine and Babylonia, during a period of roughly four centuries. As the body of rabbinic commentary evolved toward the next stage of completion—first in Jerusalem in the fifth century CE and later in Babylonia at the beginning of the sixth century CE—the Mishnah was combined with the far more elaborate text of the Gemara. Together these two scholarly works make up the Talmud. Judaism's greatest challenge during this period, however, was not simply that of preserving the teachings of its religious elite but, more important, it was that of protecting itself from a rival "sister" religion—namely, Christianity—whose political might increased throughout the Roman Empire in the course of the fourth and fifth centuries, at the same time that Judaism's power declined.

The Conflict Between Judaism and Christianity

Christianity, as you will learn in Chapter 12, began life as a splinter movement within Judaism, following the death by crucifixion of its central figure, Jesus of Nazareth, in c. 30 CE. Over the next two generations the early Christian community gradually pulled away from mainstream Judaism. Largely under the influence of Paul of Tarsus, a Pharisee who had become a leader in the early Church, Christians came to regard Jesus as the Messiah and "Son of God," the incarnate human form of YHWH. The letters of Paul and other early Christian texts indicate that most contemporary Jews viewed these teachings as heresy and banished Jewish followers of Jesus from their synagogue. By the beginning of the second century, the split between Judaism and Christianity was irreversible, and out of the matrix of Judaism a new religion had emerged.

The philosophical conflict between Judaism and Christianity sprang from a number of incompatible views on the nature of God, the covenant, salvation from sin, and the proper interpretation of biblical texts. For rabbinic Judaism, any material representation of God—either in the form of an image or a living human being—was barely acceptable, and even then only as metaphor. For Christianity, however, the embodiment of the divine in Jesus as the "Christ" soon became a central doctrine of the early Church. As for God's covenant with Israel, Paul argued that the Christian community had—at least at that moment in time—displaced the Jews as true heirs of the biblical promises made to the Patriarchs and the prophets; the Jews, he insisted, had alienated God by their rejection of Jesus and had (if only temporarily) forfeited their intimate relation to the deity. That the Christian and Jewish communities would, before long, rejoin each other in an expanded covenanted relationship with God was Paul's fervent wish and expectation. However, the first four centuries of the Common Era saw only a widening theological and social gap between the two communities.[5]

With the Roman Emperor Constantine's conversion to Christianity early in the fourth century, Judaism found itself facing not only a determined religious antagonist in the Christian Church but also an even more powerful political antagonist, as a succession of Christian emperors sought to stifle Judaism throughout the Roman Empire by imposing punitive legislation on the Jews and by condoning acts of violence against synagogues. In the eyes of the late fourth-century Christian theologian St. John Chrysostom (c. 347–407 CE), the Jews were the devil's spawn, their synagogues the dwelling places of all evils, and any civil relations between Christians and Jews, he argued, represented a betrayal of God.[6] Against such a background of institutionalized hatred, the Jews of Christian Europe struggled for the next millennium to maintain not just their faith, but their very lives.

The Age of Philosophy and Mysticism

The fourth great epoch in the history of Judaism, extending from the Early Middle Ages (sixth–seventh centuries CE) to the Early Modern period (sixteenth–seventeenth centuries CE), can be thought of as the Age of Philosophy and Mysticism.

During this period, the Jewish Diaspora stretched from China and India in the East to England in the West. Historians frequently employ the following terms to identify these historical/cultural groupings: Ashkenazim, representing those Jews living in Germany and parts of Eastern Europe; Sephardim, or Jews living in Spain, Portugal, and parts of North Africa; and Mizrachim, or Jews living in various parts of the Middle East. Each of these communities underwent periods of prosperity and decline, but throughout most of this period some of the most creative developments in Judaism took place: first in Babylonia (present-day Iraq) and later in Spain.

As the Palestinian Jewish community dwindled in numbers and prestige in the course of the sixth and seventh centuries, the center of Jewish intellectual life shifted to Babylonia and to the principal rabbinic academies of Sura and Pumpeditha. And it was Sura, in the early tenth century, that gave rise to one of the major figures in Jewish philosophy: Rabbi Saadiah ben Joseph (882–942). One unavoidable challenge faced Saadiah during his career—one from outside the Jewish community: the advent of an entirely new religion.

The Encounter with Islam   The emergence of Islam in the early seventh century (Chapter 13) posed a significant problem for Jews of Arabia and eventually throughout the Middle East. Islam arose when Muhammad (570?–632 CE) is said to have received a new work of scripture—the Qur'an—that was in the form of oral communications from God through the angel Gabriel, and that he saw as a more reliable revelation than that given to either the Christians or the Jews. Viewing himself as one in a long line of prophets that included both Moses and Jesus, Muhammad clearly expected the Jews of Arabia to accept his claim to be the last (or "seal") of the prophets and to embrace his revelation as the definitive message of God (or "Allah," as the one Creator God is referred to in Arabic) to humanity.

Although the Jews of Arabia would accept neither him nor his revelations, Muhammad found others among the Arab population to be more receptive. Muhammad's success in propagating his religious message was matched by his military success in defeating many of his more powerful enemies (which included some of the prominent Jewish tribes of Arabia), and after his death the faith of Islam spread rapidly throughout many of the lands in which Jews had settled centuries before. Although Muhammad's attitude toward the Jews, as expressed in the Qur'an, remained understandably ambivalent, from the eighth century on Jews were accorded a degree of tolerance within Muslim societies that they rarely encountered in Christian lands.

Like many Jewish scholars of his generation, Saadiah had learned a great deal from reading Muslim philosophical literature of the ninth and tenth centuries. Foremost among Saadiah's concerns, therefore, was the need to present Judaism to an educated Jewish audience already familiar with the teachings of both Islam and Greek philosophy, and to do so in a way that did not contradict Jewish Scriptures.

The result of this investigation, which Saadiah published as *The Book of Beliefs and Opinions* (933), is the earliest example of scholasticism in Jewish thought—that is, a systematic attempt to reconcile faith and reason by relating mainstream religious beliefs to contemporary philosophical arguments. Thus, Saadiah sought to prove the unique character of God's revelation to Israel, as well as the rational character of many (though not all) biblical commandments, and thereby strengthen Jewish belief in the uniquely trustworthy nature of Judaism's Scriptures.

Maimonides   The tradition of philosophical inquiry produced at least one more intellectual giant during this period: Moses ben Maimon, better known as **Maimonides** (1135–1204). In Maimonides, Judaism found one of its supreme philosophers; much of Orthodox Jewish theology derives directly from his writings. Maimonides, the son of a respected rabbinic scholar, was well prepared for this role by both his background and early education. When his family was forced to flee their native city of Cordoba, Spain, to escape the tyrannical rule of a militant Muslim regime, they found refuge in Egypt under the more tolerant rule of the celebrated Muslim ruler Salah ad-Din (c. 1138–1193). Maimonides was better known to his Muslim hosts as a physician than as a philosopher, though it is the latter role that concerns us here.

Maimonides's passion for logic and intellectual clarity is evident in all of his writings. In his *Mishneh* Torah, for example, he listed every single one of the 613 biblical commandments, revealing (even to the casual reader) that many of these mitzvot could no longer be fulfilled in the absence of the Temple in Jerusalem. Similarly, in his *Commentary to the Mishnah*, Maimonides clearly describes what he believed to be the thirteen essential "articles" of Jewish belief, thereby creating a dogmatic framework for any subsequent discussion of Judaism as a faith system.

Though not universally acceptable, even during and after Maimonides's lifetime, this compact statement of belief still serves as a useful reference point in any discussion of what today is called "Torah-true" (or "Orthodox") Judaism.

Ironically, Maimonides's most celebrated work, *The Guide for the Perplexed*, evoked considerable controversy when it finally became public, though Maimonides had not intended it originally for widespread publication. In this philosophical treatise, Maimonides attempted to grapple with some of the more problematic philosophical issues of his day: the existence and attributes of God, the nature of creation and prophecy, the problem of evil, divine providence, and the purpose of human existence. Throughout the *Guide*, Maimonides makes it clear that he distrusts any comparison between humanity and the eternal creator. At best, he argued, we can speak of God mostly in negative terms. For example, instead of saying that God is a being who lives forever, Maimonides advises that it is preferable to say that the Deity has no temporal limits. This particular approach to theology (and, inevitably, to biblical interpretation) emphasizes God's "otherness" and tends to remove God from the material world and therefore beyond the limitations of the human mind.

Like many of his Jewish contemporaries, Maimonides looked forward with some eagerness to the advent of the Messianic Age, though he was shrewd enough not to assign a date to that hoped-for event. Interestingly, however, Maimonides's view of both the Messiah and the era of his arrival is largely naturalistic, and it contrasts sharply with the more supernaturalistic traditions that both preceded and followed him:

> The "days of the Messiah" refers to a time in which sovereignty will revert to Israel and the Jewish people will revert to the land of Israel. Their king will be a very great one, with his royal palace in Zion. . . . All nations will make peace with him, and all countries will serve him out of respect for his great righteousness and the wonders which will occur through him. . . . However, except for the fact that sovereignty will revert to Israel, nothing will be essentially different from what it is now.
>
> —*Helek Sanhedrin, Ch. 10*

This demythologized version of messianic Judaism was Maimonides's principal legacy to future generations of acculturated Jews. But one important segment of the Jewish community, those drawn to mystical thinking, rejected Maimonidean scholasticism and its celebration of reason and sought to restore to Judaism some of its rich mythological past.

The Kabbalah Collectively, the many diverse traditions that make up the world of Jewish mysticism are sometimes referred to as **Kabbalah**, but when historians use that term they are thinking primarily of a school of mystics whose beginnings can be traced to twelfth-century France and thirteenth-century Spain. Common to all these writers was an acknowledgment that the hidden "essence" of YHWH—as Maimonides taught—cannot be fully grasped, and certainly never directly perceived or represented.

MAIMONIDES'S THIRTEEN ARTICLES OF JEWISH BELIEF

1. God the Creator exists.
2. God is uniquely "one."
3. God is incorporeal (and therefore all scriptural images of a divine "body" are mere figures of speech).
4. God is eternal.
5. God alone is worthy of worship and obedience.
6. The teachings of the biblical prophets are true.
7. Moses is the chief of all prophets.
8. The Torah comes directly from God (through Moses).
9. Both the Written and the Oral Torah represent the authentic word of God, and nothing can be added or taken away from either.
10. God is omniscient.
11. God rewards the good and punishes the wicked.
12. The Messiah will undoubtedly come (though no exact date can be known for his coming).
13. The resurrection of the dead will occur in the World to Come.

In a late thirteenth-century work many regard as the "bible" of Kabbalah—the **Zohar**—this entire structure of divine qualities and emanations is laid out in the form of a biblical midrash, that is, an extended interpretation of select passages from the book of Genesis. Central to this form of mystical thought is the idea that however imperfect the human race may be, we are still capable of interacting with, understanding, and even influencing God. This theology of immanence—or, more precisely, of divine–human interaction—is quite obviously at odds with Maimonides's view of a profoundly transcendent Creator. Consequently, the kabbalists felt free to evoke the Creator in explicitly anthropomorphic language (i.e., portraying God in very human terms).

By the sixteenth century, the kabbalistic system had matured to the point that a powerful and highly imaginative cosmology emerged, mainly through the teachings of one man: Rabbi **Isaac Luria** (1534–1572). The *Ari* (or "holy lion"), as he was known to his disciples, left no writings at the end of his short life, but his followers disseminated his thought throughout much of the Jewish world, and of all the many variants of Kabbalah, the "Lurianic" system is at once the most influential and the most complex. Luria taught that the individual believer could liberate the divine "spark" within by careful observance of the divine commandments and acts of self-discipline and meditation. In addition, in sharp contrast to mainstream Jewish belief, Luria envisioned each soul undergoing a series of reincarnations, as the soul constantly strives to return to its Source.

The potential danger—as well as the enormous appeal—of Lurianic Kabbalah became quite apparent a century after the Ari's death in the sensationalistic career of a messianic pretender, Shabbetai Tzevi (1626–1676). A Turkish Jew of obviously unstable temperament, Shabbetai became convinced early in life of his extraordinary spiritual powers after studying Lurianic texts. At the encouragement of one of his most fervent disciples (a self-styled prophet named Nathan of Gaza, whom he had met on a visit to Palestine), Shabbetai declared himself the "King Messiah." In 1666, he presented himself before the Sultan of Turkey, asserting his messianic credentials and his "royal" right to the historic land of Israel. The Turkish response to this would-be savior was to imprison Shabbetai for a year and then to offer him a minor position at court following his conversion to Islam. Shabbetai's acceptance of this offer not only exposed him as an apostate, but it also sent shockwaves throughout the Jewish world, particularly among those who had firmly believed that Shabbetai was indeed the messianic deliverer he claimed to be.

The Rise of Hasidism

Shabbetai Tzevi was neither the last nor even the most important religious figure to base his teachings on Lurianic thought. Within two generations of Shabbetai's death, yet another mystical teacher arose, this time in Poland. The **Baal Shem Tov** (c. 1700–1760) also taught the necessity of releasing the sparks of holiness within, thereby hastening the approach of the Messiah. His given name was Israel ben Eliezer, but his disciples commonly referred to him as the "Master of the Good Name" (Hebrew, *Baal Shem Tov*), a title that conveyed to contemporaries the belief that he possessed secret "names" of God that he could use in incantations. Orphaned as an infant, the Baal Shem Tov was given a rudimentary education, and at no time during his career as a spiritual guide was he regarded as a great scholar. Instead, his fame derived from his faith healings and exorcisms. In time, the Baal Shem Tov gave up the life of an itinerant healer and began to attract a growing number of disciples who were drawn by his reputation for wisdom and spirituality.

At the heart of the Baal Shem Tov's teachings was a profoundly immanental vision of God's omnipresence. For the Baal Shem Tov and his followers—who were soon called **Hasidim** (Hebrew, "pious ones")—God could be found everywhere, and everyone was at least potentially capable of spiritual communion with the Creator. To worship God properly, the Baal Shem Tov taught, one need not be a master scholar; the most ordinary of everyday acts, he insisted, if performed with an awareness of God's nearness and in a spirit of joy and love, become acts of spiritual devotion and serve to make everyday life sacred. No one was too humble or too depraved to turn (or return) to God, who required only a burning desire to perform his will.

At the communal level, the key to success within this system of mystical devotion lay with its leadership, and the Baal Shem Tov urged his disciples to choose a spiritual guide, or *tsaddik* (meaning "righteous one"), to provide a living example for themselves and the rest of the community of what it is like to live a life of intense religious commitment and intimacy with God. After the Baal Shem Tov's death, the Hasidic movement he helped to create spread rapidly throughout Russia and much of eastern Europe. In each major geographical center of Hasidic activity, *tsaddikim* appeared to carry on the teachings of the Baal Shem Tov. Each of these leaders formed a "court," or spiritual circle of followers. In time Hasidic dynasties appeared, as one generation followed another and as the loyalty to the father was transferred to the son. Many of these dynasties, formed in the nineteenth century, still exist today, with the result that virtually all Hasidic communities are centered around the personality and religious leadership of one man—often referred to in Yiddish as the Rebbe—whose authority in all things is largely unchallenged.

Opposition to the Hasidic movement arose soon after the Baal Shem Tov's death, and for the next two generations established rabbinic authorities in Russia and Poland sought to stifle popular interest in Hasidic teachings. Their principal fear was that Hasidism would lead to a revival of a messianic cult like the one that had formed around Shabbetai Tzevi. Yet, despite the determined opposition of the rabbinic establishment, Hasidism flourished, and by

A young Israeli Hasid with curled sideburns, commonly worn by men in his community.

the mid-nineteenth century official opposition to Hasidism waned as Europe's rabbinic leadership realized that it faced a far more formidable opponent in the Jewish reform movements that suddenly emerged in response to Enlightenment values during the late eighteenth and early nineteenth centuries.

11.4 The History of Judaism: The Modern Era

The modern era in Judaism can be studied on at least two levels—the political and the philosophical—for until the Jews of western Europe had achieved a certain degree of political emancipation, they were unable to fully acculturate within European society or benefit from the intellectual revolutions of the seventeenth and eighteenth centuries. For centuries, Jewish life in the West was characterized by both physical and cultural containment, the most visible symbol of which was the Jewish Quarter of many cities (or ghetto, as it was known after the sixteenth century), where Jews were forced to reside. By law, Jews were also restricted to certain trades and professions, especially money lending, but by the late eighteenth century many of these restrictions began to be removed. As more prosperous and highly educated Jews were permitted to intermingle (and, increasingly, to intermarry) with their Christian contemporaries, Judaism itself began to change.

Moses Mendelssohn

No better example of this pivotal transformation in Jewish life can be found than Moses Mendelssohn (1729–1786), the son of a Torah scribe and the principal Jewish representative of the Enlightenment, the eighteenth-century philosophical movement that featured growing confidence in human reason. Because Jews were not yet permitted to attend universities, Mendelssohn was largely self-taught in modern philosophy and several European languages. Before long, his philosophical writings began to attract the attention of non-Jews within his native Germany and beyond. His impact on the Jewish community was just as profound, and through his translation of the Hebrew Bible into modern German and his various other publications, Mendelssohn became one of the most effective advocates for educational reform and the modernization of Jewish intellectual life.

What Mendelssohn is best remembered for today, however, is his eloquent defense of religious freedom, coupled with a defense of the Jewish faith, in a volume entitled *Jerusalem* (1783). In this polemical masterwork, Mendelssohn entered a plea on behalf of religious tolerance and in defense of the integrity of Judaism. He argued that all higher religions share certain common beliefs (such as the existence of a benevolent Creator God or the immortality of the soul) and that because Judaism also held such beliefs, it was as much an expression of the "common religion of humanity" as Christianity or Islam.

What was distinctive to Judaism, Mendelssohn proposed, was not so much its belief system as its sacred legislation—its Torah, understood here strictly as divinely revealed law—and its emphasis on doing God's will rather than professing correct ideas about God or the afterlife. The essence of Judaism, Mendelssohn insisted, was orthopraxy (correct conduct), and not orthodoxy (correct beliefs). This interpretation of Judaism, it should be noted, was not acceptable to more conservative religious authorities, but it did appeal to more secularized Jewish readers who were prepared, in the next generation, to carry the logic of Mendelssohn's argument even further and to attempt to transform the belief structure of Judaism in more radical ways.

Reform Movements in Europe and the United States

The Enlightenment, and the revolutionary political changes it inspired, affected Judaism in various ways, but its most direct influence can be seen in the early stages of the Reform movement in the first decades of the nineteenth century. Beginning in Germany, where admirers of Moses Mendelssohn called for the political "emancipation" of European Jews and their gradual assimilation to Western society, the idea of "reforming" Judaism drew support both from lay community leaders and from a younger generation of rabbis who had been permitted to receive a university education. From the outset, the Reform movement sought to accomplish two goals: first, the modernization of Jewish thought and ritual practice, and second, the acculturation of Jews to the secular culture of nineteenth-century Europe and America. As in any "reformation," however, a split soon developed between those who were determined to achieve these objectives by radical means and those who were not.

At first, reformers seemed content with largely ceremonial innovations, insisting, for example, that rabbinic sermons be delivered in the vernacular language of the nation in which they were living (rather than in Yiddish, the Germanic language of European Jews) or that men and women be permitted to sit together in synagogue during religious services (as opposed to separate seating, which had been the norm for hundreds of years). By the 1840s, however, the demands of the more aggressive reformers became increasingly anti-traditionalist and theologically innovative, as reformist rabbis increasingly embraced the idea of Judaism as an evolving religious culture. All of these changes were opposed vigorously by more traditionalist rabbis, who, from this time forward, came to be described as "Orthodox" religious authorities.

Reform Judaism   This more radical type of reformist thinking flourished in the United States after the Civil War. By the late 1880s, Rabbi Kaufmann Kohler (1843–1926) had drafted a set of principles and objectives—known today as "The Pittsburgh Platform of 1885"—that defined the "essence" of Judaism for Kohler and many of his reformist contemporaries. The most important features of this "platform" can be found in its most negative statements, namely, that the Reform movement rejected the biblical idea of a direct, finite, and exclusive revelation from God—the traditional understanding of the concept of Torah. The reformists opted instead for the concept of an evolving (and therefore universal) revelation, an idea that was easily gleaned from the writings of Moses Mendelssohn. This way, Kohler and his colleagues were able to renounce the dietary code and all other forms of "Mosaic legislation" deemed unacceptable to the Reform rabbinate (such as circumcision and rigorous Sabbath observance) on the grounds that they were "not adapted to the views and habits of modern civilization." And in language designed specifically to suppress any sympathy for Jewish aspirations to return to the historic land of Israel, the Pittsburgh Platform declared boldly that the Jews were no longer a nation and therefore no longer desired to return to, or to restore, a nation-state in Palestine.

Conservative Judaism   However acceptable these innovations may have seemed to those American Jews who identified with the Reform movement, they were clearly unacceptable to the overwhelming majority of European Jews who began to immigrate to the United States in rapidly increasing numbers during the last two decades of the nineteenth century and the first decade of the twentieth century. As the Jewish population of America increased exponentially, the religious diversity of that community increased as well. By the middle of the twentieth century, the American Jewish community found itself largely divided into three movements: Reform, Orthodox, and Conservative. Of these three, the Conservative movement had emerged, by the 1950s, as the Reform movement's principal rival, and its appeal can be explained, historically, as a "counter-reformation" both within and outside of the Reform movement itself.

Thus, for those Jews who were initially drawn to reformist ideals but who found the more extreme changes advocated by the early Reform movement distasteful, Conservative Judaism offered a more moderate departure from traditional (or what is now called "Orthodox") beliefs and practices. Like their Reform counterparts, Conservative rabbis acknowledged the evolutionary character of Judaism and embraced the need for substantive change; unlike the leading reformists, however, they were not willing to abandon either principles of faith or religious behaviors that had defined Judaism for many centuries. The result was the formation of a "third way" of responding to the challenges facing Judaism in the modern era, in which a high level of adaptation to secular culture was combined with a selective relaxation of halacha.

In its formative stages, however, the most obvious difference between Conservative Judaism and its Reform and Orthodox counterparts was the public support of both its rabbis and laity for **Zionism**, a movement that asserts a belief in Jewish national identity and in the necessity of resuming national life within the historic land of Israel. Throughout its more than 100-year existence, the Conservative movement has been a fervent advocate for both the formation of a Jewish nation-state in what is now Israel and for the emigration of American Jews to this state.

Reconstructionist Judaism   One of the most important offshoots of Conservative Judaism first emerged in America in the 1930s. Known today as Reconstructionism, this new school of thought centered on the teachings of Rabbi

Mordecai Kaplan (1881–1983). By the 1960s, however, the Reconstructionists had formally separated themselves from Conservative Judaism, first by writing their own prayer book and later by establishing their own rabbinical seminary. Though few in number, Reconstructionists have had a far-reaching effect on the thought and religious practices of non-Orthodox Judaism in the United States.

Philosophically, Reconstructionism occupies a position somewhere between Conservatism and Reform. Unlike their Reform counterparts, Reconstructionists held firm to the concept of Jewish nationhood; in fact, for Mordecai Kaplan, the idea that Jews constituted a separate and distinctive *civilization* was central to his belief system. What followed from that assumption was a desire to retain as many traditional "folkways"—which was Kaplan's way of referring to such ritual practices as the dietary code and circumcision—as modern Jews found meaningful. As a consequence, the Reconstructionist movement tended to place greater emphasis on the historical continuity of religious customs than did Reform Judaism.

At the same time, Reconstructionism developed a much more naturalistic conception of God than either Conservativism or Reform was willing to support. For Kaplan and his followers, God could no longer be thought of as a noun—that is, as a metaphysical "entity," separate from humanity—but rather as the expression of whatever moral and spiritual potential human beings possess in their search for holiness and righteousness. Kaplan's virtual abandonment of the traditional concept of divine transcendence signaled a dramatic break with the Orthodox faith in which he was raised.

For many Jews, Reconstructionist theology seemed to be a contradiction in terms: lacking a true Judaic concept of God, it could be nothing more than a disguised form of secular humanism, and as such, a heretical rejection of Torah. Kaplan's defenders, however, insisted that, as an "evolving religious civilization," Judaism's understanding of God and of the covenant would have to change as well, and in the process absorb contemporary scientific views of the cosmos and of the human mind.

THE VARIETIES OF MODERN JUDAISM

PRACTICE OF HALACHA

ORTHODOXY: Strict observance of halacha, allowing for limited adaptation to changing conditions of life (Sabbath, family purity, and dietary laws).
CONSERVATISM: Serious commitment to observance of halacha, combined with a significant degree of adaptation to changing circumstances of modern life.

REFORM: Liberal view of halacha, generally regarding Sabbath and dietary laws as optional observances.
RECONSTRUCTIONISM: A respectful but liberal view of halacha, coupled with a view of religious practices as "folkways" and facets of Judaism as a civilization.

(continued)

GENDER SEPARATION

ORTHODOXY: Gender separation and differentiation: separate seating for women in synagogue; opposition to rabbinic ordination of women.

CONSERVATISM: Rejection of gender separation and differentiation; mixed seating in synagogue and ordination of women.

REFORM: Rejection of all forms of gender separation and differentiation; first to ordain women as rabbis and eager adoption of the Bat Mitzvah.

RECONSTRUCTIONISM: Rejection of all gender separation and differentiation; ordains women as rabbis and first movement to support the Bat Mitzvah.

HEBREW LANGUAGE IN WORSHIP

ORTHODOXY: Retention of Hebrew as language of prayer and strict adherence to traditional prayer routines.

CONSERVATISM: Retention of Hebrew as the language of prayer and preservation of most traditional prayer routines coupled with innovative practices (e.g., Bat Mitzvah).

REFORM: Initial opposition to use of Hebrew prayers changes in the course of the twentieth century to greater enthusiasm.

RECONSTRUCTIONISM: Retention of many traditional Hebrew prayers combined with an interest in innovative expressions of faith in English.

ZIONISM AND ISRAEL

ORTHODOXY: Some ambivalence toward Israel; fervent opposition toward secular Zionism.

CONSERVATISM: Enthusiastic support of Zionism and Israel.

REFORM: Initially opposed to Zionism, but support increased during the twentieth century.

RECONSTRUCTIONISM: Intense interest in Jewish "peoplehood" and enthusiastic support for cultural and political Zionism.

TORAH

ORTHODOXY: "Torah True": belief in divine revelation at Sinai and in rabbinic interpretation of Torah.

CONSERVATISM: "Positive-Historical" Judaism: belief in divine inspiration of scriptures and acceptance of historical process in the formation of halacha.

REFORM: "Progressive Judaism" committed to an evolutionary view of Jewish belief and religious practice.

RECONSTRUCTIONISM: "Humanistic Judaism" rooted in the belief that Torah is the expression of the religious creativity of the Jewish people.

AFTERLIFE, REDEMPTION, AND THE SOUL

ORTHODOXY: Literal belief in the afterlife, immortality of the soul, resurrection of the dead, messianic redemption of Israel and the world.

CONSERVATISM: Generally, nonliteral belief in the afterlife, immortality of the soul, and resurrection of the dead.

REFORM: Skeptical view of any literal belief in divine revelation, afterlife, resurrection of the dead; figurative view of immortality of the soul and messianic redemption.

RECONSTRUCTIONISM: Generally, agnostic view of any belief in a personal God, combined with a fervent belief in the creative potential of human beings.

The Shoah and the State of Israel

During the twentieth century, two of the most extraordinary events in Jewish history occurred: one traumatic, the other transformative. Both events have had a profound effect on the beliefs and practices of contemporary Judaism. The first event, referred to in Hebrew as the Shoah—or, more commonly, as the **Holocaust**—can be seen as the single greatest tragedy of modern Jewish life: the most successful attempt in history by anti-Semites to rid the world of both the religion Judaism and the Jewish people.

The Shoah   The word *Shoah* itself requires some explanation, if only because it has a different connotation than the more familiar word, *Holocaust*. In Hebrew the word *shoah* means "whirlwind," and as a metaphor it captures—as well as any image can—the insane rage of anti-Semitic hatred that was loosed on Europe's Jews during World War II. Many Jews prefer this term, unfamiliar as it may be to English-speaking audiences, precisely because it avoids the connotation of a divinely commanded sacrifice, which is exactly what the biblical term *holocaust* (or "burnt offering") brings to mind.

For centuries Jews had been the targets of Christian and occasionally Muslim hostility and persecution, but until Adolf Hitler and Nazi Germany embarked on the "Final Solution," no ruler or regime ever entertained the idea of total extermination. In Hitler's autobiography, *Mein Kampf* (1925), he described the Jews as a disease organism within the body of European society that he and his followers proposed to destroy forever. The genocidal policies that his government pursued represented a logical outcome of this essentially racist conception of the Jews and their faith. To carry out this genocidal campaign, Hitler mobilized not only the resources of Germany but also the support of willing collaborators throughout Europe. There is little doubt that had German armies defeated the United States, Britain, and the Soviet Union during World War II, the annihilation of the world's Jewish population would have been one of Hitler's proudest accomplishments. Even in defeat, however, the Nazis destroyed roughly one-third of the world's Jewish population, and the legacy of torture and mass murder they left behind has deeply scarred the Jewish consciousness.

Contemporary Jewish philosophers have responded to the tragedy of the Shoah in remarkably diverse ways. For one theologian in particular, Ignaz Maybaum (1897–1976), the slaughter of innocents can be seen as a kind of *churban* (Hebrew, "divinely willed sacrifice"), through which the Jews perform an act of vicarious atonement for the sins of the world.[7] For theologian Richard Rubenstein (b. 1924), such logic is morally insane. Rubenstein insists that the random killing of 6 million Jews (not to mention the

The entrance gate at Auschwitz.

untold suffering and murder of many more millions of non-Jews) challenges, at the most fundamental level, Judaism's belief in a just and benevolent Creator who values every single human life. In his book *After Auschwitz*, Rubenstein insisted that Judaism's historic God concept is "dead" and that no religious philosophy that is still committed to biblical ideas of divine justice and retribution can withstand scrutiny in an age of genocide and mass destruction.[8] For philosopher and rabbi Eliezer Berkovits (1908–1992),[9] however, the mystery of God's presence in history is deepened by the Shoah, not refuted by it, and ours is not the first generation to reflect on God's "hiddenness" or on the terrible consequences of human freedom. For human beings to be capable of choice, he argues, God must "restrain" himself and allow his human agents to exercise their moral will, even if the consequences of divine restraint are catastrophic.

None of these theologians, however, is willing to see the Shoah as an instance of merited (and therefore inevitable) divine punishment. Their refusal to accept that now-archaic model of God's judgment and response to human sin marks a definitive break with traditional Jewish thought. If much of the world's Jewish population can no longer declare—in the words of the traditional liturgy—"because of our sins were we exiled from the land," then what model of covenant relations can now be invoked to make both human suffering and world redemption meaningful?

For theologian Abraham Joshua Heschel, the only defensible Jewish theology after the Shoah is one that posits God's need for, and yearning after, humankind. The covenant relationship, as Heschel understands it, is a reciprocal one in which human moral intelligence and divine "pathos" join in the act of worship and of love. God's longing for us does not, Heschel insists, annul the reality of evil or the terrible freedom with which human beings have been invested. It does, however, establish what Heschel calls an "analogy of being," that is, a hint of divine likeness in every soul, and thereby the capacity to mend a broken world. If all we knew of God, Heschel argues, was a theory of omnipotence or omniscience, then the Shoah might very well sweep away that merely conceptual reality. But the truth is, he continues, that we know God at a much deeper level of moral consciousness, and that form of the divine presence abides even in the midst of the most appalling evils.[10]

Statehood for Israel

The second pivotal event of modern Jewish history is the establishment of the State of Israel in 1948, what one philosopher has called the "the Jewish return into history."[11] The Zionist philosophy on which the State of Israel rests is really several philosophical/religious arguments in one. In its earliest form, "Zionism" is simply a feeling of attachment to an ancestral homeland in which a vast majority of Jews, past and present, have never lived. Even though a comparatively small population of Jews continued to live in Palestine for centuries after the Roman dispersion of Jews in the second century CE, most Jews were content to sing "next year in Jerusalem" at the Passover Seder without ever really contemplating a return to the land of biblical Israel.

A decisive shift in such thinking occurred, however, in the course of the nineteenth century. Two Orthodox rabbis—Yehudah Hai Alkalai (1798–1878) and Zvi Hirsch Kalischer (1795–1874)—argued passionately for a messianic view of Jewish history, urging their contemporaries to emigrate to Palestine in the expectation that the redemption of Israel was about to be accomplished, but only if the Jews took the first practical step of occupying and restoring the land.[12] Their writings were largely ignored within their lifetimes, but the arguments of an assimilated Austrian Jew, writing near the end of the century, attracted much greater attention.

For Theodor Herzl (1860–1904), the rapid growth of anti-Semitism had made the condition of eastern European Jews so precarious that something had to be done—apart from continuing mass emigration to the United States—to deal with the poverty and desperation of the Jewish masses. Herzl's solution was the establishment of an internationally recognized Jewish state, either in Palestine or Argentina. He laid out his ideas in an extended tract entitled "The Jewish State" (1896)[13] and later in a utopian novel, *The Old New Land* (1902).[14] Herzl died in 1904 and never lived to see any of his ideas come to fruition. The Zionist movement he helped to found continued to solicit support for his ideas, and in 1917 British Zionists found a sympathetic advocate in the foreign minister of Great Britain, Lord Arthur Balfour (1848–1930).

Balfour's private letter (now known as the Balfour Declaration) to the most prominent Jew in England, Lord Walter Rothschild (1868–1937), is the earliest sign that any major power was willing, for whatever reason, to validate Zionist claims to a political stakehold in Palestine. In carefully guarded diplomatic language, Balfour declared his government's willingness to establish a "national home for the Jewish people," provided that "nothing shall be done which may prejudice the civil and religious rights of existing non-Jewish communities in Palestine."[15] Within a decade of this proclamation, however, both Great Britain and the rapidly growing Jewish community in Palestine discovered just how intense Palestinian Arab opposition to increased Jewish immigration really was. By the late 1930s, as Great Britain sought to limit sharply the number of Jews who could legally enter Palestine, the stage was set for a succession of wars between Arabs and Jews—wars that have continued to the present day.

As a secular ideology, Zionism rests on a few basic assumptions. The first holds that anti-Semitism may abate from time to time, but it will never disappear, and as long as Jews are hated anywhere in the world, their lives are in peril. The second assumption is that the only guarantee of physical survival in a hostile world is national sovereignty—because only a nation-state can effectively defend its citizens. Third, the guest–host relationship Jews have lived under, whether in Christian or in Muslim lands, has always

This painting of Herzl is one of many that appear on Israeli currency.

עש
שק

בנק י

been inherently unstable, and on occasion threatening to Jewish survival. If Jews are to have any hope of a secure future, they will have to regain their collective autonomy, which can be accomplished only through political means. And if one adds to all of this the specifically religious belief that the rebirth of the State of Israel represents the beginning stage of messianic redemption of the world, one has a totality of ideas that have been employed to rationalize the transformation of the world Jewish community back into a politico-religious entity. Viewed from this perspective, Jewish history has come full circle in our time, as Jews search for ways to reconnect their religious lives with their enduring sense of peoplehood.

11.5 Judaism as a Way of Life: Festivals, the Sabbath, and Life-Cycle Events

As Judaism has historically placed great emphasis on the sanctification of time, any consideration of Judaism as a "way of life" should begin with the ways in which Jews mark the passage of time. Like many ancient peoples, Jews in antiquity employed a modified lunar calendar that allowed them to celebrate each month's appearance of a new moon while at the same time periodically adjusting the lunar year to the solar year. They dated this calendar from what they presumed to be the moment of the world's creation, with the result that the year 2014 in our secular calendar overlaps with the Jewish year 5774. And within this sacred calendar, certain seasons were designated as occasions for religious celebration called "Sabbaths," during which the Jewish community reaffirms its covenant relationship with God.

Covered in a large tallit, this Yemenite Jew blows the shofar on Rosh Hashanah.

The Major Festivals

At the core of this system of seasonal religious observances are five major festivals, all linked to each other and to the cycle of nature—**Rosh Hashanah**, **Yom Kippur**, **Sukkot**, **Pesach**, and **Shavuot**—as well as minor festivals throughout the year. Each major festival is biblical in origin, and on each of these occasions Jews are commanded to cease working and devote themselves to prayer. That said, each major *chag* (Hebrew, "sacred occasion") is as individual as the season it celebrates and the ritual function it performs.

Rosh Hashanah   Commonly referred to as the Jewish New Year, Rosh Hashanah is traditionally celebrated for two days at the beginning of the month of Tishri (September–October), and it is regarded as both a solemn and joyous occasion. The year begins with a period of self-reflection, signaled by the blowing of a ram's horn (Hebrew, *shofar*) during the synagogue service. The sound of this instrument is designed to awaken the conscience of the worshiper to the need for repentance and reconciliation with God. For that reason Rosh Hashanah is referred to in the liturgy as *Yom Hazikaron*, or the Day of Remembrance—that is, remembering by way of one's conscience the sins committed in the past year and the need for the repentance of these sins. At the same time, the mood created during the two days of Rosh Hashanah is generally hopeful, and it is customary to eat a dish of apples and honey as an expression of hope that the coming year will be one of sweet fruitfulness and fulfillment. On this occasion, it is also customary for Jews to greet each other, at the conclusion of religious services, with the words *l'shanah tovah tikatevu*—"may you be inscribed for a good year." This saying alludes to the ancient belief that, during the ten-day period between Rosh Hashanah and Yom Kippur, God writes the names of those who will live for another year in a "Book of Life."

Yom Kippur
Also known as the Day of Atonement, Yom Kippur is the most solemn day in Judaism's sacred calendar and its most important fast day. The purpose of both the dusk-to-dusk fast and the penitential prayers that are recited on Yom Kippur was made clear by the rabbis centuries ago: "For transgressions against God, the Day of Atonement atones; but for transgressions of one human being against another, the Day of Atonement does not atone until they have made peace with one another" (Tractate Yoma 8:9). For repentance (Hebrew, *teshuvah*) to be effective, some restorative action must accompany prayer and self-examination. This is why the liturgy for Yom Kippur asks forgiveness for all the sins that people are likely to commit against one another, as well as all the acts of defiance that people are likely to

The Torah scroll is placed on a table where the reader will use a *yad* (a pointer) to read each word aloud.

The palm branch, the willow, and the myrtle make up the lulav; the citron and the lulav are held together during Sukkot prayers.

The Passover plate is prepared for the Seder, with an egg, a shank bone, parsley, chives, and bitter herbs.

The Star of David is a medieval symbol of Jewish identity placed in the center of the flag of Israel.

display toward God. These confessional prayers, which are recited throughout the day, are collective expressions of guilt and remorse ("Our father, our King, *we* have sinned before You"). But although it is the norm in Judaism to pray as a part of a community, each worshiper is nevertheless expected to internalize the act of repentance and strive for reconciliation with neighbors and with God.

On Yom Kippur a number of restrictions, in addition to fasting, are imposed on observers. Thus, in Orthodox communities, it is customary for married couples to abstain from intimacy, for men to wear white garments (symbolic of purification) to synagogue, and to neither shave nor bathe (as if one were in mourning). In addition, no work of any kind may be performed on Yom Kippur. People who are ill, children under thirteen years of age, and nursing mothers are generally exempt from fasting and other restrictions.

Sukkot   Five days after the conclusion of Yom Kippur, Jews undertake a week-long fall harvest celebration known as Sukkot ("booths"). As with any harvest festival, Sukkot displays symbols of the season, the most important being the palm frond (Hebrew, *lulav*), the citron, and leaves of the willow tree and the myrtle. The sukkah—or temporary hut, from which Sukkot derives its name—is adorned with these plants, and its roof is left partly open to the sky. During the seven days of this holiday, Jews are encouraged to eat and sleep in the sukkah, so as to reenact, symbolically, the biblical Exodus. Sukkot thus becomes one of three festivals (the other two being Pesach and Shavuot) that recall the Exodus narrative.

It is traditional religious practice to attend synagogue during the first two days and the last two days of the festival, offering thanksgiving prayers attuned to the fall season. The biblical book of Ecclesiastes is read on the Sabbath of Sukkot, highlighting the festival's themes of the passing of the seasons and the providence of God. At the conclusion of Sukkot, there is an eighth day of prayer and celebration, known as Shemini Atzeret (or "the Eighth Day of Assembly").

VOICES: An Interview with Rabbi Avigayil Halpern

Rabbi Avigayil Halpern is a graduate of Yale University and of the Hadar Institute, from which she received ordination last year. She is presently director of the Hillel organization in Berlin, Germany.

As a modern observant woman who is seeking semicha (rabbinic ordination), what future do you see for college-educated women within the Orthodox community? Will they be able to overcome obstacles to full religious participation in that community that have existed in the past?

I grew up in a more liberal Orthodox Judaism, and feel very connected to that community, but while I continue to practice in a way that is similar to Orthodoxy,

I no longer identify as Orthodox myself. This is because in even the most liberal streams of Orthodox Judaism today, gender division in ritual roles is central, and I practice in a gender-egalitarian way, even as I observe ritual laws like Shabbat and Kashrut to the same standards as Orthodox people. I believe that the strength of women's education in liberal/Modern Orthodoxy is to its credit, the disjunction between the opportunity to study Torah at the highest levels and the inability to participate fully in synagogue life was too jarring for me, and I sought out communities where I could have a more integrated experience of Torah study and communal religious practice. I believe that different people will seek out different ways to maximize religious participation and increase women's role in traditional forms of Judaism. For some of us, that means leaving Orthodoxy, and for others it means working within that community.

Avigayil Halpern.

Can you foresee a time when women in the rabbinate will seem commonplace to almost all Diaspora Jews?

I'll start by noting that for most American Jews, women rabbis are so commonplace as to not even be a live question anymore. Even within my short lifetime, I have seen a dramatic shift in the acceptance of women rabbis within Orthodoxy, and there is even an entire school dedicated to the ordination of women. I believe as the numbers of women within the rabbinate grow, more men and women within the Orthodox community will become accustomed to the idea of a woman in the pulpit, and it will simply start to feel less foreign.

Traditionally, Jews living outside Israel divide up Shemini Atzeret into two days, with the second day referred to as Simchat Torah (Hebrew, "Joy of the Torah"); on that day, the annual reading of the first five books of the Hebrew Bible comes to an end, and the cycle of weekly readings begins again. In Israel, and in many Reform congregations, Shemini Atzeret and Simchat Torah are combined into a single day, during which the "gift" of Torah is celebrated.

Pesach   More commonly known as "Passover" in English-speaking countries, Pesach is the second of three pilgrimage festivals, the first being Sukkot and the third being Shavuot. In ancient times, Jews made a pilgrimage to the Temple in Jerusalem to offer prayers and animal sacrifices to God. With the Roman destruction of the Second Temple in 70 CE, the practice of celebrating the Exodus from Egypt then shifted exclusively to the synagogue and to the home. It is in the home that Jews gather on the first two nights of this week-long festival to recount the Exodus story and to partake in a ceremonial meal known as a **Seder**—a practice that may well have begun in biblical times.

Like Sukkot, Pesach is celebrated for either seven or eight days during the month of Nisan (March–April). The first two and the last two days are subject to the same restrictions that govern any *chag*—no work and limited travel. In addition, however, Pesach imposes a dietary requirement: no foods containing yeast may be consumed

A decorated sukkah, ready for a midday meal.

during this period (reflecting the fact that Jewish slaves, escaping from Egypt, had no time to allow their bread to rise). Most observant Jewish households rid the home of all foods that contain leavening agents and prepare for this occasion by either boiling dishes and silverware or using a separate set of dinnerware reserved for use on Pesach alone. The dietary rules, collectively known as kashrut, are fundamentally important to Jewish practice, as the number of foods sold in supermarkets bearing a "Kosher for Passover" label demonstrates.

Observance of Pesach begins in the evening in the home, where the Seder is celebrated with family and friends, followed the next morning by a festival service in the synagogue. The Seder consists of two rituals in one: a meal, featuring biblical and seasonal foods that reflect the Exodus story, and a liturgy, found in an ancient text called the Haggadah (Hebrew, the "telling"). The Haggadah contains both the story of Israel's escape from Egypt and a collection of hymns and songs and rabbinic commentaries in praise of God, who made that deliverance possible. One of the goals of this ritualized meal is to leave each participant in the Seder with a sense of engagement with the enslaved generation that witnessed not only the liberation from bondage but also the giving of the Torah at Mount Sinai.

Because the Pesach Seder is a family event, children play a prominent role by being given questions to ask, songs to sing, and stories to listen to. During the ceremony that precedes the meal, the prayer leader takes a piece of matzah (a type of unleavened flatbread that, according to biblical writers, the escaping Israelites baked in haste while fleeing Egypt) and breaks it in half, hiding one half of this piece so that children can find it by the end of the meal and exchange it for a gift.

In addition to matzah, other foods displayed or consumed during the Seder meal include bitter herbs (a reminder of the bitterness of slavery); a mixture of wine, chopped nuts, and apples (symbolically representing the mortar used by Israelite slaves to build cities and pyramids); a roasted lamb shank bone (recalling the sacrifice of lambs by the Israelites before their departure from Egypt); and a roasted egg, a green vegetable (usually parsley), and an additional herb or vegetable. These items all reflect the ancient agricultural context of this celebration. Finally, participants consume four small symbolic cups of wine during the Seder meal, each serving as a reminder of the many blessings God bestowed upon ancient Israel and continues to bestow upon the Jewish people. A fifth cup is set aside for the prophet Elijah, whose symbolic presence at the Seder represents the hope that a messiah will someday appear and bring peace and justice into the world.

Shavuot   The last of the three pilgrimage festivals is Shavuot (Hebrew, "weeks"). Between the second day of Passover and the first day of Shavuot, it was the practice in biblical Israel to bring a sheaf of new grain to the Temple, and an obvious connection exists between this festival and the later spring harvest. However, during the rabbinic era, Shavuot became associated with the giving of the Torah on Mount Sinai, and from that moment on Shavuot became a part of the ongoing liturgical reenactment of the Exodus that we have traced through Sukkot and Pesach. Given this new historical association, we can understand why the rabbis decided that the high point of the synagogue liturgy for Shavuot would be the public reading of the Ten Commandments.

Traditionally, Shavuot is celebrated for two days (the sixth and seventh of the month of Sivan [May–June]). It is common practice on Shavuot to decorate the synagogue with flowers and to serve meatless meals with honey as a key ingredient—the idea being that the reading of the Torah should be sweet upon the lips. Also common is the public reading of the book of Ruth, which tells the story of a young Moabite widow who is welcomed into Israelite society and who, centuries later, became the prototype of the ideal convert to Judaism. Finally, there is a custom of staying up the entire first night of the festival for the purpose of studying some portion of the Torah.

The Minor Festivals

In contrast to the major festivals, several "minor" festivals serve to fill out the Jewish religious year. Despite their historically subordinate status, they are beloved by the many Jews who observe them. The observance of many of these minor festivals does not entail restrictions on labor, diet, or any other activities. In addition, while the agricultural cycle is clearly embedded within the calendar of major holidays, the minor festivals only indirectly reflect the season in which they appear.

Hanukkah   Of all of Judaism's minor holidays, Hanukkah is probably the best known throughout the Western world. Hanukkah commemorates the Maccabean rebellion that began in 167 BCE against the tyrannical rule of the Syrian monarch, Antiochus IV, who sought to suppress the practice of Judaism within Palestine and "defiled" the Temple in Jerusalem by rededicating it to the Greek gods. For the next two years, an armed insurrection, led first by a priest named Mattathias and after his death by his eldest son, Judah the Maccabee, wrested control of the Temple from Antiochus's army. Hanukkah celebrates the recovery and cleansing of the Jerusalem Temple and the miracle of the lights that Jewish tradition records. According to this legendary account, once the Temple was in Jewish hands it became necessary to rededicate the sanctuary—yet only one flask of the oil necessary to keep lamps lit could be found. Miraculously, however, this one flask continued to burn for eight days, thus attesting to the renewal of God's presence within the Temple. In commemoration of that miracle, Jews light a candle each night for eight nights until a ceremonial lamp (known in Hebrew as either a menorah or a *hanukkiah*) is completely lit. This candle-lighting ceremony is accompanied by the chanting of prayers, the singing of songs, and, in more recent times, the giving of gifts. In addition, a traditional game of chance is played with a four-sided top known as a dreidel, on whose sides are inscribed four Hebrew letters, which stand for the words meaning "a great miracle occurred there." In contemporary Israel, however, dreidels bear a slightly altered message: "a great miracle occurred here," referring to the establishment of the Jewish state in 1948.

Purim   Another history-oriented festival is Purim, which occurs on the fourteenth day of the month Adar (February–March). Purim is a carnival-like holiday whose origins can be found within the biblical book of Esther. Like Hanukkah, Purim celebrates a victory, this time over an antagonist named Haman, who appears in the book of Esther as a would-be destroyer of the Jewish people. However, unlike Hanukkah, the underlying festival narrative appears to have little or no historical basis. Still, Purim tells an interesting story of adaptation and survival against all odds, and it is a story that has gripped the Jewish imagination for centuries.

For Orthodox Jews, Purim begins with a fast on the thirteenth of the month of Adar. Once the fast is over, the festive aspects of Purim begin. These include a reading of the book of Esther. Congregants interrupt the narration with shouting and foot stamping every time Haman's name is read aloud. In addition, the rabbis, many centuries ago, sanctioned the practice of drinking to excess on Purim, thereby contributing to an atmosphere of barely controlled anarchy, while children are dressed in costumes that suggest the principal characters in the Esther story.

On the final night of Hanukkah, all the candles are lit while children play with the dreidel, a game with toy coins.

Purim also has its more sedate customs: the sending of gifts to friends, or to the poor, and the eating of triangular-shaped cookies known as hamantaschen, variously thought to represent Haman's ears, or hat, or pockets. Finally, although there is no prohibition against working on Purim, many Orthodox communities will devote the entire fourteenth of Adar to celebrating this festival.

Tu B'Shevat   The fifteenth day of the month of Shevat (Hebrew, *Tu B'Shevat*) is identified in rabbinic literature as the "New Year's Day of Trees." Typically, trees are planted on this day (especially in modern Israel), and monies are set aside for the poor. In some communities Jews hold a special Seder on Tu B'Shevat consisting of recitations from the Bible and the Talmud, combined with the eating of certain fruits and nuts that are native to the land of Israel. Tu B'Shevat is celebrated near the end of January or the beginning of February.

Tisha B'Av   The ninth day of the month of Av (Hebrew, *Tisha B'Av*) is, after Yom Kippur, the most solemn day in the Jewish calendar because it commemorates the destruction of both the First Temple by the Babylonians in 587 BCE and the Second Temple by the Romans in 70 CE. Each of these events was a tragic turning point in Jewish history, leading to the loss of national sovereignty and the subsequent exile of the Jewish masses from their homeland. On Tisha B'Av (commonly celebrated in July or August), Jews fast from sunset to sunset as they remember not only these tragedies but other terrible losses that they have suffered during their long history. Like Yom Kippur, Tisha B'Av is a day of collective contrition and virtual mourning, as Jews gather in synagogues to read from the book of Lamentations and sing hymns that reflect on the double loss of Jerusalem and Jewish nationhood.

Yom HaShoah   Holocaust Memorial Day, or *Yom HaShoah* in Hebrew, is the most recent addition to the sacred calendar in Judaism. In 1951, the Israeli Parliament selected this date (the twenty-seventh day of Nisan [March–April]) as a remembrance day for the millions of Jews who were victims of Nazi genocide during World War II. This date was chosen because it coincides with the beginning of the Warsaw Ghetto Uprising of 1943, and Jewish communities throughout the world observe this day of collective mourning and reflection. Yom HaShoah, however, is not a fast day, and unlike Tisha B'Av there are no prohibitions on work or other activities. Nevertheless, it has become customary in recent years for Jews to gather on the evening of the twenty-seventh of Nisan and to recite memorial prayers for the roughly one-third of the Jewish world population who lost their lives during the war.

The Sabbath

Although it is neither a major nor a minor festival, the weekly Sabbath (Hebrew, *Shabbat*) forms the core of the sacred calendar in Judaism. Like the major festivals, it is a day of prayer and rest, with its own liturgical tradition and pattern of observance; but, unlike any other sacred occasion in Judaism, its observance is explicitly mandated in the Ten Commandments. The Torah provides two different rationales for Shabbat: in the book of Exodus (20:8–11), it is identified as the day on which God rested from his creative labors; in the book of Deuteronomy (5:12–15), however, it is associated with the Exodus from Egypt and liberation from slavery. Each of these explanations provides a distinctive interpretation of the meaning of Shabbat; the first rationale is supernatural, whereas the second, the Exodus, is historical. For both interpretations, however, the commanding lesson of the Sabbath remains the same: God's actions, whether at the beginning of human time or at

A Jewish mother and daughter light the Sabbath candles.

a turning point in the history of Israel, serve as a model for human behavior. The Creator/Liberator has separated sacred time from ordinary time, and so must we.

Shabbat begins at dusk on Friday and concludes at sundown on Saturday. This twenty-four-hour period is ushered in by the lighting of two candles in the home, reminiscent of the first act of creation. Customarily, it is the woman of the house who lights these candles. Once the Sabbath formally begins, observance shifts to the synagogue, where the *Erev Shabbat* (Sabbath evening) service is conducted. The liturgy for Sabbath evening identifies the Sabbath itself as a "bride," and the feelings aroused by the "joy of the Sabbath" are similar to the emotions evoked by a wedding. With the return of the family from prayer, the Sabbath meal begins with a prayer of sanctification recited over wine and a blessing said over two loaves of bread. Sabbath bread is called challah, and it is usually baked in a shape that suggests a woman's braided hair (yet another allusion to the Sabbath "bride").

Sabbath morning observance shifts to the synagogue, where, in addition to the Shabbat liturgy, a weekly portion of the Torah is read, accompanied by a portion from the prophetic books. That service concluded, the remainder of the day is spent quietly until the evening, when the last two worship services of the day are celebrated, and a separation ceremony, known as Havdalah, is observed with a cup of wine, a braided candle, and a spice box—all reminiscent of the sweetness and calm of the Sabbath. The rabbis of the Talmud once observed that it was not just Israel that had kept the Sabbath but the Sabbath that had kept Israel. As the most direct link to the ancient past, Shabbat serves as one of Judaism's primary symbols of historical and spiritual continuity.

Life-Cycle Events

Judaism offers distinctive ceremonies that mark the passage through stages of the life cycle. The ultimate object of these rites of passage is the sanctification of human life and the desire to deepen the covenant relationship between Israel and God.

Birth The ritual process of entering the Jewish community begins, for male babies, on the eighth day of life with the rite of circumcision. Jews are not the only people today who circumcise male infants (nor were they in antiquity), but in Judaism circumcision is much more than a medical procedure. It is a mitzvah, a divine commandment imparted to the biblical patriarch Abraham and incumbent upon all of his male descendants from that time forward.

Historically, circumcision has been one of the distinctive physical marks of Jewish identity. Its importance for Jews can be gauged by the fact that the circumcision ritual takes precedence over the Sabbath or any other holy day in the sacred calendar. The only thing that would delay the performance of this mitzvah would be concern for the health of the child. During this ceremony, after the mohel (a ritual circumciser, who is usually a medically trained professional) has removed a portion of the infant's foreskin, the newborn receives his Hebrew name, which traditionally consists of the child's own name and that of the father (for example, Isaac son of Abraham). From this moment on, this is the name by which the child will be known in the Jewish community, particularly on ritual occasions. In many Conservative and Reform communities, it has become the custom to add the mother's name to the father's.

Baby girls enter the Jewish community under slightly different circumstances. There has never been any form of female circumcision in Judaism or any fixed naming ritual for the infant female. However, one popular custom today among Jews worldwide is the practice of bringing the newborn to the synagogue on the first (or, in some communities, the fourth) Sabbath after birth. On that occasion, either the child's father or both parents are called up to the Torah and recite the customary blessings. Then the baby girl is given a Hebrew name, and, like her male counterpart, it is the name that she will use on all ritual occasions for the rest of her life.

A table set for Shabbat: challah, candlesticks, and wine.

Bar/Bat Mitzvah and Confirmation

Jewish males traditionally enter the stage of religious maturity at the age of thirteen, whether or not they have engaged in the Bar Mitzvah ceremony. There is no reference to such a ritual in the Hebrew Bible, nor do the rabbis of the Talmud make mention of any specific rite of passage that marks a young man's assumption of responsibilities as an observant Jew. Nevertheless, by the later Middle Ages, something like the Bar Mitzvah ceremony practiced today had already begun to evolve, consisting of some demonstration of Hebrew literacy and an ability to read a weekly portion of the Torah. Of all the commonly practiced rituals of contemporary Judaism, the Bar Mitzvah is the one ritual that is likely to be familiar to non-Jews.

After years of study, the young man who becomes a Bar Mitzvah—that is, a "son of the commandment"—is taught to see himself as a scholar-in-training whose entry into adult Jewish life is just the beginning of a lifelong program of study. Although the celebration that follows is often joyous, there is a serious underlying purpose: the preparation of a young person to assume what the rabbis have called the "yoke of Torah." Thus, in addition to reading a portion from both the Torah and the prophetic literature, a Bar Mitzvah is expected to deliver a brief scholarly explanation of the portion he has just read, thereby demonstrating a mature comprehension of Jewish Scriptures.

The practice of requiring young women (between the ages of twelve and thirteen) to furnish similar proof of both literacy and religious commitment is of much more recent origin. The first Bat Mitzvah to be performed in the United States was conducted in 1922 for Judith Kaplan, daughter of Rabbi Mordecai Kaplan, the founder of the Reconstructionist movement. Beginning as a gesture designed to affirm gender equality in modern Judaism, the Bat Mitzvah soon evolved into an alternative form of the Bar Mitzvah ritual, and today the Bat Mitzvah ceremony is as common as the Bar Mitzvah in non-Orthodox communities.

Another innovative practice, known as a Confirmation, is almost as common-place today in non-Orthodox communities as the Bar and Bat Mitzvah, and it, too, involves a process of study and ritual performance by both young men and young women. The Confirmation ceremony can be traced back to the early decades of the Reform movement in nineteenth-century Germany, where some reform-minded rabbis attempted to find an alternative rite of passage for adolescents rather than the traditional Bar Mitzvah, believing that the latter had become little more than a ceremonial occasion. Their solution was to borrow a practice from the Christian church and to require sixteen-year-old males (and later females) to make a profession of faith during the Shavuot service, thus connecting their religious coming of age with the traditional celebration of the giving of the Torah at Mount Sinai. This practice was integrated into the traditional life cycle after World War II, as many Reform and several Conservative congregations added the Confirmation ceremony to the now-lengthened process of Jewish education. Thus, instead of supplanting the Bar Mitzvah, the Confirmation ceremony simply became a secondary stage of the passage to adulthood.

Marriage and Divorce

In Judaism, marriage is a contractual relationship between a man and a woman, rooted in mutual love and respect, and presumed to be both monogamous and enduring—a relationship on which divine blessings can be invoked. However, like all contracts, the marriage contract can be dissolved.

Over time, Jews have devised formal procedures for regulating and solemnizing the processes of marriage and divorce. Many centuries ago, the marriage ceremony consisted of two separate rites: the betrothal and the actual nuptials. According to this ancient custom, the future bride and groom became engaged to one another through the exchange of a ring. The couple then returned to the homes of their respective parents for a year, after which time the bride and groom gathered, along with their families, under a marriage canopy (known as the chuppah). A rabbi would recite seven blessings, praising God and sanctifying the union, and only at the conclusion of this ceremony would the marriage be consummated. Today, these two ceremonies have been combined and are accompanied by other, largely symbolic rituals: first, having the bride and groom drink from the same wine cup, and second, having the groom present the bride with her marriage contract (Hebrew, *ketuvah*). Finally, at the conclusion of the ceremony, the groom crushes a wine glass with his shoe—traditionally understood to symbolize the destruction of the two temples—whereupon the attending guests shout "Mazel Tov" (Hebrew, "good luck").

The bride and groom will stand under this chuppah during the wedding ceremony.

From a traditional point of view, the presentation of the *ketuvah* by the groom is the core of the marriage rite in Judaism because it states publicly the groom's intention to provide for his bride's well-being while he lives and her financial security after he dies, or after they divorce. Traditionally, the groom alone vows to set aside monies in escrow as "marriage insurance," but many modern Jewish couples have opted for a very different kind of *ketuvah*, vowing mutual commitment and support, symbolized by an exchange of rings.

Jewish divorce proceedings are no less formal than the marriage ceremony. After marital counseling has been tried and failed, the couple comes before a rabbinic court that hears the case. The divorce document is then drawn up, releasing both parties from any future obligation to one another. At that moment, the husband (or his representative) must hand the divorce document to his soon-to-be ex-wife. He is then declared to be free of their union and eligible to marry again—that very day, if he chooses. The wife, however, must wait three months to marry again, on the presumption that she may be pregnant and therefore carrying the child of her former spouse. Moreover, if her husband refuses to grant her a divorce—or cannot do so because he is missing—traditional Jewish law leaves her few options for dissolving the marriage. She may find herself bound by religious law to a husband who has abandoned her or who may have died without witnesses to his death. Orthodox communities continue to struggle with this legal dilemma today.

Death and Mourning
In Judaism the deceased are treated with as much dignity as the living, and the ceremonies associated with the burial of the dead

and mourning are invested with sanctity and respect. Whenever possible, a Jewish burial will take place within twenty-four hours of death (unless the Sabbath or a festival intervenes). The body is prepared for burial by being bathed and wrapped in a shroud and then traditionally placed in a simple pine box, thus discouraging ostentation. During the burial service, mourners express their sorrow by a symbolic tearing of their clothes—often facilitated by wearing a strip of torn black cloth, pinned to a garment—while reciting prayers in praise of God and for the comfort of the soul of the deceased in the afterlife.

Once burial occurs, those mourners who were closest to the deceased—parents, siblings, children, or spouse—enter into a week-long period of mourning known as shivah (Hebrew, "seven"), interrupted only by the Sabbath. During this period, mourners do not work, remain at home, and receive well-wishers who join with the mourning family in "sitting shivah." Because mourners are not expected, during this week, to attend synagogue, it is customary for friends to join the family in the home to recite morning and evening prayers.

Once shivah is over, however, mourners are expected to return to the world and everyday obligations, with the understanding that for the remainder of that month mourners will abstain from entertainments and remain in a somber state of mind. Once this thirty-day period of diminished mourning is completed, restrictions on the mourner's participation in celebratory events are lifted, though most Orthodox Jews continue a modified mourning protocol until the first anniversary of a parent's death has passed. The erecting of a tombstone does not normally occur until eleven months have passed; thereafter, close relatives are expected to visit the grave at least once a year—usually on the anniversary of the death of that family member—as well as to recite prayers in memory of the dead during memorial services held during all the major festivals. Finally, it is customary to light candles in the home at the time of the yearly anniversary of a loved one's death, and, whenever possible, to place small stones on the gravestone as a sign of one's remembrance of the deceased.

11.6 Judaism as a Way of Life: Other Sacred Practices

As a way of life, Judaism seeks to shape every facet of one's behavior: from the food one eats (or doesn't eat) to the way husbands and wives relate to one another. To those living within those traditions, these practices provide a sense of meaning and order, endowing all of life's activities with an aura of holiness.

The Dietary Code

Since antiquity, Jews have observed a restricted diet. Although the details have changed over the centuries, the underlying assumptions behind these practices have not. In the Torah, the people of Israel are told, repeatedly, that God wishes them to be in a state of "holiness," and when that principle is applied to diet, it becomes a discipline of selective food consumption and careful food preparation.

The essentials of the Jewish dietary code are as follows:

1. The only animals that may be eaten are those that have been properly slaughtered; no animal that has been killed by another or that has died a natural death may be consumed.
2. The only quadrupeds that may be eaten are those with split hooves who also chew the cud (like cows or goats), and, once properly slaughtered, their blood must be drained away.
3. No fish may be eaten that does not have both fins and scales.
4. No insects may be consumed.
5. No meat dish may be eaten at the same time as a milk dish.

The practical consequences for anyone who observes this diet are obvious: such a person will not dine at a stranger's home without first inquiring whether the food about to be served is really "kosher" (meaning in conformity to rabbinic standards of food selection and preparation) and whether the plates and cooking utensils are also completely free of contamination from forbidden foods. Within all Orthodox and many Conservative Jewish homes, it is customary to find not only kosher foodstuffs on the table but also duplicate sets of ovens, refrigerators, and dinnerware to make it easier to separate meat dishes from milk dishes. Kosher restaurants carry this process one step further by ordering only meat prepared by kosher butchers and by obtaining rabbinical certification that all food preparation procedures have been followed scrupulously. The phrase "kosher-style" is deceptive: foods and cooking processes are either kosher or non-kosher, but never both. Over the centuries, attempts have been made to rationalize this system of food taboos and culinary practices by suggesting an underlying concern with food safety and dietary well-being. But any benefits derived from not consuming infected meats are peripheral to the primary intent of the dietary code, namely, that of separating the observant Jew from a nonobservant food-consuming culture, thereby making the commonplace act of eating a religiously self-conscious event.

Family Purity

All Orthodox, and some Conservative and Reform, women, in addition to maintaining kosher homes, are also equally attentive to the practice of ritual "purity," and as a consequence attend a mikveh (Hebrew, "pool") at the conclusion of their menstrual periods. In a truly Orthodox Jewish home, husband and wife abstain from sexual intimacy not only during the entire period of menstruation but for seven days thereafter, and only then will the wife attend the mikveh. The purpose of this rite of purification, however, is not merely to bathe. Immersion in a mikveh is, rather, a symbolic act of spiritual preparation, and although it is used primarily by women preparing to resume sexual relations with their husbands, it is also used for conversion ceremonies and by Orthodox males on the afternoon before Yom Kippur.

The origin of these practices can be found in the Hebrew Bible, where men are warned against having intimate relations with a menstruating woman. Nowhere, however, in either the Hebrew Bible or in rabbinic literature does Judaism suggest that women's bodies are "unclean" in a hygienic sense. As with the dietary code, so with the laws of family purity: the ceremonial discipline of traditional Judaism requires a heightened degree of self-awareness about the routines of everyday life. Among Reform and Reconstructionist Jews, however, such practices are rarely observed, and today rigorous application of the purity laws is only a distinguishing mark of family life within the Orthodox Jewish home.

Prayer

From its earliest beginnings, Judaism developed a distinctive culture of prayer. The Hebrew Bible includes examples of the principal types of prayer that make up the traditional Judaic liturgy: prayers of praise, confession, petition, and thanksgiving. In the book of Psalms, for example, the legendary King David (to whom much of that book is attributed) petitions God in the following prayer-like poem:

> Hear my cry, O God,
> Heed my prayer.
> From the end of the earth I call to You;
> When my heart is faint,
> You lead me to a rock that is high above me.
> For you have been my refuge,
> A tower of strength against the enemy.
> O that I might dwell in Your tent forever,
> Take refuge under Your protecting wings.
>
> —*Psalms 61:2–5*

In poems like this, biblical writers addressed God in a language that is at once intimate and awestruck, praising his providential care of those who trust in him, while requesting his continued protection against evil and misfortune. But no matter what the character of any particular prayer, all prayers in Judaism are addressed directly to God, and all assume his compassion and just concern.

With the destruction of the Second Temple in 70 CE, the principal site of Jewish prayer shifted to the synagogue, where prayer alone, disconnected from animal sacrifices, became the norm. From that point on, the practice of offering prayer—now no longer primarily the privilege of temple priests—became more democratic. Each community constructed its own house of worship, and before long a recognized liturgy emerged that consisted, in part, of selections from the Hebrew Bible and prayers for various occasions composed by rabbinic authors. By the Middle Ages, these prayers were collected in the **Siddur**.

The daily routine of prayer appears to have been established during the late biblical period, where we find the exiled Daniel, living in Persia, praying three times a day while turning toward Jerusalem (Daniel 6:11). The architectural arrangement of early synagogues echoed this practice by orienting the entire building in the direction of Jerusalem, though in later centuries Jews were content with placing the Ark—a large, upright cupboard designed to hold several scrolls of the Torah—on the eastern wall. As the rabbinic protocol of prayer developed during the early Middle Ages, the rules governing thrice-daily prayer became increasingly elaborate and formalized, with an additional early afternoon service added on the Sabbath.

The most common setting for prayer in Judaism is communal, and although individual prayer is always valid, the full complement of prayers in any prayer service can only be said once a quorum of worshipers has assembled, either in the home or, more commonly, in a synagogue. That quorum is referred to in Hebrew as a *minyan*, and in Orthodox communities it consists of at least ten males thirteen years of age or older; in Conservative and Reform synagogues, a minyan consists simply of ten adults of either gender.

Holding a prayer book and wearing a tallit, tefillin, and a kipah, a young man prepares to recite morning prayers.

During the morning service, men traditionally wear a prayer shawl (Hebrew, **tallit**) and phylacteries or prayer amulets (Hebrew, **tefillin**) throughout, and then remove them at the conclusion of prayers. On the Sabbath it is customary, even in many Reform synagogues, to wear the tallit during prayer services, with tefillin worn only during weekday prayers. In most synagogues today, a head covering (known as a kipah or a yarmulke) is worn during prayer, chiefly by males, and as a sign of respect. Prayer services are conducted in the late afternoon and early evening as well.

One of the most powerful of all the prayers recited during the morning and evening services is the Shema, which consists of biblical verses that first declare the unity of God and then declare Israel's commitment to his service:

> Hear O Israel, the Lord is our God, the Lord is one!
> Blessed is God's glorious kingdom forever and ever!
> And you shall love the Lord, your God with all your heart, with all your soul, and with all your might. Set these words, which I command you this day, upon your heart. Teach them faithfully to your children; speak of them in your home and on the way, when you lie down and when you rise up. Bind them as a sign upon your hand, and let them be symbols before your eyes; inscribe them on the doorposts of your house and upon your gates.
> *—Deuteronomy 6:4–9*

This passage is one of the first prayers taught to children and it is, traditionally, the last prayer one utters before death. It is one of several prayers that are recited every day in the week, on major festivals, and on the Sabbath.

In Orthodox and many Conservative congregations, it is customary to read aloud a portion from the Torah every week, on Monday and Thursday mornings, and especially on the Sabbath (morning and late afternoon). In addition, an extra passage from the prophetic books is read on both the Sabbath and the major festivals. On each occasion, the portion selected from the prophetic books either echoes the themes of the Torah portion or reflects the themes of the festival itself. All these readings are normally recited or chanted in Hebrew, with translations in the local language available to the congregation. Today, all Jewish communities employ Hebrew in both the recitation of prayers and in readings from the Torah. Orthodox synagogues conduct services almost entirely in Hebrew, while Conservative, Reform, and Reconstructionist communities use both Hebrew and the congregation's native language.

11.7 Judaism as a Way of Life: Engaging with the World

During the last three decades of the twentieth century, and well into the new millennium, contemporary Judaism has faced a number of formidable challenges. The sheer loss of human life following the Shoah has meant more than simply a reduction in the Jewish world population. For some Jews, the very possibility of collective annihilation carried with it the secondary possibility of the "end" of Judaism itself, or at least the dwindling of what was once a global community. According to the latest demographic figures, the world Jewish population is approximately 15.7 million, with the largest centers of Jewish life being Israel and the United States. However, the threat of *cultural* extinction, following population decline, has inspired in some Jews a need to reexamine their most basic assumptions about contemporary Judaism and its role in the modern world.

The Renewal Movement

The Jewish Renewal movement is, to date, the most far-reaching attempt to breathe new life into Jewish religious institutions, and it seeks nothing less than to redefine what it means to be a committed Jew today. Advocates of this movement regard established devotional life and prayer routines—particularly in the United States—as uninspiring and obsolete, and their goal is to move Diaspora Judaism in the direction of greater religious authenticity and heightened spirituality. While the Renewal movement has had a modest impact institutionally, there are four areas of Jewish communal life where we can see the influence of Renewal ideas: congregational prayer, small study groups (Hebrew, *chavurot*), the rabbinate, and environmental politics.

The Chavurot   Beginning in the 1960s, small study groups began to appear in Reform and Reconstructionist synagogues, dedicated to a program of intellectual enrichment and spiritual revival advocated by Rabbi Zalman Schacter-Shalomi, a former Hasidic teacher and advocate of kabbalistic ideas and values. The purpose of the *chavurot*, as he understood it, was to both educate and inspire marginally committed Jews to take serious interest in Judaism's sacred texts, and to adopt a more fervent form of prayer than they were accustomed to. His associate, Rabbi Schlomo Carlebach, composed wordless melodies (Hebrew, *niggunim*) to accompany these prayers, in the hope of eliciting greater emotional intensity, and even spiritual joy, during prayer. Under Schacter-Shalomi's direction, many of his early *chavurot* engaged in meditation as well as spontaneous, improvisational prayers, treating the synagogue liturgy as something open-ended, rather than as a body of traditional declarations.

Women and the Rabbinate A growing demand to admit women to a greater role in Jewish education and synagogue leadership was apparent early in the twentieth century, decades before the Renewal movement embraced this idea, but the presence of Renewal advocates in both the Reform and Reconstructionist synagogues during the last quarter of the twentieth century hastened the day when an even more radical idea gained support in both communities: the ordination of women as rabbis with religious authority equal to that of their male counterparts. In 1972, the American Reform movement took the lead in this revisionist effort by conferring the title of Rabbi on Sally Jane Priesand (b. 1946), and shortly thereafter both the Reconstructionist and Conservative movements began to admit women to their respective rabbinical seminaries. Today, the presence of a woman Rabbi on the pulpit of a Reform or Conservative synagogue is no longer a novelty, and though most Orthodox synagogues have resisted this idea, non-Orthodox communities have endorsed this change enthusiastically.

Traditionally, the status of women in Judaism has been that of a respected but subordinate member of the religious community, and for many centuries Jewish women lived in a male-dominant culture. Although two of the books of the Hebrew Bible are named for women (the books of Ruth and Esther), and though Jewish religious identity is (traditionally) traced through the mother's line, religious leadership in Judaism has been a male prerogative. The Orthodox prayer book (Hebrew, *Siddur*) instructs Jewish males to thank God that they were not born women, while the only ritual obligations women were expected to perform were those of baking challah, lighting the Sabbath lights, and attending the mikveh. And although women were never prevented from attending a synagogue, their very presence necessitated a physical barrier, separating them from male worshipers (who, it was feared, would be distracted by the presence of their wives and daughters). As for the privilege of advanced religious study, that was reserved exclusively for men, who were thought to be better equipped by nature for the rigors of scholarly debate.

By the 1970s such views had come to be viewed as unacceptable to Jewish feminists and were categorically rejected by leaders of thee Renewal movement. As women were being admitted to the rabbinate in greater numbers, the language of prayer began to change as well. Feminist scholars began to focus on the gendered vocabulary that surrounded the biblical idea of God, as well as echoes of a distinctively masculine Deity in the prayer book as well, where God is referred to as "Father," "Lord," and "King." Renewal liturgists began to experiment with gender-neutral language such as "Eternal One" and "Source of Life" when referring to God, while eliminating altogether traditional prayers that implied male superiority or neglected female references by omission. Not all of these liturgical innovations have proven to be successful, but collectively they represent a serious effort to bring the religious discourse of Judaism into the contemporary world.[16]

Jewish Ecology　In addition to enhancing the status of women in Judaism, advocates of Jewish Renewal have also enthusiastically supported the environmentalist movement since the early 1960s, and they have found various ways to arouse a new, more reverent awareness of the environment, and of the crisis it is facing, within an observant Jewish life. Under the influence of Rabbis Arthur Waskow and Ellen Bernstein, Renewal *chavurot* began to practice a form of "eco-kashrut" (i.e., an expansion of traditional dietary laws to include a concern for farming practices and wasteful eating habits) in an attempt to deepen the Jewish commitment to social justice and personal responsibility. Under the rubric of *bal tashchit* (Hebrew, "do not destroy"), a distinctive Renewal ecological ethic has emerged that attempts to link biblical precepts to contemporary political imperatives: "Humans are guests on earth: God is our host. We are part of the web of life, and simultaneously, we have a unique task: to preserve this beautiful gift of the earth for the next generation. This responsibility is what it means to be human. For Jews, caring for the earth is our birthright and our responsibility."[17]

Zionism and the Moral Dilemmas of Nationhood

What the philosopher Emil Fackenheim once called "the Jewish return into history"[18] following the creation of the State of Israel has become, in the twenty-first century, a set of unresolved dilemmas. While a sense of attachment to the State of Israel, and a concern for its survival, remains deep-rooted in most Jewish communities throughout the world, the majority of those who practice Judaism do not live in Israel and have no plans to become citizens of that state. The very existence of a Diaspora, in fact, was something early Zionists puzzled over, and some even theorized that Judaism's Diaspora would disappear altogether with the creation of a Jewish nation-state. Clearly, that has not come to pass, and as a consequence, the relationship—both religious and political—between Israel and Diaspora communities remains problematic, and especially so in times of war between Israel and its often hostile neighbors.

Political instability and conflict within Israel itself, furthermore, often the result of profound religious differences within Israeli communities, adds to the growing anxiety Diaspora Jews experience when the question of Israel's moral legitimacy—and therefore its very right to exist—is at stake. As long as the world debates whether a specifically Jewish state *ought* to exist at all, uncertainty over the specific form of religious nationalism which Zionism represents will continue to challenge generations of Jews not yet born.

SEEKING ANSWERS

What Is Ultimate Reality?

The one God of Jewish faith is understood to be not only the source of all created things but also the highest and most complete form of reality the human mind can imagine. Jewish mystics often refer to this transcendent reality as the *Ein Sof*, or Infinite One. Traditionalists believe that God revealed himself to the people of Israel at Mount Sinai and that Jewish Scriptures provide a reliable account of that revelation. The biblical view of Creation is, initially, positive: when God views the world he has brought into being, he declares it "very good" (Genesis 1:31). However, later mystics, like Rabbi Luria, traced the evil in the world back to a mysterious cosmic error that subverted the design for the created world that God had originally intended. Nevertheless, the presence of divine "sparks" in each of us inspires us to believe that goodness and not evil will prevail.

How Should We Live in This World?

The divine commandments that make up the core of the Torah are designed to enable human beings to achieve true righteousness, that is, to bring the human moral will into conformity with God's will, and thereby ensure that justice and peace will prevail in the world. All ideas of right and wrong—such

as the Ten Commandments—must, therefore, be referred back to God's revelation of his will at Sinai and the Torah's laws that govern human conduct. Both biblical writers and their rabbinic commentators believed that human beings are created in the "image of God" and, at the same time, are torn between good and bad impulses. In the mystical tradition, this conflict can be resolved through study, prayer, and meditation, all of which draw us closer to God.

What Is Our Ultimate Purpose?

Judaism has never believed that human beings are hopelessly evil, nor does it support the view that humanity can never make moral progress. The High Holy Days are dedicated to the belief that both individuals and whole societies are capable of changing their behavior and that, through active repentance, they are even capable of drawing closer to each other and to God.

Jews have long believed that the soul is immortal and survives death. The fate of the soul in the "world to come" and God's judgment of that soul remain a subject of speculation and wonder, even today; some, however, regard these beliefs as obsolete and no longer a part of contemporary Jewish faith.

REVIEW QUESTIONS

For Review

1. What are mitzvot, and where can they be found?
2. What does the word *Torah* mean, and how many other meanings can be derived from it?
3. What are Maimonides's thirteen Principles of Faith?
4. Who was Mordecai Kaplan, and to which movement in modern Judaism is he connected?
5. What does the term *Shoah* mean, and how is it different from the word *Holocaust*?

For Further Reflection

1. What are the implications for Judaism of the concepts of election and covenant? Do Jews see themselves as the only people with whom the Creator God has communicated? Is it ever possible for a non-Jew to enter into a covenant relationship with Israel's God?
2. How did Judaism recover from the loss of the Jerusalem Temple in 70 CE? Why do you think that some Jews living today hope to rebuild the Temple and resume the practice of animal sacrifice? Why are the majority of the world's Jews content with the synagogue and its prayer routines?
3. How does Maimonides's approach to both God and Torah differ from that of the mystics? Do the kabbalists really believe that it is possible for human beings to seek union with God or to find the presence of God within oneself?
4. Among the varied responses to the Shoah that modern Jewish philosophers have proposed, which response seems the most compelling to you? If you were a Holocaust survivor, what would your view of life and of faith be now? Would you still find it possible to believe in a just and loving God?
5. What does the word *Zionism* refer to, and what role did Theodor Herzl play in promoting Zionist ideas?
6. What are the Ten Commandments, and where can they be found?
7. What is the Talmud, and how many volumes (or tractates) does the Babylonian Talmud contain?

GLOSSARY

Baal Shem Tov (1698–1760) A charismatic faith healer, mystic, and teacher (whose given name was Israel ben Eliezer) who is generally regarded as the founder of the Hasidic movement.

Bar/Bat Mitzvah (bahr/baht meets-vah') A rite of passage for adolescents in Judaism, the Bar Mitzvah (for males age thirteen) and the Bat Mitzvah (for females ages twelve to thirteen) signal their coming of age and the beginning of adult religious responsibility. These terms also refer literally to the boy or girl undergoing the rite.

covenant A biblical concept that describes the relationship between God and the Jews in contractual terms, often thought of as an eternal bond between the Creator and the descendants of the ancient Israelites.

Dead Sea Scrolls Religious literature hidden in caves near the shores of the Dead Sea (c. second–first centuries BCE).

Diaspora A Greek word in origin, it refers to those Jewish communities that live outside of the historical land of Israel.

election The belief that the biblical God "chose" the people of Israel to be his "kingdom of priests" and a "holy nation." This biblical concept is logically connected to the idea of the covenant, and it entails the belief that the Jews' relationship with God obliges them to conform to his laws and fulfill his purposes in the world.

eschatological Any belief relating to an "End Time" of divine judgment and world destruction.

ethical monotheism A core concept of Judaism: the belief that the world was created and is governed by only one transcendent Being, whose ethical attributes provide an ideal model for human behavior.

Exodus The escape (or departure) of Israelite slaves from Egypt as described in the Hebrew Bible (c. 1250 BCE).

halacha (hah-lah-khah') An authoritative formulation of traditional Jewish law.

Hasidism A popular movement within eighteenth-century eastern European Judaism, Hasidism stressed the need for spiritual restoration and deepened individual piety. In the course of the nineteenth and twentieth centuries, the Hasidic movement spawned a number of distinctive communities that have physically separated themselves from the rest of the Jewish and non-Jewish worlds and who are often recognized by their attire and their devotion to a dynasty of hereditary spiritual leaders.

Holocaust The genocidal destruction of approximately 6 million European Jews by the government of Nazi Germany during World War II. This mass slaughter is referred to in Hebrew as the Shoah.

immanence The divine attribute of in-dwelling, or God being present to human consciousness.

Kabbalah One of the dominant forms of Jewish mysticism, kabbalistic texts began to appear in Europe during the twelfth and thirteenth centuries. Mystics belonging to this tradition focus on the emanative powers of God—referred to in Hebrew as *Sephirot*—and on their role within the Godhead, as well as within the human personality.

Luria, Isaac (1534–1572) A sixteenth-century mystic who settled in Safed (Israel) and gathered around him a community of disciples. Lurianic mysticism seeks to explain the mystery surrounding both the creation of the world and its redemption from sin.

Maimonides A twelfth-century philosopher and rabbinic scholar whose codification of Jewish beliefs and religious practices set the standard for both in subsequent centuries.

messiah A possibly supernatural figure who will judge and transform the world.

mikveh (meek-veh') A ritual bath in which married Jewish women immerse themselves each month, after the end of their menstrual cycle and before resuming sexual relation with their husbands.

mitzvot (meets-voht') Literally translated, the Hebrew word *mitzvot* means "commandments," and it refers to the 613 commandments that the biblical God imparted to the Israelites in the Torah (i.e., the first five books of the Hebrew Bible).

Moses The legendary leader and prophet who led the Israelite slaves out of Egypt, Moses serves as a mediator between the people of Israel and God in the Torah and is later viewed as Israel's greatest prophet. It is to Moses that God imparts the Ten Commandments and the teachings that later became the Torah.

omnipotence The divine attribute of total and eternal power.

omniscience The divine attribute of total and eternal knowledge.

Pesach (pay'sahkh) An early spring harvest festival that celebrates the liberation of the Israelites from Egypt, Pesach (better known as "Passover" in English) is celebrated for seven days in Israel and eight days in the Diaspora. The first two nights are celebrated within a family setting.

Rosh Hashanah (rohsh hah-shah-nah') The Jewish New Year, it is celebrated for two days in the fall (on the first day of the month of Tishrai) and accompanied by the blowing of a ram's horn (a **shofar**, in Hebrew). It signals the beginning of the "ten days of repentance" that culminate with Yom Kippur.

Seder (sey'dehr) A ritualized meal, observed on the first two nights of Pesach, that recalls the Exodus from Egypt.

Shavuot (shah-vooh-oht') A later spring harvest festival that is celebrated for two days and is associated with the giving of the Torah at Mount Sinai. Along with Pesach and Sukkot, it was one of the "pilgrimage" festivals in ancient times.

Siddur (see-doohr') The prayer book that is used on weekdays and on the Sabbath.

Sukkot (sooh-koht') A fall harvest festival that is associated with the huts (in Hebrew, *sukkot*) in which the ancient Israelites sought shelter during the Exodus. It is celebrated for seven days in Israel (eight days in the Diaspora). During that time, Jews take their meals and, if possible, sleep in huts that are partly open to the sky.

synagogue Jewish houses of worship. The focal point of every synagogue is the Ark, a large cabinet where scrolls of the Torah are stored.

tallit A prayer shawl that is worn during morning prayers (traditionally by men). The fringes of this shawl represent, symbolically, the 613 mitzvot found in the Torah.

Talmud (tahl-mood') A multivolume work of commentary on the laws of the Torah and on the teachings of the entire Hebrew Bible, composed in two stages: the Mishnah (edited in approximately 200 CE) and the Gemara (edited, in its Babylonian version, around 500 CE). Traditionally, Jews refer to the Talmud as the "Oral Torah" and regard it as an extension of sacred scripture.

Tanakh An acronym standing for the entire Hebrew Bible: **T**orah (the first five books of the Hebrew Bible); **N**eviim (or "Prophets," which includes works of both prophecy and history); and **Kh**etuvim (or "Writings," a miscellaneous gathering of works in poetry and prose). Taken together, the twenty-four books that make up this collection constitute the core "scriptures" of Judaism.

tefillin (tee-fi'luhn) Two small boxes, containing biblical verses, to which leather straps are attached. Traditionally, Jewish males from the age of thirteen wear tefillin during weekday morning prayers; one box is placed on the forehead, and the other is placed on the left arm.

Torah Literally, the word *torah* means "teaching," and in its most restrictive sense it refers to the first five books of the Hebrew Bible. Less restrictively, it signifies the totality of God's revelations to the Jewish people, which includes not only the remaining books of the Hebrew Bible but also the writings contained in the Talmud.

transcendence The divine attribute of being above and beyond anything human beings can know or imagine.

YHWH These four consonants constitute the most sacred of names associated with the biblical God.

Yom Kippur Referred to as the "Day of Atonement," it is the most solemn of all of the fast days in the Jewish religious calendar.

Zionism A modern political philosophy that asserts a belief in Jewish national identity and in the necessity of resuming national life within the historic land of Israel.

Zohar A kabbalistic *midrash* based on the biblical book of Genesis (c. 1280 CE).

SUGGESTIONS FOR FURTHER READING

Akenson, Donald Herman. *Surpassing Wonder: The Invention of the Bible and the Talmuds*. Chicago: University of Chicago Press, 2001. An ambitious, and sometimes argumentative, history of the evolution of biblical and rabbinic literature.

Ariel, David. *What Do Jews Believe?* New York: Schocken Books, 1995. An accessible and nuanced account of traditional and nontraditional Jewish beliefs.

Bauer, Yehuda. *A History of the Holocaust*. New York: Franklin Watts, 2001. A well-researched and readable account of the Holocaust, written by the "dean" of contemporary Shoah historians.

Eisenberg, Ronald. *The JPS Guide to Jewish Traditions*. Philadelphia: Jewish Publication Society, 2004. A well-researched and comprehensive guide to traditional and nontraditional Jewish religious practices.

Fredricksen, Paula. *From Jesus to Christ*. New Haven, CT: Yale University Press, 1988. A close scholarly reading of the gospels that traces the separation of emergent Christianity from normative Judaism of the first four centuries.

Neusner, Jacob, and Alan J. Avery-Peck, eds. *The Blackwell Companion to Judaism*. Oxford: Blackwell, 2003. A collection of diverse articles on the history of Judaism, written by some of the leading scholars in Jewish studies.

Plaskow, Judith. *Standing Again at Sinai: Judaism from a Feminist Perspective*. San Francisco: Harper and Row, 1990. A seminal work of feminist reconceptualization of normative Judaism.

Robinson, George. *Essential Judaism: A Complete Guide to the Beliefs, Customs and Rituals.* New York: Pocket Books, 2000. A well-written and comprehensive description of Jewish beliefs and practices.

Sarna, Jonathan D. *American Judaism: A History.* New Haven, CT: Yale University Press, 2004. The best account to date of the historical development of the Jewish community in the United States.

Strassfeld, Michael. *The Jewish Holidays.* New York: HarperCollins, 1985. A nicely illustrated presentation of major and minor Jewish festivals with detailed accounts of religious observances from around the world.

ONLINE RESOURCES

My Jewish Learning

A well-researched site for historical subjects and religious practices.

The Jewish Virtual Library

A good site for contemporary subjects such as Israel and the Holocaust.

The Jewish Women's Archive

A comprehensive site for research articles on women in Judaism.

Christianity

Chapter Outline

12.1 Describe the key features of the teachings of Jesus and Paul of Tarsus.

12.2 Describe the essential teachings of Christianity about God, the world, humanity, sin, and salvation.

12.3 Describe how the Christian movement organized itself and defined its teachings in the ancient Roman world.

12.4 Describe the place of the Church in the West and East during the Middle Ages and the essential features of medieval monasticism and theology.

12.5 Describe the causes and outcomes of the Protestant and Catholic Reformations and how the Roman Catholic, Protestant, and Orthodox traditions responded to challenges in the modern era.

12.6 Describe the basic features of Christian worship and Christianity's most important devotional practices.

12.7 Describe how Christians are responding to important social, environmental, and gender-related issues.

STEVE AND RENEE WALKER have had a lot to look forward to during the past two years. First, there was the long-awaited arrival of little Simone, who brings gladness to her parents and her brother, Brent. Today there will be another exciting event as the Walkers present Simone for **baptism** into a spiritual family that Christians call the Church.

Whereas some Christians prefer to baptize adult believers who understand and accept the essential teachings of Christianity, others such as the Walkers believe that baptism is a special means by which God's love begins to grow even within small children. Wanting Simone to be touched by God in this way, they have arranged for her baptism to take place at St. James's Episcopal Church, where they have found friendship and fellowship with others.

Now the church is filled with worshipers whispering quietly in rows of pews while waiting for the service to begin. When it does, the organist fills the

A priest baptizes a baby girl as her family looks on.

building with resplendent strains of music that seem to shake its foundations, the congregation launches into a favorite hymn, and a procession of clergy makes its way to the front of the church. After welcoming everyone, the priest, Father Robert, pronounces a blessing upon them. Then all eyes turn toward the baptismal font, an elevated basin of water. Steve, Renee, and Brent are waiting there, with Renee holding Simone in her arms.

Father Robert now enters into a formal dialogue with Steve and Renee, asking if they will bring up Simone in the Christian faith, if they renounce evil in all its forms, and if they put their trust in Jesus Christ. Answering for themselves and on behalf of Simone, they respond affirmatively. Then, dipping a small silver cup into the water of the baptismal font, Father Robert pours a bit of it three times on Simone's forehead. As he does so, he says, "Simone, I baptize you in the name of the Father, and of the Son, and of the Holy Spirit. Amen." Then, placing his hand on Simone's forehead, he marks the sign of the cross and adds, "Simone, you are sealed by the Holy Spirit in baptism and marked as Christ's own forever. Amen."

Now that the baptismal ritual is complete, Simone's family returns to their seats to await the end of the service. Soon they will be on their way home to join friends and relatives for a festive dinner and celebration of the new life that Simone will live, not just with the Walker family but in communion with more than 2 billion Christians worldwide.

There are three great traditions within Christianity. Historically, the **Roman Catholic Church** has been the dominant **church** in the West. In the East (for the purposes of this chapter, the region extending from

World Christian population.

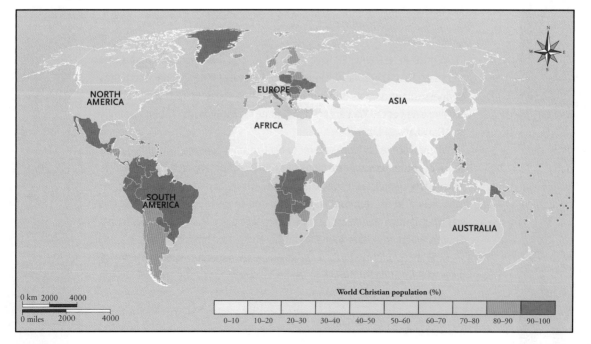

World Christian population (%)

| 0–10 | 10–20 | 20–30 | 30–40 | 40–50 | 50–60 | 60–70 | 70–80 | 80–90 | 90–100 |

the Adriatic Sea to the Middle East), most Christians have belonged to the **Orthodox Church** (also known as the Eastern Orthodox Church). **Protestant Christianity**, which consists of thousands of independent "denominations," grew out of the Roman Catholic tradition in the sixteenth century. Although these churches have been shaped in different ways by complex historical and cultural forces, they are united by shared beliefs that lie at the heart of Christianity. Christians acknowledge a personal and transcendent God, the creator and sustainer of the universe. The Christian doctrine of the **Trinity** describes God as one in essence but consisting in three "persons": Father, Son, and Holy Spirit. Christians believe that communion with God, in this life and in eternity, is the ultimate purpose of human existence. But there is an obstacle to be overcome: sin. The violation of God's will in thought or action, **sin** is common to all humanity. Worse, sin separates the individual from God. What is needed is forgiveness and restoration to a "right" relationship with God that God gives to all who have faith that the sacrificial death of Jesus Christ, the Son of God, atoned for all sin. For Christians, the sacrifice of Christ is the supreme expression of divine love. Similarly, they see in his resurrection and ascension into heaven a sign that God has overcome death for those who respond in faith to God's love. Although they remain imperfect, Christians believe that the destructive power of sin is no longer the primary force in their lives, for they have been baptized into a new "life in Christ."

We will begin our investigation of Christianity with a survey of its teachings. We will then trace the history of Christianity from the earliest days after the death of Jesus to the present time. Finally, we will explore the practices by which Christians give outward expression to their beliefs in their daily lives.

TIMELINE
Christianity

c. 30 CE	Crucifixion of Jesus.
c. 46–62	Paul's missionary journeys.
70–100	Gospels of Matthew, Mark, Luke, and John written.
313	Constantine decrees religious freedom for Christians.
325	Council of Nicea declares God the Son to be "of the same substance as God the Father."
354–430	Augustine of Hippo, first great theologian of the West and author of the *Confessions* and *City of God*.
367	Contents of New Testament established.
529	Benedict of Nursia writes the *Benedictine Rule*.
949–1022	Simeon the New Theologian and the beginning of Hesychasm.
c. 1000	Conversion of Russia to Orthodox Christianity begins.
1054	The Great Schism divides the churches of East and West.
1095–1272	Western Crusaders repeatedly attempt to free the Holy Land from Muslim rule.
1184	Pope Lucius III inaugurates the Inquisition.
1198–1216	Height of papal power under Innocent III.
1265–1274	Thomas Aquinas writes the *Summa Theologica*.
1453	Constantinople, capital of the Byzantine Empire, falls to the Ottoman Turks.
1517	The Protestant Reformation begins when Martin Luther posts his Ninety-Five Theses.
1534	King Henry VIII establishes the Church of England.
1545–1563	Council of Trent, at which the Roman Catholic Church responds to the Protestant movement.
1647	George Fox founds the Society of Friends (Quakers).
1703–1791	John Wesley, founder of the Methodist movement.
1804–1814	Napoleon, emperor of the French, acts to strip the Roman Catholic Church of its influence.
1834	The Spanish Inquisition, the last stage of the Inquisition, is formally abolished.
1869–1870	First Vatican Council declares doctrine of papal infallibility.
1948	Founding of the World Council of Churches.
1962–1965	Second Vatican Council.

12.1 The Teachings of Christianity: Foundations

By the first century, Palestinian Jews had endured centuries of oppression under foreign conquerors, struggling to preserve their unique religion and culture. Their situation became especially dangerous with the arrival of the Romans (63 BCE), whose brutality fueled a bitter resentment that ultimately led to a major Jewish rebellion. Tragically, the revolt ended with the destruction of the Jerusalem Temple, the center of Jewish religious life, in 70 CE.

As we have seen in Chapter 11, Jewish groups responded to these pressures in different ways. Pharisees defended Jewish tradition through strict observance of the Torah. Sadducees cooperated with the Romans in the hope of preserving social stability. Zealots advocated anti-Roman violence. Many Essenes withdrew to the desert lands outside Jerusalem to wait for divine deliverance.

Believing that God would soon bring an end to unrighteousness, many Jews looked for the coming of a **messiah** who would inaugurate a new era of justice and peace. Originally, messiah ("anointed one") was a title given to Israel's kings and priests, who were anointed with oil as a sign of God's favor. Later, it came to mean the deliverer God would "anoint" to save the Jewish people from oppression. Some looked for a supernatural messiah. Others watched for a descendant of David, ancient Israel's greatest king. Most believed the Messiah would rule as king and judge the wicked and the righteous.

The first Christians were Palestinian Jews who believed that Jesus of Nazareth was the Messiah—in Greek, the *Christos*, or "Christ." They proclaimed him as a deliverer not from earthly oppression but from the power of sin. In Jesus, they saw the beginning of a new era of righteousness and peace evident in his teachings, miracles, death, and resurrection.

The Life of Jesus

Our most important sources for the life and teachings of Jesus are the **gospels** of Matthew, Mark, Luke, and John. Written between 70 and 100 CE, the gospels are early Christian proclamations of the "good news" (*gospel*, from Middle English *godspel*, translates the Greek *evangelion*, "good news") about Jesus's teachings, suffering, death, and resurrection. Because their interests are more theological than biographical, the gospels leave much unsaid about the life of Jesus. Still, their essential agreement on many points allows us to establish the general outlines of his career and teachings.

The gospels report that Jesus was born in the Judean city of Bethlehem. We cannot be certain of the date; Matthew suggests that Jesus's birth occurred before 4 BCE, Luke by 1 BCE. Jesus spent his youth in

Mass baptism of Christians at Yardenit, the site on the Jordan River in northern Israel where Christian tradition says Jesus was baptized by John the Baptist.

the Galilean village of Nazareth. At about the age of thirty, he made his way south to the Judean wilderness, where he was baptized by John the Baptist in the River Jordan. A prophetic figure who warned of God's imminent judgment, John called on sinners to repent and be baptized in water as a sign of spiritual cleansing.

After his baptism, Jesus began a ministry that lasted no more than three years. The gospels say that as he traveled throughout Galilee he performed healings and miracles that testified to God's presence within him. The gospel accounts also describe Jesus as a charismatic teacher who spoke with authority on the scriptures and urged repentance and baptism in anticipation of the coming **kingdom of God**, a new era of peace and holiness. Jesus was accompanied by an inner group of disciples, sometimes called "the twelve," led by three Galilean fishermen (Peter, James, and John), as well as by people from towns, villages, and the countryside. There were also Galilean women among Jesus's disciples who supported his ministry with their own resources. Indeed, women figure prominently in the gospel accounts of Jesus's ministry.

As enthusiasm for his teachings and miracles grew, Jesus's popularity aroused resentment and opposition among members of the religious establishment. Jesus himself appears to have understood that dark days lay ahead. As he prepared to leave Galilee for Jerusalem, he warned his disciples that rejection, suffering, and death awaited him there.

Jesus arrived in the holy city just before Passover in or around 30 CE. Entering the Temple, he caused a great stir by driving out those who did business there, accusing them of making the sacred place a "den of robbers." For several days Jesus taught in the Temple, but then events took an ominous turn. After sharing a "Last Supper" with his disciples, Jesus was brought before a council of Jewish leaders and then handed over to Pontius Pilate, the Roman governor. Fearing that Jesus was a threat to public order, Pilate ordered his execution. Jesus was crucified less than a week after he had entered Jerusalem.

The gospels add theological reflections to this historical outline. Matthew and Luke assert that Jesus's mother, Mary, was a virgin who conceived miraculously in fulfillment of prophecy (Isaiah 7:14). All four of the gospels say that the Spirit of God, or the Holy Spirit, descended upon Jesus at the time of his baptism. According to Matthew, Mark, and Luke, a voice from heaven then declared: "This is my Son, the

Palestine during the time of Jesus.

Beloved, with whom I am well pleased" (Matthew 3:17). In this way, the gospels link Jesus to the Davidic king who is described in Psalms 2:1–7 as God's "anointed" and "son." The gospels also identify Jesus as the "servant" of God who would suffer for the sake of humanity, as foretold by one of Israel's prophets (Isaiah 42:1–4; 53:10–12). Finally, the gospels report that women who had followed Jesus found his tomb empty at dawn on the Sunday following his crucifixion. They and the other disciples were overjoyed when Jesus appeared to them and they remembered what he had once told them: "The Son of Man must undergo great suffering, and be rejected by the elders, chief priests, and scribes, and be killed, and on the third day rise again" (Luke 9:22). Convinced that Jesus was indeed God's Messiah, they began to proclaim the good news that God had acted through him for the salvation of the world.

According to the Acts of the Apostles, Jesus remained with his disciples for forty days after his resurrection. Then, having sent them out as **apostles** (Greek sing. *apostolos*, "one who is sent out") to preach to Jews and Gentiles alike, he ascended into heaven. Several days later, as they celebrated the Jewish holiday of **Pentecost**, Jesus's followers were suddenly "filled with the Holy Spirit," the same Spirit of God that had descended upon Jesus at his baptism (Acts 2:2–4). Empowered by the Spirit to carry out the mission Jesus had given them, they found themselves able to speak in languages they had not known before, to prophesy, and to perform miraculous healings. According to Acts, the number of believers grew rapidly, for "many wonders and signs were being done by the apostles" (Acts 2:43). Acts also reports that the first Christians spent "much time together in the temple" (Acts 2:46), reminding us that they were Jews who continued to live and worship as Jews. It did not occur to them that their belief that Jesus was the Messiah had given them a new religious identity outside of Judaism.

The Teachings of Jesus

The gospels describe Jesus as a teacher who astounded the crowds who gathered to hear him, "for he taught them as one having authority" (Matthew 7:29). Although he engaged in debate with learned Pharisees and Sadducees, Jesus also took great interest in ordinary people. He often taught them in **parables**, stories that employed vivid images from everyday life to illustrate spiritual truths.

The central theme in Jesus's teaching was the kingdom of God (in Matthew, the kingdom of heaven). For Jesus, the kingdom of God was not an ordinary realm but the state of affairs that exists when human beings recognize God's sovereignty over the world and respond in love and obedience to God's will. To put it another way, the kingdom of God means the world as it ought to be, a world in which God's love and righteous rule are fully realized. In the gospels, Jesus sometimes speaks of the kingdom as a future event to be heralded by dramatic signs such as a darkening sun and stars falling from heaven. In the midst of these cataclysmic events, the present age would pass away and the kingdom would be revealed in all its glory. But Jesus also spoke of the kingdom as already present within himself and his followers.

Asked when it would come, he replied that it was already present: "The kingdom of God is among you" (Luke 17:21). Though it was still small, Jesus expected the kingdom to grow into something great and wondrous. In one of his parables, he compared it to a tiny mustard seed that "grows up and becomes the greatest of all shrubs, and puts forth large branches, so that the birds of the air can make nests in its shade" (Mark 4:30). Whether speaking of the kingdom of God as present or future, Jesus emphasized its all-surpassing importance. Nothing can compare to the kingdom, he said, and so it is worth any price: "The kingdom of heaven is like treasure hidden in a field, which someone found and hid; then in his joy he goes and sells all that he has and buys that field" (Matthew 13:44).

Jesus taught that the kingdom of God is open to all who repent. By repentance, he meant something more than mere regret for some wrong one has done. The Greek *metanoia* ("a change of mind") found in the gospels suggests a fundamental change in attitude, a turning away from self-interest and toward doing God's will. Like other Jews, Jesus found God's will expressed in the Torah and its commandments and taught that it is through obedience to the commandments that one does God's will.

Jesus also taught that obedience to God's commandments was an expression of love. When pressed by a Pharisee to identify the greatest of the commandments, he cited two (Deuteronomy 6:5 and Leviticus 19:18), explaining that they embody the essence of scripture: "'You shall love the Lord your God with all your heart, and with all your soul, and with all your mind.' This is the greatest and first commandment. And a second is like it: 'You shall love your neighbor as yourself.' On these two commandments hang all the law and the prophets" (Matthew 22:37–40).

The nature of love is a key feature of the teaching of Jesus. He taught that genuine love knows no limits and is offered freely to everyone. Love recognizes sin but does not condemn sinners. Instead, love requires forgiveness of those who have done wrong: "For if you forgive others their trespasses, your heavenly Father will also forgive you" (Matthew 6:14). These principles are richly illustrated in Jesus's parables. The parable of the Good Samaritan (Luke 10:25–37), for example, demonstrates that even enemies deserve love and compassion. In the parable of the Prodigal Son (Luke 15:11–32), a father greets a dissolute and disrespectful son who has returned home—not with any thought of reproach, but with love and forgiveness gladly given.

The gospels describe Jesus as embodying these principles of repentance, obedience, and love. They also depict Jesus as living in the expectation of his crucifixion. In Mark, he tells his disciples that his death will be "a ransom for many" (Mark 10:45). Jesus spoke of God as Father, suggesting a relationship of special intimacy as well as obedience. He urged his followers to draw close to God as well. They were God's children, he told them. As such, they should approach God in prayer with the words "Our Father" (Matthew 6:9) and with confidence that, like a loving parent, he would provide for their needs (Luke 12:22–31).

As we will see later in this section, these fundamental teachings of Jesus lie at the heart of what Christians believe about sin, divine love, and salvation. But we first turn our attention to Paul of Tarsus, the first great interpreter of the life and teachings of Jesus, to see how Christian beliefs began to take shape in the years immediately following his crucifixion.

Paul and the Mission to the Gentiles

The most famous of the Jewish Christians who took the gospel and its teachings to Gentile lands was **Paul of Tarsus**. A Pharisee devoted to Judaism, Paul had been a persecutor of Christians, but after a dramatic experience of the risen Christ c. 31 CE (Acts 9:1–19) he dedicated himself to preaching the gospel in Asia Minor (modern Turkey), Greece, and Macedonia. In his letters to young churches in Corinth, Thessalonica, Rome, and other cities, we can see Paul emphasizing God's love for Gentiles as well as Jews and describing the significance of Jesus Christ for these very different groups. Because Paul was the first to describe the role of Jesus in the salvation of humanity from sin, some have seen him as the second founder—and even the *true* founder—of Christianity. It was due in part to his influence that Christianity was transformed in the middle of the first century from a Jewish sect into a largely Gentile movement.

At the heart of Paul's teaching was his belief that in Jesus Christ God had acted to bring salvation from sin to the world. Paul saw sin as a condition affecting all humanity: "All have sinned and fall short of the glory of God" (Romans 3:23). Controlling human beings and separating them from God, sin corrupts and ultimately destroys human life (Romans 6:23). For Paul, the good news of the gospel was that God's promise of salvation from sin, which he saw in the Jewish Scriptures, had been fulfilled in Jesus's death on the cross. Though sinless and undeserving of death, Jesus had offered himself as a perfect sacrifice in atonement for all sin.

Paul taught that the salvation made possible by Christ's sacrifice is a gift, the ultimate expression of God's love, or **grace**. God's grace enables people to have faith in the power of the death and resurrection of Jesus Christ through which God had acted to atone for human sin. It is by faith, Paul said, that people are saved from domination by sin and empowered to live as true followers of Jesus.

For Paul, faith does more than bring salvation; it unites the believer with Christ in a "newness of life" (Romans 6:4) so real that Paul could say, "It is no longer I who live, but it is Christ who lives in me" (Galatians 2:20). Like the apostles who had been filled with the Holy Spirit at Pentecost, Paul believed that the Spirit lives in believers and brings them into union with God. To the Christians at Rome he wrote: "You are in the Spirit, since the Spirit of God dwells in you" (Romans 8:9). As a divine presence within, the Spirit encourages the growth of spiritual virtues, the greatest of which is love (1 Corinthians 12:27–14:1). Paul also believed that the Spirit makes all Christians one in the Church, which he often called the "body of Christ" (1 Corinthians 12:12–27).

Like other early Christians, Paul looked forward to a time when Christ would return in glory to bring an end to evil, sin, and suffering (1 Corinthians 15:20–28). But he also believed that the transformation of the world, signaled by the resurrection of Christ, had already begun. Signs of change were especially evident in the lives of believers, who had been renewed, even re-created, through the action of God's grace. As Paul put it, "So if anyone is in Christ, there is a new creation; everything old has passed away; see, everything has become new!" (2 Corinthians 5:17).

12.2 The Teachings of Christianity: Core Precepts

What does Christianity teach about God and the world we live in? What does it say about human beings and sin, the great problem in human existence, and what God has done about it? What do Christians believe about the Church, the Bible, and the afterlife? In this section we will survey Christian teaching on these and other important issues.

God, Creation, and Original Humanity

Christian thought about God, the world, and humanity begins with the first verse in the Bible: "In the beginning God created the heavens and the earth" (Genesis 1:1). Here, and in the story of creation that follows, the Bible makes a clear distinction between created things and their Creator. God is transcendent, existing outside space, time, and the other limiting factors that give the world its order and finitude. And yet God is present in the world, sustaining and caring for all things with a loving benevolence that touches even the least of creatures.

Much as a work of art tells us something about the artist, Christians believe that creation tells us something about God. Paul made this point in his letter to the Romans: "Ever since the creation of the world his eternal power and divine nature, invisible though they are, have been understood and seen through the things he has made" (Romans 1:20). For Christians, the goodness, beauty, power, and design evident in the world are all expressions of God's nature. But it is God's goodness, and the consequent goodness of the world itself, that are emphasized in the biblical story of the world's beginnings. At the completion of each stage of creation, it says, "God saw that it was good" (Genesis 1:10, 18, 21, 25) and, ultimately, that it was "very good" (Genesis 1:31). Finally, Christianity teaches that the entire order of existing things, and especially human beings, is the deliberate and purposeful expression of a divine love that a grateful creation should return to God in praise. "Let heaven and earth praise him, the seas and everything that moves in them" (Psalms 69:34).

Andrei Rublev's icon of the Holy Trinity (1411) is considered a masterpiece of Orthodox religious art. It depicts (from left to right) God the Father, God the Son, and God the Holy Spirit. On one level, the three figures are the "angels" through whom God appeared to Abraham in the Old Testament. On a higher level, they represent the Trinity in a way that uses color, light, and imagery to give the viewer a glimpse into its unfathomable mystery.

Christians believe that, despite its original perfection, the world as we know it today falls far short of God's intentions, plagued as it is by suffering, injustice, and death. These evils cannot be attributed to God because they are completely opposed to God's perfection. Instead, Christianity points to creation itself—and, more specifically, to humanity.

The story of creation relates that "God created humankind in his image" (Genesis 1:27). For centuries, Christian thinkers have sought to understand all that is entailed by this assertion. Some have found the image of God in the human capacity for rational thought. Others have said it can be seen in the "dominion" God gave to human beings over all the earth (Genesis 1:26), which resembles God's rule over the entire universe. All Christian thought, however, acknowledges that human beings have a unique ability to love God, just as God loves them.

This idea is found in the biblical narrative that describes how God placed Adam and Eve, the first human beings, in a garden-like paradise called Eden. Whether we understand Adam and Eve as literal human beings or as symbols of original humanity—the Hebrew word *adam* means "humankind"—the point of the story remains the same. For as long as human beings related to God in loving obedience, they lived in joyous harmony with their Creator, but their eventual decision to disobey God brought an end to that harmony and, consequently, to the harmony of creation as a whole (Genesis 2:4–3:24). It was through sin that evil in all its forms became a reality in the world. Worst of all, sin separated humanity from God. In the Christian view, the salvation of creation from sin's destructive effects begins with the salvation of human beings. It is only through salvation from sin that they are restored to that original relationship with God in which they find their true place, purpose, and fulfillment. In the words of Augustine, the great fifth-century saint, "You have made us for yourself, and our hearts are restless until they find rest in you."[1]

God as Trinity

Like Judaism, Christianity is a monotheistic religion. But Christianity differs from its parent religion in defining the one God in terms of three aspects of divinity. For Christians, there is a single divine nature that expresses itself eternally in the three "persons" of Father, Son, and Holy Spirit.

The doctrine of the Trinity was not put into precise language until 381 at the Council of Constantinople, one of the meetings at which early Christian leaders assembled to establish doctrine. Building on the work of the Council of Nicea (325), the **bishops** at Constantinople produced the **Nicene Creed**, a statement of the doctrine that many Christians continue to recite in public worship:

> We believe in one God, the Father, the Almighty,
> maker of heaven and earth, of all that is seen and unseen.
> We believe in one Lord, Jesus Christ, the only Son of God,

eternally begotten of the Father,
God from God, Light from Light, true God from true God,
begotten, not made, one in Being with the Father.
Through him all things were made.
For us and for our salvation he came down from heaven:
by the power of the Holy Spirit
he was born of the Virgin Mary, and became man.
For our sake he was crucified under Pontius Pilate;
he suffered, died, and was buried.
On the third day he rose again in fulfillment of the scriptures;
he ascended into heaven and is seated at the right
    hand of the Father.
He will come again in glory to judge the living and
    the dead,
and his kingdom will have no end.
We believe in the Holy Spirit, the Lord, the giver of life,
who proceeds from the Father [*and from the Son*].
He has spoken through the prophets.
We believe in one holy catholic ["universal"] and
    apostolic Church.
We acknowledge one baptism for the forgiveness of sins.
We look for the resurrection of the dead,
and the life of the world to come. Amen.

As you can see, the Creed is divided into three parts corresponding to the three "persons" of the Trinity. It tells us about the relationships among the three persons as well as the functions of each.

The opening statement is about God the Father, the omnipotent ("almighty") Creator of all reality, spiritual as well as material, visible as well as invisible. There is one God, upon whom all things depend for their existence.

The second part of the Creed focuses on God the Son, who is "one in Being with the Father"—that is, of the same divine substance or essence as the Father. For the sake of humanity, the Son became fully human as well as fully divine. As a revelation of divinity on Earth, the Son enabled those who recognized him as such to come to a greater understanding of God: "If you know me, you will know my Father also" (John 14:7). Beyond revealing the Father, the Son has three other roles. First, recalling the Gospel of John (1:3), the Creed states that "through him all things were made."

Adam and Eve Banished from Paradise. In this fresco, the Renaissance painter Tommaso Masaccio (1401–1428) captured both the shame of Adam and Eve and the fear they felt as they were expelled from the Garden of Eden and separated from God.

Second, the suffering and death of the Son have made salvation from sin possible. Third, the Son, as the risen Christ, will one day return to judge the world.

The final part of the Creed affirms that the Holy Spirit "proceeds" from the Father, implying the Spirit's sameness in substance or essence with the Father. The addition of the Latin *filioque* ("and from the Son") by the Western church, never accepted in the East, underscores the sameness of all three persons of the Trinity. Just as the Father represents God's power in the creation of the world, and just as the Son both reveals the Father and redeems a sinful humanity, the Holy Spirit represents God's continuing presence in the world. Since the beginning, when God breathed the "breath of life" into Adam (Hebrew *ruach* means both "breath" and "spirit"), the Spirit has given life to all of creation. Christians believe that since the descent of the Holy Spirit at Pentecost it has empowered and guided the Church. Finally, it is the Spirit within that helps believers as they reach out to God in prayer (Romans 8:26) and nurtures virtues such as love, patience, kindness, gentleness, and self-control (Galatians 5:22–23).

The Consequences of Sin

Christianity emphasizes the sinfulness of human nature. This may seem a harsh way of thinking about human beings. After all, there are good reasons to believe in their essential *goodness*. Of course, Christians do acknowledge the human capacity to do good things. But they are equally aware of the human capacity for evil and the fact that people are often destructive in their thought and behavior. Christianity teaches that sin is universal; everyone sins. It also insists that the tendency to sin is far more serious than an acquired habit one might overcome through greater self-control or moral effort. The inability of human beings to rise above sin—to be as loving, humble, generous, and righteous as they should be—suggests that something has gone wrong in the perfect world God created and, perhaps, even within human nature. As we will see later in this chapter, Roman Catholic and Protestant Christians, on the one hand, and Orthodox Christians, on the other, understand this issue in different ways, though they agree that, because human beings cannot overcome sin on their own, they stand in need of salvation from its power over them—a power that cuts them off from God, the source of all good things.

Grace and Salvation

For Christianity, sin is the fundamental problem of human existence. But it is a problem solved by God's grace, the love God gives freely to human beings despite their sin. In the Christian view, it is only through reliance on divine grace that salvation from sin becomes possible.

Christians believe that God has made salvation possible through Jesus's death on the cross. They see his death as a sacrifice in which Jesus, who was sinless, made perfect atonement for sin that allows sinners to be restored to their original relationship with God. In doing so, Christians say, Jesus fulfilled the words of the Old Testament prophet Isaiah, who spoke of the "suffering servant" of God: "But he was wounded for our transgressions, crushed for our iniquities; upon him was the punishment that made us whole, and by his bruises we are healed" (Isaiah 53:5). Christians see in Christ's suffering for the salvation of humanity the supreme proof of God's grace:

> God is love. God's love was revealed among us in this way: God sent his only Son into the world so that we might live through him. In this is love, not that we loved God but that he loved us and sent his Son to be the atoning sacrifice for our sins.
>
> *—1 John 4:8*

Grace makes salvation possible, but it requires a human response in the form of faith. For Christians, faith is more than intellectual acceptance of the fact that God has made salvation possible through Jesus Christ. Faith in God involves a whole-hearted opening of oneself to God so that God's love replaces sinfulness as the prevailing power in one's life.

For Roman Catholic and Orthodox Christians, as well as for some Protestants, good works are an expression of faith, even a part of faith, for a faith that does not involve action is not faith at all. As the New Testament letter of James (2:26) puts it, "For just as the body without the spirit is dead, so faith without works is also dead." Most Protestants, in contrast, make a distinction between faith and good works. Because works, they believe, are not a part of faith, works do not contribute to salvation. In support of this view, Protestants cite New Testament passages such as Paul's letter to the Romans (3:28), "For we hold that a person is justified by faith apart from works." For those who hold this view, good works are something one does *because* one has faith. The differences here are finely nuanced, but they have profound implications that are partly responsible for the separation of the Roman Catholic, Orthodox, and Protestant traditions.

The Church

Christians do not live the Christian life in isolation. Instead, their faith and baptism unite them with all other believers. In its most basic sense, the Church is the sum of all believers, but most Christians believe that the Church is far more than this. Following Paul, they understand the Church to be the "body of Christ," a body whose diverse members are unified by the Holy Spirit: "For just as the body is one and has many members, and all the members of the body, though many, are one body, so it is with Christ. For in the one Spirit we were all baptized into one body—Jews or Greeks, slaves or free—and we were all made to drink of one Spirit" (1 Corinthians 12:13).

VOICES: An Interview with Susan H.

Susan H.

For many years, Susan H. has been a member of Trinity Episcopal Cathedral, a Christian church with roots in the Anglican tradition.

How does Christianity influence how you regard and relate to other people?

Jesus taught that the two greatest commandments are to love God and to love your neighbor. I can truly say these teachings are a part of my daily life. As part of a denomination of Protestantism that welcomes all, no matter their race, sexual orientation, or any other barrier, it is important that I do not love only on Sunday when I am with my church community but that I am involved in this way of life each and every day. I regard all people as children of God. That means I see the face of Christ when I see them; that I engage people in conversation by saying good morning; that I pray for those I know and love; that I pray particularly for those who have no home, food, or water and may not hear a kind word because I have always had those things. The mission of my church is "to love and serve." This is something I make sure I do every day.

How does Christianity help you when you experience a significant loss or disappointment in life?

In the past twenty-eight years I have lost so many in my family, including my two children. During this time I was not always attending church, but I never gave up on my faith. It has seen me through these great losses and the grieving that never goes away and has become a part of my life. I could not have come this far without knowing God is always with me. There are times when I hear these words in my head: "You are not alone." God does not always shield us from difficulties but has promised to always be with us. I have experienced this.

How does Christianity help you in your personal quest for happiness or fulfillment?

The losses I have experienced have changed my understanding of happiness. It is the little things that make me smile—birds singing, the sun shining, flowers blooming—all of these part of God's creation. I am most content when I am at a service at the cathedral, which is my happy place. Taking communion takes me back to my childhood when I attended church with my father, mother, and sister. That brings me joy. I began attending church at the cathedral between the losses of my daughter and my son. My church community has been integral in bringing me through these times. They are always there for me no matter what the circumstances. I really do not know what would have happened to me if it were not for my faith and my community. I have recently retired from my job as Formation Coordinator at the cathedral. For many years I organized classes, retreats, and speaker events to help people on their spiritual journeys. I am now discerning my next place to serve. I know that whatever God has in store for me will be fulfilling.

Scripture

When the first Christians spoke of scripture, they meant the Jewish Scriptures—the Hebrew Bible and its translation into Greek, the Septuagint. In Greek, these texts were called *ta biblia*, or "the books"—hence, our English "Bible." It was not long, however, before certain Christian writings assumed an importance equal to that of the Jewish Scriptures. By the end of the fourth century, there was general agreement that twenty-seven of these texts had greater authority than all others. These came to be known collectively as the New Testament. Since then, the Christian Bible has consisted of the Old Testament (the Jewish Scriptures) and the New Testament. In Christian interpretation, the Old Testament, which tells of God's covenant with the Jewish people, anticipates and is fulfilled by the New Testament, which reveals that the Messiah has come and established a new and universal covenant between God and the Church. Roman Catholic and Orthodox versions of the Bible also include several deuterocanonical ("secondary canon") texts, which they place in the Old Testament. Protestants call these texts the Apocrypha ("hidden texts") and sometimes place them between the Old and New Testaments in their versions of the Bible.

The first four books in the New Testament are the gospels. Although tradition attributes the gospels to specific individuals, some of them disciples of Jesus, none identifies its author by name. Each gospel portrays Jesus in its own way. In the Gospel of Mark, Jesus is a messiah who resolutely submits to suffering on behalf of humanity. In the Gospel of Matthew, Jesus is a figure reminiscent of Moses who reveals the true meaning of the Torah. The Gospel of Luke focuses on Jesus's compassion for sinners, women, the poor, and the sick. Finally, the Gospel of John emphasizes the divinity of Jesus. In describing him as God's "Word" (Greek *logos*, "word," but also "divine reason") "made flesh," John presents Jesus as a revelation of God in human form. The gospels are followed by the Acts of the Apostles, which describes the founding of the Church in Jerusalem and tells the story of Paul's missionary journeys. All but one of the texts that follow Acts are letters, many of them written by Paul. These texts describe the organization of the first Christian churches, tell us about early Christian beliefs and practices, and offer insights into the complex relationship between early Christianity and Judaism. The New Testament concludes with Revelation. Written at the end of the first century, when Christians were beginning to suffer persecution, Revelation is an apocalyptic text that employs vivid imagery in describing the coming of the kingdom of God after a climactic battle between good and evil.

Christians turn to the Bible for instruction in doctrine, ethics, and higher truths, confident that this collection of divinely inspired texts has an authority that sets it above all others. But what, exactly, does "divinely inspired" mean? More important, does the Bible make the claim of divine inspiration about itself?

As it turns out, one New Testament text speaks of scripture as "God-breathed" (2 Timothy 3:16), which comes very close to "divinely inspired." Of course, the reference here is only to the Jewish Scriptures, or Old Testament, as the New

Testament was not recognized as scripture until long after this text was written. Another New Testament passage describes the prophets of the Old Testament as men who "spoke from God as they were carried along by the Holy Spirit" (2 Peter 1:21). Two Old Testament passages say that God himself wrote the Ten Commandments (Exodus 24:12 and Deuteronomy 5:22). There are also several Old and New Testament texts that describe Old Testament figures as taking dictation from God when writing small portions of scripture (e.g., Ezekiel 11:5, Matthew 22:43). Beyond this, the Bible says little about divine inspiration.

Until the Protestant Reformation in the sixteenth century, divine inspiration was not an issue of great importance. The Roman Catholic and Orthodox traditions had always agreed that the biblical texts were *somehow* inspired by God, who chose their authors and worked *with* and *through* them, and that seems to have been enough. But Protestant reformers taught that the Bible is the only authority on which Christians can completely rely. This meant that the authority of scripture had to be raised to a level at which it was beyond question. In order to accomplish this, Protestant thinkers formulated theories of divine inspiration. Some claim that God inspired the biblical writers even to the point of determining every word they chose to use. Others say that God has ensured the truth of the message in the biblical texts but without influencing the means by which the biblical authors chose to communicate it.

Today, there is a broad range of opinion on divine inspiration and the Bible. Some Christians credit the authors of the biblical texts for their spiritual insights and leave little or no room for divine influence. Others downplay the human contribution to scripture, some to the point of attributing every word and idea to God.

The issue of divine inspiration is closely tied to that of biblical accuracy. As you might imagine, the more one emphasizes God's involvement in creating the biblical texts, the more necessary it becomes to insist on their inerrancy. After all, since God cannot lie or contradict himself, a Bible whose ultimate author is God cannot possibly contain even a single error. Of course, there do seem to be errors and contradictions in the Bible. In such cases, Christians who support absolute inerrancy use biblical, historical, and linguistic arguments to show that these are only apparent, not real. Those who endorse a limited inerrancy say that the Bible is inerrant in matters essential to faith and doctrine but may contain insignificant errors relating to geography and history. For the most part, conservative Protestants favor absolute inerrancy. Roman Catholics, Orthodox Christians, and liberal Protestants tend to support limited inerrancy.

Tradition

Tradition has great authority in the lives of most people. We look to the accumulated wisdom of the past in forms such as laws and constitutions, scientific discoveries, masterpieces of art and literature, and folklore for guidance in organizing society and understanding the world and our place in it. In a similar way, Christians have always looked to their past for guidance in matters of belief and practice.

For them, tradition is the "handing on" (Latin *traditio*) and continuing interpretation of the gospel message through the centuries. The idea of tradition is found in the Bible. In one of his letters to the Christians of Corinth, Paul wrote: "I handed on to you as of first importance what I in turn had received" (1 Corinthians 15:3). Although different groups define the content of tradition in different ways, in the broadest sense it includes creeds, forms of worship, doctrines, the decisions of church councils, the works of major theologians, and even the illustration of the gospel in art, music, and literature.

All Christians place great value on tradition. For Roman Catholics and Orthodox Christians, its authority is on the same level as scripture. Some point out that because the earliest Christians were "handing on" the faith even before the first New Testament texts were written, scripture can be seen as a *part* of tradition. Protestants set tradition below scripture but still acknowledge its importance. Most Protestants believe that tradition is helpful in understanding scripture and recognize the importance of ancient creeds, patterns of worship, and other traditional features of belief and practice.

"Last Things"

We have seen that Jesus proclaimed the coming of the kingdom of God—God's loving and righteous rule in the world. Jesus taught that the kingdom was already present in him and in his followers but that its full realization lay in the future. In doing so, he made a distinction between the present and the future that is evident throughout the New Testament. For example, Paul's letters speak of world-transforming events that had already occurred, such as the resurrection of Christ and the descent of the Holy Spirit upon his followers, but they also look forward to events that would take place at the end of the present age. Greek-speaking Christians called these events *ta eschata*, "the last things." They include eschatological events such as the Second Coming of Christ, the resurrection of the dead, the Last Judgment, and the glorious consummation of the kingdom of God.

Most early Christians assumed that these events and the end of the present age were not far off. As time passed, however, many came to believe that the consummation of the kingdom would occur within a spiritual context rather than in an earthly kingdom. There is a biblical basis for this view in the Gospel of John, whose "realized eschatology" holds that events such as judgment and resurrection into eternal life have already been realized in the interior lives of believers. Both points of view are still very much alive today, and so it is fair to say that Christians hold a wide range of opinions with respect to the time and nature of the fulfillment of God's purposes in the world.

The Afterlife

Like the adherents of many other religions, Christians believe that human existence extends beyond this life. In the afterlife, the consequences of the choices people make now in relation to God and God's grace will be fully realized. Traditionally, Christians have illustrated these consequences with images of heaven and hell. Some also believe in purgatory, an intermediate state between earthly life and heaven.

Heaven

In essence, heaven is perfect and eternal union with God, the fulfillment of the true purpose and deepest desire of human beings. Whether understood as an actual place or a state of being, as physical or spiritual, as earthly or celestial, "heaven" always means the ineffable bliss of everlasting existence in the loving presence of God.

Although New Testament texts make frequent reference to heaven, they do not describe it in detail. Instead, they provide glimpses of heaven, describing it as the city of God, the heavenly Jerusalem, life everlasting, the holy place, and the great reward. In the gospels, Jesus speaks of heaven as "paradise" (Luke 23:43) and as a place he will prepare for his followers (John 14:2–3). Paul says that Christians can be certain of heaven because their experience of the Holy Spirit in this life has already given them a taste of a future reality in which mortality will be "swallowed up by life" (2 Corinthians 5:4).

Christians today hold a wide range of views about heaven. For some, heaven is not a physical place but a purely spiritual state of being. Others understand heaven as the abode of God in the starry firmament above the Earth where the physical bodies of believers will be made perfect and immortal (1 Corinthians 15; Philippians 3:20). Following the book of Revelation, still others think of heaven as a "heavenly Jerusalem" that will become present on Earth at the end of the present age. Here, evils such as death and disease will no longer exist and God himself will live among his people.

Purgatory

One of the most striking differences between Christian views of the afterlife concerns **purgatory**. In Roman Catholic thought, purgatory is an intermediate place or state between earthly life and heaven in which the souls of the dead suffer temporal punishment due for sin. Just as a friend might forgive you for some wrong you have done but still expect you to do something to demonstrate your sorrow, Roman Catholic doctrine holds that sinners must make reparation or satisfaction for sins already forgiven by God. Traditionally imagined as a cleansing fire, purgatory offers the opportunity to complete the work of reparation left undone in earthly life. The scriptural basis for belief in purgatory is found in 2 Maccabees (12:39–45), a deuterocanonical text in which prayer is offered for the dead so that "they might be released from their sin."

Although Orthodox Christianity does not accept the Roman Catholic doctrine of purgatory, most Orthodox Christians believe that after death souls enter a "condition of waiting" in which they can benefit from prayers said on their behalf. Protestant Christians reject belief in purgatory because they find no basis for it in scripture (most Protestant Bibles do not include 2 Maccabees).

Hell   Hell is not so much God's punishment for sin as the self-imposed consequence of rejecting God's grace. Some Christians understand hell as an actual place, others think of it as a state of being, and still others do not believe in hell at all. In describing why hell must exist, one Orthodox writer has said: "God will not force us to love Him, for love is no longer love if it is not free; how then can God reconcile to Himself those who refuse all reconciliation?"[2]

The word translated as "hell" in English versions of the New Testament is *Gehenna*, the name of a valley bordering Jerusalem where many Jews in the time of Jesus expected that the worst of sinners would one day suffer torment. Thus, Gehenna works well as a way of illustrating the pain of separation from God. Although hell clearly refers to a state of existence, there is little basis in the New Testament for understanding it as an actual place. It was not until the early Middle Ages that hell was transformed in the popular imagination into a subterranean pit of fiery horrors. Although hell has long been understood as a necessary expression of divine justice, many Christian thinkers have found this idea to be inconsistent with God's love. Some have taught that God will ultimately save all people from the consequences of sin.

COMPARISON OF CHRISTIAN TRADITIONS

APOSTOLIC SUCCESSION

Orthodox: An important feature of Orthodox belief; ensures continuity with the Church established by Christ through a succession of bishops.
Roman Catholic: An important feature of Roman Catholic belief; ensures continuity with the Church established by Christ through a succession of bishops.
Protestant: Rejected by most Protestants.

AUTHORITY OF SCRIPTURE AND TRADITION

Orthodox: Tradition is the transmission of divine truth taught by Christ and the apostles. Scripture is just one form of tradition. Others include the liturgy, the Holy Mysteries (i.e., sacraments), doctrines, religious art, and texts about the lives of saints.
Roman Catholic: Divine truth taught by Christ and the apostles is transmitted by means of scripture and tradition. Apart from this distinction between scripture

and tradition, tradition is understood largely as it is in Orthodox Christianity.
Protestant: Scripture alone is an authoritative source for Christian doctrine.

BIBLE

Orthodox: Consists of the Old Testament, New Testament, and deuterocanonical books.
Roman Catholic: Consists of Old Testament, New Testament, and deuterocanonical books.
Protestant: Consists of Old and New Testaments.

CHURCH GOVERNMENT

Orthodox: Episcopal. Authority is in the hands of bishops (Greek, *episkopoi*), with the bishop or patriarch of Constantinople, the Ecumenical Patriarch, recognized as the "first among equals."
Roman Catholic: Episcopal. Authority is in the hands of bishops. The Bishop of Rome (i.e., the pope) has primacy over all other bishops.

(continued)

Protestant: Some Protestants, such as Lutherans and Methodists, recognize the authority of bishops, but most reject episcopal government in favor of other forms that place authority in the hands of individual congregations or other governing bodies.

CLERGY: GENDER AND CELIBACY

Orthodox: All clergy must be male. Priests and deacons may marry but only before ordination. Bishops must be celibate.

Roman Catholic: All clergy must be male. Priests and bishops must be celibate, with the exception of priests in the Eastern Rite of the Roman Catholic Church, who may marry.

Protestant: Many churches ordain women. Clergy may marry.

THE EUCHARIST

Orthodox: Christ is truly present in the Eucharist; the bread and wine become the body and blood of Christ by means that are a divine mystery.

Roman Catholic: Christ is truly present in the Eucharist; the bread and wine become the body and blood of Christ through "transubstantiation," the transformation of the inner substance of these elements but not their outward appearance.

Protestant: For most Protestants, the bread and wine are not changed. For some, Christ is somehow truly present in the Eucharist. For others, the bread and wine are only symbols of the body and blood of Christ.

MARY, THE MOTHER OF JESUS

Orthodox: Venerated as a saint and Theotokos (Greek, "Mother of God")

Roman Catholic: Venerated as a saint and "Mother of God"

Protestant: Regarded as a woman of great virtue chosen by God to be the mother of Christ. Protestants do not venerate Mary as a saint.

PAPACY

Orthodox: The pope is the successor of St. Peter as Bishop of Rome and so enjoys a position of honor among them, but he has no authority over other bishops.

Roman Catholic: The pope is the successor of St. Peter as Bishop of Rome and, as the Vicar (i.e., representative) of Christ, has authority over the Church. He is infallible when, through the action of the Holy Spirit, he defines doctrines relating to faith and morals.

Protestant: The pope is the leader of the Roman Catholic Church and has no authority outside the Roman Catholic Church.

SACRAMENTS

Orthodox: The sacraments, or "holy mysteries," are ways in which God discloses himself and imparts grace. Although usually said to be seven in number—Baptism, Chrismation, Eucharist, Confession, Holy Unction, Marriage, and Ordination—Orthodoxy regards all that the Church does as sacramental and has never defined the sacraments as seven.

Roman Catholic: There are seven sacraments, visible signs and channels of divine grace, which is invisible. The seven are the same as those in Orthodoxy, with some known by different names: Confirmation (Chrismation), Reconciliation (Confession), Anointing of the Sick (Holy Unction), Holy Orders (Ordination).

Protestant: Only two sacraments are generally recognized: Baptism and the Eucharist.

Christianity and Other Religions

Existing alongside other religions, Christianity has always sought to define itself in relation to them. This is particularly true of Judaism, within which it originated. We can see tension between early Christianity and Judaism in New Testament passages critical of Jewish piety and religious groups (for example, in Matthew 23 and

John 5–8). It is also evident in the gospel accounts of the crucifixion of Jesus, which place greater blame on Jewish authorities than on the Romans, who actually carried out the execution.

Tragically, the presence of anti-Jewish feeling in scripture continued to influence Christian attitudes toward Jews and Judaism long after the first century. Denounced as Christ killers and enemies of humanity, seventh-century French and Spanish Jews were subjected to forced baptism. In the late Middle Ages, Jews were expelled from England, Spain, France, and Portugal. Anti-Jewish feeling assumed its most virulent form with the rise of fascism in Germany, Italy, and other parts of Europe in the twentieth century. It was not until after the Holocaust, the genocidal murder of 6 million Jews carried out by Nazi Germany during World War II, that church leaders began working for an end to hostility toward Jews and Judaism. At its inaugural meeting in 1948, the World Council of Churches declared that anti-Semitism is incompatible with the Christian faith and "a sin against God and man." Today, many Christian groups are engaged in efforts to heal the wounds of the past and to encourage a Jewish–Christian dialogue that will foster mutual appreciation and respect.

As we will see later in this chapter, Christians have found themselves in conflict with adherents of other religions. For example, in the Middle Ages religion contributed to tensions and outright warfare between Christian Europe and the Islamic civilization of the Middle East and North Africa. Later, the expansion of European colonial powers into regions such as Africa and the Americas brought conflict between Christianity and indigenous religions.

Historically, most Christians have believed that there is no salvation outside of the Church, a view based on New Testament passages that speak of Jesus as the only way in which God has been fully revealed to humanity. But the cultural pluralism of today's global society has raised interest in other ways of understanding spiritual realities. In fact, some Christians have found a scriptural basis for the possibility of salvation in other religions. They point to Paul's letter to the Romans, which says that those who follow the dictates of their consciences will be judged as righteous on the last day (Romans 2:14–16). Similarly, the letter of James defines "pure" religion not in specifically Christian terms but as caring for the needy and keeping oneself "unstained by the world" (James 1:27). Biblical passages like these have encouraged many Christians to value the spiritual insights of other religious traditions and to enter into cooperative relationships with them. The spirit of this new attitude, expressed in formal statements by many Christian groups, is represented in the *Declaration on Non-Christian Religions* issued by the Roman Catholic bishops who assembled for the Second Vatican Council (1962–1965):

> Prudently and lovingly, through dialogue and collaboration with the followers of other religions and in witness of the Christian faith and life, we should acknowledge, preserve and promote the spiritual and moral goods found among these men, as well as the values in their society and culture.[3]

12.3 The History of Christianity: The Church in the Ancient Roman World

Christianity spread rapidly throughout the Roman Empire. As it did, Christians met with criticism and persecution that continued until Rome's emperors became Christians themselves. Also, as the Christian movement grew during these early years, it became necessary to define basic doctrines and to adopt a form of church government capable of uniting Christians and promoting uniformity of belief and practice among them.

Conflict with the Roman State

The first Christian emperor of Rome, Constantine the Great promoted the spread of Christianity throughout the Roman Empire and founded a new capital at Constantinople (modern Istanbul) in 330. He is represented here with his mother, Helena.

The Roman world was often hostile to Christians. Many suspected Christians of disloyalty to Rome because they refused to recognize its gods or participate in public events that involved pagan rituals. Localized persecutions began in the first century and expanded into empire-wide assaults in the third. Despite the terrors of mass arrests and executions, persecution failed to check the growth of Christianity. A dramatic turning point came in 312, when the Emperor Constantine (r. 306–337) defeated a rival after seeing a vision of a cross in the sky. Convinced that the God of the Christians had given him the victory, Constantine decreed religious freedom for Christians and began to promote Christianity by building churches and extending privileges to church leaders.

When Constantine transferred the imperial capital from Rome to Constantinople (modern Istanbul) in 330, he did so in the hope that it would be a truly Christian city free of paganism. Decades later, Theodosius I (r. 379–395) made Christianity the official state religion of the Roman Empire and began the suppression of other religions and schools of philosophy.

Diversity in the Early Church

During the first five centuries CE, Christians formulated many important doctrines, thereby establishing a standard of orthodoxy, or "correct belief." However, some early Christian groups challenged the emerging mainstream Church on issues as basic as the nature of God, the humanity of Christ, salvation, and ecclesiastical (Greek *ekklesia*, "church") authority.

Gnostic Christians produced mysterious gospels and other texts that did not come to light until the late nineteenth century. Many Gnostic Christians believed that Christ's body had been a mere illusion; therefore, he could not have atoned for sin by dying a physical death upon the cross. Salvation came instead from secret knowledge

(Greek, *gnosis*) that Christ gave only to a select group of *gnostics* ("knowers"), who had passed it down to others. Because Gnostic Christians saw all material reality as evil, they understood salvation as the liberation of souls from human bodies rather than as liberation from sin. Gnostics claimed that the Christianity preached publicly in churches was incomplete, as they alone understood the higher teachings of Christ.

A second group was founded by Marcion (c. 85–160 CE), a theologian who had been expelled from the church at Rome for teaching that there are two Gods: the God of the Jewish Scriptures, whom Marcion described as the unjust creator of an evil world, and the supremely good God revealed by Christ. According to Marcion, it was this good God who had sent Christ to rescue human souls. Seeking to cut Christianity off from its Jewish roots, Marcion rejected the Jewish Scriptures and all Christian texts that seemed dependent on them.

A third form of Christianity, known as Montanism, began with Montanus, a charismatic prophet of the late second century who claimed to be the mouthpiece of the Holy Spirit. Montanus prophesied that Christ would soon return to a "new Jerusalem" that was about to appear in southern Asia Minor. The greatest difficulty posed by Montanus was his claim that he preached a *new* prophecy. This raised two critical questions. First, would Christian teaching require ongoing revision in order to accommodate every new group and its revelations? Second, did claims of prophetic inspiration give charismatic figures like Montanus an authority greater than that of church leaders?

Defining Orthodoxy

Resolving questions related to correct belief, scripture, and the authority of the Church was one of the great themes in the early history of the Church. In order to establish its authority and define orthodox belief, the Church created a canon of scripture, formulated creeds, and implemented a system of ecclesiastical government that put authority into the hands of bishops.

We have already seen that a canon of scripture consisting of the Old and New Testaments was in place by the end of the fourth century. Texts widely believed to have been written by the apostles were included, as were writings from the apostolic era that were widely used in public worship. Because the Old and New Testaments were regarded as having a unique authority, they constituted a standard against which the orthodoxy of any new teaching could be judged.

The creeds developed by the early Church were formal and concise statements of essential Christian beliefs. In fact, the word *creed* itself comes from the Latin *credo*, which means "I believe." Creeds such as the Apostles' Creed and the Nicene Creed served two functions. First, they proclaimed orthodox doctrine on the incarnation, suffering, and death of Christ, as well as his resurrection and ascension into heaven. Second, the repeated recitation of the creeds by Christians throughout the empire promoted uniformity of belief within the Church.

Finally, the early Church established a form of government that concentrated power in the hands of bishops who presided over large territories called dioceses. According to the doctrine of **apostolic succession**, bishops were the successors of the apostles, who had been commissioned by Christ himself to lead the Church. Claiming to have received both their offices and correct belief through direct lines of transmission reaching back to the apostles, they held an authority that Gnostics, Montanists, and Marcionite Christians found difficult to challenge. Bishops were assisted by priests, who were responsible for individual churches, and every church was served by deacons (Greek *diakonos*, "servant") who assisted priests.

Gradually, the bishops of Rome and Constantinople emerged as the leaders of the churches of the Western and Eastern halves of the empire. Known as "popes" (Latin *papa*, "father"), the bishops of Rome were said to be the successors of the Apostle Peter, the "rock" (Greek, *petra*) upon whom Christ had said he would build his Church (Matthew 16:18–19). They claimed the same authority Christ had given to Peter. Other bishops—including the great patriarchs of Constantinople, Alexandria, Antioch, and Jerusalem—acknowledged the bishops of Rome as "first among equals" but without recognizing the right of popes to rule over them.

Early Christian Thought

The success of the early Christian movement was due in part to the work of Christian writers who produced carefully reasoned statements of Christian belief. These texts gave Christianity intellectual respectability in a world accustomed to the high standards of Greek philosophy and encouraged a search for commonalities linking Christian and pagan culture.

For example, theologians such as Clement of Alexandria (c. 150–215) and Origen (c. 185–254) taught that God had long been at work among the Greeks and Romans, preparing them for the coming of Christ. Just as God had given the Torah to the Jews, said Clement, he had given philosophy to the Greeks as a kind of "schoolmaster" in order to "bring the Greek mind . . . to Christ."[4] Like many thinkers of his time, Clement held that all truth comes from the divine "Word," or **logos**. Thus, truths found in scripture and philosophy were compatible. However, since the logos had become incarnate in Jesus Christ (John 1:18), said Clement, it was only in Christ that seekers of truth would find it fully revealed.

Controversies and Councils

Beginning in the third century, Christian theologians turned their attention to the concept of the Trinity and to the nature of Christ. Discussion of these issues led to ecumenical councils ("worldwide councils") of bishops at which doctrines were formally defined.

From the beginning, most Christians believed that God the Father, the Creator of the universe, had become present in the world in Jesus Christ, God the Son.

They also believed in the Holy Spirit as the continuing expression of God's loving presence and power in the world. But how could the one God also be three? This question was taken up by theologians such as Tertullian, who gave Latin theology its Trinitarian vocabulary by speaking of God as *tres personae, una substantia* ("three persons, one substance"). Similarly, Greek-speaking theologians described God as a single divine *ousia* ("substance" or "essence") made manifest in three *hypostases* ("subsistences").

This way of thinking about the Trinity sufficed until the early 300s, when Arius, an Egyptian priest from Alexandria, began teaching that God the Son was of a different substance than God the Father. Going further, Arius claimed that whereas the Father was eternal, the Son was created in time. Arius's views alarmed other theologians, for they seemed to undermine the unity of the Trinity. If the Father and the Son were so different, they asked, how could God be truly one?

Arius's provocative teachings soon had Alexandria buzzing as people in shops and streets argued theology with an enthusiasm that we today reserve for debates about sports and politics. Fearing that Arianism threatened the unity of the empire as well as the Church, the Emperor Constantine stepped in and convened an ecumenical council to settle the matter. The Council of Nicea (325) condemned Arius's views, ordered the burning of Arian texts, and formulated a creed affirming that God the Son is *homoousios* ("of the same substance" or "being") with God the Father. An expanded form of this creed, the Nicene Creed, produced by the Council of Constantinople (381), describes God as a Trinity of three distinct yet unified divine "persons."

Even as the Trinitarian controversy was being settled, another debate began over the person of Christ. Christians had long believed that Christ was both human and divine, but they differed in explaining how humanity and divinity coexisted in him. The orthodox position on this issue was determined at yet another ecumenical council at Chalcedon (451): in Christ, two complete and perfect natures, human and divine, were united without separation or fusion in a single person.

Augustine

The drama of the Trinitarian and Christological controversies was played out in the Greek-speaking eastern half of the Roman world and involved many leading theologians. The Latin West produced just one theological giant. This was Augustine (354–430), a North African bishop who laid the intellectual foundations for much of Western Christianity and Western civilization.

Central to Augustine's theology are his views on sin and human nature. Elaborating on the theology of Paul, Augustine argued that sinfulness is a fundamental flaw in human nature that clouds our moral vision and perverts the will by causing us to desire evil rather than good. In the *Confessions*, his spiritual autobiography, he illustrated this point by recalling the pleasure he and some teenage friends once found in stealing and throwing away pears from a neighbor's tree. According to Augustine, the tendency to sin is so deeply ingrained that we are spiritually helpless and therefore completely dependent on God for salvation.

But *how* did human nature become so corrupt? Augustine's answer came in his famous doctrine of **original sin**. All of humanity, it says, participated in the first sin: the sin of Adam and Eve, the first human beings, described in Genesis (3:1–24). At that time, Adam and Eve *were* humanity, with all future generations present in them. Thus, when they made themselves sinners by choosing to disobey God, this original sin transformed human nature in a way that was bound to affect their descendants. Every human being, said Augustine, is born with the "stain" of original sin in the form of a sinful nature. As we will see, although Augustine's teaching on original sin became a foundational feature of Roman Catholic and Protestant Christianity, it was never accepted by the Orthodox tradition.

Augustine's awareness that some people are saved from sin led him to formulate a theory of predestination. Because all human beings are sinful and therefore incapable of responding on their own to God in faith, he reasoned, God must give some people a grace that inspires faith. Divine grace is irresistible, he said, for a love that could be resisted would be incompatible with God's perfection. Thus, those whom God touches with his grace are destined to be saved. Augustine conceded that it is impossible to know *why* God extends a saving grace to some people and not to others, but he insisted that God is neither arbitrary nor unjust. Some are allowed a destiny better than they deserve, but no one receives a destiny worse than he deserves.

Augustine was never entirely comfortable with his conclusions about original sin and predestination, but his reading of scripture and observation of human behavior made them inescapable. Having seen jealousy in a baby whose brother had taken his place at their mother's breast, he felt he had no choice but to conclude that sin must be something we are born with and not simply a habit everyone happens to pick up. Similarly, though predestination seemed to be the work of an unfair God, Augustine knew that scripture taught that only some would be saved and that God's justice is not always within reach of human understanding.

Augustine's masterpiece was his *City of God*, in which he formulated a Christian philosophy of history. Writing amid the panic following the sack of Rome by a Germanic tribe in 410, he rejected the pagan claim that Rome's traditional gods allowed the city to fall because they were angry with the Romans for converting to Christianity. Augustine argued that the fall of Rome was part of God's plan for the salvation of the world. God had ordained two "cities": the earthly city, blemished by sin, and the City of God, a spiritual community grounded in love of God. Like all other manifestations of the earthly city, said Augustine, Rome must pass away so that history can move toward the full realization of the City of God on Earth. This view of history as progress toward the fulfillment of God's plan for salvation soon became standard in the Christian West.

12.4 The History of Christianity: The Middle Ages

In the fifth century, Germanic tribes overran the Western half of the Roman Empire. From the resulting chaos, a new medieval civilization emerged that combined Christianity with Roman and Germanic culture. The Eastern half of the Roman Empire survived for another thousand years. Known as the Byzantine Empire, it was Greek in its language and outlook. As the gulf between West and East widened, distinctively Western and Eastern traditions within the catholic ("universal") Church began to take shape.

The Church in the West

The most powerful of the Germanic tribes were the Franks, who controlled most of western Europe by the ninth century. The Franks supported the Roman Church and granted rich lands to bishops and monasteries. In return, the Church sanctioned the rule of the Frankish kings, supplied clergy to serve in their government, and sent missionaries to convert pagan peoples in their kingdom.

The Church's involvement in secular affairs continued after the decline of the Franks and often led to conflict between secular and spiritual rulers, especially the popes. Early medieval popes claimed that their spiritual responsibilities gave them an authority greater than that of secular rulers, but it was not until the eleventh century that the papacy rose to the level they had imagined. The most powerful of popes was Innocent III (r. 1198–1216). Intent on unifying the Christian world under the papal banner, Innocent intervened constantly in secular matters, deposing kings and emperors whenever they displeased him.

An ugly aspect of medieval Christianity in the West was the **Inquisition**, the Church's inquiry into allegations of heresy that began in the twelfth century. Working in partnership with secular rulers, who feared that religious diversity would undermine their authority, the inquisitors sought to eradicate false teachings they believed would endanger the salvation of those who accepted them. The Inquisition also targeted Jews and Muslims. Despite its use of torture and the execution of heretics by burning, the Inquisition could not stamp out heresy. Nevertheless, it persisted in various forms until its final and cruelest phase, the Spanish Inquisition, was abolished in 1834.

Completed c. 1250, the height and soaring towers of the Gothic cathedral at Chartres in France express the medieval yearning for God. For centuries, pilgrims and secular tourists have come to experience its exquisite, light-filled interior and to see its famous relic, the tunic of the Virgin Mary.

The Church in the East

In the East, the patriarchs of Constantinople governed the Church jointly with the Byzantine emperors. The Byzantine

The interior of the Cathedral of Hagia Sophia. Dedicated to the "holy wisdom" embodied by Christ, this sixth-century church is the supreme achievement of Byzantine architecture. After the capture of Constantinople by the Turks in 1453, the city was renamed Istanbul and the church first became a mosque, then a museum.

ideal was a harmony of emperor and patriarch based on their shared vision of a holy empire on Earth that reflected the glory of the celestial society of heaven. Clashes did occur, but only one threatened the symbiosis of emperor and patriarch. This was the controversy over iconoclasm, or "icon smashing." **Icons**, painted images of Christ and the saints, had long been revered by Byzantine Christians. But some saw this as idolatry. When the Emperor Leo III began removing icons from churches and other public places (726), riots erupted throughout the empire. Leo and his successors responded by deposing uncooperative patriarchs and executing monks, the leading defenders of icons. A formal end to iconoclasm came in 787, when the Second Council of Nicea determined that icons are worthy of veneration but not worship, which must be reserved for God alone.

By the twelfth century, Byzantine missionaries had brought the Slavic peoples of Russia and the Balkans into the Eastern Church. But the position of the Church became increasingly difficult in later years as the Byzantine Empire gradually collapsed under pressure from the expanding Islamic world. The empire fell in 1453 with the capture of Constantinople by the Ottoman Turks. For the next four centuries, most Eastern Christians outside Russia lived in the Ottoman Empire, an Islamic state in which they were tolerated but were denied full religious freedom.

The Great Schism: East and West Divided

The Great Schism, the split between Western and Eastern Christianity, came after centuries of gradual separation during which the two traditions developed their distinctive forms. Some of their differences were minor: baptism, for example, was performed by a sprinkling of water in the West but by full immersion in the East, and the West urged priests to be celibate whereas the East preferred them to be married. Far more divisive were the attempts of popes to control Eastern bishops and Byzantine lands. In the end, it was the West's addition of the Latin *filioque* ("and from the Son") to the Nicene Creed that brought a final break. The East rejected this move for theological reasons and because the West had acted without sanction by an ecumenical council. In 1054, angry words over the *filioque* combined with tensions over other issues to force the division of what had always been a single, universal Church into separate Roman Catholic and Orthodox churches.

The Crusades

Despite their differences, Eastern and Western Christians did share a common concern over the westward advance of Islamic armies. In 1095, Pope Urban II proclaimed a military crusade intended to push the Muslims back and liberate Jerusalem. Crying "*Deus vult!*" ("God wills it!"), armies of knights, peasants, and townspeople set out on the First Crusade. In 1099, they celebrated their capture of Jerusalem with a frenzied slaughter of Muslims and Jews. But the crusaders were unable to defend the lands they had conquered, and subsequent crusades to regain them were often military or moral disasters. Participants in the infamous Fourth Crusade (1204) never made it to the Holy Land, deciding instead to plunder Constantinople. The crusades ended at the close of the thirteenth century, having failed to deliver the Holy Land permanently into Christian hands.

Monasticism and Mysticism

One of the most visible features of medieval Christianity was monasticism, a movement that began in the third century when Christians seeking a deeper experience of God withdrew into the deserts of Egypt and Syria. Most early Christian monks and nuns lived solitary lives and practiced a severe asceticism. According to legend, Macarius of Alexandria (d. 395) remained standing for periods as long as forty days, subsisting on a weekly meal of cabbage. The nun Alexandra walled herself up in a tomb for ten years, never seeing another human face.

In the medieval period, monks and nuns were brought together in monasteries governed by "rules" that regularized monastic life and discouraged extreme forms of self-denial. Both the Eastern Rule of Basil the Great (330–379) and the Western Rule of Benedict of Nursia (480–547) required monks and nuns to take vows of chastity and poverty and to spend their days in communal worship, prayer, and labor. Although the monastic aim of pursuing holiness through the imitation of Christ meant that monks and nuns spent much time in prayer and contemplation, monasteries also served nearby communities, providing them with spiritual guidance, education, shelter for travelers, and care for the poor and sick.

The monastic movement also encouraged mysticism, the direct and intuitive experience of God beyond the limits of mere intellect. Eastern mystics emphasized the absolute "otherness" of God, whom they regarded as so utterly unlike anything else we experience that even concepts as basic as "being" and "nonbeing" are useless in describing divinity. Though remote in his incomprehensibility, they said, God is also near, touching human beings with a love that restores the sinful nature to its original state of perfection in "the image of God" (Genesis 1:26–27).

In this fresco by Giovanni Sodoma (1477–1549), Benedictine monks of the Monte Oliveto monastery in Italy eat their meal together—just as they worked and worshiped together in accordance with the Rule of St. Benedict. Note that one of the monks reads to the others from the Bible or some other holy book as they eat.

On April 29, the feast day of St. Catherine of Siena, four citizens of Siena, Italy, dress in medieval costumes and carry a casket holding the saint's relics in a procession.

"Love, the divine gift," wrote Maximus the Confessor (c. 580–662), "perfects human nature until it makes it appear in unity and identity with the divine nature."[5] Building on these ideas, Eastern monks such as Simeon the New Theologian (949–1022) and Gregory Palamas (c. 1296–1359) practiced Hesychasm, the cultivation of an inner quietude (*hesychia*) that brings an experience of God as divine light.

Western mystics also emphasized the power of divine love. Bernard of Clairvaux (1090–1153) compared Christ to a bridegroom whose love for the soul fills her with a bliss that transcends all earthly feeling. Bonaventure (1217–1274) described how divine love lifts the mind above rational thought, allowing it to unite with God in ecstasy. Many of the great Western mystics were women. Catherine of Siena (1347–1380) described a dialogue between God and a human soul seeking union with the divine in her famous *Dialogue on Divine Providence*. In her *Revelations of Divine Love*, the English recluse Julian of Norwich (1342–1416) spoke of God's love as the only means to abiding joy. "Until I am substantially united to him," she wrote, "I can never have love or rest or true happiness."[6]

Theology

In the West, early medieval theology was centered in monasteries, where learned monks and nuns engaged in debates on issues such as predestination, free will, and the sacraments. In seeking to understand how Christ can be truly present in the Eucharist, for example, medieval theologians formulated a doctrine of **transubstantiation**. According to this doctrine, the bread and wine consecrated by a priest during the Eucharist become the actual body and blood of Christ in substance, though their secondary qualities, such as taste, color, and texture, remain unchanged.

The growth of major universities in the twelfth century created a new setting for theological inquiry. Here, theologians applied the science of logic as developed by Aristotle to grasp the full meaning of truths revealed in the scripture. Known as **scholasticism**, this effort became the chief intellectual enterprise of the West in the Middle Ages. The greatest of the scholastic theologians was Thomas Aquinas (1226–1274), a professor at the University of Paris. In his *Summa Theologica*, Thomas argued that although some truths can be known through reason alone, others can be grasped only through faith. Ultimately, said Thomas, there is a perfect harmony between reason and faith, for both come from God.

The most distinctive feature of Eastern theology was its view that all essential Christian truths had been defined once and for all by seven ecumenical councils that completed their work in the eighth century. After the Second Council of Nicea (787), Orthodox theologians devoted themselves to the analysis and elaboration of the faith as articulated by the seven ecumenical councils.

One of the important ways in which Eastern theology differed from that of the West concerns Augustine's doctrine of original sin. Although both East and West agreed that the original sin of Adam had introduced sin and death into the world, the East did not accept Augustine's view that this involved a corruption of the human nature that everyone assumes at birth. By contrast, the Eastern Church taught that the natural state of human beings is one of spiritual purity. Human beings succumb to the sin and evil of the world in which we live, but this is ultimately due to the choices we make and not to a sinful nature inherited from generations reaching back to Adam that makes it impossible to live as we should. Both East and West agreed that the remedy for sin is baptism, which cleanses the individual from the effects of sin and brings salvation through union with Christ.

12.5 The History of Christianity: The Modern Era

We will begin our survey of Christianity in the modern era with the Reformation, a movement that produced Protestantism, one of the three major forms of Christianity. We will then examine some of the challenges posed to Christianity by developments in the natural and social sciences and the rise of liberalism and secularism. After taking a brief look at the missionary movement, we will turn our attention to how the Roman Catholic, Protestant, and Orthodox traditions have fared in the modern era.

Portrait of Martin Luther by Lucas Cranach the Elder (1529). It was Luther who set the Protestant Reformation in motion by posting his Ninety-Five Theses on the door of the All Saints' Church in Wittenberg, Germany.

The Reformation: Protestant Challenge and Roman Catholic Response

In the sixteenth century, a religious revolution known as the Reformation rocked Western Christianity. The Reformation's first phase is known as the Protestant Reformation because of the protests of reformers against Roman Catholic doctrines and practices. Its second phase was the Catholic Reformation, which included direct responses to Protestantism, as well as reforms undertaken independently of it. Ultimately, the Reformation left the West religiously divided, furthering the fragmentation of the Church that had begun centuries earlier with its division into the Roman Catholic and Orthodox churches.

Background to the Reformation   Throughout the Middle Ages, the Roman Catholic Church engaged in constant self-examination and reform. Even so, voices calling for change grew louder and more numerous. Some complained of corruption among the clergy. Christians north of the Alps resented taxes imposed by the Church, especially since most revenues were spent in Rome. Many were angered by the luxuries enjoyed by popes. Those who wished to emulate the simple piety of the apostles were discouraged by the example set by church leaders who seemed more interested in wealth and power than in spirituality. Calls for reform were also encouraged by the revival of humanism—a deep faith in human beings that inspired the Renaissance; this cultural movement was flourishing at the time of the Reformation. Humanists such as Desiderius Erasmus (1466–1536) argued that Christians had no need to rely on the Church. Instead, they were capable of taking charge of their spiritual lives based on their own reading and interpretation of the Bible. By the dawn of the sixteenth century, desire for religious reform was intense and widespread. The situation was volatile. In 1517, a German monk named **Martin Luther** (1483–1546) provided a spark.

The Protestant Reformation
Luther was a monk who had not found peace in monastic life. Despite his efforts to be an ideal monk, he was plagued by a sense of unworthiness and fear of God's judgment that followed him from his monastery to the University of Wittenberg, where he became a professor of theology. It was in Wittenberg that Luther, reading about "the righteousness of God" in Paul's letter to the Romans (1:17), came to believe that God's righteousness did not consist in his desire to condemn the unrighteous but in his eagerness to forgive them. God does not set before sinners the impossible task of *earning* their salvation, Luther concluded. Instead, he asks only that it be accepted, as an expression of divine grace, by faith. For Luther, it was faith alone, and not good works or sacraments, that "justified" sinners before God.

As Luther considered the implications of "justification by faith," he identified Church practices that he found objectionable. Among them was the distribution of indulgences (certificates of remission of punishment in purgatory). For centuries, popes had claimed the authority to apply the surplus merits of the saints to penitent sinners, thereby releasing them from punishment otherwise due for unconfessed sin in purgatory. By Luther's time, the outright sale of indulgences had become an important means of raising funds to finance the papal office.

In 1517, Luther called for public debate on indulgences and other issues by nailing his Ninety-Five Theses, a statement of his theological positions, to the door of the church in Wittenberg. Supporters quickly rallied behind him. When ecclesiastical and secular leaders ordered Luther to recant his views, he refused, setting the Protestant movement in motion.

Luther now began building a Protestant theology based on three principles. First, salvation is made possible by divine "grace alone." Second, it is "by faith alone" that sinners must respond to grace. Third, "scripture alone," and not the pronouncements of popes and church councils, is the only authority on which Christians can completely rely. In order to make the Bible available to the people, Luther translated it into German. Because he found no mandate in the Bible for an ecclesiastical hierarchy, he rejected the authority of popes and bishops, as well as the traditional distinction between clergy and laity. According to Luther's doctrine of the "priesthood of all believers," Christians represented themselves before God and had no need of a special class of priests.

Luther's intention had been to reform the Roman Catholic Church, not to create a new Christian movement, but his teachings cut too close to the heart of Catholicism to make this possible. Moreover, the rulers of many German territories saw in Luther a champion who might end the unwelcome influence of the pope and his ally, the Holy Roman Emperor, in their lands. They therefore encouraged a break with Rome. Fighting between Catholics and Protestants broke out. By the time it ended in 1555, Lutheranism had triumphed in northern Germany and Scandinavia.

Luther was soon joined by other reformers who expanded the geographical scope of the Reformation. In his *Institutes of the Christian Religion*, **John Calvin** (1509–1564) articulated Protestant doctrines with a power and clarity that put his life in danger in Catholic France. Welcomed by the Swiss city of Geneva, Calvin accepted the essential features of Luther's thought but gave Protestant theology his own stamp by emphasizing God's sovereignty over the universe and teaching that every honest occupation is a "calling" given by God. Calvinism quickly took root in Switzerland in the Swiss Reformed churches, in the Dutch Netherlands as the Dutch Reformed Church, and in England and Scotland as Presbyterianism.

In Zurich, the Swiss reformer Ulrich Zwingli (1484–1531) denounced all beliefs and practices that were not described in the Bible. Because the Bible makes no mention of images of Christ and the saints, candles, and incense, he removed these from Zurich's churches. A space without symbolic and decorative distractions, he reasoned, would be more likely to bring worshipers into direct communion with God. In teaching that the bread and wine used in the Eucharist were mere symbols, Zwingli went far beyond Luther and Calvin, who joined him in rejecting the doctrine of transubstantiation but retained the belief that Christ is truly in the sacrament.

Alongside the Lutheran, Calvinist, and Zwinglian movements emerged smaller, more radical groups that make up what some scholars call the Radical Reformation. Anabaptists ("*re*baptizers") insisted that Christians baptized as infants must be "born again" and baptized again as mature believers. Refusing to recognize the authority of civil governments and their laws, Anabaptists refused to take oaths and were committed to nonviolence. Other radical groups placed such great importance on the inner presence of the Holy Spirit that they saw little value in the Bible or traditional worship. Still others rejected doctrines as basic as the Trinity and the divinity of Christ.

The Reformation was brought to England by King Henry VIII, depicted here in a famous portrait by the sixteenth-century painter Hans Holbein the Younger.

In England, the Reformation began when the pope refused the request of King Henry VIII (r. 1509–1547) for an annulment of his marriage. Taking matters into his own hands, Henry prevailed upon Parliament to pass an Act of Supremacy (1534) that made the king of England, not the pope, the head of the Church in England. This break marked the beginning of the Church of England and of an Anglican tradition that was later exported to England's colonies. In America, the Anglican Church, as it is sometimes called, came to be known as the Episcopal Church.

Although Henry had wanted to effect only political change, the Church of England soon felt the impact of Protestant thought on the Continent. In the end, a kind of compromise was reached that left the Church of England very "Catholic" in its theology and patterns of worship but clearly influenced by elements of Calvinist and Lutheran theology. Although this arrangement satisfied most Anglicans, there were important groups of dissenters. Calvinist Puritans wanted to "purify" the Church of England of every vestige of Catholicism. Presbyterians, also inspired by Calvinism, wanted to replace the episcopal hierarchy with assemblies of presbyters ("elders"). Quakers rejected all formal worship and all forms of church governance.

The Catholic Reformation　The primary response of the Roman Catholic Church to Protestantism was the Council of Trent (1545–1563), where bishops reaffirmed Catholic teachings but took great care to clarify them. Against Protestant belief in the authority of scripture alone, the council held that tradition is equally authoritative. Against the Protestant reduction of the sacraments to baptism and the

Distribution of major branches of Christianity throughout the world.

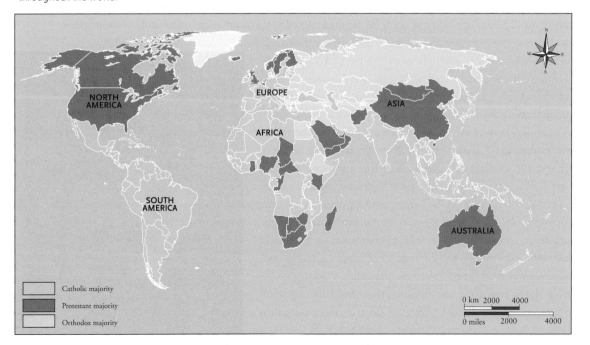

NORTH AMERICA

EUROPE

ASIA

AFRICA

SOUTH AMERICA

AUSTRALIA

Catholic majority

Protestant majority

Orthodox majority

0 km　2000　4000

0 miles　2000　4000

Eucharist, it reaffirmed the seven sacraments. In response to the Protestant doctrine of justification by faith, the council insisted that faith must be expressed by good works and cited the New Testament in support of this view (e.g., Romans 2:6; 2 Corinthians 5:10). The council also upheld transubstantiation, confession, priestly celibacy, monasticism, purgatory, and the intercession of saints in heaven on behalf of the living. Although it gave no ground to Protestantism on doctrinal issues, the Council of Trent did take decisive action to end corruption in the Church, to improve the quality of education received by priests, and to ensure that essential doctrines were made clear in the sermons, or homilies, that were a part of the Mass.

Although the Council of Trent left Catholics and Protestants divided, its reforms and clarification of doctrine did reinvigorate the Roman Catholic Church, especially in its efforts to spread the faith. New religious orders such as the Jesuits, founded by Ignatius Loyola (1491–1556), spearheaded the effort to reestablish Catholicism in lands where Protestantism had become popular and to bring it to parts of the world where Christianity had not yet established a foothold, including China, Japan, India, the Philippines, and the Americas.

Change and Challenges in the Modern Era

The Reformation was only the first challenge faced by Christianity in the modern era. Dramatic scientific, social, political, and intellectual developments also required the Church to respond to a changing world.

As early as the Reformation era, a scientific revolution was beginning to transform the traditional understanding of the universe. For centuries, the Church had endorsed the widespread belief that the universe revolves around Earth—and therefore around humanity, the supreme object of God's love. But this view was abandoned after Nicholas Copernicus (1473–1543) and Galileo Galilei (1564–1642) proved that Earth and other planets revolve around the sun. When Isaac Newton (1642–1727) demonstrated that the universe operates according to laws of nature not found in scripture, science seemed to make the Bible unnecessary to understanding the physical world. The new scientific approach also undermined old ideas about human beings. Charles Darwin's *On the Origin of Species* (1859) challenged the biblical account of the creation of humanity. Later, the work of Sigmund Freud (1856–1939) and the French sociologist Émile Durkheim (1858–1917) suggested that religion did not originate with divine revelation but in the maladjusted psyche or in the need to create order in society.

The scientific revolution was encouraged by growing confidence in the power of human reason. This was especially evident in the Enlightenment, a philosophical movement of the eighteenth century. Encouraged by Newton's description of nature as entirely rational, Enlightenment thinkers such as Voltaire (1694–1778), Jean-Jacques

This mosaic of the Virgin Mary and Christ Child is from the Annunciation Basilica in Nazareth, Israel. It is a wonderful example of the desire of Christians all over the world to understand Jesus in relation to themselves and their own cultures.

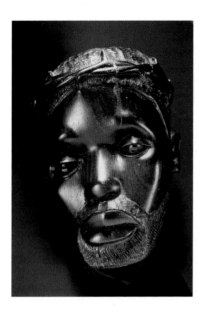

In this wood carving from West Africa, an anonymous twentieth-century artist portrays Jesus as African and manages to capture the sorrow and suffering of the Savior, who was about to face crucifixion.

Rousseau (1712–1778), and Immanuel Kant (1724–1804) believed the way to all truth was through study of the world around us. Unwilling to accept as true any idea that could not stand up under rational scrutiny, they rejected traditional Christianity except for belief in God, whose existence seemed to be implied by the orderliness of nature, and ethical ideals such as honesty and kindness to others.

In the nineteenth century, Christianity felt the effects of liberalism and secularism. Nineteenth-century liberalism held that human beings can create an ideal society if they have the freedom to think and act without interference. For this reason, liberals called for limits on the influence of both church and state. Many liberals found it difficult to reconcile Christian beliefs about the sinfulness of human nature and the revelation of truth in scripture with their own views concerning the essential goodness of human beings and the importance of independent thought. Moreover, the progress of democracy across Europe in the nineteenth century brought the implementation of liberal policies that promoted secularism—the belief that religious ideas and institutions should have much less influence in the operation of the state, and especially in public education. The American ideal of the separation of church and state is just one example of this new attitude toward the place of religion in society.

Bishops gathered at the Second Vatican Council (1962–1965) in St. Peter's Basilica.

The Missionary Movement

The geographical scope of Christianity grew dramatically in the modern era as European colonial powers expanded their influence into other continents. By the sixteenth century, Roman Catholic missionaries were active in Asia and newly discovered lands in the Americas. Orthodox Christians brought their tradition to Alaska and Japan. Protestants took the gospel to Africa, Asia, and the Americas. Most Westerners brought to foreign lands a belief in the superiority of their own culture and the conviction that they had a moral obligation to share its benefits, including Christianity, with the peoples they found there. As the British poet Rudyard Kipling (1865–1936) put it, "the white man's burden" was to civilize the world's "lesser breeds." Regrettably, the "civilizing" of non-Christians sometimes involved conversions accomplished through intimidation or outright force by colonizers.

Roman Catholicism in the Modern World

The Roman Catholic Church adapted slowly to the new realities of the modern era. Shaken by the Protestant Reformation and intent on resisting modern influences, it maintained the defensive posture adopted at the Council of Trent until the middle of the twentieth century.

Perhaps the greatest challenge faced by Catholicism was secularization. In France, the Emperor Napoleon (r. 1804–1815) stripped the Church of the authority it had enjoyed for centuries over important aspects of public life. Marriage and divorce became civil procedures and responsibility for education was assumed by the state, which promoted its own ideals in public schools. In Germany, the state seized vast tracts of land from bishops and monasteries and made priests public employees. Disturbed by the loyalty of German Catholics to Rome, Chancellor Otto von Bismarck launched an all-out attack on Catholicism known as the *Kulturkampf* ("struggle for civilization") in the 1870s.

During these difficult years, Catholics turned to Rome for decisive leadership. Intent on providing it, nineteenth-century popes asserted their spiritual authority even as their influence in secular affairs rapidly eroded. This trend culminated under Pius IX, whose *Syllabus of Errors* (1864) urged Catholics to reject modern evils such as civil marriage, separation of church and state, public education, and Marxism. The climax of Pius IX's reign came with the First Vatican Council (1869–1870), which increased the power of the papacy by proclaiming a doctrine of papal infallibility. According to this doctrine, the pope cannot err when defining doctrines relating to faith and morals.

Later popes upheld Pius IX's conception of papal authority but also attempted to address modernity in constructive ways. Leo XIII (r. 1878–1903), for example, decried the social inequities created by capitalism and industrialization and outlined principles by which justice might be achieved.

A major turning point came when John XXIII convened the Second Vatican Council (1962–1965), which called for recognition of the realities of modern culture. Vatican II urged an openness to dialogue with non-Catholic Christians and described the "high regard" of the Roman Catholic Church for other religions. It also reformed Catholic worship by requiring celebration of the Mass in modern languages instead of Latin and allowing laypeople greater participation in worship. Moving away from the traditional tendency to set the clergy above

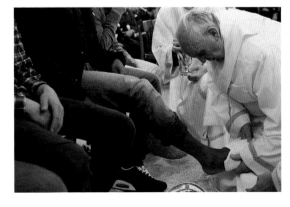

Pope Francis washed the feet of a dozen inmates, including women and Muslims, at a juvenile detention center in a Holy Thursday ritual during the first year of his papacy. Francis's boldly inclusive gesture just two weeks after his election helped define his papacy.

laypeople, the council emphasized the equality of the faithful. Since Vatican II, the Roman Catholic Church has continued to make its relevance apparent in the modern world while at the same time holding fast to tradition. Thus, Pope John Paul II (r. 1978–2005) was a driving force in bringing about the collapse of communism in Eastern Europe at the end of the twentieth century but made no concessions to Catholics who urged a greater role for women in the Church and an end to its stand against birth control.

Pope Francis (r. 2013–) has canonized both John XXIII and John Paul II as saints. A former Archbishop of Buenos Aires, Francis upholds traditional Roman Catholic teachings against abortion, contraception, and gay marriage, but he has also set an extraordinary example in his humility and has called upon all Christians to join him in service to all who are poor and marginalized.

Protestantism in the Modern World

From the beginning, Protestantism encouraged Christians to read and interpret the Bible for themselves. It also resisted the creation of any central authority capable of imposing uniformity of belief and practice. As a result, the number of Protestant denominations grew rapidly. Today, the world's 600 million Protestant Christians belong to thousands of groups. In the United States, the largest Protestant denominations are the Baptist, Methodist, Lutheran, Presbyterian, and Reformed churches.

Despite their many differences, most Protestants share basic doctrines that go back to the Reformation. Following Luther, they believe that salvation from sin is based on faith alone. Most Protestants regard the Bible as the only authority on which they can fully rely in matters of faith and practice. Finally, Protestantism allows for diverse forms of church government that give great authority to laypeople and individual congregations.

Since the early 1800s, liberalism and liberal theology have had a significant influence on older and larger Protestant denominations. Interpreting Christianity in the light of modern culture, liberal Protestants have questioned the doctrine of original sin, asked whether a loving God would allow even the worst sinners to suffer in hell, and emphasized the human element in the composition of the scriptures. Embracing the liberal idea that the essential goodness of human beings makes progress toward a better world possible, they have advocated social activism based on the teachings of Jesus as a means of making the kingdom of God a reality.

At the other end of the Protestant spectrum are three important conservative movements: fundamentalism, evangelicalism, and Pentecostalism.

Fundamentalism emerged in the early 1900s as a reaction against liberal theology, the theory of evolution, the academic study of the Bible, and other features of modern culture that conservatives found threatening. The movement takes its name from *The Fundamentals*, a series of booklets that identified five doctrines essential to Christianity: (1) the literal inerrancy of the Bible, (2) the divinity and virgin birth of Christ, (3) Christ's atonement for human sin on the cross, (4) the bodily resurrection of Christ, and (5) the imminent Second Coming of Christ. Seeking to defend these doctrines, leaders such as the television evangelist Jerry Falwell made fundamentalism a powerful force in American culture in the 1970s and 1980s. Fundamentalists also fought to defend what they called "traditional values" against feminism, gay rights, legalized abortion, and the elimination of prayer in public schools.

Fundamentalism grew out of **evangelicalism**, a much larger movement with roots in the

Pentecostal worship at the Catedral Evangelica de Chile in Santiago, Chile.

"Great Awakening," a revival of religious fervor that swept through England and North America in the eighteenth century. As its name suggests, evangelicalism encourages the preaching and sharing of the gospel (Greek, *evangelion*). It also emphasizes the need for every Christian to have a conversion experience, often described as being "born again" (John 3:3), which leads to a personal relationship with Jesus Christ. Evangelicals regard the Bible as the sole basis of faith, though they do not always insist on its literal interpretation. Like fundamentalists, many evangelicals believe that the end of the age and Second Coming of Christ will occur in the near future. Evangelicalism is a fast-growing worldwide movement that is making its presence felt both in older Protestant denominations and in new movements. It has become a major force in Africa and Asia and is particularly strong in North America. Evangelicals make up as much as one-fourth of the population of the United States,[7] where they have promoted the idea that America is an essentially Christian nation. They have had considerable success in applying their understanding of biblical principles to politics and public policy.

Pentecostalism takes its name from the holy day of Pentecost, which commemorates the descent of the Holy Spirit upon Jesus's followers after his ascension to heaven. According to Acts 1:1–4, these Spirit-filled believers were empowered to "speak in other tongues," to prophesy, and to perform healings in the name of Christ. Since its beginnings in America in the early twentieth century, the Pentecostal movement has sought to reclaim this feature of earliest Christianity. Its most essential belief is that conversion must be followed by a "baptism in the Spirit" made evident by an ability to speak in tongues and at least one of the other "spiritual gifts" described by Paul in 1 Corinthians 12–14. The belief that the ecstatic experience of God belongs at the center of Christian life is unmistakable in Pentecostal churches, where enthusiastic worshipers raise their arms in praise, speak in tongues, and sometimes dance or weep. The phenomenal growth of Pentecostalism during the last century has made it a major force in contemporary Christianity throughout the world. Today, Pentecostalism is the most popular form of Protestantism in Latin America, and it is rapidly gaining converts in Africa and Asia. In America, the most visible Pentecostal denominations include the Assemblies of God, the Church of God, and the Church of the Foursquare Gospel.

Orthodoxy in the Modern World

We saw earlier that the Ottoman Turks completed their conquest of the Byzantine Empire, the home of Orthodox Christianity, with their capture of Constantinople in 1453. The Muslim rulers of the Ottoman state tolerated the Orthodox Church, but they also brought it under government control. When Greeks, Bulgarians, Serbs, and other Orthodox peoples began declaring their independence from the declining Ottoman Empire in the early 1800s, they established independent national churches. Today's 225 million Orthodox Christians belong to fifteen autonomous churches, including the Orthodox churches of Greece and Russia and the Orthodox Church in America. The Ecumenical Patriarch of Constantinople retains an honorary primacy among Orthodox bishops but has no real authority over them. Despite this, the Orthodox churches are united by a tradition of shared theology and forms of worship they trace back to the apostles.

Orthodox Christianity resisted the influence of Western rationalism and liberalism in the eighteenth and nineteenth centuries. But Western influence in the form of Marxism had a devastating effect on Orthodoxy after the Bolshevik Revolution in Russia (1917) and the creation of a bloc of communist states in Eastern Europe after World War II. Because these states saw religion as an obstacle to the achievement of their social and political goals, they took drastic measures to strip the Church of its influence. Priests and monks were imprisoned, seminaries were closed, and church property was seized. The collapse of communism in the early 1990s brought a restoration of religious freedom and the revival of Orthodoxy. Since then, a dramatic rise in church attendance has testified to the commitment of millions of Russians, Ukrainians, Georgians, Bulgarians, Romanians, and Serbs to Orthodox Christianity.

Christianity in the Twenty-First Century

With more than 2.2 billion adherents, Christianity is the world's largest religion. Half of the world's Christians are Roman Catholics, 37 percent identify as Protestants, and 12 percent are Orthodox. The remaining 1 percent belong to other Christian groups. As of 2010, about 26 percent of Christians lived in Europe, 25 percent in Latin America and the Caribbean, 24 percent in sub-Saharan Africa, 13 percent in Asia and the Pacific, and 12 percent in North America. The global population of Christians is expected to grow to 2.9 billion by 2050, but the Christian portion of the world's population will remain stable at 31 percent.

Branches of Christianity

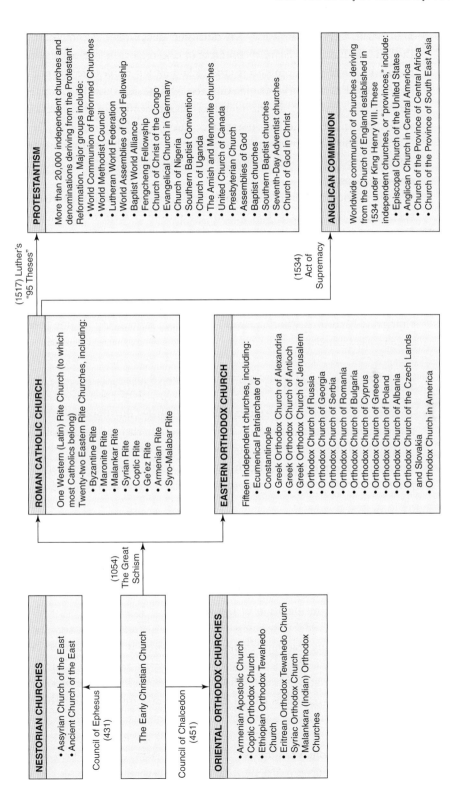

Christianity has a history of changing geography. Although it began in the Middle East, the Islamic conquest of the region in the early Middle Ages greatly diminished its presence there; today, only 4 percent of the population of the Middle East is Christian. During the Middle Ages most Christians lived in Europe, but the European exploration and colonization of the Americas, Africa, and Asia that began in the fifteenth century brought Christianity to these regions, thereby initiating another demographic shift. Christianity's steady growth in these parts of the world, far removed from its place of origin, has made it a truly global religion.

The most dramatic developments in the globalization of Christianity have occurred in recent years. Just a century ago, 80 percent of Christians lived in Europe and North America. Today, 60 percent live in Africa, Asia, and Latin America. Christianity is moving southward and, to a lesser extent, eastward. This trend will continue. According to some projections, by 2050 only 20 percent of the world's Christians will be non-Hispanic Caucasians. The vast majority will live in the Southern Hemisphere. This global shift is likely to bring significant change as African, Latin American, and Asian Christians assume greater influence in the Church.[8]

12.6 Christianity as a Way of Life: Devotional Practices

There is much more to Christianity than the beliefs Christians hold inwardly. Like the adherents of other religions, Christians express their beliefs outwardly in a variety of ways. Some are public, such as formal worship in church, participation in rituals, and the observance of holy days. Others are more personal, such as private prayer and meditation.

Worship

Christians have always made Sunday, the day of Christ's resurrection, a day set apart for communal worship. Because the first Christians were Jews, they patterned their worship on the Jewish synagogue service, which consisted of readings from scripture, prayer, and a sermon. To these elements, they added celebration of the **Eucharist**, a commemoration of the Last Supper Jesus shared with his disciples. The result was an order of worship or **liturgy** consisting of two parts: the liturgy of the word, including readings from scripture, prayer, and a sermon, and the liturgy of the Eucharist.

The Roman Catholic and Orthodox churches are highly liturgical. In worship, members of these traditions join in rhythms of praise and adoration that are similar in their essential features and reach back through two millennia to the liturgy of early church.

Roman Catholic worship, often called the "Mass," begins with a formal procession of the clergy toward the altar (a table used in celebrating the Eucharist) accompanied by the singing of an opening hymn. Next, in a penitential rite, those present confess their sins and ask God's forgiveness. The liturgy of the word that follows consists primarily of readings from scripture, a short sermon, or homily, and a recitation of the Nicene Creed. At this point, the liturgy of the Eucharist begins with the presentation of gifts of bread and wine, which are set on the altar. After the priest blesses these, there is a special Eucharistic prayer followed by a singing of the *Sanctus*, a short hymn taken from the Old Testament (Isaiah 6:3). The congregation then recites an affirmation of faith and the Lord's Prayer. In a final preparatory act, members of the congregation wish each other "the peace of the Lord." It is at this point that the bread and wine are consecrated, making Christ present upon the altar. The members of the congregation then share in the rite of communion, in which each person receives a bit of the consecrated gifts of bread and wine. Many Roman Catholic Christians say that it is in this solemn moment that they are most acutely aware of God's presence. The liturgy concludes with a final prayer, a benediction (blessing), and the formal dismissal of the congregation. The liturgy celebrated in Orthodox churches follows this general pattern, though additional processions, prayers, and blessings make it more elaborate.

Most Protestant groups have simpler and more informal patterns of worship that emphasize readings from scripture and preaching on biblical teachings. Typically, worship begins with a hymn followed by an opening prayer. After readings from scripture, worshipers might sing another hymn in preparation for the sermon, which is generally much longer than what one would find in Roman Catholic or Orthodox worship. Informal announcements of interest to the congregation

VISUAL GUIDE
Christianity

Early Christians used the "sign of the fish" as a secret symbol to identify themselves during times of persecution. The letters of the Greek word for "fish" (ΙΧΘΥΣ) are the first letters in the words that make up the phrase "Jesus Christ, Son of God, and Savior."

The cross has served as a Christian symbol since ancient times and appears in many forms. With its longer vertical and shorter horizontal arms, the Latin cross is the form favored by the Roman Catholic and Protestant churches. This one stands atop Monte Crocione in northern Italy.

Orthodox Christians use many different forms of the cross. The most common is a simple figure formed by four arms of equal length. This one decorates a small convent on the island of Mykonos, Greece.

The Celtic cross. According to legend, the Celtic cross on the left originated with St. Patrick, who brought Christianity to Ireland. This one serves as a grave marker in a cemetery in Dublin, Ireland.

(continued)

A crucifix is a cross with an image of the crucified Christ. It is used extensively in the Roman Catholic, Orthodox, Anglican, and Lutheran traditions. A vivid reminder of Christ's suffering on behalf of humanity, it is usually displayed prominently in church interiors.

The custom of using alpha and omega, the first and last letters of the Greek alphabet, to symbolize the eternity of God is based on a verse from the book of Revelation in the New Testament (1:8): "I am the Alpha and the Omega," says the Lord God, "who is, and who was, and who is to come, the Almighty."

The Chi-Rho is a symbol of Christ. Its name is based on the Greek letters chi and rho, the first two letters in the Greek word *Christos*, or "Christ." According to legend, the Chi-Rho was revealed in a dream to the Emperor Constantine, who won a military victory after marking it on the shields of his soldiers. Today, the

Chi-Rho appears on altars, plaques, vestments, and other items. It is shown here on a Christian stele from Spain, c. 600.

The "sign of the cross" is a ritual hand motion in which the shape of the cross of Christ is traced across the forehead and chest. It is used in both public worship and private prayer. The practice of "signing" oneself as an act of devotion goes back to ancient times. Writing c. 200, the North African theologian Tertullian noted that the Christians of his time "wore out their foreheads" making the sign of the cross.

might follow, along with a collection taken up for the support of the church and its charitable causes, a recitation of the Lord's Prayer, a final prayer, and a closing hymn. In some Protestant churches the Eucharist is always a part of Sunday worship; in others, it might be celebrated just once each month or even less frequently.

Sacraments

Like worship, the special rituals known as **sacraments** are central to Christian life. Understood as visible symbols of God's grace, the sacraments infuse believers with spiritual nourishment and impart a sacred character to transitional moments in their lives. The Greek word for sacrament, *musterion* ("mystery"—the term preferred by Orthodox Christians), helps to explain the significance these rituals have for Christians. Making use of ordinary elements such as bread, wine, water, and oil, they bring the individual into an experience of something extraordinary—the mystery of God's love. Roman Catholic and Orthodox Christians celebrate seven sacraments. Protestants acknowledge only two: baptism and the Eucharist.

The first sacrament celebrated in the life of a Christian is baptism, a cleansing of sin that marks the beginning of a new spiritual life in which one is united with Christ and sanctified by the Holy Spirit. Baptism can take the form of complete immersion in water or a sprinkling of water on one's head. However it is performed, the priest or minister always follows the instruction of Christ to baptize "in the name of the Father and of the Son and of the Holy Spirit" (Matthew 28:19).

After baptism, a Christian is entitled to participate in the Eucharist, also known as Holy Communion and the Lord's Supper. As we have seen, the Eucharist commemorates Christ's Last Supper with his disciples before his crucifixion. On that occasion, Christ identified the bread and wine they shared with his body and blood:

> While they were eating, he took a loaf of bread, and after blessing it he broke it and gave it to them, and said, "Take; this is my body." Then he took a cup, and after giving thanks he gave it to them, and all of them drank from it. He said to them, "This is my blood of the covenant, which is poured out for many."
> *—Mark 14:22–24*

Historically, most Christians have taken these words to mean that Christ is truly present in the Eucharist. Only with the Reformation of the sixteenth century did some Protestant groups adopt the view that the bread and wine are mere symbols of Christ's presence. Although those who believe in the "real presence" have sought to explain it in various ways, most acknowledge that it is ultimately a mystery. In a sense, it is similar to the gestures we use to communicate inward feelings in everyday life. For example, most of us believe that the love we feel for someone else can be conveyed by a hug or a kiss, but we would find it difficult to explain in precise terms how our love is present in the gesture. We can understand the Eucharist as a kind of sacred gesture in which God offers grace to human beings. Although Christians have different ways of explaining how this happens, they agree that their participation in the ritual meal of bread and wine brings them into closer union with God and each other.

A third sacrament is confirmation. In the Roman Catholic Church, confirmation is administered to adolescents who have completed formal instruction in the

This baptistery basin was built in the sixth century as part of the Basilica of St. Vitalis in what is now Sbeitla, Tunisia. Candidates for baptism were led down the steps and then baptized by full immersion in water.

In this celebration of the Eucharist, a Roman Catholic priest prays over a wafer of bread and chalices of wine, which are believed to become the body and blood of Christ.

faith. *Because* they understand its teachings, they are recognized as fully responsible members of the Church. In the Orthodox tradition, confirmation usually occurs when an infant is baptized *in order that*, nourished by grace, he or she might grow into a mature understanding of the faith and share in the work of the Church.

The four remaining sacraments are essentially the same in Catholicism and Orthodoxy. Holy matrimony gives a sacred character to marriage. For men who feel called to become priests, the sacrament of holy orders confers a grace that enables them to be effective leaders in the Church. Penance, also known as confession and reconciliation, involves confessing sin to a priest in order to receive his assurances of God's forgiveness and his prescription for the performance of an act of penance or reparation for the sin committed. The final sacrament, anointing of the sick, is meant to strengthen those who are in immediate danger of death.

Church Interiors: Sacred Space

The interior design of a church reflects its theology and liturgical style. Most Protestant churches are quite plain and have rows of seats facing a pulpit in the front as their main features. It is from the pulpit, a raised lectern, that the pastor or minister delivers the weekly sermon. Because Protestants emphasize scripture over sacraments, the pulpit generally has a more prominent position than the altar. Protestant churches make sparing use of decorative effects. There may be candles on the altar and a cross displayed on the wall, but little more. The intention behind this simplicity is to create an environment without distractions in which worshipers can meet God in prayer and in the reading and exposition of scripture.

Roman Catholic churches are more elaborate. Because Catholicism emphasizes the sacraments, and the Eucharist in particular, it is the altar rather than the pulpit that stands out from the worshiper's perspective. Religious paintings and statues of saints are commonly found, as are crucifixes, or images of Christ on the cross. To the side of some churches is a stand supporting rows of votive candles set in colored glass. When music is added to these physical features of the church, the senses are filled with sights and sounds meant to lift the mind and heart to God.

This approach to creating a sacred space is even more pronounced in Orthodox churches, whose design and decoration give worshipers a sense of entering into the heavenly presence of God. The main body of the Orthodox church is separated from the sanctuary in the front by a screen, called an iconostasis ("icon stand"), covered with painted images of Christ and the saints. Icons fill the rest of the church as well, reminding worshipers that they belong to a spiritual communion that includes the

The design and decor of this small Protestant church are simple. The attention of the congregation is directed toward the pulpit, from which the pastor delivers a sermon based on the scriptures.

Like all Roman Catholic churches, this church in St. Maarten in the Netherlands Antilles gives the most prominent place to the altar, where the Eucharist is celebrated. The priest's homily, or sermon, is delivered from a pulpit set to the side. Images of the saints that Catholics venerate can be seen along the walls.

whole company of heaven. Even the magnificent domes atop Orthodox churches display iconic murals of Christ and the saints. But the main focus of attention is the sanctuary, which can be glimpsed through several doors that provide access to the priest and his assistants. It is in this sacred space that the mystery of the Eucharist is celebrated, with chanting and incense that reveal in the material world the realities of the spiritual realm.

Prayer

For Christians, Jesus provides the ultimate example of the importance of prayer. The gospels describe him as praying frequently, often for hours and with great fervency. On one occasion, he taught his disciples to pray in this way:

> Our Father in heaven,
> hallowed be your name.
> Your kingdom come.
> Your will be done,
> on earth as it is in heaven.
> Give us this day our daily bread.
> And forgive us our debts,

The interior of an Orthodox church in Odessa, Ukraine. Note the iconostasis, or "icon screen," at the far end of the aisle. In Orthodox churches, the altar is always located behind the iconostasis. Images of Christ and the saints on the interior of the dome remind worshipers of their spiritual communion with heavenly personalities.

as we also have forgiven our debtors.
And do not bring us to the time of trial,
but deliver us from the evil one.

—*Matthew 6:9–13*

This prayer, known as the **Lord's Prayer**, is just one of many forms of prayer in Christianity. In the early Christian centuries, additional prayers were created and formally integrated into the liturgy. Of course, from the beginning, Christians also prayed privately, informally, and silently. Today, it is customary for Christians to offer a prayer of thanksgiving before meals, on rising in the morning, and before going to bed at night. When the troubles and concerns of daily life arise, they ask God for guidance, forgiveness, and peace. In the face of sickness and death, they find in prayer the assurance of God's loving presence.

Most Christian traditions include specialized forms of prayer practiced by those who wish to deepen their spiritual lives. For example, the interior walls of Roman Catholic churches display fourteen images of the passion, or suffering, of Christ during the final hours of his life. During Lent, the period before Easter, Catholics visit these Stations of the Cross in order, reciting prayers and meditating on each incident as a means of coming to a deeper understanding of Christ's suffering. Another form of Catholic devotion is praying the **rosary**. This involves recitation of a series of prayers counted on a string of beads while meditating on important moments in the lives of Jesus and his mother, Mary.

For instruction in prayer, Orthodox Christians turn to the *Philokalia*, a collection of mystical texts written between the fourth and the fifteenth centuries. Containing the words of Orthodoxy's greatest sages, the *Philokalia* is considered a treasury of wisdom concerning the practice of contemplative prayer. Whereas meditation centers on the intellect, contemplative prayer is a "prayer of the heart" in which it is not just the mind but one's whole being that reaches out to God. Its most common form is the Jesus Prayer: "Lord Jesus Christ, Son of God, have mercy on me." Ideally, the Jesus Prayer is recited continually, whether one is driving to work, standing in line, or attending to any other matter. In time, it embeds itself in one's being, and its repetition becomes as natural and effortless as breathing. According to one Orthodox saint, "even when [the practitioner] is immersed in sleep, the perfumes of prayer will breathe in his heart spontaneously."[9] In recent years, the Jesus Prayer and other forms of Orthodox contemplation have become increasingly popular among Catholics and Protestants, who share with Orthodox Christians a yearning for communion with God not only at certain times but throughout the course of each day.

The Liturgical Year

Just as the life of every Christian is punctuated by the sacraments, each year in the life of the Church is organized around celebrations of holy days and observances of religious seasons that make up the liturgical year. Built around the two great feasts of **Christmas** and **Easter**, the cycle of the liturgical year draws believers into the experience of Christ, allowing them to relive in a vicarious way the events in his life through which God brought salvation to the world.

The first great season of the liturgical year is Advent, a time of preparation and looking forward to the "coming" (Latin, *adventus*) of God into the world. Advent culminates in Christmas, a celebration of the birth of Christ on December 25, when expectation turns into rejoicing. The Christmas season ends on January 6 with a celebration of **Epiphany** (from the Greek *epiphaneia*, "manifestation"), which recalls the manifestation of Jesus's divinity as an infant (emphasized in the West) and at his baptism (emphasized in the East).

After Epiphany, the liturgical year moves forward to Easter, a springtime celebration of Christ's resurrection. Easter is preceded by the season of Lent, when many Christians practice self-denial as a way of participating vicariously in the suffering of Christ. Awareness of Christ's suffering is heightened during Holy Week, the last week of Lent, when most days have special significance. Palm Sunday recalls Christ's triumphal entry into Jerusalem, when enthusiastic crowds placed palm branches on the road before him. Maundy Thursday marks Jesus's institution of the Eucharist at the Last Supper. Good Friday commemorates the crucifixion of Jesus. Holy Week concludes with Easter, the most important Christian holiday: it is in Christ's resurrection that Christians see his triumph over death and the promise of eternal life. Easter is a truly joyous holiday, filled with signs and symbols of new life. In Orthodox countries, Easter mornings resound with the cry, "Christ is risen!" and the response, "He is risen indeed!" Rejoicing continues through the following

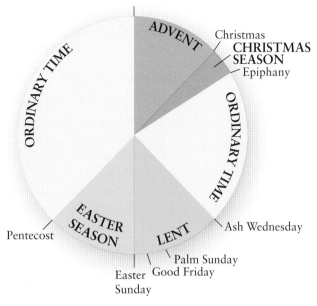

The liturgical year is an annual cycle of holy days and seasons that re-create events and times during the life of Jesus.

This Greek icon depicts Christ holding the scriptures and raising his right hand in a sign of blessing. The Greek letters outside his halo identify him as Jesus Christ. The letters inside the halo identify him as God.

weeks as Christians celebrate the ascension of Christ into heaven and the coming of the Holy Spirit at Pentecost. After Pentecost, the liturgical year moves into six months of "ordinary time" that ends with Advent, when the annual cycle begins again.

Veneration of Saints

Like the members of any group, Christians have always had their heroes. Known as **saints** ("holy ones"), they are spiritual role models who have shown how the Christian life should be lived. The greatest of saints is Mary, the virgin mother of Christ, who is considered the foremost example of what God can do in sanctifying a human life. Those who honor Mary point to her virtues of gentleness, humility, and submission to God's will and recall her expression of joy on learning that she had been chosen to bear the Christ: "Surely, from now on all generations will call me blessed" (Luke 1:48). According to Roman Catholic teaching, Mary was unique in being conceived without sin (the doctrine of the Immaculate Conception) and in being taken up bodily into heaven at her death (the doctrine of the Assumption). Orthodox Christians honor Mary with the titles *Theotokos* ("God-bearer") and *Panagia* ("All-holy").

For Protestant Christians, the significance of the saints lies almost exclusively in the inspiring examples they have set for others. In Roman Catholicism and Orthodoxy, the saints have greater significance. These traditions emphasize the eternal participation of the saints in the Church, for though they now exist in heaven, they remain within the mystical communion of believers that is "the body of Christ." Catholic and Orthodox Christians believe that Paul made this point when he wrote that Christians are "citizens with the saints and also members of the household of God" (Ephesians 2:16).

Just as the living pray for the welfare of their fellow Christians, the saints are thought to intercede for them in prayer as well. Belief in the intercession of saints is evident in early Christian literature and in ancient epitaphs found on sarcophagi and grave markers. These implore both saints and departed family members to pray for the living. "Pray for us," says one inscription, "that we may be saved." On the sarcophagus of their little boy, his mother and father wrote: "To our son Philemon, who lived happily for two years with his parents: Pray for us, together with the saints."[10] Belief in the intercession of saints remains an important part of Roman Catholicism and Orthodoxy. Strictly speaking, one does not pray *to* the saints, but *with* them. Saints are not worshiped. Instead, they are venerated with a reverential respect that recognizes their holiness.

The veneration of saints takes a variety of forms. Traditionally, Catholic and Orthodox Christians are given a saint's name at baptism, and their churches are usually named after saints. Many believers honor saints on their feast days. In addition, the physical remains of saints, known as relics, are objects of veneration. Preserved in special containers known as reliquaries, relics are found in many churches, where they bring a sense of the sacred to those who pray in their presence. The relics are often brought out for special observances or processions on the saint's feast day.

If this practice seems a bit strange to you, it might be helpful to consider how you might be affected by a more secular "relic." For example, a photograph or keepsake from a loved one you have lost can provide a sense of that person's presence. In some mysterious way, it seems, something of that person's essence remains within the item itself. So it is with the saints, whose holiness is thought to remain in the relics they have left behind.

Images of saints also produce a heightened awareness of holiness. In Roman Catholicism, images take the forms of paintings and statues whose lifelike quality is meant to underscore the experience of earthly existence that the saints share with all other believers. Meditating on a painting or statue, believers are encouraged in the spiritual life by knowing that the saint it represents once experienced the same challenges they experience. The icons of the Orthodox, who make no use of statues, are meant to have just the opposite effect. These highly stylized paintings are not intended to be lifelike. Their purpose is to represent not earthly reality but the reality of transfigured and perfected humanity in heaven. Gazing intently at their observers and communicating through symbolic gestures, the saints depicted in icons offer a glimpse of the higher, spiritual realm that is the ultimate goal of every Christian.

12.7 Christianity as a Way of Life: Engaging with the World

Christianity calls upon Christians to care for others, and in particular the poor, the excluded, and the oppressed and to serve as custodians of the world they believe God has created. In this concluding section of our survey of Christianity, we will look briefly at some of the ways in which they have responded to these challenges.

Social and Political Activism

Service to others is an important part of Christian practice. According to the New Testament (Acts 4:32–35), the earliest Christians took seriously the command to love one's neighbor as oneself: the wealthy gave all their money to the church, all property was held in common, and no one experienced great need. In the Middle Ages, the churches of the East and West provided important social services by supporting orphans, widows, and the disabled; seeking the release of prisoners of war; and caring for victims of plagues, earthquakes, and other disasters.

This tradition of social service continues today. Most congregations make significant contributions to support the poor, the sick, and the homeless in their communities. On a larger scale, there are hundreds of national and international Christian charities dedicated to fighting social and political injustice, bringing an end to poverty, and providing food, health services, and education to those in need. They include Habitat for Humanity, Bread for the World, International Orthodox Charities, Catholic Relief Services, the Salvation Army, and World Vision.

Christian activism has often brought important social and political change. American abolitionists such as Theodore Weld (1803–1895) and Harriet Beecher

Stowe (1811–1896) played leading roles in the American antislavery movement, whose aims were realized in the Emancipation Proclamation of 1863. In the 1960s, it was a Black Baptist minister, Dr. Martin Luther King Jr. (1929–1968), who championed the civil rights movement that succeeded in outlawing discrimination against minorities and women in the Civil Rights Act of 1964. Today's Christian activists are involved in causes ranging from placing water for migrants in the deserts of Arizona to protesting nuclear weapons to fighting HIV/AIDS in Africa.

Christianity and the Environment

Christians turn to the Bible in order to discern God's will concerning the environment. In the Genesis accounts of God's creation of the world (Genesis 1–2), they read that God urged original humanity to subdue the Earth and exercise dominion over all living things. The Bible does not suggest that God gave the Earth to human beings for their selfish exploitation. Instead, it affirms that the world belongs to God; for example, "The earth is the Lord's and all that is in it, the world, and those who live in it . . ." (Psalms 24:1). Ultimately, the message that emerges from the Bible is that human beings have an obligation to be good stewards of the world. These points were made in The Christian Declaration on Nature delivered at a major conference on religions and the environment held at Assisi, Italy, in 1986. It reads, in part: "Man's dominion cannot be understood as license to abuse, spoil, squander, or destroy what God has made to manifest his glory. That dominion cannot be anything other than a stewardship in symbiosis with all creatures."[11]

The cause of environmentalism has won considerable support from Christian leaders. Pope Francis has been a strong advocate of the Paris Accord on climate change and encouraged Catholic Christians to care for the environment and for the poor, who suffer disproportionately from the effects of environmental problems. Bartholomew I, the Ecumenical Patriarch of the Orthodox Church, has earned the nickname "the Green Patriarch" in recognition of his efforts to mobilize Orthodox Christians in defense of the environment. There is also support for environmental causes among Protestant leaders. In 2015, the National Association of Evangelicals issued a call to action on environmental issues. But there are significant numbers of conservative evangelical Christians who deny climate change. Christians from all three traditions have created organizations for what they often call the "care of creation." These include Earth Ministry, the North American Coalition for Christianity and the Environment, the European Christian Environmental Network, Catholic Climate Covenant, and the Evangelical Climate Initiative.

Christianity, Gender, and Inclusion

The historical development of Christianity has occurred in patriarchal cultures. Although Christian women have distinguished themselves as saints, mystics, theologians, members of religious orders, and founders of schools, hospitals, and other organizations, they have generally been excluded from positions of leadership and authority in the Church. But women's roles began to change in the nineteenth and twentieth centuries. This is especially true of the Protestant tradition, in which women are now ordained to the clergy and have even founded denominations. Although the Roman Catholic and Orthodox churches remain opposed to ordaining them, women from these traditions have found other settings in which to lead and serve. Perhaps the most notable of these is the academic world. As scholars specializing in biblical studies, ethics, and theology, women are communicating new ideas and insights that are bringing profound change to Christian thought. For example, feminist theologians have called for liberation from a Christian worldview based solely on the experience of men. In her *Beyond God the Father* (1973), Mary Daly argued that the Christian habit of thinking of God as Father allows misogyny to appear as a spiritual norm, thereby relegating women to a secondary status in the Church. In her *Sexism and God-Talk: Toward a Feminist Theology* (1983), Rosemary Radford Ruether, another influential feminist theologian, urges a new way of thinking about God as "God/ess" and has suggested the creation of churches open only to women and men committed to the rights and equality of women.

Historically, LGBTQ Christians have been denied affirmation in the Church on the basis of the popular belief that the Bible condemns homosexuality. This view has been challenged in recent years by some who argue that the Bible, when read in the original languages and with an awareness of cultural norms in the biblical period, affirms same-sex partnerships. Whatever we might make of the debate on this issue, it is clear that in recent years Christianity has begun to be more welcoming to people who identify as queer. Although some churches remain committed to traditional and exclusive views, others are enthusiastically inclusive and LGBTQ-affirming. People who identify as LGBTQ have also founded churches of their own, such as the Metropolitan Community Churches (MCC), in order to create congregations in which their needs and concerns are sure to be addressed.

In 2015 the Supreme Court of the United States ruled that the Constitution guarantees a right to same-sex marriage. The Court's decision came as significant changes in public opinion were becoming evident. According to studies conducted by the Pew Research Center,[12] in 2004 just 31 percent of all adults in the United States favored same-sex marriage. By 2015 that number had climbed to 61 percent. Similar changes in public opinion have occurred elsewhere in the world. These have not moved the Roman Catholic, Orthodox, and conservative Protestant churches from their traditional teaching that marriage is an institution only for heterosexual couples, but many Protestant and Anglican churches now sanction same-sex marriage. Many of these also ordain those who identify as gay, lesbian, bisexual, and transgender to the clergy. They include the Metropolitan Community Churches, the Evangelical Lutheran Church in America, the Presbyterian Church (USA), the United Church of Christ, the Episcopal Church in the United States, the Evangelical Church in Germany, the Swiss Reformed Church, the United Protestant Church of France, the Evangelical Lutheran Church in Canada, and many others.

SEEKING ANSWERS

What Is Ultimate Reality?

Christianity teaches that there is a single, personal, transcendent, and all-powerful God—a God who is one in essence but threefold in his manifestations as Father, Son, and Holy Spirit. God created a perfect world as an expression of divine love, but it has fallen into imperfection due to human sin. Like Jews and Muslims, Christians believe that God wants to be known in and by Creation, and especially by humanity. For Christians, the supreme revelation of the divine nature is found in Jesus Christ, who was the very incarnation of God. They also believe that God has revealed himself in other ways, such as through scripture and through the immensity and beauty of the universe.

How Should We Live in This World?

Christians believe that God has reached out in grace (love) to humanity, making atonement for sin through Jesus Christ. For those who respond to God's love in faith, a new kind of life in Christ becomes possible—a life in which the fundamental ethical principle is love. Jesus spoke of love for God and one's neighbor as the essence of scripture and described it in a radical way. Even enemies must be loved and forgiven. This demanding conception of love is one of the essential ideals in Christianity.

It is also one that requires great effort. To achieve it, Christians find inspiration in study and reflection on scripture, through prayer, and in fellowship with other Christians who take love seriously. Christians find good examples of love and other virtues in the lives of the saints, whom they seek to emulate. They also believe that the sacraments offer a spiritual nourishment that is helpful in the cultivation of lives they attempt to live in imitation of Christ.

What Is Our Ultimate Purpose?

For Christians, the ultimate goal of human existence is union with God. As Augustine wrote in the fifth century, "You have made us for yourself, O Lord, and our hearts are restless until they find rest in you." The path to reunion with God is through Jesus Christ, whose sacrificial death, an expression of God's love, atoned for all human sin. When human beings respond in faith to God's love, or grace, they are brought into union with the divine. Christians hope to share in the resurrection of Christ, which leads to eternal blessedness in union with God. But there is also the possibility of eternal separation from God. Because the Bible offers few concrete details about these two possibilities, traditionally understood as heaven and hell, they have been interpreted in many different ways.

REVIEW QUESTIONS

For Review

1. What were the means by which the Christian movement defined orthodox belief and established ecclesiastical authority in late antiquity?
2. How did the Roman Catholic, Orthodox, and Protestant traditions within Christianity emerge from the "catholic" or "universal" Christianity of the first millennium? What were the main factors that contributed to the formation of these traditions?
3. What are the seasons and holy days of the liturgical year? What is their significance for Christians? How are they observed?
4. What is the doctrine of the Trinity? Why is this doctrine central to Christianity?

5. What are the major challenges Christianity has encountered in the modern era? How has it responded to them?

For Further Reflection

1. What are some of the more important ways in which basic Christian beliefs are expressed outwardly in worship, the sacraments, prayer, and other devotional practices?

2. If asked by a friend, how would you describe the essence of Christianity? Are there teachings embraced by all (or, at least, most) forms of Christianity?

3. How do Christian beliefs about God/ultimate reality, human nature, the world, and the ultimate goal or purpose of human existence compare with those of the closely related religions of Judaism and Islam?

4. How do Christian beliefs about these same issues compare with those of religions such as Hinduism, Buddhism, Daoism, Confucianism, Sikhism, and Jainism?

5. Do you think the Christian ecumenical movement has a realistic chance of restoring the original unity of the Christian religion?

GLOSSARY

apostle (Greek *apostolos*, "one who is sent out") In the New Testament, Jesus's disciples, sent out to preach and baptize, are called apostles. Paul of Tarsus and some other early Christian leaders also claimed this title. Because of their close association with Jesus, the apostles were accorded a place of honor in the early Church.

apostolic succession According to this Roman Catholic and Orthodox doctrine, the spiritual authority conferred by Jesus on the apostles has been transmitted through an unbroken line of bishops, who are their successors.

baptism Performed by immersion in water or a sprinkling with water, baptism is a sacrament in which an individual is cleansed of sin and admitted into the Church.

bishop Responsible for supervising other priests and their congregations within specific regions known as dioceses, bishops are regarded by Roman Catholic and Orthodox Christians as successors of the apostles.

Calvin, John (1509–1564) One of the leading figures of the Protestant Reformation, Calvin is notable for his *Institutes of the Christian Religion* and his emphasis on the absolute power of God, the absolute depravity of human nature, and the absolute dependence of human beings on divine grace for salvation.

Christmas An annual holiday commemorating the birth of Jesus, Christmas is observed by Western Christians on December 25. Although many Orthodox Christians celebrate Christmas on this date, others observe the holiday on January 7.

church In the broadest sense, "church" refers to the universal community of Christians, but the term can also refer to a particular tradition within Christianity (such as the Roman Catholic Church or the Episcopal Church) or to an individual congregation of Christians.

Easter An annual holiday commemorating the resurrection of Christ, Easter is a "movable feast" whose date changes from year to year, though it is always celebrated in spring (as early as March 22 and as late as May 8).

Epiphany An annual holiday commemorating the "manifestation" of the divinity of the infant Jesus, Epiphany is celebrated by most Western Christians on January 6. Most Eastern Christians observe it on January 19.

Eucharist (yooh'kah'rist) Also known as the Lord's Supper and Holy Communion, the Eucharist is a sacrament celebrated with consecrated bread and wine in commemoration of Jesus's Last Supper with his disciples.

evangelicalism This Protestant movement stresses the importance of the conversion experience, the Bible as the only reliable authority in matters of faith, and preaching the gospel. In recent decades, evangelicalism has become a major force in North American Christianity.

fundamentalism Originating in the early 1900s, this movement in American Protestantism is dedicated to defending doctrines it identifies as fundamental to Christianity against perceived threats posed by modern culture.

gospel In its most general sense, "gospel" means the "good news" (from Old English *godspel*, which translates the Greek *evangelion*) about Jesus Christ. The New Testament gospels of Matthew, Mark, Luke, and John are proclamations of the good news concerning the life, teachings, death, and resurrection of Jesus Christ.

grace Derived from the Latin *gratia* (a "gift" or "love"), "grace" refers to God's love for humanity, expressed in Jesus Christ and through the sacraments.

icons Painted images of Christ and the saints, icons are used extensively in the Orthodox Church.

Inquisition The investigation and suppression of heresy by the Roman Catholic Church, the Inquisition began in the twelfth century and was formally concluded in the middle of the nineteenth century.

kingdom of God God's rule or dominion over the universe and human affairs. The kingdom of God is one of the primary themes in the teaching of Jesus.

liturgy The liturgy (from Greek *leitourgia*, "a work of the people" in honor of God) is the basic order of worship in Christian churches. It consists of prescribed prayers, readings, and rituals.

logos In its most basic sense, the Greek *logos* means "word," but it also means "rational principle," "reason," or "divine reason." The Gospel of John uses *logos* in the sense of the "divine reason" through which God created and sustains the universe when it states that "the Word became flesh" in Jesus Christ (John 1:14).

Lord's Prayer A prayer attributed to Jesus, the Lord's Prayer serves as a model of prayer for Christians. Also known as the "Our Father" (since it begins with these words), its most familiar form is found in the Gospel of Matthew (6:9–13).

Luther, Martin (1483–1546) A German monk who criticized Roman Catholic doctrines and practices in his Ninety-Five Theses (1517), Luther was the original leader and one of the seminal thinkers of the Protestant Reformation.

messiah In the Jewish Scriptures (Old Testament), messiah ("anointed one") refers to kings and priests, who were anointed with consecrated oil. In later Jewish literature, the Messiah is sometimes understood as a figure—in some cases, a supernatural figure—who, having been "anointed" by God, saves the Jewish people and the world from evil. Christianity understands Jesus of Nazareth as the Messiah.

Nicene Creed A profession of faith formulated by the Councils of Nicea (325) and Constantinople (381), the Nicene Creed articulates the Christian doctrine of the Trinity.

original sin Formulated by St. Augustine in the fourth century, the doctrine of original sin states that the sin of Adam and Eve affected all of humanity, so that all human beings are born with a sinful nature.

Orthodox Church Also known as the Eastern Orthodox Church and the Orthodox Catholic Church, the Orthodox Church is the Eastern branch of Christianity that separated from the Western branch (the Roman Catholic Church) in 1054.

parable According to the gospels of Matthew, Mark, and Luke, Jesus made extensive use of parables—short, fictional stories that use the language and imagery of everyday life to illustrate moral and religious truths.

Paul of Tarsus A first-century apostle who founded churches throughout Asia Minor, Macedonia, and Greece. Paul was also the author of many of the letters, or epistles, found in the New Testament.

Pentecost A holiday celebrated by Christians in commemoration of the outpouring of the Holy Spirit on the disciples of Jesus as described in the second chapter of the New Testament book of Acts.

Pentecostalism A movement that emphasizes the importance of spiritual renewal and the experience of God through baptism in the Holy Spirit, Pentecostalism is a primarily Protestant movement that has become extremely popular in recent decades.

Protestant Christianity One of the three major traditions in Christianity (along with Roman Catholicism and Orthodoxy), Protestantism began in the sixteenth century as a reaction against medieval Roman Catholic doctrines and practices.

purgatory In Roman Catholicism, purgatory is an intermediate state between earthly life and heaven in which the debt for unconfessed sin is expiated.

Roman Catholic Church One of the three major traditions within Christianity (along with Orthodoxy and Protestantism), the Roman Catholic Church, which recognizes the primacy of the Bishop of Rome, or pope, has historically been the dominant church in the West.

rosary Taking its name from the Latin *rosarium* ("garland of roses"), the rosary is a traditional form of Roman Catholic devotion in which practitioners make use of a string of beads in reciting prayers.

sacraments The sacraments are rituals in which material elements such as bread, wine, water, and oil serve as visible symbols of an invisible grace conveyed to recipients.

saint A saint is a "holy person" (Latin *sanctus*). Veneration of the saints and belief in their intercession on behalf of the living are important features of Roman Catholic and Orthodox Christianity.

scholasticism Represented by figures such as Peter Abelard, Thomas Aquinas, and William of Ockham, scholasticism was the medieval effort to reconcile faith and reason using the philosophy of Aristotle.

sin The violation of God's will in thought or action.

transubstantiation According to this Roman Catholic doctrine, the bread and wine consecrated by a priest in the Eucharist become the body and blood of Christ and retain only the appearance, not the substance, of bread and wine.

Trinity According to the Christian doctrine of the Trinity, God is a single divine substance or essence consisting in three "persons."

SUGGESTIONS FOR FURTHER READING

Bowden, John. *Encyclopedia of Christianity*. New York: Oxford University Press, 2005. A one-volume collection of short, scholarly articles on hundreds of topics.

Dowell, Graham. *The Heart Has Seasons: Travelling through the Christian Year*. Worthing, UK: Churchman, 1989. A superb introduction to the significance and celebration of the "seasons" of the liturgical year.

Dowley, Tim, and David Wright. *Introduction to the History of Christianity*. Minneapolis: Fortress Press, 1995. Includes hundreds of photos, maps, charts, and articles on topics of special interest.

Ehrman, Bart. *The New Testament: A Historical Introduction to the Early Christian Writings*. New York: Oxford University Press, 2000. An excellent introduction to the New Testament texts and selected Christian texts from the second century.

Marsden, George. *Understanding Fundamentalism and Evangelicalism*. Grand Rapids, MI: William B. Eerdmans, 1991. Describes the essential features of these two movements and their involvement in politics and science.

McGrath, Alister. *Theology: The Basics*. Malden, MA: Blackwell, 2004. Individual chapters focus on specific issues such as God, Jesus, faith, salvation, and heaven. Emphasis on Roman Catholic and Protestant thought.

Ware, Timothy (Kallistos). *The Orthodox Church*. New York: Penguin, 1993. A classic presentation of the history, thought, and practices of the Orthodox tradition by one of its greatest spokespersons.

White, James. *Introduction to Christian Worship*. 3rd ed. Nashville, TN: Abingdon Press, 2001. An ideal book for beginners interested in the history and forms of Christian worship.

ONLINE RESOURCES

Virtual Religion Index

An excellent gateway to religion-related sites of all kinds, including collections of texts, religion-specific sites, and academic program sites.

Catholic Online

This online resource provides access to information "on all things Catholic," including saints, holy days, Roman Catholic theology, and announcements from the Vatican.

Orthodox Wiki

This online resource includes nearly 4,000 articles on all aspects of Orthodox Christianity. It is a great place to begin an exploration of Orthodoxy.

Theopedia

An online "encyclopedia of biblical Christianity" with articles on hundreds of topics written from an evangelical Protestant perspective.

Islam

Chapter Outline

FAINT TRACES OF DAWN light up the tops of tall coconut palms and lush mango trees in a village in Zanzibar, an East African island in the Indian Ocean. Amina, a woman in her early thirties and a devout Muslim, rises from her bed. She was awakened by the sound of the call to prayer from the local mosque. In the open-air courtyard of her house, she begins her morning ablutions to prepare for the first of her daily prayers. She takes cool water from the cistern in the courtyard and carefully washes her face, hands, and feet, and rinses her mouth, nose, and ears. She also wets her head and hair. Before each of the five daily prayers, Amina performs similar ablutions. Although she occasionally wears eye makeup and lipstick, she is careful to avoid nail polish. She explains

Pilgrims circumambulate the Ka'ba in Mecca, Saudi Arabia. The pilgrimage to Mecca, known as the hajj, is a once-in-a-lifetime duty for devout Muslims.

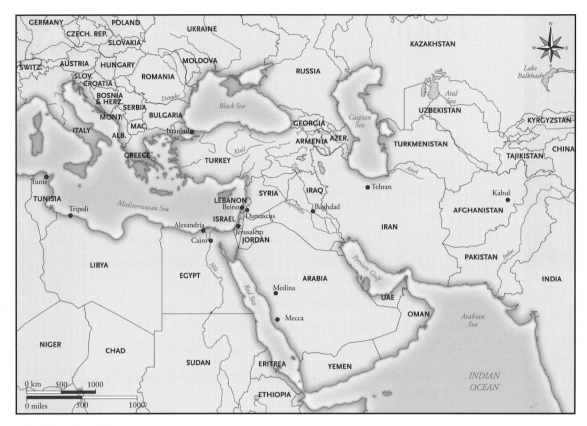

Significant sites in the history of Islam.

that all such adornment must be removed to purify herself for each prayer; makeup is easily removed with water, but nail polish is not.

After her ablutions, Amina returns to the house, covers her head and shoulders with a clean cotton wrap, and spreads a colorful woven prayer mat on the floor next to her bed. She removes her sandals, steps onto the mat, and begins the first of the five prescribed daily ritual prayers that are expected of all devout Muslims. The prayers are called *salat* and consist of the recitation of verses from the **Qur'an**, the sacred text of **Islam**, accompanied by specific bodily movements. Together, the cycles of prayer and movement are called *raka*. Amina has made her daily prayers since she was a young girl. As a child, her mother and elder sisters taught her how to pray; eventually, she will do the same for her own children. She begins the prayer standing, then kneels, bows her forehead to the ground, and kneels again in accordance with her recitation. Hand movements accompany the bodily postures. Daily prayer is an essential part of Muslim worship. Through prayer, Amina is acknowledging to herself and her community that she is submitting herself to the will of God—an important tenet of the Islamic faith. In fact, the term *Muslim* means "one who submits" in Arabic.

Amina prays alone in her modest home, but men in her community typically gather at the local mosque for each of the daily prayers, which are led by a prayer leader called an **imam**. Like Zanzibari women, most men in Zanzibar cover their heads when praying, often with a brimless, embroidered cap. Although in many parts of the Muslim world women regularly pray in mosques, in Zanzibar, particularly in rural areas, it is uncommon for women to do so. However, women often gather together at mosques for other reasons, such as Qur'an study groups and sessions in religious instruction.

When she completes her prayers, Amina rolls up her prayer mat and sets it aside for later. She reads a few verses from the Qur'an in the early morning light and then begins the first tasks of her day—making tea and sweeping the courtyard.

A mina is one of about 1.9 billion Muslims living in the world today; Islam is second only to Christianity in numbers of adherents. Amina lives in Africa, and most of the world's Muslims live in South and Southeast Asia, not in the Arabic-speaking countries of the Middle East. In fact, Arab Muslims make up less than 20 percent of the total Muslim population worldwide. The country with the largest Muslim population in the world is the Southeast Asian nation of Indonesia, followed closely by India, Pakistan, and Bangladesh. Many countries in Africa also have very large Muslim populations. Today, there are about 3.5 million Muslims in the United States,[1] and the number of Muslims in North America is increasing, mostly through immigration. Muslims also make up significant minority populations in many parts of Western Europe, especially in France, where they make up nearly 9 percent of the population.[2]

Islam developed in the Arabian Peninsula and rapidly spread through the Middle East, Asia, and Africa. Because of its global presence, Islam is practiced, understood, and interpreted in diverse ways in many different countries, cultures, and communities. However, certain beliefs and practices can be considered universal parts of Muslim religious life. First and most important of these is the monotheistic belief in the oneness of **Allah**, which is the Arabic term for God. Second, Muslims

TIMELINE
Islam

c. 570 CE	The birth of Muhammad.
610	The first revelations of the Qur'an to Muhammad.
622	The hijra (migration) from Mecca to Medina.
632	The death of Muhammad; issue of succession.
632–661	Period of the Rightly Guided Caliphs.
657	Battle of Siffin.
661	'Ali killed.
661–750	Umayyad period.
680	Battle at Karbala and martyrdom of Husayn.
750–1258	Abbasid period.
1095–1453	Crusades.
1207–1273	Jalalludin Rumi.
1281–1924	Ottoman Empire.
1483–1857	Mughal Empire.
1501–1722	Safavid Empire.
1703–1792	Ibn Abd al-Wahhab.
1849–1905	Muhammad Abduh.
1881–1938	Mustafa Kemal Ataturk.
1923	Huda Sha'rawi unveils at Egyptian train station.
1947	Partition of India and Pakistan.
1979	Iranian Revolution.
2004	France bans wearing of headscarves and other religious identifiers in schools.
2006	Keith Ellison, a Democrat from Minnesota, is first Muslim elected to US Congress.
2009	Green Movement, Iran.
2011	"Arab Spring" pro-democracy movements spread across the Middle East.

recognize **Muhammad**, who received the message of the Qur'an from God, as the final prophet in a long line of prophets sent to humanity by God. The Qur'an is believed to be the word of God and is the holy text of Muslims. In addition, Muslims around the world share the observance of the five pillars of worship practice. The term **Islam** (Arabic, "submission") reflects Muslim belief in the importance of submitting to God's will.

13.1 The Teachings of Islam: Sacred Texts

Islam arose in the Arabian Peninsula in the seventh century, when Muslims believe that a man called Muhammad began receiving communication from God. The primary source of Islamic teachings is the Qur'an, which Muslims believe is the word of God as revealed to Muhammad. According to Muslim belief, Islam was not introduced as a new religion. Rather, the revelations of the Qur'an to Muhammad were a reawakening or reintroduction of the original monotheistic faith of the prophet Abraham, a figure who is also important to Jews (Chapter 11) and Christians (Chapter 12). Islam is considered one of the Abrahamic religions, along with Judaism and Christianity, and the three religions share a great deal. Although many people in pre-Islamic Arabia were polytheists, significant numbers of Jews and Christians also lived in the region. People in Arabia were therefore familiar with biblical stories and characters, and several of these are mentioned in the Qur'an. In the Islamic view, Abraham (or Ibrahim, as Muslims call him) was the original

World Muslim population.

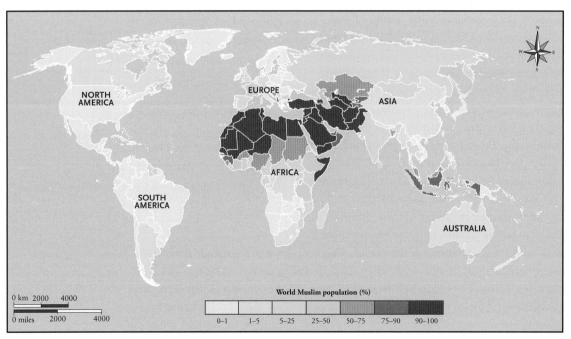

World Muslim population (%)

| 0–1 | 1–5 | 5–25 | 25–50 | 50–75 | 75–90 | 90–100 |

monotheist who received a revelation from God, a revelation that taught him the true religion centering on the oneness of God. Muslims believe that when Muhammad received the revelations of the Qur'an, he was given a reminder for humanity of what God conveyed to Abraham. This section explores what Muslims believe about the revelation of the Qur'an to Muhammad. In a later section, we explore his life, his prophecy, and his leadership roles.

The Revelation of the Qur'an to the Prophet Muhammad

Muslims consider Muhammad (c. 570–632 CE) the final messenger in a series of prophets sent by God to humanity. In addition to Abraham, these prophets include many other figures important in the Jewish and Christian traditions, such as Noah, Moses, and Jesus. In Muslim belief, all prophets are solely human—not divine. However, the importance of Muhammad to Muslims should not be underestimated. In addition to receiving the revelation of the Qur'an, Muhammad is considered an extraordinary man in all respects. He was the religious and political leader of the early Muslim community and, even today—fourteen centuries after his death—his life is considered an example for all Muslims to follow.

Some of what we know about Muhammad and his life comes from the Qur'an. We also know something of his life from biographical writings and from what his close friends, associates, and family (who are known together as his *companions*) observed about him and passed on in reports. In addition, there are many stories and legends about the Prophet. Because most of what we know about Muhammad comes from sources that were compiled by Muslims after he became a prophet, we know very little about his early life. Muslims do not believe that Muhammad was divine, but rather consider him to be *al-insan al-kamil*, the ideal human. And although he was a prophet, in many respects he lived the life of a normal man. He had a family, earned a living, and was active in his community.

Most Muslims believe that Muhammad was a spiritual man and a religious seeker even before he began receiving the revelation of the Qur'an. He was considered a devout monotheist even at a time in which many of his contemporaries were polytheists, and it is said that he often meditated alone on the oneness of God. When he reached the age of forty, in the year 610 CE, the Angel Gabriel, known in Arabic as Jibril, visited Muhammad while he was praying in an isolated cave outside Mecca. Muhammad heard a voice that told him that he was the messenger of God and commanded him to "Recite!" Muhammad is said to have been awed and bewildered. He is thought to have hesitated three times at Jibril's command because as an illiterate man he did not feel he was able to recite. Eventually, he repeated the words the angel told him to recite, and these are considered to be the first revealed verses of the Qur'an. The rest of the Qur'an was revealed to Muhammad over the next two decades.

Muhammad confided in his wife, **Khadija**, a wealthy and successful business-woman, about the revelations. She listened carefully and believed his message.

Because she was the first to believe the truth of the message received by Muhammad, Khadija is considered to be the first Muslim. Other early followers were Muhammad's close friends and family members. Muhammad's young cousin 'Ali, who later became his son-in-law when he married Muhammad's daughter **Fatima**, was the first male to become Muslim. A friend of Muhammad's called Abu Bakr was also an early Muslim, and he became Muhammad's father-in-law much later in life when, after Khadija's death, Muhammad married Abu Bakr's daughter.

After the first revelations, Muhammad began a life of preaching in Mecca. The verses of the Qur'an that he received during this time emphasized the oneness of God—the central tenet of Islam. Muhammad preached this idea to the people of Mecca and also taught about morality, social justice for the poor and downtrodden, and the inevitability of the Day of Judgment.

Muhammad was not the only prophet in the Islamic tradition. The Qur'an mentions many prophets by name and refers to the existence of many others. Muhammad, however, is known as the "seal of the prophets," which means that the door of prophecy was closed—or "sealed"—with him because he was the final prophet. Muslims believe that the revelations to Muhammad came at a time when it was necessary to reawaken understanding of God's message to humanity.

The Holy Qur'an

The Qur'an is the sacred text of Islam, and it is considered the literal word of God. The Arabic word *qur'an* means "recitation," and the book is called such because Muhammad received the Qur'an orally and taught it to his followers in the same way. When the Qur'an was eventually written down, the text was corrected by the oral knowledge of those who had committed it to memory. Even today, printed copies of the Qur'an bear the stamp of approval of a person known as *hafidh* or "keeper of the Qur'an." This is a person who knows the entire Qur'an by heart.

This illuminated Qur'an is from the thirteenth century.

The Qur'an was not revealed all at once to Muhammad, but rather gradually over a period of more than twenty years until his death. The language of the Qur'an is classical Arabic, and stylistically it resembles the beauty of the Arabic poetry of the time in which it was revealed. However, it is important to note that Muslims do not regard the Qur'an as poetry. This is because poetry is a human endeavor, and Muslims view the Qur'an as solely the word of God. Reciting, reading, and studying the Qur'an are an important part of daily life for devout Muslims today, in all parts of the world.

The Qur'an is not a narrative text, which means that it does not tell a story from beginning to end (although there are some stories within the text). The Qur'an consists of 114 chapters, each of which is called a **sura**. Each sura consists of several verses.

The suras are not organized around specific topics or time periods, and they are not arranged in the order of revelation, as one might expect. Rather, they are arranged roughly from the longest to the shortest, with the exception of the opening sura, which is quite short. Some suras are only a few verses long, and the longest has almost 300 verses. Each sura has a title. The titles were not revealed to Muhammad but were, rather, based on a distinctive element of the sura. For example, the third sura is called "The Women" because of the many verses within it that reference the status of women.

At the time of Muhammad's death, the revelations of the Qur'an had not been collected into one book. Rather, the primary mode of teaching and learning the Qur'an was oral. During the rule of the caliph 'Uthman, however, the revelations were organized into a written text. For centuries, Muslims have considered this text standard. Today, however, some secular scholars think that a number of versions of the Qur'an originally existed and that the written text of the Qur'an emerged gradually in the seventh and eighth centuries.

The most well-known sura is the first one, which is called *al-fatihah*, or "the opening." The *fatihah* is a common prayer used by Muslims in many different contexts. It is the first sura that Muslims learn when they begin studying the Qur'an as children or as adults. A devout Muslim will recite the *fatihah* several times during the day's many prayers. The sura evokes the oneness of God, the all-powerful nature of God, the Day of Judgment, and God's guidance for a righteous life.

THE OPENING (*AL FATIHAH*)

In the name of Allah, most benevolent, ever-merciful
All praise be to Allah,
Lord of all the worlds,
Most beneficent, ever merciful,
King of the Day of Judgment.
You alone we worship, and to You
alone turn for help.
Guide us (O Lord) to the path that is straight,
The path of those You have blessed,
Not of those who have earned Your anger,
Nor those who have gone astray.[3]

Today, most Muslims consider the Qur'an both inimitable and uncreated. This means that Muslims regard the holy text as unique and eternal. Today and historically, Muslims have believed that the Qur'an's equal cannot be created by human effort, which is considered proof of its divine origins. Most contemporary Muslims also believe that the Qur'an is eternal—that it has always existed. This view has not always dominated, however. The Mutazilites, a rationalist school of Islamic thought that was prominent many centuries ago, argued that the Qur'an was not eternal but was rather created by God. The Mutazilite scholars argued that the idea of an eternal Qur'an compromised the unity of God because God alone was eternal and the creator of all things—including the Qur'an. This view had some support in the tenth century, but eventually the idea of the eternal Qur'an became dominant in the Islamic tradition.[4]

Commentary on the Qur'an

The text of the Qur'an is ambiguous in some places and repetitive in others. This has resulted in a long tradition of commentary upon and interpretation of the meaning of the verses. The general Arabic term for commentary on the Qur'an is *tafsir*, which is translated in English as "interpretation." Scholars have been engaging in *tafsir* for centuries, and their commentary takes many forms. In the first few generations following Muhammad's death, scholarly commentary on the Qur'an focused primarily on grammar, language, and explanations of inconsistencies in the text. The goal of this type of *tafsir* was to clarify the meaning of the words of the Qur'an.

Muslims have not always agreed on how the Qur'an should be interpreted and understood. Some scholars have argued that the Qur'an must only be interpreted vis-à-vis itself. In other words, verses of the Qur'an should only be explained by using other passages of the text. Other scholars think that Muslims should use their own reason and rationality as believers to interpret the meaning of the verses. This method of *tafsir* is known as speculative *tafsir*.[5] A famous eleventh-century Persian scholar called Abu Hamid al-Ghazali (1058–1111) wrote that, as rational judgment is a gift from God, people should always use it when considering the meaning of the Qur'an. However, some scholars criticized his approach as preferring human reason over the words of God. Ibn Taymiyya (1263–1328), an Arab scholar, argued that using human reason was not necessary because the entire meaning of the Qur'an could be found within the text.

The Sunna: The Example of the Prophet

After the Qur'an, the second most important source of Islamic teachings is in the **sunna**, which refers to the "tradition" or way of life of the Prophet Muhammad. The sunna encompasses Muhammad's actions and words. It includes the way he handled disputes in the early community, the way he dealt with his wives, friends, and children, and the way he went about the daily business of life. This extends even to such seemingly mundane matters as how the Prophet cleaned his teeth. To Muslims, Muhammad is considered the ideal human. He is therefore the model of the best way to live. To this day, Muhammad is an inspiration to all Muslims, who strive to follow his example of conduct in their own lives. (Muhammad is discussed in more detail in the section "The History of Islam.")

The Hadith Literature
How do Muslims know how Muhammad lived his life, how he treated his family, and how he handled problems facing members of the early

Muslim community? Muslims have knowledge of Muhammad's life through a literary tradition known as the **hadith**. Hadith is a form of literature that records in brief reports the details of the life of the Prophet, including his sayings and his deeds. The hadith reports come from the observations of Muhammad's close friends and family, known as his companions. His companions realized his importance as an example of righteous behavior. They strove to remember his actions and words, and then passed them on through the generations in hadith reports.

A hadith consists of two parts: the *isnad*, or the chain of transmission of the hadith; and the *matn*, the report itself. The *matn* relates Muhammad's words or deeds, and the *isnad* names those people who transmitted the hadith from the time of the Prophet. The *isnad* always originates with one of Muhammad's close companions or a family member. One of Muhammad's wives, **'A'isha**, was one of the most important transmitters of hadith, as she passed on many reports about Muhammad's life. Muslims do not consider all hadith to be equally valid. A complex science of hadith developed in the centuries following the death of the Prophet to evaluate their reliability as true reports of Muhammad's life. Scholars ranked hadith from "solid" to "weak" based on the likelihood of authenticity. The hadith are compiled into collections of several thousand.

Reports known as *hadith qudsi*, or sacred sayings, are also important in the Islamic tradition. Although the name is similar, this is a very different sort of literary tradition from the regular hadith. The *hadith qudsi* are not reports of Muhammad's life but are believed to be words of God. Muhammad is believed to have occasionally transmitted direct words of God that were not intended to be part of the Qur'an. Many of the *hadith qudsi* are succinct and beautiful. They focus on God's love for humanity, God's mercy, and the closeness of God to creation. The following *hadith qudsi* illustrates the quality of God's mercy:

> God says: "If my Servant intends a good deed and does not do it, I write it down for him as a good deed. Then if he does it, I write it down for him as ten good deeds, or up to seven hundred times that. And if my servant intends an evil deed and does not do it, I do not write it down against him. And if he does it, I write it down for him as [only one] evil deed."[6]

13.2 The Teachings of Islam: Core Precepts

The major teachings of Islam are found in the Qur'an. The core teachings are found throughout the text, and in any number of verses we can find reference to the nature of God, the reality of the Day of Judgment, and guidelines for moral behavior.

The Oneness of God

Like the other Abrahamic religions, Islam is a monotheistic religion, and the most important principle of Islamic belief is the oneness of God. The Qur'an teaches that God, known in Arabic as "Allah," is eternal, uncreated, all-knowing, and all-powerful, and it is God alone who created the universe and humankind. God is also merciful, just, and good. God is transcendent but also present, or immanent, in the lives of believers. A much-quoted verse of the Qur'an refers to God as closer to humanity "than the jugular vein" (50:16). Muslims believe that it is impossible for God to have a partner, consort, or family because no other being shares God's divinity. Muslims believe that God is the same God of the Jews and Christians. However, to Muslims, the Christian doctrine of the Trinity compromises the unity of God. The Qur'an specifically comments on the impossibility of God begetting a son, as in the following verse:

> He to whom belongs the kingdom of the heavens and the earth: who has neither begotten a son, nor has He a partner in kingdom: (who) created everything, and determined its exact measure (25:2).[7]

The Qur'an also teaches that Muslims should strive to acknowledge the oneness of God through acts of devotion. Because the unity of God is the central tenet of Islamic belief, it follows that denying or compromising this oneness is the greatest sin. This sin of associating anything or anyone else with God is called **shirk**. In the Qur'an, *shirk* is noted as the only unforgivable sin in the eyes of Allah. This is because it denies the existence of God and the true nature of God. For the believing Muslim, the worship of God should be given to God alone, and human beings should worship nothing else. Therefore, nature, idols, images, and human beings must not be worshiped.

In Muslim belief, Allah created the universe, the world, and everything in it, including the sun and the moon, the mountains and oceans, and all living things. The natural world is mentioned throughout the Qur'an, and elements of nature are referred to as *ayat*, or signs of God: "We shall show them Our signs in every region of the earth and in themselves, until it becomes clear to them that this is the truth" (41:53). Muslims view the natural world and the entire cosmos as a type of revelation from God. (The Qur'an itself, remember, is another type of revelation.) Therefore, in Muslim belief, the natural world as a whole is evidence of the existence of God, and human beings should be able to realize this simply by observing nature. Even so, human beings cannot truly know the ultimate essence of God, God's ultimate purpose, and ultimate reality. Thus, Muslims may not be able to understand rationally why bad things happen to good people. However, they should have faith in God's purpose, even though they cannot truly know it (2:216).

Prophecy

Prophecy is also an essential component of Islamic belief, and it is mentioned several times in the Qur'an. The belief in prophecy is also important to Judaism and Christianity, and the three Abrahamic faiths share many of the same prophets. In Islam, it is through the messages revealed to prophets that humanity comes to know the desires of God and the divine laws that govern the universe and creation. The belief in revealed scripture goes hand in hand with the belief in prophecy because Muslims believe that it is through prophets that humanity obtains scripture.

Muslims recognize that there have been many prophets since the beginning of creation. Each prophet received special words from God that were appropriate for humanity at the time in which the particular prophet lived. The prophet Abraham is mentioned several times in the Qur'an. The stories of his life resemble those told by Jews and Christians, and they serve as an important basis for the annual pilgrimage to Mecca (discussed in the next section). The Qur'an also names Jesus as an important prophet (and indeed says that Jesus will return to herald the Day of Judgment), and the Gospels are considered part of God's revelation to humanity. Muslims believe that Jesus was born of the Virgin Mary, who is also mentioned in the Qur'an and is held in very high regard by Muslims. However, Muslims do not believe that Jesus was divine or the son of God. Verse 25:2, which you read earlier, reflects this idea in the passage that God has not "begotten a son."

Muslims believe that all prophets bring communication from God. The Qur'an teaches that prophets fall into different classes based on the nature of that communication. Some are said to bring simply "news" from God. Others, like Muhammad, bring a major message. In addition to Muhammad, prophets such as Moses and Jesus also received major messages. Moses received the Torah as guidance for humankind, and Muslims regard the teachings of Jesus as a major message from God. Muslims consider all scriptures, including the Torah and the gospels, to be the work of God. Although the Qur'an refers to those peoples to whom scripture was revealed as "Peoples of the Book," the Qur'an also teaches that the earlier messages have been misinterpreted or forgotten by the Christians and the Jews.

According to the Qur'an, Adam and his wife, Hawa (or Eve), were the first two humans. Adam became the first prophet in the Islamic tradition. Adam and Hawa were created separately by God from a single soul (4:1) and were made of dust or clay according to a divine model. Muslims believe that God blew spirit into humanity. Therefore, as in nature, the signs of God are also in humanity. The Qur'an teaches that human beings were created to worship God (51:56) and that the nature of humanity is to obey God and to give thankfulness for God's blessings.

You will recall that the meaning of the term *Muslim* is "one who submits." However, as part of God's creation on Earth, Muslims believe that humans should also act as responsible members of society and stewards of the natural world. The Qur'an contains a story that is similar to the one in Genesis, in which the first humans disobeyed God by tasting a forbidden fruit. In the Qur'anic story, which appears more than once in the text, Adam and Hawa are both to blame for this disobedience, and they are immediately forgiven for their transgressions by God (7:10–25; 20:114–123). Most Muslims believe that, unlike other living creatures, all human beings have free choice and thus must choose to submit to the will of God. Each individual's choices will be evaluated on the Day of Judgment.

The Day of Judgment

The coming of the Day of Judgment and the reality of the afterlife are also central teachings of the Qur'an. Many of the early suras focus on God's judgment and can be read as warnings to humanity to live a righteous life or suffer the consequences when facing God at the end of days. Despite the dire warning of some of these verses, God's justice is strongly emphasized, and the Qur'an gives details about how to live a righteous life. Greed and hypocrisy are criticized, and kindness and generosity are praised. The Qur'an teaches that all believers, men and women alike, will stand alone in front of Allah and will be judged according to their actions in life. The Qur'an teaches that, after death, a person resides in the grave in a sleeplike state until the end of days, at which time the judgment will take place. The end of days is described in the Qur'an as a time when the world turns upside down in great calamity. Sura 99 dramatically describes Judgment Day:

> When the world is shaken up by its cataclysm
> And earth throws out its burdens,
> And man enquires: "What has come over it?"
> That day it will narrate its annals,
> For your Lord will have commanded it.
> That day people will proceed separately to be shown their deeds.
> Whosoever has done even an atom's weight of good will behold it;
> And whosoever has done even an atom's weight of evil will behold that.[8]

On Judgment Day, each person will have a book that details the deeds of his or her life. The book held in the right hand indicates a righteous life, and the book held in the left hand indicates the life of a sinner. The Qur'an teaches that each individual stands alone before God and that no one can intercede on his or her behalf. However, there is debate about this issue, and some traditions in Islam suggest that Muhammad will be able to intercede on behalf of believers. Some Muslims believe that the Day of Judgment will be ushered in by a person known as the Mahdi, whose just rule will come to the Earth at the end of days. The Mahdi is not mentioned in the Qur'an. Rather, the idea developed in Islamic thought in later centuries.

Those who are judged to be righteous will enter paradise. In the Qur'an, paradise is described in much detail as a lush garden with bountiful blessings of food, drink, and beautiful young men and women. Although some take this description to be literal, other Muslims think that it is instead a metaphor for the beauties of paradise. Those who have led sinful lives will be cast into hell, which is often referred to simply as "the fire." Those who are doomed to hell include nonbelievers and Muslims who have rejected their faith by failing to live up to prescribed duties and moral standards. Some Muslims believe that sinners will eventually be forgiven and taken to paradise.

Angels and Jinn

The existence of angels is another component of Islamic belief, and angels are mentioned throughout the Qur'an. Angels are part of God's creation, without body or gender. Humans are said to be made of clay and angels from light. Angels serve as important messengers and assistants to God. The most well known of the angels in Islamic tradition is Gabriel, or Jibril. This angel is mentioned several times in the Qur'an and was instrumental in bringing the revelation of the Qur'an to Muhammad from God. Islamic tradition also recognizes supernatural beings called *jinn*, which are said to be created from fire. They are also mentioned in several places in the Qur'an. Jinn can take various forms, and, like humans, they can be both good and evil and Muslim or non-Muslim. Much folklore has developed surrounding the jinn, and they are represented in tales like *One Thousand and One Nights* as both helping and harming humans. The English term *genie* derives from the Arabic word *jinn*.

The Five Pillars

The essential teachings of Islam are closely related to Muslim worship practice. The five pillars form the basis of practice. These pillars are as follows:

1. *Shahada*: the declaration of faith
2. **Salat**: the daily prayer
3. **Zakat**: almsgiving
4. *Sawm*: fasting during the month of **Ramadan**
5. **Hajj**: pilgrimage to Mecca

Muslims believe that the foundations for the five pillars were set during the lifetime of Muhammad. The five pillars are carefully articulated in the hadith literature. All of the pillars are equally important. However, they address different elements of religious practice that must be performed at special times. For example, although prayer is a daily requirement, the Ramadan fast happens only once per year, and the hajj must be performed only once in a lifetime. The pillars are generally required of all adult Muslims. However, individuals are sometimes excused from performing the pillars. For example, someone who is ill, pregnant, or nursing an infant would not be required to fast. Devout Muslims generally aim to observe all of the pillars, but as with every religious tradition, there are variations in levels of observance. Furthermore, there has been some historical variation across communities and cultures in how much emphasis is placed on the pillars. Some Muslim scholars have even debated the relative necessity of observing the pillars, though these scholars have always been in the minority.

The Declaration of Faith   The first pillar is the declaration of faith and is called the *shahada*. This is the statement of belief: "There is no God but God and

Muhammad is the messenger of God." The other four pillars all deal directly with religious practice, but the *shahada* is different in that it is much more a statement of belief than a ritualized religious practice. To become a Muslim, all one must do is utter the *shahada* with utmost sincerity in the presence of witnesses. Most new Muslims will first declare the *shahada*, and then begin a lifetime's journey of learning the Qur'an, the sunna, and other aspects of the faith. Many people in North America and elsewhere who have converted to Islam note the simplicity of the religion as something that attracted them to Islam. This simplicity is illustrated by the succinct nature of the *shahada*.

The Daily Prayer The salat, the mandatory daily prayers, is the second pillar. You encountered the careful preparations for the daily salat of Amina at the opening of this chapter. Devout Muslims perform five daily prayers at specific times of the day. Rather than performing all the prayers at once to get them over with for the day, week, or month, Muslims should do them at the required times. The first prayer should be done at dawn every morning. The next prayer is performed at about noon. The remaining prayers are the late afternoon prayer, the sunset prayer, and the final prayer in the evening. Prayer is mentioned in several places in the Qur'an. However, the number of prayers is established not in the Qur'an but rather in the hadith. The hadith literature relates that during a miraculous journey to heaven, known as the **miraj**, Muhammad came into the presence of God. God told Muhammad he should instruct people to make fifty daily prayers. However, when Muhammad told the prophet Moses about the prayers, Moses told him to go back to God to ask for a reduction, as fifty would be too many. Eventually, the number was settled at five, although God said that every prayer would count for ten.

The salat are not individualized prayers requesting aid from God or giving thanks, although those personal prayers, called *dua*, are also common among Muslims. Rather, the salat prayers are formalized. For each prayer, specific verses of the Qur'an are recited, and special body movements accompany the recitation.

Before beginning the prayers, a Muslim must enter a state of ritual purity. As you learned from Amina at the beginning of this chapter, this purification consists of ablutions, called *wudu'*, which involve cleansing the hands, head, face, and feet. The body should be covered for prayer, and most women and men also cover their heads. The prayer begins with the *takbir*, or the declaration *Allahu Akbar*, which means "God is great." Throughout the prayer, the believer faces the direction of Mecca, where an important structure known as the Ka'ba is located (you will learn more about the Ka'ba later in this section). This means that Muslims in America pray facing the east. In prayer, a Muslim stands, kneels, and bows his head to the floor. These cycles of movements, along with the proper recitation, are called *raka* and vary in number according to the prayer. In some parts of the world, such as regions of Indonesia, the prayer opens with a declaration of intent to indicate that the Muslim is in the right frame of mind for performing the prayer.[9] Not all Muslims declare their intent to pray, but most agree that proper intention is necessary. The intention of the believer is what validates and legitimizes the action of prayer. Many Muslims believe that the intention of the prayer is even more important than the prayer itself. After reciting verses of the Qur'an, the prayer closes with a greeting of peace.

Prayers may be done anywhere—even in a park or airport. However, many Muslims perform prayers at a **mosque** (this English word is taken from the Arabic term *masjid*). A mosque is a place that is designated for prayer. Many people imagine elaborate feats of architectural workmanship when they think of mosques, but a mosque can be as simple as an unadorned room in a commercial building or even a clearing in the woods. Although mosque architecture and decoration vary from the very simple to the very ornate, mosques tend to share some features. All mosques have a prayer space, and most have a fountain so that people can perform the required ablutions. The direction of prayer, known as the *qibla*, is marked inside a mosque by a niche called a *mihrab*, which is sometimes beautifully decorated with botanical designs or Qur'anic verses. The floors of a mosque are often completely covered with colorful rugs or woven mats. Because Muslim prayer requires open space for bodily movement, there are usually no seats or pews. Many mosques, particularly those in the Middle East and North Africa, also have a tower called a minaret. The minaret is often used to broadcast the calls to prayer.

Ablution fountains outside of a mosque.

In much of the world, visitors of all faiths are welcome to enter mosques. Normally, all those entering a mosque will be asked to leave their shoes outside. Sometimes, shoes are placed in a designated cabinet watched by someone who may receive a tip and even clean the shoes. Leaving shoes outside ensures that no outside dirt will enter the mosque to violate the ritual purity of those who have made the proper ablutions for prayer. The prayer space in a mosque is open and peaceful, and people may use the mosque as a place for contemplation and rest throughout the day. When walking through the hot and dusty streets of busy Cairo, one can see men—and sometimes women—taking a break from the urban noise and bustle by resting in the serene interior of a neighborhood mosque. In many parts of the world, mosques are also used for teaching classes or for other community needs.

Friday is designated as the day for congregational prayer, known as *salat al-jum'ah*. It is incumbent upon Muslim men to attend the midday prayer together, and they may also gather at a mosque for other prayers during the day. In some areas, women also attend the communal prayer, though their attendance is not regarded as mandatory. When Muslims pray in a group in a mosque or elsewhere, it is important that one person act as the imam, or prayer leader. The imam regulates the prayer session and ensures that all believers are praying together. The Friday prayer often features a sermon, which may be delivered by the imam or another preacher. Friday should not be confused with the Christian or Jewish Sabbath. Rather than a day of rest, it is a day for group prayer. In some Muslim countries, Friday is a work day, and businesses are open. In others, businesses are closed.

The five daily prayers are announced in the words of the ***adhan***, or the call to prayer. The *adhan* is delivered by a person called a **muezzin**, who calls the faithful to prayer from the door of the mosque or the minaret, sometimes using a loudspeaker. The *adhan* is usually called in a rhythmic, recitational fashion. Hearing the *adhan* several times a day from the wee hours of the morning to evening is very much a part of life in the Muslim world. Many residents and travelers miss it enormously when they move away; non-Muslim travelers often remark that hearing the *adhan* every day is one of the most memorable experiences of visiting a Muslim country.

ADHAN

God is most great (recited four times)
I testify that there is no god but God (recited twice)
I testify that Muhammad is the messenger of God (recited twice)
Hurry to prayer (recited twice)
Hurry to success (recited twice)
Prayer is better than sleep (repeated twice before the morning prayer)
God is most great (repeated twice)
There is no god but God (once)[10]

The beautiful Shah Mosque, in Isfahan, Iran, was built in the 1600s during the Safavid period.

Like the other pillars, the salat is incumbent upon all Muslims, both male and female. In much of the Muslim world, it is more common for men to pray in mosques than women, although this is not always the case. In such places as urban Egypt and Indonesia, women often pray in mosques. Although females may serve as imam for other women,

This attractive small mosque in rural Zanzibar, Tanzania, is built in an architectural style that is similar to houses in the area.

most Muslims believe that they may not do so for men. When both women and men pray in mosques, usually the genders are separated—either in separate prayer halls or with women praying in rows behind the men. Some Muslims reason that this requirement is due to modesty and concentration. They argue that women and men should not be distracted from their prayers by the presence of the opposite gender. Others argue that men's leadership in prayer is prescribed in the Qur'an. However, some Muslim feminist scholars, such as the American professor Dr. Amina Wadud, are challenging this tradition by arguing that women can lead men in prayer.

The daily prayers are important for many Muslims on both an individual and a communal level. Many Muslims feel closest to God during prayer. Although praying five times a day may sound rigorous to non-Muslims, many Muslims welcome the breaks from mundane tasks to focus their attention completely on God. A believer must stop all activity to remember God five times every day. This indicates that submission to God is the most important part of life for a devout Muslim. On another level, praying the same prayers at the same time every day, and often in a group, draws the community of Muslims together in worship of God. Many Muslims report that, in addition to feeling an individual closeness to God during prayer, they also feel at one with the **umma**, the global community of Muslims, in the common purpose of worship. However, it is also important to remember that there is a broad range of adherence to such practices in Islam, just as in other religions. Many people certainly identify as Muslim but do not perform daily prayers for one reason or another.

Almsgiving   The third pillar, zakat, refers to required almsgiving, which is part of a believer's devotion to God and the Muslim community. The rules about zakat are very specific, and the amount of zakat is figured as a percentage (about 2.5 percent) of the value of certain types of property, including cash. Zakat is therefore something like a tax. The wealth on which zakat has been paid is considered to be pure and clean. Therefore, some Muslims describe it as a means of purifying their property. The payment of zakat also expresses a Muslim's commitment to improving his or her community in a real and concrete way. This is because the proceeds from zakat are normally distributed to the poor or are used to maintain public institutions such as mosques and

Muslim men pray together at a mosque.

schools. In some countries today, such as Pakistan, the government collects and redistributes zakat funds.[11] Elsewhere, it is up to individuals themselves to make the zakat payments. All adults should pay zakat; however, those who are mentally ill or unstable are exempt from the requirement.

Fasting During Ramadan

The fourth pillar is *sawm*, which is the mandatory fast during the month of Ramadan, the ninth month in the Islamic calendar. Muslims consider Ramadan a sacred month because it was during Ramadan that the Qur'an was first revealed to Muhammad. During Ramadan, all Muslims are required to fast from dawn to sundown. When fasting, Muslims refrain from eating, drinking, and sexual activity. Muslims also strive to avoid arguing and negative thoughts during the hours of the fast.

All adult and adolescent Muslims are generally expected to fast. However, exceptions are made for those who are traveling as well as for women who are pregnant, nursing, or menstruating. In Pakistan, curtained food stalls are set up at train stations during Ramadan. The stalls allow travelers to eat in private, where they are respectfully out of view of those who are fasting and do not wish to be tempted by the sight of someone eating. Individuals who miss fasting days or break the fast are expected to make up the days later. However, children, the sick, the mentally ill, and the very elderly are exempt from fasting entirely. Children are usually encouraged to begin fasting when they show interest, but they are only expected to fast when they are comfortable doing so.

This open-air market in Sumbawa Besar, Indonesia, is very popular during Ramadan, when people buy special foods to break the fast.

The month of Ramadan is a special time. Although the fast can be challenging, many Muslims find Ramadan to be filled with joy, sociability, and profound religious meaning. In Muslim countries or communities, the rhythm of daily life changes significantly during Ramadan. Daily activity lessens, and streets are quiet during daylight hours. However, the world awakens at sunset, when the fast ends. Many people share the evening meal with family and friends, and streets are filled late into the evening with well-wishers. Many families eat again around midnight and also before dawn to gain the strength to make it through the day.

Muslims often break the fast with dates before performing the evening prayer. This is because eating dates is sunna: Muhammad broke the fast with dates, so many Muslims follow his example. In many cultures, special treats are prepared during Ramadan. Indonesian Muslims look forward to breaking the fast with a delectable drink made with coconut milk and tropical fruits. Some Indonesians say that the drink is so sweet because it represents the beauty of a day of focusing solely on God. In Iran and in

Persian communities in the United States and Canada, a rice pudding flavored with saffron and rosewater is served during Ramadan.

During Ramadan, Muslims around the world may spend time in the evenings reciting the Qur'an. Many try to achieve the goal of reciting the entire Qur'an during this special month. People may also stay up late into the night visiting friends and enjoying the celebratory and devotional atmosphere of the month. During the last few days of Ramadan, the Night of Power occurs. This is the night when Muslims believe that the Qur'an was originally revealed to Muhammad. Many Muslims believe that a wish may be granted during this special night. The end of Ramadan is marked by an important feast day called *'Id (or Eid) al-Fitr*, the feast of fast-breaking, which we discuss later in this chapter.

Like the preceding pillars, *sawm* is important on both personal and community levels. Fasting demonstrates an individual's dependence on God, who provides for humanity. Also, by refraining from food and drink, Muslims become more sympathetic to the plight of the poor and the hungry and learn to appreciate the food they have. Like salat and zakat, fasting together also brings a sense of community to Muslims worldwide. A Muslim observing the fast in Los Angeles, for example, will know that fellow believers thousands of miles away in Malaysia are keeping the fast. In the United States, many mosques and Muslim organizations view Ramadan as a time of outreach to non-Muslim friends and neighbors and as a way of teaching people about Islam. For example, at California State University, Sacramento, the Muslim student organization holds a popular "fast for a day" event every year. Non-Muslims are invited to try fasting for a day and then breaking the fast with a special meal prepared for the entire community. These events often include guest speakers who talk about the meaning of Ramadan and the basics of the Islamic tradition. Guests are also sometimes invited to watch the evening prayer.

Hajj: Pilgrimage to Mecca

The final pillar is called the hajj, which is the holy pilgrimage to Mecca in Saudi Arabia. The Qur'an specifies the pilgrimage as incumbent upon humanity. Every year, millions of Muslims descend upon the city of Mecca in a spectacular display of devotion. The hajj is generally understood to be required of all Muslims who are physically and financially able to make it. A Muslim only needs to perform the hajj once in his or her lifetime, but many Muslims who are able to do so repeat it. Pilgrims describe the event as one of unparalleled spiritual significance, and they experience intense feelings of connection to God and humanity during the hajj. Muslims who return from the hajj often use the title hajj (for men) or hajja (for women) before their name to indicate that they have made the journey.

The hajj must be undertaken at a particular time of year, namely, during the second week of the month *Dhu al-Hajj*, which is the final month in the Islamic calendar. A person must be physically and financially able to make the trip, or else it is not valid. One may not borrow money to make the pilgrimage, but it is appropriate

Muslim pilgrims prepare for prayer at the Haram mosque in Mecca. The Ka'ba is pictured.

to accept financing for the trip as a gift. In addition, the money set aside for the hajj must be purified by paying zakat on it. As a means of organizing the millions of travelers who come for hajj, the government of Saudi Arabia today requires pilgrims to join a travel group to make the hajj. Planned excursions depart from every corner of the world, and tour companies arrange everything from air travel to bus transfers to accommodations. In Saudi Arabia, a great deal of planning is involved because of the sheer numbers of Muslims who arrive in Mecca and its environs during the week of hajj. Only Muslims may make the journey; curious tourists are not allowed to partake in the experience.

When making the hajj, pilgrims must leave behind indicators of their social and economic status to properly enter a state of ritual purity. This state is called *ihram*. All men must wear special clothing, also called *ihram*. This consists of two very simple pieces of white cloth—one is worn above the waist and one is worn below. Women may wear what they choose, and most dress in simple clothing and avoid makeup, jewelry, and perfume. Pilgrims should also refrain from sexual activity, arguing, and frivolous conversation while in a state of ihram. Ideally, these restrictions are meant to ensure that the pilgrim's mind is solely on God and the hajj. The state of ihram also emphasizes the equality of all Muslims before God because all status markers, such as expensive jewelry, are removed.

The pilgrimage involves a number of highly specific, ritualized acts. Muhammad determined the sequence of the events of the hajj before his death, and some events reenact moments from his life. Many of the rituals also recall the actions of Abraham and his family. In this way, the rituals connect the believer to the distant past and the origins of monotheism with Abraham.

Perhaps the most important focus of the hajj is the structure known as the Ka'ba, which was a focus of pilgrimage in Arabia even before the time of Muhammad. It is a cubical building about thirty feet by thirty feet, and Muslims believe it was originally built and dedicated to Allah by Abraham and his son Ismail, or Ishmael. Today, the Ka'ba is covered by a cloth embroidered with gold thread that is replaced every year by the Saudi government. When a pilgrim first arrives in Mecca, he enters the Great Mosque that encircles the Ka'ba while reciting verses of the Qur'an. The pilgrim then circumambulates the Ka'ba seven times in a counterclockwise direction. This is known as the *tawaf*. This ritual is an act of devotion that is believed to be in imitation of the angels circling God's throne. The *tawaf* is performed three times during the course of the pilgrimage.

Another important rite of the hajj is called the *sa'y*. This rite commemorates the story of Hagar, mother of Ishmael, who frantically searched for water in the desert by rushing seven times between two hills. During Hagar's search, God made a spring appear, and Hagar and Ishmael were able to quench their thirst. Pilgrims visit this spring to this day, many taking the special waters home as a symbol of Mecca. Today, the route between the two hills is enclosed as part of the Great Mosque.

Another part of the hajj involves a journey to the plain of Arafat, where a tent city is established every year to house millions of pilgrims from around the world. It is here that Muslims recollect a story about Abraham that is also prominent in Jewish and Christian traditions. In all three traditions, Abraham is believed to have been commanded by God to sacrifice his son. (Most Muslims believe he intended to sacrifice Ishmael, but Jews and Christians usually regard Isaac as the object of sacrifice; the Qur'an does not mention which son was the intended sacrifice.) As Abraham prepared to make the sacrifice, the Angel Gabriel (Jibril) appeared at the last minute, and a ram was substituted for the son. Abraham's willingness to sacrifice his beloved son is regarded as a model of faith in Islam, and this is a solemn, reflective time of the hajj. The pilgrims perform the "standing ceremony," in which they remain standing from noon until sundown in praise of Allah. The hajj ends with the most important holiday of the year, the Feast of Sacrifice, which we discuss later in the chapter.

Now that we have covered the major teachings of Islam, let us turn to the history of the religious tradition, beginning with the birth of Muhammad.

13.3 The History of Islam: Origins

What are the origins of Islam? How did the early Muslim community get its start? In this section of the chapter, we will consider the emergence of early Islam. We will begin with learning about the life of the Prophet Muhammad.

The Prophet Muhammad in Mecca

Muhammad ibn Abd Allah was born around the year 570 CE in the town of **Mecca**, a city in the southern Arabian Peninsula. At the time of his birth, the peninsula was not politically united, and much of the population was made up of nomadic herders, known as Bedouins, who lived in remote desert areas. Despite this lack of political centralization, the region was by no means isolated. The peninsula was situated between the Byzantine Empire to the northwest, the Persian Sassanian Empire to the northeast, and the Christian Abyssinian kingdom across the Red Sea in Ethiopia. In addition, the city of Mecca was a significant trading center and place of religious pilgrimage. Although there were Christians and Jews in Arabia at the time, the majority of the people living in Arabia were polytheists who worshiped several deities. Trade fairs regularly took place in Mecca, and people passing through often left representations of deities at the temple called the Ka'ba, which, as noted earlier, was a large cube-shaped building in the center of town; today, this is the site to which all Muslims turn as they pray, and toward which they make a hajj at least once in their lives, as you learned in the preceding section. Tradition holds that at the time of Muhammad, more than 300 deities and spirits were represented by idols in the Ka'ba. Muslims call this period before the revelation of the Qur'an the *jahiliyya*, or the "age of ignorance."

Muhammad was born into a tribe called Quraysh, a powerful extended family that was very influential in Mecca. His father died before he was born, and his mother died when he was a young child. After her death, Muhammad went to live with his grandfather, who was his appointed guardian. When his grandfather died, Muhammad was raised by his uncle, a man named Abu Talib. Although he spent most of his early life in the city of Mecca, as a young boy Muhammad was sent out to the desert to live with the Bedouin, who many considered to live the ideal Arab lifestyle. At the time, sending children to the Bedouin was considered an important way to impart Arab values and culture to young city dwellers.

Muhammad is known to have been a hard worker, and he was active in business and trade. Indeed, he met his first wife, Khadija, while he was working for her in a trading caravan. Khadija was a widow about fifteen years older than Muhammad, and she was so taken with the integrity and dignity of the young man that she proposed to him. They married when he was about twenty-five years old and she forty. Their marriage was thought to be one of close companionship and deep love, and they had several children together.

As was discussed earlier, Muhammad began preaching in Mecca after receiving the first revelations. His preaching was not welcomed, however, and was even controversial in some quarters of Mecca. This was because he criticized both the polytheistic beliefs held by many Meccans and the disregard that wealthy Meccans showed toward the poor. The controversy led to persecution of the small but growing community of Muslims. Because they held much power in Mecca, Muhammad's own clan, the Quraysh, stood to lose the most with the social change that Muhammad's teachings advocated. The Quraysh were thus particularly active in ridiculing and persecuting Muhammad's followers.

This persecution induced some Muslims to flee to Abyssinia (Ethiopia), where they were granted refuge by the Christian king. Others tried to resist. One well-known Muslim who resisted persecution was Bilal, an enslaved Abyssinian man who had converted to Islam. Bilal's enslaver forced him to lie in the hot sun with a stone on his chest and told him to renounce his Muslim beliefs by denying the oneness of God. Bilal refused, crying out "One! One!" until he was rescued by Abu Bakr, who purchased him from his tormentor and then freed him from slavery. Bilal is remembered by Muslims to this day for his devotion and is also known as the first muezzin—the person who calls the faithful to prayer.

The Hijra and the Growth of the Muslim Community

Because of the troubles in Mecca, Muhammad eventually encouraged his followers to leave and make a new home elsewhere. The residents of a little settlement north of Mecca with a small Jewish population welcomed him, and he encouraged his followers to go there. This town became known as **Medina** (from the term *medinat al-nabi*, which means "the city of the Prophet"). The Muslims moved from Mecca to Medina in the year 622 CE, and this migration is called the **hijra**. The hijra is a very important event in Islamic history. Indeed,, the Islamic lunar calendar begins not with Muhammad's birth but with the hijra because the hijra marked the beginning of a distinct Muslim community, or *umma*, with Muhammad as its leader.

Muhammad did not travel with the first group that went to Medina; he and some of his companions waited for a few weeks to make the trip. When they finally left for Medina, angry Meccans from the Quraysh tribe pursued them. A popular story recounts that during Muhammad's journey to Medina he hid from the Quraysh in a cave for three days. When his pursuers reached the cave, they did not look inside because a kindly spider had spun a web to hide the entrance, thus saving Muhammad. Even today, some Muslims will not kill spiders because of their appreciation for the spider's important role in protecting the Prophet from the Meccans. Stories about the hijra and the foundational period of Islam are well known and inform the way many Muslims live their lives. Today, Muslims around the world recall the hijra as a difficult but very important time.

What happened to the Muslim community with the move to Medina? With the move, the growing Muslim community took on a new political and social form. Additionally, Muhammad's role expanded over the years as he became the leader of the new community. In Mecca, Muhammad had primarily preached and taught the revelations to his followers. In Medina, however, he took on a wide variety of new roles and oversaw political, social, and religious matters. In addition to his role as prophet of God and religious leader, Muhammad became the political head of the community. He continued to receive revelations from God for twenty more years. Reflecting these changes, the verses of the Qur'an that Muslims believe were revealed to Muhammad in Medina concern the regulation of community life.

The migration to Medina did not end the Muslim community's problems with Mecca. Muhammad and the Muslims lived a perilous existence for several years as they suffered economic hardships in Medina and threats from Mecca. With the aim of providing economically for the community, the Muslims had begun to raid trade caravans bound for Mecca, though with limited success. It may sound surprising to the modern reader, but raiding was a common and even accepted economic practice in Arabia at that time, especially in times of hardship. Most often, the raids did not involve bloodshed.

Conflicts with the Meccans continued, primarily with the Quraysh tribe, who still viewed the Muslims as a threat. Furthermore, the raids caused many economic problems for the Meccans and increased the tension between the two cities. The result was one of the most famous clashes in early Muslim history, the Battle of Badr in the year 624 CE. The Muslims had planned a raid on a Meccan caravan at a place called Badr. The Meccans, learning of the plan, sent a force of more than

900 men to protect the caravan. The Muslims, though badly outnumbered at only 300 strong, soundly defeated the Meccan forces. The battle is mentioned in the Qur'an, which reports that angels helped the outnumbered Muslims win the battle (8:9). The Qur'an also notes this as a critical moment in the development of the spirit and destiny of the Muslims. After this dramatic battle, Muhammad's reputation as a great leader grew.

A few years later, in 628 CE, Muhammad attempted to lead the Muslims back to Mecca for a pilgrimage. The people of Arabia had been making pilgrimages to the Ka'ba for centuries. The Meccans, expecting an attack, proposed a negotiation with the now more powerful Muslims. Muhammad agreed, and the pilgrimage was postponed through the signing of a treaty between the Meccans and the Muslims. Two years later, in 630 CE, the Muslims returned, and the Meccans surrendered when they saw Muhammad's even greater political and military strength. Muhammad accepted the surrender and allowed the Meccan people to go free if they would convert to Islam. Upon entering Mecca, Muhammad and the Muslims destroyed the polytheistic idols housed at the Ka'ba and rededicated the building to the one and only God and the religion of Abraham.

Muhammad lived for only two more years after his victorious return to Mecca. At the time of his death, he had a large family. Khadija had died several years earlier, and after her death Muhammad married several more wives. Some of his marriages were contracted for political alliances, and others to care for widowed and divorced women who had no one else. The best known of his later wives was a woman called 'A'isha, who was the daughter of Abu Bakr. She was much younger than Muhammad, which was not unusual in marriages at the time. 'A'isha was a very important early figure in Islamic history and is thought to be one of Muhammad's most beloved wives. As mentioned earlier, she was the source of much information about Muhammad's life and was often consulted by other Muslims because of her vast knowledge of religious matters. In 632 CE, Muhammad is believed to have died peacefully in 'A'isha's arms after returning from a final journey to Mecca. He was buried under her home in Medina, and to this day, some Muslims visit this site as a place of pilgrimage.

By the time of his death, Muhammad was the political and religious leader of much of Arabia. After the move to Medina, Muslim rule had spread rapidly across the Arabian Peninsula through both nonviolent political alliances and military conquests. Many people of Arabia had converted to Islam. Some did so because they believed in the truth of Muhammad's message, and others converted for political reasons, namely, to form alliances with Muhammad and the powerful Muslim community.

Not all people living under Muslim rule converted to Islam, however. Significant Christian, Jewish, and other religious minority populations remained. From this early period, Muslims have considered Christians and Jews to be People of the Book, a designation that means that they are a people who have received scripture from God and are thus close to the Muslim community. Later, Hindus and Buddhists were also considered People of the Book, as Muslim rule spread into South Asia. Under Muslim rule, these minority communities were governed by what are termed *dhimmi* laws; the term *dhimmi* refers to their status as protected peoples. These laws allowed non-Muslims in Muslim territories to worship how they chose, provided they paid taxes and submitted to Muslim authority. The dhimmis did not enjoy all the privileges of Muslims—they were not allowed to bear arms, for example—but they were entitled to the protection of the Islamic state.

The Crisis of Succession and the Rightly Guided Caliphs

At the time of Muhammad's death, communities throughout Arabia were united under Islam, but it was unclear to Muhammad's followers who should succeed him to lead the Muslims. When he died, most Muslims thought that Muhammad had not designated a successor. The companions of the Prophet thus chose the highly respected Abu Bakr to lead the Muslim community. Recall that Abu Bakr was one of the first converts to Islam; he was also Muhammad's father-in-law. A minority of Muslims, however, believed that Muhammad had designated his cousin 'Ali to succeed him. 'Ali was also Muhammad's son-in-law because he had married Fatima, Muhammad's daughter by Khadija. Although 'Ali was highly regarded even by those who did not think Muhammad had designated him to be his successor, he was much younger than Abu Bakr, and many considered him too young to lead the community.

This controversy over leadership of the Muslim community is often known as the crisis of succession, and it led to the development of the two major branches of Islam: the **Sunni** and the **Shi'a**. The majority group became known as the Sunni, which remains the larger of the two major branches. The minority group became known as the Shi'a, a name that comes from the term *Shi'at 'Ali*, which means the "party of 'Ali," for their advocacy of 'Ali as successor to Muhammad. The Shi'a is the smaller of the two major branches of Islam. Later in the chapter, we discuss how this dispute over succession led to other differences between the Sunni and the Shi'a.

The leaders who came after Muhammad were not viewed as prophets. Each was known rather as a **caliph**, who ruled as the representatives of God and the Prophet and had both religious and political authority. This was a new form of government called a caliphate, and it remained the model for Islamic society for several hundred years. The designation of Abu Bakr as caliph started a historical period that came to be known as the time of the Rightly Guided Caliphs, who were Abu Bakr and his successors: 'Umar, 'Uthman, and finally 'Ali.

As caliph, Abu Bakr sought to strengthen relationships with the communities and tribes of Arabia who had formed alliances with Muhammad. Abu Bakr faced the potential breakdown of Muslim unity because some of these tribes, particularly those in parts of Arabia far from Medina and Mecca, wanted to sever their ties to the Muslim community when Muhammad died. After the death of Abu Bakr, which was only two years after he had been appointed caliph, the Muslims chose a man called 'Umar to lead. Like Abu Bakr, 'Umar had been close to Muhammad. Also like Abu Bakr, he was confronted with the problem of some communities wanting to break away from Islamic rule. However, he managed to preserve unity and expand Muslim rule, conquering the lands of Egypt, Syria, and Iraq. When 'Umar died in 644 CE, another of the Prophet's companions, a man called 'Uthman, was selected as the new caliph.

'Uthman led the Muslims for twelve years, from 644 to 656 CE. He continued the rapid political expansion that 'Umar had begun, but he also faced many problems. Muslim rule now extended from the Mediterranean and North Africa into Central Asia. Because the *umma* now reached beyond Arabic-speaking lands, there was a great deal of cultural and linguistic diversity among the Muslims. This situation made leadership a far more complex undertaking than it had been in the time of Muhammad and Abu Bakr, when nearly all Muslims were Arabs. This eventually led to charges that the caliphs discriminated against non-Arab Muslims. Furthermore, many accused 'Uthman of nepotism when he appointed his nephew Mu'awiya as governor of Syria. 'Uthman also placed other relatives in key posts, many of whom grew rich as a result. A few years into his rule, 'Uthman faced a number of rebellions in outer provinces of the empire, and in 656 CE he was killed by insurgents who had marched on Medina.

After 'Uthman's death, 'Ali was named caliph. During the time of the first three caliphs, 'Ali's supporters grew in numbers. Despite this growing support, 'Ali's time as caliph saw many fractures in the Muslim community. Supporters of 'Uthman were upset that 'Ali had never punished his murderers. This controversy resulted in the Battle of the Camel, a traumatic moment in Islamic history that was the first to pit Muslims against Muslims. In the battle, 'Ali defeated an army led by 'A'isha and other prominent Meccans. 'A'isha directed the battle from her mount on a camel, from which the battle took its name. 'Ali's forces attacked and brought down her camel in order to hinder her leadership, and his forces were victorious. Mu'awiya also challenged 'Ali's authority. This conflict reached a peak in the Battle of Siffin in 657 CE. When they met on the battlefield in Syria, Mu'awiya asked 'Ali for an arbitration of their dispute, and he accepted. However, some of 'Ali's followers disapproved of the arbitration, which they viewed as a surrender to Mu'awiya. This group formed a splinter group known as the Kharijites, which means "those who seceded." In 661 CE, 'Ali was murdered by a Kharijite.

13.4 The History of Islam: Development

With the death of 'Ali, the period of the Rightly Guided Caliphs was at an end. What happened to the Muslim community after this? This section of the chapter describes the expansion of Islam and early dynasties and empires.

The Umayyads and the Abbasids

After 'Ali was killed, Mu'awiya claimed the caliphate. His leadership gave birth to what is known as the **Umayyad Dynasty**. This marked the end of the period of the Rightly Guided Caliphs. The institution of the caliphate survived, but the divisions in the community of believers that had worsened under 'Ali remained.

The Umayyad period lasted nearly a century, from 661 until 750 CE. Umayyad leaders ruled from the city of Damascus in Syria. Although they were considered fairly effective leaders who expanded the Muslim Empire farther east to India and farther west to Spain, the reign of the Umayyads was controversial. For example, many Muslims thought that the Umayyads did not truly represent the diversity of the Muslim people, and favored Arab Muslims over non-Arab Muslims. Such criticism arose in part because Mu'awiya had designated his son Yazid as his successor instead of letting the community select a leader. This turned the caliphate into a dynasty.

Many Muslims who were opposed to the Umayyad Dynasty felt that the leadership of the *umma* should come from the line of Muhammad through Fatima and 'Ali and that therefore their sons, Hasan and Husayn, should lead the *umma*. With their support, **Husayn** eventually challenged the Umayyads for authority. However, he was slain in 680 CE. when Yazid's armies ambushed him on the plains of Karbala in what is now Iraq. This tragic event is referred to as the "martyrdom of Husayn." This is a moment in Shi'a history that is solemnly commemorated to the present day as Husayn's sacrifice for the Muslim people. With the death of Husayn, the number of Muslims who believed the leader of the *umma* should be from the family of the Prophet grew. It was at this point that the Shi'a movement formally broke away from the Sunnis and established a line of successors to the Prophet that remained within Muhammad's family.

In the late seventh and early eighth centuries CE, many more Muslims began to criticize the Umayyad Dynasty. This group included those who were critical of the Umayyads for their perceived discrimination against non-Arabs and also those who supported the family of 'Ali as rightful leaders of the *umma*. Muslims opposed to the Umayyads became known as the **Abbasids**, taking the name of one of Muhammad's uncles, al-Abbas ibn Abd al-Muttalib. In 750 CE, the Abbasid Revolution succeeded in removing the Umayyads from power.

The first caliph of the Abbasids was a man named Abu al-Abbas, and during his rule the Abbasids moved their capital from Damascus to Baghdad. Baghdad became a cultural capital of the world. Islamic arts and sciences flowered in this time, which became known as the classical period of Islamic civilization. One of the most well-known pieces of literature from this period is *One Thousand and One Nights*. These colorful tales celebrate the reign of the most famous Abbasid caliph, Harun al-Rashid, who ruled for twenty-five years in the late eighth century.

Many of these intellectual and artistic developments had an enormous impact on world history and the cultures of Asia and Europe. Islamic scholarship in science, philosophy, and medicine built on earlier knowledge from Greek and Persian sources and was very influential in European schools and universities for many centuries. The time of the Abbasids was also the period during which many Islamic religious doctrines were developed into forms that are still accepted today. For example, it was in this period that the Islamic legal schools of thought, which we discuss later in this chapter, were formalized.

Abbasid rule continued for several centuries, but not all Muslims were united under the Abbasid Caliphate. In 950 CE, for example, rulers in Cairo and Spain also claimed the title of caliph. Furthermore, the Abbasid period saw the influence of the Crusades in Syria and Palestine, when European Christians sought to win control of the Holy Land. Christian forces captured Jerusalem from Islamic control in 1099. The holy city was later recaptured by Salah ad-Din (also known as Saladin), a famed Muslim military leader, in 1187. The rule of the Abbasids ended in 1258 CE when Baghdad was sacked by a Mongol army from the east led by the grandson of Genghis Khan.

By the end of the Abbasid Caliphate and the beginning of the fourteenth century, Islam was the majority religion in a vast region stretching from Spain and the western edge of North Africa all the way to Iran in Central Asia. The religion was also gaining converts in sub-Saharan Africa and South and Southeast Asia. Although military conquest expanded Muslim rule in some areas, it is incorrect to think that the historical spread of Islam around the globe was solely by the sword. In the earliest years of the *umma*, many tribes in Arabia joined the Muslims through political alliance. The growth of Islam throughout much of Asia and sub-Saharan Africa was gradual and peaceful. Often, Islam was introduced largely through traveling preachers, teachers, and traders.

Later Islamic Empires: The Ottomans, the Mughals, and the Safavids

After the fall of the Abbasids, several powerful Islamic empires arose in the next few centuries. These were the Ottoman Empire in the Mediterranean region, the Safavids in Iran, and the Mughal Dynasty in India.

The Ottoman Empire spanned over 600 years, from the fourteenth to the twentieth centuries. The early empire was marked by rapid expansion, and at the height of its power, the Ottomans controlled much of the Middle East and Mediterranean, reaching into southeastern Europe and Africa. The empire reached its height during the fifteenth and sixteenth centuries, and in 1453 the Turks took the city of Constantinople, the former capital of the Byzantine Empire. The city, now called Istanbul, became the Ottoman capital and an important seat of Islamic learning and Islamic power. The Ottoman Empire did not come to an end until after World War I.

At the same time that the Ottoman Empire reached its height, another Muslim empire arose thousands of miles away in South Asia. This dynasty, known as the Mughals, ruled much of India from the early sixteenth to the eighteenth centuries, even though the Muslim population was in the minority. The Mughal Dynasty, though not as long-lived as the Ottomans, saw a growth of literary and artistic development in South Asia. Mughal architects created some of the world's most impressive buildings, such as the stunningly beautiful Taj Mahal in Agra, India. The Taj Mahal was built in the 1600s by the Mughal emperor Shah Jahan as a memorial and mausoleum for his beloved wife, Mumtaz Mahal. The Mughal Empire reached its peak in the eighteenth century, and although there was a Mughal ruler until 1857 in India, Mughal power and territory saw a decline with the advent of British occupation of South Asia.

To the west of the Mughals during the same period, the Safavid Empire flourished in Iran. Perhaps the most notable aspect of the Safavid rule was the establishment of Shi'ism as the religion of Iran; to the present day, the vast majority of Iran's Muslims are Shi'a. The Safavid period saw significant developments in Shi'ism, particularly in religious and philosophical thought. As with the Mughals, the Safavid period saw the development of great works of art and architecture.

The Sultan Ahmed Mosque in Istanbul, Turkey, was built in the 1600s and is a fine example of Ottoman architecture. It is also known as the Blue Mosque because of the blue tiling inside.

13.5 The History of Islam: The Modern Age

The modern period has seen important developments in the history of Islam. With European imperial expansion and then decline, the proliferation of new political forms came to dominate the global political landscape. What role was Islam to play in this new global world?

Islam and Nationalism

In the twentieth century, the nation-state came to dominate the political organization of the world. Muslim leaders took different positions on the ideal relationship between religion and the nation-state. In many places, religion has served as a means to unify people across ethnic, class, and social boundaries. Some Muslim nationalists and political leaders envisioned a close link between their ideals of new states and Islam. Their vision involved a state government based on the principles of Islam

The Taj Mahal, in Agra, India, was built in the 1600s by the Mughal emperor Shah Jahan as a memorial and mausoleum for his beloved wife, Mumtaz Mahal.

and Islamic law as the basis for the legal system. Other leaders sought to distance nationalist policy from Islam and favored European secular states as political models.

When the Ottoman Empire collapsed at the end of World War I, Turkey moved toward embracing European ideals of secular nationalism. A man called Mustafa Kemal, better known as Ataturk, the founder of modern Turkey, embraced this ideal. He argued that Turkey should follow the path of the western European nations and separate religion from politics. Ataturk disbanded the powerful religious brotherhoods, which had been very important in Turkey, and embraced a secular legal system that did not incorporate Islamic law at any level. He also required Turkish people to dress in a European style, which meant that women had to abandon headscarves and men had to stop wearing the traditional hat called a fez.

Although these policies were far reaching, they did not eradicate Islam from public life in Turkey. For example, although **Sufi** religious brotherhoods had been made illegal, many Turkish people still followed the mystical path known as Sufism, which we discuss later in this chapter. Although Islamic courts were no longer a part of the official legal system, Muslims still took disputes to Islamic legal authorities, particularly in rural areas. During the late twentieth and early twenty-first centuries, many Turks reembraced their Islamic heritage. The Justice and Development Party, which has been supportive of reintroducing Islam into public life, has been the majority party in the governing coalition since the early 2000s.

Other Muslim countries followed a very different path from Turkey. For example, in the Indian subcontinent, which was colonized by Great Britain, discussions of independence and nationalism early in the twentieth century focused a great deal on religious divisions in the region. With India's independence from Great Britain in 1947, two countries were formed: India and Pakistan. Pakistan was created as a Muslim homeland for the millions of Muslims who lived in South Asia. An important thinker behind the creation of Pakistan, Muhammad Iqbal, argued that Muslims needed a separate country to protect them from the Hindu majority in India. An organization called the Muslim League was instrumental in the early twentieth century in launching the idea of a separate state for the Muslim people of India. That ideal became a reality with independence. At first, Pakistan was divided into East and West Pakistan. In the 1970s, East Pakistan became the country that is now known as Bangladesh. Today, Pakistan and Bangladesh are among the largest Muslim-majority countries in the world. India's Muslim population today is even larger than in Pakistan and Bangladesh, yet they are still in the minority because India's population is so large.

Iran is an important case study of Islam and nationalism in the twentieth century. Throughout much of the century, the shah (or king) of Iran was Reza Pahlavi.

The shah embraced the ideals of the Western world and looked to Europe and the United States as models for development. However, Iran's Shi'i religious scholars were critical of the monarchy for marginalizing religious learning and religious authority in Iran. Iranian liberals and Marxists also criticized the shah as a corrupt leader who was entranced with the Western world and closely tied to Western governments, particularly the United States. In 1978, a coalition of clerics, intellectuals, and women's groups formed with the goal of removing the shah and his family from power. The revolution they staged in 1979 deposed the shah and ushered in the leadership of Islamic clerics. Not surprisingly, after the revolution, many of those people who had supported the overthrow of the shah felt neglected when the religious clerics took charge and formed an Islamic Republic.

A religious scholar known as Ayatollah Khomeini (1902–1989) headed the new government. In Shi'ism, the term *ayatollah*, which means "sign of God," refers to religious scholars who have achieved a very high level of religious learning and scholarship. Khomeini had been one of the most outspoken critics of the shah among the religious scholars, and he argued that it was the duty of the religious scholars to build an Islamic state in Iran. This is precisely what happened in the aftermath of the revolution. The new government instituted strict reforms, which they argued reflected Islamic rules of behavior. Women were required to dress in a full-length black garment known as the *chador*. Many Iranians, among them intellectuals and professionals, left the country and made their homes abroad in places such as the United States and Canada.

Today, people in Iran are divided as to how much authority religious scholars should have in the government. The supreme leader of Iran remains an ayatollah; the current supreme leader, Ayatollah Ali Khamenei, succeeded Khomeini in 1989. Iran also has a president. In 2009, huge numbers of Iranians took to the streets to protest the disputed reelection of President Mahmoud Ahmedinejad, and many have interpreted the protests as criticism of the Islamic Republic. The protest has been called the Green Movement, or Green Revolution, after the color adopted by the opposition presidential candidate, Mir-Hossein Mousavi. In 2011, Mousavi openly supported the pro-democracy Arab Spring movements in other Middle Eastern countries and called for more protests. He was then placed under house arrest for the next several years, and he remains detained at the time of writing. The current president of Iran is the moderate Masoud Pezeshkian, who was elected in 2024. In recent years, Iran has faced much internal strife, particularly over women's rights and mandatory modest dress. In 2022, the death of Mahsa Amini while she was in police custody for an inappropriate headscarf, sparked massive protests around Iran.

Islamic Reform Movements

In the last two centuries, many movements have aimed to reform local Muslim communities and the worldwide *umma*. As we discussed earlier in this chapter, in early history, Muslim states and empires rapidly grew into important world powers.

Various Muslim empires remained powerful for many centuries, through the Abbasid period and into the later Ottoman, Mughal, and Safavid sultanates. European powers were generally eclipsed by the Islamic world during this time. However, in the eighteenth century, European empires began to gain prominence as economic and political world leaders. European power continued to grow with the advent of industrialization. Eventually, the British, French, and Dutch empires colonized a great deal of the Muslim world. The British and French colonized much of Muslim Africa and the Middle East; the British and the Dutch controlled Muslim lands in South and Southeast Asia.

The "Wahhabi" Movement

During the eighteenth century, several Muslim reform movements developed. These movements were spearheaded by factions concerned about what they viewed as a decline in Muslim communities and in Muslim power worldwide. One of the most well-known reforms was the "Wahhabi" movement. It was originated by a scholar named Muhammad Ibn Abd al-Wahhab (d. 1792), and it is still influential today. Ibn Abd al-Wahhab disapproved of Muslim practices that he perceived as falling outside of the Qur'an and sunna and that had developed after the time of Muhammad. The Wahhabi movement was especially critical of venerating saints and visiting tombs. Al-Wahhab argued that these practices and others were inappropriate innovations and had contributed to the decline of Islam and the Muslim world. As a result, al-Wahhab's followers razed many saints' tombs and shrines, and also those of Muhammad, his companions, and Husayn.

In the late eighteenth century, followers of al-Wahhab formed significant ties with the ruling family of Arabia. To this day, the movement remains influential in Saudi Arabia and in other parts of the Muslim world where it has sent teachers and established schools. Followers of the movement call themselves Muwahiddun, though they are commonly called "Wahhabis" in the news media. Sometimes movements like the Wahhabis that advocate living according to models from the past are known as Salafi or Salafist, from the Arabic term *salaf al-salih*, which means "righteous ancestors."

The Wahhabi movement is often characterized as very conservative or "fundamentalist." However, we must be careful in using the term "fundamentalist" when discussing any religious movement. This is because not all movements called fundamentalist are the same. The Wahhabi movement is often termed "fundamentalist" because of its emphasis on the primacy of the Qur'an and the sunna and its criticism of later developments in Muslim thought and practice. The movement thus emphasizes the "fundamentals" of Islam—the Qur'an and the model of the Prophet. Today, the Wahhabi movement is often portrayed negatively in the Western media, owing to its influence on notorious extremists such as Osama bin Laden and the emphasis some Wahhabis place on bringing their version of

Islam to other parts of the Muslim world. Although followers of Wahhabi Islam are generally more conservative than other Muslims, not all embrace a political version of Islam.

Resisting Colonialism and Westernization

During the nineteenth century, European powers increasingly dominated Muslim lands. Many Muslim thinkers lamented the loss of a cohesive and powerful *umma* and regretted the decline of several important Muslim empires. The Mughals had dominated much of South Asia for several generations, but the introduction of British rule in the nineteenth century saw the end of the Mughals. The Ottoman Empire, too, had thrived in the eastern Mediterranean and North Africa, but by the early nineteenth century it was threatened by increasing European power.

As a result, many reformist movements prioritized revitalizing the *umma*. Some focused on trying to revive the lost glory and power of the *umma*. Other movements directly resisted European imperialism and, later, American expansion and influence. And some reformers tried to deflect the criticism of the Islamic world that was coming from powerful Western governments. European leaders and scholars were often quick to criticize Islam and Muslim cultures as being "backward," and some Muslim reformers made concerted efforts to combat these developing stereotypes.

These movements took several forms. One reformer was Muhammad Ahmed ibn Abdallah (1844–1885), more commonly known as the Sudanese Mahdi. The Sudanese Mahdi organized a powerful military uprising against the Egyptian and British forces that occupied the Sudan in the nineteenth century. Many people have claimed the title of Mahdi over the years, and Abdallah convinced people that he was indeed the Mahdi heralding the end of days. In this way, he was able to recruit a large number of followers. His movement emphasized social equality, and he entirely revamped the five pillars. For example, he incorporated a declaration of himself as Mahdi in the *shahada*, and he dropped the hajj as a requirement. His revamping of the pillars was highly controversial, and many Sudanese Muslims did not support his efforts. However, his aims were more political than religious, and he successfully took the city of Khartoum in 1885 from the British and Egyptian armies.

Jamal al-din al-Afghani (1838–1897) was a reformer who sought to inspire Muslims by convincing them that the roots of revitalization were within their own faith and their own history. Born in Iran, al-Afghani traveled extensively in the Middle East and Central Asia and advocated the idea that all Muslims worldwide should join together with the goal of revitalizing the *umma* and defeating Western imperialism. He called upon his fellow Muslims to unify against Western influence. Al-Afghani is often considered the originator of the anti-imperialist sentiment among many Muslim thinkers of the time. In addition, he argued that Islam was the religion most amenable to scientific knowledge. Al-Afghani was also well known as an activist for the poor and downtrodden, and he called for social reform in Muslim countries to alleviate their plight.

Through calling for unification of the *umma*, al-Afghani is often considered the father of pan-Islamism, and he was a great inspiration to other reformers. Perhaps the best known of his followers is Muhammad Abduh (1849–1905), who was born in Egypt and achieved great renown as an advocate of Egyptian nationalism. Like al-Afghani, Abduh saw no conflict between religion and science, and he asserted that Islam had always embraced scientific methodologies. And like many reformers of his time, Abduh thought that the Qur'an should be interpreted in light of social changes. Abduh argued that although certain Islamic doctrines were absolute and unchangeable, some teachings should change with the times. For example, he is well known for his criticisms of polygamy, discussed in more detail later in this chapter.

A third reformer of the same period was the modernist thinker Sayyid Ahmed Khan (1817–1898). Khan is best known for his educational reforms in South Asia and his support of the British. Unlike reformers such as al-Afghani, Khan admired the West, particularly the British, and attempted to bring Western ways of thought and education to his native India. Although he did not advocate imperial rule, he believed that the Muslims of South Asia could only move forward through embracing certain Western ways. In light of these views, it is not surprising that he was criticized by other reformers of his time as being too sympathetic with the British. He is also known for advocating interpretation of the Qur'an in a rational way in light of social changes. Like Abduh and Afghani, he embraced developments in science and argued that there was no conflict between Islam and science.

The Muslim Brotherhood

The reformist spirit of the nineteenth century carried over into the twentieth. Several important and wide-reaching twentieth-century movements responded to and built on the developments of the nineteenth century. A key goal for many twentieth-century reformers involved finding a path to economic development for Muslim countries that did not follow Western models. More specifically, many thinkers have sought a path that allows Muslim countries and cultures to maintain their Muslim identities and still embrace certain ideas and technologies that originated in the West. Even in the postcolonial world, Europe and the United States are criticized for cultural imperialism because Western cultural models and products are spread throughout the world, particularly through business and media.

One of the most influential contemporary movements has been the Muslim Brotherhood. The Brotherhood has been in existence for several decades. It is based in Egypt, though it has been influential all over the globe. The founder was Hassan al-Banna, who organized the movement in 1928 to revitalize Islam from within by focusing on a return to the Qur'an and the sunna. Like other reformers of his time, al-Banna was opposed to Western imperialism. He argued that encroaching Western values were contributing to the decline of Islamic societies.

Sayyid Qutb, one of the more influential members of the Brotherhood and an outspoken critic of Western influence, aimed to revitalize the Islamic world solely through Islamic principles. Qutb was executed in 1966 by the Egyptian government after being repeatedly accused of treason, terrorism, and a plot to kill President Gamal Abdel Nasser. Qutb's writings have continued to influence certain Islamic activists and some extremists, including those highly critical of Western influence on the Muslim world, such as Osama bin Laden and members of al-Qaeda. However, it is important to note that many members of the Muslim Brotherhood have been very critical of Sayyid Qutb's radical views.

Throughout its existence, the Brotherhood has had a fractured relationship with the Egyptian government. It was banned in the 1950s, after members of the Broterhood attempted to assassinate Egyptian President Nasser. Despite this ban, the Brotherhood remained active, and in later years it attempted to reconcile with the government of President Hosni Mubarak, who was deposed in 2011. In 2012, Muhammad Morsi was the first member of the Brotherhood to be elected president in Egypt. He was ousted in 2013, however, and the Brotherhood was again banned by the new government.

Muslims in North America

Today, about 3.5 million Muslims live in the United States, and about 1 million live in Canada. Both populations are growing rapidly, primarily through immigration. American Muslims are making social contributions in both their home communities and regional and national politics. Many Muslims live in large urban areas, but significant populations also live in smaller towns and more rural areas. The Muslim population in the United States is not limited to one particular city or even one particular region. Muslims live everywhere, from Los Angeles to Salt Lake City to Dearborn, Michigan, the city that has the largest Muslim population in the United States.

The African American Muslim population grew significantly in the twentieth century. Scholars estimate that from 10 to 30 percent of the Africans who were enslaved and brought to the United States from the seventeenth to the nineteenth centuries were Muslims. Once in the United States, however, many enslaved people were not permitted to freely practice their religion, although some were literate in Arabic and tried to maintain their religious practice. Many were also forced to convert to Christianity or converted by choice.

In the twentieth century, Black Americans were attracted to Islam and converted for a variety of reasons. For example, many people regarded Islam as the likely religion of their African ancestors. Thus, Muslim religious leaders often stressed these ties to Africa; some claimed that Islam was a more "authentic" religion for African Americans, for Islam was not the religion of the European

An American Muslim soldier praying.

American slave owners. Today, about half of the Muslims in the United States are African Americans.[12] The Nation of Islam has played an important role in the US Muslim community. However, the majority of African American Muslims are not members of the organization but are rather Sunni Muslims whose beliefs and practices are like those of other Sunni Muslims around the world. The Nation was founded by a man who was known by several different names, among them Wallace Ford and Wali D. Fard. In the 1930s, Fard established the Temple of Islam in Detroit, Michigan, and he preached that all Black people were originally Muslims. Eventually, a student of his named Elijah Muhammad succeeded him as the leader of the Nation of Islam. The Nation differs from mainstream Islam on several key teachings. Most significantly, followers regard Fard as God incarnate, and Elijah is considered his prophet. The Nation of Islam has been controversial in the United States because of teachings that suggest the natural supremacy of Black people and encourage the rejection of white society. Despite its controversial nature, the Nation has been active in improving the lives of Black Americans.

When Elijah Muhammad died in 1975, the Nation of Islam split. One group, led by his son Warith Deen Muhammad, moved away from the teachings of the Nation toward mainstream Sunni Islam and became known as the American Muslim Mission. This is the largest organized group of African American Muslims today. Louis Farrakhan, a radical preacher who is very controversial for his espousal of Black supremacist ideas and politics, has led the other group, which retained the name Nation of Islam, for many years.

Malcolm X, a leader in the Black Power movement of the 1960s, was perhaps the most famous American Muslim and the most famous member of the Nation of Islam. He was raised a Christian with the name Malcolm Little and converted to Islam while serving a prison sentence. He took the name X as a statement decrying his "slave name" of Little, in reference to the historical practice of enslaved people being given the surnames of their masters. He eventually took the name Malik al-Shabazz. Malcolm X was affiliated with the Nation of Islam for several years and became an influential public figure. However, after he made the hajj to Mecca in the 1960s, he moved toward mainstream Islam and eventually separated himself from the Nation. In his autobiography, he movingly describes the sense of harmony and unity he felt while on hajj with Muslims of all colors, ethnicities, and cultural backgrounds.[13]

Many American Muslims today are either immigrants or the descendants of immigrants. Like all immigrants to the United States, Muslims have come in waves from many parts of the world. In the late nineteenth century, Muslims migrated from the Middle East, namely, Syria, Jordan, and Lebanon, to the Americas for economic reasons. Most of them were uneducated, and most were single men. This resulted in much intermarriage between these Muslim newcomers and people of varied cultural and religious backgrounds.

In the middle of the twentieth century, Muslim immigrants began to come from other areas of the Middle East, the Soviet Union, and Eastern Europe. Many in this wave of immigrants were educated and from wealthy families, and many had a great interest in assimilating to the wider American population. In later years, Muslim peoples came to the United States from South Asia, Iran, and other parts of the world. Many in this most recent wave have had less interest in assimilating to mainstream American culture, instead hoping to preserve their cultural and religious heritage while still engaging productively in American community life; we'll return to this later in the chapter.

In 2015, several hundred members of the Muslim community of Hamtramck, Michigan, rallied at City Hall to condemn terrorism and ISIS.

Islam and Politics in the Twenty-First Century

In the twenty-first century, Muslims face questions about the role of religion in private and public life and relationships with other religious communities in plural environments. In many countries, as exemplified by participants in the "Arab Spring" demonstrations of early 2011, Muslims are considering the relationship between Islam and democracy. Although many thinkers and activists argue that Islam is inherently compatible with democracy because of examples such as the historical emphasis on consensus, some have suggested that democracy is a Western concept that is not compatible with an Islamic system of government.

In Chapter 1, we considered Bruce Lincoln's theory regarding the potential of religion to facilitate violent conflict. And as nearly every chapter in this book shows, individuals, groups, and states have invoked religion to engage in or to justify warfare, colonization, and other forms of violence. In recent years, ISIS (Islamic State in Iraq and Syria) has been frequently in the news. Like al-Qaeda before it, ISIS has claimed responsibility for many terrorist attacks around the world, including suicide bombings. Political scientists define terrorism as a premeditated act of violence, often against civilians, that has a specific political goal. Perpetrators may believe that there is a religious basis or reward for their violent actions, or they may attempt to justify the violence with religious ideologies. In the 9/11 attacks on the United States, Osama bin Laden and al-Qaeda used religion to explain their actions, and bin Laden claimed to be influenced by the writings of Sayyid Qutb.

In the early 2000s, ISIS was established as an umbrella movement for al-Qaeda in Iraq and other Sunni insurgent groups. In 2014, ISIS leaders claimed to have established a "caliphate" in northern Iraq and to be applying Islamic law. However, ISIS has taken an extremely violent approach to dealing with adversaries (both Muslim and non-Muslim) and even journalists. Muslims worldwide have denounced ISIS, just as they did with al-Qaeda. And although al-Qaeda and ISIS claim to be founded on Islamic principles, it is important to understand the rise of such groups in their historical and political context. Many political scientists think that the war in Iraq, launched in 2003, further destabilized an already precarious state, exacerbated interreligious tensions, and contributed to the devastating conditions under which ISIS arose and gained support.

Muslims around the world have expressed dismay at the use of Islam to facilitate or justify violence, contending that terrorist attacks are antithetical to the teachings of Islam, which prohibit the killing of innocents. Muslims cite scriptural evidence for this stance in a Qur'anic verse (5:32) that equates the killing of one innocent person to the killing of all of humanity. Empirical evidence also exists showing that contemporary Muslims condemn violence committed in the name of Islam. For example, in 2014, Heraa Hashmi, a student at the University of Colorado, began compiling a spreadsheet of Muslim activists, leaders, and thinkers worldwide who have condemned such violence. Her project recorded nearly 6,000 public statements of condemnation by Muslim political leaders, religious leaders, thinkers, and activists.

In the twenty-first century, numerous political conflicts around the globe have oppressed and imperiled Muslims. In Buddhist-majority Myanmar, a Muslim-minority ethnic community known as the Rohingya has faced severe persecution from the state since 2017. Rohingya are denied citizenship, and many have been killed and displaced from their homes. Hundreds of thousands of Rohingya have fled as refugees, mostly to neighboring Bangladesh. In 2018, a United Nations report called Myanmar's military assault on Rohingyas as having "genocidal intent."

In China, an ethnic-minority Muslim community called the Uighurs currently faces persecution and detention in western China's Xinjiang region. Since 2016, up to 1 million Uighur Muslims have been detained without charge in so-called reeducation camps. The Chinese state's position has been that it is combating religious extremism, although journalists report that Muslims are being detained for basic religious practices like prayer and modest dress.

13.6 The History of Islam: Different Ways of Being Muslim

Most of what we discuss in this chapter is applicable to both major branches of Islam, the Sunni and the Shi'a. Although the essential beliefs of the two branches are the same—notably, the oneness of God, the Qur'an as the word of God, and Muhammad as the messenger of God—there are some important differences between them.

Who Are the Sunni?

Sunnis make up the majority of Muslims worldwide, about 85 to 90 percent, and the Shi'a make up about 10 percent of the global Muslim population. As you learned earlier, the Sunni and Shi'a split began over the leadership of the Muslim community after the death of the Prophet Muhammad. The majority of Muhammad's companions thought that he had not chosen a successor, and so they supported Abu Bakr as the next leader. However, Sunnism did not develop into a distinct branch of Islam until about 300 years later. At that point, certain scholars emphasized that Muslims should primarily follow the example of the Prophet Muhammad, the Qur'an, and the opinions of earlier scholars with regard to engaging in rationalist thought like that of the Mutazilites. The word *sunni* comes from this emphasis on the sunna of the Prophet.

One of the differences between the Sunni and the Shi'a concerns the sources of Islamic law, which we discuss in more detail in a later section. In short, although both branches agree on the importance of the Qur'an and the sunna, in Sunni Islam an additional source is the consensus of the community. This became a source of law because of a hadith that reported the Prophet saying, "My community will never agree upon an error." Of course, it is impossible to solicit the opinion of every Muslim on a particular legal question, so Sunnis have generally agreed that the community in question consists of the ulama, or legal scholars.

Who Are the Shi'a?

The Shi'a are in the majority in Iran and Iraq, and they form significant minorities in other countries, including Pakistan and India. In addition to believing that Muhammad designated 'Ali to be his successor, the Shi'a believe that Muhammad passed on special religious knowledge to his relatives through 'Ali. Therefore, to the Shi'a, only Muhammad's family and their descendants should lead the Muslim community. This belief in a continuing spiritual leadership of the Muslim community through the line of successors is the most significant contrast between Sunni and Shi'i Islam (the term *Shi'a* is the plural form of *Shi'i*; *Shi'i* is also the adjectival form). For the Shi'a, the rightful leaders of the Muslim community are known as imams, the same term used for someone who leads prayer. For the Shi'a, the imam is both the political and the religious leader of the community, and he possesses the special religious knowledge that Muhammad passed on to the members of his family. 'Ali is regarded as the first imam. It is important to note that, although the imam has a very prominent role in Shi'ism, he is not a prophet.

The authority of the Shi'i imams has a special role in Shi'i law that we do not see in Sunni approaches to Islamic law. The Shi'i schools do not recognize consensus as a source of law but instead focus on the infallibility of the imam. Islamic scholarship is highly important in the Shi'i tradition. Also, although scholarship and learning

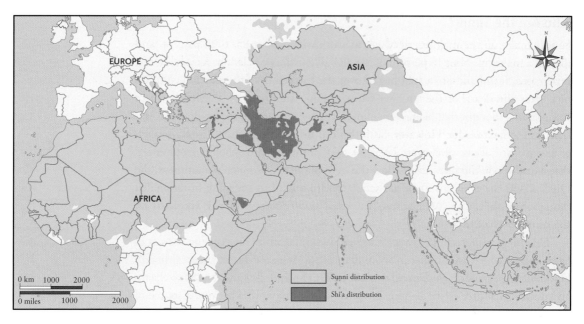

World Sunni and Shi'a distribution.

are valued among Sunni Muslims, there is a more formal religious authority structure in Shi'ism that we do not find in Sunni Islam.

Shi'ism itself has several branches, which differ in how they trace the line of imams in descent from 'Ali. The largest branch is known as the Twelvers, who make up the majority of Muslims in Iran and Iraq. The Twelvers believe that the line of imams went through several generations until the twelfth imam disappeared in the ninth century. This twelfth imam is considered to be in "occultation," or hiding. Twelvers believe that he will eventually return. In the meantime, the Islamic scholars are considered responsible for the leadership of the Muslim community. This idea was important in the new government set up in Iran after the 1979 revolution.

An Iraqi soldier stands guard as Shi'i pilgrims approach the holy city of Karbala.

Another branch of Shi'ism, known as the *Ismailis*, believes that there has been an unbroken line of imams from 'Ali until the present day. They take their name from the seventh imam, a man named Ismail, whom the Twelvers do not recognize as an imam.

Sufism

Muslims have sometimes described the shari'a, or Islamic law, as the "outer" way to God because it regulates a person's "outer" existence: how he or she should handle relationships with other people, how he or she should live in a community, and how he or she should worship. (We will discuss shari'a later in this chapter.) For many Muslims, however, there is also an "inner" way to God. This is the mystical tradition of Islam, which is known as Sufism. Like traditions of mysticism in other religions, the goal of a follower of Sufism, a Sufi, is to draw close to and personally experience God. However, unlike mystics of other religions, Sufis base this spiritual quest on the sources of Islam, namely, the Qur'an and the example of Muhammad. Sufism is not a "branch" of Islam so much as a way of being Muslim, and Sufis are found in both in the Sunni and Shi'a traditions.

It is likely that Sufism arose in the years after the death of Muhammad as a response to the worldly excesses and materialism of the Umayyad Dynasty. Many early Sufis were ascetics who taught that a simple way of life was in keeping with the way Muhammad lived. One famous eighth-century Sufi was Hasan of Basra. (Basra is a city in Iraq.) He was known for preaching asceticism and for his constant weeping out of fear of God. A renowned early female Sufi was Rabi'a al-'Adawiyya, also of Basra. Rabi'a was known for her almost giddy happiness in the love of God. There are many wonderful stories about Rabi'a. In one, she criticized Hasan of Basra by telling him that his constant weeping and fear of God drew the focus to himself rather than to God. This theme is echoed in another story, in which she walks through the streets of Basra carrying a pitcher of water and a flaming torch. When asked why she was doing this, she explained that she wanted to set paradise ablaze and put out the fires of hell so people would love God solely for the sake of God—not out of hope of paradise or fear of hell.

After Rabi'a's time, this ideal of intense love for God became a primary focus for Sufis. Love is often expressed in Sufi poetry, which is one of the premier art forms in Islamic history. The following poem, by the great thirteenth-century Sufi poet Jalal-ludin Rumi (1207–1273), describes the beauty of submitting to God. Those who love and submit to God are compared to a moth who is drawn to a candle's flame.

> Love whispers in my ear,
> "Better to be a prey than a hunter,
> Make yourself My fool.
> Stop trying to be the sun and become a speck!
> Dwell at My door and be homeless.
> Don't pretend to be a candle, be a moth,
> so you may taste the savor of Life
> and know the power hidden in serving."[14]

Sufis ground their belief and worship practice in the teachings of the Qur'an. Sufi readings of the Qur'an have often searched for the inner, or hidden, meaning.

The Dome of the Rock in Jerusalem.

This approach to interpreting the Qur'an often focuses on God's love for creation and God's closeness to humanity. Sufis often emphasize the teachings of the *hadith qudsi*, which focus on these themes.

Sufis consider Muhammad the ideal human, and they strive to emulate the way he lived his life. Sufis emphasize the story of the miraculous night when Muhammad journeyed from Mecca to Jerusalem and from there ascended to heaven to meet God. The ascension to heaven is known as the *miraj*. Muslims believe that the Angel Gabriel came to Muhammad one night while he was sleeping and took him to Jerusalem. From there, Muhammad ascended upward through the many levels of heaven. He met earlier prophets like Jesus and Moses. Eventually, Muhammad came into the presence of God. God gave him significant blessings and special spiritual knowledge that he later passed on to his companions, particularly 'Ali. Because Muhammad is believed to have personally experienced the presence of God, Sufis consider him to be the first Sufi and the source of the special spiritual knowledge they seek. In East Africa and the Middle East, Muslims learn of the *miraj* through epic poems, which are recited on special occasions like *Mawlid al-Nabi*, a celebration of the birth of the Prophet.

The night journey is mentioned in the Qur'an (17:1) and the hadith literature and is considered by many Muslims to be the greatest of all Muhammad's spiritual experiences. Because Muhammad ascended to heaven from Jerusalem, the city holds a special place in Islam, and it is one of the three Muslim holy cities, along with Mecca and Medina. In the year 691 CE, the beautiful shrine known as the Dome of the Rock was built over the spot from which Muhammad ascended to heaven. The Dome of the Rock is located on the place known as the Temple Mount, where the ancient Jewish temples were located. It is therefore easy to understand why this place in the center of Jerusalem is special to both Muslims and Jews. This is one of the primary reasons that the status of Jerusalem is so central to the Arab-Israeli conflict today: practitioners of both faiths (as well as Christians) consider the city to be holy and thus want to have unfettered access to it.

Most Sufis agree that an individual needs guidance along the spiritual path to God. As a result, a master–disciple relationship is very important in Sufism. The shaykh, or master, directs the spiritual training of the novices. In the early centuries of Islam, respected shaykhs would guide several pupils, and as a result a number of Sufi orders, known as *tariqas*, developed around particular Sufi masters. Each order traces a spiritual lineage of learned leaders back to Muhammad and from Muhammad to God. Muhammad is believed to have passed on his special religious knowledge to his companions, who then passed it down through the generations from master to disciple.

Sufi orders emphasize the necessity of some type of *dhikr*. *Dhikr* means "recollection" and refers to Sufi practice in which the believers strive to "recollect" God so completely that they forget themselves. Dhikr can take many forms and varies from order to order; some forms are similar to meditation. Sometimes dhikr is as simple as the recitation of the shahada, and sometimes it is much more elaborate. The Mevlevi order, based on the teachings of Rumi, has an elaborate practice. In the West, they are often called the "Whirling Dervishes" because their spiritual practice involves controlled whirling.

Not all Sufi practice takes place in the formal context of the orders. In many parts of the world, Muslims may participate in Sufi practice without affiliation to an order. A good example is the practice of saint veneration. Many Sufis venerate shaykhs or saints who were well known and respected for their religious learning and spirituality. In some areas, such as Pakistan and northern India, the tombs of deceased shaykhs have become

Mevlevi dhikr; Mevlevis are sometimes known as Whirling Dervishes.

places of pilgrimage. At the tombs, people seek blessings from the saints. Tomb visitation is very common in South Asia, when the celebration of the saints' death date can draw thousands of pilgrims. Many pilgrims are not affiliated with a Sufi order, and some are not even Muslim; people of all faiths may recognize the power of a saint.

Throughout Islamic history, occasional tension has arisen between Sufis and other Muslims. For example, the practice of saint veneration has drawn criticism from some, who argue that the celebration of saints compromises the oneness of God by raising

Pilgrims at the shrine of Hazrat Mu'in ud-Din Chishti in Ajmer (Rajasthan), India.

mere mortals to the level of the divine (recall al-Wahhab's criticism of saint veneration). Those who participate in saint veneration do not regard saints as divine. Rather, they view saints as close friends of God, who are filled with blessings that can be transferred to others. Historically, Sufis have sometimes been criticized by other Muslims for neglecting the five pillars in favor of more esoteric religious knowledge and practice. However, this was never a majority opinion among Sufis. Indeed, some Sufis have made a specific effort to reconcile the shari'a and Sufism; in the eleventh century, the scholar al-Ghazali established Sufism as a branch of formal learning in the Islamic sciences.

VOICES: An Interview with Hadi Eltahlawi

Hadi Eltahlawi is a graduate student in journalism. He moved to the United States from Egypt in 2022 for his studies. Hadi is planning to earn a PhD in journalism and work as a full-time university professor in the future.

Hadi Eltahlawi.

How does Islam help you in your personal quest for happiness or fulfillment?

There is a verse in the Quran that provides an understanding of my own experience with happiness. It is in 13:28 "Those who have believed and whose hearts are assured by the remembrance of Allah. Unquestionably, by the remembrance of Allah hearts are assured." The sense of assurance and reliance on Allah once I read or listen to the Quran just brings me peace. Apart from this, Islam guides my search of happiness through other ways. Islam allows the pursuit of happiness though worldly pleasures, but has created limits and rules as to not be enslaved by one's desires. It also encourages brotherhood and solidarity among Muslims which creates a sense of belonging wherever I go.

How do the teachings and values of Islam shape your life, especially when you make major life decisions involving such things as education, career, marriage, or partnership?

The priority whenever I am about to make a major life decision is to make sure that it is not against, in any way, the teachings of Islam. To me, no matter what the decision is, or its mundane value, if I disobey Allah in any way, my conscience would trouble me. And I do believe firmly that if I disobey Allah in the pursuit of anything, it won't end well. And Islam's values are related to every aspect of my life. I try not to abandon them as best as I can. And I found that my life is balanced and stable in that way. But once I deviate, things start to crumble somehow, and my mental state gets deeply affected.

How does Islam help you when you experience a significant loss or disappointment in life?

Whenever that happens, I always try to remind myself of the essence of Islam, in the most basic sense. It is the complete surrender to the will of Allah. And I mean an unshakeable belief that Allah has a plan for everyone, and whatever he wills should be accepted no matter what it is. I do grieve whenever I face a huge loss, but knowing that this life isn't the end of it relieves me. This life is nothing but a small point in the eternal life of my soul. And I know that what I should be worried about is the afterlife, which is the goal of every Muslim. But this life is just ephemeral and will end eventually. The Prophet Muhammad (peace be upon him) did grieve, when he lost his son Ibrahim for instance, but never said something that would anger Allah. At the end of the day, He loves us more than our mothers, so why fear or lose hope? He knows best and I just trust him unconditionally.

13.7 Islam as a Way of Life: Observances

What does it mean to be a practicing Muslim? What does one do on a daily basis? In this section, we discuss worship practice, the Islamic year and important holidays, and Islamic law. We also explore gender roles and family life and the complex concept of jihad.

The Qur'an in Daily Life

The Qur'an is an important part of the daily life of all Muslims, and the text itself is treated with great reverence and respect. To Muslims, the Qur'an is authentic only in the original Arabic. This means that a translation, such as an English version of the Qur'an, is not the holy book itself but merely an interpretation of the meaning. In many Muslim countries, children are encouraged to attend Qur'an schools, where they are often introduced to religious study through learning to memorize and recite sections of the Qur'an. In most communities, both boys and girls study the Qur'an, and people will often continue to study the Qur'an throughout adulthood. Indeed, Muhammad encouraged all Muslims to pursue a life of learning.

To Muslims, the true meaning of the Qur'an can only be understood in the original Arabic. The beauty of the language is said to lend itself to the spiritual nature of the words of God. Thus, Muslims around the world learn to recite the Qur'an in Arabic—even if they do not speak or understand the language. (Often, a teacher will explain the meaning of the text in the local language.) Verses of the Qur'an are recited during the daily prayers, and the Qur'an is also recited at numerous other occasions, including weddings, funerals, birth celebrations, holidays, and political events.

Hearing the Qur'an recited by a talented person can be a moving experience for people of all faiths, even if they do not understand the words. Although people can achieve great fame for their ability to recite beautifully, Muslims do not normally regard recitation as entertainment or singing. In many places, children and adults recite the Qur'an in highly organized competitions that can resemble an American spelling bee.

What Is Jihad?

The term **jihad** comes from an Arabic verb meaning to "struggle" or "strive" and has historically had complex meanings. The concept of jihad is often distorted in contemporary Western media. In general, the term *jihad* means exerting oneself in the name of God. Jihad can refer to several types of struggle on both personal and social levels. The term is used only rarely in the Qur'an, and nowhere is it explicitly linked to armed struggle. Rather, it was early in Islamic history that the term became associated with defensive military endeavors against the enemies of the growing Muslim community. Some Muslim groups both today and throughout history have called for a military jihad against nonbelievers, even out of the context of defense of the Muslim community. You can see how the term is used in different verses of the Qur'an:

> O Believers, go out in the cause of God, (whether) light or heavy, and strive (jihad) in the service of God, wealth and soul. This is better for you if you understand.
>
> —9:41

> And strive (jihad) in the way of God with a service worthy of Him. He has chosen you and laid no hardship on you in the way of faith, the faith of your forebear Abraham. He named you Muslim earlier, and in this (Qur'an) in order that the Prophet be witness over you, and you be witness over mankind. So be firm in devotion, pay the zakat, and hold on firmly to God. He is your friend: How excellent a friend is He, how excellent a helper!
>
> —22:78

> So do not listen to unbelievers and strive (jihad) against them with greater effort.
>
> —25:52

Muslims often refer to the *greater* jihad as one's struggle to become a better person by striving against one's own sinful tendencies and to live in accordance with the will of God. Although we often see the term *jihad* translated into English as "holy war," Muslims regard the military connotations of the term as the *lesser* jihad. The idea of "greater and lesser" jihad comes from the hadith literature. Muhammad is reported to have said, upon returning home from a battle, "We return from the little jihad to the greater jihad."

The Shari'a: Islamic Law

Muslims believe that God, as the creator of the universe and humanity, established a wide-ranging set of guidelines for human beings to follow. These guidelines are known as the **shari'a**. The literal translation of the Arabic term *shari'a* is the "road" or "way." In English, it is most often translated as "law." However, the shari'a encompasses a much broader range of law and legal activity than what is normally associated with law in the Western world. The shari'a regulates almost every aspect of daily life for believers. Proper religious practice is included in the shari'a, and so are areas of law that North Americans find more familiar, such as marriage and divorce, inheritance, commerce, and crime. However, few countries have actually applied Islamic law in full, either today or in the past.

In Islamic belief, God is the sole legislator. In theory, this means that while humanity can interpret law, humans cannot legislate or make new laws. The shari'a is drawn from several sources. The Qur'an is the primary legal source. In the early Meccan suras, general legal principles are introduced. These include the importance of generosity, of obeying God's commands, and of performing prayer and religious duties with sincerity. In the later Medinan suras, many technical legal matters are presented in great detail. Some of these suras contain specific laws governing community relations, marriage and family, and inheritance and commerce.

Islamic scholars throughout history have recognized that the Qur'an does not address every legal situation. As a result, there are also other sources of Islamic law. Different branches of Islam, such as the Sunni and Shi'a traditions, and different schools of thought within them have recognized different sources as more or less important. For example, in Sunni Islam, many scholars have referenced the sunna as a very important additional legal source, which is second only to the Qur'an in importance. For centuries and up to the present day, Islamic jurists have consulted the sunna for answers to legal questions that are not explicitly addressed by the Qur'an. The sunna is important because Muhammad is considered the ideal human, the person closest to God, and the recipient of the revelation of the Qur'an. For that reason, his words and actions became an important legal source as a model for human behavior. Furthermore, Muhammad acted as a judge and a mediator of disputes in Medina, and the way he resolved legal conflicts is recorded in the hadith.

This building in Zanzibar, Tanzania, has been used to house both Islamic and secular primary courts, as well as government offices.

There are also other sources of Islamic law. In the sections on Sunni and Shi'a Islam, we discussed sources of law that are distinct to each. For example, many Sunni scholars agree that if a legal matter is not addressed by the Qur'an or the sunna, then it is appropriate to use human reason to find an analogous situation; reasoning by analogy is known as *qiyas*. In addition, Sunni Muslims recognize the consensus of the Muslim community as a source of law; this is known as *ijma* and is recognized as a source of law because a hadith reports that Muhammad said, "My community will never agree upon an error." Law for Shi'a Muslims is somewhat different. For example, Shi'a legal traditions do not recognize consensus as a source of law but do recognize the imams as an important source of law, as they are considered infallible.

Both historically and today, studying shari'a is an important part of Islamic education. Those who gain expertise in the law may have a special status in the community. The term *ulama* refers to Islamic legal scholars. Among these scholars are legal practitioners known as *qadis*, court judges who issue rulings on various matters. A *mufti* is an expert in Islamic law who is qualified to give nonbinding legal opinions, known as *fatwas*.

Today, many Muslim-majority states include Islamic law and courts in the state legal systems. However, in most countries in which Islamic law is applied,

Case files from an
Islamic court in East
Africa.

Islamic courts handle only matters of family law and only for Muslims. Family law includes issues such as marriage, divorce, child custody, and inheritance. Only a very few countries, such as Iran and Saudi Arabia, recognize Islamic criminal law in the state legal system. One reason is that many countries that were colonized by European powers adopted European legal codes for criminal matters. Also, some countries have determined that centuries-old laws are not appropriate for modern contexts.

Many Muslims try to live in accordance with Islamic law in their personal lives, even if they do not live in a country that recognizes Islamic law. Other Muslims, however, do not feel that it is important to do so. As noted earlier, Islamic law informs the daily life of the believer and regulates how a Muslim worships God. In addition, much like Jewish law, Islamic law regulates what a believer should eat and drink. For example, Muslims are prohibited from consuming pork and alcohol. Much of the legal basis for the prohibition on pork comes from the Qur'an. The prohibition on alcohol, though mentioned in the Qur'an, is more thoroughly developed in the hadith literature. It is important to remember, however, that not all Muslims adhere strictly to dietary codes or consider this to be an essential part of Muslim practice. As with every religious tradition, there is a wide range of commitment to ideals and required practices among those who consider themselves Muslims.

13.8 Islam as a Way of Life: The Islamic Year and Holidays

The Islamic calendar begins with the hijra, that is, the migration of Muhammad and the early Muslim community from Mecca to Medina in 622 CE. The Islamic calendar is lunar because the Qur'an stipulates that the moon should be the measure of time. In most of the Muslim world, however, people use both the lunar and solar calendars. The Qur'an also designates the names of the twelve months of the year.

Several important celebrations and feast days occur throughout the Islamic year, and Muslims around the world celebrate these days in a variety of ways. The Feast of Sacrifice, or ʿId (or Eid) al-Adha, is the primary holiday of the Muslim year. The feast takes place at the end of the hajj season, and it is celebrated by all Muslims—not just those who made the pilgrimage that year. The feast commemorates Abraham's willingness to sacrifice his son at God's command. In many countries, offices and shops close for two days, and people spend time with their families and friends. In commemoration of the ram that was sacrificed instead of Ishmael, Muslims are expected to slaughter an animal to mark the holiday. However, because this is not always possible, Muslims may make charitable donations as a substitute.

The second most significant holiday in the Muslim calendar is ʿId al-Fitr, the Feast of Fast-Breaking. This holiday marks the end of the month of Ramadan.

This feast is a time of joy and forgiveness and is celebrated in many different ways around the world. Muslims mark the day by attending congregational prayers, visiting friends and family, or celebrating in public festivals and carnivals. Often, Muslims will wear elegant clothing for the holiday, and children are dressed in their finest new clothes. In some places, children are also given special treats, money, or gifts.

The Prophet Muhammad's birth is also an occasion for celebration in many parts of the Muslim world, such as North Africa, East Africa, and South Asia. This celebration is known as *Mawlid al-Nabi* and takes place around the twelfth day of the third month of the Islamic calendar. The birth of the Prophet may be marked by state-sponsored ceremonies. Elsewhere, the birthday is marked by all-night recitation sessions, at which participants recite the Qur'an and devotional poetry. Some Muslims criticize the celebration of the Prophet's birth. They argue that such celebration of Muhammad risks elevating the Prophet to the status of God. Muslims in Saudi Arabia, for example, do not generally celebrate *Mawlid al-Nabi*.

The month of the Islamic calendar known as Muharram is especially significant to the Shi'a. This is because the martyrdom of Muhammad's grandson Husayn, discussed earlier in this chapter, is recalled on the tenth of the month. This date is called **'Ashura**, and the entire month of Muharram is recognized as an important and somber time. At this time of year, the death of Husayn is commemorated in many ways by the Shi'a in places such as Iran and Iraq. Husayn's story is retold through passion plays and street processions, called Ta'ziya, in which Muslims re-enact the events of Husayn's death.

For the Shi'a, the tombs of the Prophet's family are popular sites for pilgrimages. Through these pilgrimages, Muslims commemorate and honor the Prophet's family. Karbala, where Husayn was martyred and is said to be buried, is an important pilgrimage site in Iraq.

13.9 Islam as a Way of Life: Family And Community

Marriage and family life are the cornerstones of Muslim communities. In this section of the chapter, we will consider the nature of family and community in Muslim contexts by looking specifically at marriage, divorce, and conceptions of gender identity and gender roles.

Marriage

Devout Muslims, who strive to follow the example of the Prophet in their daily lives, consider Muhammad to have set the example of marriage and to have been the ideal husband and father. As a result, marriage is generally regarded as incumbent upon all Muslim men and women when they reach adulthood. Celibacy is not normally encouraged, and sexual pleasure is considered a gift from God to be enjoyed within a marriage.

Much variation exists throughout the Muslim world concerning marriage arrangements, weddings, and the organization of the family life. In some areas, marriages for young people are arranged by their parents, whereas in others, women and men select their own marriage partners. However, in most Muslim communities, dating is not an acceptable practice—even among Muslims living in North America. Furthermore, adult children in many Muslim families live with their parents until they marry, even if they are financially able to live on their own. Regardless of the method of arranging marriages, according to the shari'a, young men and women may reject a marriage partner they deem unsuitable; the consent of both the bride and the groom is necessary for the marriage to take place. However, this legal right does not always coincide with community or cultural norms. In some cultures, a bride's silence about her parents' choice of a marriage partner is considered to indicate acceptance of the proposal.

In Islam, a marriage is considered a contractual relationship. For the marriage to be valid, the bride, the groom, and witnesses must sign a marriage contract. The contract designates the *mahr*, which is the gift a bride will receive from the groom and his family. The gift may be cash or other property. The marriage contract may be considered invalid without the *mahr*, though the amount may vary greatly from family to family and culture to culture. The amount depends not only on the family's wealth but also on community norms. For example, urban Muslims in the Middle East might give a *mahr* of thousands of dollars, whereas the normal amount in a small village might be much less. According to shari'a, the *mahr* is solely the property of the bride. However, in many cultures, a bride's parents may take some of the *mahr* due to customary practices and local expectations.

In Muslim weddings, the bride and groom may be separated for most of the festivities on the wedding day. The groom usually signs the marriage contract in a mosque in the company of his male friends and relatives. The marriage official, often an imam, then takes the contract to the bride in her family's home, where she is accompanied by her female relatives and friends. Wedding celebrations are often large affairs, and feasting, Qur'an recitation, and sometimes music and dancing may accompany the signing of the contract. In many communities, men and women celebrate entirely separately. This is because some Muslims do not consider it acceptable for men and women to socialize together. In some cultures, the bride is taken to the groom's home in a big procession at the end of the day. There, the new couple shares a special meal and begins their life together.

According to most interpretations of Islamic law, Muslim men are allowed to marry up to four wives. However, this is only under certain conditions, and only if the man can support all his wives and treat them equally. For example, the verses in the Qur'an concerning polygamy suggest that the practice is appropriate in times of warfare when there may be many unmarried women. Furthermore, the Qur'an states, "Marry such women as seem good to you, two, three, four; but if you fear you will not be equitable, then marry only one" (4:3). A later verse says that "You will not be equitable between your wives, even if you try" (4:129). Some thinkers, such as the Egyptian reformer Muhammad Abduh (about whom you read earlier in this chapter), argued that these two verses actually prohibited polygamy because the later verse stated that no man could possibly treat multiple wives equitably, which is a necessary condition of polygamy. Abduh also contended that although polygamy may have been necessary in the time of the Prophet to protect women who had no one to care for

A Muslim bride signs her marriage contract.

them, it was destructive in the modern context. However, most Muslims have considered polygamy legal, though the occurrence of the practice varies tremendously around the world, and some countries, like Tunisia, have banned it entirely.

Divorce   Several types of divorce are permitted in Islam. Guidelines for divorce come from both the Qur'an and hadith literature. One type is divorce by male unilateral repudiation. In this type of divorce, a man writes or pronounces the formula "I, (the man's name), divorce you, (the wife's name)." In classical Islamic law, this type of divorce does not need the approval of the wife or a legal authority. However, in many countries today, unilateral divorce is no longer permissible, and men and women must both file for divorce in court. According to shari'a, women may seek divorce from Islamic judges on a variety of grounds. Stipulations for divorce are occasionally written into the marriage contract. For example, a woman may specify that she can divorce her husband if he marries another wife. Divorce is common in some Muslim countries and uncommon in others. In some places, a divorced man or woman is dishonored and finds it difficult to remarry, whereas in others there is little or no stigma attached to divorce.

Gender and Sexuality

There is much variation in how gender roles are perceived and interpreted throughout Muslim cultures. As in other religious traditions, such as Judaism, Christianity, and Hinduism, patriarchal cultural norms are sometimes justified in terms of religion. When we consider the historical context in which it was revealed, the Qur'an introduced many legal rights and privileges to women that they had not previously enjoyed. For example, women were given the right to divorce their husbands on a variety of grounds, they were allowed to inherit and hold property that remained theirs even in marriage (women in England did not gain this right until the late nineteenth century), and they were given the right to refuse arranged marriages. The Qur'an also prohibited female infanticide.

According to Islamic belief, women and men are viewed as equals in the eyes of God and will be judged on their own accord. In the Qur'an, verse 35 of sura 33 addresses this issue:

> Verily for all men and women who have come to submission,
> Men and women who are believers,
> Men and women who are devout,
> Truthful men and truthful women.
> Men and women with endurance,
> Men and women who are modest,
> Men and women who give alms,
> Men and women who observe fasting,
> Men and women who guard their private parts,
> And those men and women who remember God a great deal,
> For them God has forgiveness and a great reward.[15]

The Qur'an requires all Muslims, women and men, to live a righteous life and to seek education. Women may work outside the home, though this is still uncommon in some areas. According to religious law, all of a woman's earnings remain her property. Thus, women are not required to use their earnings to support the family and maintain the home; it is a man's legal duty to provide for his family, even if his wife is wealthier than he is. Of course, in practice, many women contribute their earnings to the household.

Despite all these rights, the place of women in Islam has sometimes been interpreted in very strict fashion. For example, in Afghanistan, the Taliban have denied women the right to work outside the home, the right to be educated, and even the right to walk freely in the street. However, this strict interpretation of religious texts and traditions is far from mainstream. Most Muslims view the Taliban's orders as radical and even religiously unlawful.

Along these same lines, much cultural variation exists in the practices regarding interaction between Muslim men and women. In some parts of the world, Muslim men and women live very separate lives. The seclusion of women is called *purdah* in South Asia and is practiced by some Hindus and Sikhs, as well as some Muslims. Elsewhere, as in many parts of Southeast Asia and Africa, Muslim men and women intermingle freely.

The Qur'an encourages both men and women to dress and behave modestly. The verses concerning dress—particularly that of women—are interpreted in many ways. Modest men's and women's dress takes many different cultural forms. In some cultures, modest dress is interpreted as long pants and a modest shirt or tunic for both men and women. In other contexts, Muslim women wear a type of cloak over their clothing when they leave the home. And some Muslim women choose to cover their heads and hair with a scarf. But this is not solely a Muslim practice: in the Middle East and Mediterranean, women covered their heads long before the time of Muhammad.[16] Covering the head has also been common practice among many Christian, Jewish, Hindu, and Sikh women. Although the word *veil* is often used in the West as a catch-all

Muslim family in modest attire.

term for modest head coverings, the terms used for elements of modest clothing vary from culture to culture. Even so, several terms derived from Arabic are commonly recognized around the world. For example, the Arabic term *hijab* may refer simply to modest dress or more specifically to a scarf that covers the hair and neck. The term *niqab*, also from Arabic, normally refers to a covering of the nose and mouth. The Arabic term *abaya* refers to a full-length cloak-like garment. A *burqa*, also from Arabic, usually refers to a garment that covers the head, body, and most of the face.

Many Muslim women dress modestly strictly out of religious commitment. For others, wearing modest dress is an important move toward gender equality in the work-

Three young Palestinian students in modest dress.

place and the public sphere. Such women believe that when they are dressed modestly, they are valued by others on their merit alone, not on their appearance. To others, wearing modest dress makes a statement of resistance to Western scholars and activists by demonstrating that feminism can be defined in myriad ways in different cultural and religious contexts. Some Muslim women say they pity Western women, whom they believe must dress in a way that serves men's pleasure in viewing the female form. One matter that has received much attention in the

twenty-first-century press is that of "Islamic dress" in Western Europe. In France in 2004, schoolgirls were prohibited from wearing headscarves because officials argued it violated France's commitment to secularism. Many Muslims thought this was a violation of their freedom to practice religion. In 2015, Germany's highest court reversed its 2003 ban on female teachers wearing headscarves. Today, German teachers can wear headscarves as long as they are not disruptive.

We should not consider the status of women in any religious tradition without also considering historical change; this is particularly true of Islam because of the many negative stereotypes Muslim women have faced in recent years. As we discussed earlier in this chapter, several important reformers in the nineteenth and twentieth centuries sought to improve women's status in Muslim countries and cultures. As we learned, many of these reformers focused on proper understanding of religious sources and Islamic law concerning women.

In much of the twentieth century, particularly in the first half, Muslim feminists were upper-class women who had the time and leisure to deliberate these issues, not working-class women whose labor was necessary to support their families. One of the most famous of these early Muslim feminists was Huda Shaarawi (1879–1947), an educated upper-class Egyptian woman who symbolically removed her face veil in an Alexandria train station in 1923. Shaarawi was president and founder of the Egyptian Feminist Union and did not believe that veiling was an Islamic requirement. When she removed her veil, she had just returned from a women's conference in Rome. She encouraged women to cast off their headscarves in a quest for liberation. Many Egyptian women, particularly educated and elite women, were inspired by her example and ceased wearing face veils and headscarves. Shaarawi remained an activist and feminist leader throughout her life. She founded schools and medical facilities in Egypt and also advocated for women's rights throughout the Arab world.

In the twenty-first century, Muslim women in most countries around the world are free to choose how modestly they will dress. In 2018, even the generally conservative country of Saudi Arabia eliminated a law requiring head coverings and abayas for women. As discussed earlier in this chapter, in recent years, huge crowds have protested Iran's strict enforcement of women's modest dress following the 2022 death of Mahsa Amini while in custody.

Sexuality   In the Islamic tradition, sexuality is something to be enjoyed and embraced within a marriage. Islam is often described as a "sex positive" religion, in that sexuality is seen as an aspect of the wonder of God's creation. Throughout the ages, Islamic scholars have emphasized the importance of sexual activity for pleasure and spiritual development, not simply for procreation.[17]

As with other religious traditions, Muslims have a variety of views related to sexual orientation and identity. Historically, Islamic societies have often acknowledged same-sex love and attraction, and the Arabic and Persian literary traditions are rife with such references. In the modern period, many conservative Muslims have condemned homosexuality on religious grounds. However, the Qur'an has little to say on the subject. Some Muslims interpret the Qur'anic story of Lut (Lot) and the destruction of Sodom (similar to the story in the Bible) as prohibiting male homosexuality (for example, 7: 81–82). However, others argue that the narrative indicates God's displeasure with the city's lack of faith, not homosexuality.[18]

Many Muslims have advocated for a wider acceptance of LGBTQ identities and orientations. In the 1980s, scholars at a leading Sunni Islamic institution, Al-Azhar University in Egypt, supported gender reassignment as permissible under Islamic law. This surgery is also permitted in Shi'a-majority Iran, as per a fatwa from Ayatollah Khomeni in 1987. However, transgender Muslims, as other transgender people, still suffer discrimination in many societies. In the United States, an organization called Muslims for Progressive Values (MPV) advocates for gender and sexual diversity in Muslim communities, as embodied in the following issue statement: "MPV endorses the human and civil rights of lesbian, gay, bisexual, transgender, intersex, and queer (LGBTIQ) individuals. We affirm our commitment to ending discrimination based on sexual orientation and gender identity and we support full equality and inclusion of all individuals, regardless of sexual orientation or gender identity, in society and in the Muslim community" (https://www.mpvusa.org/lgbtqi-resources).

VISUAL GUIDE
Islam

Calligraphy developed as an important art form in Islam because of a widespread understanding that imagery is prohibited by the sacred sources of Islam. This example is the word *Allah*. Beautiful calligraphy decorates pages of the Qur'an, mosques, and other items.

Throughout the daily prayer, the believer faces the Ka'ba in Mecca and stands, kneels, and bows his head to the floor. These cycles of movements, along with the proper recitation, are called *raka* and vary in number according to the prayer.

The direction of prayer, known as the *qibla*, is marked in a mosque by a niche called a *mihrab*, which is sometimes highly decorated with designs or Qur'anic verses, like this *mihrab* at a mosque in Cairo, Egypt.

The Ka'ba, a cubical building in Mecca that measures about thirty feet by thirty feet. Many Muslims believe it was built and dedicated to the one God by Abraham and Ishmael.

13.10 Islam as a Way of Life: Engaging with the World

Islam is truly a global religion, and it is one of the largest and fastest growing religions. Today, there are about 1.9 billion Muslims living all over the world. About 85–90 percent of Muslims are Sunni, 10 percent are Shi'a, and the rest belong to a variety of smaller sects. The largest Muslim populations are found in Asia—about 62 percent of the world's Muslims live in Indonesia, Pakistan, India, or Bangladesh—and the Middle East and North Africa (about 20 percent).[19] According to Pew Research, "Muslims make up a majority of the population in 49 countries around the world."[20] Muslims everywhere are responding to a rapidly changing world and increased globalization.

Muslim Engagement in the West

In the United States, Muslims represent only about 1 percent of the population. In Western Europe, the numbers are higher. Muslims make up 6 percent of the population in United Kingdom and 9 percent in France. Demographers project that "10% of all Europeans will be Muslims by 2050."[21] The global Muslim community is growing for a variety of reasons, including demographics—Muslims typically have more children than other religious communities—and conversions. One of the most marked characteristics of the Muslim world today—its regional, ethnic, and political diversity—is likely to increase in the twenty-first century.

As their populations grow in countries like the United States and Canada, Muslims are playing an increasingly important public role. In 2006, the United States saw the election of the first Muslim member of Congress, Representative Keith Ellison of Minnesota. Mr. Ellison remained in Congress until January 2019, when he became the Attorney General of Minnesota. In 2018, the United States elected two Muslim women to Congress, Representative Rashida Tlaib of Michigan and Representative Ilhan Omar of Minnesota. It is notable that Ms. Omar follows Mr. Ellis as the second Muslim elected to Congress representing Minnesota's 5th district, which is predominantly Christian. In 2015, eleven Muslims were elected to the Canadian Parliament—the highest number ever. Muslim politicians are also increasingly prominent in the United Kingdom and Europe. In 2024, the mayors of both London in the United Kingdom and Rotterdam in the Netherlands are Muslim. However, as with many immigrant groups before them, immigrants from the Muslim world face challenges in Europe and North America.

In the United States, Muslims must contend with the difficulty of an American population that does not know much about Islam. In the aftermath of 9/11, North American Muslims faced suspicion and hostility from their non-Muslim neighbors. Some non-Muslim Americans mistakenly viewed the terrorist attacks as representative of Islam and Muslims and, in turn, targeted Muslim communities, breaking windows in mosques and threatening teachers at Islamic elementary schools. In 2010, a controversy about the building of an Islamic center in lower Manhattan turned especially heated. Many non-Muslim Americans were vehemently opposed to the center because it was a few blocks away from the site of the September 11 attacks on New York.

Despite these difficulties, in recent years, many Americans have expressed increased interest in understanding other faiths and cultures—particularly Islam. Also, many American Muslim individuals and communities have made concerted efforts to educate other Americans about their faith, beliefs, and religious practices. Through these outreach efforts and the efforts of non-Muslim Americans to understand Islam and Muslim peoples and cultures, meaningful religious diversity in the United States can be possible.

Islam and Social Justice

In the modern era, Muslims around the world have been active in social justice movements. In the nineteenth and first part of the twentieth century, many of these movements focused on anticolonialism and resistance to European imperialism. Reformers of the time advocated a consideration of Islamic sources in light of contemporary problems and issues. They argued that traditional scholars had not focused as much on social welfare as Islam requires. A number of the reformers discussed earlier in this chapter, such as Jamal al-Din al-Afghani, Muhammad Abduh, Hassan al-Banna, and Sayyid Qutb, had a strong social justice component to their teachings and activism. In his writings, al-Afghani advocated that devout Muslims should be focusing on improving life in this world, rather than simply focusing on the next:

> Islam . . . is concerned with its believers' interests in the world here below and with allowing them to realize success in this life as well as peace in the next life. It seeks "good fortune in two worlds." In its teachings it decrees equality among different peoples and nations. (al-Afghani, 2007: 19)[22]

Hassan al-Banna argued that it was necessary for Islamic societies to work for and maintain justice. A key part of this was the necessity of a moral approach to economics, and the Muslim Brotherhood emphasized Islamic economics as a means to ensure social justice. Sayyid Qutb, also a member of the Muslim Brotherhood, wrote a book called *Social Justice in Islam* (1948), in which he argues that Islam is inherently concerned with earthly matters and "prescribes the basic principles of social justice" (1948), which are built on freedom of conscience, equality, and mutual responsibility in society.[23]

Since the early twentieth century, gender justice has been a focus of many Muslims around the world. Many Muslim feminists have sought paths to gender equality that diverge from Western models. In their view, Islam itself provides the necessary means for women to achieve equality, and thus there is no need to follow a Western model. Many argue that the Qur'an must be reinterpreted in an attempt to eradicate cultural practices that are detrimental to women but have been justified as appropriate Islamic practice. Some have argued that women's status would be much improved only if Islamic laws were properly followed. Some Muslim women in recent decades have reembraced modest dress as a feminist statement. In Egypt, this idea became prominent in the 1980s, and many mothers and grandmothers who had consciously decided against wearing veils or headscarves were dismayed that their daughters were wearing them, ironically with the same rationale their grandmothers used to discard it.

Muslim feminists differ in their approaches to Islam. The Egyptian feminist Zaynab al-Ghazali (1917–2005) advocated increasing women's rights and improving women's status through Islam. Nawal al-Saadawi (1931–2021), also Egyptian, maintained that women can achieve equality only by rejecting what she views as the patriarchal tendencies of religion. Al-Saadawi was both a medical doctor and a writer, and her novels and stories have been both influential and controversial in the Arab world because of her focus on feminist issues and problems facing Arab women. Dr. al-Saadawi was active in the 2011 Egyptian revolution that overthrew the thirty-year presidency of Hosni Mubarak.

In the twenty-first century, gender justice efforts have often focused on reforming Islamic family law as it is applied in practice. In the early 2000s, Egypt, Jordan, and other Muslim-majority Arab countries made state-level changes to divorce law to permit no-fault divorces initiated by women through a divorce procedure known as *khul'*; Pakistan had done something similar in the late twentieth century. Other states have limited or prohibited men's rights to unilateral divorce, known as *talaq*. In 2017, the Indian Supreme Court banned what is known as "triple talaq," or an instant divorce by repudiation. Although women's rights organizations lauded this, when the Supreme Court also criminalized triple talaq in 2019, many interpreted this decision as discriminatory against the Muslim community.

In recent years, Saudi Arabia has loosened or abrogated laws that had restricted women's activities and dress. Iran has seen huge demonstrations in favour of enhanced women's rights and in protest of strict laws of dress for women.

Islam and the Environment

In the Islamic tradition, the natural world provides *ayat* ("signs," i.e., proof) of God. The Qur'an repeatedly indicates that signs of God are discernible in the natural world (e.g., 13:3, 30:24, 16:11, 16:13). This is evident in the following verse, in which numerous aspects of the natural world are described as signs of God:

> Creation of the heavens and the earth, alternation of night and day, and sailing of ships across the ocean with what is useful to man, and the rain that God sends from the sky enlivening the earth that was dead, and the scattering of beasts of all kinds upon it, and the changing of the winds, and the clouds which remain obedient between earth and sky, are surely signs for the wise (2:164)[24]

The Qur'an asserts humanity's stewardship of the Earth, as in the following: "It is He who made you trustees on the earth" (6:165). The Qur'an also frequently instructs humanity not to abuse or corrupt the Earth: "So, O my people, weigh and measure with justness, and do not withhold things due to men, and do not spread corruption in the land, despoiling it" (11:85; also 2:205; 7:74), and not to live in extravagance (7:31). Other verses emphasize the importance of balance in the natural world, such as the following:

> The sun and moon revolve to a computation;
> And the grasses and the trees bow (to Him) in adoration.
> He raised the sky and set the Balance
> So that none may err against the scales
> And observe correct measure, weigh with justice, and not cheat the
>   balance (55:5–10)[25]

Modern environmental awareness and activism among Muslims have deep roots in the Qur'an. Today, numerous thinkers have emphasized the importance of protecting the environment as a part of both a Muslim's religious obligation and the obligation to seek justice in the world. Beginning in the 1960s, the influential philosopher Seyyed Hossein Nasr led this movement with his arguments that the West lacked respect for the natural world, and he called for a reconsideration of humanity's relationship to nature in light of the teachings of Islam and other religious traditions.[26] Recently, scholars like Yasin Dutton have argued that environmental degradation is due to interest-based global capitalism, which is un-Islamic since Islam prohibits usury.[27]

Muslim-majority states have also taken steps to work toward environmental change from a religious basis in the twenty-first century. In Indonesia, numerous Islamic nongovernmental organizations (NGOs) have utilized the Qur'an and hadith as the basis for environmental activism in encouraging reforestation, recycling, and limiting waste. In 2014, the Indonesian Uleme Council (MUI) issued a fatwa prohibiting the poaching of endangered species. In 2018, the country's largest Islamic NGOs, Muhammadiyah and Nadhlatul Ulama, collaborated with the MUI, Greenpeace, and the Indonesian government to discourage plastic waste. One of their projects aimed to curb the use of single-use plastics during Ramadan festivities by enlisting local imams to preach this message in their communities. In Zanzibar, an island state of Tanzania, NGOs have recently collaborated with local Islamic leaders to discourage fishermen from fishing with explosives; imams have pointed out that this is impermissible from an Islamic perspective because the Qur'an enjoins believers not to waste natural resources.

In the West, numerous Islamic organizations are also encouraging environmental protection. The Islamic Foundation for Ecology and Environmental Sciences (IFEES) is a nonprofit organization based in the United Kingdom that encourages

SEEKING ANSWERS

What Is Ultimate Reality?

Muslims believe that God is the creator and sustainer of the universe, the world, and all that is in it. Muslims believe that elements of the beautiful natural world are signs of God. Humans can learn something about ultimate reality through God's revelations, which are communicated to humanity through prophets. The Qur'an is the source of God's teachings about the nature of ultimate reality and the nature of the world.

How Should We Live in This World?

Muslims believe that human beings are part of God's creation. The Islamic tradition offers many guidelines concerning the right way for human beings to live. People should worship God, be generous to the needy, and live righteously. The life of the Prophet Muhammad, especially as related in the sunna, serves as an example for Muslims of how to live. The five pillars of Muslim worship practice are the foundation for how Muslims live their faith.

What Is Our Ultimate Purpose?

Muslims believe in an afterlife and a Day of Judgment, when all humans will be judged on their actions and deeds in this life. Those who have lived righteously will enter paradise, and those who have led sinful lives will be cast into the fire. Some Muslims think that human beings have free choice and must choose to submit to the will of God. The choices that individuals make will be evaluated on the Day of Judgment, when God will judge each person independently. Other Muslims do not adhere to an idea of free will. Devout Muslims aim to live righteous lives by submitting to the will of God, adhering to the five pillars, and following the example of the Prophet Muhammad.

Muslims to "live up to their responsibilities as guardians of Allah's creation."[28] The Canadian organization Khaleafa (from the Arabic term *khalifa*, "guardian or steward") is dedicated to "raising awareness of environmental issues through and Islamic lens" (www.khaleafa.com). In partnership with other NGOs, Khaleafa aims to educate Canadian Muslims about living green in Islamic fashion; for example, the NGO has published guidelines for a more environmentally friendly way to observe Ramadan.

We have learned that Islam is a truly global religion, and both historically and today, there is variation in how Muslims interpret the sacred sources and practices of Islam. Without a doubt, Islam has been an astonishingly influential global force, giving rise to great civilizations, and scientific, philosophical, and artistic developments that have shaped the world. Although it is difficult to predict what the future will bring, it is clear that Islam will continue to grow and will certainly remain a dynamic and diverse religious tradition.

REVIEW QUESTIONS

For Review

1. What are the essential principles of belief in the Islamic religion?

2. What are the key religious practices in Islam? How do beliefs relate to religious practice and expression?

3. What are the most important sources of spirituality for Muslims?

4. What is a prophet in the Islamic tradition? What role does Muhammad play in Islam and in the life of Muslims today? How do Muslims know about the life of Muhammad, and how does he differ from other prophets?

5. What is Sufism, and how is it rooted in the Islamic tradition?

For Further Reflection

1. How do the teachings of Islam inform religious practice? How might the daily life of Muslims reflect their commitment to Islamic ideals? How do Islamic teachings about God compare with those of other monotheistic traditions?

2. What important challenges do Muslims face in the modern world? Why do you think Islam has been so stereotyped in North America and the West?

3. How have Muslims tackled issues of social and environmental justice from a religious perspective in the modern period?

GLOSSARY

Abbasids (uh-ba'sids) An important Muslim empire that ruled from 750 to 1258 CE.

adhan (ah-dahn'; Arabic) The call to prayer.

'A'isha (a'ee-shuh) A beloved wife of Muhammad who is known for transmitting many hadith.

'Ali Son-in-law of Muhammad; one of the Rightly Guided Caliphs.

Allah (ahl'lah; Arabic, "God") The Arabic term for God.

'Ashura (ah-shooh-ra') The tenth day of the month of Muharram, recognized by the Shi'a as the anniversary of the martyrdom of Husayn.

caliph (kay'lif; Arabic) Leader of the Muslim community after the death of Muhammad.

Fatima Daughter of the Prophet Muhammad.

hadith (hah-deeth'; Arabic) Literary tradition recording the sayings and deeds of the Prophet Muhammad.

hajj (hahj; Arabic) The annual pilgrimage to Mecca, one of the five pillars of Islam.

hijra (hij'ruh; Arabic) Sometimes spelled hegira. The migration of the early Muslim community from Mecca to Medina in 622 CE; the Islamic calendar dates from this year.

Husayn (hoo-sayn') Grandson of Muhammad who was killed while challenging the Umayyads.

imam (ee-mahm'; Arabic) Prayer leader; in Shi'ism, one of the leaders of the Muslim community following the death of the Prophet Muhammad.

Islam (is-lahm'; Arabic, "submission") Specifically, the religious tradition based on the revealed Qur'an as word of God.

jahiliyya (jah'hil'lee'yah; Arabic) The "age of ignorance," which refers to the time before the revelation of the Qur'an.

jihad (ji-had'; Arabic, "striving") The greater jihad is the struggle with one's self to become a better person; the lesser jihad is associated with military conflict in defense of the faith.

Khadija (kha-dee'juh) Muhammad's beloved first wife.

Mecca The city in which Muhammad was born; place of pilgrimage for Muslims.

Medina The city to which Muhammad and his early followers migrated to escape persecution in Mecca.

miraj (mir-ahj'; Arabic) Muhammad's Night Journey from Mecca to Jerusalem and from there to heaven, where he met with God.

mosque (mosk; from the Arabic term *masjid*) Place of prayer.

muezzin (mooh-ez'-zin; Arabic) The person who calls the *adhan*.

Muhammad The prophet who received the revelation of the Qur'an from God; the final prophet in a long line of prophets sent by God to humanity.

Qur'an (kuh-rahn' or koo-rahn'; Arabic) The holy text of Muslims; the word of God as revealed to Muhammad.

Ramadan (rah'muh-dahn; Arabic) The month in which Muslims must fast daily from dawn until dusk; the fast is one of the five pillars of Islam; also the month in which the Qur'an is believed to have been revealed to Muhammad.

salat (suh-laht'; Arabic) The daily prayers, which are one of the five pillars of Islam.

sawm (sohm; Arabic) The mandatory fast during the month of Ramadan; one of the five pillars of Islam.

shahada (shah-hah'dah; Arabic) The declaration of faith: "There is no God but God and Muhammad is the Messenger of God"; the first of the five pillars.

shari'a (sha-ree'ah; Arabic, "the way to the water hole") Islamic law.

Shi'a (pl.), Shi'i (n. adj.) (shee'ah, shee'ee; Arabic) One of the two major branches of Islam. The Shi'a believed that 'Ali should have succeeded as leader of the Muslim community after the death of Muhammad.

shirk (sherk; Arabic) The sin of idolatry, of worshiping anything other than God, the one unforgivable sin in Islam.

Sufi (soof'ee) A follower of the mystical tradition of Islam, Sufism, which focuses on the believer's personal experience of God and goal of union with God.

sunna (soon'nuh; Arabic, "way of life" or "custom") Specifically refers to the example of the life of the Prophet Muhammad; important religious source for Muslims.

Sunni (soon'nee; Arabic) One of the two main branches of Islam. The Sunnis believed that the Muslim community should decide on a successor to lead after the death of Muhammad.

sura (soo'rah; Arabic) Chapter of the Qur'an; there are 114 suras in the Qur'an.

tafsir (taf-seer'; Arabic) Interpretation of or commentary on the Qur'an. There are several types of *tafsir*, which aim to explain the meaning of the Qur'an.

Umayyad Dynasty (oo-may'yad) Muslim dynasty that ruled from 661 to 750 CE.

umma (oom'muh; Arabic) The worldwide Muslim community.

zakat (za'kat; Arabic) Regulated almsgiving; one of the five pillars of Islam.

SUGGESTIONS FOR FURTHER READING

Denny, Frederick M. *An Introduction to Islam.* 4th ed. Englewood Cliffs, NJ: Pearson Prentice Hall, 2011. A thorough introduction to Islam aimed at college students.

Ernst, Carl W. *Following Muhammad: Rethinking Islam in the Contemporary World.* Chapel Hill: University of North Carolina Press, 2003. A readable introduction to Islam for the general public, focusing on Islam in the modern world.

Renard, John, ed. *Windows on the House of Islam.* Berkeley: University of California Press, 1998. A collection of primary source materials from early Islamic history until the present; includes poetry, essays, philosophical writings, and more.

Safi, Omid. *Memories of Muhammad: Why the Prophet Matters*. New York: HarperOne, 2009. A biographical account of the Prophet Muhammad from his lifetime to the present day; includes his significance to Muslims today and throughout history.

Schimmel, Annemarie. *Mystical Dimension of Islam*. Chapel Hill: University of North Carolina Press, 1975. A classic and comprehensive overview of Sufism.

Sells, Michael. *Approaching the Qur'an: The Early Revelations*. Ashland, OR: White Cloud Press, 2002. Translation and explanation of the earliest suras of the Qur'an.

Wadud, Amina *Qur'an and Women: Re-reading the Sacred Text from a Woman's Perspective*. Oxford: Oxford University Press, 1999.

ONLINE RESOURCES

Oxford Islamic Studies Online

A comprehensive source with contributions from top scholars on all topics related to Islam.

Center for Muslim-Jewish Engagement

Useful site from the University of Southern California with databases for searching English translations of the Qur'an and hadith collections.

New Religious Movements

IT IS THE EVENING of August 1, and Barbara Z. is preparing an altar for the celebration of **Lughnassadh**, a fall harvest festival celebrated by practitioners of Wicca. For centuries, European men and women who worshiped the forces of nature, or who believed that they could perform acts of magical power by communing with these forces, were often referred to as "witches," a term contemporary Wiccans often use to describe themselves. Unlike the witches of fairy tales and films, however, Barbara Z. is a successful business professional who was raised as an Episcopalian and who had never heard of Wicca until a close friend suggested she read *The Spiral Dance* by Miriam Simos (better known by her Wiccan name of "Starhawk").

Reading that book, and many others that described the beliefs of Wicca, changed Barbara's life. She soon established a personal connection with a local coven, or witches' circle. In their company, she discovered a community

An offering of wine to the Earth spirits is a common feature of Wiccan ceremonies.

of like-minded men and women whose worldviews were remarkably similar to her own. For Wiccans, the natural universe is alive with sacred energy, a power that is often represented in Wiccan ritual as the worship of a specific god, and by paying homage to that deity, Wiccans believe they are celebrating the beauty and wonder of nature itself. **Lughnassadh** (also known as *Lammas*), named for the Celtic god Lugh, is one such festival. Wiccans take a particular interest in pre-Christian European deities, and many of their sacred festivals are dedicated to one or another of these pagan gods. Like many of those who have joined a new religious movement, Barbara thinks of Wicca as a break with her Christian upbringing and as an essential part of a journey of spiritual self-discovery.

The celebration of Lughnassadh entails several ritual acts, all of them related symbolically to the fall harvest. Part of the day is spent baking a loaf of bread, which is to be used later that evening during the Lughnassadh ceremony. Wiccans customarily share this bread in celebration of the grain harvest, and it is from this practice that the name *Lammas*—meaning "loaf-mass"—is derived. At dusk, Barbara will create a magic circle of lights, placing her altar at the center of this circle. On that altar Barbara will place a sheaf of wheat and several cornbread figures, representing the god Lugh and his worshipers, and a basket of star-shaped cookies. Each member of the coven will be asked, in turn, what they most fear and what they most desire from the coming year, and they will then perform a dance in honor of the dying year that will soon be reborn. Having tossed the cornbread figures into a fire, the participants in this ceremony will then eat the star-shaped cookies in anticipation of a bountiful year to come. Following the conclusion of this ritual, the members of the coven will sit down to a celebratory meal, at which time the witches will address each other by their "craft" names. As a third-degree Wiccan priestess, Barbara will be addressed as Lady Sparrow, combining a title of honor with the name she chose on entering the Wiccan community.

Ritual practices will differ from one Wiccan community to another, the great constant being the underlying conviction that each act performed by the coven brings their community—and every member of that circle—closer to the indestructible source of life that is nature itself.

14.1 What Is "New" about New Religious Movements?

Anyone who has searched the Internet using terms such as *cults* and *sects*,[1] or who has ventured into a bookstore in search of works on astrology, witchcraft, or non-traditional methods of healing, must be aware of how diverse the audience for religious information has grown. Social scientists and historians have estimated that, globally, no fewer than 14,000 new religious communities have come into existence in the course of the twentieth and early twenty-first centuries. While not everyone agrees on what constitutes a "new" religious movement, most students of religion in the modern era are aware of both an exponential growth of new religious communities worldwide and of the often aggressively nontraditional (and even countercultural) character exhibited by many of these new religions. It will be useful, therefore, to begin with some general observations about the larger cultural milieu within which these new religions arose and then to identify what is really innovative in their teachings and practices. However, readers of this volume should already recognize that, at some point in history, practically *every* religious movement or philosophy has been perceived as "new" by its contemporaries and oftentimes rejected for that very reason.

In this chapter, we will use terms such as *cult* and *sect* more precisely than those words are used in the media, or in casual conversation. When employed by contemporary sociologists, the term *sect* designates a subgroup within an established religious community, one whose belief system differs somewhat from the beliefs of that community. The term *cult*, however, describes a *radically* innovative religious community that exists outside of any established organizational structure, and one whose beliefs are often perceived by society as strange or even threatening. Beginning with the 1970s, and in the decades that followed, a number of religious groups were called "cults" if their leaders were perceived as mentally unstable, or if their teachings promoted violence or other kinds of extreme behavior. Understandably, the notoriety such communities attracted gave a pejorative meaning to the word *cult* that clings to it even today. Nevertheless, we will attempt to describe such groups with as much objectivity as possible—and particularly those at the very margins of social acceptability—while recognizing their problematic status within the larger religious community.

Modernization, Globalization, and Secularization

In Chapter 1, we considered several interrelated phenomena that have brought about profound changes in religious thought and behavior, particularly during the last two centuries. The first, and arguably the most important, of these phenomena is **modernization**, which historians identify with the condition of postindustrial Europe and America in the nineteenth and twentieth centuries. Modernized societies, as we noted, exhibit higher levels of literacy and advanced technological capabilities. These societies have witnessed both the growth of scientific knowledge and a greater diffusion of political power, with a corresponding erosion of traditional authority and respect for the past, in politics as well as religion. Therefore, because of the long-term effect of modernization, not only have established religious institutions lost influence and credibility, but the number of new religious movements empowered by cultural change has increased dramatically. This was especially true of nineteenth-century America, where "communities of dissent" (in Stephen Stein's phrase[2]) suddenly began to flourish after the Civil War and where a culture of religious liberalism and experimentation increasingly took root in American soil. Collectively, these new religious leaders (as well as their followers) often referred to themselves as **seekers**, and their quest for new spiritual insights led thousands to explore nontraditional beliefs and social ideals. The new technology of mass communications ensured that the dissemination of information about any innovative teaching or social organization would be both rapid and widespread.

Globalization is another important factor in the growth of new religious movements. Even before the creation of the Internet, the pace of cultural interaction had increased as a result of Western imperialism and of colonialist encounters between Western and non-Western peoples. Evidence of such interactions within the religious domain can be seen in the **World's Parliament of Religions**, held in Chicago in 1893 as part of an International Trade Exposition. Representatives of such non-Western religious traditions as Vedanta, Zoroastrianism, Jainism, and Buddhism shared the stage with liberal Protestants, Reform Jews, and spokespersons for various types of Spiritualist and Theosophical belief systems, with the aim of achieving some form of global understanding of human religious diversity. When, in 1993, a second Parliament was held in Chicago (this one, and others that have been held subsequently, called the Parliament of the World's Religions), an even larger number of religious communities were represented, and a special effort was made to include those (such as Native Americans) who had been excluded a century earlier.

These gatherings demonstrated the exponential growth of interest in the West in religious cultures that had earlier been ignored or marginalized (or even demonized) by the West but that were now accorded a much greater measure of respect. This movement toward a multicultural perspective on religion was enhanced significantly in the United States by the repeal of the Asian Exclusion Act in 1965 and the resulting immigration of increasing numbers of non-Western peoples to America over the following decades. But even before this demographic shift occurred, greater numbers of thoughtful, spiritually oriented persons had already embraced a pluralistic view of religious diversity; that is, a view of modern society that presupposes multiple forms of religious experience and expression as the *normal* condition of life in the contemporary world.

Along with these changes in outlook and socialization in the modern era, the phenomenon of **secularization** should be discussed. A secular society is one in which the values and methodologies of science are viewed as culturally dominant and in which religious beliefs and worldviews are seen as largely subjective or simply lacking in intellectual authority. This subordination of religion to science is one of the immediate consequences of what historians call the scientific revolution, and ongoing disputes between conservative Christians (and more recently, conservative Muslims as well) and biologists who support a Darwinian model of species evolution provide ample evidence that the struggle between science and religion that began with Galileo's new astronomy in the sixteenth century is still being waged today. However, the difference between a Galileo, who challenged the prevailing geocentric view of the solar system, and a contemporary biologist, who challenges the biblical portrait of divine creation, is profound: the weight of educated opinion in most modern societies is on the side of the scientist, whose cosmology is seen as more credible than that of his fundamentalist adversary. Moreover, the prevalence of materialist values in modern societies and the persistent view that religious belief is a matter of personal choice reinforce the often critical perspective from which all religious ideas and institutions are regarded. It follows, therefore, that if all religious teachings are equally problematic from a secular point of view, then any new form of religious belief has as much, or as little, claim to credibility (in the eyes of a skeptical observer) as any more established religious tradition. The secularization of modern societies thereby creates an opportunity for new religious ideas to develop without fear of overwhelming cultural rejection, and for many new religious communities the need to "reenchant" the world is the most pressing spiritual need of our time.

This need is particularly evident in religious communities that have been linked to **New Age** thought and to counterculture movements growing out of the 1960s and 1970s that embrace a belief in magic and in esoteric wisdom. New Age religious practices include (though are not limited to) the **channeling** of disembodied spirits, the use of crystals and magnets for healing purposes, and a reliance on astrological calculations to determine one's fate and fortune. While secularists view these practices as culturally obsolete and empirically invalid efforts at controlling the natural environment, New Age advocates argue that science has neglected or suppressed ancient teachings about the human body or the physical universe that cannot be reconciled to any current model of truth. And although it is impossible to speak of a single, coherent New Age philosophy, many groups that fall under this rubric are clearly in search of an alternative worldview that will allow a "transformation of consciousness," or at the very least a renewed sense of wonder and reverence for those hidden forces of nature, or of the human spirit, that contemporary science refuses to acknowledge.

Theoretical Models and Social Typologies

Over several decades attempts have been made to categorize the kinds of new or "alternative" religions (as they are sometimes called) that have developed during the twentieth and early twenty-first centuries. One popular theoretical model has been proposed by Roy Wallis (*The Elementary Forms of the New Religious Life*, 1984),[3] who classifies new religious movements in relation to their perception of the world and of human destiny. For Wallis, new religions can be understood as either "world-affirming," "world-renouncing," or "world-accommodating." Thus, a world-affirming religion is one that attributes positive value to human existence and whose goal is to improve the conditions of life wherever it is possible to do so through human effort. Consequently, removing oneself from society or longing for self-annihilation consequently has no value for someone who has embraced this point of view. A world-renouncing religion, in contrast, takes the opposite position, proceeding instead from the assumption that human society is irredeemably evil and that life itself is too filled with pain and futility to be worth improving. Adherents of this religious philosophy, such as the Japanese cult Aum Shinrikyo (discussed later in this chapter), typically envision an imminent and destructive end to the world and even devise strategies for bringing about that end, either to the social order or to one's individual existence. World-accommodating religions, as the term suggests, are

TIMELINE
New Religious Movements

1830 CE   Publication of the Book of Mormon and beginnings of the Church of Jesus Christ of Latter-day Saints.

1853   Mirza Husayn Ali Nuri (Baha'u'llah) declares himself a "Messenger of God": the beginnings of the Baha'i faith.

1875   Establishment of the Theosophical Society by Helena Blavatsky and Henry Steel Olcott.

1876   Founding of the Christian Science movement.

1881   Establishment of the Watchtower Society (Jehovah's Witnesses).

1914   The International New Thought Alliance formed.

1933   Founding of the Worldwide Church of God.

1954   Beginnings of Wicca, the Unification Church, and the Church of Scientology.

1957   Establishment of a center for Transcendental Meditation by the Maharishi Mahesh Yogi.

1965   Founding of ISKCON and Eckankar.

1974   Claude Vorilhon ("Rael") creates the Raelian movement.

1975   Marshall Herff Applewhite and Bonnie Nettles found the Heaven's Gate community (collective suicide, 1997).

1999   Collective protest by Falun Gong practitioners against Chinese government; suppression of their movement.

prepared to adapt to a world that is manifestly deficient in goodness or grace, while at the same time asserting their belief in a higher goal for humankind (which it cannot, at present, attain). The merit of these typologies is that they focus our attention on the relationship between a core perception of social reality and a corresponding metaphysical view that surrounds it. The basic weakness of Wallis's system, however, is that it tends to oversimplify the often eclectic teachings and social ideals of the religious movements it seeks to categorize. Many of the new religions we will consider in this chapter, in fact, exhibit a certain ambivalence toward the evils of this world, for which they devise a means of either overcoming or escaping, thereby becoming at once world-renouncing and world-accommodating.

Another theoretical overview is that of Peter Clarke,[4] who emphasizes the theme of "social transformation" that runs through nearly all of those religious movements thought of as "new" or "alternative." Many of these new movements, Clarke notes, fix on the inner life as the primary agency of transformation, hoping that through the attainment of a true Self, the individual can either begin to change the conditions of life for the better or begin the process of disengagement from life altogether. In either case, the individual who enters a new religious community is likely to be searching for an ideology of change that is not to be found within existing religious cultures. Such individuals, Clarke observes, are inclined to describe themselves as spiritual rather than as religious, with an implicit acknowledgment that the only personally valid religious experience these seekers are likely to find acceptable is one that lies outside the framework of established religious institutions or systems of thought.

Neither of the preceding systems of classification, or others that have been proposed, can claim to be exhaustive or universally applicable. However, they do provide some insight into the social/intellectual dynamic of the innovative religious cultures that we are about to examine. What follows is a series of historical vignettes of contemporary religious movements and philosophies that sociologists of religion such as Wallis and Clarke have identified as demonstrably "new" and therefore representative of the latest phase of global religious expression. We have chosen to focus on the new religions of the West, partly because these communities are likely to be more familiar to our readers and partly because the sheer number of alternative religions worldwide is so large that no single chapter in a book could honestly claim to represent all of them.

14.2 Alternative Christianities and Their Offshoots

Some of the most successful new religious movements of the modern era are churches that derived from recognizably Christian sources and whose beginnings can be traced back to nineteenth-century America. Then, as now, religious culture in the United States was pluralistic, and although most Americans professed some form of Christian belief, no single Christian denomination was dominant. What historians refer to as the **Second Great Awakening**—a nationwide evangelical movement that evoked intense religious fervor in many communities—continued to affect Christian thought in the United States up through the mid-1800s. One manifestation of this upsurge in religious enthusiasm can be found in the formation of new Christian churches, some claiming new revelations of divine truth and many looking forward eagerly to the imminent Second Coming of Christ. The following discussion focuses on those groups whose influence continues to be felt today: the Church of Jesus Christ of Latter-day Saints, Christian Science, Seventh-day Adventists, and Jehovah's Witnesses.

The Church of Jesus Christ of Latter-day Saints

The Church of Jesus Christ of Latter-day Saints (LDS) was founded by Joseph Smith (1805–1844) in 1830 in Fayette, New York. Although its members are commonly referred to as Mormons, many prefer to be known as Latter-day Saints. According to Joseph Smith's account, he was fourteen years old when, in 1820, he withdrew to the woods near his home and asked God which church he should join. While praying for guidance, he was approached by two figures who identified themselves as God the Father and Jesus Christ. They informed Smith that he should not join any existing church but rather establish his own and that he had been chosen to restore the one true faith of Jesus Christ. Three years later, Smith was visited by the Angel Moroni, who revealed to him the location of two thin golden plates covered with strange writing. His translation of these plates, accomplished "by the gift and power of God," resulted in the writing of the Book of Mormon, one of the principal scriptures of the Church of Latter-day Saints. Although these plates were later taken away by an angel, witnesses testified to having seen and touched them.

Published in 1830, the Book of Mormon tells how the prophet Lehi and his followers fled Jerusalem around the year 600 BCE and migrated to America, where they founded a great civilization. During subsequent centuries, their descendants recorded their history on metal plates. These plates described how conflict eventually divided the people into two groups, the Nephites and the Lamanites. These plates also included prophecies of the birth and crucifixion of Jesus Christ and described how, after his resurrection, Jesus appeared to the peoples of North America and established his church among them. In 421 CE, the Lamanites (ancestors of the people we know as Native Americans) annihilated the Nephites, whose memory was preserved only in the history they had written. A surviving Nephite, the prophet Mormon, wrote an abridgment of that history on two golden plates and gave them to his son, the prophet Moroni, who hid them. Fourteen centuries later, Moroni—who by then had become an angel—revealed their location to Joseph Smith. Mormons believe that the Book of Mormon is divinely inspired scripture and recognize it as having an authority equal to that of the Old and New Testaments. They also make extensive use of two other texts: *Doctrines and Covenants* (1835) and *The Pearl of Great Price* (1842), both of which consist of revelations, statements, translations, and other writings, many by Joseph Smith.

The discovery of the Book of Mormon soon attracted followers to Joseph Smith and his church. At the same time, conflict with their detractors soon forced the Mormons to leave New York. After settling briefly in Kirtland, Ohio, continued opposition to Smith's teachings forced the Mormons to move on, first to Jackson County, Missouri, and then to Nauvoo, Illinois. For a time the Mormons prospered in Nauvoo, but their practice of polygamy (abolished in 1890) aroused the animosity of their neighbors. On June 24, 1844, Joseph Smith was killed by an angry mob opposed to the Mormon way of life. The leadership of the movement then fell to Brigham Young (1801–1877), who led the Mormons on an epic trek from Nauvoo to the Great Salt Basin of Utah, where they settled and established their church headquarters at a site known today as Salt Lake City.

The Angel Moroni delivering the plates of the Book of Mormon to Joseph Smith.

Mormons accept many familiar Christian doctrines, though often with radical (and, to most Christians, unacceptable) changes. Like mainstream Christians, the Mormons believe in a Trinity, consisting of God, the Heavenly Father; his Son, Jesus Christ; and the Holy Ghost (sometimes referred to as the Holy Spirit). However, Mormons understand these figures to be three separate gods. Moreover, Mormons believe that the Heavenly Father was once a mortal man. Descended from human beings who themselves had become gods, the Heavenly Father attained divinity and became the ruler of our region of the universe. Through intercourse with a celestial wife, he produced a Son, Jesus Christ, who also progressed from humanity to divinity, and finally the Holy Ghost. Whereas the Heavenly Father and Jesus Christ possess material bodies (albeit perfect and immortal), the Holy Ghost is pure spirit.

Mormons also believe that all human beings are "spirit children" of the Heavenly Father, who sends us to Earth so that we can receive physical bodies and gain both knowledge and experience that are essential for spiritual progress. We are guided in this life by the perfect example of Jesus Christ and by the Holy Ghost that dwells within believers and helps them to grasp eternal truths. Ultimately, we can return to dwell eternally with the Heavenly Father, become gods ourselves, and have spirit children of our own. Sin can prevent us from achieving this goal, but it need not do so, for Jesus Christ atoned for our sins through his suffering and death. We can therefore achieve salvation if we have faith in Christ's atonement, repent our sins, accept baptism, and receive "the gift of the Holy Ghost." The critical factor, for Mormons, in determining who can or cannot be saved from sin is the acceptance of "the Gospel of Jesus Christ in its fullness," and that form of Christian teaching can only be found within the Church of Latter-day Saints. However, it is possible for Mormons to obtain baptism (by proxy) on behalf of deceased family members who were not Latter-day Saints—and therefore ensure their retroactive salvation; this explains the extraordinary interest Mormons take in genealogical research. Finally, Mormons abstain from the consumption of alcohol, tobacco, coffee, tea, caffeinated soft drinks, and illegal drugs, believing that such abstentions are not only conducive to good health but are also part of the revelation given to Joseph Smith in 1833.

The Salt Lake Temple in Salt Lake City, Utah.

Mormons are millennialists who believe that one day Christ will return to judge and rule the world for a thousand years. Although they acknowledge the existence of a hell, where some will suffer temporary punishments, Mormons are convinced that, in the end, all people will be saved. However, the final destiny of every individual will be determined by the extent of his or her obedience to God's commandments. Accordingly, there are two distinct levels of salvation: Mormons who faithfully follow the teachings of their church will attain divinity and eternal life in the presence of the Heavenly Father; non-Mormons will receive lesser rewards and will therefore enter lesser "kingdoms" in eternity. Mormons also believe in continuing divine revelation and, more specifically, they believe that God's will is revealed through the senior leadership of their church. Its president (often referred to as "the prophet"), his two counselors, and the members of the Quorum of the Twelve Apostles are all recognized as having prophetic abilities, and together they possess the same authority as the prophets and apostles described in the Bible. This link with the biblical past underlies the Mormon Church's conception of itself as the *restored* church of Jesus Christ, and because other churches have corrupted the teachings of Christ, the Mormon Church is therefore the only true and living church upon the Earth. Needless to say, no other Christian community is prepared to accept this claim.

The LDS Church is one of the most energetically proselytizing churches in the world today, with over 70,000 full-time missionaries serving in missions throughout the world. This is particularly true in Africa where the church has established no fewer than thirty-one missions. Interest in Africa began gradually in the 1850s, when LDS missionaries sought to promote the Book of Mormon among the white, English-speaking residents of Cape Town. Outreach to Black Africans, however, throughout the nineteenth and much of the twentieth centuries, was hampered by the church's refusal to admit persons of African descent to the priesthood. It was not until June 9, 1978, in fact, that the leadership of the LDS Church decided, in response to a new revelation, to reverse a policy that dated back to the time of Brigham Young, and began admitting Mormon converts to the priesthood without regard to race or skin color. This decision—referred to as the "Revelation on Priesthood"—made it possible to actively missionize among the native African population and to choose Black African elders for leadership positions within the church.

Christian Science and New Thought

The religious philosophy known as Christian Science has its origins in the life experiences and teachings of Mary Baker Eddy (1821–1910). As a young woman, Eddy suffered from illnesses and nervous disorders for which the physicians and hypnotists she consulted could offer no lasting relief. In 1866, however, she claimed to have been completely cured while reading an account of one of the miraculous healings effected by Jesus in the New Testament. This led her to discover the Science of Christianity, or Christian Science, which she later described in her book *Science and Health with Key to the Scriptures* (published in 1875). A skilled organizer, Mrs. Eddy (as church members prefer to call her) established the Church of Christ, Scientist, in 1879 with its headquarters in Boston. Today there are nearly 2,500 Christian Science communities throughout the world, and the newspaper she helped establish, *The Christian Science Monitor*, is a well-known and respected publication.

Like many offshoot Christian communities, including the Mormons, Christian Scientists regard their church as a restored form of primitive Christianity. Although they acknowledge the Bible as the inspired word of God, they nevertheless maintain that its full meaning can only be grasped through studying *Science and Health*, which they believe was written under divine inspiration. But what truly distinguishes Christian Science is its foundational belief that all reality is spiritual, for it derives from the purely spiritual nature of God. Matter and the body do not really exist, nor do the evils associated with them, such as disease, deformity, and death. These are nothing more than mental errors created by our limited minds. We experience pain and illness only as long as we *think* we are suffering from these things, and as long as we attribute objective reality to these illusions, we will find ourselves cut off from God. To achieve salvation from this delusional state, we must follow the example of Jesus Christ, the "Way-shower," whose awareness of God and God's goodness allowed him to overcome all forms of suffering and to perform miraculous healings of body and mind.

Because Christian Scientists deny the existence of material reality, they do not accept the traditional Christian doctrine of the Incarnation. Instead, they believe in Christ as the divine idea of "sonship" to God and in Jesus as the one in whom that idea was perfectly expressed. God is the Father–Mother of all, while the Holy Spirit is God's loving relationship with creation. Christian Science teaches that prayer based on a correct understanding of God and reality as spiritual existence is the key to improving human life. Prayer is therefore not so much a matter of asking God for healing as it is a yielding of the individual mind to the Divine Mind and to the truth that whenever God's presence and loving power are recognized, health and healing are sure to follow. For example, Christian Scientists trust in God's love rather than in vaccinations for the prevention of diseases; when they do become ill, they turn to prayer for healing, often with the assistance of "practitioners," that is, church members who devote themselves full time to teach others how to use "scientific prayer" in gaining access to God's healing love. Nevertheless, church members remain free to obtain help from medical professionals if they so choose, and they have broadened their understanding of the principle of spiritual healing to include the elimination of major social problems.

Mary Baker Eddy was the founder of the Church of Christ, Scientist (Christian Science).

Christian Science is viewed by historians as just one of the forms taken by a larger American religious movement known as **New Thought**. Though more a philosophical current within late nineteenth-century religious thought than an actual creed, New Thought advocates embraced a transcendentalist belief in the presence of the divine within nature, and especially within the human mind. In 1914, the International New Thought Alliance was formed, dedicated to the constructive power of the mind and the "freedom of each soul as to choice and as to belief." Within that larger community of optimistic faith in the human spirit various groups took root, particularly the Unity School of Christianity. Founded by Charles Fillmore (1854–1948) and his wife, Myrtle (1845–1931), in 1903, Unity was originally based on the concept of "mind cure," or the relief from illness through the exercise of mind over matter. A prime example of this phenomenon occurred in 1886, when Myrtle Fillmore was cured of tuberculosis after repeating inwardly, for two years, "I am a child of God and therefore I do not inherit sickness." Today, Unity practitioners describe themselves as engaged in a positive and practical form of Christianity in which the daily application of the principles exemplified by Jesus Christ promotes health, prosperity, and happiness. Unity teaches that the spirit of God lived in Jesus Christ, just as it lives in everyone. By living as Christ did, we overcome sin—which

Unity understands to be separation from God in our consciousness—as well as illness, depression, and doubt. Like many New Thought churches, Unity believes that a heightened awareness of God's presence will bring peace, health, and happiness to the human race.

Adventism

The Adventist movement, based on the belief that Christ would soon return to Earth, represents one of the more radical tendencies of nineteenth-century Christian thought. By midcentury a number of Adventist denominations became increasingly prominent in American religious life. The first of these groups gathered around a Baptist minister named William Miller (1782–1849), whose experience at a revival meeting led him to undertake the study of biblical prophecy. In 1835, Miller announced that Christ would return to Earth between March 21, 1843, and March 21, 1844, to preside over a final judgment, destroy the world, and inaugurate a new heaven and a new Earth. The failure of this Second Coming to materialize prompted recalculations and predictions of new dates, but when these, too, passed without incident, many Millerites gave up their hope of seeing Christ's return. Others, sometimes scorned and ridiculed in their churches, emulated Miller by forming new ones, most of which were organized as part of the Evangelical Adventist Association.

The largest of the Adventist churches to emerge from what the Millerites called **The Great Disappointment** was that of the Seventh-day Adventists, founded by Ellen White (1827–1915). White became a follower of Miller in 1842, but after the Great Disappointment of 1844 White taught that the Second Coming of Christ had been delayed by the failure of Christians to obey the Ten Commandments—especially the fourth commandment, which requires observance of the Sabbath on the seventh day of the week (that is, Saturday). In addition, White believed (like her counterparts in Christian Science) that scripture contains rules for physical, as well as spiritual, health: "Disease," she wrote, "is the result of violating God's laws, both natural and spiritual" and would not exist if people lived "in harmony with the Creator's plan." For this reason, and because they consider the body a "temple" of the Holy Spirit, Seventh-day Adventists practice vegetarianism, abstain from alcohol and tobacco, and prefer natural remedies to drugs when ill. It was in hope of creating a health food that would meet the standards White discerned in scripture that Dr. John Kellogg, one of her disciples, invented his famous cornflakes.

Today there are more than 10 million Seventh-day Adventists worldwide, the great majority of whom live outside of North America (principally in Africa and Central and South America). Emphasizing the apocalyptic books of Daniel and Revelation in the Bible, they preach that the world must be prepared for the Second Coming, which will occur after the gospel has been spread to all parts of the world. The returning Christ will raise the faithful from their present state of unconsciousness, make them immortal, and bring them back to heaven for his millennial reign. At the conclusion of the millennium, Satan will be destroyed, along with sinners who indicate they have no wish to live in Christ's presence. The saints will then descend from heaven to live forever on an Earth restored to its original perfection.

Most Christian denominations consider the Seventh-day Adventist Church to be a genuine Christian church, although they may not share its preoccupation with Christ's Second Coming or recognize the legitimacy of a Saturday Sabbath worship tradition. However, some groups with roots in Seventh-day Adventism are much further from the Christian mainstream. The Worldwide Church of God, for example, urges its members to observe the dietary laws and many of the other commandments found in the Hebrew Bible. Moreover, its leaders (Herbert Armstrong [1892–1986] and his son Garner Ted Armstrong [1930–2003]) believed that the English-speaking peoples were the literal descendants of the "lost tribes" of ancient Israel. The Davidian Seventh-day Adventists, founded in the 1930s by a Bulgarian immigrant, Victor Houteff, also observe many of the ritual requirements found in the Hebrew Bible; however, they criticize traditional Seventh-day Adventists for claiming that prophecy came to an end with the death of Ellen White. God, the Davidians say, continues to guide their church through the prophets he sends. One particular splinter group, the Branch Davidian Church (founded by Benjamin Roden in the 1960s), achieved tragic notoriety in 1993 when David Koresh (born Vernon Howell in 1959), who had taken control of a Branch Davidian community located in Waco, Texas, in the 1980s, convinced his followers that he was the Messiah and that Armageddon would take place in the United States rather than in Israel. When federal agents raided the Branch Davidian compound on February 28, 1993, a shootout and fifty-one-day siege followed, culminating in an assault and fire that left eighty members of the Waco community (including Koresh himself) dead.

Jehovah's Witnesses

Another millennialist church that succeeded the Millerites was founded in 1881 by the lay preacher Charles Taze Russell (1852–1916). Officially called Zion's Watch Tower Bible and Tract Society, it is more commonly known as the Jehovah's Witnesses. Russell's study of the Bible led him to conclude that the Second Coming would occur in 1874, when Christ would return to prepare for the kingdom of God. This event was to be followed by the battle of Armageddon and the end of the world in 1914, after which Christ would begin his millennial reign over the Earth. Russell published a more detailed account of his thought in a work titled *Studies in Scripture*, and in 1879 he began the publication of a magazine called *The Watchtower*. Russell's followers were at first referred to as Bible Students and Watchtower People, but once Joseph Franklin Rutherford (1869–1942) had succeeded Russell as the head of the Watchtower organization, members of that community were officially known as Jehovah's Witnesses.

Under Rutherford's leadership, centralized control both of the Watchtower organization and of its teachings increased. At the same time, its membership grew, and today there are approximately 4 million Witnesses in 200 countries. As the most "world-renouncing" of the Adventist churches of the modern era, the Witnesses continued to predict the end of history and the imminent rule of Christ and his saints. More recently, Witnesses have become wary of fixing dates for the apocalypse and are generally content to proclaim that Christ's return to Earth will come sooner than later.

Jehovah's Witnesses take their name from the name of God commonly found in earlier English translations of the Hebrew Bible. Although they understand Jesus Christ as God's "Son," they reject the doctrine of the Trinity and insist that the Son is simply the first of God's creations. As for the Holy Spirit, that is understood as "God's active force" within persons of true Christian faith. Witnesses continue to believe that a "great tribulation" is imminent and that, after destroying the present world system, the elect (whose core number is fixed at 144,000) will experience full salvation. These elect individuals, who alone have immortal souls, will ultimately be taken up into heaven. All others may be saved through obedience to God and faith in the efficacy of Christ's sacrificial death, but their reward will be eternal life on Earth, which will be restored to its original, paradisiacal condition. As for the wicked, they will perish in the cataclysmic end-time battle (that is, Armageddon), but only after they have been given fair warning of their fate. The familiar practice of going door to door, which brings teams of Witnesses into thousands of neighborhoods every year, is premised on the belief that they have a responsibility to warn their fellow human beings that the world—which they believe to be under the present dominion of Satan—will soon come to an end. Witnesses also refuse military service and will not salute the flag or hold government offices, believing these practices to be a compromise with worldly evil. Their refusal to accept blood transfusions, based on their interpretation of biblical precepts forbidding the consumption of blood (Genesis 9:4), has often placed the Witnesses in opposition to contemporary medical practice and public policy. Finally, since they regard other churches as having fallen into gross error, they have little contact with other Christian denominations and do not join in celebrating holidays such as Christmas and Easter.

The Unification Church

At an even greater remove from traditional Christianity is the Unification Church, officially known today as "The Family Federation for World Peace and Unification." First established in 1954 by the Reverend Sun Myung Moon (1920–2012), the "**Moonies**," as they are popularly called, constitute a particularly aggressive and theologically eclectic Adventist community. Within this community, the Reverend Moon occupies a position of honor and spiritual influence equal to that of Jesus, and it is therefore arguable whether the Unification Church can be considered a historically legitimate form of Christianity. Though often derided during the 1970s as a "cult," the Unification Church has consistently denied charges of exploitation of its members. The organization has recently sought mainstream acceptance by devoting considerable sums to the promotion of international peace gatherings and interfaith conferences and by purchasing major newspapers such as the *Washington Times*. Still, at the heart of this movement we find both the personal presence and teachings of Sun Myung Moon, whose followers consider him the Messiah of our age.

Moon's spiritual journey began in 1936 in what is now North Korea, when he received a vision of Jesus at Easter time. In that vision, Jesus informed Moon that he was to take up the mission of world redemption where Jesus had left off, succeeding where the

The Reverend Sun Myung Moon blessing a mass wedding ceremony in Madison Square Garden, New York.

Christian savior had failed. Believing himself a successor to Jesus Christ, Moon constructed a belief system that combines Christian scriptures with Buddhist, Daoist, and shamanistic elements. Moon's principal publication, entitled *Divine Principle*, claims that he has completed the Testaments and represents the next stage in the progression of Christian thought. Thus, according to Moon, God can be thought of as an invisible essence, from which all life flows. God's original plans for the biblical Adam and Eve were thwarted, however, when the Serpent (Satan) seduced Eve, inspiring her to have intercourse with Adam "prematurely," thus leading in turn to the fall of the human race. Because the sins of our first parents extend to every generation, the salvation of humankind depends on the appearance of a messiah, who, along with his wife (who serves as a second Eve), will restore the purity of the family and reconcile the world to God's will. Unificationists refer to Moon's second wife, Hak Ja Han, as the "True Mother" who is a model of authentic motherhood and spiritual guidance.

The ability to receive new revelations extends beyond the Reverend Moon himself to at least one other member of his family. In 1984, Moon's second son, Heung Jin, was fatally injured in an auto accident, but almost immediately after his funeral, Moon announced that his son had become a "commander in chief" in the spirit world to those who had died unmarried. To ensure that Heung Jin would not remain a bachelor through eternity, a postmortem marriage was arranged between the daughter of one of Moon's aides and the spirit of Heung Jin, whereupon members of the Unification Church began receiving revelations from him. Perhaps the most important of these messages are those that confirm the status in heaven of both Moon and his wife, who are spoken of as the "True Parents" before whom even Jesus bows in humility and reverence. Additional testimonials from the spirit realm, celebrating Moon's cosmic preeminence, have come not only from Heung Jin but also from a deceased Unification scholar, Dr. Sang Hun Lee, who informed a Unification receptor that Buddha, Confucius, Muhammad, and Jesus all acknowledge Moon's role as the ultimate redemptive "parent" of humanity. Charles Taze Russell, Mary Baker Eddy, Joseph Smith, and no fewer than thirty-six deceased presidents of the United States have added their voices to this swelling chorus of affirmation. Critics of the Unification Church have seized upon such statements as proof of a "personality cult" at the heart of Moon's gospel, and it is clear that Moon's redeemer persona is central to the salvific claims made by the Unification Church and its defenders.

Rastafarianism

The Rastafarian movement, which can be traced back to Kingston, Jamaica, during the 1920s and 1930s, exhibits only the most tenuous relationship to either Christianity or the advent movements that grew out of Christian thought in the nineteenth and twentieth centuries. However, like the Unification Church, it shows unmistakable signs of millenarian thought. Combining elements of Black nationalist ideology and liberation theology, the Rastafari religious culture attempted to lift up the African diaspora of the Caribbean out of poverty and despair and to inspire both a pride in African ancestry and a desire for repatriation to an Africa freed from white colonial oppression.

An important influence on Rastafarian thought is Marcus Garvey (1887–1940), a militant Jamaican socialist leader. In his writings, Garvey expressed indignation over the plight of the island's poor and disdain for the shallow materialism of the West and its racist hatred of Africans. Regarding the enslavement of Blacks as a form of divine punishment, Garvey concluded that the African diaspora's period of tribulation was drawing to an end and that a king would emerge in Africa who would lead the disenfranchised Black masses back to their homelands and to a life of dignity and prosperity.

A simple Rastafarian food shop named Lion House in Stony Hill, Jamaica, features paintings of Rasta heroes Marcus Garvey, Haile Selassie, and Bob Marley.

The ascension of the Ethiopian prince Ras Tafari Makonnen—better known by his throne name as Haile Selassie (1891–1975)—to the position of emperor of Ethiopia in 1930 seemed to give concrete shape to Garvey's prophecy. Jamaicans who were influenced by the teachings of the Jamaican priest and mystic Leonard Howell (1898–1981) became convinced that the moment of collective liberation from white rule had finally come. For Howell, and others who now began to speak of themselves as followers of Ras Tafari—hence "Rastafarians"—Haile Selassie was more than a mortal ruler: he was either Christ returned to Earth or God incarnate.

When Selassie first visited Jamaica in the 1950s and met with Rastafarian leaders, many in the movement concluded that Howell's "Adventist" view of Selassie had been validated and that this visit signaled the final move back to "Ethiopia" (understood as a metaphor for the whole of Africa). However, the few thousand Jamaicans who did emigrate to Ethiopia in the 1960s soon found that their dreams of apocalyptic fulfillment were not to be realized and that the moment of divine deliverance had to be deferred.

The overthrow of Selassie in 1974 and his death a year later shook the Rastafarian movement to its core. Some followers denied that Selassie had really died, and others were convinced that his spirit would return to his earthly body at some point in the future. Today, most Rastafarians speak of "liberation before repatriation"—signifying a demand for social justice within the countries they reside in—and although many still revere Haile Selassie and believe that his spirit lives on in Rastafarian artists and teachers, they are prepared to wait some time for the Day of Final Judgment against "Babylon" (i.e., Anglo-European society) to arrive.

Rastafarians have adopted distinctive religious practices that—to those outside the movement—typify the behavior of all Rastafarians. This is particularly true of the practice of smoking marijuana (or "ganja"). Though not universal, this practice is encouraged within the Rastafarian community in the belief that it both enhances one's health and opens the mind to greater sources of spiritual influence. Similarly, the practice of wearing one's hair in dreadlocks (particularly among men) reflects the Rastafarian belief that they have adopted the behavior of the biblical Nazirites (Samson, for example), whose uncut hair was a sign of strength and devotion to God. In addition, and out of the desire to live a "natural" life, many Rastafarians have adopted a vegetarian diet consisting only of organically grown foods. Avoidance of pork and alcohol are also common, once again reflecting the influence of Old Testament mores on Rastafarian thought.

Most Rastafarian festivals revolve around important dates in the life of Haile Selassie, particularly the date of his accession to the throne of Ethiopia (November 2, 1930). In addition, Rastafarians will gather together for informal discussions called "reasonings" or for celebratory dances connected to formal holidays (known as "nyabinghis"). The smoking of ganja is common to both occasions.

The most popular cultural icon of the Rastafarian movement, even today, remains the 1970s reggae singer and Jamaican political activist Bob Marley (1945–1981). As the front man of a band called The Wailers, Marley became a charismatic advocate for Rasta values throughout the Caribbean during his short lifetime, and since his death his songs have become an anthem for young Jamaicans—and young people everywhere—who long for a world without racism and injustice.

14.3 Reinterpretations of Asian Religious Thought

As early as the 1890s, liberal intellectuals and religious seekers in the United States came under the spell of a charismatic Hindu reformer and writer named Swami Vivekananda (1863–1902), who was one of the more memorable speakers at the World's Parliament of Religions held in Chicago in 1893. Vivekananda saw himself

as a cultural ambassador for Indian religion generally, and his influence in the West was felt by a number of alternative religious communities, including those attracted to "New Thought." Through his speaking tours and the formation of the Vedanta Society (Chapter 4), Vivekananda popularized knowledge of Hindu metaphysics and encouraged an appreciation for yoga and meditative disciplines. The constant theme of his writings and lectures was the need to liberate the spirit from the material world. In the historical vignettes that follow, we focus on some of the more notable religious movements that reflect the encounter between Asian religious thought and practice and Westerners in search of sources of religious enlightenment.

Madame Helena Blavatsky, founder of the theosophy movement.

The Theosophical Society

The Theosophical Society, founded in 1875 by Helena Petrovna Blavatsky (1831–1891) and Henry S. Olcott (1832–1907), was an attempt to combine Hindu and Buddhist ideas in a new approach to the spiritual life, which Blavatsky and Olcott termed **theosophy** (i.e., "divine wisdom"). The Society sought to popularize these ideas in the West. Blavatsky and Olcott not only wanted to make Asian spirituality accessible to religious seekers of the late nineteenth century but also to create a bridge between Western and occult and mystical thought. Blavatsky and Olcott claimed to have knowledge of the secret teachings of the "Ascended Masters" of India and Tibet, whom they claimed to have "channeled."

Blavatsky, the principal theorist of the Theosophical Society, became notorious in the United States when she promoted the practice of séances, through which she claimed to contact the spirits of the dead. Her critics dismissed her as a fraud, but for a time her writings—particularly *Isis Unveiled* (1877) and *The Secret Doctrine* (1889)—had considerable influence on "spiritualists" of this period.

The Theosophical Society believed that all religions reveal a common source, often referred to as "perennial wisdom." Its mission statement reflected its global view of religion, designed to promote a belief in the unity of all peoples and cultures:

1. To form the nucleus of a universal brotherhood of humanity, without distinction of race, creed, sex, caste, or color.
2. [To promote] the study of ancient and modern religions, philosophies, and sciences, and the demonstration of the importance of such study.
3. [To encourage] the investigation of the unexplained laws of nature and the psychical powers latent in man.[5]

Of these three goals, the last was the most important to theosophists. The anti-materialist character of Blavatsky's speculative writings defined the philosophical character of the Theosophical Society for decades to come. Believing that a philosophy based on psychic powers could best be propagated by a Hindu sage, Blavatsky's successors—C. W. Leadbeater and Annie Besant—encouraged their followers to embrace a young Indian mystic named Jiddu Krishnamurti (1895–1986). Leadbeater and Besant regarded Krishnamurti as the "Maitreya" (or "World Teacher") who would succeed in bringing together all of the world's religious leaders under the banner of theosophy. This great enterprise failed in the late 1920s when Krishnamurti himself withdrew his support from the Society and renounced all of the titles and claims it had bestowed upon him.

Today, the Society's headquarters are in Pasadena, California, and it still has many adherents in

Members of a Hare Krishna community dancing on a London street.

India, as well as the United States. It continues to promote a belief in the "oneness of life" and familiar concepts such as karma and reincarnation.

ISKCON: The International Society for Krishna Consciousness

Better known in North America as the Hare Krishna movement, **ISKCON** derives its religious philosophy from the teachings of A. C. Bhaktivedanta Swami (1896–1977), a follower of the sixteenth-century Hindu reformer and mystic Sri Chaitnaya Mahaprabhu. Chaitnaya's disciples regarded him as a divine avatar, and his particular form of Hinduism stressed devotion to the god Krishna, through whom all peoples, regardless of caste or origin, could achieve spiritual fulfillment. Bhaktivedanta (referred to as Prabhupada by his closest followers) brought this message to the West in 1965 when he sought to establish a center for the study of Chaitnayan devotional practices in New York. Two years later, Prabhupada was drawn to San Francisco and its emergent counterculture, where he developed a communalistic movement dedicated to both Krishna worship and an austere code of conduct. Since then, Prabhupada's disciples have established ISKCON centers in more than 300 communities worldwide, and the movement appears to have survived the death of its founder in 1977.

At the heart of the ISKCON philosophy is the belief that Krishna is the sole, supreme deity in the universe and that the highest goal of human life is to achieve "Krishna consciousness," through which the soul can return to its Creator. One of the central rituals of the movement, through which the attainment of Krishna consciousness is facilitated, is the repetitive chanting of one particular mantra—*Hare Krishna, Hare Krishna, Krishna Krishna, Hare Hare, Hare Rama, Hare Rama, Rama Rama, Hare Hare*—accompanied by the rosary-like counting of prayer beads, sixteen times each day. To serve Krishna, Prabhupada taught, one must adopt a strictly vegetarian diet and abstain from violence, gambling, alcohol, tobacco, and drugs. Sexual relations outside of marriage are forbidden, and even within marriage, sexual relations are intended for procreation alone. During the early stages of the movement, ISKCON members committed themselves to selling translations of Prabhupada's commentaries on the Vedas, and the presence of Hare Krishnas (as they were called) at airports and other public locales became a familiar sight during the 1970s.

Prabhupada's death in 1977 occasioned a crisis within the movement, as the eleven gurus he had chosen to lead ISKCON proved too inexperienced (or, in some cases, corrupt), and widespread criticism of the institution of the guru was voiced, both within and outside the movement. There are now approximately 100 ISKCON gurus throughout the world, and though their activities are supposed to be monitored by a governing body, the organizational structure within the movement is fairly loose. Increasingly, local ISKCON temples are independent of policies established by the main Indian congregation in Mayapur (Bengal). Nevertheless, ISKCON continues to maintain a missionary outlook and thinks of itself as an international religious movement.

Transcendental Meditation

At an even further remove from traditional Hindu thought is a meditative discipline that denies it is a religious philosophy at all: Transcendental Meditation. "TM," as it is popularly known, was founded by the Maharishi Mahesh Yogi (1918?–2008), a figure surrounded by mystery (which includes uncertainty about his given name or actual date of birth). A graduate of India's prestigious Allahabad University (in physics), he spent thirteen years at a monastery in northern India studying under Swami Brahmananda Saraswan, commonly called Guru Dev. After Guru Dev's death in 1953, the Maharishi (a self-appointed title meaning "Great Seer") went into seclusion. When he emerged, he set out to share the techniques of meditation he had learned from Guru Dev with the world. Having first established a meditation center that he named the Spiritual Regeneration Movement in Madras in 1958, the Maharishi went on to open similar centers in Los Angeles and in London in 1960, which led to the founding of the International Meditation Society in 1961 and (a decade later) the opening of the Maharishi International University in Iowa in 1971. Each of these institutions was designed both to disseminate the Maharishi's teachings and to promote greater understanding among diverse peoples. In the 1990s, TM renamed itself the Maharishi Foundation, and as part of its plan to promote world peace, it sponsored the creation (in Great Britain) of the Natural Law Party, whose manifesto calls for bringing existing political systems into line with "the intelligence and infinite organizing power that silently maintains and guides the evolution of everything in the universe."[6]

Those who promote TM as the solution to all human problems define it, variably, as a "technology of consciousness" and as a "Science of Creative Intelligence," though its presumed benefits have been questioned by skeptical observers who find little objective evidence to support TM's claims to enhance physical well-being and conflict resolution. This is particularly true of the technique known as **yogic flying**, during which the TM practitioner rocks back and forth with legs crossed, hoping to levitate a few inches. The object of this exercise is to maximize mind–body coordination; TM literature suggests that the key to future spiritual and moral evolution lies in this yogic form of physical transcendence. In addition, TM students are given a special mantra to recite—consisting of a sacred sound rather than a word—with the expectation that reciting this mantra will facilitate a transformation of consciousness leading to greater peace of mind. Those who have benefited from this procedure insist that it has led to significant stress reduction.

The question remains whether this is merely a therapeutic procedure of possible psychological value or a spiritual discipline of personal growth. Unlike Christian Science and other religious philosophies influenced by New Thought, TM offers its disciples no dogmas, and its view of life is entirely "world affirming."

Falun Gong

The influence of Asian religious thought on contemporary seekers is not confined to philosophical influences emanating from India. One recent movement that traces its descent from traditional Chinese sources—and one that has aroused both interest and controversy—is the movement known as Falun Gong or Falun Dafa. Falun Gong is often described as a "cultivation system," one that employs a variation of qigong (martial art) exercises (Chapter 8). But important as meditational and physical routines are to Falun Gong practice, most followers of this movement and of the teachings of its founder, Li Hongzhi, would insist that it offers a discipline of spiritual restoration and a path to philosophical enlightenment.

At the heart of the Falun Gong belief system is a triad of ethical principles designed to guide human beings toward a fuller life, one that is in harmony with nature and the underlying forces of the universe: truthfulness, benevolence, and forbearance. Cultivation of these moral attributes on a collective, and not just personal, level leads to what Master Li calls a "divine culture," whereby an entire society pursues the highest goals humanity is capable of. Seen in this light, Falun Gong resembles a form of redemptive theology, leading its practitioners toward something like salvation. Leaders of the movement take a very dim view of Chinese communism, seeing Marxism as an alien Western ideology, and regarding any form of materialism as a rejection of Daoist first principles. When thousands of Li Hongzhi's followers assembled outside a Chinese government compound in Beijing on April 25, 1999, in silent protest against the government crackdown against the movement, the action provoked an even more severe suppression of Falun Gong teachings and practices. The Chinese government declared Falun Gong to be subversive and "heretical," leading to long prison sentences and reports of torture for those who persisted in public adherence to Falun Gong ideas and rituals. Since then, Falun Gong practitioners appear to have gone underground in China, while interest

Falun Gong devotees in New York City protest the Chinese government's repression of their movement.

in the movement has grown elsewhere, particularly in the West.

Although its roots are in Chinese philosophy and religious practice, Falun Gong also borrows ideas from Buddhism, and the very name of the movement reflects that influence: Falun Gong means "the Dharma Wheel of Practice." Stressing the importance of counteracting the effects of karma (personal and ancestral) upon one's health and moral well-being, Falun Gong practitioners note that the accumulation of such karma affects not only the health of individuals but also society at large. At some point, Master Li insists, entire civilizations perish from an accumulation of moral sickness; in fact, he believes that humanity has undergone eighty-one such destructions of advanced societies, and that our own world civilization may be on the brink of yet another catastrophic collapse unless we can arrest this cycle of growth and decline through personal and collective purification.

In 1994, Li published a summation of his teachings, the **Zhuan Falun**, that is carefully studied by followers of the movement and serves as a guide to right thinking and restorative living for practitioners. In 1997, Li emigrated from China to the United States, where he has since received asylum and from which he continues to guide the movement he helped to create.[7]

VOICES: An Interview with Dr. Xinyu David Zhang

Dr. Xinyu David Zhang.

Dr. Zhang is a senior database administrator for the California Commission on Teacher Credentialing and has a PhD in organizational psychology. He is a practitioner of Falun Gong.

Is it appropriate to think of Falun Gong as a religion, or should we think of it as something similar to hatha yoga or tai chi?

For people in the West, it may very well resemble a religion, but most Chinese think of it as a cultivation system, that is, as a body of teachings designed to improve both mind and body. In China the word *religion* is unfamiliar and Western sounding—and even has a pejorative meaning—but aside from the unfamiliarity of the concept, Falun Gong has none of the trappings of Western religions: no sanctuaries, no clerical hierarchy, no sacred rituals, and practitioners are free to enter or leave the movement, as they please.

Nevertheless, Falun Gong does seem to possess a sacred text in the *Zhuan Falun*.

Once again, your Western analogy is a bit misleading. The *Zhuan Falun* (meaning "The Turning of the Wheel of the Law") contains Master Li's thoughts on the importance of mindfulness in the search for the moral life. His recent teachings place particular stress on the need for social justice, the restoration of human rights denied by the communist regime, and the necessity of bringing back a "divine culture" to China. We in Falun Gong have come to regard Chinese communism as a wholly foreign materialist philosophy that can only increase the amount of bad karma in the world. Our ultimate aim, therefore, is the restoration of moral health to both the individual and the world.

Aum Shinrikyo: A Cult of Redemptive Violence?

Aum Shinrikyo (Japanese, "religion of supreme truth") was established in 1986 by Matsumoto Chizuo (1955–2018), known to his followers as Shoko Asahara. Aum has been described as a doomsday cult, yet it initially appeared to be one of many cultivation disciplines (like yoga and meditation) to emerge from East Asia, blending Buddhism and Hinduism. After traveling to the Himalayas, Asahara became convinced that the Hindu god of destruction, Shiva, had spoken to him and that he was destined to rescue humankind from impending catastrophe. Asahara's readings of the Christian book of Revelation and the sixteenth-century French prophet Nostradamus further reinforced his obsession with the end time. He fixated upon 1999 as the final time of reckoning for the human race, believing that only his teachings stood between planetary annihilation and world salvation.

Aum Shinrikyo founder Shoko Asahara.

During the 1990s, Asahara's messianic ideas became darker and more paranoid. After failing to attract enough votes for Aum to enter the Japanese Parliament, Asahara concluded that Japan was no longer receptive to Aum's redemptive message. Instead of averting disaster, Asahara reasoned, the time had come to bring on the Apocalypse, believing that destruction on a massive scale would cleanse the world of its accumulated evils and lead to the establishment of a utopian order. He persuaded his followers to build bomb shelters and procure military weapons in preparation for the impending world doom. Like many of the more maniacal religious leaders Bruce Lincoln discusses in his book *Holy Terrors*, Asahara had long since convinced himself that his voice was the voice of God.[8]

On March 20, 1995, Asahara ordered Aum members to release sarin gas on a Tokyo subway station, killing twelve and injuring thousands. Further investigation revealed that Asahara and his disciples had not only committed earlier crimes against their opponents—and against defectors

In the weeks after the 1995 deadly sarin gas attack on a Tokyo commuter train, Japanese police raided an Aum Shinrikyo compound near Mount Fuji and confiscated chemical and biological weapons as well as explosives.

from their movement—but that they had been stockpiling even more lethal weapons in anticipation of a final struggle for world supremacy. Asahara and several close associates were tried and finally put to death in 2018. Asahara's followers, however, have since formed two new groups in Japan ("Aleph" and "Circle of Rainbow Light"). Although both groups claim to have renounced Asahara's advocacy of violence, they remain under close surveillance by the Japanese government.

It is difficult to explain how a man of limited education and extreme views could attract thousands of followers and inspire them to engage in criminal activities bordering on genocide. While Aum's worldview resembles other "world-renouncing" religious philosophies in its desire to separate from a perceived corrupt social order, in its advocacy of mass murder as the path to salvation, Aum stands alone.

In the weeks after the 1995 deadly sarin gas attack on a Tokyo commuter train, Japanese police raided an Aum Shinrikyo compound near Mount Fuji and confiscated chemical and biological weapons as well as explosives.

14.4 The Revival of Esoteric and Neo-Pagan Thought

The religious philosophies we turn to next combine many of the ideas and behaviors sociologists commonly refer to as esoteric. In fact, what all of these alternative communities share is the belief that a superior kind of spiritual knowledge—known in antiquity as *gnosis* (Greek, "knowledge")—is available to everyone in the modern world, often due to the presence of enlightened intermediaries in our midst. Once one is in possession of such knowledge, the world we presently call real appears very different—whether enhanced or diminished—depending on how "world affirming" or "world denying" one's experience of a greater reality turns out to be. The belief that the world of common, everyday perception is only a fragment (or a shadowy reflection) of something much more real is a recurrent insight of most of the world's religions. Nevertheless, the conviction that direct knowledge of that greater reality is a guarded secret that only a few initiates can grasp is the core presumption behind all forms of esoteric thought in the West.

Eckankar

Though first established as a distinctive religious community in 1965, Eckankar claims to be the most ancient of all religions and, therefore, the spiritual "root" from which all later religious traditions have descended. In his book *Eckankar: The Key to Secret Worlds* (1969), Eckankar's founder, Paul Twitchell (1908?–1971), endorses a belief in **astral voyages** (the projection of the mind or spirit onto higher levels of experience) and asserts that we can inhabit two different planes of reality at the same time. Through the exercise of ancient meditational techniques, Twitchell taught, it is possible for the soul to travel outside of the body and to free itself from both the prison world of ordinary perception and the cycle of reincarnations. These same spiritual exercises allow one to experience God's voice as a form of light and sound and thereby draw closer to the source of all being. Only the *chela*, or student of Eckankar-based wisdom, can make this spiritual ascent, and a lengthy period of initiation is required before the movement of the mind to this astral plane can be accomplished successively.

Because emanative forces from God flow through the consciousness of the living Eck Master, his influence is vital if one is to experience the divine reality. Twitchell believed himself to be such a Master—the 971st Eck Master—which placed him in a long line of spiritual guides going back to remote antiquity, one that included Jesus and St. Paul. Twitchell believed that they, too, had been influenced by Eck Masters and that Christianity could therefore be viewed as an offshoot of Eck teachings. Further, he believed that any living Eck Master can not only "channel" the thinking of deceased Masters but can also correct any mistaken notions proclaimed by his immediate predecessors. The words of the living Master, therefore, are determinative of whatever doctrines emerge, at any given time, from the Eckankar community—an assumption that has led to institutional instability.

Upon Twitchell's death in 1971, leadership of the movement fell to Darwin Gross (1928–2008), who, despite some opposition within the Eckankar community, immediately declared himself to be Living Master No. 972. That claim was later disputed by his successor, Harold Klemp (b. 1942), who, as Living Master No. 973, declared that Gross was no longer an Eck Master. This power struggle within the Eckankar leadership led to a splintering of the community and public attacks on Twitchell's claims to credibility. Several critics of the movement have even demonstrated Twitchell's literal indebtedness—often in the form of outright plagiarism—to earlier writers of the Sant Mat tradition (which combines elements of Hindu and Sikh mysticism). Today, Twitchell's followers generally acknowledge similarities between his revelations and earlier religious texts and traditions, but they insist that he was merely echoing truths that have been revealed to all great religious teachers. Since the 1980s, the movement has been headquartered in Chanhassen, Minnesota, where the Temple of Eck was constructed in 1990. The number of Eckists, as members of this community are known, may be as high as 20,000.

The Raelian Movement

Another expression of contemporary esoteric religious thought can be found in movements committed to a belief in extraterrestrial beings. Popularly dubbed

"UFO cults," many of these communities have assumed the concerns—and in some cases the language—of millenarian Christian theology, namely, a visionary future in which believers will be rescued from a dying Earth by visitors from outer space, who will transport the chosen few to a blissful life on a distant planet. One recurrent article of faith among such groups is the belief that human civilization is the result of interaction with beings from another planetary system who have used our world as a laboratory for genetic and cultural experimentation. Within the context of this quasi-religious creed—which sociologists refer to as **Ufology**—spiritual enlightenment consists of the realization that our collective destinies are ultimately in the hands of unearthly beings whose power and intelligence vastly exceed our own and whose immediate goal is to make contact with those few human beings capable of receiving their secret (and ultimately world-redeeming) revelations.

The Raelian movement, which was given its name and its creed by its founder, Claude "Rael" Vorilhon (b. 1946), is one of the better known communities of UFO worshipers. Its belief system should be at once familiar and strange to anyone living within a Judeo-Christian culture. In his book *The Message Given to Me by Extraterrestrials: They Took Me to Their Planet* (1978), Rael revisits the various accounts of divine–human interaction in the Hebrew Bible and identifies the **Elohim**—a term used in the Hebrew Bible to identify the Creator God—as the true creators of our planet and of the human race. However, the Elohim are not supernatural beings, Rael insists, but rather an advanced race of extraterrestrials. It was the Elohim who renamed Vorilhon "Rael," and it was one of the Elohim who impregnated Mary of Nazareth and fathered Jesus centuries ago. Rael believes that he, too, is the result of human–extraterrestrial mating, which places him among a select group of prophets and teachers that includes, among others, Buddha, Jesus, and Muhammad. Believing himself to be the Messiah of our age, Rael founded the Raelian religion in 1974 (known formally as "The Movement to Welcome the Elohim, Creators of Humanity") as a means of publicizing the presence of the Elohim within our planetary system and in anticipation of the day when the peoples of Earth will be able to receive the Elohim in peace. Only then will a new world order be possible and the global reign of men and women of superior intelligence commence.

Rael's flair for publicity is one of the reasons that the Raelians have achieved a larger measure of public recognition than most UFO religions. In 2002, Dr. Brigitte Boisselier (b. 1956) announced that she and her fellow Raelians had successfully cloned a human baby in fulfillment of the Raelian goal of achieving immortality through scientific means. No proof has been offered confirming this claim, but it did succeed in drawing international attention. Rael himself has organized a conference promoting masturbation, arguing that "self-love" would stimulate the growth of new brain cells and thereby make it possible for humans to experience sexual pleasure without guilt. Rael has repeatedly sought public confrontations with the Catholic Church, insisting, for example, that his followers address him as "Your Holiness"—a title normally reserved for the Pope.

Many of the Raelian teachings that have provoked controversy can be found in other UFO-oriented organizations and in esoteric religious communities generally. Critics of Vorilhon's writings have accused him of having "borrowed" Erich von Daniken's mythic account of the extraterrestrial origins of human civilization (*Chariots of the Gods*, 1968) for his own purposes and have focused on his advocacy of various kinds of sexual "liberation" as proof of the inherently antisocial character of the movement (though a belief in "free love" is not uncommon among alternative religions). But in his own defense, Rael has pointed out that his belief in superior beings from another galaxy or in spaceships circling Earth is no stranger than believing in supernatural "guides" who direct the course of human history. From his perspective, all he has done is offer a more "scientific" version of a belief that, in one form or another, has been embraced by most of the world's religions. As for the Raelians' promotion of cloning (for pets as well as humans) as a legitimate response to the dilemma of mortality, it was never the desire of the Elohim, they argue, that the human race remain forever limited to a single lifespan, nor that we should suffer from the ravages of disease. The Elohim, the Raelians teach, remain poised, waiting for the next evolutionary leap in human development to occur, at which time they will share with us the superior knowledge and technological expertise they have accumulated over eons of time.

Critics insist that what is particularly disturbing about this movement (and other dedicated UFO communities) is the potential for socially destructive behavior. Anticult activists point to the collective suicides of the Heaven's Gate community in 1997—whose thirty-nine members took their lives in the belief that, having shed their bodies, their spirits would ascend into the heavens and join the "mother ship"—as proof that Ufology, carried to its extreme conclusion, can generate a pathological form of world renunciation. Still, although it is not possible to assert that the Raelian community will never adopt a radical and apocalyptic view of the human condition, Vorilhon has yet to display any sign of the psychopathology that compelled Marshall Herff Applewhite (1931–1997), the leader of the Heaven's Gate movement, and his followers to take their lives as an act of spiritual liberation.

The Church of Scientology

Of all the new religious movements we have discussed thus far, none has aroused as much opposition, or public curiosity, as the movement founded by Lafayette Ron Hubbard (1911–1986) in 1954. Hubbard's personality, as well as the extraordinary claims made on his behalf by his

Rael is seated in front of a model of a double helix as he announces the supposed cloning of a human child.

followers, has been the focus of much of the criticism directed at the Church of Scientology. But even if Hubbard had not played such a visible role in the formation of Scientology, its teachings alone would have stirred controversy. At its beginnings, Scientology was presented to the public as a new form of mental healing. Hubbard's best known publication, *Dianetics: The Modern Science of Mental Health* (1950), offered its readers an alternative view of the self and the dynamic forces at work within the subconscious mind. Yet, even at this early stage in the development of his largely esoteric belief system, Hubbard was committed to a view of the "true" self—or **thetan** as it is called in his writings—that stresses the immaterial nature of what most Western religions would call the "soul." Thus, even though the thetan inhabits the body during an individual's lifespan, and even though it interacts with matter and energy, it possesses an eternal and independent reality and can therefore survive death and pass on to other bodies. To attain enlightenment, Hubbard believed, one must first acknowledge the primary reality of the thetan before passing on to higher levels of spiritual understanding.

The critical moment, Scientologists believe, in this search for expanded consciousness comes when the presence of "**engrams**"—traumatic events stored as images in the "reactive" or subconscious mind—is made evident to both the subject of mental analysis and the "auditor" engaged in detecting unsettling memories and deeply irrational feelings. One of the primary purposes of Scientology's form of counseling is to release the troubled individual—referred to as "pre-clear" in Scientological literature—from emotionally crippling past experiences. Indeed, once one is declared "clear" of whatever destructive engrams have accumulated in the mind, one's health (physical and mental) will improve dramatically, and those who have benefited from the process of "auditing" have testified to its liberating effects.

But Scientology is more than the sum of its therapeutic promises and procedures. Beginning in the 1950s, Hubbard evolved a complex mythology in which the thetans—now thought of as a race of super-beings—were creators of our material universe who gradually lost their creative powers and fell victim to the reactive mind, which grew in influence as their powers waned. To recover the energy and imagination once possessed by these primordial thetans has become the mission of Scientology's elite cadres, and at the highest levels of spiritual and intellectual development within the movement, the secrets of continued progressive evolution are revealed. Such emphasis on secrecy and hidden truths, disclosed only to the initiated, is one of the persistent characteristics of esoteric movements generally, and it is only within their movement, Scientologists insist, that one can achieve the status of a spiritually evolved individual (or an "Operating Thetan," in Scientological terminology). Ironically, by tightly controlling the means of progressive self-development, Scientology has committed itself to the same kind of therapeutic monopoly that Hubbard denounced in his attacks on modern psychiatry.

Critics of Scientology have attacked the movement on several fronts.[9] The official biography of its founder, they argue, is filled with distortions and lies.

In reality, they insist, L. Ron Hubbard was nothing like the hero of the mind portrayed in movement literature but a scheming science-fiction writer whose cravings for power and wealth led him to fabricate a mock religion of mental health. As for the E-meter—used to detect the presence of engrams in the pre-clear mind—it is no more effective, these critics charge, than an ordinary lie detector (which it resembles) in eliminating the reactive mind or in tracing the effects of negative mental energy. Counseling of practically any kind, they point

An E-meter and a display of Hubbard's *Dianetics.*

out, can accomplish much of what Scientologists attribute to their methodology, and without the trappings of a science-fiction cult. Scientology's twenty-six-year struggle with the Internal Revenue Service to have itself recognized as a legitimate religious organization was finally resolved in the church's favor by 1993. Still, the testimonies of former Scientologists to the authoritarian nature of its leadership and to the suppression of criticism within the movement seem to indicate a fundamental discrepancy between the aspirations of the church and its actual policies.

In response to such critics, Scientologists point out that apostates from any religious movement often bear tales of deception and mistreatment and just as often misrepresent the very teachings they have come to reject. The ultimate goals of the Church of Scientology, its defenders insist, have not changed in the half-century or so in which the movement has existed. Its goals, they claim, clearly reflect the redemptive mission of its founder: to achieve "a civilization without insanity, without criminals and without war, where the able can prosper and honest beings can have rights, and where man is free to rise to greater heights." At present, there are well over 100 Scientology churches worldwide, in at least as many countries. While the precise number of members still actively affiliated with the church is difficult to determine, its presence within the contemporary religious landscape appears to be well established, at least in the United States. In Europe, however, Scientology's insistence on being seen as an authentic religion—or in Hubbard's words as an "applied religious philosophy"—has been met with much greater skepticism and resistance.

Wicca and the Return to Neo-Paganism

Witches have long figured in the popular imagination and in much of Western folklore, but the contemporary nature religion known as *Wicca* is a far cry from the literary incarnations of the archetypal embodiment of evil. Contemporary witches, or *Wiccans*, as they prefer to be called, do not cast harmful spells, do not communicate with spirits of the underworld, and most especially do not worship the Devil. They do claim to practice various types of magic, however, and they often worship various pre-Christian deities, particularly those associated with natural forces and phenomena. Contemporary Wiccans prefer to be thought of as pagans, or more precisely, "neo-pagans," since the ensemble of beliefs and practices that characterizes witchcraft today is so eclectic that no direct link between Wicca and pre-Christian religious cultures can be said to exist.

The Wiccan movement appears to have been the brainchild of one British enthusiast, Gerald B. Gardner (1884–1964), who, after a career as a civil servant in Southeast Asia, returned to England to pursue an interest in folklore and esoteric religious thought. In concert with Margaret Murray (1863–1963), an anthropologist and Egyptologist (as well as a prominent early feminist) whose book *The Witch Cult in Western Europe* (1921) argued that the witch cults of medieval Europe were survivors of an indigenous fertility religion, Gardner sought to prove that remnants of these ancient pagan rituals could still be found in the modern world. Although anthropologists have since rejected both Murray's research and Gardner's more extravagant claims, the modern form of Wicca seems to have been born out of their collaboration. Following the repeal in 1954 of England's 1735 Witchcraft Act, Gardner set out to revive interest in "the Craft" by describing ancient pagan beliefs in his landmark book *Witchcraft Today* (1954), which both legitimated the pursuit of once-forbidden practices and opened the door to future development of Wiccan principles and ritual acts. Gardner's critics have since cast doubts on the authenticity of his claims to have recovered the secrets of ancient witch cults. Nevertheless, his work has inspired Wiccans whose interpretations of Gardnerian lore have led to distinct schools of Wiccan thought.

At the heart of Wiccan teachings is the neo-pagan belief that divine magic and mystery lie within ourselves and within the natural world. The Wiccan concept of the sacred is almost entirely immanental—that is, dwelling *within* nature rather than outside or above it. Although many Wiccan communities have chosen to worship a variety of pre-Christian deities, these gods are generally viewed as personifications of the power and grandeur that resides within nature and within the human imagination. When Wiccans speak of "the God" or "the Goddess," they are not referring to the transcendent Creator of the Abrahamic religions but rather to a creative force that lies within all existing things, to which human cultures attribute gender and personality. Wiccans are not content, however, simply to worship the powers that permeate our universe; they also seek to access those powers through ritualized acts of magic (or "magick" as most Wiccans prefer to spell that word). It is this more assertive aspect of Wicca that places it within Melton's "magical" family of new religions. The only constraint that Wiccans acknowledge upon the exercise of such power is embodied in the **Wiccan Rede**—that is, those principles of ethical behavior that virtually all modern witches accept as binding—which teaches: "And it harm none, do what you will." For

Wiccan communities, that rule entails the use of "magick" to achieve positive ends, and many Wiccan authors urge their readers to practice deeds that will be of benefit to humanity. In addition, many versions of the Wiccan "Rede" (or "rule" in modern English) teach a belief in some form of karma; thus, Wiccans are cautioned to expect that harmful acts will return to afflict the witch who inflicts them on others.

As indicated in the vignette with which this chapter began, Wiccans celebrate the change of seasons, as well as the phases of the moon. Two common ceremonies within the Wiccan community are the *Esbat* and the *Sabbat*, which are designed, respectively, to pay honor to the Goddess of the Moon and the God of the Sun. On one hand, Esbats most often occur when the moon is full, though custom varies from community to community. Sabbats, on the other hand, are seasonal and mark the occurrence of equinoxes and solstices, or midpoints between them. There are eight Sabbats within the Wiccan calendar, the most familiar of which is Yule (or "Yuletide," as it is known in many Christian cultures). The ceremonies associated with Esbats and Sabbats differ considerably: during an Esbat celebration, for example, some attempt to "draw down the moon" (that is, draw the moon's energy into oneself) is the ritual's focus; on a Sabbat, however, it is customary to light bonfires and to decorate an altar in a way that pays tribute to the character of the particular god who is being honored that season. In each case, Wiccans hope to align themselves with the hidden energies of nature and to confer blessings on themselves and their loved ones through such acts of natural communion.

Wicca is one of the most decentralized of new religious communities. Wiccans generally gather in small groups known as **covens**, though some witches prefer to practice their "Craft" in isolation. One of the more influential schools of Wiccan thought is the Reclaiming movement, founded by Miriam Simos (b. 1951; better known in Wiccan circles as "Starhawk") in the 1970s. The Reclaiming philosophy is more overtly political than most varieties of Wicca, and in her writings Simos blends feminist, anti-capitalist, and ecological concerns in an attempt to reclaim Earth from political forces that have despoiled the planet and oppressed its population. Most Wiccans, however, prefer not to align their communities with a specific political agenda, though the formation of the Witches' League for Public Awareness in 1986 and other lobbying organizations (such as the Alternative Religious Education Network) have received widespread support in the Wiccan movement. One of the more organized

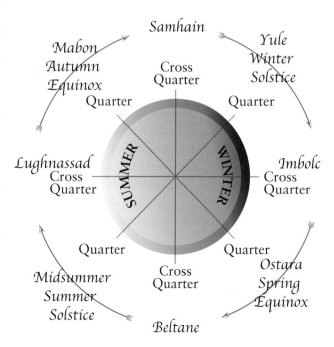

Wiccan wheel of the year.

Wiccan communities, the Church and School of Wicca (founded in 1968), estimates the number of its adherents to be around 200,000. Although it is impossible to extrapolate the number of Wiccans worldwide, the movement has benefited from court decisions in the United States that conferred legal status on the practice of witchcraft, allowing individuals to claim Wicca as their legally acknowledged religion.

14.5 Universalist Religious Thought

The global presence of both Christianity and Islam ensured that, by the late nineteenth century, emergent religions throughout the world would reflect the influence and prestige of these Abrahamic traditions. The most direct manifestation of this influence can be found in their embrace of a monotheistic paradigm, in which the idea of a single and singular "God" becomes a core precept in their offshoot theology. But no less direct an influence can be found in the belief—shared by so many "universalist" religions, and in particular by Baha'i and Unitarianism—that their teachings reach beyond the boundaries of time and geography and therefore speak to the whole of humankind.

The Baha'i Faith

As the last of the Abrahamic religions that traces its origins to the Middle East, Islam presents itself as the final and decisive revelation of divine truth to humankind. This belief has been challenged not only by the two Abrahamic religions that preceded it, Judaism and Christianity, but by later monotheistic religions as well. Perhaps the most significant challenge to Islam's belief in the finality of the Qur'an, however (at least within the context of Middle Eastern religious culture), occurred in mid-nineteenth-century Iran, where Sayyid Ali-Muhammad Shirazi (1819–1850) saw himself as a successor to Muhammad and as the recipient of new revelations from Allah. His followers called him the *Bab*—meaning the "Gate" through which the Twelfth Imam of Shi'ism would enter the world—and his teachings were soon declared heretical by Muslim authorities. His imprisonment and death failed to stifle the messianic movement he had ignited, and in 1853 one of his most devoted followers, Mirza Husayn Ali Nuri (1817–1892)—better known by the title he later bore, Baha'u'llah—declared himself to be a "Messenger of God" and therefore the legitimate successor to the Bab. Many of the followers of the Bab subsequently pledged their allegiance to Baha'u'llah and their adherence to his teachings, and thus began the new religious movement known as Baha'i.

Baha'i is both a monotheistic and a universalistic faith, based on a belief in one Creator God who is the source of all existence and goodness in the universe and the ultimate object of worship for all peoples. Because this God is a wholly transcendent, eternal, and unknowable Being, "he" cannot be described or comprehended by human minds, but his representatives or chosen "messengers" on Earth can at least impart something of his will for humankind. According to Baha'u'llah, there has been a succession of such messengers in history (including Moses, Zoroaster, Buddha, Jesus, and Muhammad), each one serving as a prophet for his respective faith community. Baha'u'llah saw himself as the most recent of these manifestations of divine wisdom, and for his followers no future messenger from God is expected for another thousand years. Because divine revelation for Baha'is is progressive, each of these prophets advances human understanding of the divine with each successive revelation. For Baha'is, the teachings of Baha'u'llah and his successors within the Baha'i movement constitute the most complete understanding of divine thought that human beings have yet attained. As for the writings of Baha'u'llah, they have become for Baha'is part of an unfolding authoritative "scripture," and as a written revelation they have the advantage of having no competing oral tradition (unlike the hadith in Islam, for example).

The core truth that Baha'u'llah sought to impart to his followers and to the world was this: that because God is one, humanity must also be one. Baha'u'llah believed that all the barriers that separate people from one another (such as differences of race, nationality, gender, wealth, and religious belief) must give way to an awakened sense that the human race has at last "come of age" and that the world is ripe for political structures and cultural values that unite rather than divide. World government (and world peace) is finally attainable, he insisted, but only if we are willing to embrace twelve principles of thought and behavior:

1. The oneness of God and the common foundation of all religions
2. The oneness of humanity
3. The equality of men and women
4. The need to eliminate all types of prejudice
5. The need to eliminate all extremes of wealth and poverty
6. A belief in the harmony of science and religion
7. The need for compulsory universal education
8. The need for a common language spoken by all peoples
9. The need for independent inquiries into truth
10. The pursuit of spiritual solutions to political and social problems
11. Obedience to one's government coupled with avoidance of partisan politics
12. The establishment of a world government as the guarantor of world peace

The mission of the Baha'i community, as Baha'u'llah understood it, was to promote these teachings and to become a role model for the world's religious communities, demonstrating in their communal life that diverse cultures can embrace a vision of universal harmony and mutual understanding.

The Baha'i community has evolved a body of scripture, religious practices, and governing structure that have given their faith a distinctive character. Chief among the texts that Baha'is consider holy are the writings of the Bab, Baha'u'llah, Abdul-Baha (1844–1921, Baha'u'llah's eldest son), and Shoghi Effendi (1897–1957),

Referred to as the Lotus Temple, this structure borrows its design from Hindu iconography.

Abdul-Baha's eldest grandson and the last individual leader of the Baha'i community. Baha'is study these writings throughout the year and integrate readings from them in their religious services. Daily prayer is obligatory for Baha'is over the age of fifteen, and because there are no Baha'i clergy, any member sufficiently familiar with the liturgy can lead these services.

The Baha'i religious calendar is made up of nineteen months, each of which has nineteen days, with an additional four days added to bring it into line with the solar year. The first day of each month is a feast day, consisting of both prayers and social events. Baha'is also celebrate eleven holy days, the most important of which are the birthday of the Bab (October 20) and his martyrdom (July 9) and three days marking the declaration of Baha'u'llah's divine mission in 1863 (April 21 and 29 and May 2). Like Muslims, Baha'is fast once a year (for nineteen days, from March 2 to March 20) and abstain from alcohol. Marriage and family life are important aspects of Baha'i life, and, as in most Middle Eastern societies, parental consent is necessary for any marriage to take place and to be recognized by the community.

There are eight major Baha'i Houses of Worship, the most striking of which is the temple in New Delhi—its shape is that of a lotus flower—and an administrative center in Haifa, Israel. The Universal House of Justice is also located there, and since 1963 its elected members have served as the governing body for all members of the Baha'i community. At present, there are over 5 million Baha'is worldwide.

Unitarian Universalism

The Unitarian Universalist Association came into being in 1961 as the result of a merger of two previously independent institutions: the American Unitarian Association (founded in 1825) and the Universalist Church of America (established in 1866). Each of these religious communities represented, within the context of nineteenth-century Christianity, a radical deviation from the more familiar forms of Christianity: the Unitarians denied the Trinity, and the Universalists denied any belief in eternal damnation. As both groups evolved, they moved closer to a humanist worldview in which the rule of reason and the authority of science displaced religious dogmas as an acceptable basis for understanding the universe, as well as human nature. By the time of their merger, neither the Unitarians nor the Universalists saw themselves as definably (or exclusively) Christian any longer, though Unitarian Universalists feel free to adapt specific Christian ideas—such as the Golden Rule or the forgiveness of one's enemies—to their own developing system of ethics.

At the heart of Unitarian Universalist teachings today, we find seven "principles and purposes" that constitute the spiritual core of the Association's belief system:

1. A belief in the inherent dignity and worth of every human being
2. A need for justice, equity, and compassion in all human relationships
3. Toleration and respect for each other as the basis for spiritual growth
4. A need for a free and responsible search for truth and meaning
5. The right of the individual conscience and a commitment to the democratic process
6. The goal of a world community based on peace, liberty, and justice for all
7. Recognition of the "web" of all living things and the interdependence of all life forms, human and nonhuman

None of these teachings amounts to a creed. Instead, they can be viewed as guidelines for moral conduct and social relationships, accompanied by an enduring respect for the *mysterium tremendum* (Chapter 1) that is common to many of the world's religions.

Unitarian Universalists have adopted rituals to embody these teachings, depending on the cultural and religious backgrounds of any particular congregation. Thus, any given Unitarian Universalist community may observe some version of a Passover Seder, a Muslim Iftar, a Buddhist meditation, or a Christmas Eve celebration (possibly combined with a winter solstice rite). Such eclecticism reflects both the openness of Unitarian Universalist society and the recognition of religious diversity, seen from a global perspective.

Spiritual Ecology

For many of those who are committed to saving our planet from any further destruction of natural resources, the contemporary ecological movement lies at the intersection of science and religion, and possesses the same concern for the welfare of humankind that other, more established religious communities do. This is particularly true for those persons of faith who have embraced—to a greater or lesser degree of literalness—the Gaia hypothesis of James Lovelock and Lynn Margulis. As stated first in the 1970s, and later revised in the 1990s, this revolutionary theory rests on the assumption that our planet can best be understood as a "self-regulating complex system" whose ultimate goal is to achieve homeostasis (i.e., "optimal conditions for life"). Both Lovelock, a chemist, and his colleague Lynn Margulis, a microbiologist, attribute something like intentionality to the various systems that make life possible on Earth: hence the choice of the mythical name "Gaia" (in Greek mythology the goddess of Earth) as the composite term for all of the phenomena which Earth science has identified as prerequisite for all living organisms on this planet. Indeed, what makes their thesis so revolutionary is the tendency to see the evolving history of Earth as the story of a single organism, endowed with purposefulness and self-awareness, and capable of progressive adaptation.[10]

Needless to say, this theory has been challenged again and again by scientists who insist that Lovelock and Margulis have done nothing more than literalize a metaphor, treating "Mother Nature" as something more than an image. However, various contemporary religious philosophers, and particularly those who are committed to the principles of the ecological movement, have found in the Gaia hypothesis a clue to the divine unity and manifest purpose of life on Earth, albeit, one that has eluded empirical sciences in the West until now. This confluence of scientific and religious discourse—often termed "spiritual ecology"—can be found, for example, in Pope Francis's 2015 encyclical entitled "Laudato Si': On Care for Our Common Home" in which he argues that the present ecological crisis of global warming that we are witnessing today is essentially a *spiritual* crisis, stemming from the fact that we have forgotten the fact that Earth itself is a "gift from God," who has instructed us to assume a burden of "stewardship" toward all living things. Pope Francis's plea was later echoed at a meeting of the Parliament of the World's Religions, held that same year, and the view that emerged from that gathering of clerical and academic representatives was that the need to confront climate change was the principal moral and spiritual challenge of our time.

A more radical and far-reaching version of this same argument, however, can be found in Rosemary Radford Reuther's book *Gaia and God: An Ecofeminist Theology of Earth Healing* (1992), in which the author brings together several diverse strands of ecological spirituality. Thus, taking as her objective the need to "rebuild human society for a sustainable earth," Reuther insists, like Pope Francis, that the ecological crisis is, in reality, a spiritual crisis, brought about by a civilization that views the natural world as something inhuman and devoid of spiritual value. Moreover, the dominant God concept of the West, she insists, is both utterly transcendent and hopelessly patriarchal, and therefore one that serves as the theological foundation of our present technological culture: a culture that both legitimizes the destruction of Nature and the exploitative domination of non-Western societies. In its place, Reuther proposes a revisionist, post-Christian understanding of humankind—one that places human beings within, rather than outside, the biosphere—and a concept of divinity that finds "God" both within human consciousness and within the world of natural process. Taking her cue from the Jesuit philosopher Teilhard de Chardin, Reuther envisions a newly sacralized universe in which matter and spirit have finally become one, and in which the human mind is at last understood to be the site of cosmic thought. If Gaia and God are not simply interchangeable terms in Reuther's worldview, then they are at least complementary forms of the same divine mystery.[11]

The political imperatives that follow logically from this visionary reconstruction of Western religious thought are undeniably utopian in character: the redeemed world she envisions is a world without competition or aggression, in which poverty and injustice no longer flourish. Male domination in all its forms will have ceased to exist, and new creative forms of parenting and governing will have arisen. Like the biblical prophet Isaiah, Reuther envisions a future in which nation will not take up sword against nation, nor make war anymore. Once we have moved beyond patriarchy and the subjection of non-Western peoples, she insists, humankind will experience a kind of *metanoia*, or reversal of consciousness, that will allow for a final falling away of the self and the emergence of spiritually transformed societies at peace with themselves and with nature.

The Findhorn Foundation

If there is any community that has at least tried to embrace this vision of a reclaimed planet and a redeemed human race, it is, perhaps, the Findhorn Foundation in Scotland. Like so many New Age communities, Findhorn was a product of the political turmoil and revolutionary expectations of the 1960s. When its founders, Peter and Eileen Caddy, withdrew to a quiet Scottish village named Findhorn in 1962, they hoped to establish there a communitarian way of life that would be open to new forms of religious experience. Eileen Caddy had long believed that she had received messages from God, and that the end of the present world order was at hand. Her hope, then, was that the alternative society she and her husband planned to create would outlast the apocalypse and become a model for a small-scale agricultural way of life. As time went on, and as the Findhorn community grew, its subsequent leadership moved away from a postapocalyptic/survivalist mode of thinking to something more adaptive and progressive. This shift in self-understanding and political perspective—corresponding to Wallis's distinction between a world-renouncing and a world-accommodating ideology—was accompanied by the physical expansion of the original Findhorn colony and the development of residential educational programs designed to promote "planetary cleansing."

Today Findhorn is the site of one of the more successful ecovillages in any Western nation. It boasts that it has the "smallest ecological footprint" of any community in the postindustrial world, but even more remarkably it serves as a haven for spiritually minded persons who wish to pursue a nondogmatic contemplative life with active community engagement. In the nineteenth century the typical Findhorn resident would have

Members of Findhorn Foundation engaged in Sacred Dance.

been described as a "seeker," and the fluid population of the entire Findhorn community makes it unlikely that it will ever become anything more than a village in size and composition.[12]

14.6 The New Atheism

Strange though it may seem to conclude a discussion of modern trends and movements in religious thought with a reference to systems of *disbelief,* any analysis of contemporary spirituality would be incomplete without some recognition of a recent groundswell of oppositional voices representing those—particularly in the West—who view any and all religious ideas as delusional and politically dangerous. And although some form of atheism—understood as the denial of belief in any supernatural being or agency—has been a fact of cultural life in both the East and the West since antiquity, the term *atheist* is most commonly applied today to those who reject the idea of a God who is presumed to be the Creator of the universe and of humankind.

Since the Enlightenment of the eighteenth century, Western cultures have seen the rise of philosophical opponents of Christianity who have sought to refute the very basis of Christian faith by denying either the validity or the rationality of any and all theistic beliefs. Baron d'Holbach's (1723–1789) *The System of Nature* (1770) is an example of this type of Enlightenment atheism in its most aggressive form. His argument against religion proceeds from the belief, supported by the science of his day, that the universe consists of nothing but matter and energy. From that premise it follows, d'Holbach insists, that there is neither a soul nor an afterlife, neither a heaven nor a hell, and that all ideas about God are nothing but human attributes projected onto a cosmos that obeys only the laws of physics. This argument on behalf of a materialistic antitheism remains the essential narrative of atheism today. In the words of the modern French philosopher Jean-Paul Sartre (1905–1980), atheism has left a "God-shaped hole"[13] in the cultural consciousness of the West, and nothing, he argues, has emerged to fill that void.

That was the position of a number of later twentieth-century theological skeptics—known collectively as the "Death of God" movement—who took up the cry of the nineteenth-century German philosopher Friedrich Nietzsche (1844–1900) that God was "dead." God *was* dead, for them, at least in the sense that it was no longer possible, in the modern world, to maintain a belief in a Deity of rewards and punishments, of Creation and of a Judgment Day. In the words of one representative voice of this movement, Thomas J. J. Altizer (b. 1927):

> We shall understand the death of God as an historical event: God has died in *our* time, in *our* history, in *our* existence. The man who chooses to live in our destiny can neither know the reality of God's presence nor understand the world as his creation; or at least he can no longer respond . . . to the classical Christian images of the Creator and the creation.[14]

In contrast to their eighteenth- and nineteenth-century counterparts, these religiously oriented atheists hoped that old images of a transcendent, omnipotent, and benevolent deity—which, they argued, are no longer supportable in an age of scientific skepticism and mass murder—will give way to a renewed faith in the creative potentialities of the human imagination. This faith-infused humanism is not Christianity, nor is it really compatible with the theistic assumptions that underlie any of the Abrahamic religions. To its defenders, it represented instead a response to the nihilism that followed decades of global warfare, as well as an alternative to the fear that, without some form of life-affirming faith, humanity would finally succeed in exterminating itself.

More recently, a new school of polemical atheists (or "positive" atheists as they are sometimes called) has taken up d'Holbach's campaign against religion in the name of both contemporary science and enlightened political values. Unlike their Death of God predecessors, they betray no sorrow over the loss of religious conviction among their secularized contemporaries. Chief among these writers is the biologist Richard Dawkins (b. 1941), whose book *The God Delusion* (2006) offers the following critique of the claim that religious values promote human welfare:

> Religious behavior is a writ-large human equivalent of anting or bower-building. It is time-consuming, energy-consuming, often as extravagantly ornate as the plumage of a bird of paradise. Religion can endanger the life of the pious individual, as well as the lives of others. Thousands of people have been tortured for their loyalty to a religion, persecuted by zealots for what is in many cases a scarcely distinguishable alternative faith. Religion devours resources, sometimes on a massive scale. . . . Devout people have died for their gods and killed for them; whipped blood from their backs, sworn themselves to a lifetime of celibacy or to lonely silence, all in the service of religion. What is it all for? What is the benefit of religion?[15]

For Dawkins, religion has no utility at all: it is merely a divisive social force, and its presence in society guarantees some form of conflict and, not infrequently, sectarian violence. For Dawkins, no religion is ultimately a religion of peace.

But on a very different level of intellectual dissent, Dawkins's objections to religion—and those of fellow atheists such as Sam Harris (b. 1967) (*The End of Faith*, 2005) and Daniel Dennett (b. 1942) (*Breaking the Spell*, 2006)—spring from the perception that a religious worldview, and specifically belief in an Intelligent Designer, is untenable and that science provides a truer understanding of how the universe came into existence and how humankind evolved from less complex life forms. For centuries, Dawkins insists, religious authorities have made pronouncements on the nature of physical reality that have since been disproved and advanced claims of inerrancy on behalf of their sacred texts that are no longer believable and, in any case, mutually contradictory. And although scientists cannot answer every question the human mind can pose about the nature of reality, Dawkins concedes, they are bound by a self-correcting process of inquiry that will bring us closer to truth than any dogmatic system of beliefs that has ever been devised.

Critics of the "New Atheists," as Dawkins and those who echo his arguments have been dubbed, often observe that the zeal and certitude that this intellectual community displays are remarkably similar to the dogmatic certainty of traditional religionists. In place of God and revelation, these atheists (their critics say) substitute a materialist worldview and an empirical process of inquiry, thereby turning science into a kind of surrogate religion, with its own peculiar dogmas from which no one in the scientific community is allowed to dissent.[16] Defenders of the atheist position reply that scientific theories are always open to disconfirmation, which religious beliefs are not, and therefore any similarities between the convictions of scientists and those of religionists are either exaggerated or mistakenly applied. Of course, the future of this debate, like the future of the global phenomenon we have termed "religion," has yet to be written.

14.7 New Religious Movements: Engaging with the World

The variety of religions in the modern world suggests that, despite the influence of secular thought and the challenge of scientific rationalism, religious cultures continue to be born anew, to survive and even flourish. Whatever needs religion may be thought to satisfy—the desire to identify with a being or power greater than oneself, for example, or a curiosity about humanity's place and purpose in the universe which scientific speculation cannot gratify—the teachings and social organization of religious traditions continue to draw adherents all over the globe. Even those who are reluctant to identify themselves as persons of any particular faith or creed can be seen to express an interest in "spirituality," and no one who has lived through the first decades of the twenty-first century can doubt the enduring power of religious emotions and ideas, or fail to see how they continue to shape our world. Whether human beings possess a "religious instinct"—as some cognitive scientists and evolutionary anthropologists have suggested—is likely to remain an unanswered question, or simply a recurrent theme of speculative literature.

What we can observe, however, is a persistent need within human societies to move beyond the social and material worlds we are familiar with, and to identify with reality as a whole. For some, this need can only be satisfied through a belief system that enables the human imagination to transcend all particularities of time space, while for others, a sense of identification with the natural world or "biosphere" provides a new sense of being. In either case, the finite, solitary self can be left behind, while an enlarged, transcendent reality is allowed to take its place. The more urgent this need becomes in contemporary society, the more likely it is that new forms of religious thought will emerge to satisfy it. This is, perhaps, as close to an answer to Dawkins's question—"What is religion *for*?"—as we can hope for. Whether future generations will see the present time as an Age of Faith or an Era of Disbelief has yet to be determined.

SEEKING ANSWERS

What Is Ultimate Reality?

Virtually all of the new religious movements we have studied reveal a desire to move beyond the world of common, material existence, and many of them attempt to reach out to some higher plane of reality. For example, the followers of Paul Twitchell (the founder of Eckankar) believe that there are two distinct levels of reality and that through techniques of spiritual ascent we can access a higher plane of reality and release the soul from its imprisoned condition in the material world. Followers of Bhaktivedanta Prabhupada, whose teachings have their origin in Hindu mysticism, also believe that the soul can achieve release and return to its Creator—in this case the Hindu god Krishna. The Hare Krishnas, as they are commonly known, engage in devotional and meditative practices designed to raise the individual consciousness to the level of divine awareness and self-transcendence. For Christian communities, however—and especially those influenced by Adventist thought—ultimate reality is to be found in the biblical God and the soul's deepest longing is to be united with him. That union, for Adventists, will occur once this world has vanished or been destroyed, to be replaced at last by the Kingdom of God.

How Should We Live in This World?

New religious movements emerge in response to a rapidly changing world, in which traditional certainties about society and culture are subject to swift and sometimes brutal challenges. Each of the broad categories of movements we have studied in this chapter has developed tenets by which adherents should live in this world and with each other. Some alternative Christianities, such as Christian Scientists, hold that human life can be made better by first acknowledging that we are spirit beings rather than simply material organisms. Only then can we draw near the Divine Mind and experience God's love in the form of real healing of body and mind. For followers of the Guru Prabhupada (or Hare Krishnas), whose beliefs are based in Eastern thought, the purest life is attained only when one has achieved Krishna consciousness, which entails a strict vegetarian diet and equally strict avoidance of such vices as alcohol, tobacco, drugs, gambling, and sexual immorality. The diversity of neo-pagan systems reflects the fractured state of contemporary society. Wiccans emphasize the need for humans to live in a respectful and harmonious relationship with the natural world, whereas Scientologists believe in the power of the human mind, assisted by specific technologies, to overcome unnecessary repression of the "true" self (or thetan) and recover those creative energies which the "reactive" mind stifles or distorts. Once free from such repression, Scientologists believe, humanity can free itself from insanity, crime, and war. The Baha'i faith looks to the perfection of social and political structures in order to help all of humanity live together peacefully, whereas the New Atheists believe that the triumph of reason over faith would allow humans to coexist peacefully without succumbing to ancient prejudices.

What Is Our Ultimate Purpose?

Virtually all religious communities invest human existence with some ultimate end or purpose, though not all rationalize that belief by appealing to the will of a higher power. Scientologists, for example, believe that, as a species, we have the potential to attain enlightenment and to allow the true self (or "thetan") to grow in understanding. Similarly,

(continued)

SEEKING ANSWERS (*Continued*)

practitioners of Transcendental Meditation believe that the enhancement of well-being through the meditative unification of body and mind will enable all of humanity to become one with the creative intelligence that lies behind everything in the universe. For members of the Church of Jesus Christ of Latter-day Saints (or Mormons), however, the purpose of human life is defined in more nearly Christian terms: to return to the Heavenly Father after death and even to become divine oneself, by embracing

the teachings of the Mormon Church. Ultimately, all people, Mormons believe, will enter one of the eternal kingdoms and enjoy immortality. Members of the Unification Church (or "Moonies"), another alternative form of the Christian faith, similarly believe that the goal of life is to advance beyond our present fallen state and to enter a condition of spiritual purity, guided by the teachings of the Reverend Sun Myung Moon, whose messianic role (like that of Jesus) is to lead the world back to God.

REVIEW QUESTIONS

For Review

1. What does the term *esoteric* mean, and why is it applied to movements like Eckankar?
2. What are engrams, and how do Scientologists claim to be rid of them?
3. What is New Thought, and which religious communities embody its principles?
4. Who are the Moonies, and who does the founder of this religious community claim to be?
5. What is the Gaia hypothesis, and how is it related to the principles of spiritual ecology?
6. What did nineteenth-century Unitarians and Universalists reject in traditional Christian thought?
7. On which points of faith does the Bah'ai community differ from mainstream Islam?

For Further Reflection

1. How sharply do Adventist churches differ in their outlook from mainstream Christianity? Are they more

"world renouncing," or are they simply closer to early Christian thought?
2. If another Parliament of the World's Religions were held sometime in the near future, which religious communities would you like to see invited to attend? Why?
3. What is the appeal of religious movements that focus on the personality of a powerful and charismatic leader? Are such larger-than-life figures essential to the growth of new religions?
4. Are communities that embrace some form of Ufology (that is, a belief in the existence of extraterrestrials) really religious organizations? Is there a difference between communicating with angels, or other spiritual beings, and talking with visitors from outer space?
5. Of all of the religious movements we have studied in this chapter, which one appears to be the most "world accommodating"? What are the advantages in belonging to such a community?

GLOSSARY

astral voyages Visionary experience of a mind or spirit projection through space and time.

channeling The ability to receive and transmit messages sent by spiritual beings not of this world.

coven A community of witches.

Elohim (el-loh-heem') One of several terms used in the Hebrew Bible to identify the Creator God; the name of alien creators responsible for the creation of the human race and culture in Raelian teachings.

engrams In Scientology, traumatic events stored as images in the subconscious mind.

globalization Any movement, within commerce or culture, toward the internationalization of human interchange.

The Great Disappointment Disillusionment and shock following the failure, in 1844, of William Miller's prediction of the Second Advent.

ISKCON The official name of the Hare Krishna movement founded by A. C. Bhaktivedanta Swami.

Lughnassadh (looh-nah'sah) A summer harvest festival (August 2) celebrated by Wiccans, honoring the Celtic god Lugh.

modernization Any transformation of postindustrial Western society that leads to the abandonment of traditional religious beliefs and values.

Moonies A slang term for members of the Unification Church.

New Age An umbrella term for various religious and quasi-religious practices based on a belief in the transformation of both nature and human consciousness.

New Thought A philosophical school of thought, popular in the late nineteenth century, that stressed the power of the human mind to discover the divine within nature and to control material reality.

Second Great Awakening An evangelical movement popular in the United States from the early nineteenth century to the 1880s.

secularization Any tendency in modern society that devalues religious worldviews or seeks to substitute scientific theories for religious beliefs.

seekers A popular term, current in the late nineteenth century, for individuals who cannot find spiritual satisfaction in mainstream religious institutions and who describe themselves as spiritual rather than religious.

theosophy Any religious philosophy that entails communication with deceased "spiritual masters" and emphasizes the superiority of "spirit" to "matter."

thetan (thay'tuhn) A term used by Scientologists to identify the immortal self and source of creativity in the human mind.

Ufology Any systematized belief in extraterrestrials.

Wiccan Rede A traditional set of rules and ethical values cherished by Wiccans.

World's Parliament of Religions Worldwide gathering of religious leaders held in Chicago in 1893; gatherings under the name Parliament of the World's Religions have been held subsequently, beginning in 1993 in Chicago.

yogic flying A meditational practice, similar to levitation, attributed to members of the Transcendental Meditation community.

Zhuan Falun (zyahn-fay'luhn) The collected writings of Li Hongzhi, the founder of Falun Gong. First published in 1994.

SUGGESTIONS FOR FURTHER READING

Barrett, David V. *The New Believers*. London: Cassell & Co., 2001. A comprehensive (and often polemical) overview of alternative religious movements, with extensive historical and biographical information.

Chevannes, Barry. *Rastafari: Roots and Ideology*. New York: Syracuse University Press, 1994. A historical analysis of the development of Rastafarian culture combined with field research into contemporary Rastafarian self-understanding.

Clarke, Peter B., ed. *Encyclopedia of New Religious Movements*. London: Routledge, 2006. Brief but comprehensive essays on new religious movements, arranged alphabetically.

Clifton, Chas S. *Her Hidden Children: The Rise of Wicca and Paganism in America*. Lanham, MD: AltaMira Press, 2006. A carefully documented, chronologically organized account of paganism in North America.

Hinnells, John R., ed. *A New Handbook of Living Religions*. London: Penguin Books, 1997. A popular resource work, this provides a global view of the religious landscape with essays on all of the world's principal religions, including new religious movements in Western and non-Western cultures.

Klemp, Harold. *Autobiography of a Modern Prophet.* Minneapolis: Eckankar, 2000. The present Eck Master's account of his spiritual journey toward "God-Realization."

Lachman, Gary. *Madame Blavatsky: The Mother of Modern Spirituality.* New York: Penguin Group, 2012. A thoroughly researched account of Mme. Blavatsky's spiritual development and close analysis of her writings.

Lewis, James R., ed. *The Oxford Handbook of New Religious Movements.* New York: Oxford University Press, 2004. A scholarly survey of sociological research on some of the most widely studied new religions.

Lewis, James R., and Jesper A. Petersen, eds. *Controversial New Religions.* New York: Oxford University Press, 2005. A collection of essays focusing on new religions that have exhibited violent and antisocial tendencies.

Palmer, Susan. *Aliens Adored: Rael's UFO Religion.* New Brunswick, NJ: Rutgers University Press, 2004. Extensive background information on the UFO phenomenon, coupled with a largely sympathetic analysis of the Raelian movement.

Partridge, Christopher, ed. *New Religions: A Guide.* New York: Oxford University Press, 2004. The most extensive collection of brief scholarly vignettes of new religions, combined with lengthier articles of a historical and analytical nature. Cross-referenced and arranged by religious "families."

Roderick, Timothy. *Wicca: A Year and a Day.* Saint-Paul, MN: Llewellyn Publications, 2005. A detailed and reliable portrait of Wiccan beliefs and practices.

Schmidt, Leigh Eric. *Restless Souls: The Making of American Spirituality.* San Francisco: Harper-Collins, 2005. In-depth biographical accounts of leading spokespersons for "liberal" religious causes and alternative spiritualities.

Stein, Stephen J. *Communities of Dissent: A History of Alternative Religions in America.* New York: Oxford University Press, 2003. A readable overview of religious nonconformity in nineteenth- and twentieth-century America.

Urban, Hugh B. *The Church of Scientology: A History of a New Religion.* Princeton, NJ: Princeton University Press, 2011. A thorough and remarkably objective view of L. R. Hubbard and Scientology's place in American culture.

ONLINE RESOURCES

Hartford Institute for Religion Research

A selective website maintained by the Hartford Institute for Religion Research, which provides a wide-ranging list of sites and journals for new religious movements.

Religion Facts

A compendium of brief articles on world religions, ancient and modern.

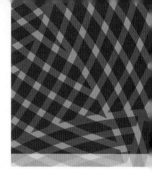

NOTES

Chapter 1

1. See especially Tomoko Masuzawa, *The Invention of World Religions: Or, How European Universalism Was Preserved in the Language of Pluralism* (Chicago: University of Chicago Press, 2005).

2. See especially Immanuel Kant, Religion *Within the Limits of Reason Alone*, trans. Theodore M. Greene and Hoyt H. Hudson (New York: Harper & Row, 1960).

3. Émile Durkheim, *Elementary Forms of the Religious Life*, trans. J. W. Swain (1912; repr., New York: Free Press, 1965), 62.

4. William James, *The Varieties of Religious Experience* (1902; repr., London: Penguin Books, 1985), 31.

5. Paul Tillich, *Theology of Culture*, ed. Robert C. Kimball (New York: Oxford University Press, 1959), 7–8.

6. Jonathan Z. Smith, ed., *HarperCollins Dictionary of Religion* (New York: HarperCollins, 1995), 893.

7. Bruce Lincoln, *Holy Terrors: Thinking about Religion after September 11* (Chicago: University of Chicago Press, 2003), 5–7.

8. Peter Berger, *The Sacred Canopy* (New York: Doubleday, 1967), 175.

9. Sigmund Freud, *The Future of an Illusion*, trans. James Strachey (1927; repr., New York: W. W. Norton, 1961), 55.

10. Karl Marx, "Contribution to the Critique of Hegel's Philosophy of Right," in *On Religion* (Chico, CA: Scholars Press, 1964), 41–42.

11. The term *transtheistic* is used for Jainism by Heinrich Zimmer, *Philosophies of India*, ed. Joseph Campbell (Princeton, NJ: Princeton University Press, 1951), 182.

12. Mircea Eliade, *The Sacred and the Profane: The Nature of Religion*, trans. Willard Trask (London: Harcourt Brace, 1959), 11.

13. Matthew 7:12. New Revised Standard Version of the Bible.

14. Lincoln, *Holy Terrors*, 95.

15. Barna Group, "Number of Female Senior Pastors in Protestant Churches Doubles in Past Decade," September 14, 2009, https://www.barna.com/research/number-of-female-senior-pastors-in-protestant-churches-doubles-in-past-decade/.

16. October 12, 2020, https://eileencampbellreed.org/state-of-clergy/.

17. Rice University Office of Public Affairs, "Misconceptions of Science and Religion Found in New Study," news release, February 16, 2004, https://news.rice.edu/2014/02/16/misconceptions-of-science-and-religion-found-in-new-study/.

18. See especially Smart's *Dimensions of the Sacred: An Anatomy of the World's Beliefs* (Berkeley: University of California Press, 1999) and his earlier and very popular *Worldviews: Crosscultural Explanations of Human Belief* (New York: Scribner's, 1983), which details six of the dimensions (Smart later separated out the material dimension as a seventh).

19. This analogy is drawn from Wilfred Cantwell Smith, *The Meaning and End of Religion* (San Francisco: Harper & Row, 1964), 7.

Chapter 2

1. Denise Lardner Carmody and John Tully Carmody, *Native American Religions: An Introduction* (New York: Paulist Press, 2003).

2. Dennis Tedlock, trans., *Popol Vuh: The Definitive Edition of the Mayan Book of the Dawn of Life and the Glories of Gods and Kings* (New York: Simon and Schuster, 1985).

3. Sam Gill, *Native American Religions: An Introduction* (Belmont, CA: Wadsworth/Thomson Learning, 2005).

4. Sam Gill, *Sacred Worlds: A Study of Navajo Religion and Prayer* (Westport, CT: Greenwood Press, 1981), 54–55.

5. John D. Loftin, *Religion and Hopi Life* (Bloomington: Indiana University Press, 2003), 110.

6. Richard Erdoes and Alfonso Ortiz, *American Indian Myths and Legends* (New York: Pantheon Books, 1984), 346.

7. Gill, *Native American Religions*, 64.

8. Ibid., 96.

9. Tedlock, *Popol Vuh*.

10. John Neihardt and Black Elk, *Black Elk Speaks: Being an Account of the Life of a Holy Man of the Oglala Sioux* (Lincoln: University of Nebraska Press, 1972), 1.

11. Erdoes and Ortiz, *American Indian Myths and Legends*, 85.

12. Joseph Epes Brown, *Teaching Spirits: Understanding Native American Religious Tradition* (London: Oxford University Press, 2001), 87.

13. Keith Basso, *Wisdom Sits in Places: Landscape and Language among the Western Apache* (Albuquerque: University of New Mexico Press, 1996).

14. Brown, *Teaching Spirits*, 36.

15. Ibid., 15.

16. Ibid., 49.

17. Robert Franklin and Pamela Bunte, "Animals and Humans, Sex and Death: Toward a Symbolic Analysis of Four Southern Numic Rituals," *Journal of California and Great Basin Anthropology* 18, no. 2 (1966): 178–203.

18. Forrest S. Cuch, *A History of Utah's American Indians* (Logan: Utah State University Press, 2003).

19. Alexandra Witze, "Religion and the Rise of Cahokia," *American Archaeology* 20, no. 1 (2016): 18–25.

20. Thomas J. Nevins and M. Eleanor Nevins, "'We Have Always Had the Bible': Christianity and the Composition of White Mountain Apache Heritage," *Heritage Management* 2, no. 1 (2009): 11–34.

21. Ibid.

22. Helen McCarthy, "Assaulting California's Sacred Mountains: Shamans vs. New Age Merchants of Nirvana," in *Beyond Primitivism: Indigenous Religions and Modernity*, ed. Jacob Olopuna (New York: Routledge, 2004), 172–178.

23. Arlene Hirschfelder and Paulette Molin, *An Encyclopedia of Native American Religions* (New York: Facts on File, 1992), 176.

24. Greg Sarris, *Mabel McKay: Weaving the Dream* (Berkeley: University of California Press, 1997).

25. Brown, *Teaching Spirits*, 17.

26. Carmody and Carmody, *Native American Religions*, 73.

27. Hirschfelder and Molin, *Encyclopedia of Native American Religions*, 287.

28. Loftin, *Religion and Hopi Life*, 37.

29. Gill, *Native American Religions*.

30. Ibid., 98.

31. Ibid., 72.

32. Annemarie Shimony, "Iroquois Religion and Women in Historical Perspective," in *Women, Religion and Social Change*, ed. Y. Haddad and E. Finley (Albany: State University of New York Press, 1985), 412.

33. Hirschfelder and Molin, *Encyclopedia of Native American Religions*, 130, 328.

34. January 23, 2024, https://www.theguardian.com/commentisfree/2020/sep/16/california-wildfires-cultural-burns-indigenous-people.

Chapter 3

1. Tepilit Ole Saitoti, *Worlds of a Maasai Warrior: An Autobiography* (Berkeley: University of California Press, 1988), 67.

2. Ibid., 69.

3. Ibid., 71.

4. Bilinda Straight, *Miracles and Extraordinary Experience in Northern Kenya* (Philadelphia: University of Pennsylvania Press, 2009), 56.

5. Marcel Griaule, *Conversations with Ogotemmeli* (London: Oxford University Press, 1965).

6. Rowland Abiodun, "Hidden Power: Osun, the Seventeenth Odu," in *Osun Across the Waters: A Yoruba Goddess in Africa and the Americas*, ed. Joseph M. Murphy and Mei-Mei Sanford (Bloomington: Indiana University Press, 2001), 17–18.

7. E. E. Evans-Pritchard, *Nuer Religion* (London: Oxford University Press, 1971).

8. John S. Mbiti, *African Religions and Philosophy* (New York: Praeger, 1969), 85–86.

9. Ibid., 89–90.

10. Ibid., 84–85.

11. Ibid., 92.

12. Graham Connah, *Forgotten Africa: An Introduction to Its Archaeology* (New York: Routledge, 2004), 31–32.

13. Benjamin C. Ray, *African Religions: Symbol, Ritual, and Community* (Upper Saddle River, NJ: Prentice Hall, 2000), 170–171.

14. Beverly B. Mack and Jean Boyd, *One Woman's Jihad: Nana Asma'u, Scholar and Scribe* (Bloomington: Indiana University Press, 2000).

15. Ray, *African Religions*, 171.

16. Ibid., 184–191.

17. Cynthia Hoehler-Fatton, "Christianity: Independent and Charismatic Churches in Africa," in *Encyclopedia of Africa*, ed. K. A. Appiah and H. L. Gates (New York: Oxford University Press, 2010), 273–274.

18. Brigid M. Sackey, *New Directions in Gender and Religion: The Changing Status of Women in African Independent Churches* (Lanham, MD: Lexington Books, 2006), 30–32.

19. Ray, *African Religions*, 85–88.

20. Ibid., 53.

21. Adeline Masquelier, *Prayer Has Spoiled Everything: Possession, Power and Identity in an Islamic Town of Niger* (Durham, NC: Duke University Press, 2002).

22. Ibid.
23. For example, Marion Kilson, "Women in African Traditional Religions," *Journal of Religion in Africa* 8, no. 2 (1976): 133–143.
24. Paula Girshick Ben-Amos, "The Promise of Greatness: Women and Power in a Benin Spirit Possession Cult," in *Religion in Africa: Experience and Expression*, ed. T. D. Blakely, W. E. A. Van Beek, and D. L. Thomson (London: James Currey, 1994), 118–134.
25. E. E. Evans-Pritchard, *Witchcraft, Oracles and Magic among the Azande* (London: Oxford University Press, 1976).
26. Ray, *African Religions*, 58–59, citing Edith Turner, *Experiencing Ritual* (Philadelphia: University of Pennsylvania Press, 1992).
27. Mbiti, *African Religions and Philosophy*, 113.
28. Ibid., 114–115.
29. Ibid., 120.
30. Margaret Drewal, *Yoruba Ritual: Performers, Play, Agency* (Bloomington: Indiana University Press, 1992), 53.
31. Ellen Gruenbaum, *The Female Circumcision Controversy: An Anthropological Perspective* (Philadelphia: University of Pennsylvania Press, 2000).
32. Ifi Amadiume, *Male Daughters and Female Husbands: Gender and Society in a West African Town* (London: Zed Books, 1987).
33. Jack Goody, *Death, Property and the Ancestors: A Study of the Mortuary Customs of the LoDagaa of West Africa* (Palo Alto, CA: Stanford University Press, 1962), 239.
34. Ray, *African Religions*, 102–103.
35. Ibid., 61.
36. Jacob Olupona, "Religion and Ecology in African Cultural and Society," in *The Oxford Handbook of Religion and Ecology*, edited by Roger S. Gottlieb (New York: Oxford University Press, 2009), 259–282. DOI:10.1093/oxfordhb/9780195178722.003.0012.
37. Ibid., 11.
38. Bolaji Bateye, "Rethinking Women, Nature, and Ritual Purity in Yoruba Religious Tradition," in *African Traditions in the Study of Religion, Diaspora and Gendered Societies*, ed. E. Chitando, A. Adogame, and B. Bataye (New York: Routledge, 2013), 147–161.

Chapter 4

1. *Brhadaranyaka Upanishad* 3.9.1–3.9.2. In Sarvepalli Radhakrishnan and Charles A. Moore, *A Sourcebook in Indian Philosophy* (Princeton, NJ: Princeton University Press, 1957), 85.
2. Sarvepalli Radhakrishnan and Charles A. Moore, *A Sourcebook in Indian Philosophy* (Princeton, NJ: Princeton University Press, 1957), 77.
3. *Bhagavad Gita* 4.6–8. In Barbara Stoler Miller, trans., *The Bhagavad-Gita: Krishna's Counsel in Time of War* (New York: Bantam Books, 1986), 52.
4. David M. Knipe, *Hinduism: Experiments in the Sacred* (New York: HarperCollins, 1991), 44–45. The passage appears repeatedly in the *Chandogya Upanishad* 6.9–6.6.13.
5. *Bhagavad Gita* 2.71. In Radhakrishnan and Moore, *Sourcebook in Indian Philosophy*, 112.
6. *Bhagavad Gita* 5.11–12. In Miller, *Bhagavad-Gita*, 60.
7. *Bhagavad Gita* 12.6–8. In Miller, *Bhagavad-Gita*, 110.
8. *Bhagavad Gita* 4.38–39. In Miller, *Bhagavad-Gita*, 56.
9. Laws of Manu II.36. In Radhakrishnan and Moore, *Sourcebook in Indian Philosophy*, 177.
10. Thomas J. Hopkins, *The Hindu Religious Tradition* (Belmont, CA: Dickenson, 1971), 139. Cited in Arvind Sharma, "Hinduism," in *Our Religions*, ed. Arvind Sharma (New York: HarperCollins, 1993), 13.
11. An oft-quoted line from Major-General Charles Stuart's (1758–1828) *Vindication of the Hindoos*, which was published in 1808.
12. Pew-Templeton Global Religious Futures Project: Data Explorer, September 30, 2020, http://globalreligious-futures.org/explorer#/?subtopic=15&chartType=bar&year=2020 &data_type=number&religious_affiliation=all&destination=to&countries=Worldwide&age_group=all&gender=all&pdfMode=false.
13. Pew-Templeton Global Religious Futures Project: Countries: Hindus, September 30, 2020, http://www.globalreligiousfutures.org/religions/hindus.
14. Diana Eck, *Darsan: Seeing the Divine Image in India* (New York: Columbia University Press, 1998).
15. *Laws of Manu* III.56. In Radhakrishnan and Moore, *Sourcebook in Indian Philosophy*, 189.
16. The ensuing discussion is much indebted to the scholarship of David L. Haberman, who authored the Overview Essay on Hinduism for the Yale Forum on Religion and Ecology, September 30, 2020, https://fore.yale.edu/World-Religions/Hinduism/Over view-Essay.

Chapter 5

1. "The Global Religious Landscape," December 18, 2012, Pew Research Center: Religion and Public Life, www.pewforum.org/2012/12/18/global-religious-landscape-exec.
2. Juan Mascaró, trans., *The Dhammapada: The Path of Perfection* (London: Penguin Books, 1973), 35.
3. Stephen Beyer, *The Cult of Tara: Magic and Ritual in Tibet* (Berkeley: University of California Press, 1973), 92.
4. The demographic data cited here are available at "The Global Religious Landscape," December 18, 2012,

Pew Research Center: Religion and Public Life (www.pewforum.org/2012/12/18/global-religious-landscape-exec.) and the Pew-Templeton Religious Futures Project (www.globalreligiousfutures.org).

5. The conference, sponsored by the World Wildlife Fund, produced The Assisi Declarations. The Buddhist declaration was delivered by the Venerable Lungrig Lamgyal Rinpoche, abbot of Gyuto Tantric University. The full text can be found at www.arcworld.org.

Chapter 6

1. *Acarangasutra* 1.4.1.1–2, trans. Hermann Jacobi, in *Sacred Books of the East*, vol. 20, ed. Friedrich Max Müller (Oxford: Oxford University Press, 1884).

2. Yogendra Jain, *Jain Way of Life: A Guide to Compassionate, Healthy, and Happy Living* (Boston: Federation of Jain Associations of North America, 2007), i.

3. *Tattvarthadhigama Sutra*, Chapter II, 22–23, trans. J. L. Jaini, in *A Sourcebook in Indian Philosophy*, ed. Sarvepalli Radhakrishnan and Charles A. Moore (Princeton, NJ: Princeton University Press, 1957), 254.

4. Heinrich Zimmer uses this term for Jainism in *Philosophies of India*, ed. Joseph Campbell (Princeton, NJ: Princeton University Press, 1951), 182.

5. Paul Dundas, *The Jains* (New York: Routledge, 1992), 47; the text referenced here is the *Sthānānga* 171.

6. *Avashyakasutra* 32; cited in Dundas, *The Jains*, 171.

7. Padmanabh S. Jaini, *The Jaina Path of Purification* (Berkeley: University of California Press, 1979), 196–197.

8. Dundas, *The Jains*, 55–56; the text referenced here is the *Kalpasutra*.

9. L. M. Singhvi, "The Jain Declaration on Nature," in *Jainism and Ecology: Nonviolence in the Web of Life*, ed. Christopher Key Chapple (Cambridge, MA: Center for the Study of World Religions, Harvard Divinity School, 2002), 224. Originally published in 1990.

10. Consideration of both Declarations and much more with regard to Jain environmentalism is provided by Christopher K. Chapple in his overview article on Jainism for the Yale Forum on Religion and Ecology, October 10, 2020, https://fore.yale.edu/World-Religions/Jainism. The full text of the Declaration is accessible through the JAINA website, October 10, 2020: https://cdn.ymaws.com/www.jaina.org/resource/resmgr/jaindeclarationonclimatechange/Update_Jain_Declaration_on_C.pdf.

Chapter 7

1. Hew McLeod, *Sikhism* (London: Penguin, 1997), 219.

2. Mann, *Sikhism*, 14.

3. Adapted from a quotation in W. Owen Cole and Piara Singh Sambhi, *The Sikhs: Their Religious Beliefs and Practices* (London: Routledge & Kegan Paul, 1978), 9.

4. Quoted in ibid., 10.

5. Quoted in Khushwant Singh, "Sikhism," *Encyclopedia of Religion* (New York: Simon & Schuster Macmillan, 1995), 13:316.

6. Quoted in ibid., 316.

7. From *Puratan Janam-sakhi*, cited in W. H. McLeod, ed. and trans., *Textual Sources for the Study of Sikhism* (Totowa, NJ: Barnes & Noble Books, 1984), 25.

8. Khushwant Singh, "Sikhism," 319.

9. Cited in McLeod, *Sikhism*, 271.

10. Ibid., 272.

11. Ibid., 98.

12. Gopal Singh, *A History of the Sikh People* (New Delhi, India: World Sikh University Press, 1979), 263–264.

13. Teja Singh and Ganda Singh, *A Short History of the Sikhs: Volume One (1469–1765)*, 3rd ed. (Patiala, India: Punjabi University, 1999), 67.

14. McLeod, *Sikhism*, 203.

15. Cited in McLeod, *Textual Sources*, 79–80.

16. Cited in McLeod, *Sikhism*, 216.

17. October 10, 2020, https://www.bbc.co.uk/bitesize/guides/znnv87h/revision/3.

18. October 10, 2020, https://www.huffpost.com/entry/sikh-environment-day-the-ecological-roots-of-sikhism_b_2884402.

19. *Āsā ki Vār* 19:2, Adi Granth, 473. Cited in McLeod, *Textual Sources*, 109.

20. Mann, *Sikhism*, 106.

21. Ibid., 14.

Chapter 8

1. This term is not found in the *Book of Changes* itself but is in fact a later Daoist rendition of the idea of the primordial one.

2. See Tu Wei-ming, "Li as a Process of Humanization," *Philosophy East and West* 22, no. 2 (April 1972): 187–201.

3. See Herbert Fingarette's *Confucius: The Secular as Sacred* (New York: Harper Torchbooks, 1972), 7.

4. See Xinzhong Yao, *An Introduction to Confucianism* (Cambridge: Cambridge University Press, 2000), 46.

5. See Robert C. Neville, *Boston Confucianism* (New York: SUNY Press, 2000). Prominent members of this group include Robert Neville, John Berthrong, and Wei-ming Tu.

6. Summary based on Patricia Buckley Ebrey, ed., *Chinese Civilization: A Sourcebook*, 2nd ed. (New York: Free Press, 1993), 157–163.

7. This summary of the *jiao* liturgy is based on a composite description of two separate ceremonies conducted, respectively, in 1994 and 2005 in Hong Kong. A DVD depicting the rites and explaining their religious meaning was produced in 2009 by the Center for the Study of Daoist Culture of the Department of Culture and Religion, Chinese University of Hong Kong.

8. Several recent publications address the issue of Chinese religions and ecology. See Mary E. Tucker and John Berthrong, eds., *Confucianism and Ecology: The Interrelation of Heaven, Earth, and Humans* (Cambridge, MA: Harvard University Press, 1998); N. J. Girardot, James Miller, and Xiaogan Liu, eds., *Daoism and Ecology: Ways Within a Cosmic Landscape* (Cambridge, MA: Harvard University Press, 2001); James Miller, *China's Green Religion: Daoism and the Quest for a Sustainable Future* (New York: Columbia University Press, 2020).

9. See the highly nuanced discussion of the topic by Li-Hsiang Lisa Rosenlee, in her *Confucianism and Women: A Philosophical Interpretation* (Albany: State University of New York Press, 2006). See also Chenyang Li, ed., *The Sage and the Second Sex: Confucianism, Ethics, and Gender* (Chicago: Open Court, 2000). Deborah Achtenberg's "Aristotelian Resources in Feminist Thinking," in *Feminism and Ancient Philosophy*, ed. Julie K. Ward (London: Routledge, 1996), 97, is also very suggestive.

Chapter 9

1. Quoted in William Theodore de Bary et al., eds., *Sources of Japanese Tradition* (New York: Columbia University Press, 2001), 1:259.

2. Quoted in ibid., 2:498, 512.

Chapter 10

1. Mary Boyce, ed. and trans., *Textual Sources for the Study of Zoroastrianism* (Manchester, UK: Manchester University Press, 1984), 35.

2. Ibid., 48.

3. Roshan Rivetna, "The Zarathushti World—A Demographic Picture," September 29, 2020, www.fezana.org, and Pew Research Center: Religion & Public Life, citing World Religion Database, September 29, 2020, https://www.pewforum.org/2015/04/02/other-religions/.

Chapter 11

1. Richard Rubenstein, *The Cunning of History* (New York: Harper and Row), 90–97.

2. Martin Buber, *The Eclipse of God: Studies in the Relation Between Religion and Philosophy* (New York: Harper and Row, 1957), 13–24.

3. See Roger Kamenetz, *Stalking Elijah: Adventures with Today's Jewish Mystical Masters* (San Francisco: Harper and Row, 1998), for an engaging first-person perspective on the Renewal movement in Judaism. A more scholarly approach can be found in George W. Wilkes, "Jewish Renewal," in *Modern Judaism: An Oxford Guide*, ed. Nicholas de Lange and Miri Freud-Kandel (Oxford: Oxford University Press, 2005), 114–125.

4. Stephen Hodge, *The Dead Sea Scrolls Rediscovered* (Berkeley, CA: Ulysses Press, 2003), 158–210.

5. Paula Fredricksen, *From Jesus to Christ: The Origins of the New Testament Images of Jesus* (New Haven, CT: Yale University Press, 1988), 160–176.

6. Wayne A. Meeks and Robert L. Wilken, *Jews and Christians in Antioch: In the First Four Centuries of the Common Era* (Missoula, MT: Scholars Press, 1978), 85–126.

7. Ignaz Maybaum, "The Face of God after Auschwitz," in *Holocaust Theology: A Reader*, ed. Dan Cohn-Sherbok (New York: New York University Press, 2002), 96–98.

8. Richard Rubenstein, *After Auschwitz: History, Theology, and Contemporary Judaism* (Baltimore, MD: Johns Hopkins University Press, 1992), 171–174.

9. Eliezer Berkovits, "Free Will and the Hidden God," in *Holocaust Teology*, 153–156.

10. Abraham Joshua Heschel, "No Religion Is an Island," in *Moral Grandeur and Spiritual Audacity*, ed. Susannah Heschel (New York: Farrar, Straus and Giroux, 1997), 235–250.

11. Emil L. Fackenheim, *The Jewish Return into History* (New York: Schocken Books, 1978), 129–143. See also *God's Presence in History* (New York: Harper and Row, 1970), 67–79, for Fackenheim's reflections on the significance of the Shoah as the pivotal event in modern Jewish history.

12. Arthur Hertzberg, ed., *The Zionist Idea* (New York: Atheneum, 1984), 103–114.

13. Theodor Herzl, "The Jewish State," in *The Zionist Idea*, 204–230.

14. Theodor Herzl, *The Old New Land*, trans. Lotta Levensohn (Princeton, NJ: Marcus Wiener, 2000).

15. "The Balfour Declaration," in *The Jew in the Modern World*, ed. Paul Mendes-Flohr and Jehuda Reinharz (Oxford: Oxford University Press, 1995), 582. See also Jonathan Schneer, *The Balfour Declaration* (New York: Random House, 2010).

16. See Judith Plaskow, *Standing Again at Sinai: Judaism from a Feminist Perspective* (San Francisco: Harper and Row, 1990) for a groundbreaking feminist critique of male dominance in Jewish thought and religious practice. To date, the most radical attempt at rewriting the Siddur from a feminist perspective is Marcia Falk's *The Book of Blessings* (Boston: Beacon Press, 1996).

17. Ellen Bernstein and Dan Fink, "Blessings and Praise" and "Bal Tashchit" in *This Sacred Earth: Religion, Nature, Environment*, ed. Roger S. Gottlieb (New York: Routledge, 2004), 525–526. See also Ellen Bernstein, ed., *Ecology and the Jewish Spirit: Where Nature and the Sacred Meet* (Woodstock, VT: Jewish Lights Publishing, 2000).

18. Emil L. Fackenheim, *The Jewish Return into History: Reflections in the Age of Auschwitz and a New Jerusalem* (New York: Schocken Books, 1978).

Chapter 12

1. Augustine, *Confessions* 1.1. Author's translation.

2. Timothy (Kallistos) Ware, *The Orthodox Church* (New York: Penguin Books, 1997), 261.

3. *Declaration on Non-Christian Religions*, no. 2, quoted in Anthony Wilhelm, *Christ among Us*, 2nd ed. (New York: Paulist Press, 1975), 396.

4. Clement of Alexandria, *Stromata* 1.5.28. Author's translation.

5. Maximus the Confessor, *Book of Ambiguities* 41, quoted in Vladimir Lossky, *The Mystical Theology of the Eastern Church* (London: James Clarke, 1957), 214. The idea that Christians participate in the divine nature is found in the New Testament (e.g., 2 Peter 1:4) and is supported by the doctrine that the Holy Spirit is at work in every believer (e.g., Romans 8).

6. Julian of Norwich, *Revelations of Divine Love* 4 (short text), in *Julian of Norwich: Showings*, trans. E. Colledge and J. Walsh (New York: Paulist Press, 1978), 131.

7. "The Religious Composition of the United States," Pew Forum on Religion and Public Life/U.S. Religious Landscape Survey, at https://www.pewforum.org/religious-land scape-study/.

8. The demographic data found in this section are taken from the Pew-Templeton "Global Religious Futures Project" (www.globalreligious futures.org) and "The Changing Global Religious Landscape," a study by the Pew Research Center (www.pewforum.org).

9. Quoted in Ware, *The Orthodox Church*, 305.

10. See Orazio Marucchi, *Christian Epigraphy*, trans. J. Willis (Chicago: Ares Press, 1974), 153–155.

11. The conference, sponsored by the World Wildlife Fund, produced The Assisi Declarations. The Christian declaration was delivered by Father Lanfranco Serrini, a Roman Catholic priest. The full text can be found at http://www.arcworld.org.

12. "Majority of Public Favors Same-Sex Marriage, But Divisions Persist," Pew Research Forum, at pewresearch.org.

Chapter 13

1. Pew Research Center, http://pewresearch.org.

2. Ibid.

3. All translations from the Qur'an are from Ahmed Ali, trans., *al-Qur'an* (Princeton, NJ: Princeton University Press, 1993).

4. Frederick Mathewson Denny, *An Introduction to Islam* (New York: Pearson Prentice Hall, 2006), 174–175.

5. Ibid., 110–111.

6. William A. Graham, *Divine Word and Prophetic Word in Early Islam* (The Hague: Mouton, 1977), 157.

7. Ali, *al-Qur'an*.

8. Ibid.

9. John R. Bowen, *Muslims Through Discourse* (Princeton, NJ: Princeton University Press, 1993).

10. Denny, *An Introduction to Islam*, 110–111.

11. Abdallah al-Shiekh, "Zakat," in *Oxford Encyclopedia of the Modern Islamic World* (New York: Oxford University Press, 1995), 366–370.

12. Sherman A. Jackson, *Islam and the Blackamerican: Looking Toward the Third Resurrection* (New York: Oxford University Press, 2005).

13. Malcolm X, *The Autobiography of Malcolm X: As Told to Alex Haley* (New York: Ballatine Books, 1965).

14. *Mathnawi* V, 411–414. In *The Rumi Collection*, trans. Kabir Helminski (Boston: Shambala Press, 2005), 165.

15. Ali, *al-Qur'an*.

16. Leila Ahmed, *Women and Gender in Islam* (New Haven, CT: Yale University Press, 1992).

17. Scott Siraj a-Haqq Kugle, "Sexuality, Diversity, and Ethics in the Agenda of Progressive Muslims," in *Progressive Muslims on Gender, Justice, and Pluralism*, ed. Omid Safi (Oxford, Oneworld Publications, 2003), 190–234.

18. Scott Kugle and Stephen Hunt, "Masculinity, Homosexuality and the Defense of Islam: A Case Study of Yusuf al-Qaradawi's Media Fatwa," *Religion and Gender* 2, no. 2 (2012): 254–279.

19. January 23, 2024, https://www.pewresearch.org/short-reads/2017/08/09/muslims-and-islam-key-findings-in-the-u-s-and-around-the-world/.

20. Ibid.

21. Ibid.

22. Jamal al-Din al-Afghani, Islamic Solidarity, in *Islam in Transition: Muslim Perspectives*, ed. John J. Donohue and John L. Esposito (Oxford: Oxford University Press, 2007), 16–19.

23. Sayyid Qutb, *Social Justice in Islam* (Islamic Publications International, [1948] 2000).

24. Ali, *al-Qur'an*.

25. Ali, *al-Qur'an*.

26. Seyyid Hossein Nasr, "Religion and the Environmenal Crisis," in *The Essential Seyyid Hossein Nasr*, ed. William Chittick (Bloomington, IN: World Wisdom, 2007).

27. Yasin Dutton, "The Environmental Crisis of Our Time: A Muslim Response," in *Islam and Ecology: A Bestowed Trust*, ed. Richard C. Folz (Cambridge, MA: Harvard University Press, 2003), 323–340.

28. January 23, 2024, http://www.ifees.org.uk.

Chapter 14

1. The cult controversy has engaged the attention of religious studies scholars and journalists alike for several decades. One of the best accounts of this controversy—from a sociological and legal perspective—can be found in James R. Lewis, ed., *Odd Gods: New Religions and the Cult Controversy* (Amherst, NY: Prometheus Books, 2001).

2. Stephen Stein, *Communities of Dissent: A History of Alternative Religions in America* (Oxford: Oxford University Press, 2003).

3. Roy Wallis, *The Elementary Forms of Religious Life* (London: Routledge and Kegan Paul, 1984).

4. Peter B. Clarke, ed., *Encyclopedia of New Religious Movements* (London: Routledge, 2006).

5. Gary Lachman, *Madame Blavatsky: The Mother of Modern Spirituality* (New York: Penguin Group, 2012), 134.

6. Christopher Partridge, ed., *New Religions: A Guide* (Oxford: Oxford University Press, 2004), 184.

7. To date, the fullest account of the origins and teachings of Falun Gong can be found in Maria Hsia Chang's *Falun Gong: The End of Days* (New Haven, CT: Yale University Press, 2004).

8. See Bruce Lincoln, *Holy Terrors: Thinking about Religion after September 11* (Chicago: University of Chicago Press, 2006), 94.

9. See Janet Treitman, *Inside Scientology* (Boston: Houghton Mifflin Harcourt, 2011). Treitman's study of the organizational history and dynamics of Scientology is the most complete to date.

10. See James E. Lovelock, *The Ages of Gaia: A Biography of Our Living Earth* (New York: Bantam Books, 1990). Lovelock's penultimate chapter, entitled "God and Gaia," may well have inspired Reuther's later attempt to correlate theism and earth science.

11. Rosemary Radford Reuther, *Gaia and God: An Ecofeminist Theology of Earth Healing* (San Francisco: HarperSanFrancisco, 1992).

12. Clarke, *Encyclopedia of New Religious Movements*, 189–190.

13. See Karen Armstrong, *The Battle for God* (New York: Ballantine Books, 2001), 199.

14. Thomas J. J. Altizer and William Hamilton, *Radical Theology and the Death of God* (New York: Bobbs-Merrill, 1966), 95.

15. Richard Dawkins, *The God Delusion* (Boston: Houghton Mifflin, 2006), 164–165.

16. See William A. Stahl, "One-Dimensional Rage: The Social Epistemology of the New Atheism and Fundamentalism," in *Religion and the New Atheism: A Critical Appraisal*, ed. Amarnath Amarasingam (Leiden, The Netherlands: Brill, 2010), 97–108.

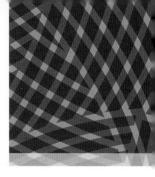

GLOSSARY

Note: The guides to pronunciation adhere for the most part to the commonsense approach utilized in the *HarperCollins Dictionary of Religion* (1995) and are intended to be straightforward without need of a key. One exception involves the long "i" sound (as in "mine"), which herein is represented by "ai."

Abbasids (uh-ba'sids) An important Muslim empire that ruled from 750 to 1258 CE.

adhan (ah-dahn'; Arabic) The call to prayer.

Adi Granth (ah'dee gruhnth; Punjabi, "first book") Sikhism's most important sacred text and, since the death of Guru Gobind Singh in 1708, Sikhism's primary earthly authority; traditionally known as Sri Guru Granth Sahib.

ahimsa (ah-him'suh; Sanskrit, "nonviolence," "not desiring to harm") Both the avoidance of violence toward other life forms and an active sense of compassion toward them; a basic principle of Jainism, Hinduism, and Buddhism.

Ahura Mazda (ah-hoo'reh maz'dah; Avestan, "Wise Lord") The God of Zoroastrianism; also known as Ohrmazd.

'A'isha (a'ee-shuh) A beloved wife of Muhammad who is known for transmitting many hadith.

ajiva (uh-jee'vuh; Sanskrit, "nonsoul") Nonliving components of the Jain universe: space, time, motion, rest, and all forms of matter.

'Ali Son-in-law of Muhammad; one of the Rightly Guided Caliphs.

Allah (ahl'lah; Arabic, "God") The Arabic term for God.

Amaterasu (ah-mah-teh-rah-sooh; Japanese, "deity that shines in the sky") The sun goddess in Shinto. Enshrined at Ise, Amaterasu is the kami of the imperial family. As the sun goddess, she is the most august of all deities. Her descendants are considered the only rightful rulers of Japan.

American Indian Religious Freedom Act 1978 US law to guarantee freedom of religious practice for Native Americans.

Amesha Spentas (ah-may'shah spen'taz; Avestan, "Beneficial Immortals") Seven angels—including Spenta Mainyu, the Holy Spirit of Ahura Mazda—who help Ahura Mazda govern creation.

Amma (ah'muh; Dogon) The High God of the Dogon people.

amrit (am'rit; Punjabi, "immortalizing fluid") A special drink made from water and sugar crystals, used in the Khalsa initiation ceremony.

anatman (ahn-aht'muhn, Sanskrit; anatta, ahn-aht'tah, Pali) "No-self." The Buddha's doctrine that there is no independent and eternal self or soul underlying personal existence.

Angra Mainyu (an'grah main'yoo; "Foul Spirit") Evil adversary of Ahura Mazda; also called Ahriman.

apostle (Greek *apostolos*, "one who is sent out") In the New Testament, Jesus's disciples, sent out to preach and baptize, are called apostles. Paul of Tarsus and some other early Christian leaders also claimed this title. Because of their close association with Jesus, the apostles were accorded a place of honor in the early Church.

apostolic succession According to this Roman Catholic and Orthodox doctrine, the spiritual authority conferred by Jesus on the apostles has been transmitted through an unbroken line of bishops, who are their successors.

arati (ah-rah'tee; Sanskrit) Worship with light, involving the waving of a lamp in front of the deity.

arhat (ahr'huht; Sanskrit, "one who is worthy") In Theravada Buddhism, one who has attained nirvana and is not subject to rebirth.

asha (ah'shuh) The true, cosmic order that pervades both the natural and social spheres of reality, encompassing the moral and religious life of individuals; opposed to *druj*. When capitalized, the term refers to the *Amesha Spenta* Asha Vahishta.

'Ashura (ah-shooh-ra') The tenth day of the month of Muharram, recognized by the Shi'a as the anniversary of the martyrdom of Husayn.

astral voyages Visionary experience of a mind or spirit projection through space and time.

atheism Perspective that denies the existence of God or gods.

atman (aht'-muhn; Sanskrit) The eternal self or soul that is successively reincarnated until released from samsara through moksha.

avatar (a'vuh-tahr; from Sanskrit *avatara*, "descent") A "descent" of God (usually Vishnu) to Earth in a physical form with the specific goal of aiding the world.

Avesta (a-ves'tuh) The oldest and most important of Zoroastrian scriptures, consisting of a collection of texts including the Yasna and Gathas.

axis mundi (ak'suhs moon'dee; Latin) An academic term for the center of the world, which connects the Earth with the heavens.

Baal Shem Tov (1698–1760) A charismatic faith healer, mystic, and teacher (whose given name was Israel ben Eliezer) who is generally regarded as the founder of the Hasidic movement.

baptism Performed by immersion in water or a sprinkling with water, baptism is a sacrament in which an individual is cleansed of sin and admitted into the Church.

Bar/Bat Mitzvah (bahr/baht meets-vah') A rite of passage for adolescents in Judaism, the Bar Mitzvah (for males age thirteen) and the Bat Mitzvah (for females ages twelve to thirteen) signal their coming of age and the beginning of adult religious responsibility. These terms also refer literally to the boy or girl undergoing the rite.

bhakti marga (bhuhk'tee mahr'guh; Sanskrit) The path of devotion.

bishop Responsible for supervising other priests and their congregations within specific regions known as dioceses, bishops are regarded by Roman Catholic and Orthodox Christians as successors of the apostles.

Black Elk Famous Lakota religious leader.

bodhisattva (boh-dee-saht'vah; Sanskrit) "One who aspires to awakening."

bori (boh-ree'; various languages) A term for West African spirits.

Brahman (brah'muhn; Sanskrit, "expansive") For monistic Hinduism, the supreme, unitary reality, the ground of all being; for dualistic Hinduism, Brahman can refer to the supreme God (e.g., Vishnu).

brahmin (brah'min; Sanskrit) A member of the priestly class of the *varna* or caste system.

Buddha (booh'duh; Sanskrit) An "awakened one" or "enlightened one."

buddha nature In Mahayana teaching, the awakened awareness of the Buddha, which is the true nature of the Buddha and, in fact, the true nature of all reality.

caliph (kay'lif; Arabic) Leader of the Muslim community after the death of Muhammad.

Calvin, John (1509–1564) One of the leading figures of the Protestant Reformation, Calvin is notable for his *Institutes of the Christian Religion* and his emphasis on the absolute power of God, the absolute depravity of human nature, and the absolute dependence of human beings on divine grace for salvation.

Candomblé New World religion with roots in West Africa—particularly Yoruba culture—which is prominent in Brazil.

Chan Buddhism See **Zen Buddhism**.

Changing Woman Mythic ancestor of the Navajo people who created the first humans.

channeling The ability to receive and transmit messages sent by spiritual beings not of this world.

chantway The basis of Navajo ceremonial practice; includes chants, prayers, songs, and other ritual practice.

Chinvat Bridge The bridge that needs to be crossed by the soul in order to reach the afterlife—wide and easy to cross for the good, razor-thin and impossible to cross for the evil.

Christmas An annual holiday commemorating the birth of Jesus, Christmas is observed by Western Christians on December 25. Although many Orthodox Christians celebrate Christmas on this date, others observe the holiday on January 7.

church In the broadest sense, "church" refers to the universal community of Christians, but the term can also refer to a particular tradition within Christianity (such as the Roman Catholic Church or the Episcopal Church) or to an individual congregation of Christians.

cosmology Understanding of the nature of the world that typically explains its origin and how it is ordered.

coven A community of witches.

covenant A biblical concept that describes the relationship between God and the Jews in contractual terms, often thought of as an eternal bond between the Creator and the descendants of the ancient Israelites.

cry ceremony Sacred mourning ceremony involving songs, dances, and stories about the deceased, all of which aid the spirit of the deceased in transition to the next world.

Daena (dai'nuh) The feminine being who embodies the individual's ethical quality and who appears to the soul after death.

daevas (dai'vuhs) The various demonic powers aligned with Angra Mainyu.

dalit (dah'lit; Sanskrit, "oppressed"; Marathi, "broken") Self-designation of people who had traditionally been classified as untouchables or outcastes.

dama (dah'mah; Dogon) A Dogon rite of passage marking the transition to adulthood and to the afterlife.

dan (dahn) In Daoism, literally a pill, but understood as the essence of immortality.

dana (dah'nuh; Sanskrit, Pali, "giving") Ritual of giving.

dantian (dahn'tee-an) "Fields for the refinement of the immortal pill"; major nodal points in the human body where the "pill" of immortality can be refined through alchemical means.

Dao (dow) A fundamental concept in Chinese religion, literally meaning the "path" or the "way." In Confucianism, it specifically refers to the entire ideal human order ordained by the Absolute, *Tian*. In Daoism, it is the primary source of the cosmos, the very ground of all beings.

Daodejing (dow-duh-jing) Foundational Daoist text, lit. "The Scripture of the Way and Its Potent Manifestation"; also known as the Book of *Laozi*, the name of its purported author.

Daozang (dow-dzahng) Literally "Treasury of the Dao," this is the Daoist Canon that contains the entire corpus of Daoist texts. The most complete version, still in use today, was first published in 1445.

darshan (duhr'shuhn; from Sanskrit *darshana*, "to see") Worship through simultaneously seeing and being seen by a deity in the presence of its image.

de (duh) Another fundamental concept in Chinese religions, meaning "virtue" or "potency." In Confucianism, it is the charismatic power of the ruler or the man of virtue, while in Daoism it means the concrete manifestation of the Dao.

Dead Sea Scrolls Religious literature hidden in caves near the shores of the Dead Sea (c. second–first centuries BCE).

Dharma (dahr'muh; Sanskrit) In Buddhism, the teachings of the Buddha.

dharma (dahr'muh; Sanskrit) Duty, righteousness, "religion"; basis for living in a way that upholds cosmic and social order.

Diaspora A Greek word in origin, this term refers to those Jewish communities that live outside of the historical land of Israel.

Digambara (di'guhm-buh-ruh; Sanskrit, "those whose garment is the sky") The second largest Jain sect, whose monks go about naked so as to help abolish any ties to society; generally more conservative than the Shvetambara sect.

divination The attempt to learn about events that will happen in the future through supernatural means.

druj (droohj; Avestan, "lie") Cosmic principle of chaos and evil, opposed to *asha*.

dualism In Zoroastrianism, of two types: cosmic dualism of order and chaos (or good and evil); dualism of spirit and matter (or thought and body).

dukkha (dook'kuh; Pali) Usually translated as "suffering," *dukkha* can also be understood as anxiety, unease, or dissatisfaction caused by the ignorance, attachment, and aversion that lead to unwholesome desire.

Easter An annual holiday commemorating the resurrection of Christ, Easter is a "movable feast" whose date changes from year to year, though it is always celebrated in spring (as early as March 22 and as late as May 8).

election The belief that the biblical God "chose" the people of Israel to be his "kingdom of priests" and a "holy nation." This biblical concept is logically connected to the idea of the covenant, and it entails the belief that the Jews' relationship with God obliges them to conform to his laws and fulfill his purposes in the world.

Elohim (el-loh-heem') One of several terms used in the Hebrew Bible to identify the Creator God; the name of alien creators responsible for the creation of the human race and culture in Raelian teachings.

ema (e'mah) Wooden tablets expressing pleadings to kami for success in life.

empathy The capacity for seeing things from another's perspective, and an important methodological approach for studying religions.

emptiness A Mahayana doctrine according to which all things are empty of any inherent existence. Also known as **shunyata** (shoon'yuh-tah; Sanskrit, "emptiness").

engrams In Scientology, traumatic events stored as images in the subconscious mind.

Epiphany An annual holiday commemorating the "manifestation" of the divinity of the infant Jesus, Epiphany is celebrated by most Western Christians on January 6. Most Eastern Christians observe it on January 19.

eschatological Any belief relating to an "End Time" of divine judgment and world destruction.

ethical monotheism A core concept of Judaism: it is the belief that the world was created and is governed by only one transcendent Being, whose ethical attributes provide an ideal model for human behavior.

Eucharist (yooh'kah'rist) Also known as the Lord's Supper and Holy Communion, the Eucharist is a sacrament celebrated with consecrated bread and wine in commemoration of Jesus's Last Supper with his disciples.

evangelicalism This Protestant movement stresses the importance of the conversion experience, the Bible as the only reliable authority in matters of faith, and preaching the gospel. In recent decades, evangelicalism has become a major force in North American Christianity.

Exodus The escape (or departure) of Israelite slaves from Egypt as described in the Hebrew Bible (c. 1250 BCE).

fangshi (fahng-shuhr) In Daoism, "magicians" who allegedly possessed the recipe for immortality.

Fatima Daughter of Muhammad.

Five Classics The five canonical works of Confucianism designated in the Han Dynasty: *Book of Odes, Book of History, Book of Changes, Record of Rites,* and *Spring and Autumn Annals.*

Four Books The four texts identified by the Neo-Confucian Zhu Xi as fundamental in understanding the Confucian teaching. Between 1313 and 1905, they made up the curriculum for the civil service examination. They are *Analects, Mencius, Great Learning,* and *Doctrine of the Mean.*

Four Noble Truths The four truths that form the basis of the Dharma in Buddhism: suffering is inherent in human life, suffering is caused by desire, there can be an end to desire, and the way to end desire is the Noble Eightfold Path.

fravashis (fruh-vah'sheez) Preexisting higher souls and guardian spirits of individual human beings.

fundamentalism Originating in the early 1900s, this movement in American Protestantism was dedicated to defending doctrines it identified as fundamental to Christianity against perceived threats posed by modern culture.

Ghost Dance Religious resistance movements in 1870 and 1890 that originated in Nevada among Paiute peoples.

globalization The linking and intermixing of cultures; any process that moves a society toward an internationalization of religious discourse; any movement, within commerce or culture, toward the internationalization of human interchange.

gospel In its most general sense, "gospel" means the "good news" (from Old English *godspel*, which translates the Greek *evangelion*) about Jesus Christ. The New Testament gospels of Matthew, Mark, Luke, and John are proclamations of the good news concerning the life, teachings, death, and resurrection of Jesus Christ.

grace Derived from the Latin *gratia* (a "gift" or "love"), "grace" refers to God's love for humanity, expressed in Jesus Christ and through the sacraments.

The Great Disappointment Disillusionment and shock following the failure, in 1844, of William Miller's prediction of the Second Advent.

gui (gwee) Ghosts and demons, malevolent spirits.

gurdwara (goor'dwah-ruh; Punjabi, "doorway of the Guru" or "by means of the Guru's [grace]") A building for Sikh worship that houses a copy of the Adi Granth; the central structure of any Sikh community.

guru (gooh'rooh; Sanskrit, "venerable person") A spiritual teacher and revealer of truth, common to Hinduism,

Sikhism, and some forms of Buddhism. When the word *Guru* is capitalized, it refers to the ten historical leaders of Sikhism, to the sacred text (Sri Guru Granth Sahib, or Adi Granth), and to God (often as True Guru).

hadith (hah-deeth'; Arabic) Literary tradition recording the sayings and deeds of the Prophet Muhammad.

hajj (hahj; Arabic) The annual pilgrimage to Mecca, one of the five pillars of Islam.

halacha (hah-lah-khah') An authoritative formulation of traditional Jewish law.

haoma (how'meh) Sacred drink made in ancient times from the sour, milky juice of the soma plant; in modern times from water, pomegranate, ephedra, and goat's milk.

harae (hah-rah'eh) Shinto purification.

Hasidism A popular movement within eighteenth-century eastern European Judaism, Hasidism stressed the need for spiritual restoration and deepened individual piety. In the course of the nineteenth and twentieth centuries, the Hasidic movement spawned a number of distinctive communities that have physically separated themselves from the rest of the Jewish and non-Jewish worlds and who are often recognized by their attire and their devotion to a dynasty of hereditary spiritual leaders.

haumai (how-mai; Punjabi, "self-centeredness") In Sikhism, the human inclination toward being self-centered rather than God-centered, which increases the distance between the individual and God.

henotheism The belief that acknowledges a plurality of gods but elevates one of them to special status.

hijra (hij'ruh; Arabic) Sometimes spelled hegira. The migration of the early Muslim community from Mecca to Medina in 622 CE; the Islamic calendar dates from this year.

hindutva (hin-doot'vuh; Sanskrit, "Hindu-ness") A modern term that encompasses the ideology of Hindu nationalism.

hogan (hoh'gahn; Pueblo) A sacred structure of Pueblo peoples.

Holocaust The genocidal destruction of approximately 6 million European Jews by the government of Nazi Germany during World War II. This mass slaughter is referred to in Hebrew as the Shoah.

Holy People Ancestors to the Navajo people, described in mythic narratives.

Holy Wind Navajo conception of a spiritual force that inhabits every element of creation.

hukam (hooh'kahm; Punjabi, "order") In Sikhism, the divine order of the universe.

Husayn (hoo-sayn') Grandson of Muhammad who was killed while challenging the Umayyads.

icons Painted images of Christ and the saints, icons are used extensively in the Orthodox Church.

Ifa (ee'fah; Yoruba) The divination system of the Yoruba religion, believed to be revealed to humanity by the gods.

imam (ee-mahm'; Arabic) Prayer leader; in Shi'ism, one of the leaders of the Muslim community following the death of the Prophet Muhammad.

immanence The divine attribute of indwelling, or God being present to human consciousness.

Inquisition The investigation and suppression of heresy by the Roman Catholic Church, the Inquisition began in the twelfth century and was formally concluded in the middle of the nineteenth century.

interdependent origination The Buddha's teaching that reality is a complex of interdependent phenomena in which the origin or coming-into-existence of all things depends on all other things.

ISKCON The official name of the Hare Krishna movement founded by A. C. Bhaktivedanta Swami.

Islam (is-lahm'; Arabic, "submission") Specifically, the religious tradition based on the revealed Qur'an as word of God.

Izanagi (ee-zah-nah-gee) The male kami who is the pro-creator of the Japanese islands as well as many other kami.

Izanami (ee-zah-nah-mee) The female kami who is the procreator of the Japanese islands as well as some of the kami.

jahiliyya (jah'hil'lee'yah; Arabic) The "age of ignorance," which refers to the time before the revelation of the Qur'an.

jati (jah'tee; Sanskrit, "birth group") One of thousands of endogamous groups or subcastes, each equal in social and ritual status.

jiao (jee-ow') Daoist communal sacrificial offerings to signal cosmic renewal and collective cohesion.

jihad (ji-had'; Arabic, "striving") The greater jihad is the struggle with one's self to become a better person; the lesser jihad is associated with military conflict in defense of the faith.

jinas (ji'nuh; Sanskrit, "conquerors") Jain title for those who have "conquered" samsara; synonymous with tirthankaras.

jinja (jin'juh) Shinto shrine.

jiva (jee'vuh; Sanskrit, "soul") The finite and eternal soul; also the category of living, as opposed to nonliving, entities of the universe.

jnana marga (juh-nah'nuh mahr'guh) The path of knowledge.

Jump Dance Renewal dance of Yurok people.

junzi (joon'zee) The personality ideal in Confucianism; the noble person.

Kabbalah One of the dominant forms of Jewish mysticism, kabbalistic texts begin to appear in Europe during the twelfth and thirteenth centuries. Mystics belonging to this tradition focus on the emanative powers of God—referred to in Hebrew as *Sephirot*—and on their role within the Godhead, as well as within the human personality.

kachinas (kah-chee'nah; Hopi) Pueblo spiritual beings.

kami (kah-mee) Shinto deity and spirit with awe-inspiring power.

karma (kahr'muh; Sanskrit, "action") "Action" and the consequences of action; determines the nature of one's reincarnation. In Buddhism, because Buddhism emphasizes the intentions that precede actions, karma can be understood as "intentional action" and its consequences. In Jainism, all activity is believed to involve various forms of matter that weigh down the soul (jiva) and thus hinder the quest for liberation.

karma marga (kahr'muh mahr'guh) The path of ethical and ritual works, or "action."

kevala (kay'vuh-luh; shortened form of Sanskrit *kevala-jnana*, "isolated knowledge" or "absolute knowledge") The perfect and complete knowledge or omniscience that is Jain enlightenment; marks the point at which one is free from the damaging effects of karma and is liberated from samsara.

Khadija (kha-dee'juh) Muhammad's beloved first wife.

Khalsa (khal'sah; Punjabi, "pure ones") An order within Sikhism to which the majority of Sikhs belong, founded by Guru Gobind Singh in 1699.

Kinaalda (kee-nahl'dah) Rite of passage for young Navajo women.

kingdom of God God's rule or dominion over the universe and human affairs. The kingdom of God is one of the primary themes in the teaching of Jesus.

Kinjiketele (kin-jee-ke-te'le) The leader of the Maji Maji rebellion in Tanganyika (today's Tanzania).

Kojiki (koh-jee-kee) *Record of Ancient Matters*, compiled in the eighth century CE.

kshatriya (ksha'tree-uh; Sanskrit) A member of the warrior and administrator class of the *varna* or caste system.

kusti (koo'stee) Sacred cord that is to be worn daily by Zoroastrians who have undergone the initiatory rite of the investiture ceremony.

lama (lahm'ah; Tibetan, "guru" or "teacher") In Tibetan Buddhism, an authoritative teacher.

langar A gurdwara's community kitchen that is used for the preparation of meals for anyone who visits, regardless of religious or caste identity.

li (lee) In Confucianism, etiquette and proper manners; rituals and holy rites.

liturgy (from Greek, *leitourgia*, "a work of the people" in honor of God) The basic order of worship in Christian churches consisting of prescribed prayers, readings, and rituals.

logos In its most basic sense, the Greek *logos* means "word," but it also means "rational principle," "reason," or "divine reason." The Gospel of John uses *logos* in the sense of the "divine reason" through which God created and sustains the universe when it states that "the Word became flesh" in Jesus Christ (John 1:14).

loka (loh'kah; Sanskrit, "world") The Jain universe, often depicted as having the shape of a giant man.

Lord's Prayer A prayer attributed to Jesus, the Lord's Prayer serves as a model of prayer for Christians. Also known as the "Our Father" (since it begins with these words), its most familiar form is found in the Gospel of Matthew (6:9–13).

Lughnassadh (looh-nah'sah) A summer harvest festival (August 2) celebrated by Wiccans, honoring the Celtic god Lugh.

Luria, Isaac (1534–1572) A sixteenth-century mystic who settled in Safed (Israel) and gathered around him a community of disciples. Lurianic mysticism seeks to explain the mystery surrounding both the creation of the world and its redemption from sin.

Luther, Martin (1483–1546) A German monk who criticized Roman Catholic doctrines and practices in his Ninety-Five Theses (1517), Luther was the original leader and one of the seminal thinkers of the Protestant Reformation.

Mahayana Buddhism (mah-hah-yah'nah; Sanskrit, "Great Vehicle") The form of Buddhism most prominent in China, Tibet, Mongolia, Japan, South Korea, Vietnam, Indonesia, Malaysia, and Taiwan.

Maimonides A twelfth-century philosopher and rabbinic scholar whose codification of Jewish beliefs and religious practices set the standard for both in subsequent centuries.

Maji Maji (mah-jee mah-jee; Swahili) A 1905 rebellion against German colonizers in Tanganyika (today's Tanzania).

mandala (mahn'duh-luh; Sanskrit, "disk") A geometric figure, usually a circle, that makes use of elaborate symbolism to represent buddhahood.

mantra (mahn'truh; Sanskrit, "sacred utterance") A word or sound thought to have spiritual power.

matsuri (mah-tsooh-ree) Shinto religious festival.

maya (mah'yah; Sanskrit, "magic" or "illusion") In the Vedas, the magical power the gods used to create this world; in Vedanta philosophy, illusion that veils the mind.

McKay, Mabel (1907–1993) A Pomo woman who was well known as a healer and basket weaver.

Mecca The city in which Muhammad was born; place of pilgrimage for Muslims.

Medina The city to which Muhammad and his early followers migrated to escape persecution in Mecca.

medium A person who is possessed by a spirit and thus mediates between the human and spirit worlds.

messiah In the Jewish Scriptures (Old Testament), the term *messiah* ("anointed one") refers to kings and priests, who were anointed with consecrated oil. In later Jewish literature, the Messiah is sometimes understood as a figure—in some cases, a supernatural figure—who, having been "anointed" by God, saves the Jewish people and the world from evil. Christianity understands Jesus of Nazareth as the Messiah.

Middle Way In the teaching of the Buddha, the path to awakening between the extremes of asceticism and self-indulgence.

miko (mee-koh) Unmarried female Shinto shrine attendants.

mikoshi (mee-koh-shee) Portable shrine temporarily housing a Shinto deity.

mikveh (meek-veh') A ritual bath in which married Jewish women immerse themselves each month, after the end of their menstrual cycle and before resuming sexual relations with their husbands.

ming See *Tianming*.

miraj (mir-ahj'; Arabic) Muhammad's Night Journey from Mecca to Jerusalem and from there to heaven, where he met with God.

misogi (mee-soh'gee) Shinto ritual of purification with water.

mitzvot (meets-voht') Literally translated, the Hebrew word *mitzvot* means "commandments," and it refers to the 613 commandments that the biblical God imparted to the Israelites in the Torah (i.e., the first five books of the Hebrew Bible).

modernization The general process through which societies transform economically, socially, and culturally to become more industrial, urban, and secular; any transformation of societies and cultures that leads to the abandonment of traditional religious beliefs and values.

moksha (mohk'shuh; Sanskrit, "release") Liberation, the final release from samsara.

monism The belief that all reality is ultimately one.

monotheism The belief in only one god.

Moonies A slang term for members of the Unification Church.

moran (mor-an; Samburu and Maasai) A young man in Samburu or Maasai culture who has been circumcised and thus has special cultural and religious duties.

Moses The legendary leader and prophet who leads the Israelite slaves out of Egypt, Moses serves as a mediator between the people of Israel and God in the Torah and is later viewed as Israel's greatest prophet. It is to Moses that God imparts the Ten Commandments and the teachings that later became the Torah.

mosque (mosk; from the Arabic term *masjid*) Place of prayer, from the Arabic term *masjid*.

muezzin (mooh-ez'-zin; Arabic) The person who calls the *adhan*.

Muhammad The prophet who received the revelation of the Qur'an from God; the final prophet in a long line of prophets sent by God to humanity.

mukti (mook'tee; Punjabi, "liberation") In Sikhism, spiritual liberation bringing on the eternal and infinitely blissful state of being in the presence of God; sometimes the Sanskrit term *moksha* is used instead.

Mul Mantra (mool mahn'truh) The summary of Sikh doctrine that comprises the opening lines of the *Japji*, Guru Nanak's composition that in turn comprises the opening section of the Adi Granth. (See p. 245 for an English translation of the full text.)

multiculturalism The coexistence of different peoples and their cultural ways in one time and place.

mysterium tremendum **and** *fascinans* The contrasting feelings of awe-inspiring mystery and of overwhelming attraction that are said by Rudolf Otto to characterize the numinous experience.

mystical experience A general category of religious experience characterized in various ways, for example, as the uniting with the divine through inward contemplation or as the dissolution of the sense of individual selfhood.

myth A story or narrative, originally conveyed orally, that sets forth basic truths of a religious tradition; myths often involve events of primordial time that describe the origins of things.

Native American Church A church founded in the early twentieth century based on peyote religion.

Navjote (nahv'-yoht) For Parsis, the name of the ceremony of initiation into the community of Zoroastrians. See also **Sedreh Pushi**.

neidan (nay-dahn) Daoist "internal" alchemical regimens designed to attain immortality through meditation, breath control, gymnastics, diet, and massage.

neisheng waiwang (nay-sheng wai'wahng) Neo-Confucian ideal of "inner moral cultivation and external skillful management of society and state."

New Age An umbrella term for various religious and quasi-religious practices based on a belief in the transformation of both nature and human consciousness.

New Thought A philosophical school of thought, popular in the late nineteenth century, that stressed the power of the human mind to discover the divine within nature and to control material reality.

Nicene Creed A profession of faith formulated by the Councils of Nicea (325) and Constantinople (381), the Nicene Creed articulates the Christian doctrine of the Trinity.

Nichiren Buddhism (nee-chee-ren) A form of Mahayana Buddhism with origins in Japan.

Nihon shoki (nee-hohn shoh-kee) *Chronicles of [the Land Where] the Sun Originates*, eighth century CE text.

nirvana (neer-vah'nuh, Sanskrit; nibbana, Pali) The ultimate goal of Buddhist practice, nirvana is the extinguishing of unwholesome desire and suffering.

Noble Eightfold Path The Buddha's prescription for a way of life that leads to enlightenment, it consists of the practice of eight ideals.

nontheistic Term denoting a religion that does not maintain belief in God or gods.

norito (noh-ree-toh) Invocational prayer offered by Shinto priests to the kami.

Nowruz (now-rooz') Zoroastrian New Year's Day coinciding with the vernal equinox, the most popularly observed annual holy day; celebrated in varying ways throughout western Asia by people of all religious and ethnic backgrounds.

numinous experience Rudolf Otto's term for describing an encounter with "the Holy"; it is characterized by two powerful and contending forces, *mysterium tremendum* and *fascinans*.

Odu (oh-doo; Yoruba) The original prophets in Yoruba religion.

OM (ohm; from three Sanskrit letters: *A-U-M*) The primordial sound through which the universe is manifested.

omikuji (oh-mee'koo-jee) Paper fortunes found at shrines.

omnipotence The divine attribute of total and eternal power.

omniscience The divine attribute of total and eternal knowledge.

original sin Formulated by St. Augustine in the fourth century, the doctrine of original sin states that the sin of Adam and Eve affected all of humanity, so that all human beings are born with a sinful nature.

orisha (aw-ree-shah'; Yoruba) Lesser deities in Yoruba religion.

Orthodox Church Also known as the Eastern Orthodox Church and the Orthodox Catholic Church, the Orthodox Church is the Eastern branch of Christianity that separated from the Western branch (the Roman Catholic Church) in 1054.

Oshun (oh'shoon; Yoruba) A Yoruba goddess.

Pali Canon Also known as the *Tipitaka*, the Theravada canon is the first canon of Buddhist texts consisting of three "baskets" or collections of sutras.

Panth (puhnth; Sanskrit, "path") The Sikh community. In lowercase, *panth* ("path") is a term applied to any number of Indian (primarily Hindu) religious traditions.

pantheism The belief that the divine reality is identical to nature or the material world.

pantheon A group of deities or spirits.

parable According to the gospels of Matthew, Mark, and Luke, Jesus made extensive use of parables—short, fictional stories that use the language and imagery of everyday life to illustrate moral and religious truths.

parinirvana (pah'ree-neer-vah'nuh; Sanskrit) The full entry into nirvana at death of one who has attained nirvana, *parinirvana* brings release from samsara and rebirth.

Parker, Quanah Comanche man who called for embrace of peyote religion.

Paul of Tarsus A first-century apostle who founded churches throughout Asia Minor, Macedonia, and Greece. Paul was also the author of many of the letters, or epistles, found in the New Testament.

Pentecost A holiday celebrated by Christians in commemoration of the outpouring of the Holy Spirit on the disciples of Jesus as described in the second chapter of the New Testament book of Acts.

Pentecostalism A movement that emphasizes the importance of spiritual renewal and the experience of God through baptism in the Holy Spirit, Pentecostalism is a primarily Protestant movement that has become extremely popular in recent decades.

Pesach (pay'sahkh) An early spring harvest festival that celebrates the liberation of the Israelites from Egypt, Pesach (better known as "Passover" in English) is celebrated for seven days in Israel and eight days in the Diaspora. The first two nights are celebrated within a family setting.

peyote (pay-oh'tee) Hallucinogenic cactus used in many Native American religions.

polytheism The belief in many gods.

Popol Vuh (poh-pohl voo'; Quiché Mayan, "council book") The Quiché Mayan book of creation.

Protestant Christianity One of the three major traditions in Christianity (along with Roman Catholicism and Orthodoxy), Protestantism began in the sixteenth century as a reaction against medieval Roman Catholic doctrines and practices.

puja (pooh'jah; Sanskrit, "worship") Generally, worship; usually the offering before an image of the deity of fruit, incense, or flowers.

Purana (poo-rah'nuh; Sanskrit, "ancient") A compendium of myth, usually with a sectarian emphasis.

Pure Land Buddhism A form of Mahayana Buddhism that emphasizes devotion to Amitabha Buddha.

purgatory In Roman Catholicism, purgatory is an intermediate state between earthly life and heaven in which the debt for unconfessed sin is expiated.

qi (chee) Breath, force, power, material energy.

Quetzalcoatl (ket-zuhl-kuh-wah'tuhl; Aztec) Aztec god and important culture hero in Mexico.

Qur'an (kuh-rahn' or koo-rahn'; Arabic) The holy text of Muslims; the word of God as revealed to Muhammad.

Rahit (rah-hit'; Punjabi) The *rahit-nama*, a collection of scripture that specifies ideals of belief and conduct for members of the Khalsa and, by extension, for Sikhism generally.

Ramadan (rah'muh-dahn; Arabic) The month in which Muslims must fast daily from dawn until dusk; the fast is one of the five pillars of Islam; also the month in which the Qur'an is believed to have been revealed to Muhammad.

ren (ruhn) In Confucianism, human-heartedness, benevolence; the unique moral inclination of humans.

revealed ethics Truth regarding right behavior believed to be divinely established and intentionally made known to human beings.

revelation The expression of the divine will, commonly recorded in sacred texts.

rites of passage Rituals that mark the transition from one life stage or social stage to another.

rites of renewal Rituals that seek to enhance natural processes, like rain or fertility, or to enhance the solidarity of a group.

ritual Formal worship practice.

Roman Catholic Church One of the three major traditions within Christianity (along with Orthodoxy and Protestantism), the Roman Catholic Church, which recognizes the primacy of the Bishop of Rome, or the pope, has historically been the dominant church in the West.

rosary Taking its name from the Latin *rosarium* ("garland of roses"), the rosary is a traditional form of Roman Catholic devotion in which practitioners make use of a string of beads in reciting prayers.

Rosh Hashanah (rohsh hah-shah-nah') The Jewish New Year, it is celebrated for two days in the fall (on the first day of the month of Tishrai) and accompanied by the blowing of a ram's horn (a *shofar*, in Hebrew). It signals the beginning of the "ten days of repentance" that culminate with Yom Kippur.

Ru (rooh) Scribes and ritual performers of the Zhou period; later used exclusively to refer to followers and practitioners of Confucius's teachings.

sacraments In Christianity, rituals in which material elements such as bread, wine, water, and oil serve as visible symbols of an invisible grace conveyed to recipients.

saint A "holy person" (Latin *sanctus*). Veneration of the saints and belief in their intercession on behalf of the living are important features of Roman Catholic and Orthodox Christianity.

salat (suh-laht'; Arabic) The daily prayers, which are one of the pillars of Islam.

samsara (sahm-sah'ruh; Sanskrit) The continuing cycle of birth, death, and rebirth; also the this-worldly realm in which the cycle recurs.

sand painting A painting made with sand used by Navajo healers to treat ailments.

sangha (sahn'guh; Sanskrit, "community") The community of Buddhist monks and nuns. Sangha can also denote individual communities of Buddhists or the worldwide community of Buddhists.

sannyasi (suhn-yah'see; Sanskrit) Renouncer in the fourth stage (ashrama) of life.

Santería (sahn-teh-ree'ah; Spanish) New World religion with roots in West Africa; prominent in Cuba.

sawm (sohm; Arabic) The mandatory fast during the month of Ramadan; one of the pillars of Islam.

scholasticism Represented by figures such as Peter Abelard, Thomas Aquinas, and William of Ockham, scholasticism was the medieval effort to reconcile faith and reason using the philosophy of Aristotle.

Second Great Awakening An evangelical movement popular in the United States from the early nineteenth century to the 1880s.

secularization The general turning away from traditional religious authority and institutions; any tendency in modern society that devalues religious worldviews or seeks to substitute scientific theories for religious beliefs.

Seder (sey'dehr) A ritualized meal, observed on the first two nights of Pesach, that recalls the Exodus from Egypt.

sedreh (sed'reh) White cotton vest worn by Zoroastrians that symbolizes the path of righteousness.

Sedreh Pushi (sed'reh poo'shee) For Iranis, the name of the ceremony of initiation into the community of Zoroastrians. See also **Navjote**.

seekers A popular term, current in the late nineteenth century, for individuals who cannot find spiritual satisfaction in "mainstream" religious institutions and who describe themselves as "spiritual" rather than "religious."

shahada (shah-hah'dah; Arabic) The declaration of faith: "There is no God but God and Muhammad is the Messenger of God"; the first of the five pillars.

Shaiva (shai'vuh; Sanskrit) A devotee of Shiva.

Shakta (shahk'tah; Sanskrit) A devotee of the Great Goddess, Devi.

Shangdi (shahng-dee) The August Lord on High of the Shang period.

shari'a (sha-ree'ah; Arabic, "the way to the water hole") Islamic law.

Shavuot (shah-vooh-oht') A later spring harvest festival that is celebrated for two days and is associated with the giving of the Torah at Mount Sinai. Along with Pesach and Sukkot, it was one of the "pilgrimage" festivals in ancient times.

shen (shen) Gods and deities; benevolent spirits.

shengren (sheng-ren) (or *sheng*) The Confucian sage, the epitome of humanity.

shi (shir) Men of service; lower-ranking civil and military officials in the Zhou period.

Shi'a (pl.), Shi'i (n. adj.) (shee'ah, shee'ee; Arabic) One of the two major branches of Islam. The Shi'a believed that 'Ali, the Prophet's son-in-law, should have succeeded as leader of the Muslim community after the death of Muhammad.

shimenawa (shee-meh-na-wah) Huge rope hung in front of the worship hall to mark sacred spaces and objects at a shrine.

shintai (shin-tai) The "body" of a kami housed in a public shrine, a family shrine, or temporarily in a *mikoshi*.

Shinto (shin-toh) "The way of the gods." Traditional Japanese religion that acknowledges the power of the kami.

shirk (sherk; Arabic) The sin of idolatry, that is, of worshiping anything other than God, the one unforgivable sin in Islam.

shruti (shroo'tee; Sanskrit, "that which is heard") Term denoting the category of Vedic literature accepted by orthodox Hindus as revealed truth.

shudra (shooh'druh; Sanskrit) A member of the servant class of the *varna* or caste system.

shunyata (shoon'yuh-tah; Sanskrit) A Mahayana doctrine according to which all things are empty of any inherent existence. Also known as **emptiness**.

Shvetambara (shvayt-ahm'buh-ruh; Sanskrit, "those whose garment is white") The largest Jain sect, whose monks and nuns wear white robes; generally more liberal than the Digambara sect.

Siddur (see-doohr') The prayer book that is used on weekdays and on the Sabbath.

sin The violation of God's will in thought or action.

skandhas (skahn'duhs; Sanskrit, "bundles" or "heaps") In Buddhism, transitory phenomena (material form, feelings, perceptions, mental constructions, and awareness) that give rise to a sense of self.

skillful means The Mahayana doctrine that in teaching or demonstrating the Dharma one should adapt one's words and actions to the needs of one's audience.

smriti (smree'tee; Sanskrit, "tradition") Term denoting the vast category of Hindu sacred texts that is not shruti.

Spenta Mainyu (spen'tah mine'yoo) Ahura Mazda's Holy Spirit; one of the seven *Amesha Spentas*.

stupas (stooh'puhs; Sanskrit) Reliquary mounds or other structures in which the relics of the Buddhas are buried preserved and venerated.

Sufi (soo'fee) A follower of the mystical tradition of Islam, Sufism, which focuses on the believer's personal experience of God and goal of union with God.

Sukkot (sooh-koht') A fall harvest festival that is associated with the huts (in Hebrew, *sukkot*) in which the ancient Israelites sought shelter during the Exodus. It is celebrated for seven days in Israel (eight days in the Diaspora).

Sun Dance Midsummer ritual common to many Native American religions; details vary across cultures.

sunna (soon'nuh; Arabic, "way of life" or "custom") Specifically refers to example of the life of the Prophet Muhammad; important religious source for Muslims.

Sunni (soon'nee; Arabic) One of the two main branches of Islam. The Sunnis believed that the Muslim community should decide on a successor to lead after the death of Muhammad.

sura (soo'rah; Arabic) Chapter of the Qur'an; there are 114 suras in the Qur'an.

sutra (sooh'truh, Sanskrit; *sutta*, Pali) A text containing a discourse or sermon of the Buddha.

sweat lodge A structure built by Native Americans for ritually cleansing and purifying the body.

synagogue Jewish house of worship. The focal point of every synagogue is the Ark, a large cabinet where scrolls of the Torah are stored.

tafsir (taf-seer'; Arabic) Interpretation of or commentary on the Qur'an. There are several types of *tafsir*, which aim to explain the meaning of the Qur'an.

tallit A prayer shawl that is worn during morning prayers (traditionally by men). The fringes of this shawl represent, symbolically, the 613 mitzvot found in the Torah.

Talmud (tahl-mood') A multivolume work of commentary on the laws of the Torah and on the teachings of the entire Hebrew Bible, composed in two stages:

the Mishnah (edited in approximately 200 CE) and the Gemara (edited, in its Babylonian version, around 500 CE). Traditionally, Jews refer to the Talmud as the "Oral Torah" and regard it as an extension of sacred scripture.

Tanakh An acronym standing for the entire Hebrew Bible: **T**orah (the first five books of the Hebrew Bible); **N**eviim (or "Prophets," which includes works of both prophecy and history); and **Kh**etuvim (or "Writings," a miscellaneous gathering of works in poetry and prose). Taken together, the twenty-four books that make up this collection constitute the core "scriptures" of Judaism.

Tantra (tuhn'truh; Sanskrit, "loom") System of ideas and practices that potentiate sudden liberation from samsara; also a form of sacred text detailing the ideas and practices.

tefillin (tee-fi'luhn) Two small boxes, containing biblical verses, to which leather straps are attached. Traditionally, Jewish males from the age of thirteen wear tefillin during weekday morning prayers; one box is placed on the forehead, and the other is placed on the left arm.

temizuya (te-mee'zoo-yah) Purification fountain at a shrine.

theistic Term denoting a religion that maintains belief in God or gods.

theocracy A governmental system that claims power and guidance based on divine authority.

theosophy Any religious philosophy that entails communication with deceased "spiritual masters" and emphasizes the superiority of "spirit" to "matter."

Theravada Buddhism (thai-ruh-vah'duh) The form of Buddhism that is most prominent in Sri Lanka, Thailand, Cambodia, Myanmar (Burma), and Laos.

thetan (thay'tuhn) A term used by Scientologists to identify the immortal self and source of creativity in the human mind.

Three Refuges Also known as the Three Jewels. Buddhists proclaim their identification as such by saying that they take refuge in, or place their trust in, the Buddha, the Dharma, and the Sangha.

Tian (tee-yahn') The Ultimate Absolute of Confucian teaching; the conscious Will that regulates the cosmos and intervenes in human affairs; in Daoist usage, it means nature itself; conventionally but misleadingly translated as "Heaven."

Tianming The mandate or command of *Tian* that confers political legitimacy to the ruler; also understood by Confucians as the calling to morally improve oneself and to transform the world.

Tianshi (tee-yahn'shir) "Celestial Master"; reference to a Daoist salvational figure, as well as an organized movement.

Tiantai Buddhism (tyen-tai, Chinese; ten-dai, Japanese) Known as Tendai in Japan, Tiantai is a form of Mahayana Buddhism with origins in China.

tipi (also teepee) A typical conical structure of the tribes of the Great Plains which is often constructed with a sacred blueprint.

Tipitaka (ti-pee'tah-kah; Pali, "three baskets") The Pali Canon of Buddhist texts.

tirthankaras (teer-tuhn'kuhr-uhs; Sanskrit, "makers of the river crossing") The Jain spiritual heroes, such as Parshva and Mahavira, who have shown the way to salvation; synonymous with jinas.

Torah Literally, the word *torah* means "teaching," and in its most restrictive sense it refers to the first five books of the Hebrew Bible. Less restrictively, it signifies the totality of God's revelations to the Jewish people, which includes not only the remaining books of the Hebrew Bible but also the writings contained in the Talmud.

torii (toh-ree-ee) Crossbar gateway leading up to the Shinto shrine.

transcendence The divine attribute of being above and beyond anything human beings can know or imagine.

transtheistic Term denoting a theological perspective that acknowledges the existence of gods while denying that the gods are vital with regard to the most crucial religious issues, such as the quest for salvation.

transubstantiation According to this Roman Catholic doctrine, the bread and wine consecrated by a priest in the Eucharist become the body and blood of Christ and retain only the appearance, not the substance, of bread and wine.

trickster A common figure in North American mythologies; trickster tales often teach important moral lessons.

trikaya (treh-kai'ya; Sanskrit, "three bodies") The Mahayana doctrine of the three "bodies" or modes of existence of the Buddha.

Trinity According to the Christian doctrine of the Trinity, God is a single divine substance or essence consisting of three "persons."

Two Spirit An additional gender identity in many Native North American cultures; often thought to have special spiritual powers.

Ufology Any systematized belief in extraterrestrials.

Umayyad Dynasty (oo-may'yad) Muslim dynasty that ruled from 661 to 750 CE.

umma (oom'muh; Arabic) The worldwide Muslim community.

Upanishads (oo-pah'nee-shuhds; Sanskrit, "sitting down near [a teacher]") Philosophical texts from the later period of Vedic literature, also called Vedanta ("end of the Vedas").

urbanization The shift of population centers from rural, agricultural settings to cities.

Vaishnava (vaish'nuh-vuh; Sanskrit) A devotee of Vishnu and his avatars.

vaishya (vaish'yuh; Sanskrit) A member of the producer (farmer and merchant) class of the *varna* or caste system.

Vajrayana Buddhism (vuhj-ruh-yah'nuh; Sanskrit, "Thunderbolt" or "Diamond Vehicle") The most prominent form of Mahayana Buddhism in Tibet, Nepal, Bhutan, and Mongolia.

varna (vahr'nuh; Sanskrit, "color") Caste or class; the four main classes form the basis of the traditional hierarchical organization of Hindu society.

Vedanta (vay-dahn'tuh; Sanskrit, "end of the Vedas") Synonym for Upanishads; prominent Hindu philosophical school.

Vedas (vay'duhz; from Sanskrit *veda*, "knowledge") Broadly, all Vedic literature; narrowly, four ancient collections (samhitas) of hymns and other religious material.

vision quest A ritual attempt by an individual to communicate with the spirit world.

Vodou (vo-doo'; Fon and French) New World religion with roots in West Africa; prominent in Haiti and the Haitian diaspora.

waidan (wai'dahn) Daoist "external" alchemical regimens involving refining of "pills" with herbs and minerals for ingestion so that immortality can be attained.

Wiccan Rede A traditional set of rules and ethical values cherished by Wiccans.

witchcraft A contested term used by Western scholars to describe the use of supernatural powers to harm others.

World's Parliament of Religions Worldwide gathering of religious leaders held in Chicago in 1893; gatherings under the name Parliament of the World's Religions have been held subsequently, beginning in 1993 in Chicago.

Wovoka A Paiute man whose visions started the Ghost Dance of 1890.

wuwei (wooh-way) Daoist notion of action without intention; actionless action.

xian (shee-ahn') Daoist immortals and perfected individuals.

xiao (shee-ow') Filial piety; respect and care for parents and ancestors.

xinzhai (shin'jai) "Fasting of the Mind" in the *Zhuangzi*.

yang (yahng) Lit. the south-facing side of a mountain, representing the energy that is bright, warm, dry, and masculine.

yangsheng (yahng-sheng) Daoist techniques of nourishing life and attaining immortality.

Yasna (yas'nuh) Seventy-two-chapter section of the Avesta containing material recited by priests in rituals; includes the *Gathas*. The Yasna liturgy, an important ritual, is the sacrifice of the sacred drink haoma before a fire.

yazatas (yah-zah'tahs; "ones worthy of worship") A large number, eventually fixed at thirty, of deities on the side of Ahura Mazda and order/good.

YHWH These four consonants constitute the most sacred of names associated with the biblical God.

yin Lit. the north-facing side of a mountain, representing the energy that is dark, cold, wet, and feminine.

yoga (yoh'guh; Sanskrit, "yoking" or "uniting") Generally, uniting of the self with God; sometimes used as an alternative to marga when referring to the three main paths to liberation; also (normally capitalized: Yoga) one of the six philosophical schools, focusing on moral, physical, and spiritual practices leading to liberation.

yogic flying A meditational practice, similar to levitation, attributed to members of the Transcendental Meditation community.

Yom Kippur (yohm' kee-poohr') Referred to as the "Day of Atonement," it is the most solemn of all of the fast days in the Jewish religious calendar.

zakat (za'kat; Arabic) Regulated almsgiving; one of the five pillars of Islam.

zar (zahr; various languages) A term for spirits in East Africa.

Zarathushtra (za-ruh-thoosh'truh) (Also spelled "Zarathustra") Called Zoroaster by the ancient Greeks; ancient Iranian prophet and poet, founder of the Zoroastrian religion; dates uncertain (between 1300 and 800 BCE).

Zen Buddhism Known as Chan Buddhism in China, Zen Buddhism (as it is known in Japan) is a Mahayana school that emphasizes meditation over doctrine.

zhai (jai) Daoist "fasts" designed to seek redemption of transgressions by the gods.

Zhuan Falun (zyahn-fay'luhn) The collected writings of Li Hongzhi, the founder of Falun Gong. First published in 1994.

Zionism A modern political philosophy that asserts a belief in the Jewish national identity and in the necessity of resuming national life within the historic land of Israel.

ziran (zee'rahn) Daoist notion of natural spontaneity.

Zohar A kabbalistic *midrash* based on the biblical book of Genesis (c. 1280 CE).

zuowang (zoh'wahng) Practice of "sitting and forgetting" in the *Zhuangzi*.

CREDITS

INDEX

Note: Page numbers followed by "m" refer to maps.